Switzerland
Without a Car

the Bradt Travel Guide

Anthony Lambert

edition
5

www.bradtguides.com

Bradt Travel Guides Ltd, UK
The Globe Pequot Press Inc, USA

KEY

- ■ Capital city
- ● Main town
- ○ Other town
- ✈ Airport
- ══ Main road
- — Other road
- ┼┼┼ Railway
- ─·─·─ International boundary

F R A N C E

Mulhouse → Freiburg

Belfort →

BASEL

Belfort →

Olten

Jura

La Chaux-de-Fonds

Biel/Bienne

Solothurn

Burgdorf

Neuchâtel

BERN ✈

Besançon →

Yverdon-les-Bains

Lac de Neuchâtel

Fribourg

Thunersee

Vallorbe

Spiez

Interlaken

Meirin

Lausanne

Lauterbrunnen

Grindelw

Lötschberg Base Tunnel

Eiger 3970m

Berner Alpen

Jungfrau 4158m

Lac Léman

Montreux

Lenk

Lötschberg Tunnel

Brig

Lyon →

Genève

Simplon Pass

Lyon →

Chamonix →

✈ Sion

Martigny

Chamonix →

Zermatt

Matterhorn 4478m

Dufourspitze 4634m

N

Bradt

Mont Blanc 4807m

→ Aosta

I T A L Y

0 ——— 80km
0 ——— 50 miles

Switzerland Don't miss...

Stunning mountain scenery
With such varied alpine landscapes, gorgeous views come as standard in Switzerland — wind around precipitous bends on the Zermatt–Gornergrat line and catch unparalleled views of the famous Matterhorn
(WM/S) page 305

Lake Luzern
Cruise around one of the most beautiful inland lakes in Europe aboard one of five old-fashioned paddle steamers
(G/DT) page 173

Breathtaking high mountain passes

The train that links Göschenen and Andermatt climbs the spectacularly precipitous Schöllenen gorge, scene of a fierce battle during the Napoleonic Wars

(AC/S) page 311

Exploring the Bernese Oberland

Whether by foot or by bike, the Bernese Oberland abounds with opportunities for outdoor adventure, with exceptional winter sports facilities, miles of walking and cycling trails and some of Europe's favourite climbing peaks

(INEH/FLPA) page 143

Old Town Bern

Recognised as a UNESCO World Heritage Site, the charming Old Town is famous for its towers, bridges and geranium-filled window-boxes

(IK/DT) page 93

Switzerland in colour

left   Switzerland boasts more than 600 funiculars, cable cars, rack railways and chairlifts — Muottas Muragl funicular in Graubünden offers inspiring views over the Engadine lakes (AM/W) page 355

above   Climb to the top of Mount Titlis (10,000ft) by cable car and gaze across the Titlis Glacier — this ride offers the highest viewpoint in central Switzerland (BS/F) page 185

below   The Swiss postbus system covers a network of 738 routes totalling more than 11,000km — the distinctive yellow coaches can be spotted across the country (CE/DT) page 21

above left   Two railways climb up Mount Rigi, central Switzerland's panorama peak – from Vitznau on Lake Luzern and, seen here, from Arth (S/DT) page 177

above right   With 12 navigable lakes in the country, travel by water is a picturesque method of getting from one place to the next, especially on the sizeable Lake Luzern (AM/W) page 173

right   The only mountain railway with daily steam operation in season is the Brienz-Rothorn Bahn above Lake Brienz, worked by ten steam locomotives dating from 1892 to 1996 (A/DT) page 194

below   Curving around the Landwasser Viaduct, the scenic Glacier Express averages about 36km/h (F/DT) page 26

A seemingly daunting proposition in a country known for its peaks, cycling in Switzerland can be enjoyed by all, from those looking for a leisurely pedal to those keen to tackle the heights (INEH/FLPA and AT) page 31

AUTHOR

Anthony Lambert has been visiting Switzerland since childhood and has written 15 books about railways and travel. He has contributed to half a dozen books on great railway journeys and written about travel and railway journeys for such newspapers and magazines as *The Independent, Orient-Express Magazine, New York Times, The Daily Telegraph, The Sunday Times* and *Wanderlust*. He was consultant editor for the nine-volume part work, *The World of Trains*, and has travelled on the railways of over 50 countries.

Anthony's part-time work for the National Trust reflects an interest in architecture and cultural history, and he is also a keen cyclist and walker. He has talked on railways and travel to a wide range of audiences, including the Royal Geographical Society, of which he is a Fellow.

AUTHOR'S STORY

My love of Switzerland stems from childhood holidays. We went every third year and I was even then captivated by the sheer scale of the mountain landscapes in which we walked, as well as being enthralled by the character and number of mountain railways, cablecars and chairlifts – much more fun than cablecars.

Returning in my twenties, I realised that, quite apart from the fact that Switzerland has far more than its fair share of Europe's finest landscapes, the country is a paradigm for responsible tourism. Environmental considerations are generally to the fore in the planning and execution of any developments, and it has unquestionably the finest public transport system in the world.

Most mountain areas are thankfully roadless so a car is a pointless encumbrance. It's much better to rely on the Swiss Travel System and the range of passes, which are excellent value. Swiss precision applies to all forms of transport, which are admirably integrated and reliable. During research for the book I often took up to 25 separate journeys in a day, switching from train to bus to funicular to lake steamer, generally with connections of under ten or even five minutes. In many months of travel, I missed one connection.

My purpose in writing the book was to encourage travellers to have a much more rewarding experience while minimising their footprint. Writers seldom receive feedback unless they commit a howler, but one day a letter in spidery handwriting arrived via the publisher. It was from a retired gentleman who said that he had never managed to persuade his wife to venture abroad; this book convinced her to give Switzerland a try, and since the first successful visit they had been going every year. No writer could ask for a better reward.

PUBLISHER'S FOREWORD — Hilary Bradt

I first met Anthony Lambert in the 1980s, and quickly learned of his passion for the railway both as transport and as the best way of seeing a country. Our discussions led to the publication of the first version of this guide, *Switzerland by Rail* – and, with a few title changes on the way, it's been steaming along for over a decade. Of course you can drive in Switzerland, but you'll be missing a heck of a lot if you do. The Swiss Travel System is probably the best in the world, and is genuinely integrated – visitors can use bicycles, trains, postbuses and ferries to explore the peaks, valleys and waters of this stunning country. There's no place more readily travelled in an environmentally friendly way than Tolkien-esque Switzerland.

Reprinted September 2015
Fifth edition published March 2013   First published in 1996

Bradt Travel Guides Ltd
IDC House, The Vale, Chalfont St Peter, Bucks SL9 9RZ, England
www.bradtguides.com
Print edition published in the USA by The Globe Pequot Press Inc, PO Box 480, Guilford, Connecticut 06437-0480

Text copyright © 2013 Anthony Lambert
Maps copyright © 2013 Bradt Travel Guides Ltd
Photographs copyright © 2013 individual photographers (see below)
Project Managers: Kelly Randell and Maisie Fitzpatrick

The author and publisher have made every effort to ensure the accuracy of the information in this book at the time of going to press. However, they cannot accept any responsibility for any loss, injury or inconvenience resulting from the use of information contained in this guide. All rights reserved. No part of this publication may be reproduced, stored in a retrieval system, or transmitted in any form or by any means, electronic, mechanical, photocopying, recording or otherwise without the prior consent of the publisher. Requests for permission should be addressed to Bradt Travel Guides Ltd in the UK (print and digital editions), or to The Globe Pequot Press Inc in North and South America (print edition only).

British Library Cataloguing in Publication Data
A catalogue record for this book is available from the British Library

ISBN: 978 1 84162 447 1 (print)   e-ISBN: 978 1 84162 757 1 (e-pub)   e-ISBN: 978 1 84162 659 8 (mobi)

Photographs Alamy: Phil Rees (PR/A); Appenzellerland Tourist Board (AT); Basel Tourism: Friedrich Reinhart Verlag (FRV/BT), Michael Will (MW/BT); Dreamstime: Akulamatiau (A/DT), Daniel Boiteau (DB/DT), Olga Demchishina (OD/DT), Christa Eder (CE/DT), Fotoember (F/DT), Gepapix (GP/DT), Gevisions (G/DT), Igor Korsunski (IK/DT), Mihai-Bogdan Lazar (MBL/DT), Ulrich Müller (UM/DT), Noamfein (N/DT), Swisshippo (S/DT); Flickr: Erik Charlton (EC/F), Björn Söderqvist (BS/F); FLPA: Imagebroker, Norbert Eisele-Hein (INEH/FLPA); Getty Images: Altrendo (A/GI); Shutterstock: Bertl123 (B123/S), Alexander Chaikin (AC/S), Martin Lehmann (ML/S), Wei Ming (WM/S), Nikos Psychogios (NP/S) Travelpeter (T/S); Wikimedia Commons: Ad Meskens (AD/W), Adrian Michael (AM/W)
Front cover Train passing through the Alps (A/GI)
Front cover picture research Pepi Bluck, Perfect Picture
Back cover Weggis (T/S); façade of an old building in Luzern (NP/S)
Title page Mont Blanc hiking trail (N/DT); Gruyères Castle (GP/DT); façade of an old building in Luzern (NP/S)

Maps David McCutcheon FBCart.S, with regional maps compiled from Philip's 1:1,000,000 Europe Mapping (*www.philips-maps.co.uk*); includes map data © Open Street Map (open Database Licence)
Colour map Relief map base by Nick Rowland FRGS

Typeset from the author's disc by Wakewing, High Wycombe
Production managed by Jellyfish Print Solutions and manufactured in India
Digital conversion by the Firsty Group

Acknowledgements

Inevitably a book of this nature depends upon the help of numerous people in providing advice, information and hospitality. To the following I extend my thanks for their kindness:

Peter Anderegg, Ernst Bachmann, Daniel Bachofner, Virgine Baeriswyl, Eveline Bandi, Erich Bapst, Ernst Baumberger, Corinne Baume, Ina Bauspiess, Patrick Belloncle, Peter Bernhard, Helmut Biner, Olivier Bovet, Christa Branchi-Müller, Manu Broccard, Robert Brookes, Dominic Brühwiler, Frank Bumann, Daniel Burckhardt, Lisbeth Cardis, Aurelia Carlen, Claudia Cattaneo, Alison Chambers, Corinne Chevallaz-Chappuis, Xavier Collange, Barbara Compton, Domitille Cornaro, Paola Corazza, Stefano Crivelli, Dr Hans P Danuser, Kurt A Diermeier, Jean-Vital Domézon, Katrin Dürrenberger, Urs Eberhard, Beatrice Ellenberger, Douglas Ellison, H-P Ernst, Adeline Favre, Olivier Federspiel, Ursula Fischer, Christine Flück, Sandrine Foschia, Hans Peter Frank, Mike Frei, Anina Fromm, Daniela Fuchs, Cédric Fuhrer, Dominique Fumeaux, Hugo Furrer, Robert Gander, Bruno Gantenbein, Cécile Gardaz, Oliver Garnett, Barbara Gasser, Raymond Gertschen, Andrew Gordon, Robi Guglielmetti, Monika Haecki, Toni Hählen, Martina Hänzi, Peider Härtli, Christine Hartmann, Isabella Hefti, Philipp Heinzelmann, Ines Hentz, Philipp Hermann, Andrea Herzog, Isabelle Hesse, George M Hoekstra, Roland Huber, Ueli Hug, Bruno Huggler, I Jeckelmann, Ursula Känel, Nicole Kaufmann, Karin Kelly, Xavier Kempf, Natalie Kenmeugni-Schmid, David Kestens, Daniela Kiser, Samuel Kocher, Matthias Kögl, Roswitha Koller, Christian Kräuchi, Jolanda Kruckner, Lisa Krummen, Philippe Kühne, Jrène Küng-Schmocker, Hansueli Kunz, Claudia Lansel, Peter Lehner, Peter Lemmey, Cornelia Lindner, Danny Löwensberg, Rolf Luethi, Andrea Lüthi, Cornelia Mainetti, Barbara Marti, Peter Mills, Jean-François Morerod, Dominique Moritz, Sabine Moser, Simon Mouttet, Adrian K Müller, Jürg Müller, Monica Müller, Barbara Mürner, Hans and Sylvia Neururer, Sir John and Lady Osborn, Adrian Ott, Nicole Pandiscia, Marcel Perren, Amadé Perrig, Eddy Peter, Beat Pfammatter, Sylviane Putallaz, Beni Rach, Willy Raess, Robert Reich, Sylvia Reinert, Heidi Reisz, Véronique Robyr, Ivan Rodrigues, Biba Roesti, Kathrin Rohrbach, Margaret Ross, Reto Rostetter, Stefanie Rother, Monika Rüthermann, George Saudan, René Schaetti, Douglas Schatz, Urs Schenk, Jean-Louis Scherz, Max Schlumpf, Susy Schuppli, Kaspar Schürch, Dorle Schürmann, Hans Rudolf Schmidt, Gieri Spescha, Jan Steiner, Andrea Stettler, Edith Strub, Gaudenz Thoma, Barbara Thommen, Jurg Tschopp-James, W Twerenbold, A Ulrich, Hans van Well, Myriam Vils, Carol Voeffray, Katherine von Ah Tall, Corinne von Allmen, Nora von Däniken, Christine Waetli, Michael Whitehouse, Rolf Wild, Hans Wismann, Marc Woodtli and Roland and Heidi Wyss.

My particular thanks to Eva Brechtbuehl, who was Director of the London office of Switzerland Tourism while the research was being done, and to the former

Director, Evelyn Lafone, without whose help and organisation the book would never have been written; and to the ever-helpful staff at Switzerland Tourism in London led by Marcelline Kuonen – Julie Melet, Roland Minder, Anne Pedersen, Heidi Reisz and Katja Walser for their particular help with subsequent editions.

Many thanks to the original editor of the book, Tricia Hayne, and to the publisher, Hilary Bradt, for having the confidence in the book to keep it in print. My thanks, too, to Sally Brock for the design, and to David McCutcheon for the maps.

Finally, my thanks to Marilyn and Gabriel for sharing my passion for the country.

DEDICATION

For Gabriel and Marilyn

Contents

LIST OF MAPS

USING THIS BOOK

Each section heading indicates the full extent of the relevant train service, but the text in that section describes only that part of the line between the places in capital letters (eg: the section headed LUZERN–AIROLO–Lugano–Chiasso describes only Luzern to Airolo). In the text, place names in **bold** refer to stations. Cross-referencing is usually by table number – the numbers applied by SBB to each train service and by which the printed rail timetable is organised; a list of tables and page numbers is given in *Appendix 3*, page 370.

Introduction

Switzerland is synonymous with some of the most beautiful mountain landscapes on Earth. It is primarily to see sights such as the Jungfrau, Eiger and Matterhorn that over 8.5 million people a year visit Switzerland, with UK visitors second only to Germany. Tourism promotion is the catalyst for most visitors today, but curiously it was mainly the writings of poets and playwrights which encouraged the early tourists to visit the country – the third canto of Byron's *Childe Harolde*, Schiller's *Wilhelm Tell* and Rossini's opera based on it did more for Swiss tourism in the first half of the 19th century than any official promotion. This celebration of the country's natural beauty by writers and painters has, however, distorted the view of what Switzerland has to offer.

Because the landscape dominates most visitors' perceptions of the country, its architectural and cultural attractions have been relatively neglected. The principal art galleries, for example, have collections of paintings that would hold their own with most capital cities. The country has thousands of fine museums, castles, mansions and outstanding churches, as well as delightful vernacular buildings. The country's cities are a pleasure to visit, largely because the impact of motor traffic has been minimised. Mercer's 2011 Quality of Life Survey ranked the cities of Zürich, Geneva and Bern respectively as second, eighth and ninth, making Switzerland the most successful country in the world. Zürich has been in first or second position for over ten consecutive years. As the Swiss comedian Dom Jolly put it, the country 'somehow enthuses one with a feeling everything is right with the world'.

It is a neat and tidy land where everything works as it should and where, by and large, its people feel strongly about their patrimony and the quality of their environment. Inexplicably there are some who find this dull; others see in the Swiss the perfect combination of northern efficiency and southern vitality. A love of nature is deeply embedded in the national psyche, and many take every opportunity to enjoy it on foot or by bike. Ostentatious displays of wealth are widely regarded as vulgar.

One of the country's greatest challenges is the increase in second homes, many of which lie empty for most of the year and contribute nothing to the life of the community or the economy. The phenomenon of 'cold beds' is sucking the life out of well-known resorts such as Verbier and smaller villages like Ernen in the Valais; estate agent Savills estimates that 35% of all properties in the canton are second homes. It became such a contentious issue that in March 2012 the Swiss people voted in a referendum for a limit of 20% of second homes in a town or village.

Switzerland is a paradise for those who prefer peace and solitude to noise and crowds, although the larger cities have plenty of opportunities for those in search of lively and cutting-edge nightlife. Even in high summer it is easy to escape the throng on summits of mountains like Pilatus and the Stanserhorn by walking for five minutes. Equally there are many relatively undiscovered places that would be major tourist attractions in countries less well endowed with natural beauty.

This book is a guide to exploring the country by public transport, describing every railway line and what there is to see from each station, as well as connecting journeys by steamer, postbus, funicular, cableway, bicycle and on foot. It does not attempt to provide a history of the country – though there is much history in it – nor to portray its character; books to be read before a visit, such as the Insight Guide to Switzerland, are suggested in *Appendix 4, Further Information*, page 372.

WHY CHOOSE PUBLIC TRANSPORT?

Three factors combine to make public transport the best way to travel round Switzerland: the country has much of Europe's finest alpine scenery, a good part of which thankfully cannot be reached by road; it has without question the best national public transport system in the world; and the Swiss Pass which entitles visitors to unlimited travel over most of the system, discounts on almost all the rest, and confers free admission to 450 museums, is very good value. This combination is enough to persuade many tourists to rely wholly upon public transport, but there are other compelling reasons for doing so.

Principal amongst the positive reasons is the pleasure of travelling by train in Switzerland. For those accustomed to public transport systems starved of investment, the Swiss Travel System will be something of a revelation: its every aspect seems to be designed and operated to a standard rather than a price. Trains are modern, clean and punctual. Larger stations offer facilities that smooth the traveller's path, such as luggage forwarding, cycle hire, money changing and a restaurant or café that is often used by locals because of its quality.

But what probably impresses visitors most is the way that Swiss public transport is planned to offer a seamless, integrated service. Trains connect with each other, buses meet and feed trains, and both are timed to complement a boat or funicular service. At each station, timetables give clear information about all local transport, walks are signposted from most stations and many stations offer cycling routes and bike hire.

Then there is the view from the window. Some suburban lines apart, it is hard to find a train journey that does not offer attractive scenery, and Switzerland has more than its fair share of the world's really spectacular train journeys. Although the best known are deservedly popular, there are some little-known journeys through equally fine landscapes to provide that sense of surprise which is part of the joy of travel.

TOURISM AND SUSTAINABLE TRANSPORT

Concern about the impact of tourism on environments has focused largely on developing countries, but there are equally strong if different reasons why the principles of sustainable tourism should be applied to developed countries. The impact of climate change is nowhere more evident than in the Alps, where glaciers are in steady retreat, forest trees show increasingly severe evidence of atmospheric pollution and people living in ski resorts on the margins of dependable snow grow more worried by the year. The Swiss Academy of Sciences reports that of the 91 glaciers being monitored (out of 1,800), 84 are in retreat, while the other seven are static. Europe's longest glacier at 23km, the Aletsch, has lost an average length of 50m a year over the last 30 years. A Swiss geomorphologist estimates that at this rate 80% of the surface of the glacier will be gone by 2100. Global warming is having a potentially catastrophic effect on Europe's permafrost: air temperature increases are being magnified fivefold underground. This will increase the instability of mountainsides and undermine the foundations of buildings at high altitude, including most of the skiing industry infrastructure.

The impact of vehicle pollution along Swiss transit corridors – turning entire valleys into 'traffic centres asphyxiated by pollution' as one Swiss writer put it – was the principal reason why the Swiss voted in favour of alpine base tunnels to carry lorries on trains and accelerate passenger train timings. But transport remains the fastest-growing source of carbon dioxide and some other greenhouse gases. As Anna Pavord wrote in a series of articles on ecotourism in the *Independent*, the first lesson is not to hire a car. Still worse is to drive your own car across Europe.

Green reasons aside, there are other disadvantages to using a car. Driving requires total concentration from the driver, especially on twisty mountain roads, so he or she will obtain little or no pleasure from the scenery. Unless you are experienced in driving on snow or ice, the roads in winter present a particular hazard. As travel insurance statistics show, traffic accidents are the major killer of travellers, whereas travelling by train is statistically safer than staying in your own home.

There is probably no other railway in the world that can boast such an environmentally friendly source of power. Not only is most of the electricity used by Swiss railways generated by water, but the technical sophistication of Swiss railway engineering is reflected in the high proportion of trains equipped with regenerative braking. This exploits the steep gradients of many Swiss railways to combine braking with electrical generation; traction motors are turned into dynamos to feed current back into the overhead lines while checking the speed of the train. As a rule of thumb, two descending trains provide enough power for one to climb the gradient.

Public transport in Switzerland remains good value, and, as one US writer put it, 'the word "excellent" doesn't begin to describe the Swiss rail and bus system'. For the sake of Switzerland, its people and its visitors, let us hope it remains worthy of such praise and that more and more visitors use it.

FEEDBACK REQUEST

At Bradt Travel Guides we're aware that guidebooks start to go out of date on the day they're published – and that you, our readers, are out there in the field doing research of your own. Any information regarding such changes, or relating to your experiences in Switzerland – good or bad – would be very gratefully received. Such feedback is invaluable when compiling further editions. Contact us on ☏ 01753 893444 or e info@bradtguides.com. We will forward emails to the author who may post 'one-off updates' on the Bradt website at www.bradtguides.com/guidebook-updates. You can also visit this website for updates to information in this guide. Alternatively you can add a review of the book to www.bradtguides.com or Amazon.

Part One

GENERAL INFORMATION

Location Central Europe
Neighbouring countries France, Italy, Germany, Liechtenstein, Austria
Size 41,285km^2
Climate Temperate, but varies with altitude
Status Democracy
Population 7,870,500
Capital Bern
Other main towns Zürich, Geneva, Basel
Life expectancy 79.4 years (men), 84.2 years (women)
Economy Modern market economy
GDP US$635.7 billion
Languages German is spoken in north, central and eastern Switzerland, French in the west, Italian in the south and Romansch in the southeast.
Religion Christian
Currency Swiss franc (SFr)
Exchange rate £1 = SFr1.49, US$1 = Sfr0.92, €1 = SFr1.21 (January 2013)
National airline Swiss
International telephone code +41
Time GMT+1
Electricity 220V, 50Hz
Weights and measures Metric, using a comma rather than a decimal point and denoting thousands by a full point rather than a comma (eg: 1,6kg = 1.6kg).
Flag White cross on red background
National anthem *Swiss Psalm*, officially confirmed in 1981 but first performed in 1843
National flower Edelweiss
Public holidays 1 August (National Day); many local holidays/festivals

1

Practical Information

For a first visit to any country there is a great temptation to try to see as much as possible in the time available. Even if it means that there is little time to savour the atmosphere of a place or explore anywhere in detail, this approach has much to commend it. If you don't expect to return to the country, then at least you will have seen as many different areas as time permits; if it is intended to be the first of a number of visits, a whistle-stop tour is a good way to decide which parts of the country appeal most and where you would like to spend more time on the next occasion.

Switzerland is not a large country, and the speed and frequency of main-line trains make it easy to traverse the whole country in a matter of hours – Geneva to St Gallen, or Basel to Lugano, for example, takes about four hours. Moreover, armed with a Swiss Pass, there is no additional cost for intensive use of the Swiss Travel System.

Ardent travellers excepted, however, most visitors prefer to be selective, or at least to pause for two or three nights at carefully chosen bases. Choices are obviously subjective affairs, but it is easy to explore regions like the Bernese Oberland or the Ticino from a single base.

WHEN TO VISIT

There is almost no time in the year when a visit to Switzerland is inadvisable. Even in the unpopular month of November, one can be lucky and have glorious sunshine – and benefit from low season prices. Much depends on the area and altitude. May in the mountains, for example, is often not a good time to visit: many of the major hotels, mountain cableways and funiculars will be closed because it is too late for skiing and too early for walking or spring flowers. June and even July are the best months to see the mass of colour on unsprayed mountain slopes.

It is wrong to think of Swiss alpine resorts in winter as being devoted solely to the needs of skiers: about 40% of winter visitors are non-skiers, though most participate in other outdoor activities such as hiking, snowshoe trekking, paragliding or sledging.

Skiing at the higher resorts can be good right into April, and even into June at Saas Fee and Zermatt. Rainfall in spring and autumn is generally higher than during the winter or summer, but rain often serves to clear the air, producing a clarity that is rare in summer when haze can obstruct views. The Jura region, in particular, is noted for its high spring rainfall. Although some hotels close for a couple of months in late September or October, the autumn can be a delightful time: the summer crowds are gone, the colours of the trees are glorious and the views can be much clearer than during the summer. Most mountain cable cars and chairlifts close at the end of October to allow maintenance before the winter sports season begins.

The mountain ranges that criss-cross the country often act as a dividing line between two very different sets of weather conditions: the passage of the Gotthard

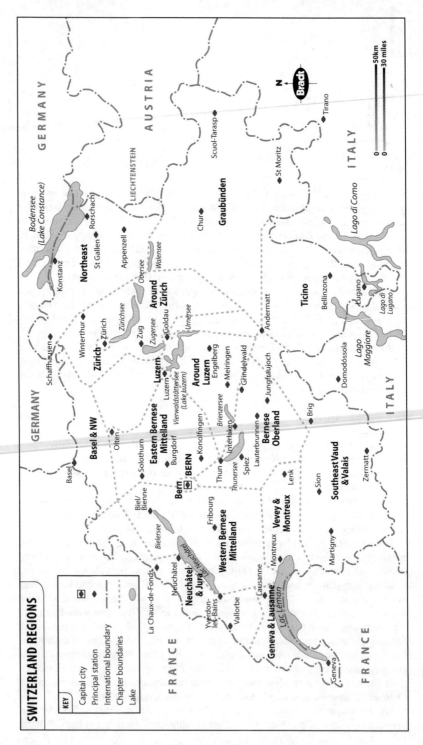

SWITZERLAND REGIONS

KEY

⊡ Capital city
◆ Principal station
— · — International boundary
----- Chapter boundaries
Lake

GERMANY

AUSTRIA

LIECHTENSTEIN

ITALY

FRANCE

N

Bradt

50km
30 miles
0
0

*Bodensee
(Lake Constance)*

Konstanz

Northeast

Rorschach
St Gallen
Appenzell

Obersee
Walensee

Schaffhausen

Winterthur

Zürich
Zürich

Zürichsee

Zug
Zugersee

**Around
Zürich**
Goldau
Urnersee

Graubünden

Chur

Scuol-Tarasp

Tirano

St Moritz

Andermatt

Ticino

Bellinzona

Lago di Como

*Lago di
Lugano*
Lugano

*Lago
Maggiore*

Domodóssola

ITALY

Basel & NW

Olten

Basel

Solothurn

**Eastern Bernese
Mittelland**

Burgdorf

Konolfingen

BERN
Bern ⊡

Luzern
Luzern
*Vierwaldstättersee
(Lake Luzern)*

**Around
Luzern**
Engelberg
Meiringen
Grindelwald
Jungfraujoch

Brienzersee

Interlaken

Lauterbrunnen

**Bernese
Oberland**

Brig

Thun
Spiez
Thunersee

Lenk

Sion

**Southeast Vaud
& Valais**

Zermatt

Biel/
Bienne

Bielersee

Fribourg

**Western Bernese
Mittelland**

La Chaux-de-Fonds

Neuchâtel

**Neuchâtel
& Jura**

Yverdon-
les-Bains

Vallorbe

Lac Neuchâtel

**Vevey &
Montreux**

Montreux

Martigny

Lausanne

Geneva & Lausanne

Lac Léman

Geneva

FRANCE

GERMANY

Tunnel can mark a transition from grey skies to bright sunshine. South of the Alps, the number of hours of sunshine is higher and precipitation lower, so those wanting a warm holiday at the margins of the summer may want to consider a few days in Ticino.

HIGHLIGHTS

In terms of Switzerland's great railway journeys, it is easy to recommend something of a hierarchy. The popularity of the Glacier Express between Zermatt and St Moritz is wholly deserved, and this is probably *the* journey not to be missed. Other outstanding and well-known scenic journeys are:

- Montreux–Zweisimmen
- Luzern–Interlaken
- Interlaken–Jungfraujoch
- St Moritz–Tirano
- Locarno–Domodóssola

But there is a host of other lines, some used by hardly anyone except local people, that would warrant inclusion in a pantheon of great railway journeys for most other countries:

- St Gallen–Gais–Altstätten
- Gais–Appenzell–Wasserauen
- Luzern–Bern
- Luzern–Engelberg
- Luzern–Andermatt–Lugano
- St Moritz–Scuol-Tarasp
- Martigny–Vallorcine
- Bex–Villars
- Aigle–Les Diablerets
- Yverdon-les-Bains–Ste-Croix
- Neuchâtel–Buttes
- La Chaux-de-Fonds–Glovelier

That said, there are very few lines in Switzerland that are actually dull, blessed as the country is with a profusion of picturesque landscapes.

TOURIST INFORMATION

The principal source of information in the UK is **Switzerland Tourism** (*Swiss Centre, 30 Bedford St, London WC2E 9ED;* \ *0800 100 200 30;* e *info.uk@myswitzerland. com; www.myswitzerland.com*) and, at the same address, the **Swiss Travel Centre** (\ *020 7420 4934;* e *sales@stc.co.uk; www.stc.co.uk*).

Contact details for other Switzerland Tourism offices around the world are given on page 368. More specialised information can be obtained from the various regional tourist offices:

Z Basel Tourism Aeschenvorstadt 36, Basel CH-4010; \ 061 268 68 68; e info@basel.com; www. basel.com

Z Bernese Oberland Tourism Jungfraustrasse 38, Interlaken CH-380; \ 033 823 03 03; e info@ berneroberland.ch; www.berneroberland.ch

Z Canton Vaud Avenue d'Ouchy 60, Lausanne CH-1000; ☏ 021 613 26 26; e info@lake-geneva-region.ch; www.lake-geneva-region.ch

Z Central Switzerland/Vierwaldstättersee Tourismus Bahnhofplatz 4, Stans CH-6371; ☏ 041 610 88 33; e info@lakeluzern.ch; www.lakeluzern.ch

Z Eastern Switzerland Fürstenlandstrasse 53, St Gallen CH-9000; ☏ 071 274 99 00; e info@ostschweiz.ch; www.ostschweiz.ch

Z Geneva Tourism Rue du Mont Blanc 18, Case postale 1602, Geneva 1 CH-1211; ☏ 022 909 70 70; e info@geneve-tourisme.ch; www.geneve-tourisme.ch

Z Graubünden Holiday Alexanderstrasse 24, Chur CH-7001; ☏ 081 254 24 24; e contact@graubuenden.ch; www.graubuenden.ch

Z Jura Tourism Pl du 23 Juin 6, Sagnelégier CH-2350; ☏ 032 420 47 74; e administration@juratourisme.ch; www.juratourisme.ch

Z Office du tourisme du Jura bernois Av de la Gare 9, Moutier CH-2740; ☏ 032 493 53 43; e info@jurabernois.ch; www.jurabernois.ch

Z Pays de Fribourg Le Restoroute 174, Avry-le-Pont CH-1644; ☏ 026 915 92 92; e information@fribourgregion.ch; www.fribourgregion.ch

Z Schweizer Mittelland Tourism c/o Bernese Tourism, Laupenstrasse 20, Bern CH-3001; ☏ 031 328 12 28; e info@smit.ch; www.smit.ch

Z Ticino Tourism Via Lugano 12, Postfach 1441, Bellinzona CH-6501; ☏ 091 825 70 56; e info@ticino.ch; www.ticino.ch

Z Tourisme Neuchâtelois – Littoral Hôtel des Postes, Case Postale 1374, Neuchâtel CH-2001; ☏ 032 889 68 90; e info@ne.ch; www.neuchateltourisme.ch

Z Valais Tourism Rue Pré-Fleuri 6, Case Postale 1469, Sion CH-1951; ☏ 027 327 35 70; e info@valais.ch; www.valaistourism.ch

Z Zürich Tourism Bahnhofbrücke 1, Zürich CH-8023; ☏ 041 215 40 00; e information@zuerich.com; www.zuerich.com

RED TAPE

Tourist visits of less than 90 days by nationals of the EU, Australia, Canada, New Zealand and the US do not require a visa.

EMBASSIES AND CONSULATES

Australia ☏ 022 799 91 00
Austria ☏ 031 356 52 52
Belgium ☏ 031 350 01 50
Brazil ☏ 031 371 85 15
Canada ☏ 031 357 32 00
China ☏ 031 352 73 33
Denmark ☏ 031 350 54 54
Finland ☏ 031 351 41 00
France ☏ 031 359 21 11
Germany ☏ 031 359 41 11
Great Britain ☏ 031 359 77 00
Hungary ☏ 031 352 85 72
India ☏ 031 350 11 30
Ireland ☏ 031 352 14 42
Israel ☏ 031 356 35 00

Italy ☏ 031 350 07 77
Japan ☏ 031 300 22 22
Korea (South) ☏ 031 356 24 44
Luxembourg ☏ 031 311 47 32
Netherlands ☏ 031 350 87 00
New Zealand ☏ 022 929 03 50
Norway ☏ 031 310 55 55
Poland ☏ 031 352 04 52
Portugal ☏ 031 351 17 73
Russia ☏ 031 352 05 66
South Africa ☏ 031 350 13 13
Spain ☏ 031 350 52 52
Sweden ☏ 031 328 70 00
USA ☏ 031 357 70 11

GETTING THERE AND AWAY

BY RAIL The Channel Tunnel and Eurostar services to Lille, Paris Gare du Nord and Brussels have transformed the rail map of Europe, opening up new possibilities for practical day journeys to Switzerland. TGV services to Switzerland are operated by Lyria, a Swiss and French railways joint venture, which began in June 2007. Trains leave from Gare de Lyon, reached from Gare du Nord by taking RER Line D for just two stops (direction Melun/Malesherbes). The opening of the high-speed LGV Rhine/Rhone in December 2011 reduced journey times between Paris and Basel/Zürich by half an hour. Journey time from the French capital to Basel is 3 hours, to Zürich is 4 hours, Geneva in 3¼ hours, Lausanne in under 4 hours and Bern in 4½ hours. Passengers travelling first class on Lyria trains are given light meals and drinks at no extra charge.

For those combining a visit to Switzerland with other countries, the range of trans-European trains is impressive. The following principal stations in Switzerland are linked by direct services with the cities that follow:

- **Basel** Amsterdam, Berlin (ICE), Bologna, Bonn, Brussels, Cologne, Dortmund, Dresden, Düsseldorf, Frankfurt (ICE), Hamburg (ICE), Hanover, Leipzig, Luxembourg, Milan, Moscow, Paris (TGV), Prague, Rome, Strasbourg (TGV), Venice, Warsaw
- **Bern** Amsterdam, Barcelona, Berlin (ICE), Bologna, Cologne, Florence, Frankfurt, Hamburg, Hanover, Milan, Paris (TGV), Rome
- **Geneva** Barcelona, Bologna, Grenoble, Lyon (TGV), Marseille (TGV), Milan, Montpellier (TGV), Nice (TGV), Paris (TGV), Valence, Venice
- **Interlaken** Berlin (ICE), Frankfurt (ICE)
- **Lausanne** Barcelona, Bologna, Milan, Paris (TGV), Venice
- **Zürich** Amsterdam, Barcelona, Belgrade, Brussels, Budapest, Dresden, Frankfurt (ICE), Hamburg (ICE), Innsbruck, Koblenz, Leipzig, Ljubljana, Milan, Munich, Paris (TGV), Prague, Salzburg, Strasbourg, Stuttgart, Vienna, Zagreb

Some of these are overnight trains operated by **City Night Line** (*www.citynightline. ch*) with very well-appointed sleeping cars. First-class passengers have en-suite shower and WC.

High-speed rail links with France
TGVs (French high-speed trains) operate daily return trains between Paris and Basel (five trains), Bern (one train), Zürich (six), Geneva (seven) and Lausanne (four). There are one or two fewer departures at weekends.

High-speed rail links with Italy
Rail links with Italy have been transformed by the opening in 2007 of the Lötschberg Base Tunnel, cutting half an hour off the times between Basel/Bern, the Valais at Brig, and Milan. The appalling unreliability of the Pendolino tilting trains has led to the decision to replace the entire fleet, but it will be some years before new trains are in service. In the meantime some trains have reverted to locomotive-hauled coaching stock.

European rail passes
For those planning extensive rail travel in countries neighbouring Switzerland, it may be sensible to think of a rail pass for Europe. An invaluable guide to the pros and cons of the various passes is available at www. seat61.com.

InterRail/InterRail 26+
Originally devised as a pass only for young people up to 26 years old, the InterRail pass is now available to all, priced on a band basis. It allows unlimited travel on second-class national rail services for under-26s and either first- or second-class travel for those over 26. The pass brings with it discounts

on certain shipping services and on some privately owned railways, particularly in Switzerland, and free admission to various transport museums. The InterRail Global Pass covers all participating countries (currently 30) for any five days in ten, ten days in 22 (a FlexiPass), or 15 or 22 days or one month of consecutive use. The InterRail One Country Pass (available for 27 countries) offers three, four, six or eight days of travel within a month.

A valid passport and proof of residence in Europe for at least six months are required to purchase a pass, but the country of residence is excluded from the pass. For details, see www.interrailnet.com.

The price bands, in descending order of cost, are as follows:

1 France, Germany, Great Britain (excluding Northern Ireland)
2 Austria, Benelux (Belgium, Luxembourg, the Netherlands), Italy, Norway, Spain (national railway only), Sweden
3 Denmark, Finland, Greece Plus (including ferries to Italy), Ireland Switzerland
4 Croatia, Czech Republic, Greece, Hungary, Poland, Portugal, Romania, Slovakia, Slovenia
5 Bulgaria, FYR Macedonia, Serbia, Turkey

Supplements for travel on many of the fastest train services are required, and seat, couchette and sleeper reservations are extra.

Eurail Pass The range of Eurail passes is designed for those who have been resident outside Europe for at least six months prior to the validity of the pass. Generally passes should be bought before you leave the country of residence, but they can be purchased from Rail Europe (see page 369). They offer unlimited travel over the national railways of 23 European countries. The countries covered are: Austria (including Liechtenstein), Belgium, Bulgaria, Croatia, Czech Republic, Denmark, Finland, France (including Monaco), Germany, Greece, Hungary, Ireland, Italy, Luxembourg, the Netherlands, Norway, Portugal, Romania, Slovakia, Slovenia, Spain, Sweden and Switzerland. The Eurail Global Pass offers continuous travel over 15 or 21 days, one, two or three months. For more flexible use, there are three other types of Eurail Pass.

The Eurail Select Pass covers three, four or five countries and allows five to ten days of travel within a two-month period. The Eurail Regional Pass covers two bordering countries in 24 combinations and allows four to ten days of travel within two months. Finally, the One Country Pass is valid for one month and the number of days' travel varies from one country to another. With each of the flexible passes, you choose the start date and the days on which you wish to use the pass.

Special youth rates for those under 26 are available for Eurail passes in second class only, and there are also special rates for children aged four to 11; proof of age and a passport are required when purchasing tickets (*www.eurail.com/eurail-passes*).

Senior discounts Most train operators offer discounts to those over 60. For example, the SNCF Senior Card entitles you to 50% off rail tickets for many long-distance and local train services, and Lyria offers discounts on its services from Paris to Lausanne, Basel, Zürich and Geneva.

Useful addresses

⚊ **Eurostar** ☏ 08432 186 186 (UK), +44 123 361 7575 (from outside UK); www.eurostar.com

⚊ **European Rail Ltd** Unit 25, Tileyard Studios, Tileyard Rd, London N7 9AH; ☏ 020 7619 1083;

e sales@europeanrail.com; www.europeanrail.
co.uk (for holidays), www.europeanrail.com (for
tickets). Booking service for rail tickets throughout
Europe, much of the former USSR & Yugoslavia but
not Albania.

☸ Rail Europe Ltd 193 Piccadilly, London W1J
9EU; ☏0844 848 4078; www.raileurope.co.uk.
Also sells rail passes & tickets to 5,000 European
stations.

☸ German Railways (DB) PO Box 687A,
Surbiton, Surrey KT6 6UB; ☏08718 808066;
e sales@bahn.co.uk; www.bahn.co.uk

☸ Railbookers 14 Bonhill St, London EC2A 4BX;
☏020 3327 0800; e info@railbookers.com; www.
railbookers.com. Individual holiday itineraries.

☸ Swiss Railways (SBB) Switzerland Travel
Centre, 30 Bedford St, London WC2E 9ED; ☏020
7420 4934; e sales@stc.co.uk; www.stc.co.uk

See also the travel companies listed on page 369.

BY AIR Four Swiss airports receive flights from the British Isles: Basel, Bern,
Geneva and Zürich. The easiest connections between air terminal and railway
station are at Zürich and Geneva where the two facilities are adjacent. Both have
frequent train services to many parts of Switzerland. Currently there are flights to:

- **Basel** from: Edinburgh, London City, London Gatwick, London Heathrow and
  Manchester
- **Bern** from: London City
- **Geneva** from: Belfast, Birmingham, Bournemouth, Bristol, Cardiff, Cork,
  Dublin, East Midlands, Edinburgh, Glasgow, Leeds Bradford, Liverpool,
  London City, London Gatwick, London Heathrow, London Luton, London
  Stansted, Manchester, Newcastle, Southampton and Southend
- **Zürich** from: Birmingham, Bristol, Cardiff, Dublin, Edinburgh, Guernsey,
  Inverness, Jersey, London City, London Gatwick, London Heathrow, London
  Luton, Manchester and Shannon

✈ British Airways 0844 493 0787;
www.ba.com
✈ Easyjet www.easyjet.com

✈ SkyWork ☏0871 977 6088; www.flyskywork.
com (London City–Bern only)
✈ Swiss ☏0845 601 0956; www.swiss.com/uk

North America airports served by Swiss:

Atlanta, Boston, Calgary, Chicago, Cincinnati, Cleveland, Dallas/Fort Worth,
Denver, Detroit, Fort Lauderdale, Greensboro, Halifax, Honolulu, Las Vegas, Los
Angeles, Miami, Minneapolis/St Paul, Montréal, New York/Newark, Orlando,
Ottawa, Phoenix/Scottsdale, Pittsburgh, Portland, Québec, Salt Lake City, San
Diego, San Francisco, Seattle/Tacoma, Tampa/St Petersburg, Toronto, Vancouver,
Washington.

The toll-free reservation number for Swiss in the United States and Canada, unless
otherwise stated, is ☏877 359 7947.

MAPS

For planning a holiday based on use of the Swiss Travel System (see *Chapter
2*, page 15), Kümmerly + Frey's map of the railway and postbus networks is
invaluable. The most detailed maps of the country are produced by the Swiss
equivalent of Britain's Ordnance Survey, the Federal Office of Topography,
and are to 1:25,000 scale. Most visitors will find the 1:50,000 series adequately

detailed, and the Office also produces specialised maps showing hiking routes (see *Chapter 4*, page 29), ski routes, cultural heritage, museums and castles. The Federal Office of Topography symbols and signs are explained in a separate free A5 leaflet, *Conventional Signs*.

These maps can be obtained from **Stanfords** (*12–14 Long Acre, Covent Garden, London WC2E 9LP; mail order service* \ *020 7836 1321;* e *sales@stanfords.co.uk; www.stanfords.co.uk*).

HEALTH

Since there is no state health service in Switzerland, nor reciprocal agreements for free treatment with other countries, it is imperative that you take out health insurance, especially if you are taking part in sports or mountain walking.

Switzerland has very high standards of hygiene so neither food nor tap water should pose any hazard, but it is not advisable to drink from mountain streams, however clear they may look.

In parts of the country, the mosquitoes can gather in rather dense clouds during the summer. Apply a DEET-based product to prevent being bitten and consider a hat with a net to keep them away from your nose and eyes.

DISABLED TRAVELLERS

Switzerland caters well for disabled travellers, though difficulties do arise from the low platform levels common throughout much of the Continent. Larger stations have hoists that will elevate a wheelchair to the level of the coach floor, and wheelchairs are available at a smaller number. There is a large and exemplary section in English on the Swiss Federal Railways website (*www.sbb.ch*) devoted to helping passengers with disabilities. Click on 'Stations & Services'.

The **Royal Association for Disability & Rehabilitation** (*Unit 12, 12 City Forum, 250 City Road, London EC1V 8AF;* \ *020 7250 3222*) and Switzerland Tourism can provide information. Hotels of three stars and above can be expected to have lifts.

Provision for disabled access inevitably varies widely on mountain cableways and railways. Chairlifts and gondola lifts, which are usually boarded while in continuous motion, are obviously difficult if not impossible, but modern or rebuilt cable cars can sometimes accept wheelchairs.

ELECTRICITY

Electricity in Switzerland is 220V, 50Hz. Most appliances set for 240V will operate on 220V, but alter the setting if possible.

MONEY

Banks are open Monday to Friday 08.30–16.30 as a rule. The currency is the Swiss franc (SFr). Notes are available in denominations of SFr10, 20, 50, 100, 200 and 1,000. Currency can be changed at airports and large stations daily between 08.30 and 22.00. Travellers' cheques may be cashed at banks and large hotels (albeit at an inferior rate). Although all major travellers' cheques are acceptable, the 'instant replacement' policy of American Express, Thomas Cook or Visa may be an advantage. Keep the numbers of your travellers' cheques in a separate wallet.

BUDGETING

Switzerland's strong currency can make it an expensive country to visit, but there are still some remarkably good value accommodation offers, both online and through travel agents. There are ways to save money:

- Although the Swiss Pass is discussed in *Chapter 2* (see page 16), it is worth emphasising here that it represents excellent value for money if you are on a touring holiday. There are few places you cannot reach with it, and it also confers free admission to over 450 museums.
- If you can, avoid the busiest months – usually July and August in summer and the school holidays in winter – when prices of accommodation are highest.
- Eating in a mountain restaurant, perhaps on an open terrace overlooking a panorama of surrounding peaks, is part of the Swiss experience, but the prices can be high for the very good reason that it costs a lot to bring in the provisions. Some mountain restaurants even have to heat the pipes carrying away waste water. If you are on a tight budget, it is worth buying the ingredients for a picnic at a grocery before departure.
- Hotels outside the main resorts and towns are often considerably cheaper than those near the centre, and with a Swiss Pass there is no additional cost in travelling in from an outlying station. Many resorts have created 'guest cards' which are issued to hotel guests and which entitle holders to free use of public transport and discounts at a wide range of shops and services.
- Renting an apartment or chalet can also save money, especially if it is at a discounted rate (see *Accommodation*, below).

ACCOMMODATION

Swiss hotels reflect the high standards which characterise most aspects of Swiss public services. Whether a five-star hotel or a simple country inn, standards seldom disappoint. Swiss hotels are given the customary ranking of up to five stars, but a small number of hotels are deemed to have 'unique' qualities that make conventional star ranking inappropriate. Equally, inns or small hotels without even a single star should not be considered in any way sub-standard; they will have fewer facilities and simpler furnishings, but may well have a homely quality that will appeal to anyone whose holiday won't be ruined by the absence of a trouser press.

For those in search of character and atmosphere, the number of large, grand hotels put up for the huge influx of Victorian visitors has diminished steadily since World War I; hotels like the Schreiber on Mount Rigi, the Axenfels in Morschach and the Bristol in Lugano have succumbed to a sea-change in tourist requirements. Nonetheless there are still some magnificent hotels redolent of the days when the Gotthard Express was steam-hauled and guests often stayed for months.

A selection of hotels and restaurants near stations is to be found throughout the book. An '(H)' after the hotel name indicates that its building has historic interest or character. An association called **Swiss Historic Hotels** (*Gurtenweg 17, CH-3074 Muri b. Bern;* \ *+41 31 302 32 26; www.swiss-historic-hotels.com*) was formed in 2004 to promote historic hotels. Several books devoted to hotels and inns are listed in *Appendix 4* (page 372), and the Swiss Hotels Association publishes the annual *Swiss Hotel Guide*, with illustrations of most of the establishments listed.

For those wanting a sense of place, **Typically Swiss Hotels** (accessed through www.MySwitzerland.com) offers over 250 hotels that provide exactly that. They can be old or modern buildings, in a city or on a mountain, but they all have qualities that will delight visitors in search of the distinctive: architecture that reflects the region; interior design that says 'Swiss', whether traditional or modern; they are not part of a chain; they are in attractive locations; the service is personal and warm as well as competent; and regional specialities form at least 30% of the menu, and Swiss wines 20% of the wine list.

There are huge differentials in the highest and lowest prices charged by hotels within the same star ranking, partly reflecting the difference between high and low season rates and between 'fashionable' resorts and equally attractive, but less pretentious, resorts. A service charge of 15% is added to hotel, restaurant and bar bills by law so tipping is neither expected nor desirable.

The largest agency offering apartments or chalets for rent is **Interhome** (*Morie St Studios, Wandsworth Town, 5 Morie St, London SW18 1SL;* \ *020 8877 6370; www. interhome.co.uk*), with over 4,000 properties available throughout Switzerland. Minimum rental periods are three nights in low season, seven nights in high season. The free brochure describes and illustrates all properties on offer. If you are going to Switzerland at short notice, it is worth contacting Interhome on a Saturday when a sale of rentals at up to one-third discount is held for the week commencing the following Saturday; this can produce some real bargains out of season. Interhome also represents some Swiss hotels.

Bed and breakfast is becoming increasingly popular. The principal sources of information are the annual publication and website of **Bed and Breakfast Switzerland**, which give details of over 1,000 establishments (e *english@bnb. ch; www.bnb.ch*). Details of holidays on over 210 Swiss farms are available from **Bauernhof Ferien**, an organisation that supports farming enterprises (e *info@ bauernhof-ferien.ch; www.agrotourismus.ch or www.bauernhof-ferien.ch*).

Youth hostel accommodation is available to visitors up to 25 years of age, but older people are accepted if room is available. A membership card of the national organisation in the visitor's country of residence must be shown, and intending visitors should check with youth hostels just as they would for a hotel. A list of the 52 Swiss youth hostels is available at www.youthhostel.ch; bookings can also be made on \ 044 360 14 14.

CAR-FREE RESORTS
Switzerland has nine car-free resorts that have formed the Society for Car-free Swiss Holiday Resorts. Some have made a virtue out of necessity, turning the near impossibility of road access into an asset, but the environmental conscience of many Swiss makes the absence of cars more than simply a cause of clean air and safety for children. The nine resorts are Bettmeralp, Braunwald, Mürren, Riederalp, Rigi-Kaltbad, Saas Fee, Stoos, Wengen and Zermatt.

Zermatt is the largest of these resorts and exceptional in that road access could have been feasible; however, local people felt that the quality of life and character of the place would have been ruined by the work necessary to accommodate cars. As the road up the valley from St Niklaus was gradually enlarged, a referendum was taken in Zermatt to determine whether the last stage from Täsch into Zermatt should be widened; 92% voted against it. Consequently the decision was taken to operate a rail shuttle service from Täsch. Most freight to Zermatt also travels by train, and movement within Zermatt is largely by electric vehicles, the only exceptions being rubbish collection, ambulances and snowploughs. Even police vehicles are electric.

Towards the arrival time of trains, the square outside the station is lined with small electric vehicles, slightly smaller than British milkfloats, which each serve a particular hotel. The drivers wear identifying caps, and load the luggage on to the back platform while passengers seat themselves in the cab. The two five-star hotels have horse-drawn buses or open carriages, which are lavishly decorated with flowers for newly married couples.

The measures taken in the other resorts to carry luggage and fulfil other services are similar but smaller in scale.

Information about the resorts can be found on the website of the Association of Car-free Resorts (*www.auto-frei.ch*).

DRINKING

It is illegal to drink alcohol under the age of 16. Those aged 16–18 may drink beer, cider or wine.

SHOPPING

Hours are usually 09.00–12.15, 13.30–18.00 on weekdays; 08.30–16.00 on Saturdays. Monday morning is often a half day.

ARTS AND ENTERTAINMENT

ART GALLERIES Art collections of international repute may be found in Baden, Basel, Bern, Lugano, Winterthur and Zürich. Collections of largely Swiss interest or lesser European works are in Geneva, Lausanne, Locarno and Solothurn.

CASTLES The country has numerous castles. Amongst the finest that still have military pretensions are Aigle, Bellinzona, Burgdorf, Chillon, Grandson, Hagenwil, La Sarraz, Lenzburg, Lucens, Morges, Munot (Schaffhausen), Nyon, Oron, Porrentruy, Sion, Soyhières and Thun.

COUNTRY MANSIONS Among the most attractive houses open to visitors are some that were once castles, but have been rebuilt in such a way that they retain only symbols of their defensive origins: Bottmingen, Brig, Bubikon, Chur, Colombier, Coppet, Gruyères, Hallwil, Jegenstorf, Kyburg, Landshut, Oberhofen, Spiez, Tarasp and Werdenberg.

MUSEUMS The Swiss Pass confers free entry to over 400 museums. An inferior alternative is to buy a Museum Pass (*www.museumspass.com*), which gives free admission to over 230 museums, castles and parks in Switzerland, Germany and France for one year. The cost is discounted for students, apprentices, unemployed or disabled persons, teachers and friends of the museums. A single adult pass includes five children under 18.

ARCHITECTURE There is so much good vernacular and ecclesiastical architecture in Switzerland that it is invidious to select a few places for special mention. Some indication of the interest of a town or village is inevitably reflected by the length given to it in this book. Many tourist offices organise guided walks taking in the best buildings and sometimes visiting some not normally open to visitors.

Switzerland boasts the work of some of Europe's leading modern architects as well as home-grown figures such as Mario Botta, Jacques Herzog, Pierre de Meuron and Peter Zumthor. Among recent outstanding buildings are Renzo Piano's Zentrum

Paul Klee in Bern, Jean Nouvel's KKL Cultural and Convention Centre in Luzern, Mario Botta's spa at the Tschuggen Grand Hotel in Arosa, Norman Foster's Chesa Futura in St Moritz (with Kuchel Architects) and Santiago Calatrava's Stadelhofen station in Zürich.

LANGUAGE

Switzerland has four national languages – French, German, Italian and Romansch – which influences both cultural and culinary traditions. Swiss German or Schwyzerdütsch is spoken by about two-thirds of the population, in the north and central regions. Within this are dialects that can be hard to understand for speakers of High German, or Hochdeutsch, which is the written language. French is the language of cantons Geneva, Vaud, Neuchâtel and Jura and parts of Bern, and the Valais. Italian is spoken in Ticino and in the Val Poschiavo enclave of Graubünden, while Romansch is confined to the country's largest canton, Graubünden. Romansch is a Rhaeto-Romance language derived from the Vulgar Latin spoken by the Roman-era occupiers of the region. Most people in the tourism industry speak at least some English.

MEDIA AND COMMUNICATIONS

POST OFFICES Core hours are usually Monday to Friday 07.30–noon and 13.45–18.30; Saturday 08.00–11.00. Mail sent 'Poste restante' to a post office is held for 30 days and surrendered on production of a passport.

TELEPHONES Some large post offices have telephone sections where you pay for a call after making it. Calls made from hotel rooms are likely to be more expensive, since the hotel determines the rate. Lower-rate calls can be made between 17.00 and 07.00.

Emergency numbers

Police ✆117
Fire brigade ✆118
Ambulance ✆144

On-duty doctors ✆111
Mountain rescue ✆1415

English-speaking information line Anglo-Phone is a 24-hour English-speaking information line. Dial ✆ 157 5014 from anywhere in Switzerland and someone will even be able to provide advice on finding an English-speaking babysitter, as well as events, excursions and activities.

2

The Swiss Travel System

Switzerland has the densest network of public transport in the world. For two-thirds of Swiss people it is less than five minutes' walk from their homes to the nearest public transport; 97.5% live less than a kilometre away. Besides just over 5,000km (3,125 miles) of state- and privately owned railways, there are 812 postal-coach routes operated by 2,145 vehicles and over 600 funiculars, cable cars, rack railways and chairlifts. With local transport and steamer services, this amounts to a public transport network of about 20,500km (12,812 miles).

Only Japanese railways are used more frequently per person than those in Switzerland, but the Swiss on average travel more kilometres by train than any other nation. With at least an hourly service on most Swiss routes, and half-hourly on the busiest routes, a long wait is a rare occurrence.

Most of the standard-gauge network is operated by Swiss Federal Railways, which is abbreviated on coach sides to SBB, CFF or FFS, standing for Schweizerische Bundesbahnen, Chemins de Fer Fédéraux Suisses or Ferrovie Federali Svizzere in the three main languages of the Swiss Confederation. The second major operator is the Bern-Lötschberg-Simplon (BLS) railway. On top of this, there are over 50 private railway companies, most of which operate narrow-gauge railways.

Many countries have a good public transport infrastructure, but all too often multiple ownership militates against the evolution of an integrated, complementary network within and between different modes of transport. Switzerland not only has the finest public transport infrastructure in the world, it also has the most integrated, making it fully deserving of the term 'system'. Despite multiple ownership, trains, buses, steamers, funiculars and cable railways are carefully timetabled to connect with admirable precision.

As one would expect of the Swiss, timekeeping is usually exemplary: if a train is a few minutes late, it causes palpable concern among waiting passengers. This dependability, the frequency of services (except on the remoter postal-bus routes) and the ease of connections makes public transport a pleasure to use and the most stress-free way to travel.

GENERAL ADVICE

The best starting point for detailed advice on the facilities described in this chapter is the excellent **SBB** website (*www.sbb.ch*). Click on the sitemap for quick access to the information required. The offices of Switzerland Tourism/Swiss Travel Centres (see page 5 for London and *Appendix 2*, page 368) are able to provide further information as well as selling passes and tickets. They can also make reservations for trains and postbuses where necessary, including dining cars (Rail-and-Dine).

There is a SFr5 charge for dining reservations in the form of a voucher, but this sum is deducted from the bill.

Railway and postbus timetables are available online, but for those wanting the easier accessibility of paper, they can be obtained from **European Rail Timetables** (*39 Kilton Glade, Worksop, Nottinghamshire S81 0PX;* ✆ *01909 485855;* e *ghertmpp@ hotmail.com*).

TRAINS

RAIL CARDS AND PASSES A range of passes has been created to suit the travel requirements of most visitors. These not only make use of the system much easier; they also represent excellent value.

The **Swiss Pass** entitles the holder to unlimited travel for four, eight, 15 or 22 days or one month on more than 16,000km (10,000 miles) of railway, boat and

---

THE TRAIN TIMETABLE

The Swiss train timetable, known as the Kursbuch (see sample opposite), is a model of clarity. Each service is given a three-digit number; these numbers are given alongside the headings for the route descriptions throughout this book. They also appear alongside the synoptic map at the beginning of the timetable and alongside the route on the Kümmerly + Frey railway map.

At the beginning of the timetable is a list of all places served by any form of public transport. To the right of each place name, **bold three-digit numerals** (eg: 300) refer to train services, numbers like 31.021 to connecting bus services, four-digit numbers beginning with 2 to cableways or 3 to steamer services. These services are listed separately at the end of the train section in the Kursbuch.

The **bold arrows** beneath the number of the timetable tell you in which direction to turn the page(s) to find the times of services in the opposite direction.

If the operation is seasonal (as for many cableways), the dates are given. Times given alongside stations are departure times unless a **circle** precedes the time, in which case it is the arrival time.

A **number** beside a station name indicates the table number of the main connecting service. A **numeral in a box** beside a station name indicates how many minutes you should allow to change trains.

At the head of the column of times is the train number; this number is used on the boards that indicate the location of carriages on the train. Fast trains are in bold type; regional (stopping) trains are in normal type.

A **dotted vertical line** to the right of the service indicates that a supplementary charge is made (a rare stipulation). A wavy line to the left means that the train does not run every day, so a careful check should be made.

A **small 'x'** beside a station name means that it is a request stop, at which passengers have either to tell the guard that they wish to alight or, if they are at the station, to inform the driver that they wish to board the train by pressing a button on the platform (see page 20).

The timetable is issued once a year in early December and may be purchased from railway stations and offices of Switzerland Tourism. Free pocket timetables for individual lines are available from Swiss stations.

256 Palézieux–Châtel-St-Denis–Bulle–Gruyères–**Montbovon** ⑳

		553	X614	710	814		853	1010	1053		1210	1214	1253
Lausanne		553	X614	710	814		853	1010	1053		1210	1214	1253
Palézieux	o	615	X632	725	838		914	1025	1114		1225	1238	1314

		542	544	546	548	550	552	554	556	558	562	566	568	572
Palézieux	x				X618	X654	736	843	936	1030	1136	1228	(A)1257	1336
Granges (Veveyse)	x				{620	{656	738	845	938	1032	1138	1230	{1259	1338
Bossonnens				x	{622	{658	740	847	940	1034	1140	1232	{1302	1340
Tatroz	x				{623	{659	742	848	941	1035	1141	1233	{1303	1341
Remaufens	x				{624	701	744	850	943	1037	1143	1235	{1305	1343
Au Moulin	x				{626	703	746	852	945	1039	1145	1237	{1307	1345
Châtel-St-Denis	o				X629	705	749	854	947	1041	1147	1238	(A)1311	1347
Châtel-St-Denis			X605			{711	754	856	950	1044	1150		(A)1249	1350
Prayoud	x		{608			{715	757	859	953	1047	1153		{1252	1353
Semsales			x{612			{719	801	903	957	1051	1157		{1256	1357
La Verrerie			x{615			{722	803	905	1000	1053	1159		{1300	1400
Le Crêt	x		{618			{725	806	908	1002	1056	1202		{1302	1402
Les Ponts	x		{620			{729	809	911	1005	1059	1205		{1305	1405
Vaulruz-Sud	x		{622			{731	810	912	1006	1100	1206		{1308	1406
Les Colombettes	x		{624			{733	812	914	1008	1102	1208		{1310	1408
Vuadens-Sud			{627			{736	814	916	1010	1104	1210		{1314	1410
Planchy	x		{629			{738	816	918	1012	1106	1212		{1316	1412
Bulle	o		X634			X742	820	922	1016	1110	1216		(A)1320	1416
Bulle		X527	639	708			832	927	1017	1117	1217		1327	1432
La Tour-de-Trême	x	{530	642	711			835	930	1020	1120	1220		1330	1435
Le Pâquier-Montbarry	x	{532	644	713			837	932	1022	1122	1222		1332	1437
Gruyères	o	{533	645	714			838	934	1024	1123	1223		1334	1438
Gruyères		{534	646	715			839	935		1124	1224		1335	1439
Estavannens	x	{537	649	718			842	937		1127	1227		1337	1442
Enney	x	{538	650	719			843	938		1128	1228		1338	1443
Grandvillard		x{542	654	723			847	942		1132	1232		1342	1447
Neirivue	x	{545	657	726			850	945		1135	1235		1345	1450
Albeuve	x	{547	659	728			852	947		1137	1237		1347	1452
Lessoc	x	{549	701	731			854	949		1139	1239		1349	1454
Montbovon	o	X554	706	737			859	954		1144	1244		1354	1459
Montbovon		(A)600		746			904			1146	1304			1504
Château-d'Oex 120	o	(A)616		804			919			1204	1319			1519

				1410		1514	1614		1710	1814	1910			2110
Lausanne				1410		1514	1614		1710	1814	1910			2110
Palézieux	o			1425		1538	1638		1725	1838	1925			2125

		34 [R]✸ PA (D)	574	38 [R]✸ PA (D)	576	580	592 [R]✸ PA	582	588	590	590	594
Palézieux			1430		1543	1643		1736	1843	1936		2136
Granges (Veveyse)	x		1432		1545	1645		1738	1845	1938		2138
Bossonnens			1434		1547	1647		1740	1847	1940		x2140
Tatroz	x		1435		1548	1648		1742	1848	1941		2141
Remaufens	x		1437		1550	1650		1744	1850	1943		2143
Au Moulin	x		1439		1552	1652		1746	1852	1945		2145
Châtel-St-Denis	o		1441		1554	1654		1749	1854	1947		2147
Châtel-St-Denis			1444		1556	1656		1754	1858	1950		2150
Prayoud	x		1447		1559	1659		1757	1901	1953		2153
Semsales			1451		1603	1703		1801	1905	1957		x2157
La Verrerie			1453		1605	1705		1803	1907	2000		x2159
Le Crêt	x		1456		1608	1708		1806	1910	2002		2202
Les Ponts	x		1459		1611	1711		1809	1913	2005		2205
Vaulruz-Sud	x		1500		1612	1712		1810	1914	2006		2206
Les Colombettes	x		1502		1614	1714		1812	1916	2008		x2210
Vuadens-Sud			1504		1616	1716		1814	1918	2010		2212
Planchy	x		1506		1618	1718		1816	1920	2012		2214
Bulle	o		1510		1622	1722		1820	1924	2016		2216
Bulle		[R]1438:		1618:	1627	1727	[R]1755:	1832	1927		2022	
La Tour-de-Trême	x				1630	1730		1835	1930		[12]2026	
Le Pâquier-Montbarry	x				1632	1732		1837	1932		[12]2028	
Gruyères	o	[R]1444:		1623:	1636	1736	1801:	1838	1934		[12]2030	
Gruyères				1624:	1637	1737	1802:	1839	1935		[12]2031	
Estavannens	x				1640	1737		1842	1937		[12]2036	
Enney	x				1641	1740		1843	1938		[12]2038	
Grandvillard					1645	1742		1847	1942		[12]2041	
Neirivue	x				1648	1745		1850	1945		[12]2044	
Albeuve	x				1650	1747		1852	1947		[12]2046	
Lessoc	x				1653	1749		1854	1949		[12]2048	
Montbovon	o			[R]1643:	1659	1754	[R]1835:	1859	1954		2053	
Montbovon						1704			1904			
Château-d'Oex 120	o					1719			1919			

(Vertical text in columns: "Bulle-Gruyères" · "Bulle-Montbovon" · "Château-d'Oex-Montreux")

◼ SUPERTRAIN DU CHOCOLAT / SUPERPANORAMIC-EXPRESS ③ du 3 août – 19 oct
◼ FONDUE-TRAIN ⑤ du 5 nov–17 déc, 7 jan–25 mars
[12] Les arrêts sont déplacés en bordure de la route cantonale
Voie étroite. Classe unique
GFM, Fribourg

postal bus networks and on the municipal transport systems of 41 towns and cities. It also entitles the holder to 50% discounts on nearly all mountain railways and aerial cableways. A few of the smaller railways are excluded but offer a 25% or 50% reduction. There is a 25% discount on the Swiss Pass purchase price of a **Youth Pass** for those aged up to 26.

The **Swiss Flexi Pass** is ideal for those wanting to walk or cycle from a few centres: choose any three, four, five or six non-consecutive days within a month and enjoy the same benefits as the Swiss Pass. On other days, the Flexi Pass entitles the holder to a 50% discount. No youth discount is available.

If two or more people are travelling together, a 15% saving can be gained on the purchase of a Swiss Pass or Swiss Flexi Pass.

The **Swiss Card** is valid for one month and provides a round-trip ticket for the most direct route from the border point or airport to any Swiss resort. It gives the holder unlimited half-fare trips on all other train, bus and steamer services, as well as excursions to most mountain tops.

The **Swiss Transfer Ticket** is of particular benefit to winter sports travellers who will be likely to obtain a ski pass of some kind covering local transport, but would not wish to go further afield. Valid for one month, the Transfer Ticket covers a one-day transfer from a border station or airport to any station in Switzerland and back. It is available only from Switzerland Tourism.

Holders of the Swiss Pass, Flexi Pass, Swiss Card or Swiss Transfer Ticket may also obtain a **Junior Card** which allows children under 16 to travel free provided that they are accompanied by at least one parent. The Junior Card is available free to holders of these cards, on the condition that they are bought outside Switzerland. Non-family members aged between six and 16 receive a 50% discount.

The **Swiss Half Fare Card** allows unlimited purchase of train, bus, boat and some cable car tickets at half price within the one-month validity.

Regional passes

There is a wide range of regional passes which usually cover trains, buses and boats, but the precise scope and conditions should be checked. The passes are available from railway and steamer stations in the areas concerned and from local tourist offices. Variously covering between two and ten days but offering 50% discounts on the other days, these passes cover the following regions: Bernese Oberland, Erlebnis (Upper Valais/Gotthard), Golden Pass (Léman/Alpes), Léman/Pays de Vaud, Tell Pass (Zentral Schweiz) and Graubünden (summer and winter passes). Most are only available from spring to autumn.

There is also a range of regional rovers, mostly valid for a single day, giving unlimited use of public transport, but most urban areas also sell weekly and monthly passes:

- **Arc Jurassien Carte Journalière** – a wide area south of Basel
- **Basel TNW Tageskarte** – the TNW area around Basel
- **Bern–Solothurn Libero Tageskarte** – covers a wide area around Bern and Solothurn
- **Erlebnis Card (Oberwallis/Gotthard)** – covers canton the MGB bounded by Zermatt and Göschenen/Disentis-Mustér, postbuses in the Upper Valais and 50% discounts on over 70 mountain railways and cableways
- **Fribourg (Frimobil)** – covers canton Fribourg
- **Genève Carte Journalière** – services within the canton
- **Graubünden Pass** – RhB network between Chur–Disentis-Mustér/St Moritz/ Tirano
- **Jungfraubahnen Pass** – available between May and October, it is valid for six days and gives unlimited travel over all transport infrastructure in the area except the Jungfraubahn itself, on which there is a 50% discount
- **Lausanne Carte Journalière** – covers all eight zones of the city's public transport
- **Passepartout Tageskarte (Luzern)** – all public transport around the city in zones 10, 20 and 40

- **Ostwind Tageskarte** – most of northeast Switzerland
- **Regional Pass Berner Oberland** – covers an area bounded by Thun, Gstaad, Grindelwald and Brig
- **Schwyz Tageskarte** – all public transport in canton Schwyz except the Rigibahn
- **Tell Pass (Zentral Schwyz)** – covers Luzern, Meiringen, Schwyz and Zug
- **Zugerland Tageskarte** – all public transport in canton Zug; can be combined with Schwyz
- **Zürich Tageskarte** – all public transport in canton Zürich, on a zonal basis

USEFUL ADDRESSES

European Rail Ltd Unit 25, Tileyard Studios, Tileyard Rd, London N7 9AH; 020 7619 1083; e sales@europeanrail.com; www.europeanrail.co.uk. Railway travel specialists.

Ffestiniog Travel 1st Fl, Unit 6, Snowdonia Business Park, Penrhyndeudraeth, Gwynedd LL48 6LD; 01766 772030; e info@ffestiniogtravel.co.uk; www.ffestiniogtravel.com. Sister company to the Ffestiniog Railway (so travel profit helps to support the railway) with over 30 years' experience of specialised help with rail travel. Organises escorted & unescorted railway-based tours.

Great Rail Journeys Ltd Saviour Hse, 9 St Saviourgate, York YO1 8NL; 01904 521900; e grj@greatrail.com; www.greatrail.com. Organises escorted railway-based tours.

Rail Europe 193 Piccadilly, London W1J 9EU; 0844 848 4075; www.raileurope.co.uk. Sells rail passes & tickets to 5,000 European stations.

Swiss Travel Centre 30 Bedford St, London WC2E 9ED; 0800 100 200 30 (freephone), 020 7420 4900; e sales@stc.co.uk; www.switzerlandtravelcentre.co.uk. The Swiss experts.

Trainseurope Ltd 4 Station Approach, March, Cambs PE15 8SJ; 0871 700 7722; e info@trainseurope.co.uk; www.trainseurope.co.uk

FLY-RAIL This marvellous facility enables you to send your bags from any airport in the world right through to certain destinations when you check in to fly to Switzerland via Zürich or Geneva airports, or from the station of departure when you begin the journey home via these two airports.

For a charge equivalent to SFr22, a special green label obtainable from Switzerland Tourism and Swiss (airline) offices should be attached to the case (but not bicycles or unwieldy objects) before it is checked in abroad. This label also serves as a customs declaration. You will next see your case at the station at your Swiss destination.

On your return, cases can be sent from Fly-Rail stations through to the airport at home, though e-tickets are seldom accepted and the facility does not apply to any flights to the US.

Moreover, rail passengers can check in not less than 24 hours before take-off and reserve a seat long before other passengers. To obtain a boarding card, you need to show your train ticket, airline ticket with OK status and passport. This facility applies to most airlines.

The stations/destinations to which luggage can be sent/dispatched and where passengers may check in are: Aarau, Adelboden, Arosa, Baden, Basel, Bellinzona, Belp, Bern, Biel/Bienne, Brig, Buchs SG, Burgdorf, Chur, Davos Dorf, Davos Platz, Engelberg, Fleurier, Frauenfeld, Fribourg, Genève, Grenchen Süd, Grindelwald, Gstaad, Interlaken Ost, Interlaken West, Kandersteg, Klosters, Kreuzlingen, La Chaux-de-Fonds, Langenthal, Lausanne, Locarno, Lugano, Luzern, Montreux, Mürren, Neuchâtel, Olten, Rapperswil, St Gallen, St Margrethen, St Moritz, Saas Fee, Sargans, Schaffhausen, Sion, Solothurn, Spiez, Thun, Wädenswil, Wengen, Wil, Winterthur, Zermatt, Zug, Zürich HB.

At some remote, unstaffed stations and halts, particularly on narrow-gauge railways, there is a system for waiting passengers to indicate that they wish to board the train. A button has to be pressed to activate a signal that instructs the driver to stop to pick up passengers. Notes adjacent (usually in several languages) explain the procedure. If you do not follow the correct procedure, the train will not stop unless there are passengers wishing to get off. Flagging it down by hand as one might a bus will have no effect. In the timetable such stations are marked by a small 'x'.

FAST BAGGAGE This facility (*www.rail.ch/baggage*) was introduced in 2005 to enable passengers to forward their luggage between 45 tourist destinations within the country. This is of particular benefit to those planning holidays with more than one centre, or for those walking or cycling.

Passengers hand in their luggage no later than 09.00 and collect it at their destination from 18.00 the same day (or a little later in some places). A train ticket or pass is necessary to make use of this service, which costs SFr20. Obviously the opening and closing times of the ticket offices should be checked; these are available on the SBB website (*www.sbb.ch*). Even prams, skis and sledges can be sent by this service, but not bicycles. Discounts are available for families and groups. The following destinations participate: Adelboden, Arosa, Basel SBB, Bellinzona, Bern, Bettmeralp, Biel/Bienne, Brig, Chur, Davos Dorf, Davos Platz, Engelberg, Genève, Grindelwald, Gstaad, Interlaken Ost and West, Kandersteg, Klosters, Lausanne, Lauterbrunnen, Lenk, Lenzerheide, Leukerbad, Locarno, Lugano, Luzern, Meiringen, Montana-Vermala, Montreux, Mürren, Pontresina, St Gallen, St Moritz, Saas Fee, Samedan, Scuol-Tarasp, Sion, Spiez, Thun, Visp, Wengen, Zermatt, Zürich HB and Zweisimmen.

STATION FACILITIES The principal Swiss stations offer a good range of facilities, especially at those most used by tourists. For example, a large number of stations change money, provide general information about the town as well as railway matters, hire bicycles (see *Chapter 4*, page 31), handle luggage etc.

Luggage trolleys Some of the largest stations, such as Geneva Aéroport and Zürich Flughafen, have luggage trolleys that are designed to go on to escalators. The first experience of wheeling a trolley on to one can be daunting, but rubber grips prevent movement once the handle is released to secure the brake. In particular, these trolleys make the long haul from airport carousel to train much easier.

At stations of any size there are rows of trolleys both outside and at several points along the platform. A deposit of a SFr2 coin in a slide mechanism is required to release a trolley; it can be recovered by returning the trolley to a row and inserting the key into the adjacent trolley.

Left luggage Most large stations have both an office for left luggage and banks of lockers. The latter are usually in two sizes: the smaller at SFr5 is suitable for smaller cases and items; the larger at SFr6 is for suitcases. The coin slots take SFr1, 2 and 5 coins. Many stations have lockers only.

Credit cards Swiss Federal Railways (and most private railways) accept American Express, Diners Club, Eurocard/MasterCard and Visa.

Refreshments Swiss railway stations are a hub of local life, and an astonishing number of even quite small stations have cafés of such quality that they are used by people not travelling by train. At the largest stations such as Olten and Chiasso, there are restaurants with table service. Most of the larger stations and junctions have at least a buffet, and most stations have vending machines that dispense fruit juice cartons, canned drinks, chocolate, biscuits and snacks.

It is rare for an express train not to have at least a trolley selling hot and cold drinks, rolls, chocolate, etc. The more important standard-gauge trains have restaurant cars, reintroduced after an unpopular flirtation with bistros.

Platform information Platforms in Switzerland are referred to as 'tracks' in announcements. Timetables displayed on platform boards are colour coded: the yellow table shows departing trains (*Abfahrt, Départ, Partenza*); the white table shows arriving trains (*Ankunft, Arrivée, Arrivo*). Stations served by inter-city trains of some length have blue boards that show the composition of trains – where the first- and second-class coaches and any restaurant or sleeping cars may be found. This board should be consulted and the direction of travel established (it's usually obvious) so that you can wait in the appropriate sector of the platform (generally A–D). The legendary punctuality of Swiss trains depends upon station stops not being exceeded, and it is no pleasure having to race a trolley of cases down the platform at the last minute.

However, since seat reservations are generally unnecessary, except for groups of ten or more and for such trains as the Glacier Express (as detailed in the relevant descriptions in this book, *Chapter 3*, page 25), it is usually a question only of finding the correct class of coach rather than a specific carriage.

POSTBUSES

The Swiss postbus system, operated by Swiss Post (PTT), has a network of 738 routes covering over 11,102km (6,939 miles) with 2,145 vehicles. It evolved from the 19th-century mail coach service which in 1913 was using 2,523 horses, 2,231 coaches and 1,059 sleighs, and on which the first motor service between Bern and Detligen was introduced in 1906.

Because the Swiss believe, quite rightly, that the only sensible way to organise public transport services is to achieve the maximum degree of integration between modes, bus services are complementary to the rail network. The majority of services therefore connect with trains, steamers or mountain cableways, 'so switching from one to the other is child's play' as the postbus timetable puts it, without exaggeration.

The timetable is laid out in a similar manner to the rail timetable (see *The Train Timetable* box, page 16). Note that an 'R' in a square box means that seats have to be reserved, but this condition applies to very few routes, other than the Route Express Lines. Some of the routes over the passes operate during the summer months only.

The Swiss Pass (see *Rail cards and passes*, page 16) allows unlimited free travel on postbuses (as well as on all other public transport), though there is a small supplement (Alpine Ticket) on some of the mountain pass routes that are patronised primarily by tourists. There is a small range of passes, some in conjunction with rail companies, for Graubünden, Haslital, Saastal, Ticino, Valais and Upper Valais (Erlebnis); visit www.postauto.ch and click on 'On the road daily' followed by 'Special tickets'. Children under six years old travel free and those between six and 16 pay half fare. Postbuses operate all non-urban services and are painted in distinctive yellow livery with a red band.

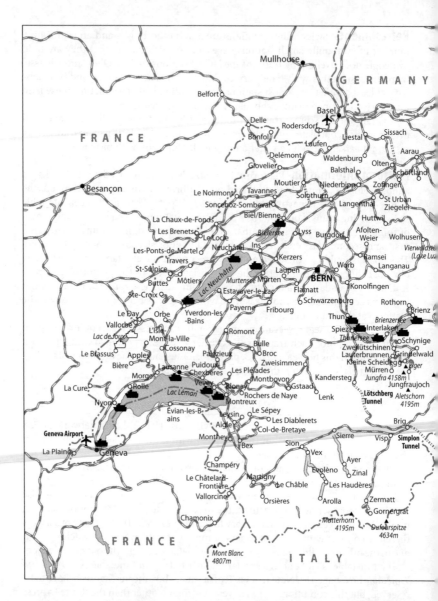

Bikes are carried whenever there is room (which is normally the case as PostBus has expanded its capacity with bike racks and trailers, especially in cantons Graubünden, Valais and Bern), but a phone call to check is officially recommended – telephone numbers for operators are given alongside each table in the timetable.

It almost goes without saying that the quality of the buses and their cleanliness is extremely high.

PostBus Switzerland ☏0848 888 888; e see
contact form on website; www.postauto.ch.

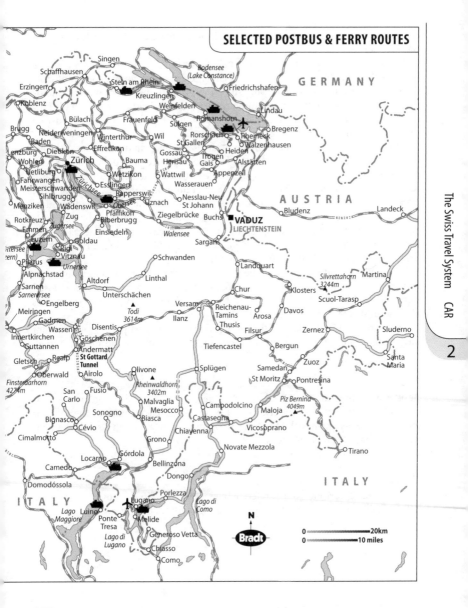

CAR

Given the extent of Swiss public transport, there is almost nowhere that cannot be reached by it and a short walk. However, if using a car is unavoidable, 1,000 Click & Drive hire cars are available at 360 SBB railway stations – provided by Mobility at attractive prices and even for short-hire periods of less than three hours. To use Click & Drive, an initial registration must first be completed at any of 75 SBB stations around Switzerland – you will then be handed the Mobility card, which serves as the key to all of the hire cars. After completing this procedure, you will be able to reserve your car online. There are ten different categories of vehicle to choose from, including Smart car, Honda Hybrid and BMW 1-series.

Access to Swiss motorways has to be paid for by purchasing a vignette (available from Switzerland Tourism). Although a Green Card is not compulsory, motorists are strongly advised to acquire one, since the protection offered by most motor insurance policies is only to a minimum requirement. Drivers are required to show a vehicle registration certificate at the border and a full driving licence must be carried at all times.

The minimum driving age in Switzerland is 18, and children under 12 must travel in the rear seats. A warning triangle must be carried, and police radar speed trap detectors are illegal. On-the-spot fines can be collected for failing to wear a seat belt or for exceeding the speed limits of 120km/h (75mph) on motorways, 100km/h (62.5mph) on major roads, 80km/h (50mph) on other roads (unless otherwise signed) and 50km/h (31mph) in built-up areas, whether or not there are signs indicating this speed. Speeding fines may be based on income, as a Swiss millionaire discovered in 2011 when he was fined $290,000 (then £180,000) for driving at 137km/h (85mph) through a village.

The driver should not expect to be able to enjoy the scenery, as mountain roads in particular require vigilance. Some roads across the higher or more exposed passes are closed during the winter months, although tunnels or car-carrying trains act as a substitute on the principal arteries.

There are 23 alpine passes and tunnels with varying dates of opening and different tariff systems. Tickets for tunnels are purchased from booths on the approach road.

TOURIST OFFICES

Besides providing information about what there is to see and do in an area, tourist offices (indicated by **𝒊** in the text) usually provide excellent maps of the town or locality. Some also help with obtaining accommodation, although a small charge is normally made for this service.

USING THIS BOOK

For a detailed description of the referencing method used in this guide, see page ix. A list of tables and page numbers is given in *Appendix 3*, page 370.

3

Special Trains

In addition to the expresses that bisect Switzerland, there are a number of special trains, including those travelling from one region to another. Some of these, like the Voralpen Express, are used by many locals, while others have been devised specifically for tourists. All journeys can be made in either direction.

WILLIAM TELL EXPRESS: Luzern–Lugano/Locarno

One of the best-known tourist services is the William Tell Express, which combines a paddle-steamer for the length of Lake Luzern with a reserved first-class coach on the train from Flüelen to Lugano or Locarno (change at Bellinzona). Included in the ticket is lunch in the steamer's first-class restaurant, an English guide to the sights en route and a souvenir of the journey. There are two departures a day in each direction between May and mid-October, and the journey takes five to six hours to either destination. (See *Chapter 13*, page 195 and table 600 (pages 49, 195, 315 and 334) for the journey.)

WILLIAM TELL/CENTOVALLI ROUNDTRIP: any station– Luzern–Lugano–Domodóssola–Montreux–any station

A package sold by SBB, this three-day excursion begins at any station in Switzerland to reach Luzern to connect with the William Tell Express (see above). After a night in Lugano, you take the train for Locarno and the delightful journey by narrow-gauge train to Domodóssola and a train to Montreux for the final night before returning to your station of choice.

GOLDEN PASS LINE

One of the main promotions by Switzerland Tourism is the Golden Pass Line linking Lac Léman and central Switzerland. The train (see below) operates between Luzern, Interlaken and Montreux. At present it is necessary to change trains at Zweisimmen and Interlaken Ost, but a project to introduce coaches with gauge-changing bogies may allow through running.

GOLDEN PASS PANORAMIC: Montreux–Zweisimmen

This name is given to the tourist trains operated by the Montreux–Oberland Bernois railway over its scenic route. The trains have observation cars at each end with an elevated driver's cab so that passengers have an unobstructed view of the track ahead or behind. They also include a lounge bar car. The service runs five to seven times a day, and the journey takes 1¾ hours. Seat reservations, obtainable through offices of Switzerland Tourism, are strongly advisable in the high season. Booking for groups is obligatory (✆ *0840 245 245;* e *info@goldenpass.ch; www.goldenpass. ch*). See table 120 for the journey, page 269. For those wanting a more leisurely journey redolent of the inter-war years, the summer-only **Golden Pass Classic** uses restored coaches from the 1930s Golden Mountain Pullman Express.

GLACIER EXPRESS: Zermatt–St Moritz

The first Glacier Express between Zermatt and St Moritz ran on 25 June 1930, only a few weeks after the section between Visp and Brig was opened. Originally a summer-only service, the train now runs throughout the year, thanks to elaborate avalanche-protection works and the Furka Base Tunnel. See tables 140, 142, 143, 920 and 940 for the journey. Table 144 encapsulates the Glacier Express train times.

The **Glacier Express** (e *info@glacierexpress.ch; www.glacierexpress.ch*) is the slowest express in the world, averaging 36km/h (22mph), but it is such a remarkably scenic and varied journey that few passengers would want to lose a minute of the 7½-hour journey. It is the most popular of the tourist trains and has become one of the 'must do' experiences in Europe. There are three trains a day in each direction, with a fourth between Davos Platz and Zermatt, made up of special coaches with panoramic windows and restaurant car. A headphone commentary in six languages is provided, and an at-seat lunch is served in first class. A supplementary fare is payable and seat reservations are mandatory. Early booking for the high season is advised.

Rhaetian Railways (e *see website for contact form; www.rhb.ch*) also operates a luxury train called the Alpine Classic Pullman Express, which runs about ten times a year from St Moritz to Zermatt. The package includes a gourmet lunch in the period dining car en route.

PALM EXPRESS: St Moritz–Lugano

This 3¾-hour journey is covered by postbus (e *see website for contact form; www. postauto.ch/en*), taking a route southwest from St Moritz through the lovely Bregaglia Valley (which is not on the railway) and over the Maloja Pass. The route winds down into the Bergeli Valley with its lovely chestnut woods to reach Italy and the market town of Chiavenna, where a stop is made. The bus follows the shores of Lake Como and then Lake Lugano.

BERNINA EXPRESS: Chur–St Moritz–Tirano (–Lugano)

This train takes in the final part of the Glacier Express route (travelling from Zermatt) and continues over the Bernina Pass, the highest rail crossing of the Alps, to Tirano in Italy. The journey takes 4½ hours, so the return trip can be made in a day with over 2 hours in Tirano for lunch. In summer, there is the option of continuing by bus to Lugano station and town centre, which takes a further 3 hours. See tables 940 and 950 for the journey, pages 345 and 355.

PRE-ALPINE EXPRESS/VORALPEN EXPRESS: Luzern–Romanshorn

Linking two of Switzerland's largest expanses of water, lakes Luzern (Vierwaldstättersee) and Constance (Bodensee), the **Voralpen Express** (e *see* *website for contact form; www.voralpen-express.ch*) runs at hourly intervals, takes 2½ hours and has a bistro car. First-class coaches also have panoramic windows. It provides connections to Einsiedeln at Biberbrugg and to the Appenzeller Bahn at Herisau and St Gallen. See tables 600, 670, 672, 671 and 870 for the journey.

CHOCOLATE TRAIN: Montreux–Gruyère–Broc–Montreux

Operated by the Montreux–Oberland Bernois Railway, the **Chocolate Train** is a perfect day-out for families. It follows the route of tables 120 and 256 (pages 269 and 276) from Montreux to the Gruyère region to visit the delightful eponymous town and factories making Cailler chocolate and Gruyère cheese. Travel is in first-class 'Belle Epoque Pullman' carriages of 1914–15 or in modern panoramic coaches. The Gruyère tour shows how the cheese is made, and includes a film and tasting at Broc chocolate factory – it's astonishing how few of the tempting chocolates most people can manage. The Chocolate Train runs every Monday, Wednesday and Thursday from May to October and every day in July and August. Reservations are mandatory and can be made at Montreux station through Swiss Travel Centre or online (*visit www.goldenpass.ch; click Golden Pass Line, then 'From Montreux–Zweisimmen', followed by 'Chocolate Train'*). The package includes coffee and croissants on the train, bus transfers and a tour of Gruyère castle, as well as visits to the demonstration cheese dairy and the chocolate factory.

Special Trains **CHOCOLATE TRAIN**

3

Bradt Travel Guides

Claim 20% discount on your next Bradt book when you order from www.bradtguides.com quoting the code BRADT20

Africa

Africa Overland	£16.99
Algeria	£15.99
Angola	£18.99
Botswana	£16.99
Burkina Faso	£17.99
Cameroon	£15.99
Cape Verde	£15.99
Congo	£16.99
Eritrea	£15.99
Ethiopia	£17.99
Ethiopia Highlights	£15.99
Ghana	£15.99
Kenya Highlights	£15.99
Madagascar	£16.99
Madagascar Highlights	£15.99
Malawi	£15.99
Mali	£14.99
Mauritius, Rodrigues & Réunion	£16.99
Mozambique	£15.99
Namibia	£15.99
Nigeria	£17.99
North Africa: Roman Coast	£15.99
Rwanda	£16.99
São Tomé & Príncipe	£14.99
Seychelles	£16.99
Sierra Leone	£16.99
Somaliland	£15.99
South Africa Highlights	£15.99
Sudan	£16.99
Swaziland	£15.99
Tanzania Safari Guide	£17.99
Tanzania, Northern	£14.99
Uganda	£16.99
Zambia	£18.99
Zanzibar	£15.99
Zimbabwe	£15.99

The Americas and the Caribbean

Alaska	£15.99
Amazon Highlights	£15.99
Argentina	£16.99
Bahia	£14.99
Cayman Islands	£14.99
Chile Highlights	£15.99
Colombia	£17.99
Dominica	£15.99
Grenada, Carriacou & Petite Martinique	£15.99
Guyana	£15.99
Haiti	£16.99
Nova Scotia	£15.99
Panama	£14.99
Paraguay	£15.99
Peru Highlights	£15.99
Turks & Caicos Islands	£14.99
Uruguay	£15.99
USA by Rail	£15.99
Venezuela	£16.99
Yukon	£14.99

British Isles

Britain from the Rails	£14.99
Bus-Pass Britain	£15.99
Eccentric Britain	£16.99
Eccentric Cambridge	£9.99
Eccentric London	£14.99
Eccentric Oxford	£9.99
Sacred Britain	£16.99
Slow: Cornwall	£14.99
Slow: Cotswolds	£14.99
Slow: Devon & Exmoor	£14.99
Slow: Dorset	£14.99
Slow: New Forest	£9.99
Slow: Norfolk & Suffolk	£14.99
Slow: North Yorkshire	£14.99
Slow: Northumberland	£14.99
Slow: Sussex & South Downs National Park	£14.99

Europe

Abruzzo	£16.99
Albania	£16.99
Armenia	£15.99
Azores	£14.99
Belarus	£15.99
Bosnia & Herzegovina	£15.99
Bratislava	£9.99
Budapest	£9.99
Croatia	£15.99
Cross-Channel France: Nord-Pas de Calais	£13.99
Cyprus see North Cyprus	
Estonia	£14.99
Faroe Islands	£16.99
Flanders	£15.99
Georgia	£15.99
Greece: The Peloponnese	£14.99
Hungary	£15.99
Iceland	£15.99
Istria	£13.99
Kosovo	£15.99
Lapland	£15.99
Liguria	£15.99
Lille	£9.99
Lithuania	£14.99
Luxembourg	£14.99
Macedonia	£16.99
Malta & Gozo	£14.99
Montenegro	£14.99
North Cyprus	£13.99
Serbia	£15.99
Slovakia	£14.99
Slovenia	£13.99
Svalbard: Spitsbergen, Jan Mayen, Franz Jozef Land	£17.99
Switzerland Without a Car	£15.99
Transylvania	£15.99
Ukraine	£16.99

Middle East, Asia and Australasia

Bangladesh	£17.99
Borneo	£17.99
Eastern Turkey	£16.99
Iran	£15.99
Israel	£15.99
Jordan	£16.99
Kazakhstan	£16.99
Kyrgyzstan	£16.99
Lake Baikal	£15.99
Lebanon	£15.99
Maldives	£15.99
Mongolia	£16.99
North Korea	£14.99
Oman	£15.99
Palestine	£15.99
Shangri-La: A Travel Guide to the Himalayan Dream	£14.99
Sri Lanka	£15.99
Syria	£15.99
Taiwan	£16.99
Tajikistan	£15.99
Tibet	£17.99
Yemen	£14.99

Wildlife

Antarctica: A Guide to the Wildlife	£15.99
Arctic: A Guide to Coastal Wildlife	£16.99
Australian Wildlife	£14.99
East African Wildlife	£19.99
Galápagos Wildlife	£16.99
Madagascar Wildlife	£16.99
Pantanal Wildlife	£16.99
Southern African Wildlife	£19.99
Sri Lankan Wildlife	£15.99

Pictorials and other guides

100 Alien Invaders	£16.99
100 Animals to See Before They Die	£16.99
100 Bizarre Animals	£16.99
Eccentric Australia	£12.99
Northern Lights	£6.99
Swimming with Dolphins, Tracking Gorillas	£15.99
The Northwest Passage	£14.99
Tips on Tipping	£6.99
Total Solar Eclipse 2012 & 2013	£6.99
Wildlife & Conservation Volunteering: The Complete Guide	£13.99

Travel literature

A Glimpse of Eternal Snows	£11.99
A Tourist in the Arab Spring	£9.99
Connemara Mollie	£9.99
Fakirs, Feluccas and Femmes Fatales	£9.99
Madagascar: The Eighth Continent	£11.99
The Marsh Lions	£9.99
The Two-Year Mountain	£9.99
The Urban Circus	£9.99
Up the Creek	£9.99

4

Walking and Cycling

Switzerland is a paradise for walkers and cyclists, whether on road or mountain-bike terrain. Facilities for both are exemplary. A major improvement for tourists was initiated in 2008 with the launch of the organisation SwitzerlandMobility.

SWITZERLANDMOBILITY

SwitzerlandMobility (*www.schweizmobil.ch/en*; for booking, see *www.swisstrails.ch*) has formalised new facilities over a non-motorised network of almost 20,000km. Itineraries for walkers (6,300km), touring cyclists (8,500km), mountain bikers (3,300km), inline skaters (1,000km) and canoeists (1,000km) have been devised, with standardised signposting and a range of services including accommodation, luggage transportation, equipment rental and travel by public transport. All of these arrangements are made for you, making it simple to book a holiday based on the routes. Full details of the itineraries are published in 57 route guides in English as well as German and French. SwitzerlandMobility routes are accessible through over 18,000 stops on the public transport network.

WALKING

It would be hard to find a country with better provision for the walker than Switzerland. The superb public transport system takes you to even the remotest of places to begin a walk, and the country has almost 64,000km (40,000 miles) of uniformly marked paths. Virtually every station in the country has a number of suggested walks, indicated by small yellow signposts with black lettering listing destinations, usually with walking times. The use of yellow as an identifier appears again in the occasional arrow markings indicating the path if there may be doubt regarding the direction, and on small boards making special requests, such as not to leave the path through a nature reserve. Sometimes there is simply a sign saying *Wanderweg*, meaning 'footpath', without a destination being given.

Even on these paths, for which no particular knowledge or experience is required, it is advisable to wear at least proper walking shoes or walking trainers. It is always sensible to take weatherproof clothing appropriate for the season, sufficient food and drink for a longer walk, and a small first aid kit. In summer and during all seasons at higher altitudes, it is wise to take a high-factor sunscreen or sunblock and to wear a hat – especially children with sensitive skin or fair hair. The lips should also be protected. Always take sunglasses or goggles. Don't attempt to do too much; try to maintain a steady even pace: walking fast with frequent stops induces fatigue.

The next category of path is the mountain route (*Bergweg*), denoted by a red horizontal flash at the end of the yellow signposts. For these walks it is necessary to

PRECAUTIONS FOR MOUNTAIN WALKS

- Hiking boots are essential.
- Plan routes bearing in mind the limitations of the weakest member of the party, and do not go alone unless you are highly experienced.
- A first aid kit, provisions, protective clothing, a small torch and topographic maps are essential.
- A telescopic walking stick will help with descents.
- The weather in mountain areas can change rapidly, so it is advisable to obtain a forecast before setting out and to be prepared for deteriorating conditions.
- Always tell someone where you are going and what time you expect to return.
- Set off early and plan to return early, allowing time to return if you encounter difficulties.
- Be careful if lighting a fire, and never do so in dry weather.
- Close gates behind you, be careful of plants and animals and do not leave any litter.

be fit and well prepared and to have a head for heights, since sections of the paths may be narrow with long drops. In mountain areas, a pink circle embossed with a white snowflake beside a destination on the yellow signs denotes a path that is cleared for winter walks.

The most difficult category of route is indicated by direction signs with a blue background and white typography. These are alpine walks which lead into trackless terrain, across snowfields and glaciers or up short sections of rock climbing or scrambling. These should be attempted only by those who have experience in such terrain and are extremely fit; even then, it is unwise to go without a mountain guide who is aware of localised dangers and the risk of avalanches. In addition to the above equipment, it is vital to take an altimeter, compass, rope and ice axe.

SPECIAL WALKS OR COMBINED WALKING AND CYCLING ITINERARIES Less commonly seen are brown signs with white typography; these denote cultural walks which might follow a Roman road, pilgrim route or packhorse trail. Alternatively, they may have a theme such as viticulture, castles or mills.

Some of these are very long routes that could form the basis of walking holidays taking several weeks or much shorter tours tackling a section of the route. Equally, some can be covered by bike, either using the railway to send your bike on when you come to a walking section or by hiring a bike on-site. Six types of longer-distance footpaths include:

- Roman roads, the route describes a letter 'n' through the country from the St Bernard Pass, through Martigny, Lausanne, Payerne, Murten, Augst (near Basel), Zürich and south to the Septimer Pass and Chiasso
- The pilgrimage routes of St James, stretching from Geneva in the southwest to St Gallen in the northeast, with various branches and alternative routes
- The Great Walser Route, which links the settlements of this medieval nomadic tribe and takes in some of Switzerland's loveliest areas, from Zermatt and Saas Fee to the border with Austria beyond Klosters. This fairly taxing route is for more experienced walkers.

- Mule tracks and long-distance trade routes, a series of suggested journeys rather than one itinerary. These take in some of the great mountain passes.
- The Swiss Path, the easiest and shortest, created to mark the 700th anniversary of the Swiss Confederation, and described in *Chapter 13* (see page 176).
- Paths from the Steam Age: three historical north–south routes giving an insight into the industrial past, from Vallorbe to Bex, Basel to Lake Lugano and Winterthur to Sargans.

Swiss Post (see *Postbuses*, page 21) produces English-language leaflets describing walks that can be planned in conjunction with postal buses.

CYCLING

Cycling in Switzerland is not as laughable a proposition as the faint-hearted might think, and even they may gain courage with the offer of an electric or e-bike. Switzerland has become a major centre of electric bike manufacture and a large number of e-bike hire points are now available. Even without the boost of an e-bike, there is plenty of gently undulating countryside, and many of the alpine valleys have cycle routes along their bottom. Half of the Swiss population own bicycles, and most cities and towns have good networks of cycle tracks and lanes. The general population also has a highly developed environmental conscience which has encouraged greater consideration of transport choices, and cycling – in urban areas especially – makes a tangible impact on pollution reduction. In Basel, for example, 40% of journeys using some form of mechanical transport are by bike (compared with 30% public transport, 30% car). In canton Zürich there are spaces for 4,040 cars at stations, but accommodation for 12,000 bikes.

The consequence for the visitor is a developed infrastructure of cycle tracks, signs, maps and rental facilities. The railways, too, are keen to exploit the natural synergy between bike and train: most trains carry bikes, and there is covered accommodation for bikes at the majority of stations. On the Brünig line between Luzern and Interlaken, for example, the twice-daily Brünig Panoramic Express has an entire car adapted for cycle carriage. There are a few lines that do not carry bicycles, such as the Centovalli in Ticino, so it is important to check. Most SBB trains carry bikes; those that do not are indicated in the timetable by a bike symbol crossed through, and there are permanent restrictions on the carriage of bikes by Zürich and Bern S-bahn trains during the morning and evening peak hours. A multiple-day card for bikes, obtainable from railway stations, offers the best value: a six-day pass costs SFr60.

The blue train information board on station platforms shows where carriages with a bike compartment will stop, and a bike symbol on the door indicates the precise location.

Bikes can be hired from over 80 railway stations (a list of the stations can be downloaded from www.sbb.ch/en/station-services/car-bike/hire-or-borrow/rent-a-bike.html). Up to seven types of bike are often available, including: a city/country (on-road) bike with seven gears; a mountain bike with 21 gears; electric bikes; tandems; and a child's mountain bike with seven gears. Trailers for young children can also be hired. The bikes are of good quality, with Shimano gears. It is advisable to reserve bikes a day or two ahead, especially in July and August, but not later than 18.00 the previous day. Rates are based on ½, 1 or 7 day rentals. Bikes hired for a full day can be returned to a different station (enabling you to cycle downhill only) for which a small charge is levied; bikes taken for a half day have to be returned to the hiring station. A family package is available for the hire of two city/country bikes and one bike for a child under 16 years of age. Helmets can also be hired.

At many stations there are cycling information boards, usually denoted by a red 'i'. A map illustrates the area's cycling routes with gradients and other useful information. Bike routes are marked by red signs with white lettering.

An excellent website with information about cycling in Switzerland is available through the SwitzerlandMobility site or directly at www.veloland.ch.

CYCLE ROUTES With so many cycle routes, it is almost invidious singling out a few for mention.

There are nine long-distance national routes ranging from 128–505km (80–316 miles), 53 regional and 45 local cycle routes with the signing and mapping you would expect.

From the edge of Zürich there is a separate cycling path beside the River Glatt to Oberglatt, Höri, Niederglatt, Bülach, Glattfelden, Zweidlen and Eglisau. In the Bernese Oberland, there is a route from Kandersteg to Spiez which continues on through Thun, Bern, Aarberg, Solothurn and Olten to Aarau. Also in the Bernese Oberland are some lovely paths through the valleys of the Black and White Lütschine to Grindelwald and Lauterbrunnen respectively, and some good paths around Interlaken.

Canton Solothurn has developed some attractive long-distance routes through easy cycling terrain, and, in common with most of the cycling initiatives in the country, there are good leaflets and maps to promote their use. These are available at tourist offices and online at www.veloland.ch.

One of the best areas for cycling is the Upper Engadine and along the routes of the Rhätische Bahn in Graubünden. Two days' notice is all that is required to pick up a hire bike at any station on their system. Along the valley of the Upper Engadine between Samedan and Scuol-Tarasp is a 60km (37 mile) cycle route linking the villages along the valley – one of the loveliest in all Switzerland and a cyclist's dream.

Another, much longer journey in the area lies between Thusis and Bellinzona. The old road is almost free of traffic now that a motorway has been driven through this beautiful series of valleys and tunnelled under the San Bernardino Pass.

OFF-ROAD CYCLING Mountain bike riders will find that Switzerland offers spectacular opportunities. The bike trails in the Bernese Oberland, for example, are surrounded by views that would be hard to beat anywhere you're likely to take a mountain bike. Dedicated mountain bike trails are indicated by roadside symbols similar to the conventional bike routes, but with the bike's front wheel raised.

CYCLISTS' CODE

The Swiss ask cyclists to follow a simple code:

- Mountain bike riders should stick to existing tracks, roads and specially marked mountain bike routes.
- Cyclists should give way to walkers in all circumstances and be polite and considerate towards them.
- Cyclists should respect all forms of plant and animal life, shut gates behind them and not ride cross-country.
- Cyclists must not leave litter behind.

TAKING YOUR BIKE TO SWITZERLAND The easiest way is probably by Eurostar from London St Pancras to Gare du Nord in Paris, taking a quiet route (if you can find one) to Gare de Lyon and taking the TGV to Bern or Lausanne. Cyclists can reserve a place for their bikes on the same train they are travelling on (as long as there is space in Eurostar's luggage holds) by calling ☏ 0844 822 5822. The new service costs £30 for a one-way journey and is available between London, Paris and Brussels. In addition, many cyclists who have folding bikes or who can dismantle their bike and place it in a bike bag can choose to carry them onboard the train as part of their normal luggage allowance, provided the overall size is no more than 120cm in length.

The cheaper £25 registered baggage service does not guarantee that your bike will travel on the same train as you but every effort is made to send it on the next available service, space permitting. It is guaranteed that your bike will be available to collect at your Eurostar destination within 24 hours after registration. This service can be booked on the day of travel or your bike can be sent before your journey so it will be ready to collect when you arrive.

Bikes are accommodated on TGV and long-distance coaches free of charge providing they can be folded or their wheels removed to fit into special covers that measure no more than 120 x 90cm. Bikes in these covers can be taken on the train as hand luggage. Most luggage vans on regional trains in France accept bikes, though the capacity of many is limited to three. Bikes are not allowed on the Paris Métro system or the central sections of the cross-Paris RER routes.

Alternatively you can take your bike on the Eurotunnel Shuttle trains from Folkestone to Coquelles, which use a specially adapted trailer to ferry up to six bikes and their riders through the tunnel twice a day in each direction. They leave from the Holiday Inn Express at Folkestone – Channel Tunnel at 08.00 and 15.30 and from Ciffco, Boulevard de l'Europe, 62904 Coquelles in France at 12.30 and 18.00. Reservations are compulsory (☏ 01303 282201; www.eurotunnel.com).

MAPS AND GUIDES FOR WALKING AND CYCLING

Switzerland's two principal cartographic companies, Kümmerly + Frey (K+F) and the Federal Office of Topography, produce excellent ranges of maps for walkers and cyclists. These maps and other maps of the country may be obtained from travel bookshop Stanfords (*12–14 Long Acre, Covent Garden, London WC2E 9LP; mail-order service* ☏ *020 7836 1321; www.stanfords.co.uk*).

The best detailed mapping of Switzerland comes from swisstopo (*www.swisstopo. ch*), the country's national survey organisation, and from Kümmerly + Frey. Swisstopo produces three series of maps at 1:50,000. Its standard topographic survey at that scale covers the country on 78 sheets, each showing an area of 35 x 24km. Twenty-five of the country's most popular regions are also covered by larger sheets, each designed to show major holiday resorts and the surrounding countryside on one map. All but a handful of the standard sheets are now also available in a special hiking edition, overprinted with routes waymarked and maintained by SAW (Swiss Hiking Federation). The whole country is also covered by swisstopo on 247 maps at 1:25,000, each showing a quarter of the corresponding standard 1:50,000 sheet. Larger maps are again available for 18 popular regions, but there is no 1:25,000 series with SAW routes. All information, including detailed grids for all the scales, is shown on their website at www.swisstopo.ch.

Kümmerly + Frey has an excellent hiking series at 1:60,000, with large contoured maps showing plenty of local paths and tourist information, including postbus routes with stops. The series includes maps for the central part of the country, including the Bernese Oberland, Michabel with the Mattertal and the Saastal, and the Engadine Valleys. For the latest information, see available maps on www. stanfords.co.uk.

Hallwag K+F has launched a new series of Valser 1:50,000 hiking maps, beginning with the ten most popular walking areas of the country: Valsertal, Chasseral, Appenzell, Vierwaldstättersee, Haslital, Montreux, Adelboden/Lenk, St Moritz, Zermatt and Lugano/Malcontone.

K+F holiday maps at 1:120,000, published for the Bernese Oberland and the cantons of Valais, Graubünden and Ticino, are useful for more general planning, showing both hiking routes and public transport.

K+F also publish a cycling series at 1:60,000, covering most of the country north of the Rhone and the Rhine, plus the southern part of Ticino, in 22 maps. The maps show not only a large selection of national and cantonal routes for cycles and mountain bikes, indicating road surfaces, gradients, density of motorised traffic etc, but even chairlifts and cable cars carrying bikes. They also feature useful additional information such as places of interest, accommodation and restaurants. K+F also do a general cycling map of the whole of Switzerland at 1:301,000, with similar detailed grading of routes and tourist information, including 'velotels' – special accommodation for cyclists.

All visitors to Switzerland will welcome the return of the very popular railway map of the country at 1:301,000, published jointly by Kümmerly + Frey and SBB. It is available as *Switzerland – The Official Map of Public Transport*, and includes a booklet with public transport maps for all the main cities. The map shows everything from railway lines and bus routes to lake boat routes, cable cars and chairlifts. Maps are avaialble from principal railway stations and good map shops.

Part Two

THE GUIDE

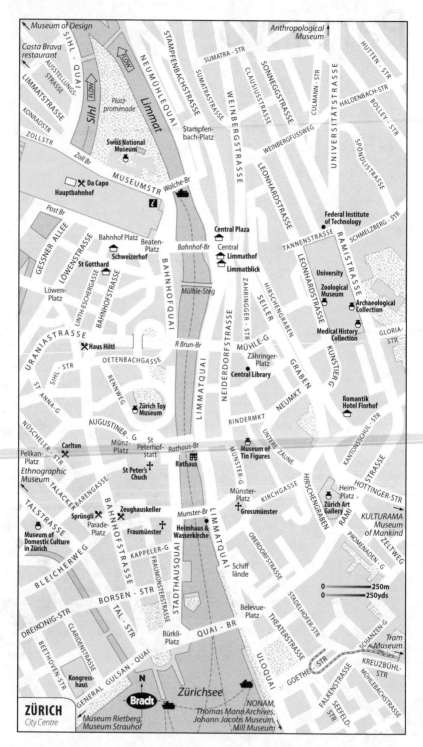

5

Zürich

Switzerland's largest city has become a popular destination for weekend and longer breaks thanks to its famously vibrant culture and nightlife, with over 500 night spots, to match its international reputation as one of the world's foremost financial centres. For those who know the city, it comes as no surprise that Zürich consistently ranks first among world cities in the Mercer's Quality of Life Survey. With a delightful old town straddling the Limmat River, some most attractive streets of good shops, over 50 museums, 14 theatres, 51 cinemas, an opera house and many concert halls, the city has a great deal to offer the visitor.

The city's origins pre-date the birth of Christ: in 15BC the Romans established a customs post here, though the first record of Zürich as a town was in AD929. The government of the city was taken over by the Guilds in 1336, and it joined the Swiss Confederation in 1351. It was in Zürich in 1523 that the great reformer Zwingli sparked off the Reformation in Switzerland. The first purely Swiss railway opened for traffic between Zürich and Baden in 1847, and 30 years later the city's stock exchange opened, growing to become one of the most important in the world today. Zürich is the world's second-biggest gold trading centre.

Culturally the city's most vibrant years were probably around World War I when political and artistic refugees swelled the ranks of the intelligentsia, among them James Joyce. He moved to Zürich from Trieste in 1915 and wrote much of *Ulysses* before leaving in 1919, only to return in 1940. He died the following year and is buried in the Fluntern Cemetery. The most tangible product of the World War I years was the founding of Dadaism in 1916 at the Cabaret Voltaire on Spiegelgasse.

The 21st century has seen the previously industrial area of Zürich West transformed with cafés, trendy shops such as Freitag at Geroldstrasse 17, and cultural venues, reached by a new tram route (17) to Werdhölzli. Nearby is Im Viadukt, a linear shopping district created along an attractive stone railway viaduct with shops selling designer clothes and funky accessories. An indoor market has 50 stalls selling produce from local farms, which provide ingredients for the city's restaurants.

The size of the city is modest (a population of 380,000), and the compact central area is easy to explore on foot. The region enjoys outstandingly good and well-integrated public transport, as well as facilities for cyclists and walkers. A measure of its efficiency is that only 25% of commuters use cars for their journeys to work, helping to make Zürich's air quality among the best in urban Europe.

GETTING THERE

Whether travelling by train from elsewhere in Switzerland, by international train or from the airport, passengers arrive at the imposing terminus of Zürich

Hauptbahnhof (HB), opened in 1871. To reach the tourist office when you arrive, go straight ahead from the end of the platforms into what would be the choir of a cathedral, and the tourist office is on the far left-hand side. Ask for a map of the S-Bahn network, which shows all the railway lines and connecting bus routes on one side and on the other the tram network and connecting buses, as well as the train and bus network around Winterthur. The office supplies two maps: a Cityplan of the centre and a Stadtplan showing most of Zürich. Also ask for the monthly *Zürich Events*.

GETTING AROUND

USING PUBLIC TRANSPORT Public transport in Zürich is organised by the Zürcher Verkehrsverbund (ZVW); the booklet *Tickets and prices* explains the ticket options and where and how to buy tickets. Single tickets are of course available, but the best value is the range of day or multiple-day passes. The latter can be used by one person on six days, or by several people travelling together, validating one section of the pass per person. The city is divided into tariff zones, which are shown on the S-Bahn map. Children under six travel free, and those between six and 16 travel for half price. Tickets cannot be purchased on trams or buses, and a surcharge is imposed on anyone travelling without a ticket.

Holders of Swiss and Flexi Passes can use the whole network and boat services free; Eurailpasses and Swiss Cards are valid on S-Bahn lines and on the lake.

The ZürichCARD confers not only free use of public transport within the city and even up the Üetliburg mountain, but also free admission to over 40 museums, a wide range of discounts and a free drink at some restaurants. It is valid for 24 or 72 hours and can be bought at Zürich Airport, railway stations and at the tourist office at the main station.

During 2014 four new underground platforms will be added to the existing four beneath the main station. The new station is called Löwenstrasse and will allow through running of more suburban and inter-city trains, such as Geneva–Zürich–St Gallen services.

Besides the railways, trams and buses, there are three funiculars in Zürich. From the area called Central – one of the principal tram junctions just the other side of Bahnhof Bridge from the station – the Polybahn funicular ascends to the Institute of Technology and the university. From Römerhofplatz (on tram lines 3, 8 and 15) a funicular rises to the Dolder area, where there are wooded walks, tennis courts and a golf course. The largest area of woods above the city, on the Zürichberg, can be reached by funicular from Rigiplatz (tram lines 9 and 10 or bus route 33) to Rigiblick, so named because the Rigi (see *Chapter 13*, page 177) can be seen from there.

CYCLING Free bikes and bike trailers (only at Velogate) can be 'hired' from Velogate (⊕ *Nov–Apr 08.00–19.00 daily, May–Oct 07.00–21.30 daily*) on platform 18 at Zürich HBF. You need to present some form of ID and a SFr20 deposit. If you use a vehicle for longer than six hours, it costs SFr5 or SFr20 overnight.

TOURIST INFORMATION

🄘 Station concourse; ☏ 044 215 40 44;
e information@zuerich.com; www.zuerich.com;
⊕ May–Oct 08.00–20.30 Mon–Sat, 08.30–18.30

Sun; Nov–Apr 08.30–19.00 Mon–Sat, 09.00–
18.00 Sun. Guided tours.

WHERE TO STAY

The majority of central hotels are on the east bank of the River Limmat, and therefore a tram ride across the Bahnhof Bridge to Central (tram 3, 6, 7 or 10). However, directly opposite the main exit from the station is the:

Schweizerhof****** (H)** Bahnhofplatz 7, CH-8021; 044 218 88 88; e info@hotelschweizerhof.com; www.hotelschweizerhof.com

A hotel only a little further away is the:

St Gotthard******** Bahnhofstrasse 87, CH-8021; 044 227 77 00; e reservation@hotelstgotthard.ch; www.hotelstgotthard.ch

Most of the hotels are on or just off Limmatquai or in the fork between Limmatquai and Seilergraben, the closest to the station being:

Central Plaza******** Central 1, CH-8001; 044 256 56 56; e info@central.ch; www.central.ch

Limmatblick******* Limmatquai 136, CH-8001; 044 254 60 00; e reception@limmatblick.ch; www.limmatblick.ch

Limmathof****** Limmatquai 142, CH-8001; 044 267 60 40; e info@limmathof.com; www.limmathof.com

For those in search of a quiet hotel within a few minutes' walk of the old town, the Florhof has no passing traffic, a good restaurant and is an attractively restored building dating from 1576 (two stops to Neumarkt on tram 3 or bus 31).

Romantik Hotel Florhof***** (H)** Florhofgasse 4, CH-8001; 044 250 26 26; e info@florhof.ch; www.florhof.ch

WHERE TO EAT

Restaurants near the station are:

Carlton Bahnhofstrasse 41; 044 227 19 19. French. Art Deco building. Tram stop Paradeplatz, lines 2, 6, 7, 8, 11, 13.

Costa Brava Limmatstrasse 267; 044 272 27 71. Spanish. Tram stop Dammweg, lines 4, 13.

Da Capo In station; 044 217 15 15. Mediterranean.

Haus Hiltl Sihlstrasse 28; 044 227 70 00. Top-quality vegetarian restaurant founded in 1898. Tram stop Rennweg, lines 6, 7, 11, 13 or Sihlstrasse, lines 2, 9.

Confisserie Sprüngli Bahnhofstrasse 21; 044 224 46 46. Famous café founded in 1836 selling breakfast & light lunches. Tram stop Paradeplatz, lines 2, 6, 7, 8, 9, 11, 13.

Zeughauskeller Bahnhofstrasse 28a at Paradeplatz; 044 220 15 15. City's top beer hall with wood-ceilinged 15th-century cellar serving hearty meat dishes. Tram stop Paradeplatz, lines 2, 6, 7, 8, 11, 13.

WHAT TO SEE

EXPLORING THE OLD TOWN The best way to see the old town is on foot, not least because many of its streets have restricted access for motor vehicles. The *City Map* provided by the tourist office has a suggested walking route which takes in most of the centre's main sights. The order is immaterial, but there are some streets and buildings that should not be missed.

Before leaving the station it is worth spending a few minutes admiring it and the statue outside to the right; this tribute to the great railway magnate Alfred Escher was created by Richard Kissling in 1889. You can reach the old town in minutes either by taking a tram (6, 7, 11 or 13) or by walking down Bahnhofstrasse, the city's principal shopping street, which was built on the site of the city walls. Softened by trees and mostly free of traffic, it is a pleasure to walk along. Turn left into Augustinergasse which is lined with 17th- and 18th-century houses, many with bay windows. The street is broken by Münzplatz on which stands the Augustinerkirche, built in the late 13th century and secularised in 1525; its choir was later converted into the mint. The nave was returned to religious use in 1842 and the whole building was restored in

1958–59. There is also a fountain in the square, one of 1,030 in the city – the water is safe to drink, as it is in all of Zürich's fountains. At No 9 Augustinergasse is Museum Strauhof, which hosts temporary exhibitions on literary themes.

The street leads into the delightful St Peterhofstatt (St Peter's Square). Sitting in the quiet shade of its central tree, surrounded by historic buildings and with the only sound coming from the modern sculptural fountain, it is hard to believe one is in the centre of the country's largest city. On one side is St Peter's, Zürich's oldest parish church, though this is the fourth building on the site. The tower dates from c1450 and has the largest church clock face in Europe, at 8.7m (28½ft), which was installed in 1534. Restoration in the 1970s returned the church to its 1705 state when the nave was rebuilt. The barrel vault has fine stucco, the pulpit is oddly positioned in the arch of the apse, and stalls line the perimeter of the whole church. The church contains the grave of the theologian Johann Caspar Lavater (1741–1801) whose house (No 6) is on the opposite side of the square; he was visited here by Goethe. The pastor of St Peter's for 23 years, Lavater was shot by a French soldier while tending the wounded during the seizure of the city.

To the north of St Peter's Square is the Lindenhof, a raised area on which the Roman customs post was sited, followed by a ten-towered fort. This was enlarged c800 by Charlemagne into a palace that was occupied by German kings and emperors in the following century, law being administered from under the linden tree. The palace was destroyed in 1218 when Zürich became a free, imperial city. Today it is a park with a giant chess board and views across the Limmat.

To the south of St Peter's Square is the Fraumünster, founded in 853 as a convent for noble ladies by the German King Ludwig, whose daughter Hildegard was the first abbess. Having been suppressed in 1534 and adapted to become the Stadthaus, the convent has been reduced to a few remains: part of the Romanesque south tower, with blind arcading; part of the cloister; and most importantly the choir, with its screen of 1470, and the transept, both of which have stained glass by Marc Chagall, installed in 1970 and 1978. The keystones in the vaults of the transept are also noteworthy.

Adjacent to the Fraumünster is the Zunfthaus zur Meisen, the vintners' guild house that was built in Rococo style in the mid 18th century. This now contains the ceramic collection of the National Museum (see opposite).

Across the Münster Bridge, at the end on the right is the neo-classical Helmhaus of 1791–94, which is now used for exhibitions. Adjacent to it towards the lake is the Wasserkirche, which was on an island until the extension of Limmatquai in 1839. The late Gothic church was built in 1479–84 on the site of a much earlier church. It was secularised in 1521, and for nearly 300 years from 1631 was used as the city library. It reverted to being a church in 1942 and has stained glass by A Giacometti.

Continuing into Münsterplatz, the Grossmünster (🕐 Mar–Oct 09.00–18.00 Mon–Sat; Nov–Mar 10.00–17.00 Mon–Sat, after service on Sun) is the largest church in the city, its twin towers with their octagonal lanterns dominating the skyline. Built on the site of an earlier building, the present Romanesque basilica was begun before 1100 and largely completed by 1230. It was here that Zwingli preached. The nave is unusually high, and the church contains complete and fragmented wall-paintings of the 13th and 14th centuries. In the crypt is a statue made in 1460 of Charlemagne, the founder of the original church on this site. The stained glass designed by A Giacometti was installed in 1932. The cloisters of c1200, which are now part of the university theological faculty, should not be missed for the grotesque faces, monkeys, dragons and centaurs which decorate the 12th-century capitals and spandrels of the arched windows.

A little to the northwest is the Rathaus (Town Hall), built in 1694–98 on the barrel vault of the old one. Along the Limmatquai between Münster and Bahnhof bridges is a series of guildhalls, some with origins in the 13th century but mostly rebuilt in the 16th to 18th centuries.

Turning right up Mühlegasse to Zähringerplatz is the Central Library, built in 1915–17 on the site of a Dominican monastery. The state archives are housed in the adjacent former Predigerkirche, completed in 1269 with a Gothic choir added in the following century.

All the streets to the south of the library are worth exploring, as nearly all have buildings of interest. Neumarkt and Rindermarkt form the longest street of the old town. Speigelgasse has a 14th-century tower (No 26). No 11 was the home of Lavater in the 1740s, No 12 was the house in which the German poet Georg Büchner, author of *Wozzeck*, died in 1837 and No 14 was Lenin's home from February 1916 until his portentous return to Russia in April 1917.

MUSEUMS Zürich has over 50 museums, and a separate guide to them is available from the tourist office. Unless otherwise stated, entrance is free.

Swiss National Museum (Schweizerische Landesmuseum) (*Museumstrasse 2, opposite railway station on north side, connected by subway;* ✆ *044 218 65 11;* ⏰ *10.00–17.00 Tue–Sun; admission charge; tram 4, 11, 13 or 14*) As its name suggests, this is the most wide-ranging museum in Zürich, housed in a purpose-built neo-Gothic edifice designed to fuse various Swiss styles to resemble a castle. Completed in 1898, the museum has artefacts dating from the Stone Age to the 19th century. The entrance is to the left of the archway, just beyond the St Gotthard stage-coach. Its sections include pre- and early history, weapons, flags, uniforms and costumes, metalwork from pewter to gold, glass, jewellery, textiles, ceramics, sculpture, paintings, musical instruments, watches and farming implements. There are also entire rooms from medieval and Renaissance buildings that have been dismantled and reconstructed.

Zürich Art Gallery (Kunsthaus Zürich) (*Heimplatz 1;* ✆ *044 253 84 84;* ⏰ *10.00– 20.00 Wed–Fri, 10.00–18.00 Sat–Sun & Tue; admission charge; tram 3, 5, 8 or 9 or bus 31 to Kunsthaus*) The gallery has been successively enlarged since 1910 to house a large collection ranging from 15th-century religious works to late 20th-century paintings. Amongst the international artists represented are El Greco, Bellotto, Guardi, Canaletto, Hals, Hobbema, Cranach the Elder, Jan Breughel the Elder, Renoir, Courbet, Seurat, Manet, Corot, Bonnard, Rodin, Gauguin, Klee, Kandinsky, Chagall, Van Gogh, Picasso, Magritte, Ernst, Miró, Munch and Kokoschka. Swiss painters include Angelica Kauffmann, Böcklin, Füssli, Segantini, Koller, Anker and Hodler. There are changing exhibitions of international and local artists.

Among the best-known paintings is the *Gotthard Post*, painted in 1873 by Rudolf Koller, which was commissioned as a present for Alfred Escher, whose statue stands beside the station. It has been described as the most popular painting in Swiss art.

Aathal Dinosaur Museum See table 740/S14, pages 60–1.

Museum Rietberg (*Gablerstrasse 15;* ✆ *044 206 31 31;* ⏰ *10.00–17.00 Tue–Sun, 10.00–20.00 Wed & Thu; admission charge; tram 7 to Museum Rietberg*) Housed in a neo-classical mansion built in 1857, this collection of non-European art includes sculpture from India, China, Japan, Africa and South America.

Collection of Prints and Drawings of the Federal Institute of Technology (Graphische Sammlung der ETH) *(ETH, Rämistrasse 101, entrance on Künstlergasse;* ☏ *044 632 40 46;* ☉ *10.00–17.00 Mon–Fri, 10.00–19.00 Wed) during exhibitions; admission charge; tram 6, 9 or 10 to ETH-Zentrum)* Large collection of woodcuts, etchings and engravings by European masters such as Mantegna, Dürer, Rembrandt, Canaletto, Piranesi, Goya and Picasso.

Museum of Domestic Culture in Zürich (Museum Bärengasse) *(Bärengasse 20–22, entrance on Basteiplatz;* ☏ *044 211 17 16;* ☉ *10.30–17.00 Tue–Sun; admission charge; tram 2, 6, 7, 8, 9, 11 or 13 to Paradeplatz)* Situated in two re-erected houses of the 16th and 17th centuries, the museum's rooms are furnished to reflect the decorative arts from 1650 to 1840. Special exhibitions. Doll collection.

Archaeological Collection of the University (Archäologische Sammlung) *(Rämistrasse 73;* ☏ *044 634 28 11;* ☉ *13.00–18.00 Tue–Fri, 11.00–17.00 Sat–Sun; admission charge; tram 6 or 9 to ETH-Zentrum)* Collection of original objects found in Egypt, Mesopotamia, Assyria, Persia, Greece and Etruria (objects found in Switzerland are in the National Museum).

North American Native Museum (NONAM) *(Seefeldstrasse 317;* ☏ *043 499 24 40;* ☉ *13.00–17.00 Tue–Fri, 10.00–17.00 Sat–Sun; admission charge; trains S6, 7, 16 or tram 2 or 4 to Zürich Tiefenbrunnen)* Containing 1,400 artefacts relating to the native peoples of North America, this is the only museum devoted to the subject in western Europe.

Museum of Design (Museum für Gestaltung) *(Ausstellungsstrasse 60;* ☏ *043 446 67 67;* ☉ *10.00–17.00 Tue–Sun; admission charge; tram 4, 13, 17 to Museum für Gestaltung)* Changing exhibitions of everyday design and visual communication in 1930s listed building. Collection of graphics, design and 200,000 Swiss posters.

Central Library (Zentralbibliothek Zürich) *(Zähringerplatz 6;* ☏ *044 268 31 00;* ☉ *08.00–20.00 Mon–Fri, 08.00–16.00 Sat; tram 4 or 15 to Rudolf-Brun-Brücke; tram 3 or bus 31 to Neumarkt)* Reading room. Collection of manuscripts, maps and music. North American Library.

Thomas Mann Archives *(Schönberggasse 15, 2nd floor;* ☏ *044 632 40 45;* ☉ *14.00–16.00 Wed & Sat, or by telephone appointment; tram 6 or 9 to ETH-Zentrum, 5 to Kantonsschule)* The study and library of the German novelist, with documents of his life and work. Mann left Germany for Switzerland in 1933 after expressing opposition to the Nazis; he lived in Küsnacht until moving to the United States before World War II. He returned to Switzerland after the war and died in hospital in Zürich in 1955. He is buried at Kilchberg.

Collection of the Cultural History of Coffee (Johann Jacobs Museum) *(Seefeldquai 17, corner of Feldeggstrasse;* ☏ *044 388 61 51;* ☉ *14.00–19.00 Fri, 14.00–17.00 Sat, 10.00–17.00 Sun; admission charge; tram 2 or 4 to Feldeggstrasse)* Artefacts, books, paintings and special exhibitions on the history of coffee since the 16th century.

Mill Museum (Mühlerama) *(Seefeldstrasse 231;* ☏ *044 422 76 60;* ☉ *14.00–17.00 Tue–Sat, 10.00–17.00 Sun; admission charge; tram 2 or 4 to Wildbachstrasse or train/*

Zollikerbus to Tiefenbrunnen) Housed in a *belle époque*-style former brewery that was converted to a mill in 1913, the museum is devoted to the history of milling, following the course of the grain through the building's four storeys until it emerges as flour. Sections on nutrition and storage.

Museum of Tin Figures (Zinnfiguren-Museum) (*Obere Zäune 19;* ☎ *044 262 57 20;* ⊕ *11.00–16.00 Sun; admission charge; tram 4 or 15 to Rathaus*) Collection of 40,000 tin toys and figures, and Swiss history in tin figures.

Zürich Toy Museum (Zürcher Spielzeugmuseum) (*Ecke Fortunagasse 15, 5th floor;* ☎ *044 211 93 05;* ⊕ *14.00–17.00 Mon–Fri, 13.00–16.00 Sat; admission charge; tram 6, 7, 11 or 13 to Renneweg/Augustinergasse*) All manner of European toys from the end of the 18th to the early 20th centuries.

Tram Museum (*Forchstrasse 260;* ☎ *044 380 21 62;* ⊕ *13.00–17.00 Wed–Sun; admission charge; tram 11 to Burgweis, direction Rehalp*) Collection of old trams (the oldest from 1897) with historical and technical exhibitions.

Zoological Museum of the University (Zoologisches Museum) (*Karl Schmid-strasse 4;* ☎ *044 634 38 38;* ⊕ *09.00–17.00 Tue–Fri, 10.00–17.00 Sat–Sun; tram 6, 9 or 10 to ETH-Zentrum*) Exhibits depicting Ice Age mammals, birds and mammals of the world, insects, slide and film shows.

Anthropological Museum of the University (Anthropologisches Museum) (*Winterthurerstrasse 190;* ☎ *044 635 49 54;* ⊕ *noon–18.00 Tue–Sun; tram 7 or 14 to Milchbuck or 10 to Irchel*) The foundations of human development portrayed in diagrams, charts, audio-visual presentations and videos.

Medical History Collection of the University (Medizinhistorisches Museum) (*Rämistrasse 69;* ☎ *01 634 20 73;* ⊕ *13.00–18.00 Tue–Fri, 11.00–17.00 Sat–Sun; tram 5 or 9 to Kantonsschule*) History of traditional and Western medicine and surgery, with reconstructed rooms such as a children's ward from c1850 and a chemist from c1750.

Collection of Geology and Mineralogy of the Federal Institute of Technology (Geologisch-Mineralogische Ausstellung) (*Sonneggstrasse 5, Floor E;* ☎ *044 632 37 87;* ⊕ *10.00–18.00 Mon–Fri, 10.00–16.00 Sat; tram 6, 9 or 10 to ETH-Zentrum*) Collection of minerals, rocks and fossils. Reliefs, maps and changing exhibitions.

University of Zürich Ethnographic Museum (Das Völkerkundemuseum der Universität Zürich) (*Pelikanstrasse 40;* ☎ *044 634 90 11;* ⊕ *10.00–13.00 & 14.00–17.00 Tue–Fri, 14.00–17.00 Sat, 11.00–17.00 Sun; tram 7, 7, 11, 13 to Rennweg or 9 to Sihlstrasse or 8 to Selnau*) Changing exhibitions on non-European cultures covering social, technical and philosophical subjects.

KULTURAMA Museum of Mankind (Museum des Menschen) (*Englischviertelstrasse 9;* ☎ *044 260 60 44;* ⊕ *13.00–17.00 Tue–Sun; admission charge; tram 3, 8 to Hottingerplatz or 15 to Englischviertelstrasse*) Chronological survey of evolution ranging over 600 million years through fossils, dinosaurs and skeletons. Part of the museum covers the development of the human body.

EVENTS The city's principal event usually takes place on the third Sunday and Monday of April when the Guilds and citizens celebrate their spring festival, the Sechseläuten. Both days see parades of up to 7,000 participants in historical dress, 500 horses and floats and carriages. The Monday evening concludes with the burning of the *Böögg*, a white scarecrow symbolising winter, which is stuffed with firecrackers. On the second Saturday of August (usually) the city reverberates to the sounds of the Street Parade, one of the largest techno and dance music festivals in the world, with over a million participants.

PARKS The city is well endowed with green spaces, of which the most notable are:

Belvoirpark (*tram 7 to Brunaustrasse*) The largest park, with huge collection of irises.

Chinese Garden (⊕ *11.00–19.00 daily mid-Mar–Oct; tram 2, 4 or bus 33 to Höschgasse or Fröhlichstrasse*) A gift from the city of Kunming.

Irchel (*tram 9 or 10 to Irchel or Milchbruck or 7 or 14 to Milchbruck*)

Rieterpark (*tram 7 to Museum Rietberg*) With fine old trees.

Muralengut (*near Belvoirpark & Rieterpark*) With rose garden.

Arboretum (*tram 11 to Bürkliplatz, then walk in direction of Enge*) Part of lakeside gardens.

Quaianlagen A delightful walk beside the lake from near Bellevueplatz (*tram 4, 6, 8, 9 or 15*) to the rhododendron garden at the Zürichhorn.

City Hall Park (*Bürkliplatz; tram 11*) Holds a fleamarket on Saturdays in summer.

Of more specialist interest are:

Botanical Garden of the University (Botanischer Garten) (*Zollikerstrasse 107;* ☏ *044 634 84 61;* ⊕ *08.00–18.00 Mon–Fri, 08.00–17.00 Sat–Sun; plant houses 09.30–16.00 daily; tram 2 or 4 to Höschgasse or bus 31, tram 11 to Hegibachplatz*) Large garden divided into areas according to the ecological zone or botanical theme.

Municipal Garden, Display Garden and Greenhouses (Stadtgärtnerei) (*Sackzelg 25–27/Gutstrasse;* ☏ *044 492 14 23;* ⊕ *09.00–11.30 & 13.30–16.30 daily; tram 3 or bus 89 to Hubertus*) Peaceful park with conservatories and greenhouses of plants from all over the world, with a special display of orchids.

Municipal Succulent Collection (Städtische Sukkulentensammlung) (*Mythenquai 88;* ☏ *043 344 34 80;* ⊕ *09.00–11.30 & 13.30–16.30 daily; tram 7 to Brunaustrasse*) Succulents from the old and new world, with over 25,000 cacti.

Zoo (Zoologischer Garten) (*Zürichbergstrasse 221;* ☏ *0848 966 983;* ⊕ *Mar–Oct 09.00–18.00 daily; Nov–Feb 09.00–17.00 daily; admission charge; tram 5 or 6 to Zoo or bus 751 to Zoo/Forrenweid*) Over 1,500 animals of about 250 species with a rainforest hall, aquarium, big cats area and a mini zoo for children.

6

Around Zürich

There is plenty of scope for day excursions from Zürich, given the modest distances of most Swiss journeys and the efficiency of the railways. The tourist office suggests that day trips as far afield as Graubünden and the Ticino are perfectly feasible. The S-Bahn and outer suburban services from Zürich are frequent and most are operated by double-deck coaches that give excellent views from the upper level. For details of ticket arrangements around Zürich, see page 38.

ZÜRICHSEE (LAKE ZÜRICH)

The lake is Switzerland's third largest completely within its borders, covering 88.5km² (34.2 square miles). Boat services on the Zürichsee operate from the pier at Bürkliplatz (trams 2, 5, 8, 9, 11) between the beginning of April and late October. A variety of trips are available: 1½-hour short excursions; half-lake tours of 2½ hours; and longer trips down to Rapperswil and beyond. There are 32 piers the length of the lake to Schmerikon, enabling travellers to devise circular journeys using rail for one leg.

From May to the end of September, two paddle steamers with restaurants, *Stadt Rapperswil* (1914) and *Stadt Zürich* (1909), operate cruises between Zürich and Rapperswil. Evening fondue, Schnitzel, salsa, gay and oldies cruises are run on summer evenings.

Information and tickets are available at the tourist office, from the pier at Bürkliplatz or from boat operator ZSG (*044 487 13 33; www.zsg.ch*).

ZÜRICH HB–ÜETLIBERG Table 713/S10

A short and pleasant way to reach woodland walks and enjoy panoramic views over the city and lake with the Alps in the distance is to take the standard-gauge railway up to the 871m (2,857ft) peak at Üetliberg, a journey of 20 minutes.

Trains leave from the underground platforms on the west side of the station and follow the River Sihl for a short distance before starting to climb steeply after **Binz**. The suburbs of Zürich are soon left behind and the line climbs through woodland laced with footpaths.

From the summit terminus at **Üetliberg** (with buffet and adjacent children's playground), a path leads up through the woods to the summit hotel and terrace restaurant/café, built in 1879 in chalet style and recently refurbished. The path passes the first of the planets on a planetary trail that leads to Felsenegg, and on the left-hand side is the site of a huge Victorian hotel with cast-iron viewing tower and elaborate gardens; a picture of it may be seen in the small museum adjacent to the

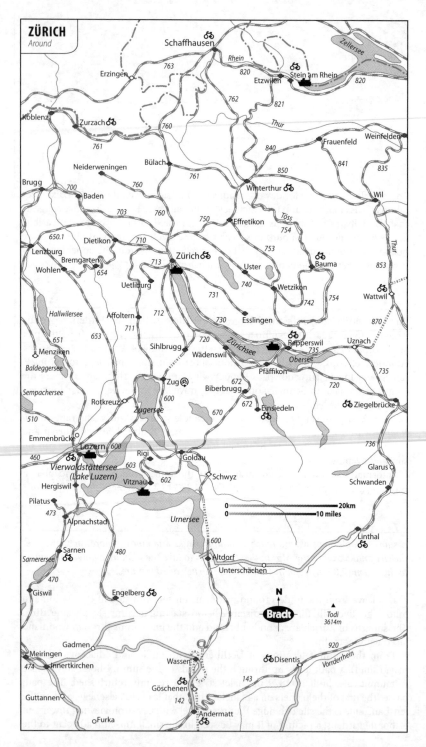

hotel which is devoted primarily to the Roman occupation of this strategic hilltop. A viewing platform on a huge telecommunications tower close to the hotel offers an even more impressive view for fit visitors – it is reached by 179 steps.

From Üetliberg it is a 1½–2-hour walk along the wooded ridge to Felsenegg, where there is a restaurant, for the cable car down to Adliswil (table 2705/line 26). It is an eight-minute walk to Adliswil station on the S-Bahn line S4 to Sihlbrugg (table 712) for a train back to Zürich, taking 16 minutes.

ÜETLIBERG
Where to stay

The hotel can be reached only by public transport so is in a peaceful location.

🏠 **Hotel Uto Kulm****** CH-8143; ☎044/457 66 66; e info@utokulm.ch; www.utokulm.ch

ZÜRICH HB–SIHLBRUGG Table 712/S4

The exit from Zürich provides a depressing example of the way urban space has often been ruined by trying to cater for the motor car: for a mile or more beside the railway the River Sihl is in permanent shade from a monstrous viaduct carried on pillars that are sunk into the riverbed.

Once Zürich has been left behind, the attractiveness of the river valley progressively improves. At **Adliswil** a cable car ascending to Felsenegg (table 2705/line 26) is eight minutes' walk from the station, and **Wildpark-Höfli** serves a wildlife park. Some trains terminate at **Langnau-Gattikon** from where there is a 1¾-hour walk or shorter cycle ride along the remarkably unspoilt riverbank to Sihlwald, Switzerland's largest natural beech wood, and Sihlbrugg. At **Sihlbrugg** numerous walks are signed from the top of the stairs from platforms 3 and 4, and a map indicates the routes.

A steam train with historic carriages hauled by two tank engines, of 1899 and 1911 vintages, can be hired for use between Giesshübel or Wiedikon stations in Zürich and Sihlbrugg (☎ *0848 962 962; www.museumsbahn.ch*).

ZÜRICH HB–ZUG Table 720

Zug is served by frequent InterRegio trains from Zürich and deserves a visit, with its lovely old town and lakeside setting.

This service shares with trains to Ziegelbrücke the line as far as **Thalwill** (also shown on table 720). At Thalwill the Zug line heads west through two long tunnels separated by a short stretch beside the River Sihl near **Sihlbrugg**. At the former textile town of **Baar**, St Martin's Catholic parish church has an attractive Romanesque tower with 17th-century cupola, and the half-timbered Rathaus on Hauptstrasse dates from 1676. The town has expanded rapidly over recent decades; the companies with headquarters here include the global commodities company Glencore. Low taxation in canton Zug has also encouraged many international companies to set up their European headquarters in the canton's capital. Though mostly bland modern buildings surround the station at **Zug**, the station itself offers a spectacular sight after dark when a lighting installation by the American light artist James Turrell creates changing effects using the primary colours. Ten minutes' walk brings you to one of Switzerland's loveliest and largely pedestrianised old towns. Zug is situated in the lee of the wooded plateau of Zugerberg, which has caused problems with periodic landslides, and at the northwest corner of the Zugersee, dominated at its southern end by Mount Rigi.

From the station, walk directly ahead down Alpenstrasse to reach the lake and walk along Seestrasse into Landsgegemeindeplatz, a pleasant tree-fringed square with cafés and restricted car access. Continue along Seestrasse to reach the old town, and turn left into Fischmarkt. Ahead you will see one of the old town's entrance towers, the **Zytturm**, built c1200, with blue and white tiles reflecting the canton's colours and incorporating an astronomical clock (open to visitors); on the right is the late Gothic **Rathaus** from 1505 with elaborate carving on the upper storey.

Running south from Fischmarkt are two parallel streets – Ober and Unter Altsadt (a third parallel street sank into the lake in 1435) – lined with delightful shuttered houses; their heavy overhanging eaves, dormer windows, window boxes and, in Ober, jetties along one side, give them a pleasingly homogeneous though not uniform character. Between the two streets are connecting walkways with fountains and trees, and at the southern end the streets meet beside the **Liebfrauenkapelle**. This church, dating from c1266, was restored in a restrained Baroque style between 1725 and 1728, and has an imposing organ gallery at the rear of the nave.

On the other side of busy Grabenstrasse from the Liebfrauenkapelle is Zugerbergstrasse. Take the first turning on the left into St Oswald-Gasse; at **No 17**, a painted house dating from c1540, there is a museum of masks and carvings from central Africa (*Afrikamuseum*; ⊕ *09.00–11.30 & 14.00–17.00 Mon–Fri*), and the Gothic **St Oswald's Catholic church**. Built between 1478 and 1545, the church is dedicated to the Northumbrian king and martyr, who gave to Bishop Aidan the island of Lindisfarne as a site for a monastery. The diffusion of the cult of St Oswald was largely due to the dismemberment of his body by the pagan King Penda, who defeated and killed Oswald in battle in 642. Inside the church at Zug is a painting of Oswald praying before this fatal battle. The late 15th-century choir-stalls are of exceptional quality and beauty.

Turn right into Kirchenstrasse to the half-timbered early 13th-century **castle**, which contains the town and cantonal museum (⊕ *14.00–17.00 Tue–Sat, 10.00–17.00 Sun*), with displays of silver, gold, archaeology, arms and armour, paintings, costumes, furniture, pewter and stained glass. The size of the stones making up the rough courses of the cylindrical tower of the castle diminishes as they rise. On Dorfstrasse to the right of the castle is the **Kunsthaus** (⊕ *noon–18.00 Tue–Fri, 10.00–17.00 Sat–Sun*), with a collection of largely 20th-century paintings, including work by Swiss Surrealists.

Return via Kolinplatz, on which there are some lovely town houses with a particularly fine carved-stone doorcase dated 1689 on the corner with Grabenstrasse, and Zeughausgasse for the **Münz**, which housed the town's mint and the Master's residence.

Boats on the Zugersee serve various piers around the lake that make possible circular tours using trains for one leg of the journey; they include Cham, Oberwil, Walchwil, Arth and Immensee. Boats leave from the pier on Vorstadt, at the end of Alpenstrasse, directly ahead from the station (*information ☎ 041 728 58 58; www. zugersee-schifffahrt.ch*).

From Zug station, bus 12 passes Hofstrasse 15 where the **Museum of Pre-History** (Museum für Urgeschichte) is located in a large former industrial building (⊕ *14.00–17.00 Tue–Sun; admission charge*). Archaeological finds from the Ice Age to the Early Middle Ages are presented in a lively manner with settlement models and a children's gallery reached by rope ladder. Bus 2 from the station (table 60.602, direction Menzingen) reaches the spectacular limestone caverns of Höllgrotten

(*Hell's Cavern*; ☉ *Apr–Oct 09.00–17.30 daily*) and the funicular that ascends the Zugerberg from Schönegg (table 2562 for bus and funicular).

PRACTICALITIES Bike hire is available two minutes from Zug station at the SBB site Eichi Ökibahnhof.

ZUG

Tourist information

🛈 **Reisenzentrum Zug** Bahnhofplatz, CH-6304; ✆ 041 723 68 00; e tourism@zug.ch; www.zug-tourismus.ch; ☉ 09.00–19.00 Mon–Fri, 09.00–noon, 12.30–16.00 Sat, Apr–Oct 09.00–15.00, Nov–Mar 09.00–noon Sun. Guided tours.

Where to stay

A hotel five minutes' walk from the station is:
🛏 **Zugertor***** Baarerstrasse 97, CH-6300; ✆ 041 729 38 38; e info@zugertor.ch; www.zugertor.ch

The next closest is:
🛏 **Parkhotel****** Industriestrasse 14, CH-6304; ✆ 041 727 48 48; e info@parkhotel.ch; www.parkhotel.ch
An attractive, quiet hotel overlooking the lake is:
🛏 **Löwen am See***** Landsgemeindeplatz 1, CH-6300; ✆ 041 725 22 22; e info@loewen-zug.ch; www.loewen-zug.ch

ZUG–ARTH-GOLDAU Table 600

This section of the through journey from Zürich to the Gotthard and Ticino is constantly in view of the Zugersee, with steep orchard- and vine-covered slopes to the left. **Walchwil** is a quiet fishing village served by lake boats. For **Arth-Goldau**, see table 600, pages 195–9.

ZUG–ZÜRICH HB VIA AFFOLTERN Table 711/S9

A largely suburban route offering little of interest. At **Knonau** is a Gothic church and castle, both from the early 15th century, and at **Mettmenstetten** is an early 16th-century church with carved wooden ceiling.

ZÜRICH HB–BRUGG Table 710/S12

The section of this route along the Limmat river valley as far as Baden was the first railway entirely within Switzerland, opened in 1847. It is probably the only railway in the world that received a nickname based on food: because of the penchant by Zürich people for a particular type of roll made in Baden, a special train was run early each morning to convey fresh rolls. The line was consequently christened the Spanischbrötlibahn – the Spanish roll line.

As part of the main line between Zürich and Basel, this section is one of the busiest on Swiss railways, serving the industrial corridor through **Schlieren** to **Dietikon**, junction for the appealing tram to Wohlen (see table 654/line S17). A small tank engine is preserved under an awning on the north side of the line at Dietikon. At **Wettingen** is a former Cistercian abbey, founded in 1227 and now used as a school. The cloister has stained glass dating from the Renaissance to the Baroque, and the choir of the church has some fine late Renaissance carving.

Although **Baden** has become an industrial centre, the old town remains relatively unspoilt and is largely traffic-free. The town's hot springs were used by the Romans and are still an attraction, with several hotels offering health programmes, but the town did not develop until the 13th century. Little remains of the fortifications except the 15th-century Gothic gate-tower, its corner turrets framing a clock. The arch leads to the Stadthaus, where the Old Confederation met between 1424 and 1712.

Although the castle of Stein above the town is in ruins, the Landvogteischloss (bailiff's castle) survives intact beside a covered bridge over the Limmat. Dating from the 13th century with later additions, it is now a historical museum with a collection of Roman finds, arms, furniture, paintings and local history (⊕ *13.00–17.00 Tue–Fri, 10.00–17.00 Sat–Sun*). It also contains on loan an elaborate late 17th-century metal bowl depicting the town's fortifications that was owned by the American magnate J Pierpont Morgan.

In 1891, the Swiss-born son of a British engineer, named Charles Brown after his father, set up what was to become the internationally famous Brown, Boveri & Co in Baden to make electrical railway equipment. A magnificent legacy of this decision is the Langmatt Foundation (*Römerstrasse 30;* ✆ *056 200 86 70;* ⊕ *Mar–Nov 14.00–17.00 Tue–Fri, 11.00–17.00 Sat–Sun*), which contains many French Impressionist paintings collected by Sidney and Jenny Brown since 1908, including works by Boudin, Bonnard, Cézanne, Corot, Courbet, Degas, Gauguin, Monet, Pissarro, Renoir, Sisley and Van Gogh. The Foundation is seven minutes' walk from the station.

Children will enjoy the Swiss Children's Museum (*Kindermuseum; Ländliweg 7;* ⊕ *14.00–17.00 Tue–Sat, 10.00–17.00 Sun*), which has displays of toys and learning materials as well as a programme of activities and playrooms.

Brugg is situated on the River Aare close to the two places where it is joined by the rivers Limmat and Reuss. Three towers have survived: the Schwarze Turm, Archivturm and Storchenturm, and to the west of the town overlooking the Aare is Altenburg Castle, now a youth hostel. Adjoining the Schwarze Turm is the Gothic Rathaus from 1579, and around the cobbled Hofstatt is a cluster of former civic buildings such as the turreted arsenal (Zeughaus), salt store (Sallzhaus) and Kornhaus, as well as a local history museum. On the east façade of the former Latin School are allegorical wall paintings dating from 1640. The house where the educational reformer Pestalozzi (see page 231) died in 1827 still stands. At Museumstrasse 1, the town's Roman connections are evident in the Vindonissa Museum (⊕ *13.00–17.00 Tue–Sat, 10.00–17.00 Sun*); it is called Vindonissa after the name the Romans gave to the guardhouse and camp that they occupied from 15BC to AD260, which was across the river from Brugg in Windisch.

Beside this separate town are the remains of sections of wall, a 10,000-seat amphitheatre – the largest in Switzerland – and a gateway close to the abbey of Königsfelden. This was founded in 1310 by the widow of Albrecht of Habsburg on the spot where he was assassinated in 1308. Much of the original structure was demolished between 1868 and 1871 to enlarge the mental hospital that the abbey had become in 1804, but the 14th-century church survived with its outstanding stained-glass windows (1325–30) in the choir.

From Brugg station, a PostBus (table 50.366) ascends to Habsburg and the remains of the castle which was the seat of the famous House of Habsburg from the 11th to 13th centuries. The keep dates from its foundation in 1020, and the castle now houses a restaurant (✆ *056 /441 16 73;* e *info@schlosshabsburg.ch*).

BADEN
Tourist information
🚩 **Oberer** Bahnhofplatz 1, CH-5401; ✆ 056 200 87 87; e info@baden.ag.ch; www.baden.ch;   ⊕ noon–18.30 Mon, 09.00–18.30 Tue–Fri, 09.00–16.00 Sat

Where to stay

None of the hotels are close to the station, the majority clustering around Kurplatz on the bend of the Limmat. Those of historic or architectural interest include:

BRUGG
Where to stay

⌂ **Terminus Brugg*** Bahnhofplatz 1, CH-5200; ☎056 460 25 25; e info@terminus-brugg.ch; www.terminus-brugg.ch

⌂ **Limmathof****(H)** Limmatpromenade 28, CH-5400; ☎056/200 17 17; e info@limmathof.ch; www.limmathof.ch. Designer hotel with spa.

⌂ **Atrium-Hotel Blume*** (H)** Kurplatz 4, CH-5400; ☎056/200 02 00; e info@blume-baden. ch; www.blume-baden.ch. Listed building with unusual Roman-style atrium.

DIETIKON–WOHLEN Table 654/S17

This metre-gauge roadside tramway is a delight for connoisseurs of such forms of travel and serves the relatively undiscovered riverside town of Bremgarten.

Trains of the Bremgarten–Dietikon-Bahn leave from platform 11 on the west side of **Dietikon** station in Bahnhofplatz. Trains leave the station in a northerly direction along the street before turning west and climbing out of the town. The houses on the outskirts betray their rural origins with their adjoining barns and orchards. After **Rudolfstetten Hofacker**, the first of a series of exceptionally tight U-shaped curves takes the line steeply uphill to **Berikon-Widen**, after which the line drops down through equally tortuous curves to **Bremgarten**.

Situated on the east bank of the Reuss, Bremgarten is well endowed with medieval and Baroque buildings. Turn left outside the station (lockers and good buffet) until you see the sign to the Aldstadt where you turn right, soon passing a remnant of the town walls with covered wall-walk. Nearby is a handsome town house with coat of arms in the centre of a broken pediment and the date 1641 carved on the doorcase. Three towers survive, one of which, the Spittelturm at the head of Antonigasse, is dated 1557 and has a Renaissance coat of arms.

The 13th-century Catholic church of St Nikolaus is late Gothic. The river is crossed by a covered wooden bridge incorporating two chapels originally built in the 1540s and restored in the 1950s. On the west bank is a church dating from 1618 to 1621, which was once part of a Capuchin monastery that became a children's home in 1889.

A large number of walks are suggested from Bremgarten station, both on a map and by yellow signs. Amongst destinations with stations are Wohlen and Üetliberg (4¾ hours), and the banks of the River Reuss offer attractive walks.

Leaving Bremgarten and just before crossing the river, the tram calls at a tiny halt, **Bremgarten Obertor**, which is only two minutes' walk from the main street. The line climbs steeply out of the Reuss valley to **Bremgarten West** and through attractive woods in which there is a small halt for walkers. The tram draws to a halt beside the SBB station in **Wohlen**, on the line between Lenzburg and Rotkreuz (see page 52).

BREMGARTEN
Tourist information

🅴 Züricherstrasse 10, CH-5620; ☎056 648 42 00; e info@bremgarten.ch; www.bremgarten.ch; ⊕ 07.00–19.30 daily

Where to stay

⌂ **Sonne*** (H)** Marktgasse 1, CH-5620; ☎056 648 80 40; e hotel@sonne-bremgarten.ch; www. sonne-bremgarten.ch

Most services over this line operate between Aarau and Zug.

For Lenzburg, see table 651. **Wohlen** is the junction for Dietikon to the east, and has a terraced buffet shaded by trees at the south end of platform 1. The line passes through gently undulating farmland and coniferous forests to **Muri**, where there is an outstanding Swiss Baroque church that once formed part of the Benedictine abbey founded in 1027. The nave of the Romanesque basilica was pierced between 1695 and 1697 by an octagonal dome 25m (82ft) high, and the interior was lavishly decorated. The church has two early 17th-century Baroque organs. Beneath the choir is an 11th-century crypt, and in the cloister is some Renaissance stained glass.

At **Sins** and **Oberrüti** are delightful timber-framed station buildings. **Rotkreuz** is the junction for Luzern, Arth-Goldau and Zug, and has a buffet on platform 1.

For Zug, see table 720. From Zug the train skirts the northern shore of the Zugersee, paralleling cycle and foot paths beside the lake. Close to **Cham** station is the Hirstgarten park overlooking the lake. On a promontory stands Schloss St Andreas and its chapel, the former first documented in 1282 but much altered, and the chapel dating from 1488 to 1489 with Baroque alterations dating from 1675. The late Baroque Catholic church of St Jacob (1783–94) was given a zinc-covered spire in 1853 on a Gothic tower from an older building.

As the line makes for **Rotkreuz** (see table 653), it turns to the west away from the lake to follow the valley of the River Reuss, which comes into view on the right before **Gisikon-Root**. Part of the Renaissance cloister from 1591 survives at the former Cistercian monastery. For Luzern see *Chapter 12*, page 165.

Skirting the southern shore of the Zürichsee and offering fine views over the lake, the line serves a number of villages at which steamers call, facilitating circular journeys. It is also the route to the magnificent monastery at Einsiedeln. Sit on the left.

Leaving Zürich HB, the line curves south through the striking station at **Zürich Enge**, its frontage being formed by a curving arched colonnade topped by a clock framed by two flying female figures. It was built between 1925 and 1927 to the design of Otto and Werner Pfister. The writer Thomas Mann spent the last 15 months of his life at No 39 Alte Landstrasse in **Kilchberg** and was buried here after his death in 1955.

Thalwil, once the centre of Switzerland's silk industry, is the junction for Zug to the west, the Ziegelbrücke line continuing along the lake. At **Oberrieden**, the Reformed parish church of 1761 is by Johann Ulrich Grubenmann, and at **Horgen** the Reformed parish church has an almost oval shape and idiosyncratic fenestration, dating from 1780 to 1782. A short walk from the station at Bergwerkstrasse 27 is a coal-mining museum (☉ *Apr–Nov 13.00–16.30 Sat*) with a 1.4km underground ride.

At **Au**, part of the small peninsula jutting into the lake is a nature reserve with orchards and vineyards; it is looked after by a college devoted to viticulture and fruit growing which occupies the much-altered 16th-century castle in **Wädenswil**, a few kilometres to the south. Here, some timber-framed houses survive in the old town and the Reformed parish church (1764–67) is another building by J U Grubenmann. The station is the junction for services to Arth-Goldau and Einsiedeln and the departure point for the postbus service to Horgen station (table 70.150); this passes through Hirzel, birthplace of Johanna Spyri (1827–1901), who wrote *Heidi*. The large house where she lived still stands, and the delightful school she attended at Dorfstrasse 48 is now a museum (🕐 *14.00–16.00 Sun*).

Besides a pretty, unspoilt centre, **Richterswil** has an interesting group of buildings around a mill that dates from the 13th century; they have been adapted to become a craft school. Of the boat piers on the west shore of the lake, Richterswil is closest to the island of Ufenau, where the 12th-century Romanesque church of SS Peter and Paul stands on the site of a 1st- or 2nd-century Roman temple. The Chapel of St Martin was built in 1141, although its wall-paintings date from various centuries. Near the lake at Freienbach is a 13th-century castle which became the property of the abbey at Einsiedeln.

Pfäffikon is the junction for trains across the causeway to Rapperswil (see table 730). Just to the west of the station is the 13th-century fortified keep which housed part of the administration of Einsiedeln monastery; a moat and extensions were added in the 14th century. Leaving the town, a line forks off to the left to Rapperswil and the Zürichsee becomes the Obersee, connected by a channel through the causeway that divides the two.

Altendorf is served by boats on the Obersee, as is **Lachen**, where the large Catholic church was built between 1707 and 1710, its twin towers surmounted by sugar-castor domes. Just before the junction at **Ziegelbrücke**, the railway crosses the Linthkanal that connects Obersee with Walensee. Expresses continue beyond Ziegelbrücke to Chur, and branches go off to Uznach/Rapperswil and to Linthal.

THALWIL
Where to stay
🏠 **Sedartis****** Bahnhofstrasse 15/16, CH-8800; ☎ 043 388 33 00; e info@sedartis.ch; www.sedartis.ch

HORGEN
Where to stay
🏠 **Hotel Meierhof****** Bahnhofstrasse 4, CH-8810; ☎ 01 728 91 91; e mail@hotelmeierhof.ch; www.hotelmeierhof.ch

ZIEGELBRÜCKE–LINTHAL Table 736

This line keeps close company with the River Linth, which bisects the canton of Glarus, and serves some spectacular walking country around Linthal. It is one of those byways that deserves to be better known.

The northern part of the line is surprisingly industrial, the railway serving many factories as it heads south into the U-shaped ring of mountains that make up the southern part of the small canton. It is a 25 minute walk from **Niederurnen** to the small cable car that goes up to Morgenholz (table 2825).

The town of Näfels (station **Näfels-Mollis**) is best known in Switzerland for the extraordinary victory won in 1388 by 600 men of Glarus over an overwhelmingly superior Austrian force; the losses were supposed to have been 54 and 2,500 respectively. The battlefield lies to the east of the railway. The town's Schlachtkapelle, behind the Baroque Catholic parish church of St Fridolin and Hilary (1778–81) was created as a memorial to the men who fell in battle. The cantonal museum is housed in the Freulerpalast, built as a house between 1642 and 1647 with some fine Renaissance carving in stone outside and wood inside. The museum (⊕ Apr–Oct 10.00–noon & 14.00–17.30 Tue–Sun) contains examples of printed textiles, an important industry in the canton.

Netstal has a concrete Catholic church built between 1933 and 1934. The Linth is crossed just before the cantonal capital of **Glarus**, dominated by a series of peaks forming the Glärnisch mountain, the highest of which is 2,914m (9,560ft). The town's large neo-Gothic stone station from 1903 reflects the town's status rather than the needs of its relatively modest population. Zwingli, who was parish priest here for ten years from 1506, would recognise few of the buildings since fire fanned by the notorious Föhn wind laid waste the town in 1861. It was then rebuilt on a grid pattern, giving a neo-classical unity to much of the town's architecture.

A few buildings that survived the fire may be found around Landsgemeindeplatz, where the annual assembly takes place in May, and further away from the town centre. A fine example is the tall house built for the founder of the local textile industry (1746–48), the Haus in der Wies. To the north is the Spielhofplatz where some of the civic buildings built after the fire may be seen, such as the courthouse and school. The Reformed church was built between 1864 and 1865 to the design of Ferdinand Stadler. Near the Stadtpark, laid out between 1874 and 1878, is the Kunsthaus (⊕ 14.00–18.00 Tue–Fri, 11.00–17.00 Sat–Sun; admission charge), with paintings by Swiss artists.

A summer bus service (table 72.504) from the station serves one of the area's scenic delights, the small deep blue Klöntalersee, ringed by precipitous slopes. The Russian General Suvarov came past the lake in 1799 on his way through the Pragelpass beyond, heading for Schwyz.

Beyond Glarus, the valley floor is formed of rolling hills between the high mountains on each side. During the 19th century, **Ennenda** became a busy manufacturing village, and has some fine villas and housing from that era. While the train pauses at **Mitlödi**, you can admire the ducks and geese that live on a narrow strip between the station and river. The school here is located in a neo-classical house (1829–30), while on the hillside is a half-timbered house with façade paintings.

Schwanden is an industrial town, though the map at the south end of the station charts the extensive network of footpaths in the area. It was from Schwanden that Burkhardt Tschudi (1718–73) came to London and became one of the most eminent harpsichord-makers, providing instruments for Haydn, the Prince of Wales and Frederick the Great. John Broadwood, who later founded the English piano-manufacturing firm, was an apprentice to Tschudi and married his daughter. It was also a native of Schwanden who introduced the potato to Switzerland from Ireland in 1697. Near Schwanden is the country's oldest wildlife reserve, the Kärpf, set up in 1569 to provide two chamoix for each man in the canton when he married. From the station, a bus (table 72.541) goes up the valley of Sernftal to Elm, stopping at Matt, from where it is a five-minute walk to the cable car up to Weissenberg (table 2835). Another bus from Schwanden (table 72.544) goes to Kies for the cable car to Mettmen (table 2830). The Reformed church from 1753 at Schwanden is by J U Grubenmann.

Beyond the village of Luchsingen (station **Luchsingen-Hätzingen**), the valley narrows to reach **Linthal Braunwaldbahn**, where a station links the SBB with the steep funicular (table 2840) through woods and a bare rock tunnel to Braunwald at 1,257m (4,123ft). It was in this traffic-free resort that the idea for the Society for

Car-free Swiss Holiday Resorts was born. Built along a terrace affording marvellous views of the area's tallest mountain, the Tödi at 3,614m (11,854ft), Braunwald is popular for summer and winter sports, having eight hotels and many chalets. Besides 50km (31 miles) of footpaths through nature reserves, the resort has Europe's highest rose garden, which is a mass of colour when over 4,000 rose bushes of over 500 varieties are in bloom between July and September. From Braunwald, a chairlift ascends to Kleiner Gumen (table 2841) and from nearby Niederschlacht, a cable car goes to Grotzenbüel (table 2843).

It is only a short distance to the terminus of the line at **Linthal**, head of the valley and gateway to the Urnerboden valley, through which a road climbs across the border with Canton Uri to the Klausen Pass, Switzerland's longest pass. From the summit at 1,948m (6,389ft) the road drops down to the cantonal capital of Altdorf (see table 600). This is one of the most spectacular postbus journeys, the Historic Route Express (table 60.409), the service connecting Linthal with Flüelen station and pier (see table 600), but it is necessary to reserve seats (✆ 058 448 06 22; e *zentralschweiz@postauto.ch*).

From the station at Linthal numerous walks are signed, most with the white and red markings indicating that heavy walking boots and appropriate clothing and equipment are required. Destinations amongst the high-level walks include the Kisten, Richetli and Klausen passes, and there are a number of mountain lodges for hikers. In Linthal the Catholic church (1906–07) has a tower that dates from 1283.

Many trains serving Linthal start or finish at Rapperswil.

PRACTICALITIES Bicycle hire from Ziegelbrücke and Linthal stations.

GLARUS
Tourist information
🛈 Bahnhofstrasse 23, CH-8750; ✆055 650 23 23; e info@glarussell.com; www.glarnusnet.com; ⏰ 09.00–noon & 13.30–18.30 Tue–Fri, 09.00–16.00 Sat, 09.00–13.00 Sun

Where to stay
🏠 **Glarnerhof***** Bahnhofstrasse 2, CH-8750; ✆055 645 75 75; e info@glarnerhof.ch; www.glarnerhof.ch

BRAUNWALD
Tourist information
🛈 **Braunwald-Klausenpass Tourismus** Dorfstrasse 2, CH-8784; ✆055 653 65 65; e info@braunwald.ch; www.braunwald.ch; ⏰ mid-Jun–mid-Oct, early Dec–Mar 08.00–noon & 13.30–17.00 Mon–Fri, 08.00–noon Sat; mid-Oct–early Dec 09.00–noon, 14.00–16.00 Mon–Fri

Where to stay
🏠 **Märchenhotel Bellevue****** CH-8784; ✆055 653 71 71; e info@maerchenhotel.ch; www.maerchenhotel.ch. Supervised nursery.
🏠 **Alexander's Tödiblick***** CH-8784; ✆055 653 63 63; e toediblick@bluewin.ch; www.toediblick.ch
🏠 **Cristal***** CH-8784; ✆055 643 10 45; e info@hotel.cristal.ch; www.hotel-cristal.ch
🏠 **Resort Hotel Alpenblick***** CH-8784; ✆055 653 54 55; e info@klausen-resort.ch; www.klausen-resort.ch

LINTHAL
Where to stay
🏠 **Bahnhof*** CH-8783; ✆055 643 15 22; e info@hotelbahnhof-linthal.ch; www.hotelbahnhof-linthal.ch. Newly renovated.

Although this line serves commuter towns along the north shore of Zürichsee, it has some attractive sections with good views over the lake and to the vineyards covering the hills inland. The elevated position of the upper level of the double-deck trains is a novelty for many visitors.

Trains thread through the suburbs to **Küsnacht**, where a Romanesque keep has been adapted beyond recognition into a house, its top two timber-framed storeys built on a stone base of three storeys. At Tobelweg 1 is a regional museum (*Ortsmuseum;* ⊕ *14.00–17.00 Wed & Sat–Sun*) based in an early industrial building complex. Beside the lake is a venerable building called the Trottengebaüde where the villagers used to press the grapes. A former tithe barn that was once part of the Cistercian abbey of Kappel has frescoes from c1410. Thomas Mann lived in Küsnacht at Schiedhaldenstrasse 33 from 1933 to 1938. He also lived at adjacent **Erlenbach** between 1953 and 1954.

In Feldmeilen (**Herrliberg-Feldmeilen** station) is a 17th-century country house and estate named Landgut Mariafeld where the composers Franz Liszt and Richard Wagner were among members of the 'Round Table of Mariafeld'. Wagner completed his celebration of the simple man, *Die Meistersinger von Nürnberg*, while staying here. There follows a pretty stretch of line as it runs close to the lake shore.

It is worth breaking the journey at **Meilen**, where there are two fine 18th-century country houses, Seehalde and Seehof. Some of the wrought ironwork made for the latter is in the National Museum in Zürich; in the 1870s, Seehof was the home of the poet and novelist Conrad Ferdinand Meyer. The Reformed parish church is a much-extended building dating back to c700.

Rapperswil can also be reached by boat in 1¾–2¼ hours depending upon route. The town was founded c1200 and the older part is attractively situated on a peninsula dominated by the late 12th-century castle. A circular walk can be made by first turning left outside the station and right at the end of Bahnhofplatz into Fischmarktplatz to walk beside the lake (the town's fish restaurants are renowned). At Fischmarkplatz 1 is Switzerland's only circus museum (⊕ *Apr–Oct 10.00–17.00 Mon–Sun; Nov–Mar 13.00–17.00 Mon–Sat*). Beyond the square, continuing beside the tree-fringed lake, is Seequai, in which the tourist office can be found on the right near Hotel Schwanen.

The lakeside promenade becomes Bühler-Allee with a rose garden on the right, just before the much-altered buildings of the Capuchin monastery, begun in 1606. A flight of steps on the right leads up to the Lindenhof. At the top of the steps, turn right through the trees towards the castle. Deer can be seen in the field that slopes down to the lake on the left.

The waterfront was enhanced in 2001 by the opening of a new 841m wooden bridge – Switzerland's longest – to Hurden, forming part of Jakobsweg, or Way of St James, to Santiago de Compostela. During construction of the bridge, timber piles were discovered dating from 1523AD.

Parallel to Bühler-Allee away from the lake is Herrenberg, where at 30/40 is the Stadtmuseum Rapperswil-Jona (⊕ *14.00–17.00 Wed–Fri, 11.00–17.00 Sat–Sun*), covering a millennium of the town's history.

Rapperswil's castle was built c1230 by the Count of Rapperswil, destroyed by an army from Zürich in 1350 but quickly rebuilt. A square keep, round powder tower and five-sided clock tower are at the corners of the unusually shaped triangular courtyard (with all its castles, Britain has only one of this shape). Although the castle has been rather clinically restored – only the remnants of the gatehouse have the patina of antiquity – it contains the interesting Polish Museum (⊕ *Apr–Oct 13.00–17.00 daily; Mar, Nov–Dec 13.00–17.00 Sat–Sun*) illustrating the long-standing connections between Poland and Switzerland. A series of rooms illustrates the story behind Poland's struggle for independence and freedom between the 18th century and the rise of Solidarity from 1980 to independence in 1989. Many of the displays are devoted to Polish culture and arts, including a whole section on the pianist (and Prime Minister) Paderewski. Many Swiss craftsmen emigrated to Poland in the late 17th century and Swiss served at the Polish court until the mid 18th century. There were once 163 Swiss-run cafés in Poland. A Swiss designed the town hall in Poznan, of which there is a model in the museum. Set up in 1870, the museum at Rapperswil Castle became a bastion of Polish national aspirations and culture at a time when the country was partitioned by Prussia, Russia and Austria. The castle also houses a restaurant.

Leave the castle by walking beside its southern front, along the wall from which there are fine views overlooking the old town and lake, and walk through the tiny gatehouse. The smaller church on the left is the Liebfrauenkapelle, a late Gothic chapel from c1489 which serves the cemetery. The larger church on the right is the Catholic parish church of St Johannes; it was originally built in the 13th century, but had to be rebuilt after a fire in 1883. Its two asymmetrical towers were raised, rivalling in height those of the castle.

Between the parish church and the castle, a double flight of stairs flanks a fountain to descend into the pedestrianised main square, Hauptplatz. On the right is Hintergasse, with arcaded buildings, and at No 16 the Bleulerhaus from 1606; this street leads down to Endingerplatz in which you can turn left along Marktgasse to return to Hauptplatz with the early 15th-century town hall on the corner. Turn right to return to Bahnhofplatz. The station building itself, with octagonal turret and asymmetrical gables, is worth a glance, though it has been insensitively extended.

The town also has a children's zoo (*Knies Kinderzoo;* ⊕ *Mar–Oct 09.00–18.00*), which includes pigs, cows, rhinoceros, giraffes, zebra, emus, performing dolphins and elephants that give rides. Some may find the small size of enclosures and the repetitive behaviour of their occupants dismaying. Also on display is a small tank engine built in Winterthur in 1910. The zoo is ten minutes' walk from the station. Turn right outside the station and proceed past the bicycle racks, keeping as close to the railway as possible. A footbridge across the railway may be seen ahead. Cross it, proceed straight ahead at the foot of the stairs and a sign directs you down a street on the right to the entrance.

RAPPERSWIL

Tourist information

ℹ Fischmarkplatz 1, CH-8640; ☏ 055 220 57 57; info@vvrj.ch; www.vvrj.ch; ⊕ Apr–Jun & Oct 10.00–17.00 daily, 10.00–19.00 Jul–Aug daily, Nov–Mar 13.00–17.00 daily

Where to stay

⌂ **Schwanen**** (H)** Seequai 1, CH-8640; ☏ 055 220 85 00; e reservation@schwanen.ch; www.schwanen.ch

⌂ **Hirschen*** (H)** Fischmarkplatz 7, CH-8640; ☏ 055 220 61 80; e sleep@hirschen-rapperswil.ch; www.hirschen-rapperswil.ch

⌂ **Historisches Hotel Jakob*** (H)** Hauptplatz 11, CH-8640; ☏ 055 220 00 50; e info@jakob-hotel.ch; www.jakob-hotel.ch

Where to eat

✘ **Manora Restaurant** Neue Jonastrasse 20; ☏ 055 220 46 99. Emphasis on dishes prepared with fresh local produce.

✘ **Restaurant Rathaus** Hauptplatz 1; ☏ 055 210 11 14. Classic French cuisine & regional specialities in historic setting dating from 16th century.

✘ **Schloss Restaurant** Lindenhügel; ☏ 055 210 18 28. Mediterranean cuisine.

These routes form a letter 'X' and interconnect at Samstegern or Biberbrugg, enabling travellers from any direction to reach the monastery at Einsiedeln, one of the most important in Switzerland.

Taking the line from Rapperswil first, Zürichsee was first divided by a wooden bridge in the 14th century, which has been gradually rebuilt and enlarged into today's causeway with a channel for boats that serve Altendorf, Lachen and Schmerikon on the Obersee. For **Pfäffikon**, see table 720. The line to Arth-Goldau and Einsiedeln, once part of the Bodensee–Toggenburg-Bahn, climbs to the left through **Wollerau**, where there is a lovely church on the left overlooking the railway.

If you have to change trains for Einsiedeln, it is better to do so at **Biberbrugg** than at **Samstagern** since there is more shelter at the former. The line continues to climb through sparsely populated country on to a pastoral plateau. At **Rothenthurm** is a 13th-century tower left over from the conflicts between the monastery of Einsiedeln and Schwyz. Ten minutes' walk from **Sattel-Aegeri** is a chairlift to Mostelberg (table 2586.1). As the line begins to drop steeply down to Arth-Goldau, a magnificent view opens up to the south with Vierwaldstättersee in the distance. For **Arth-Goldau**, see table 600.

To return to the second route, from **Wädenswil**, the line climbs steeply to the junction at **Samstagern** (see above). Leaving Biberbrugg, the **Einsiedeln** branch swings east through the sinuous valley of the River Alp, soon reaching the town made famous by its Benedictine monastery. Proceed slightly to the left out of the terminus to gain the main street and turn left; the tourist office is at Hauptstrasse 85 on the left-hand side. The monastery is at the end of this street, about ten minutes' walk from the station.

The monastic community at Einsiedeln grew up around the place where St Meinrad was murdered by robbers in 861. Meinrad was educated at the island monastery of Reichenau near Kreuzlingen and ordained there before taking his vows as a Benedictine monk. Later desiring solitude, he chose the hill of Etzel, a little to the northwest of Einsiedeln. A stream of visitors seeking advice drove him further into the forest where he lived by a spring; it was at his cell here that he was murdered.

The first community was founded on the site in 934, and the pilgrimage to it was blessed by papal bull in 964. The monastery received the protection of, successively, the counts of Rapperswil, the Habsburgs and the house of Schwyz. It was during the period of Habsburg protection, in 1314, that the monastery was ransacked one night by a group of Schwyz men, angered by long-running disputes over grazing rights; they drank enough of the contents of the cellar to go on the rampage, smashing treasures and relics and departing the next morning with the monks and cattle as prisoners.

Perhaps the most famous priest here was Zwingli, between 1516 and 1518. Fires and sparse information prevent a clear picture being given of the five or six successive buildings on the site until the late 17th and 18th centuries, when a growth in both the monastic community and the number of pilgrims necessitated expansion. The decision to build a new monastery was taken in 1702 and the work was planned by Brother Kaspar Moosbrugger, though he had to incorporate two relatively recent buildings, the confessional chapel and the adjacent choir. He created a cruciform ensemble and four courtyards enclosed within a huge rectangle, which bears comparison in size with the Escorial near Madrid.

By 1718, the monastery was finished and work began on the new church, again to plans by Moosbrugger. The convex west façade overlooking the square was finished in 1724, followed by the two flanking towers in 1726, but it was 1735 before the rest of the work was completed to allow consecration of the new church. The square in front, the Klosterplatz, was laid out between 1745 and 1747.

The object of pilgrimage, the late 15th-century Black Madonna (replacing an earlier figure ruined by fire), stands in the octagon devised by Moosbrugger on the site of the ancient cell and first chapel. Although the monastery was plundered by the French in 1798, the Madonna had been carried to safety in the Tirol by the monks.

The sumptuous decoration of the church, much of it by the Asam brothers from Munich, makes it one of the finest Baroque buildings in Switzerland. Angels dangle legs over broken pediments while branch-waving cherubs gaze down on the congregation. The historian Edward Gibbon came here in 1755 and 'was astonished by the profuse ostentation of riches in the poorest corner of Europe; amidst a savage scene of woods and mountains, a palace appears to have been erected by magic'.

The courtyards should not be missed – those to the right of the entrance are open to visitors. Made up of barns and stables, some are still home to horses, their names or those of their predecessors given on enamel plates above the stalls. Through the archway at the end are rising hills with waymarked paths.

Einsiedeln has few other sights of note, but its oldest building is not even signed. Turn right out of the church along Klosterplatz, and straight ahead, over a traffic island, is a small stone church with tiny six-sided bell tower. This is the chapel of St Gangolf, begun shortly after 1029.

From Einsiedeln station, a bus (table 60.554) goes south along the valley of the River Alp to Brunni for the cable car up to Holzegg (table 2576), and a series of buses (tables 60.552/3/5) serves the villages beside the Sihlsee, now a reservoir.

PRACTICALITIES Bicycle hire from Einsiedeln station.

EINSIEDELN
Tourist information
ℹ Hauptstrasse 85, CH-8840; 📞055 418 44 88; e info@einsiedeln-tourismus.ch; www.einsiedeln. ch; ⊕ 09.00–noon & 13.00–17.00 Mon–Fri, 09.00–noon & 13.00–16.00 Sat, 10.00–13.00 Sun

Where to stay
Hotels overlooking the monastery, within ten minutes' walk of the station, are:
🏠 **Linde*** (H)** Schmiedenstrasse 28, CH-8840; 📞055 418 48 48; e hotel@linde-einsiedeln. ch; www.linde-einsiedeln.ch

🏠 **Rot Hut**** Hauptstrasse 80, CH-8840; 📞055 412 22 41
🏠 **Sonne**** Hauptstrasse 82, CH-8840; 📞055 412 28 21; e info@hotel-sonne.ch; www.hotel-sonne.ch
🏠 **Zunfthaus Bären (H)** Am Klosterplatz, CH-8840; 📞055 418 72 72; e info@hotel-baeren.ch; www.hotel-baeren.ch

RAPPERSWIL–WINTERTHUR Table 754/S26

Although part of Zürich's S-Bahn network, the Tösstalbahn has not a trace of suburban character and passes through attractive countryside that offers good walking.

The exit from Rapperswil overlaps the final section of line S5 through **Jona** to **Rüti** (see table 740), where S26 curves sharply away to the east towards the pleasant market town of **Wald**, where the Reformed church (1686–87) has a contemporary inlaid pulpit and balustraded gallery. Near **Steg** the line joins the River Töss, which it follows for most of the way to Winterthur.

At **Bauma** a preserved railway to Hinwil (see table 740) is operated by the Dampfbahn-Verein Zürcher Oberland (DVZO; ☏ 052 386 17 71; www.dvzo.ch) which has a collection of historic steam locomotives and electrics at Bauma. Three or five return trains are run on varying weekends between May and October over the steeply graded and scenic line to Bäretswil and Hinwil.

The popularity of this hilly area for walkers is testified by the numbers that use stations such as **Wila** and **Turbenthal**. A little to the north of Turbenthal at Hutzlikon are the remains of an early 14th-century castle, Breitlandenberg Burg. At Zell (**Rämismühle-Zell** station), some mid 14th-century wall-paintings can be seen in the bell tower of the Gothic Reformed parish church. From **Kollbrunn** it is a walk of about 2km (1½ miles) to the spectacular castle of Kyburg (though a longer distance, it can also be reached by postbus from the Zürich–Winterthur line; see opposite). The largest medieval stronghold in eastern Switzerland, Kyburg is magnificently positioned on a rock above the Töss and retains its 11th–13th-century buildings. Now a museum (www.schlosskyburg.ch; ☉ Nov–late Mar 10.30–16.30 Sat–Sun; late Mar–Oct 10.30–17.30 Tue–Sun) with collections of furniture, arms and armour, it conveys a vivid impression of feudal life with rooms on view from cellars to attic. The chapel has 13th–15th-century wall-paintings.

For **Winterthur,** see table 750 opposite.

ZÜRICH STADELHOFEN–ESSLINGEN Table 731/S18

More of a tramway than a suburban railway, the Forchbahn climbs into hills that offer walks through farmland. The generous space allowed for bicycles on the trams reflects the opportunity for cycling en route, for example a cycle route from Waldburg station to Zollikon.

The modern trams leave from an attractive leafy square outside **Stadelhofen** SBB station (on tram lines 11 and 15). The suburbs are soon left behind as the line enters wooded country with views over fields to Zürichsee to the right, although there is a return to the urban tram with a long section of tunnel near **Zumikon**. Some of the line's historic vehicles, used on special occasions, may be seen at **Forch**, the summit of the line where many walkers leave the train at weekends.

Beyond **Scheuren** views open up to the east over Greifensee and the large town of Uster on its eastern side. Buzzards and red kites are often seen. From Scheuren the line falls towards the terminus, pausing at **Emmat**, where walks are signed through neighbouring woods and farmland.

ZÜRICH HB–HINWIL/RAPPERSWIL Table 740/S5 and S14

The departure from Zürich gives an attractive illustration of progressive lineside management: near **Zürich Wipkingen** is a deep cutting in which the vegetation is kept in check by goats and sheep. There is little else of interest until **Nänikon-Greifensee**, where an attractive, early 12th-century castle, much rebuilt, is owned by the canton and privately let. In an angle of the lakeside town's walls is an unusual triangular church from c1350.

Above the industrial town of **Uster** stands the much-altered medieval stronghold built in the 11th century. The keep, topped by crow-stepped gables, is surrounded by mid 18th-century residential accommodation which is now a college of domestic science. Uster is also the start of a history trail that takes in sites of interest to industrial archaeologists on its way to Bauma. A short walk from **Aathal** is the Sauriermuseum (*Dinosaur Museum*; ⊕ *10.00–17.00 Tue–Sat, 10.00–18.00 Sun*) where you can see the biggest and smallest of dinosaurs, experience a dig and watch dinosaur films.

Wetzikon is junction for the lines to Effretikon, Hinwil and Rapperswil, and has the remains of a medieval castle. **Hinwil** is the end of S-Bahn services and start of the historic steam trains that run to Bauma on two or three Sundays a month from May to October (see table 754).

Taking the Rapperswil line, at **Bubikon** is the impressive Ritterhaus (*knights' residence*; *www.ritterhaus.ch*), the only surviving Swiss Commandery of the Knights of Malta. Founded in 1192, it has been through such vicissitudes as becoming a cotton mill, but is now cared for by a local society which has also created a Crusader Museum (⊕ *Apr–Oct 13.00–17.00 Tue–Fri, 10.00–17.00 Sat–Sun*).

The Reformed parish church at **Rüti** incorporates parts of a Premonstratensian monastery from which paintings of 1492 have become part of the choir. The Premonstratensians are an order of canons, founded by St Norbert in 1119 at Prémontré near Laon in France. Beyond Rüti the line passes through a thickly wooded river gorge with craggy rock faces towards **Rapperswil** (see table 730).

WETZIKON–EFFRETIKON Table 753/S3

Leaving Wetzikon, the line veers east to loop around Pfäffikonsee. A little inland on the outskirts of **Pfäffikon** are the well-conserved stone walls of the late 3rd-century Roman camp of Irgenhausen, their largest defensive site in Switzerland, with the remains of four corner and three additional towers. The Reformed parish church (1484–88) has late Gothic frescoes.

ZÜRICH HB–WINTERTHUR Table 750/S7 & 12

Although the journey has little of note, Winterthur should not be missed. Despite its industrial background, it retains an attractive, largely pedestrianised old city, and its prosperity has endowed the city with one of the world's finest art collections.

It is only 15 minutes by train from Zürich to **Winterthur**. In many countries, this proximity would militate against the smaller town having a vibrant cultural life. But Winterthur, with a population of only 89,000, can offer a variety and quality that would be the envy of much larger cities. Besides art collections, there is an aggressively modern theatre, a symphony orchestra that sometimes gives free concerts, and the Swiss Technorama.

The town's origins go back to a Gallo-Roman colony named Vitudurum, which was on the site of today's Oberwinterthur to the east of the centre. The present city was founded in 1170 by the Kyburgs, whose castles can be found in the surrounding countryside. Rivalry with Zürich has been a theme of its subsequent history, encouraging the entrepreneurship that gave Winterthur an early lead in Swiss industrial development. The city established a reputation first for textiles and then for heavy engineering; the name of Schweizerische Locomotiv & Maschinen-Fabrik, founded by a Middlesex-born Englishman, appears on the worksplates of steam and electric locomotives all over the world, while that of Sulzer can be seen in the engine rooms of ships – including many of the steamers on Swiss lakes. The money made through industry and commerce found its way into civic projects and the arts, creating some fine buildings and the collections that enrich the city and attract visitors. The City Hall in Stadthausstrasse was built between 1865 and 1870 and designed by Gottfried Semper; it is one of Switzerland's finest neo-classical buildings and hosts concerts in the main hall.

Leaving the station by the main entrance, the old town lies immediately to the east of the station. Walk down Stadthausstrasse from Bahnhofplatz; on the left is Museum Stiftung Oskar Reinhart (see opposite) and on the right is the Rathaus (1782–84), which was altered between 1872 and 1874 to create an elegant shopping arcade between this street and Marktgasse. In the latter is the Waaghaus, built in 1503 in a Moorish-Gothic style and now serving as an exhibition centre. Behind it in Kirchplatz is the Reformed town church with elements built between the 16th and 19th centuries.

The museum bus operates hourly from Winterthur station, from 09.45 during museum opening hours, to the Oskar Reinhart Foundation; this is also the stop for the Briner and Kern Museum. The bus then continues on to the Art Museum (Kunstmuseum) and the Oskar Reinhart Collection am Römerholz. On Sundays it also stops at the Villa Flora Hahnloser Collection and the Photograph Museum.

PRACTICALITIES Bicycle hire from Winterthur station.

WINTERTHUR
Tourist information
i Bahnhof, CH-8401; ✆ 052 267 67 00; e tourismus@win.ch; www.winterthur-tourismus. ch; ☉ 08.30–18.30 Mon–Fri, 08.30–16.00 Sat

Where to stay
The following hotels are within five minutes' walk of the station:
🏠 **Sorrell Hotel Krone*** (H)** Marktgasse 49, CH-8401; ✆ 052 208 18 18; e info@ kronewinterthur.ch; www.kronewinterthur.ch
🏠 **Wartmann*** ** Rudolfstrasse 15, CH-8400; ✆ 052 260 07 07; e wartmann@wartmann.ch; www.wartmann.ch

What to see
The Briner and Kern Museum (*Rathaus, Stadthausstrasse 57/Marktgasse 20; ✆ 052 267 51 26; ☉ 14.00–17.00 Tue–Sat, 10.00–noon & 14.00–17.00 Sun; admission charge; bus 1 or 5 to Stadthaus, or 7min walk from station*) Landscapes, still lifes and portraits by 17th-century Dutch masters and their influence on English, French and German painters of the 19th century are the themes of the Jacob Briner Foundation. It is supplemented by miniature portraits from the 16th to 19th centuries from the E S Kern donation.

Art Gallery (Kunstmuseum) (*Museumstrasse 52; ✆ 052 267 51 62; ☉ 10.00– 20.00 Tue, 10.00–17.00 Wed–Sun; admission charge; bus 1, 3 or 6 to Stadthaus, or 7min walk from station*) The municipal collection has works by artists from the 19th century to the present, including Van Gogh, Bonnard, Léger, Fuseli, Kokoschka, Rousseau, Braque, Monet, Pissarro, Renoir, Vuillard, Gris, Klee, Mondrian and Arp.

Oskar Reinhart Collection (Sammlung Oskar Reinhart) (*'Am Römerholz', Haldenstrasse 95; ✆ 052 269 27 40; ☉ 10.00–17.00 Tue–Sun, until 20.00 Wed; admission charge; bus 3 to Spital or 10 to Haldengut*) Winterthur's most important art collection was built up by the son of the head of the trading company Volkart Brothers, which was so successful that it spawned banks and insurance companies.

Its Swiss headquarters were in Winterthur and its main trading office in Bombay. From 1924 until his death in 1965, Oskar Reinhart built up one of the world's finest collections, which he gave to the Swiss Confederation in 1958. The collection includes works by Cranach, Holbein, Brueghel, Rubens, Rembrandt, Hals, Poussin, Chardin, El Greco, Goya, Watteau, Constable (*Hampstead Heath*), Delacroix, Daumier, Corot, Courbet, Manet, Renoir, Cézanne, Van Gogh, Degas, Picasso and Gauguin.

Oskar Reinhart Foundation (Museum Stiftung Oskar Reinhart) (*Stadthausstrasse 6;* ✆ *052 267 51 72;* ⊕ *10.00–20.00 Tue, 10.00–17.00 Wed–Sun; admission charge; bus 1 or 3 to Schmidgasse, or 5min walk from station*) A collection of over 500 paintings by Swiss, Austrian and German artists from the 18th to early 20th centuries, such as Friedrich, Böcklin, Hodler, Giacometti, Anker and Fuseli.

Photograph Museum (Fotomuseum) (*Grüzenstrasse 44;* ✆ *052 234 10 60;* ⊕ *11.00–18.00 Tue–Sun, 11.00–20.00 Wed; admission charge; bus 2 to Schleife*) Located in a former factory, the museum hosts five large temporary exhibitions each year and is the only institution of its kind in the German-speaking part of the country.

Swiss Technorama (Technorama der Schweiz) (*Technoramastrasse 1;* ✆ *052 244 08 44;* ⊕ *10.00–17.00 Tue–Sun; admission charge; bus 5 to Technorama*) Science and technology presented in an accessible and entertaining way, with sections on water, nature, physics, mathematics, automation, textiles, materials and music boxes. Plenty of interactive opportunities and historic industrial machinery, including operative steam engines.

Villa Flora Winterthur (*Tösstalstrasse 44;* ✆ *052 212 99 66;* ⊕ *14.00–17.00 Tue–Sat, 11.00–15.00 Sun; admission charge; bus 2 to Fotozentrum from station or 15 mins' walk*) Created between 1907 and 1930, this collection of Swiss and French art focuses on young Swiss artists and on the works of the Nabis (Bonnard, Vallotton, Vuillard) and Fauves (Matisse, Rouault, Manguin) groups as well as their forerunners (Cézanne, van Gogh, Redon). The Villa Flora retains the charming atmosphere of the former home of the collectors, Hedy and Arthur Hahnloser-Bühler.

WINTERTHUR–BÜLACH–KOBLENZ Table 761/S41

A cross-country line that follows the Rhine for its western half.

Leaving Winterthur, the line briefly follows the River Töss as far as **Winterthur Wülflingen**, where at Wueflingerstrasse 214 there is a plain 17th-century manor house with crow-stepped gables now in use as a restaurant (✆ *052 222 18 67;* ⊕ *Wed–Sun; bus line 2*). The building was saved by a benevolent society in the early 20th century and presented to the city of Winterthur. The interiors have finely carved and painted panels and a coffered ceiling.

Although **Bülach** was documented as a town as early as 811, most of today's buildings in the old town date from after its third and last major fire in 1506. To the west the town walls survive in the form of a line of houses. The Rathaus was built between 1672 and 1673 incorporating parts of an older building, and the large half-timbered Gasthof Goldenen Kopf was carefully rebuilt after a fire between 1965 and 1966.

Part of the riverside village of **Eglisau** was submerged when the level of the Rhine was raised artificially, but the group of half-timbered buildings and church by the riverside is delightful. The Romanesque church has a choir from 1350 and some late 15th-century frescoes, and there is a well-restored almshouse from 1682. Leaving the village, the line to Schaffhausen continues north as the Koblenz line turns west. Kaiserstuhl (**Weiach-Kaiserstuhl** station) was founded in the mid 13th century on an unusual triangular plan and has retained a medieval atmosphere with parts of the town wall, fortified towers and houses on Hauptgasse. At **Rümikon-Mellikon** are the restored remains of a 4th-century lookout tower.

Bad Zurzach has long been an important crossing place of the Rhine. The Romans built a large fort, of which there are substantial remains. In the Middle Ages it became the venue of one of Europe's most important fairs, and since the discovery in 1955 of thermal springs, it has developed as the spa of Bad Zurzach. Its principal building of interest is the Collegiate church of St Verena, once the focus of pilgrimage to the grave of the Christian nurse who is thought to have come from Egypt with the Roman legions and died here in 344 after 20 years of work. The 10th-century Romanesque nave was unfortunately given a Baroque refacing in the 18th century, but the choir and tower (1294–1347) and the Gothic hall-crypt underneath were spared. A 19th-century manufacturer's house overlooking the Rhine has been converted into an art gallery with terraced restaurant.

PRACTICALITIES Bicycle hire from Bad Zurzach station.

BÜLACH
Where to stay
⌂ **Zum Goldenen Kopf*** (H)** Marktgasse 9, CH-8180; ☏ 044 872 46 46; e info@zum-goldenen-kopf.ch; www.zum-goldenen-kopf.ch

BAD ZURZACH
Tourist information
✓ Quellenstrasse 1, CH-5330; ☏ 056 269 00 60; e info@badzurzach.ch; www.badzurzach.ch; ⊕ 09.00–noon & 13.30–17.30 Mon–Fri

Where to stay
⌂ **Park-Hotel***** Badstrasse 44, CH-5330; ☏ 056 269 88 11; e info@park-hotel-zurzach.ch; www.park-hotel-zurzach.ch

ZÜRICH HB–NIEDERWENINGEN/BÜLACH–SCHAFFHAUSEN
Table 760/S5 & 22

The principal route to Schaffhausen (there is a secondary route via Winterthur) and the branch to Niederweningen share the same line as far as Oberglatt. The latter gives access to the medieval town of Regensberg.

On the branch to Niederweningen, the second station is **Dielsdorf**, from which an hourly bus (table 70.593) runs to the fine medieval town of Regensberg, founded in 1244 and situated on an attractive hill-top site. It has Switzerland's deepest well at 56m (184ft) and a castle with a circular keep – although the castle is a children's home, the keep is open to visitors daily.

The line to Schaffhausen briefly crosses into Germany, taking a route through an area in which the border seems perversely sinuous. For **Bülach** and **Eglisau**, see above; for **Schaffhausen**, see table 820. Just after the Schaffhausen line leaves

Eglisau, the railway crosses over the Rhine by a very high bridge with wonderful views west, shortly before **Hüntwangen-Wil** station.

PRACTICALITIES Bicycle hire from Schaffhausen station.

ZÜRICH–BADEN Table 703/S6

This suburban route to Baden (fast trains go via Dietikon) takes in one site of interest: about 7km (4 miles) from **Würenlos** is the Benedictine convent of Fahr, which has long been linked with the abbey of Einsiedeln. Both the convent church and buildings date from the 18th century. For **Baden**, see table 710.

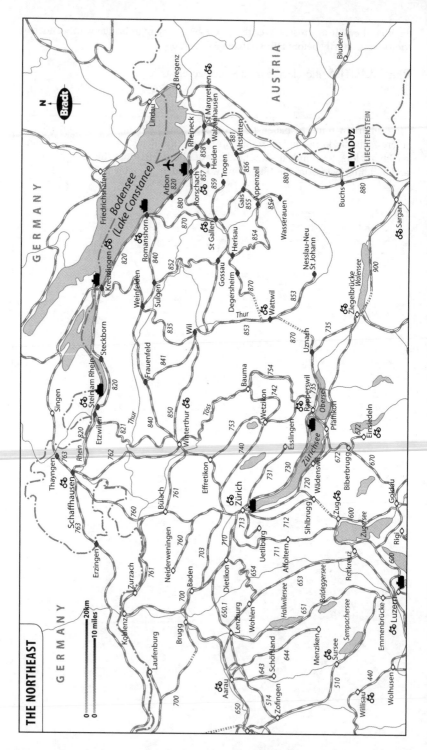

THE NORTHEAST

7

The Northeast

The northeastern cantons of Appenzell, St Gallen, Schaffhausen and Thurgau are not as well known as most other parts of Switzerland. Yet they have much to offer, both culturally and scenically. The Appenzell, for example, offers some of the country's most attractive terrain for walking and cycling, and the whole region has many delightful towns and villages.

WINTERTHUR–ST GALLEN Table 850

Baedeker dismissed this principal route with the terse comment: 'The St Gallen railway is unattractive.' It is an unnecessarily harsh judgement on farming country of orchards, market gardens and woods dotted with characteristic farmhouses of red-painted timber framing.

For **Winterthur**, see page 62. The first town of note after leaving industrial Winterthur is **Elgg** where the tall spire of the Reformed parish church dominates the late medieval town and its castle (not open to the public). The late Gothic church dates from 1508 to 1518, though the tower is thought to be c1370.

Midway between Winterthur and St Gallen is the large junction of **Wil**, from where lines to Frauenfeld and Weinfelden head north (see tables 841 and 835, page 90) and the line to Nesslau-Neu St Johann runs south (see table 853, page 78). Wil has some distinguished buildings in the old town. The outer oval ring of mostly domestic buildings stands fortress-like on a hill, similar to the northeastern side of Avanches, while an inner ring has a section of arcades. At the centre is the largely 15th-century but much-altered Catholic parish church of St Nikolaus, while to the north is the Hof. This late 12th-century castle was rebuilt between the 15th and 16th centuries and is joined to the town gate by the former residence of St Gallen Abbey, the late 15th-century Haus zum Toggenburg. Wil has the most important neo-classical house in the canton of St Gallen: the arcaded Baronenhaus dating from 1795 stands on Marktplatz and has a hipped roof and turrets.

Continuing east, the old choir tower of the Catholic parish church of Mariä Himmelfahrt at Henau (**Algetshausen-Henau** station) is considered the finest Gothic tower in the canton. Admirers of Arts and Crafts architecture can find an example of the work of the English architect M H Baillie Scott in **Uzwil**, where he designed the Langhaus Waldbühl between 1907 and 1911. From the station at **Flawil** it is only about 2km (1¼ miles) south to the beautifully situated Cistercian convent at Magdenau, founded in 1244 and periodically rebuilt and enlarged. About 2km to the east of Flawil is **Burgau**, which has some fine 17th-century timber buildings, including the Rathaus, which was built onto a 1632 farmhouse.

Gossau is a junction for the Appenzellerbahn (see table 854, page 76) and for Weinfelden. Within walking distance of the station is **Schloss Oberberg**. Built in the mid 13th century, it was rebuilt in 1406 after being destroyed in the Appenzell war. It later became the seat of the bailiffs of the abbots of St Gall, and was restored after a fire in 1955.

St Gallen

For anyone interested in architecture, **St Gallen** deserves at least a day, with its old town and the cathedral with its magnificent library, ranked by UNESCO as a World Heritage Site. The capital of the eponymous canton, its name is derived from the Irish monk Gall or Gallus, a pioneer of Christianity in Switzerland, who built a hermitage c612 in the Steinach valley. Between 719 and 752, an abbey was built on the site of his cell and flourished to become one of the most important religious communities in the area. The Benedictine abbey was encircled by a wall following a Hungarian invasion in 926, and by the second half of the 12th century markets were being held within it. The town's prosperity was founded on the linen and later cotton industries, its allegiance to the abbot ending in 1454 when St Gallen joined the Swiss Confederation. The Reformation was brought to the town in 1524 by its mayor and great scholar, Vadian, whose statue, recalling the appearance of Henry VIII, dominates the junction of Marktgasse and Neugasse. The town wall was removed in the early 19th century, and the monastery was dissolved in 1805, becoming the cathedral of the new diocese of St Gallen in 1847.

What to see and do Leaving the station by the main columned exit, go straight ahead across the square to the tourist office on the corner of Bahnhofplatz and St Leonhardstrasse. To reach the old town and cathedral, turn left out of the tourist office along St Leonhardstrasse towards the **Broderbrunnen monument** (1894). Beside it, turn right along Oberer Graben and almost immediately left into Webergasse to enter the largely pedestrianised quarter of the old town in Multergasse, straight ahead. Continue along Webergasse for Gallus-Platz; the cathedral is to the left.

Several architects had a hand in designing the **abbey**, which was built between 1755 and 1769, one of the last monumental buildings of the late Baroque. The long nave and central rotunda were designed by Peter Thumb, and the imposing twin-towered east front was a collaboration between J M Beer, Brother Gabriel Loser and J F Feuchtmayer, who also designed the confessionals.

With no stained glass and columns in off-white, the interior has a light, open feeling. The paintings in the rotunda depicting the advent of Christ in the presence of the blessed and those representing the monastery's patron saints in the domes of the nave bays are by Joseph Wannenmacher. The elaborate pulpit is decorated with four figures, while each wooden pew end has a different carved decoration. The intricate gilt wrought-iron choir screen was made in 1771 by J Mayer.

The interior of the adjacent **Collegiate Library** (*Stiftsbibliothek;* ☉ *10.00–17.00 Mon–Sat, 10.00–16.00 Sun, closed for 3 weeks in Nov; adult/child SFr10/7; for information about special opening times, see www.stiftsbibliothek.ch*) has been described as the country's most beautiful secular Rococo interior. The ceiling of the two-storey room was again decorated by Joseph Wannenmacher. Built between 1758 and 1767 following designs by Peter Thumb, the library contains one of the most important collections in Europe; particularly rare amongst the 130,000 volumes, 2,000 illuminated manuscripts and 1,650 early printed works are some 7th–12th-century Irish manuscripts, early scores of Gregorian chant, an 8th-century Virgil manuscript and a plan of the abbey made c820. Most of the buildings

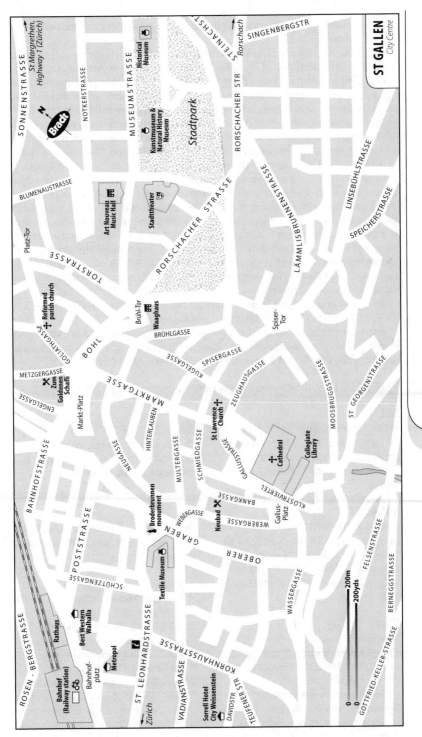

ST GALLEN
City Centre

Rorschach

SINGENBERGSTR

Historical
Museum

Kunstmuseum &
Natural History
Museum

Stadtpark

MUSEUMSTRASSE

NOTKERSTRASSE

SONNENSTRASSE

St Margrethen,
Highway 1 (Zürich)

N

BLUMENAUSTRASSE

Platz-Tor

TORSTRASSE

RORSCHACHER STRASSE

Art Nouveau
Music Hall

Stadttheater

Reformed
parish church

GOLIATHGASSE

BOHL

Brühl-Tor

Waaghaus

BRÜHLGASSE

LÄMMLISBRUNNENSTRASSE

LINSEBÜHLSTRASSE

SPEICHERSTRASSE

RORSCHACHER STR

STEINACHSTR

METZGERGASSE

Zum
Goldenen
Schäfli

ENGELGASSE

BAHNHOFSTRASSE

Markt-Platz

NEUGASSE

MARKTGASSE

HINTERLAUBEN

MULTERGASSE

SCHMIEDGASSE

SPISERGASSE

KUGELGASSE

ZEUGHAUSGASSE

Spiser-
Tor

MOOSBRUGGSTRASSE

ST GEORGENSTRASSE

St Lawrence
Church

GALLUSSTRASSE

Cathedral

Collegiate
Library

KLOSTERVIERTEL

POSTSTRASSE

SCHÜTZENGASSE

Textile Museum

GRABEN

OBERER

Broderbrunnen
monument

WEBERGASSE

Neubad

BANKGASSE

Gallus-
Platz

WEBERGASSE

WASSERGASSE

FELSENSTRASSE

BERNEGGSTRASSE

Rathaus

Bahnhof
(Railway station)

Bahnhof-
platz

Best Western
Walhalla

Metropol

Sorrell Hotel
City Weissenstein

ST LEONHARDSTRASSE

KORNHAUSSTRASSE

VADIANSTRASSE

DAVIDSTR

TEUFENER STR

GOTTFRIED-KELLER-STRASSE

ROSEN - BERGSTRASSE

Zürich

200m
200yds

0
0

in the monastery precincts were built between the 17th century and the first half of the 19th century.

The **old town** is a warren of narrow streets whose dominant feature is the profusion of glorious oriel windows – 111 of them – in a most public-spirited display of one-upmanship. A rewarding hour or two can be spent ambling through these streets, in which there are plenty of cafés and restaurants. On the northeast side of the old town, on a broad street named Bohl, is the **Waaghaus**, a merchants' hall dating from 1584. From the adjacent Markt-Platz, Goliathgasse leads to the **Reformed parish church of St Mangen**, founded in 898 and rebuilt c1100. Its Gothic tower dates from 1505.

Among the town's museums is the **Historical Museum** (*Museumstrasse 50; ⊕ 10.00–17.00 Tue–Sun; from the station, bus 1, 4, 7, 11 to Theater or bus 12 to Athletik Zentrum*), which contains models of the town, paintings, reassembled rooms, furniture, sculpture, arms and armour, musical instruments and stamps. The **Kunstmuseum** (*Museumstrasse 32; ⊕ 10.00–17.00 Tue–Sun, 10.00–20.00 Wed*) contains works by Teniers, Delacroix, Millet, Monet, Corot, Courbet, Pissarro and Sisley, and by eminent Swiss artists such as Angelica Kauffmann, Hodler and Boecklin, as well as naïve paintings by local artists. The **Natural History Museum** (*Museumstrasse 32; ⊕ 10.00–17.00 Tue–Sun, 10.00–20.00 Wed; from the station, bus 1, 4, 7, 11 to Theater*) has an exhibition of indigenous mammals and birds, living wood ants, dinosaur, geology and mineralogy.

At Vadianstrasse 2, off Oberer Graben, is the **Textile Museum** (⊕ 10.00–17.00 daily, 10.00–19.00 Thu), devoted to lace, embroidery and linen.

For those staying in St Gallen, the town's opera is highly regarded in Switzerland, performing in the **Stadttheater** on Museumstrasse, built in 1968. The municipal orchestra plays in the **Art Nouveau Music Hall** (Tonhalle) opposite.

PRACTICALITIES Bicycle hire from St Gallen station.

WIL
Tourist information
ℹ Bahnhofplatz 6, CH-9500; ☎071 913 53 00; e touristinfo@stadtwil.ch; www.stadtwil.ch; ⊕ 09.00–noon & 14.00–17.30 Mon–Fri, 09.30–noon Sat

Where to stay
⌂ **Schwanen** *** Obere Bahnhofstrasse 21, CH-9500; ☎071 913 05 10; e info@hotel-schwanen.ch; www.hotel-schwanen.ch

ST GALLEN
Tourist information
ℹ Bahnhofplatz 1A, CH-9001; ☎071 227 37 37; e info@stgallen-bodensee.ch; www.stgallen-bodensee.ch; ⊕ May–Oct 09.00–18.00 Mon–Fri, 10.00–15.00 Sat; Nov–Apr 09.00–18.00 Mon–Fri, 10.00–13.00 Sat

Where to stay
Numerous hotels; close to the station are:
⌂ **Best Western Walhalla** **** Bahnhofplatz, CH-9001; ☎071 228 28 00; e info@hotelwalhalla.ch; www.hotelwalhalla.ch
⌂ **Sorrell Hotel City Weissenstein***** Davidstrasse 22, CH-9000; ☎071 228 06 28; e info@cityweissenstein.ch; www.cityweissenstein.ch

⌂ **Metropol** *** Bahnhofplatz 3, CH-9001; ☎071 228 32 32; e info@hotel-metropol.ch; www.hotel-metropol.ch

Where to eat
✗ **Restaurant Neubad** Bankgasse 6; ☎071 222 86 83; www.restaurant-neubad.ch; ⊕ 10.00–14.30 & 17.00–00.00 Mon–Fri. Traditional Swiss cuisine in a 16th-century house with 1st-floor dining room. Closed w/ends.
✗ **Zum Goldenen Schäfli** Metzgergasse 5; ☎071 223 37 37; www.zumgoldenenschaefli.ch; ⊕ 11.00–14.30 & 18.00–00.00 Mon–Sat (& Sun, Sep–Apr). Specialising in fish, the restaurant occupies the 2nd floor of the 17th-century Butchers' Guildhall.

ST GALLEN–TROGEN Table 859

This delightful 10km (6¼ miles) roadside tramway begins at a separate platform outside and to the right of St Gallen station and is of particular use for walkers. Services are being extended westwards over the Appenzellerbahn. Sit on the left.

The streets through St Gallen accommodate both the twin metre-gauge tracks and road traffic until the outskirts at **Schülerhaus** where the tracks become single. The line climbs for much of the way to Trogen, affording marvellous views to the left over St Gallen and the increasingly deep drops into the valley floor. At **Schwarzer Bären** signposts for walks radiate in all directions, some taking you back to St Gallen, others sending you past the lake on the right. Soon after **Rank** (more walks), Bodensee comes into view. Just before **Schützerngarten** is a good view to the left of the attractive church sited on a knoll. The small health resort of **Speicher** has some good buildings, including a neo-classical Reformed church, as well as the railway's headquarters and depot.

Trogen is built on a hill and is the venue in even years of a meeting of the Landsgemeinde (on the last Sunday of April) in which local people can vote on the affairs of the half-canton of Appenzell Ausserrhoden – providing they are wearing a sabre. The Dorfplatz, where the meeting takes place, is a testimony to the town's prosperity since the 18th century, lined with affluent houses and two double palaces. The Reformed church dating from 1779 to 1782 in the northeast corner is a highly-regarded work by Hans Ulrich Grubenmann, one of a family of master builders who built many churches in the region. Uphill to the south of the town is a group of chalets known as Pestalozzidorf, named after the Swiss educational reformer. This children's village was built between 1944 and 1957 for European orphans of World War II; it continues to fulfil a similar role. The village has skiing in winter, including illuminated slopes.

From Trogen station a postbus (tables 80.229 and 80.230) connects with some trains for the well-wooded journey to Heiden (table 857), enabling a circular tour to be made via Rorschach.

SPEICHER
Where to stay

⌂ **Idyll Hotel Appenzellerhof**
Trogenerstrasse, CH-9042; ☎071 343 71 10;
e reservation@appenzellerhof.ch; www.
appenzellerhof.ch. Serves organic food.

TROGEN
Where to stay

⌂ **Krone** **(H)** Landsgemeindeplatz 3, CH-9043; ☎071 340 09 75; e info@kronetrogen.ch;
www.krone-trogen.ch

ST GALLEN–WATTWIL–RAPPERSWIL Table 870

The eastern half of this line is part of the Bodensee–Toggenburg-Bahn, along which the Voralpen Express runs on its journey between Romanshorn and Luzern. It crosses the highest bridge in Switzerland and passes through one of the longest tunnels in the country.

Leaving St Gallen, the train is soon above the level of the Winterthur line as it starts to climb up the deep gorge that carries the River Sitter down from the Appenzell towards Bodensee. The railway crosses the river on the outskirts of the town by the tallest bridge in Switzerland. Opened in 1910, the steel truss span of 120m (394ft) is supported by two slender stone piers 99m (324ft) high.

Shortly after **Gübensee** the lake of the same name can be seen on the right, and the junction of **Herisau** is soon reached (see table 854 for the town, page 76). Here you can change on to the Appenzeller Bahn. A historic train and steam locomotive (Bodensee–Toggenburg-Bahn 2-6-2 tank No 9, built by Maffei in 1910) is kept here and runs special trains, entitled the 'Amor Express', to Nesslau-Neu St Johann between April and October (*www.sob.ch*). Leaving Herisau the line swings briefly to the north, crossing a long stone viaduct before weaving through a series of deeply folded and forested valleys. To the right beyond the platform at **Degersheim** is a 2-6-2 tank engine on display, built in 1910; it once worked over the Bodensee–Toggenburg-Bahn. In the town is a Jugendstil Reformed church dating from 1908.

Immediately after **Brunnadern-Neckertal** the line enters the Wasserfluh Tunnel – at over 3.5km (2.2 miles), it is the second longest of the many tunnels on this railway. The train emerges at the junction of **Lichensteig**, a town founded c1200 by the Toggenburgs and built on an unusual triangular plan. Arcaded half-timbered houses and the former Rathaus can be seen in Hauptgasse. Close to the old town hall at Hauptgasse 1 is the Toggenburger Heimatmuseum (✆ *071 988 81 81;* ⊕ *Apr-Oct 13.00–17.00 Sat–Sun*). To the north of the town is the Baroque Loreto chapel dating from 1677 to 1680.

Wattwil is another junction for Nesslau-Neu St Johann, and a better place than Lichensteig to change for northbound trains to Wil. The River Thur flows through this small textile town on its way to the Rhein. Regarded as the 'capital' of Toggenburg, Wattwil has a reformed church dating from 1845 to 1848 with the rare feature of a nave wider than its length. Ringstrasse has several timber-framed houses and an old people's home converted from a factory and given a Biedermeier-style roof. Above the town to the north are the walled Franciscan nunnery of St Maria der Engel, with a church built between 1622 and 1780 and buildings from 1730 to 1782, and the much-altered and repaired Iberg Castle, built c1240.

Soon after turning southeast from Wattwil, the line enters the single-bore 8.6km (5½ miles) **Ricken Tunnel**, which developed a notorious reputation in the days of steam traction: a locomotive hauling a heavy freight train stalled on the gradient and the crew died of asphyxiation.

At **Uznach** a line from Ziegelbrücke trails in from the left. Laid out in an oval form with two rings lined by houses, Uznach has two fine buildings built for travellers: the timber-framed Zum Hof Inn built c1734 and the classical Linthhof, constructed as a hotel in 1834 but now used as offices. The Catholic church of the Holy Cross, built between 1494 and 1505 and altered in 1775, has an integral polygonal choir.

The Obersee comes into view on the left at **Schmerikon**, from where there is a lakeside path to **Bollingen**, which passes the lovely house built by Carl Jung with his own hands between 1923 and 1955. However it looks much older, as he said: 'I can live as in olden times in my Bollingen tower. It will survive me, with an atmosphere and style reminiscent of centuries long past.'

Both the path and the railway continue along the lake shore to **Rapperswil** (see table 730, page 56).

PRACTICALITIES Bicycle hire from Wattwil and Rapperswil stations.

ST GALLEN–ROMANSHORN Table 870

The line taken by the Voralpen Express on its last leg from Luzern to Romanshorn.

After a long tunnel entered on the outskirts of St Gallen, the railway passes **Wittenbach**, where the Baroque Catholic parish church of St Ulrich was built c1675. To the east of the chapel of St Johannes Nepomuk (1758) is a farmhouse that has been repeatedly altered to become Egg Castle.

Less than 2km (1¼ miles) from **Roggwil-Berg** is the extraordinary castle of Mammertshofen (not open to the public) with a 16th-century wooden upper storey that overhangs the stone curtain wall. The keep dates from the 13th century. The castle can also be reached by a frequent bus service from St Gallen or Arbon stations (table 80.200).

From **Häggenschwil-Winden** station a bus (table 80.205) can be taken to Häggenschwil; about 2km (1¼ miles) to the west of the village lies the ruined Burg Ramschwag on the bank of the River Sitter. The keep, a tower and a section of wall survive.

Another castle can be reached by bus from **Muolen** station: a service between there and Amriswil station (table 80.942) passes close to one of Switzerland's few remaining moated castles and one of its most picturesque. Hagenwil was first documented in 1277 and was built by the Crusader Rudolf von Hagenwil, though parts are over a thousand years old. The half-timbered castle is built on stone walls. The gallery is a restaurant (☏ *071 411 19 13; www.schloss-hagenwil.ch;* ⊕ *daily except Wed*). For **Romanshorn**, see table 820, page 82.

PRACTICALITIES Bicycle hire from Romanshorn station.

ST GALLEN–GAIS–APPENZELL Table 855

Connecting with the Appenzeller Bahnen from Wasserauen to Gossau at Appenzell, this line forms part of a near circuit of metre-gauge lines, offering good walks and cycling. The delightful countryside with snow-covered mountains in the distance is relatively undiscovered. At some intermediate stations on the Appenzeller Bahnen, you need to indicate to the driver that you wish to catch the train by pressing a clearly marked button on the platform (for instructions, see box, page 20). Work is in hand to link the Appenzeller Bahnen with the Trogenerbahn to provide through services. Sit on the right.

Leaving from a separate platform outside and to the right of St Gallen station, adjacent to the Trogenerbahn, trains for Appenzell head southwest parallel to the main line for a short distance before swinging south. The rack mechanism is engaged and the train climbs through a series of horseshoe curves at a gradient that will astonish those still unaccustomed to the mountain climbing abilities of Swiss trains (though a new section of line is being built to eliminate the rack section).

Once the upland has been reached and the train has emerged from steeply sloped woods, the open, rolling Appenzeller countryside is spread out to the south, with the dominant peak of Säntis in the distance. The train twists from one valley into another, past streams, waterfalls and small farms scattered over the hills. At **Niederteufen** is the Capuchin convent of Mariä Rosengarten founded in 1397; both church and monastery were rebuilt in 1687. It is worth breaking the journey at **Teufen** to explore this ribbon village, which is a good walking centre as well as a health resort. The Reformed church was rebuilt between 1776 and 1778 by Hans

Ulrich Grubenmann; in the old station is a museum celebrating the work of the Grubenmann family, who were also responsible for many of the wooden bridges that still span the Sitter and Wattbach rivers.

Bühler's main street is lined with solid stone houses of the 18th and 19th centuries; one incorporates the former Rathaus in Trogen, the upper part of which was dismantled and re-erected on a new base. **Gais** is the junction for Altstätten Stadt (see table 856, opposite) and a good centre for hiking and cross-country skiing. A fire in 1780 devastated much of the village so most of the houses date from this period, those around the village square displaying extraordinarily shaped gables.

Leaving Gais the line describes a 'U', passing the junction for Altstätten on the left, and drops down towards Appenzell. A characteristic of many of the farm buildings passed on the way is a T-shaped layout with the barn forming the vertical bar and the farmhouse the horizontal one. The line describes another horseshoe curve, with a great cliff of rock on the right-hand side of the valley, before crossing the River Sitter on a long girder bridge.

The first port of call in **Appenzell**, capital of the Catholic half-canton of Appenzell Innerrhoden – the smallest in Switzerland – should be the tourist office in Hauptgasse (see *Tourist information*, opposite), which is reached by walking directly north through Postplatz from the station. It has information on the whole of Appenzeller and exceptionally good information and maps about the area's cycle routes and 1,200km (750 miles) of footpaths. It also contains a museum about the customs and history of the Appenzell region.

Although a capital, Appenzell is little more than a large village of 5,700 inhabitants and it enjoys a surprising range of holiday facilities for its size. Much of its centre is pedestrianised, enabling visitors to admire the ornately decorated houses that line Hauptgasse and neighbouring streets safely. Many have intricately painted panels on the front and even painted, curved eaves. As so often in Switzerland, a fire in the village's history marks the start of a concentrated period of reconstruction, in this case after 1560. Having been spared another catastrophe, Appenzell now has an outstanding collection of late 16th-century houses.

Amongst other important buildings are the Catholic church of St Mauritius, dating from the 16th century with a nave from 1823; the Heiligkreuzkapelle, dating from 1561, near the tourist office on Hauptgasse with a portico from 1787 and an immense organ that also fills the width of the church; the Capuchin monastery of Maria Lichtmess, dating from 1586 to 1587, with a church rebuilt in 1688; and the Capuchin convent of Maria der Engel with a church from 1621 to 1622. The Rathaus, built between 1561 and 1563, is decorated with frescoes on the façade depicting the history of Appenzell, painted in 1928.

It is in the Landsgemeindeplatz that the annual open-air meeting of the cantonal parliament takes place on the last Sunday in April, locals voting by a show of hands. Traditional dress is *de rigueur*, and many of the men wear swords or daggers. Other ceremonial occasions occur on unspecified days when herdsmen move their cattle up to the alpine pastures in early summer and back again in the autumn. These traditional processions take place wherever this transhumance is practised in Switzerland, though the way the cattle are decorated and the particular details of the custom vary by region.

TEUFEN
Tourist information
🛈 In the station. Ebni 1, CH-9053; 📞 071 333 38 73; 🕐 08.00–noon & 13.00–18.00 Mon–Sat

Where to stay

🏠 **Anker** Dorf 10, CH-9053; 📞 071 333 13 45; ✉ info@anker-teufen.ch; www.anker-teufen.ch

🏠 **Linde***** Bühlerstrasse 87, CH-9053; 📞 071 335 07 37; ✉ info@hotelzurlinde.ch; www.hotelzurlinde.ch

GAIS

Where to stay

🏠 **Zur Krone** (H)** Dorfplatz 6, CH-9056; 📞 071 790 06 90; ✉ info@krone-gais.ch; www.krone-gais.ch

APPENZELL

Tourist information

ℹ Hauptgasse 4, CH-9050; 📞 071 788 96 41; ✉ info.ai@appenzell.ch; www.appenzell.ch; 🕐 08.00–noon & 13.30–17.30 Mon–Fri, 09.00–noon Sat

Where to stay

🏠 **Säntis**** (H)** Landsgemeindeplatz, CH-9050; 📞 071 788 11 11; ✉ info@saentis-appenzell.ch; www.saentis-appenzell.ch

🏠 **Adler***** Weisbadstrasse 2, CH-9050; 📞 071 787 13 89; ✉ info@adlerhotel.ch; www.adlerhotel.ch

🏠 **Appenzell*** (H)** am Landsgemeindeplatz, CH-9050; 📞 071 788 15 15; ✉ info@hotel-appenzell.ch; www.hotel-appenzell.ch

🏠 **Gasthaus Hof (H)** Engelgasse 4, CH-9050; 📞 071 787 40 30; ✉ info@gasthaus-hof.ch; www.gasthaus-hof.ch

GAIS–ALTSTÄTTEN STADT Table 856

Changes in the landscape are usually gradual, but this short journey provides a real surprise and passes through charming farming country. Sit on the right.

Leaving Gais, the train turns sharply to the left and passes a couple of request stops before **Rietli**, where an extraordinary panorama suddenly opens up to the right. The ground drops away steeply to reveal the broad valley of the Rhein, with mountains in the distance. The train engages the rack for the steep descent to Altstätten and tilts down past farms with wood piles under the eaves, the logs stacked as carefully as the pieces of a mosaic. Outside a barn surrounded by orchards of pears and apples, you may see sheep being sheared or a cluster of rabbit hutches.

Altstätten station is close to the centre of the attractive small town, with cobbled streets and arcades. Half-hourly buses link it with Altstätten SG station on the Rorschach–Sargans main line (table 80.300). Most of the town's houses date from the 18th century and one of the town's original four gates, the Untertor, survives in Engelplatz. The local history museum on Obergasse (🕐 *10.00–16.00 Sat–Sun*) is one of the oldest in Switzerland, founded in 1895 (three years before the Swiss National Museum) and displays items from the daily lives of the middle class, including furniture, pictures, porcelain, glass and pewter.occupies part of the Prestegg, the oldest part of which was built in 1488. In Merktgasse is the Placiduskapelle dating from 1646.

ALTSTÄTTEN

Tourist information

ℹ Breite 9, CH-9450; 📞 071 750 00 23; ✉ reisetreff.steiger@bluewin.ch; www.altstaetten.ch; 🕐 08.30–noon & 13.30–18.30 Mon–Fri, 08.30–noon Sat

Where to stay
🏠 **Untertor***** Engelgasse 13, CH-9450;
📞 071 757 50 50; e info@hotel-untertor.ch; www.
hotel-untertor.ch

GOSSAU–HERISAU–APPENZELL–WASSERAUEN Table 854

The Appenzeller Bahnen's second route to Appenzell leaves the main line between Winterthur and Rorschach at Gossau. It provides access to some of the finest parts of the Appenzell, including the Ebenalp and Säntis mountains. The rolling hills are often wooded, and the popularity of this area for walking and cycling is obvious from the number of hikers who use the trains and the cyclists on adjacent roads and tracks.

Curving south away from the main line, the Appenzell line climbs across the St Gallen–Rapperswil line shortly before reaching **Herisau** station. Herisau is the capital of the Protestant half-canton of Appenzell Ausserrhoden and was first documented in 837. An important textile centre, the town has some fine houses around the square, which was laid out following a fire in 1559. A small historical museum (⊕ *May–Dec 13.00–17.00 Wed–Sun*) occupies the former Rathaus in Oberdorfstrasse.

Buses from the station serve one of the few Appenzell towns not on the railway, including Stein (tables 80.180 and 80.181). In addition to its attractive central square, Grubenmann church dating from 1749, covered bridges and the highest footbridge in Europe, it has a working craft museum (⊕ *10.00–17.00 Tue–Sun*) with demonstrations of embroidery and weaving, and a cheese centre with specialist restaurant.

Leaving Herisau, there is a fine view of the huge stone Glattal Viaduct to the north. The line climbs steeply through **Wilen** to **Waldstatt**, where the Reformed church dates from 1720 to 1721. The railway follows the mountain contours to reach **Urnäsch**, a good walking centre with 120km (75 miles) of paths and well endowed with colourful 17th- and 18th-century houses around a picturesque main square. The Reformed church was built on the foundations of an older church following a fire that devastated the village in 1641. The Säntis Skiing School complements the area's seven ski lifts. A museum of Appenzell folklore with replica Alpine dairy in Dorfplatz (⊕ *Apr–Oct 09.00–11.30, 13.30–17.00 Mon–Sat, 13.30–17.00 Sun; Nov–Mar 09.00–11.30 Mon–Sat*, 📞 *071 364 23 22*) gives an introduction to traditional wood-carving, costumes, dancing and music.

A bus from the station climbs up to **Schwägalp** (table 80.791) for one of Switzerland's most impressive cable car journeys, to Säntis (table 2730). It ascends the sheer precipice by a cable span of 960m (3,150ft), from a pylon close to the base to one on top of the rock wall. The view from the 2,503m (8,209ft) summit of Säntis is spectacular, especially in mid-winter when the air is at its clearest and you can see as far as the Jura in western Switzerland and even the Vosges in France. A network of paths gives various options for the return, including a walk for seasoned hikers along the ridge to Ebenalp via Seealpsee (*4 hrs*). From Schwägalp the same bus (table 80.791) can be taken to the station at Nesslau-Neu St Johann (see table 853, page 78).

The railway describes a 'U' after leaving Urnäsch, climbing to **Jakobsbad** and the adjacent cable car station for the **Kronberg** (table 2725) at 1,663m (5,455ft). A 1km *Bobbahn* (sledges on rails) descends the mountain. The pretty village of **Gonten**, where the neo-Gothic Catholic church of St Verena was built in 1863, derives its name from *Gunton*, meaning 'mountain marshland'. For **Appenzell**, see page 74.

Leaving Appenzell, the line to St Gallen veers off to the left and the Wasserauen heads up the Sitter valley. The hills on either side of the line rise steadily as the journey progresses until the terminus at Wasserauen, where sunlight reaches the valley floor for only a few hours a day. At **Steinegg** the delightful small church of St Magdalena, consecrated in 1590, stands beside the level crossing, its windows deeply recessed and the doorway surrounded by painted decoration.

From **Weissbad** a bus to Brülisau (table 80.192) connects with certain trains. At Brülisau, it is a minute's walk to the cable car up the Hoher Kasten (table 2745) at 1,795m (5,889ft). From the summit, where there is a revolving restaurant and an alpine garden, you can see mountains in four countries. At **Schwende** is the Catholic parish church of St Martin, built as recently as 1928 to 1929 by Alfred Gaudy, and combining Jugendstil (German Art Nouveau) with the neo-Baroque.

The approach to **Wasserauen** is dramatic as the valley sides close in and steepen into rock walls. On the opposite side of the road from the station is the cable car for the eight-minute journey to **Ebenalp** (table 2740) at 1,596m (5,236ft). On the way up you can see the Wildkirchli, the St Michael hermitage which was founded in 1658 and dissolved in 1853, perched on the edge of a cliff. Nearby are caves in which the remains of pre-glacial bears, wolves and lions have been found, plus evidence of human occupation. Some of the finds are displayed in the hermit's dwelling. The Wildkirchli is a short walk from the viewing platform at Ebenalp. Built into a cliff is the early 19th-century Äscher guest house. Well-shod and equipped hikers can walk along the ridge to the highest mountain in the region, the Säntis, at 2,503m (8,209ft) (see opposite) or descend to Wasserauen via the picturesque lake at Seealpsee.

HERISAU
Where to stay

⌂ **Herisau*** ** Bahnhofstrasse 14, CH-9100; ☎071 353 83 83; e info@hotelherisau.ch; www. hotelherisau.ch

URNÄSCH
Where to stay

⌂ **Krone (H)** Appenzellerstrasse 2, CH-9107; ☎071 365 64 00; e info@krone-urnaesch.ch; www.krone-urnaesch.ch

GONTEN
Where to stay

⌂ **Jakobsbad*** (H)** Hauptstrasse, CH-9108; ☎071 794 12 33; e info@hotel-jakobsbad.ch; www.hotel-jakobsbad.ch

⌂ **Gasthaus Bären (H)** Dorfstrasse 40, CH-9108; ☎071 795 40 10; e info@baeren-gonten.ch; www.baeren-gonten.ch

WEISSBAD
Where to stay

⌂ **Gemsle Weissbad*** Weissbadstrasse, CH-9057; ☎071 798 90 30; e gemsle@bluewin.ch

⌂ **Hof Weissbad** Im Park 1, CH-9057; ☎071 798 80 80; e hotel@hofweissbad.ch; www. hofweissbad.ch

SCHWENDE
Where to stay

⌂ **Hotel Frohe Aussicht** Küchenrain 11, CH-9057; ☎071 799 11 74; e hotel@froheaussicht.ch; www.froheaussicht.ch. Quiet, 5min from station.

⌂ **Landgasthof Edelweiss** CH-9057; ☎071 799 11 59; e info@edelweiss-appenzell.ch; www. edelweiss-appenzell.ch

EBENALP

Where to stay

⌂ **Berggasthaus Äscher** Wildkirchli, Ebenalp,
Weissbad CH-9057; ☎ 071 799 11 42. No shower,
but an extraordinary place to stay.

SCHWÄGALP

Where to stay

⌂ **Schwägalp*** (H)** CH-9107; ☎ 071 365 66
00; e hotel@saentisbahn.ch; www.saentisbahn.ch

St Gallen–GOSSAU–SULGEN–Weinfelden Table 852

Operated as a service from St Gallen to Weinfelden, this extraordinarily sinuous branch leaves the main line at Gossau and joins the Winterthur–Romanshorn line at Sulgen.

For **Gossau**, see table 850, pages 67–70. The 1664–65 country house of Oberes Schloss at **Hauptwil** is an early Baroque design, but the setting leaves something to be desired. The village has some fine half-timbered houses from the 17th and 18th centuries.

The line between **Bischofszell Stadt** and **Bischofszell Nord** stations describes such a large horseshoe curve that there is an intermediate station between them, at **Sitterdorf**. Though a centre of brewing and the food industry, Bischofszell should not be missed: the delightful old town stands on high ground above the confluence of the Sitter and Thur rivers, the former spanned by an important late medieval eight-arched bridge from 1487. The town was fortified before 1000 by the Bishops of Constance, and as so often happened in Switzerland, the outer defensive wall of the town became the walls of a ring of houses. After a fire in 1743 destroyed about 70 buildings, the town was rebuilt to plans by the three Grubenmann brothers who were responsible for numerous buildings in the region.

Of the fortifications, the Bogenturm to the east became a bell and clock tower when this suburb was fortified in 1437, and the castle was once a 13th-century bishop's residence, with the upper part dating from the mid 15th century.

The Catholic church of St Pelagius is a basilica with rebuilt 15th-century nave and a 14th-century chapel. The pink Baroque Rathaus dating from 1747 to 1750 has a double staircase and ground-floor windows decorated by elaborate wrought ironwork.

WIL–NESSLAU-NEU ST JOHANN Table 853

The line follows the River Thur all the way, mostly on the left-hand side.

Turning south from the Winterthur–St Gallen line, the branch quickly enters hilly country with the higher ground to the west. At **Lütisburg** the Catholic church of St Michael stands on a former castle mound and is partly built with stone from the remains. A wooden covered bridge from 1790 spans the river.

Between the junctions of **Lichtensteig** and **Wattwil** (see table 870, page 71), the branch joins the St Gallen–Rapperswil line. Between April and October, steam-hauled trains marketed as the 'Amor Express' run periodically over this onward section to Nesslau; they start at **Herisau** (see table 870, page 71). At **Ebnat-Kappel**, in Eich, are some Toggenburg wooden houses, and Acker has a 1752 house that was re-erected here for Albert Edelmann, who founded the Heimatmuseum Ackerhus at Ackerhusweg 16 (⏲ *10.00–noon & 14.00–17.00 Thu–Fri, 14.00–17.00 2nd and 4th Sun in month*). **Krummenau** also has some Toggenburg wooden buildings. A footpath follows the wooded banks of the Thur.

The valley widens as the line nears the terminus at **Nesslau-Neu St Johann**, a popular centre for walking, cycling and skiing. A path beside the River Thur provides a pleasant three-hour walk to Stein and Alt St Johann. The former Benedictine abbey was moved to its present site in Neu St Johann in 1626; the Baroque church was built between c1641 and 1680. Buses leave from the railway station for Rietbad and Schwägalp (see bus table 80.791, train table 854) and for Wildhaus and Buchs station on the Rorschach–Sargans line (table 80.790). This calls at Alt St Johann, where a glorious chairlift (table 2765) ascends to Alp Sellmatt and the small resort of Unterwasser. Four minutes' walk from the bus stop, a funicular followed by a cable car ascends from Iltios to Chäserrugg (table 2767).

At the larger resort of **Wildhaus**, the next major stop, the wooden birthplace of the liberal reformer and priest Zwingli (1484–1531) can be visited (⏲ *Jan–mid-Apr, Jun–mid-Nov 14.00–16.00 Tue–Sun*). It is behind Hotel Friedegg and is one of Switzerland's oldest wooden buildings, dating from the 15th century.

NESSLAU-NEU ST JOHANN
Tourist information
i Hauptstrasse 3, Nesslau, CH-9650; ☏ 071 994 17 22; e neslau@toggenburg.org; www.nesslau-krummenau.info; ⏲ 08.00–noon & 14.00–18.00 Mon, Tue, Thu & Fri, 08.00–noon Wed, 08.00–14.00 Sat

WILDHAUS
Tourist information
i Hauptstrasse Ligishaus, CH-9658; ☏ 071 999 27 27; e kontakt@toggenburg.ch; www.toggenburg.org; ⏲ 08.00–noon & 13.30–17.30 Mon–Fri, 08.00–16.00, mid-Dec–Apr also 08.00–noon Sun

Where to stay
⌂ **Hirschen***** CH-9658; ☏ 071 998 54 54; e info@hirschen-wildhaus.ch; www.hirschen-wildhaus.ch

Where to stay
⌂ **Sternen***** Hauptstrasse 28, CH-9650; ☏ 071 994 19 13; e sternen-nesslau@bluewin.ch; www.sternen-nesslau.ch. 5 mins from the station.

⌂ **Sonne***** CH-9658; ☏ 071 999 23 33; e sonne@beutler-hotels.ch; www.beutler-hotels.ch

⌂ **Toggenburg***** Lisighaus, CH-9658; ☏ 071 998 50 10; e toggenburg@beutler-hotels.ch; www.beutler-hotels.ch

⌂ **Friedegg**** Lisighaus, CH-9658; ☏ 071 999 13 13; e info@hotel-friedegg.ch; www.hotel-friedegg.ch

ST GALLEN–RORSCHACH Table 880

This section is part of the route between Zürich, Sargans and Chur.

Heading east from St Gallen towards the Bodensee (Lake Constance), Schloss Sulzberg at **Goldach** was built c1230 but has been much altered for residential use. Rorschach is Switzerland's largest port on Bodensee, served by ferries that cross the lake to Lindau in Germany and along the Swiss shore to Arbon, Romanshorn and Kreuzlingen. **Rorschach** station is the junction where the line from St Gallen meets the line beside Bodensee from Romanshorn. It is also the junction for the rack railway to Heiden. For **Rorschach**, see table 845, page 80.

The southern terminus of suburban trains over this line beside Bodensee is Heerbrugg on the main line to Chur (see table 880, page 91).

Leaving the junction station of **Rorschach**, the first stop is **Rorschach Hafen**, which serves the town centre and is situated on Hauptstrasse; on the corner with Mariabergstrasse to the right is the tourist office. To the left of the station is the Rathaus from 1681 to 1689 and 1747, and close by are some fine oriel windows decorating houses of the 16th to 18th centuries. Equally close to the station is the Kornhaus, reached by turning right outside the station, crossing the railway and turning left. Picturesquely situated beside the harbour, the Baroque Kornhaus in Hafenplatz was built between 1746 and 1748 as a grain store but resembles a palace. Today it houses an art gallery and museum displaying lace and embroidery as well as exhibits about the town's history (⊕ *Apr–Oct 10.00–17.00 daily*).

About a mile to the south of the station, directly at the end of Mariabergstrasse on which there are numerous Baroque houses, is a former Benedictine convent. Regarded as one of Switzerland's finest late-medieval monastic buildings, it was begun in 1487 and has magnificent stellar and net vaulting in the cloisters.

The town is dominated by the forest-covered slopes of the Rorschacherberg (3,000ft, 914m), which can be reached by postbus from the post office (tables 80.240 and 80.248). This is in Neugasse just outside the station across the road and to the right. Three castles stand on the Rorschacherberg: the 15th–16th-century St Anna-Schloss, the heavily rebuilt Schloss Wartensee and the equally altered Schloss Wartegg, now a hotel (see *Where to stay*, opposite).

Leaving Rorschach, the train passes a municipal garden with large fountains and water jets before entering a countryside of market gardens and fruit farms. A train can be taken back to Rorschach from **Horn** after a delightful walk or bike ride along the lake.

Although **Arbon** is an important industrial town, its Roman origins and development make it worth a visit, as its fort has been incorporated into the 13th-century castle. Turn left outside the station down Bahnhofstrasse (in which the tourist office is situated) to reach Hauptstrasse on which stands the Stadthaus, once the home of linen manufacturers but adapted in 1941 to become the town hall. The Rathaus in Promenadenstrasse dates from 1791 and is one of many half-timbered houses in the old quarter which lies to the west of the castle. The enclosure of the Roman fort, named Arbor Felix ('happy tree'), is preserved by the later castle walls. By the southeast tower is the Galluskapelle, marking the place where St Gallus and St Columban are said to have stepped ashore in 612. The chapel has a Romanesque nave and polygonal apse. The upper part of the keep was added in 1520 and can be easily distinguished from the 13th-century base.

Before reaching **Romanshorn**, the branch line from St Gallen trails in from the west. For Romanshorn, see table 840, page 88.

PRACTICALITIES Bicycle hire from Rorschach station.

RORSCHACH

Tourist information

ℹ Hauptstrasse 56, Hafenbahnhof, CH-9401; ☏ 071 841 70 34; ℮ info@tourist-rorschach.ch; www.tourist-rorschach.ch; ⊕ May–Jun, early to mid-Sep 08.30–noon & 13.30–18.00 Mon–Fri, 09.00–14.00 Sat; Jul–Aug 08.30–18.00 Mon–Fri, 09.00–14.45 Sat–Sun; mid-Sep–Apr 08.30–noon, 13.30–18.00 Mon–Fri

Where to stay

🏠 **Mozart***** Hafenzentrum, CH-9400; ☏071 844 47 47; e info@mozart-rorschach.ch; www. mozart-rorschach.ch

🏠 **Hotel Rorschacherhof** Bahnplatz 15, CH-9400; ☏071 841 43 48

🏠 **Schloss Wartegg (H)** Rorschacherberg, CH-9404; ☏071 858 62 62; e schloss@wartegg. ch; www.wartegg.ch. Built in 1557 & situated in English-style parkland; the restaurant uses largely organic produce.

RORSCHACH–HEIDEN Table 857

This rack line provides marvellous views over Bodensee and serves a health resort noted for its Biedermeier houses. Apart from the Rigi system, it is the only standard-gauge rack railway in Switzerland. Sit on the left.

Leaving from Hafen station and stopping at Rorschach's principal station, the trains of the Rorschach–Heiden-Bergbahn climb 394m (1,292ft) in 7km (4½ miles). It was one of the country's first rack-and-pinion railways, opening in 1875, using the Riggenbach rack system.

Trains ascend through vine-covered slopes near **Weinacht-Tobel**, past fields of pumpkins, orchards and farms, and through pretty woods as they near **Heiden**. A model of the station in the days when steam locomotives propelled trains up the hill can be seen in the booking hall. Turn left outside the station up the hill to reach the village square.

A large part of Heiden was badly damaged by fire in 1838, after which the town was laid out on a grid and the houses built in the Biedermeier style, which was in vogue in Germany and Austria between the Congress of Vienna in 1815 and the revolutions of 1848. The style emphasised the qualities of utility and good proportions at the expense of decoration or pronounced forms.

People have come here for over a century for health cures, which today include electrotherapy. The most celebrated Heiden figure was Henri Dunant (1828–1910) who was instrumental in founding the Red Cross after witnessing the plight of the wounded at Solferino in 1859 during the war between Austria and an alliance of France and Piedmont. He spent the last 23 years of his life in Heiden and was living in poverty when he received the first Nobel Peace Prize in 1901. He died at Heiden, where a museum at Am Kirchplatz 2 commemorates his work (⊕ *Apr–Oct 13.15–16.30 Tue–Sat, 10.00–noon & 13.15–16.30 Sun, Nov–Mar 13.30–16.30 Wed & Sat*).

A postbus (table 80.223) leaves the post office in the main square for **Walzenhausen**, where the Bergbahn Rheineck–Walzenhausen (see table 858, page 92) can be taken down to Rheineck for a steamer down the Alter Rhein and along Bodensee back to Rorschach. Buses also leave for Altstätten SG Rathaus and Heerbrugg station (table 80.226), Rheineck station (table 80.222), St Anton (table 80.229), St Gallen station (tables 80.120 and 80.221), Trogen station (table 80.230) and for Walzenhausen and St Margrethen stations (table 80.224).

HEIDEN

Tourist information

ℹ️ Bahnhofstrasse 2, CH-9410; ☏071 898 33 01; e heiden@appenzellerland.ch; www.heiden.ch; ⊕ May–Sep 09.00–17.00 Mon–Fri, 10.00–14.30 Sat–Sun, 10.00–14.30; Oct–Apr 09.00–noon & 13.00–17.00 Mon–Fri

Where to stay

🏠 **Aparthotel Krone (H)** Biedermeier-Dorfplatz 9, CH-9410; ☏071 891 11 27; e kroneheiden@bluewin.ch; www.kroneheiden.ch

🏠 **Linde*** (H)** Poststrasse 11, CH-9410; ☏071 898 34 00; e info@lindeheiden.ch; www. lindeheiden.ch

A scenic delight since either Bodensee or Untersee is seldom out of view until the beginning of the Rhine at Stein am Rhein. Harbours for yachts punctuate the shore, which is lined with market gardens and vineyards. Sit on the right.

Leaving Romanshorn beside Bodensee, the first station is **Uttwil** where there is a much-altered 17th–18th-century castle. **Kesswil** was the birthplace of the psychiatrist Carl Gustav Jung (1875–1961), and at **Altnau** the Landschlacht Chapel is notable for its 14th- and 15th-century murals. The chapel was built between the 11th and 12th centuries on the pilgrim route between Constance and St Gallen. The former Benedictine nunnery at **Münsterlingen** was rebuilt in 1716 and now serves as a hospital, though the Baroque church remains in use.

The town of **Kreuzlingen** is contiguous with Konstanz in Germany through which there is a railway line to Singen and Engen (see table 835, page 90). Kreuzlingen is also the junction for trains to Weinfelden and Wil, and the departure point for boat services to over a dozen piers in Germany. In Hauptstrasse is the former Augustinian monastery church of St Ulrich, built between 1650 and 1653; it was devastated by fire in 1963, but retains sumptuous Rococo decoration and the 'Kreuzlingen Passion' (1720–30), which contains over 300 carved figures in wood, of which about 250 are original. The monastery buildings of c1660 have been converted into a teachers' training college.

Ermatingen offers no less than four castles: Hard, dating from 1520 but altered several times; Wolfsberg from c1571, altered and extended; Lilienberg, built in 1830; and at Fruthwilen (four minutes by bus from Ermatingen station, table 80.833), the partially half-timbered Hubberg from 1596. The town also boasts the oldest hotel in the canton of Thurgau, Hotel Adler, where Alexandre Dumas, Hermann Hesse, Thomas Mann and Graf Zeppelin (born in Konstanz) have dined. Postbus line 833 (table 80.833) goes from Ermatingen station to the richly historic castle of Arenenberg (see below).

The railway line is particularly close to the Untersee during the section to **Mannenbach-Salenstein**, where even more illustrious castles can be found. Less than 1km from the station and a 15-minute walk through vineyards is Schloss Arenenberg. Originating in 1546 to 1548, the castle was bought and rebuilt in 1817 by Hortense de Beauharnais, Napoleon's stepdaughter. She had been queen of Holland through her marriage to Napoleon's third brother, Louis, who abdicated in 1810. Their son Prince Louis Napoleon, later Napoleon III, was brought up at Arenenberg. Here Queen Hortense received Chateaubriand, Dumas père and Mme Récamier. After Napoleon III's death in exile in England, his widow Eugénie sometimes lived here until she gave the castle to the canton of Thurgau in 1906 together with the Napoleonic collections. Today it is a museum (*Napoleonmuseum;* ☉ *Apr–mid-Oct 10.00–17.00 daily; mid-Oct–Mar 10.00–17.00 Tue–Sun*) with fine portraits, Empire furniture and sculptures by Canova. The castle is surrounded by a fine landscape park. Also at Salenstein are Schloss Salenstein, much altered though with 11th-century remnants, and Schloss Eugensberg dating from 1821.

At the lovely village of **Berlingen**, with its lakeside timber-framed houses, the Untersee is at its greatest width of 8km (5 miles). A cycle route parallels the railway for much of its path beside the lake. **Steckborn** grew from a monastic farm into a town, receiving its charter in 1313 when the walls and Turmhof beside the lake were begun. Both survive, the latter as a local museum (✆ *052 761 29 03;* ☉ *mid-May– mid-Oct 15.00–17.00 Wed–Thu & Sat–Sun*) with Roman and Alemannic finds. The half-timbered Rathaus was rebuilt in 1667, and Schloss Glarisegg was built between 1772 and 1774.

The small lakeside village of **Mammern** is blessed with a large park surrounding Schloss Mammern, once the home of the abbots of Rheinau, described in the 1895 Baedeker as a 'Hydropathic Establishment' and still functioning as a clinic. The Baroque chapel (1749–50) has *trompe-l'oeil* decoration on the ceiling. Above the village is the ruined 13th-century tower of Neuburg.

Although the small town of **Stein am Rhein** is overrun by visitors in high season, they come for a good reason. Try to spend at least one night there; once the coach trippers have gone, those living or staying there reclaim the place and by late afternoon it is relatively quiet. It is only a short walk from the station to the centre: proceed straight ahead from the station, turn right at the T-junction and immediately left to cross the Rhine.

As you cross the bridge you can see the landing stage for boats to the left, reached by Bäregass, while to the right is the Reformed church and former monastery of St George. Cars are excluded from much of the town centre, making the compact historic quarter a pleasure to explore on foot, protected by its 14th-century gate-towers. The centre of the town is Rathausplatz, reached by turning left at the T-junction shortly after crossing the bridge, where many of the house façades are graced with oriel windows and decorated with paintings depicting biblical or moral themes and subjects from Swiss history. The half-timbered upper storey of the Rathaus was added in 1745 above the two storeys dating from 1539 and 1542, and the whole building was restored between 1898 and 1900, by which time the value of Stein am Rhein's legacy of fine buildings had begun to be appreciated (earlier in the century a 17th-century star-shaped redoubt had been blown up).

Rathausplatz becomes Understadt, and at No 33 is the Museum Lindwurm (⊕ *Mar–Oct 10.00–17.00 daily*), which should not be missed. In a building with elements dating from 1279, the rooms of the house have been superbly restored to illustrate the life of a bourgeois family and its servants in the mid 19th century. Each room has cards in English, French, Italian and Japanese to explain what you are seeing, and there is an even more detailed description which can be borrowed on request at the entrance. Reflecting the interest in 'below stairs' life, all of the ancillary rooms such as the basement, laundry, tannery, nursery, attic with meat-smoking chamber, barn and wagon shed have been restored and opened to the public.

Down Chirchhofplatz (to the right of the Rathaus) and to the right lies the Benedictine monastery of St George. Founded in 1005, the monastery's oldest buildings date from the 11th century, including the Romanesque basilica which was altered between 1583 and 1584 to become a Reformed church. The monastery is composed of 12th–16th-century buildings and now functions as a local history museum (⊕ *Apr–Oct 10.00–17.00 daily except Mon*) with frescoes and wood-carving, but there are no guidebooks or labels in English. The panelled interiors, old glass and decoration of the abbot's lodging are nonetheless worth seeing.

The town is overlooked by the well-preserved and largely intact castle of Hohenklingen, dating from the 11th century, though most of what stands is 16th-century. The walls and keep offer a panoramic view of the Rhine, and there has been a restaurant in the castle since 1865.

Beyond Stein am Rhein, the river is out of sight of the railway as it runs through a flat area of intensive market gardening. At **Etzwilen** is the junction for a branch line to Winterthur, though services run through to Stein am Rhein. **Diessenhofen** is noted for its 16th–18th-century houses and other buildings, many in Gothic style, and for its frequently rebuilt wooden bridge over the Rhine, most recently following its destruction by the Russians in 1799 and by American bombing during World War II. Surviving fortified buildings in Obere Kirchgasse include the much-rebuilt 12th-century Unterhof and the Siegelturm, built between 1545 and 1546 as an inner gate.

Schaffhausen

The approach to Schaffhausen is impressive, crossing the Rhine on a tall viaduct and curving round the north of the town in a tunnel to enter the large station. The sizeable historic quarter is straight in front of you, beginning on the other side of the road from the bus station, and it takes at least a day to do it justice. Cars are thankfully excluded from much of the area. To reach the tourist office, turn right outside the station parallel with the railway and turn left into Schwertstrasse; turn right into Fronwagplatz and the tourist office is in the Fronwagturm on the far side of the square.

Given its city charter in 1045, Schaffhausen owes its prosperity to one of its principal tourist sights: the nearby **Rhine Falls**. This impassable section of the river compelled carriers to unload their goods on to waggons at Schaffhausen; the expansion of trade during the Middle Ages encouraged its development as a centre of commerce and industry. The affluence of the town's merchants is reflected by the magnificent façades and oriel windows – over 170 of them – that decorate many of the older houses. Statues and fountains adorn many of the streets, helping to make the old town one of the loveliest in Switzerland.

What to see and do   The falls in particular have attracted visitors for centuries. In 1563, the Holy Roman Emperor Ferdinand I visited the town, throwing the assembled burghers into confusion by arriving at the wrong gate following an impromptu detour to see the falls. It was from Schaffhausen that Ruskin, as a child, had his first, distant view of the Alps and from where D H Lawrence set out in 1913 to walk the width of Switzerland, over the Gotthard Pass to Bellinzona and Lugano. His experiences are described in *Twilight in Italy and Other Essays*.

The best view of the town can be had from the walls of the **Munot**, the largest circular fortress in Switzerland, which was built between 1564 and 1585. It is unique in being the only castle based on the ideas of Albrecht Dürer, which he set out in his *Treatise on Fortification*, published in Nuremberg in 1527. The 5m-thick walls (16ft) of the Munot are reached by long flights of steps up a vine-covered hillside from either Bachstrasse or Unterstadt. Inside the dominant, cylindrical tower, with caretaker's flat under its pinnacled roof, is a spiral ramp which allowed cannon and carts of supplies to be taken up to the battlements. In summer, concerts, dancing and a Munot Ball are held in the open space inside the wall-walk.

Beneath the Munot and beside the Rhine on Freierplatz is the **Güterhof** (1785–87), an imposing warehouse and reminder of the town's trading origins. Also recalling its mercantile past are the 12 guildhalls, some now restaurants. Most notable amongst the dozens of distinguished houses in the old town are the **Haus zum Ritter**, No 65 Vordergasse, with its scenes from Roman history and mythology by the town's native artist Tobias Stimmer – remnants of the originals can be seen in Allerheiligen Museum at All Saints; the **Haus zum Goldenen Ochsen** from c1600 in Vorstadt, which has one of the most ornate oriel windows and allegorical representations of the five senses on the 1609 Renaissance façade; and the **Grosse Haus** on Fronwagplatz, with outstanding oriel windows from 1685.

The largest of the churches is the Romanesque **All Saints**, founded in 1048 as part of the Benedictine abbey which was begun in the 11th century and extended between the 13th and 16th centuries. In 1052, Leo IX came to consecrate the abbey church, which was not completed until 1104. Today the abbey complex with its 12th-century cloisters houses a variety of activities. The **Allerheiligen Museum** (*Baumgartenstrasse 6; www.allerheiligen.ch;* ⊕ *11.00–17.00 Tue–Sun*) has an exhibition of prehistoric, Roman and medieval antiquities, reconstructed rooms, ceramics, costumes, local industry, topographical and modern Swiss paintings, and 16th–20th-century copper engravings. The city library is housed in the former granary, while the sound of music may betray the presence of a music school. The air is often scented by fragrances from the medieval herb garden.

Just to the south of the abbey on the corner of Baumgartenstrasse and Klosterstrasse is a large former textile factory that has been converted into a gallery of international contemporary art, the **Hallen für Neue Kunst** (⊕ *15.00–17.00 Sat, 11.00–17.00 Sun*). It was one of the first industrial buildings to be transformed into an art gallery anywhere in the world, becoming a model for others.

Beside Vordergasse is the **Reformed parish church** of St Johann, thought to have been founded in the 11th century. A 15th-century rebuild gave it a nave and pair of aisles, to which were added another two aisles, making it the third-widest church in Switzerland after Basel and Bern. On the fourth storey of the 1350 bell tower can be seen the crenellations of the former guard house.

Other fortified towers on the periphery of the old town are, to the north, the 14th-century **Schwabentor**, the successively raised 13th-century **Obertor** near the station, the **Frontwagturm** with its astronomical clock from 1564, and the **Diebsturm** to the southwest.

To reach the Rhine Falls, take bus No 1 towards Neuhausen/Herbstäcker (*every 10 mins*), get off at Neuhausen Zentrum and follow the brown signs down to the Rhine Falls (*walking time about 20 mins*). The sound of Europe's most powerful falls can be heard long before they are in sight. The volume of water is greatest in June and July when it is augmented by snow melt, and on 1 August (Swiss National Day) a firework display illuminates the sky above the falls. Statistics are impressive – an average of 1,200 tonnes of water a second, 700m3 (916 cubic yards) a second, 150m (492ft) wide – but it is no wonder that the experience of watching and listening to the cataract has inspired so many painters and poets. You can see the falls from several vantage points. Steps down from the bus stop at Neuhausen lead to a riverside walk past Restaurant Park to the former customs post at Wörth, thought to date from the 12th century and now a restaurant. Schloss Laufen (another restaurant and probably Europe's most dramatically sited youth hostel) has two nearby belvederes overlooking the falls; it can be reached by train (table 762) to the halt at Schloss Laufen am Rheinfall, by local bus or by walking across the railway bridge taking the Schaffhausen–Winterthur line over the Rhine just above the falls. In season, boats take visitors to a rock in the middle of the falls up which a staircase ascends to a viewing platform. The spray is such that waterproof clothing is needed for all vantage points except Schloss Laufen.

A journey east along the Rhine should not be missed, whether by boat (services to Kreuzlingen and Constance with many ports of call), by bicycle or on foot, since this is one of the most highly regarded stretches of the river.

PRACTICALITIES Bicycle hire from Romanshorn, Kreuzlingen, Stein am Rhein and Schaffhausen stations.

ARBON
Tourist information
🇮 Schmiedgasse 5, CH-9320; ☏ 071 440 13 80; e info@infocenter-arbon.ch; www.infocenter- arbon.ch; ⊕ 09.00–11.30 & 14.00–18.00 Mon–Fri; mid-Jun–Aug also 09.00–11.30 Sat

Where to stay

🏠 **Seegarten***** Seestrasse 66, CH-9320;
📞071 447 57 57; e info@hotelseegarten.ch; www.hotelseegarten.ch

ERMATINGEN
Tourist information

ℹ️ see Hotel Ermatingerhof below

STECKBORN
Where to stay

🏠 **See & Park Hotel Feldbach*** (H)**
Feldbachareal, CH-8266; 📞052 762 21 21; e info@hotel-feldbach.ch; www.hotel-feldbach.ch

STEIN AM RHEIN
Tourist information

ℹ️ Oberstadt 3, CH-8260; 📞052 742 20 90; e tourist-service@steinamrhein.ch; www.steinamrhein.ch; ⊕ 09.30–noon & 13.30–17.00 Mon–Fri; Jun–Aug also 09.30–noon & 13.30–16.00 Sat

SCHAFFHAUSEN
Tourist information

ℹ️ Herrenacker 15, CH-8200; 📞052 632 40 20; e info@schaffhausen-tourismus.ch; www.schaffhauserland.ch; ⊕ May–Sep 09.30–18.00 Mon–Fri, 09.30–16.00 Sat, 09.30–14.00 Sun; Oct–Apr 09.30–17.00 Mon–Fri, 09.30–14.00 Sat

🏠 **Rotes Kreuz**** Hafenstrasse 3, CH-9320; 📞071 446 19 18; e info@hotelroteskreuz.ch; www.hotelroteskreuz.ch

Where to stay

🏠 **Ermatingerhof*** (H)** Hauptstrasse 82, CH-8272; 📞071 663 20 20; e info@ermatingerhof.ch; www.ermatingerhof.ch

🏠 **Adler (H)** Fruthwilerstrasse 2/4, CH-8272; 📞071 664 11 33; e adlerermatingen@bluewin.ch; www.adler-ermatingen.ch

Where to stay

The hotel nearest the station is about ten minutes' walk:

🏠 **Rheinfels*** (H)** Rhigass 8, CH-8260; 📞052 741 21 44; e rheinfels@bluewin.ch; www.rheinfels.ch. Occupies 16th-century guild building.

In the old town is:

🏠 **Adler*** (H)** Rathausplatz 2, CH-8260; 📞052 742 61 61; e hotel-adler@bluewin.ch; www.adlersteinamrhein.ch

Where to stay

🏠 **Best Western Hotel Bahnhof******
Bahnhofstrasse 46, CH-8201; 📞052 630 35 35; e mail@hotelbahnhof.ch; www.hotelbahnhof.ch

🏠 **Park Villa*** (H)** Parkstrasse 18, CH-8200; 📞052 635 60 60; e hotel@parkvilla.ch; www.parkvilla.ch. Unspoilt fin-de-siècle villa in a quiet street with park behind, 10mins' walk from station.

SCHAFFHAUSEN–ERZINGEN Table 763

The principal place of interest on this short line that runs to the German border at Erzingen is **Neunkirch**. This delightful walled town was laid out on a grid pattern in the late 13th century and retains much of its medieval appearance. Defensive buildings include the Obertor (1574) and the castle, extended in the 16th century and now housing a local history museum at Hintergasse 9 (*Ortsmuseum*, ⊕ *Apr–Oct 14.00–17.00 1st Sun in month*). The high ground on which stands the largely late 14th-century Reformed Bergkirche makes it a landmark for miles around.

Also worth visiting is Wilchingen, a short walk to the southeast of the station named **Wilchingen-Hallau**. A curious feature of this wine village is its covered passages running between houses to connect adjoining roads or alleys.

SCHAFFHAUSEN–THAYNGEN Table 763

Local trains to Singen cross the border with Germany at **Thayngen**. The Reformed parish church (c1500–04) has a defensive tower on the north side. The village was once well endowed with guesthouses: the Adler was built between 1711 and 1712, the Rebstock was documented in the Middle Ages and enlarged in 1701, and the Sternen is a neo-classical building from 1792. At nearby Kesserloch is a major Palaeolithic site; the items found in the caves are on display in the Allerheiligen Museum in Schaffhausen (page 85).

SCHAFFHAUSEN–WINTERTHUR Table 762

Heading south from Schaffhausen, the train offers a glimpse of the Rhine Falls as it crosses the river on a stone-arched bridge before plunging into a tunnel. In summer, trains stop at **Schloss Laufen am Rheinfall**. From **Marthalen** station, an hourly bus (table 70.620, line 620) serves the small town of Rheinau where a Benedictine abbey church and complex stands on a peninsula (once an island) on the Rhine. The largely Baroque church is built on the grave of an Irish missionary from Leinster, St Fintan, who died here in 879. The church is considered one of Switzerland's finest examples of high Baroque, having been rebuilt in the early 18th century. In addition to the extensive abbey buildings there is a covered bridge from 1804 over the Rhine and a Roman watchtower in Köpferplatz. Marthalen itself is worth an hour or two to admire its fine half-timbered houses.

The railway passes between vine-covered slopes to **Andelfingen**, the centre of this wine-growing region. From the train you can see the Reformed parish church dating from 1666 to 1667 with its colourfully tiled tower roof. In the centre, the castle, built between 1780 and 1782, is now an old people's home, and overlooks the River Thur across which there is a covered wooden bridge dating from 1814 to 1815. The Rhine comes into view on the approach to **Schloss Laufen**, from which there are steps up to the castle. There is a magnificent view of the Rhine Falls to the left upon leaving the station.

For **Winterthur**, see table 750, pages 61–3.

PRACTICALITIES Bicycle hire from Winterthur station.

WINTERTHUR–ETZWILEN/STEIN AM RHEIN Table 821

This sinuous single-track branch is used by two S-Bahn services: S12 from Zürich as far as Seuzach and S29 from Winterthur to Stein am Rhein.

A few minutes' walk from **Oberwinterthur** station is the attractive medieval stronghold of Hegi, at Hegifeldstrasse 125. The once-moated castle has a keep dating from c1200 and now houses a youth hostel and museum (⊕ *Mar–Oct 14.00–17.00 Tue–Thu & Sat, 10.00–noon & 14.00–17.00 Sun*) with displays of furniture, stoves, ceramic objects, stained glass and weaponry from the 15th to 18th centuries. A 30–40-minute hiking trail from **Reutlingen** leads to the 11th–13th-century castle of Mörsburg. The large rectangular tower was taken over by the town of Winterthur as early as 1598 and is now a museum of furniture and everyday objects from the 17th and 18th centuries, as well as an outstanding collection of arms and armour (⊕ *Mar–Oct 10.00–noon & 13.30–17.00 Tue–Sun; Nov–Feb 10.00–noon & 13.30–17.00 Sun*).

At **Dinhard** is a late Gothic Reformed parish church dating from 1511 to 1515. On the approach to **Ossingen** the line crosses the River Thur by the Thurbrücke Ossingen, a 332m (1,089 ft) long five-span truss bridge. Ossingen has some fine 16th–18th-century half-timbered houses around the 1651 Reformed parish church. The privately owned medieval Schloss Widen, to the west of the town overlooking the Thur, had to be rebuilt after a US bomber crashed here in 1944.

The station at **Stammheim** serves the separate parishes of Unterstammheim, around the station, and Oberstammheim, less than a kilometre to the east, served by bus from the station (table 70.605). Both are delightful villages with fine half-timbered vernacular buildings. The timbered Gasthof Hirschen at Oberstammheim has an unusual three-storey oriel.

For **Stein am Rhein**, see table 820, pages 82–6.

PRACTICALITIES Bicycle hire from Stein am Rhein station.

OBERSTAMMHEIM
Where to stay
⌂ **Gasthof zum Hirschen (H)** CH-8477; ☎052 745 11 24; e info@hirschenstammheim.ch; www. hirschenstammheim.ch. One of the most attractive and historic places to stay in Switzerland.

WINTERTHUR–ROMANSHORN Table 840

The eastern section of the main line between Zürich and Bodensee.

This service shares the line as far **Oberwinterthur** with trains to Stein am Rhein (see page 83) and then heads northeast to **Wiesendangen**, where the choir of the Reformed parish church from 1480 has 21 wall-paintings. **Issikon** began to develop as a centre of dyeing and fabric printing in the late 18th century, some of the buildings being in the Biedermeier style. Less than a kilometre to the northwest of the station, at Kefikon, is a much-altered, formerly moated castle.

The origins of **Frauenfeld**, capital of canton Thurgau since 1803, go back to 1227 when the counts of Kyburg began to build their castle. To the keep were added residential buildings at Freie Strasse 24 that now house the Thurgau Historical Museum (⊕ *14.00–17.00 daily except Mon*). However, the historical interest of the town was diminished by two fires in the late 18th century that laid waste most of the town. Neighbouring cantons came to the town's aid and helped to rebuild it, giving it a variety of Baroque frontages that can be identified as the work of craftsmen from Zürich, Bern or Luzern. Nonetheless some medieval buildings remain between the neo-classical Rathaus dating from 1790 to 1794 and the Reformed church. In Oberkirch is the non-denominational church of St Laurence, the oldest part of which is 10th century; it has some important stained glass from c1330. At Freiestrasse 26 is a natural history museum (⊕ *14.00–17.00 Tue–Sat, noon–17.00 Sun*). The railway station building itself at Frauenfeld is one of the country's older stations, built in 1855.

Near **Felben-Wellhausen** is Schloss Wellenberg with a 13th-century keep, 16th-century residential building and staircase tower from 1768. The village centre of **Weinfelden** has some interesting buildings, including the early Baroque Gasthaus zum Trauben from 1649. On the Ottenberg to the north stands a castle with a 12th-century keep and living quarters rebuilt in 1860. The station is the junction for trains to Kreuzlingen and Wil (see table 835 for both, page 90).

The keep of the castle at **Bürglen** dates from the 12th to 13th centuries. Between 1888 and 1889, it became a school and was further converted and enlarged between 1950 and 1951. The River Thur is close to the line on the right after Bürglen, making it a pretty stretch. The Reformed church is the castle's chapel. **Sulgen** is the junction for St Gallen, though the train service starts at Weinfelden and runs through to St Gallen (table 852). The village of **Erlen** has half-timbered houses and a church built by Johann Ulrich Grubenmann in 1764. **Oberaach** contains one of the most elaborate half-timbered houses in Switzerland: the Gasthaus zum Goldenen Löwen. It has a courtroom on the first floor with coffered ceiling and intarsia work (a picture made out of different coloured inlaid woods or other materials).

The industrial town of **Amriswil** has some half-timbered buildings and a modern Catholic church, built of concrete in 1939. The castle of Hagenwil (see table 870, page 73) can be reached by bus from the station (table 80.942).

A succession of fires and the industrial development of **Romanshorn** have left few buildings of note, but it has a fine park and the ecumenical Old Church has 14th-century murals. The tower of the Catholic church of St Johann, built between 1911 and 1913, was based on St Mark's in Venice. The station is the junction for services to Winterthur (table 840) and St Gallen (see table 870, page 73). To the south of the station at Egnacherweg 1 in the former SBB depot is the Locorama museum (\ *071 460 24 27*; e *office@locorama.org*; *www.locorama.ch*; ⊕ *May–Sep 14.00–17.00 Sat–Sun*), with reconstructed signal-box and a variety of Swiss locomotives and carriages.

PRACTICALITIES Bicycle hire from Romanshorn station.

FRAUENFELD
Tourist information
🛈 Railway Station, Bahnhofplatz 75, CH-8500; \052 721 31 28; e tourismus@regiofrauenfeld. ch; www.regiofrauenfeld.ch; ⊕ 09.00–noon & 14.00–18.00 Mon–Fri

Where to stay
⌂ **Blumenstein***** Bahnhofplatz, CH-8500; \052 721 47 28; e info@hotel-blumenstein.ch; www.hotel-blumenstein.ch

WEINFELDEN
Tourist information
🛈 Frauenfelderstrasse 10, CH-8570; \071 626 83 85; e kultur.tourismus@weinfelden.ch: www. weinfelden.ch; ⊕ 09.00–11.30 Mon–Fri

Where to stay
⌂ **Gasthaus zum Trauben (H)** Rathausstrasse 1, CH-8570; \072 622 44 44; e info@trauben-weinfelden.ch; www.trauben-weinfelden.ch
⌂ **Rössli** Amriswilerstrasse 3, CH-8570; \071 622 30 90; e mail@roessli-weinfelden.ch; www. roessli-weinfelden.ch

AMRISWIL
Tourist information
🛈 Arbonerstrasse 2, CH-8580; \071 414 11 11; e info@amriswil.ch; www.verkehrsverein-amriswil.ch; ⊕ 08.00–noon & 14.00–17.00 Mon–Fri

Where to stay
⌂ **Gasthaus zum Ochsen** Bahnhofstrasse 2, CH-8580; \071 411 18 71; www.ochsen-amriswil.ch
⌂ **Landgasthof Hirschen (H)** Weinfelderstrasse 80, CH-8580; \071 412 70 70; e info@hirschen-amriswil.ch; www.hirschen-amriswil.net

ROMANSHORN

Tourist information

🚉 Railway Station, CH-8590; ✆071 463 32 32; e touristik@romanshorn.ch; www.romanshorn.ch; 🕐 Apr–Sep 08.00–18.00 daily; Oct–Mar 08.00–17.30 Mon–Fri, 09.00–11.00 & 14.00–17.00 Sat–Sun

Where to stay

🏠 **Bahnhof** Löwenstrasse 1, CH-8590; ✆071 463 17 26; e info@hotel-bahnhof-romanshorn.ch; www.hotel-bahnhof-romanshorn.ch

FRAUENFELD–WIL Table 841

This single-track metre-gauge roadside railway follows the River Murg for most of its 17km (11 miles), though the scenery is unremarkable. Sit on the right.

The train for **Wil** leaves from a separate platform to the right outside Frauenfeld station. It weaves its way through the picturesque streets of the town, many of them pedestrianised, past some fine civic buildings. On the outskirts of town, an area of immaculately tended allotment gardens can be seen on the right. **Wängi** has a pretty timber-framed station.

St Margaretha's chapel in **Münchwilen** dates from 1641 and has three Baroque altars contemporaneous with the building. The train terminates at a platform outside **Wil** main station. For Wil, see table 850, page 70.

WIL–WEINFELDEN–KREUZLINGEN–(Konstanz–Singen–Engen) Table 835

Although this route has the character of a branch line, it is operated as an international service into Germany, connecting with trains to Frankfurt and Kassel.

At **Bronschofen** is an exceptionally fine former parish church, which was acquired by the monastery of Rüti in 1280. Becoming the pilgrimage church of Our Lady of Dreibrunnen, it was rebuilt in 1672 with an attractive demi-octagonal, colonnaded porch. Paintings of battles with the Turks at Lepanto and Vienna decorate the ceiling. At Tobel – alight at **Tobel-Affeltrangen** – is a Commandery of the Knights of the Order of St John, built in 1228 and successively rebuilt and enlarged. Buses leave from the station to Stettfurt (table 80.837), from which it is about 40 minutes' walk to the castle at Sonnenberg. First documented in 1242, the impressive structure visible today is the result of rebuilding after a fire in 1596. It was acquired by the monastery of Einsiedeln (see table 672, page 58) in 1678 and remains in its possession.

The line weaves through rolling pastoral hills dotted with large farmhouses. On the approach to **Bussnang,** a distinctive, almost circular modern church can be seen to the left.

Weinfelden (see table 840, pages 88–9) is a junction on the Winterthur–Romanshorn line.

After a sinuous section of railway, the train reaches **Berg**, where there are several notable buildings. The three-storey Schloss Pfauenmoos was built c1564 and altered in the late 18th century. The Grosser Hahnberg was built c1616 and rebuilt c1770, while the Kleiner Hahnberg is a 16th-century half-timbered building with tall staircase tower. The Catholic parish church of St Michael was rebuilt between 1775 and 1776, incorporating the medieval tower.

PRACTICALITIES Bicycle hire from Kreuzlingen station.

With sections of this route used by international expresses to such destinations as Vienna, Graz and Munich, there is a wide choice of trains through the Rhine valley, though the river is barely visible.

Heading east, the first station of note is **Rheineck**, close to the Rhine delta – this is the easterly end of Swiss lake services. Rheineck is the junction for the 2km (1¼ miles) rack line up to Walzenhausen (see table 858, page 92). The small town has a Rathaus dating from 1553 to 1555, one of the country's first modern churches – the Catholic parish church of St Theresia (1932–33) – and the Baroque Custerhof from 1750 to 1753, which has been an agricultural college since 1896. The huge three-storey Löwenhof, with mansard roof and dormer windows, was built between 1746 and 1748 for a wealthy merchant.

St Margrethen is an industrial frontier village and junction for the line to Bregenz in Austria. At the junction to the east of the station, the line turns to the south to parallel the broad Rhine valley. On the site of an 11th-century fortress at **Heerbrugg** is a Baroque residence dating from 1774 to 1778 with a tower built in 1911. Less than a kilometre to the southwest is Balgach, which has a former Rathaus from 1566, and to the southwest again and visible from the railway is the rebuilt 13th-century Schloss Grünenstein.

Above the station at **Rebstein-Marbach** is the castle of Weinstein. First documented in 1375 and rebuilt in 1479, the castle (at Weinsteingass 219) is now a gourmet, wood-panelled restaurant (✆ 071 777 11 07; www.schlossweinstein.ch; ⊕ daily). However, it is about 2km (1¼ miles) from the station, so a bus from Heerbrugg (table 80.301) may be preferred. For **Altstätten**, see table 856, page 75.

From **Buchs** buses head east into **Liechtenstein** (the Swiss franc is the country's currency). The buses (table 88.012) run through Liechtenstein's capital of Vaduz on their way to Feldkirch on the main Aarlberg railway line to Innsbruck and Vienna. On the western edge of Buchs lies the village and castle of Werdenberg, served by the bus from the station to Gams (table 80.410). Built beside an ornamental lake, the village claims to be Switzerland's, if not Europe's, oldest wooden housing settlement. Built around a market square dominated by a half-timbered house resting on three arches with huge pillars, the village is overlooked by the magnificent castle built c1230 by Count Rudolf of Montfort. It is now a museum (⊕ Apr–Oct 11.30–18.00 Tue–Fri, 10.00–18.00 Sat–Sun) with reconstructed rooms and 17th–18th-century furniture.

Just to the west of **Sevelen** are the ruins of the 13th-century castle of Herrenberg. The village is connected to Liechtenstein by a wooden bridge. About a kilometre from **Weite** is the ruined 13th-century castle of Wartau; the five-storey keep survives with some residential buildings on a hill above the railway.

The approach to the junction of **Sargans** is dominated by the 13th-century castle that overlooks the town, its keep soaring above the cluster of residential buildings. The property of the town authorities since 1899, it now houses a youth hostel, restaurant and museum of local history (⊕ 10.00–noon & 13.30–16.00 Mon, 10.00–noon & 13.30–17.00 Tue–Sun), including an exhibition about the nearby Gonzen iron-ore mine. The mine itself can be visited by underground train (✆ 081 723 12 17; www.bergwerk-gonzen.ch). Few buildings in Sargans pre-date 1811, when a fire destroyed most of the town within the walls. Of note are the Neo-classical Rathaus and the chapel of St Sebastian, dating from 1502. Sargans is on the Zürich–Chur main line (see table 900).

PRACTICALITIES Bicycle hire from St Margrethen and Sargans stations.

BUCHS
Tourist information
i Bahnhofplatz 2, CH-9471; ☎ 081 740 05 40;
e touristinfo@werdenberg.ch; www.werdenberg.
ch; ⏰ 09.00–noon & 14.00–17.00 Mon–Fri

SARGANS
Tourist information
i Städtchenstrasse 45, CH-7320; ☎ 081 720 03
33; *e* info@sargans-tourismus.ch; www.sargans-
tourismus.ch; ⏰ 08.00–11.30 & 14.00–18.00
Mon, 08.00–11.30 & 14.00–16.00 Tue–Fri

Where to stay
🏠 **Zum Ritterhof***** (H) Bahnofstrasse 12, CH-
7320; ☎ 081 710 68 30; *e* info@hotel-ritterhofch;
www.hotel-ritterhof.ch

RHEINECK–WALZENHAUSEN Table 858

Built to the unusual gauge of 1,200mm (3ft 11¼in), this 2km (1¼ miles) line
uses the Riggenbach rack system to climb up to the village and health resort of
Walzenhausen, overlooking Bodensee. Before the railway opened in 1896, it took
a stagecoach one hour and five minutes; today it takes the train just six minutes. A
Capuchin monastery was established here in 1424 and rebuilt in 1724. A bus from
the station (tables 80.223 and 80.224) goes to Heiden, enabling a circular journey
to be made back to Rorschach.

WALZENHAUSEN
Tourist information
i Dorf 48, CH-9428; ☎ 071 888 24 70;
e verkehrsverein@walzenhausen.ch; www.
walzenhausen.ch

Where to stay
A hotel adjacent to the station is:
🏠 **Walzenhausen****** CH-9428; ☎ 071 886 21
21; *e* info@hotel-walzenhausen.ch; www.hotel-
walzenhausen.ch

8

Bern

Although Bern has been the capital of the Swiss Confederation since 1848, it is only the fourth-largest city, after Zürich, Basel and Geneva, with a population of 134,000. Few cities in Europe can rival Bern for the way that it has kept its medieval centre intact; UNESCO has recognised this and placed the city on its list of world cultural landmarks, on a par with the centres of Rome, Florence and Havana. It is renowned for its fountains, towers and bridges, the profusion of geranium-filled windowboxes and the 6km (4 miles) of arcades, the *Lauben*, that line many of the streets of greenish-grey sandstone buildings.

Its position on a high peninsula in a meander of the River Aare was chosen by Berchtold V, Duke of Zähringen, for its easily defensible location. Although he was certainly the city's founder, there was already a small settlement in existence by c1155, clustered around Nydegg Castle at the eastern end of the peninsula. Legend has it that the name came from Berchtold saying that the new settlement would have the name of the first wild animal caught on the peninsula. Whatever the validity of the story about the ensuing hunt, the bear has been the city's emblem since at least 1224, when it was used on the city's seal. It also gave rise to the tradition of keeping bears in the former moats from at least 1480 to 1857, when they were moved to the current bear pits beside the River Aare close to the Nydegg Bridge.

The city grew in a westerly direction towards what is now Bahnhofplatz, two moats being successively filled in to form the north–south squares of Kornhausplatz and Bärenplatz/Waisenhausplatz and new walls built. On each occasion the main east–west street was extended. The first wall, built on Berchtold's orders, was divided by the Clock Tower (Zeitglockenturm); the main gateway-tower of the second wall, built c1250, was the Prison Tower; and the third wall, begun in 1346 on the site of today's railway station and completed in a mere 18 months, was dominated by the Christoffel Tower. The first two towers thankfully survive, but the last was torn down in 1865 after a referendum narrowly sanctioned its demolition.

From the completion of the third wall until the early 19th century, the city boundaries did not change, though defences were strengthened by a series of entrenchments built in the 17th century on the site of the present university. However, one event transformed Bern's appearance. At sunset on 14 May 1405, fire broke out near the Clock Tower. Fanned by a strong wind, the fire consumed 600 houses – almost all of the city's largely wooden structures. What visitors to the city see today is chiefly the product of reconstruction in stone, clay and plaster that followed, helped by such neighbouring towns as Fribourg, which sent 12 waggons and 100 people for nearly a month.

An equally harrowing experience was the occupation of the city by French troops in 1798 following defeat of the city's forces at Grauholz. The town was systematically plundered of all its treasures – even the bears were carried off. Its

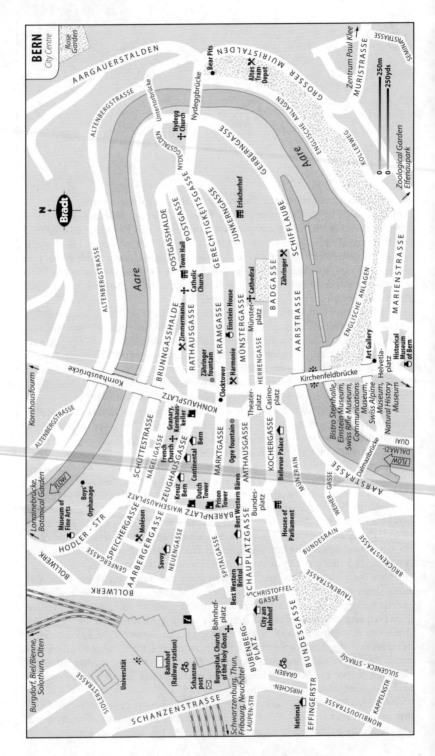

BERN
City Centre

Rose Garden

AARGAUERSTALDEN

ALTENBERGSTRASSE

Aare

Kornhausbrücke

Kornhausforum

ALTENBERGSTRASSE

Lorainebrücke,
Botanical Garden

FLOW

Museum of
Fine Arts

Boys'
Orphanage

HODLER - STR

BOLLWERK

GENFERGASSE

SCHÜTTESTRASSE

NÄGELIGASSE

SPEICHERGASSE

Granary
French
Church

Kornhaus-
keller

Continental
Bern

Kreuz
Bern

Dutch
Tower

Prison
Tower

ZEUGHAUSGASSE

WAISENHAUSPLATZ

BÄRENPLATZ

Molèson

AARBERGERGASSE

NEUENGASSE

Savoy

Best Western
Bristol

SCHAUPLATZGASSE

SPITALGASSE

Best Western Bären

Bundes-
platz

Houses of
Parliament

BOLLWERK

Burgdorf, Biel/Bienne,
Solothurn, Olten

Universität

SIDLERSTRASSE

Bahnhof
(Railway station)

Schanzen-
post

Burgspital, Church
of the Holy Ghost

Bahnhof-
platz

BUBENBERG-
PLATZ

City an
Bahnhof

SCHRISTOFFEL-
GASSE

CHRISTOFFEL-
GASSE

SCHANZENSTRASSE

Schwarzenburg, Thun,
Fribourg, Neuchâtel

LAUPEN-STR

HIRSCHEN-
GRABEN

National

EFFINGERSTR

MONBIJOUSTRASSE

BUNDESGASSE

BUNDESRAIN

TAUBENSTRASSE

SULGENECK - STRASSE

KAPPELNSTR

BRÜCKENSTRASSE

N

Bradt

BRUNNGASSHALDE

RATHAUSGASSE

POSTGASSHALDE

Town Hall

Catholic
Church

Zimmermania

KRAMGASSE

Zähringer
fountain

Clocktower

Harmonie

Einstein House

MÜNSTERGASSE

Münster/
platz

Cathedral

HERRENGASSE

KONHAUSPLATZ

MARKTGASSE

Ogre fountain

AMTHAUSGASSE

Theater-
platz

Casino-
platz

KOCHERGASSE

Bellevue Palace

MONZRAIN

WEIHER - GASSE

Kirchenfeldbrücke

POSTGASSE

Nydegg
Church

Untertorbrücke

Nydeggbrücke

RATHAUSGASSE

GERECHTIGKEITSGASSE

JUNKERNGASSE

Erlacherhof

Zähringer

BADGASSE

SCHIFFLAUBE

AARSTRASSE

Bear Pits

GROSSER MURISTALDEN

GERBERNGASSE

Aare

ENGLISCHE ANLAGEN

Altes
Tram
Depot

MURISTRASSE

Zentrum Paul Klee

SEMINARSTRASSE

0   250m
0   250yds

Zoological Garden
Elfenaupark

KOLLERWEG

ENGLISCHE ANLAGEN

MARIENSTRASSE

Art Gallery

Helvetia-
platz

Historical
Museum
of Bern

Bistro Steinhalle,
Einstein Museum,
Swiss Rifle Museum,
Communications
Museum,
Swiss Alpine
Museum,
Natural History
Museum

Dalmazibrücke

AARSTRASSE

DALMAZI-
QUAI

FLOW

BRÜCKENSTRASSE

94

impoverishment was matched by a loss of political power which it did not regain until 1848 when Bern was chosen by the first Swiss Parliament as the capital of the Confederation. The different-coloured street signs and house numbers are a legacy of the French occupation: many of Napoleon's soldiers could neither read nor write, so streets were coded red, green, blue and white to assist identification. The same system was used in Vienna.

The key to Bern's expansion has naturally been a series of bridges over the River Aare (see page 101). Until 1844 the only crossing was the Untertorbrücke, but new structures made possible the construction of large civic buildings that could not otherwise have been accommodated in the old town without extensive demolition.

Regrettably, the feature of Bern's environs that most impressed visitors was swept away when roads were adapted for motor traffic. Bern's prosperous families had country houses accessible by roads radiating from the city that were often built in the 17th century for military purposes; these roads were characterised by avenues of elm trees planted to provide shade for travellers and the landed families. Their destruction was keenly felt by the Bernese, who had enjoyed walks out of the city.

In addition to its exceptional buildings, Bern has numerous museums, art galleries and theatres, and a vibrant musical life, helped by being home to the Swiss Jazz School and an International Jazz Festival, held every year from March to May (*www.jazzfestivalbern.ch*). Bern's mountain is home to the Gurtenfestival (*www. gurtenfestival.ch*), four days in July featuring over 60 live acts from rock and soul to blues and country. The arcaded shopping streets were astutely misaligned by the builders to prevent them from becoming wind tunnels, but their scale has a benefit that has become apparent only in the late 20th century: their modest proportions have kept out all but a few supermarkets, making the shops a delight even for those who normally abhor shopping. Aside from specialist shops and antique dealers of all kinds, the residential use of the upper storeys throughout the old town has helped to retain grocers, delicatessens and cafés, as well as restaurants. The consequence is a variety of shops and entertainment that has been lost in many towns and cities thanks to anodyne out-of-town developments.

GETTING THERE

The city's principal railway station, Bern HB, is perfectly situated on the western edge of the old town, and is the focal point of the tram and bus networks. The station's platforms are connected by a subway in which lockers can be found, as well as showcases of city shops and businesses and various shops selling provisions.

The tourist office stands in the bland complex erected over the station in 1970, which includes ticket and luggage offices and bicycle hire.

GETTING AROUND

PUBLIC TRANSPORT Bernmobil operates five tram lines and 13 bus or trolley lines. Several maps are available with varying degrees of detail showing just the urban network or the entire network of tram, bus and railway lines. For visitors without a Swiss Pass, day tickets covering all forms of city public transport are available from the tourist office, hotels and Bernmobil ticket offices. Alternatively, the Bern Card provides free admission to permanent museum exhibitions, unlimited free use of the city's public transport, and a 25% discount on guided walking tours of the old town, the Clock Tower tour, and rental of an audio guide. Cards are valid for 24, 48 or 72 hours.

Like Zürich, Bern has an S-Bahn network with routes denoted by 'S' and a numeral, and also like Zürich HB, it contains a separate underground station of four platforms (U1–U4) which serves an extensive metre-gauge suburban network with trains to Jegenstorf and Solothurn (both S8), Unterzollikofen (S9) and Worb Dorf (S7). Line 6 to Gümligen and Worb Dorf starts at Bern Fischermätteli, passing through the main station.

BICYCLE Bern is particularly well suited to exploration by bicycle and has created a good 400km (250 miles) network of cycle lanes (marked on the road by yellow lines) and paths, which are indicated on a special cycling map and by the usual red direction signs. For example, there are routes to Thun, Aarberg, Laupen, Olten and Biel/Bienne. Bikes can be hired free of charge from Bern Rollt (*Bahnhofplatz;* \ *079 277 28 57; www.bernrollt.ch*); a refundable deposit and ID are required. Bicycles can be hired from SBB at Bern HB (\ *051 220 23 74*). Another rental outlet is Ski- and Velocenter (*Hirschengraben 7;* \ *031 321 00 31*).

TOURIST INFORMATION

🚹 Railway Station, Bahnhofplatz 10a, CH-3011; \ 031 328 12 12; e info@bern.com; www.bern. com; ⊕ 09.00–19.00 daily; 09.00–18.00 Sun

WHERE TO STAY

There are many hotels in the old town close to the railway station, but beware of those on or close to main squares – the combination of 24-hour underground car parks, delivery lorries from 05.00 and late-night revellers on scooters can make for short and broken sleep. Ask for a quiet room. Those within easy reach of the station (but not necessarily in a quiet location) are:

🏠 **Bellevue Palace******* **(H)** Kochergasse 3–5, CH-3000; \ 031 320 45 45; e info@bellevue-palace.ch; www.bellevuepalace.ch

🏠 **Hotel Bern****** **(H)** Zeughausgasse 9, CH-3011; \ 031 329 22 22; e reception@hotelbern.ch; www.hotelbern.ch

🏠 **Best Western Hotel Bären****** Schauplatzgasse 4, CH-3011; \ 031 311 33 67; e reception@baerenbern.ch; www. baerenbern.ch

🏠 **Best Western Hotel Bristol****** Schauplatzgasse 10, CH-3011; \ 031 311 01 01; e reception@bristolbern.ch; www.bristolbern.ch

🏠 **Savoy Bern****** Neuengasse 26, CH-3011; \ 031 311 44 05; e reservation-sav@zghotels.ch; www.hotel-savoy-bern.ch

🏠 **City am Bahnhof***** Bubenbergplatz, CH-3011; \ 031 311 53 77; e cityab@fhotels.ch; www. fassbindhotels.ch

🏠 **Hotel Continental***** Zeughausgasse 27, CH-3011; \ 031 329 21 21; e info@hotel-continental.ch; www.hotel-continental.ch

🏠 **Kreuz Bern***** Zeughausgasse 41, CH-3000; \ 031 329 95 95; e info@kreuzbern.ch; www. kreuzbern.ch

🏠 **National**** **(H)** Hirschengraben 24, CH-3011; \ 031 381 19 88; e info@nationalbern.ch; www.nationalbern.ch

WHERE TO EAT

Bern has a large number of good restaurants, listed in a leaflet available from the tourist office. Some in the old city have unusual entrances – angled double doors underneath the arches of the arcades, leading down into converted cellars.

✗ **Altes Tram Depot (Old tram depot)** GR Muristalden 6; ☏031 368 14 15; www. altestramdepot.ch; ☉ 10.00–00.30 Mon–Sun (summer), 11.00–00.30 Mon–Sun (winter). Great view of the old town as you sample Tram Beer brewed in the middle of the restaurant.

✗ **Bistro Steinhalle** Helvetiaplatz 5; ☏031 351 51 00; www.steinhalle.ch; ☉ 9.00–22.00 Tue–Fri, 10.00–17.00 Sat–Sun. Lovely open-air terrace beside museum annex with works of art enhancing the atmosphere.

✗ **Kornhauskeller** Kornhausplatz 18; ☏031 327 72 72; www.bindella.ch; ☉ 11.45–14.30 & 18.00–00.30 Mon–Sun (from 15.00 Sat & Sun, early Oct–mid-Mar). Spectacular atmosphere in this historic granary building with a barrel that holds over 40,000 litres. Traditional Bernese food.

✗ **Moléson Gourmanderie** Aarbergergasse 24; ☏031 311 44 63; www.moleson-bern. ch; ☉ 11.30–14.30 & 18.00–23.30 Mon–Fri, 18.00–23.30 Sat (hot meals until 22.00, 22.30 in summer). An emphasis on good ingredients matched with good cooking – Charolais beef, fish, Fribourg cheese fondue.

✗ **Restaurant Harmonie** Hotelgasse 3; ☏031 313 11 41. Traditional restaurant with Swiss specialities.

✗ **Restaurant Zähringer** Badgasse 1; ☏031 312 08 88; www.restaurant-zaehringer.ch. Mostly Mediterranean dishes are served in the four areas of varying formality.

✗ **Zimmermania** Brunngasse 19; ☏031 311 15 42; www.zimmermania.ch; ☉ 11.00–14.30 & 17.00–23.30 Tue–Sat. Small French bistro with 13 GaultMillau points & lovely period atmosphere.

WHAT TO SEE AND DO

EXPLORING THE OLD TOWN Thanks partly to its modest size and partly to the confined location of the old town, Bern is a city that can be properly explored only on foot or by bicycle. The following walking itinerary takes in nearly all of the principal buildings, and would take anything from half to one day depending on the walker's interest in architecture. For the bridges, see the separate section on page 101. The tourist office has a very brief folded A4 sheet and longer booklet on historic monuments in the old town.

A remnant of the old town can be seen even before leaving Bern HB: when the station was reconstructed in the 1970s, the decision was taken to preserve the foundations of the third of Bern's walls and the Christoffel Tower as part of the huge shopping area and station complex underneath Bahnhofplatz.

Above ground the square has two buildings of note. To the right of the station is the **citizens' hospital** (Burgerspital), a rectangular building built between 1734 and 1742, with a central courtyard like the Hotel des Invalides in Paris (1734–42). Opposite is the **Church of the Holy Ghost** (Heiliggeistkirche), which has been described as the most important Protestant Baroque church in Switzerland. The vast columns, stuccoed vaults and galleries were put up between 1726 and 1729.

When leaving the church, turn left into Spitalgasse. Halfway down the street is the first of 11 Renaissance fountains for which the original figures were created in the mid 16th century. It is hard now to comprehend the importance of these water supplies, centuries before piped water was introduced into houses. For many of the population they would have been the focus of street life, where news and gossip was exchanged. The significance of the figure on the Piper Fountain is unknown.

In Bärenplatz lies the **Prison Tower** (Käfigturm) which was built between 1641 and 1643 on the site of the second west gate (1256). It remained a prison until 1897. Turn right into Bundesplatz and straight ahead are the **Houses of Parliament** (Bundeshäuser), built in stages between 1851 and 1902. The interior is open to the public for guided tours outside of parliamentary sessions (*tours leave at 14.00 Mon & Thu, in English; book one day in advance;* ☏ *031 322 85 22; passport required)* and includes the two debating chambers. The square was revamped in 2004 with new lights and a water display (*11.00–23.00 on the hour & half hour*) of 26 fountains representing the cantons.

From the south side of the Parliament building, walk along the terrace overlooking the Aare to the end of the Kirchenfeldbrücke at the south end of **Casinoplatz**, named after the 1909 casino on the opposite side of the road. Turn left (north) into Casinoplatz and proceed to the contiguous **Theaterplatz**, where the unusual single-storey, columned building with gabled roof was erected between 1766 and 1768 as a guard room and later became the police headquarters (1832–1910). The square is dominated by the **Hôtel de Musique,** built between 1767 and 1770 as a concert hall, theatre and venue for social gatherings by one of Bern's most successful and prolific architects, Niklaus Sprüngli.

Turn right into Münstergasse and on the corner is the **City and University Library**, which was built between 1755 and 1760 as a granary. The magnificent three-storey oriel window at No 62 is part of the **May House**, built in 1515 for Bartlome May. Oriel windows are a rarity in Bern – its bourgeoisie thought they would prove too great a distraction for women.

Immediately on the right as you enter Münsterplatz is the **Moses Fountain**; the figure is a replacement from 1790 to 1791 on the site of the 1544 original. The square in front of the **cathedral** is the old city's only purpose-built square (the others having been the result of filling in the moats). Bern's most impressive church began construction on 11 March 1421 on the site of an existing church, which was gradually surrounded by the new edifice but which remained in use for over 30 years before being dismantled and carried out stone by stone through the new portal. Work began under Matthäus Ensinger, one of a family of cathedral builders from Ulm who had proved their worth in Ulm, Strasbourg and Esslingen. By 1517, much of the main work had been finished, but during the Reformation many of its treasures were destroyed.

However, the magnificent tympanum over the principal entrance was spared, perhaps, it has been conjectured, because the extraordinary mélange of 238 individually-sculptured figures includes depictions of the Last Judgement. The Apostles and the wise and foolish virgins may also be seen. It was designed with a sense of humour: the lord mayor of Bern is shown attaining paradise whereas his counterpart in Zürich is banished to hell! The conditions of the figures are, of course, the result of restoration necessitated by the friable sandstone, and 47 of the originals may be seen in the **Historical Museum of Bern** (*Bernisches Historisches Museum*, see page 102).

Inside, the reticulated vaulting over the nave contains 87 keystones, some incorporating the arms of old Bernese families. The figures on the choir-stalls are worth closer attention: carved between 1523 and 1525, they depict not only religious figures but also the tradespeople of contemporary Bern, such as the dairymaid, baker and tailor. Three of the nine cathedral bells were re-used from the old church on site and they rang in 1339 in celebration of the Bernese victory at the Battle of Laupen; they have been rung since then on comparable occasions in the city's history. One of these bells is the largest in Switzerland, weighing 10.5 tonnes and cast in 1611 with a frieze of dancing bears and cherubs.

Nearly all of the stained glass in the choir dates from 1441 to 1450, except for the two to the right of the centre window, which date from 1868. The central window is known as the Passion window, and to its left is the Bible window, followed by the Three Kings window to its left. The latter is notable for its early depiction of landscape, which was an unusual subject at the time.

The 254 steps to the first platform of the stair turret in the tower can be climbed, followed by another 90 to the second, both of which offer magnificent views over the city. The tower was only half its present height at the Reformation and only reached its current height of 100m (328ft) in 1893 with the addition of an octagon and spire, making it the highest church tower in Switzerland.

Leaving the cathedral, turn left and left again through the terraced garden beside it. Before turning left behind the east end, there is a fine view along the houses that line Junkerngasse, many of which have their main façades overlooking the Aare, including the fourth house along, **Béatrice von Wattenwyl House**, with its classical front (1705). Turn right into Junkerngasse; on the right (No 59) is the plainer street front of Béatrice von Wattenwyl House, built between 1446 and 1449. The house was given to the Confederation in 1934 and is used for official receptions.

The imposing **Erlacherhof** at No 47 is the only courtyard house in Bern, built by Mayor von Erlach between 1746 and 1752. It has been the seat of municipal government since 1832 and was the centre of the Federal Council for ten years from 1848.

At the end of the street, in a horseshoe of houses beside the west end of Nydeggbrücke, stands the **Nydegg Church**. It was partly built on the site of Bern's original castle, which predated the city's foundation and was pulled down c1260–70. Most of the late Gothic church was built between 1341 and 1500. Near the church is an **1847 statue** commemorating Berchtold V of Zähringen, the city's founder. To the left of the Untertorbrücke is the Messenger Fountain, where men would wait to deliver messages brought over the bridge from the Bernese Oberland and Aarau, which were the only two roads to Bern for many years. The figure is a replica of the original (1545), which is in the Historical Museum.

Cross either bridge and turn right to the **bear pits** beside the end of the Nydeggbrücke. Their small size was a source of constant criticism, so they were substantially enlarged to 6,000 square metres and reopened in 2009 (*www. baerenpark-bern.ch*). They are accessible at all times, but the keepers are there from 08.00 to 17.00 and the shop is open 08.00–16.30.

Cross the road and ascend a narrow footpath that veers to the left, passing in front of a few houses. This leads to the **Rose Garden** and one of the best views of the city. Much of the sandstone for Bern's reconstruction after the fire of 1405 was taken from the area below the Rose Garden, which accounts for the width of the road at the foot of the slope. Return across Nydeggbrücke and proceed straight ahead into Gerechtigkeitsgasse. The figure on the **Justice Fountain** holds the scales of justice and a sword while the pope, the sultan, the Holy Roman emperor and the mayor of Bern sit at her feet, representing theocracy, monarchy, autocracy and democracy, respectively.

Gerechtigkeitsgasse is lined with elegant classical façades built for Bern's patrician families. Notable are **Marcaud House** at No 40 (1741–42) and **Sinner House** at No 81 (1767). On the corner of Kramgasse (No 2) is the **oldest pharmacy** in Bern, established in 1571. Kramgasse also has several guildhalls, such as the **Company of Merchants** at No 29 (1720–22) and the **Butchers** at No 45 (1769–70). The figure on the Samson Fountain (1544) is based on a fountain of the same name in Solothurn. A short distance before the Clock Tower is the **Zähringer Fountain** dating from 1535, another tribute to the city's founder, this time in the form of an armoured bear carrying the family coat of arms.

The **Clock Tower** (Zeitglockenturm) is Bern's oldest building and probably its best known. It formed the main gateway to the town's first western wall, its earliest stonework dating back to the 12th century. The side facing the city was open and made of wood until reconstructed in stone after the fire of 1405. The clock was not only the official time by which other clocks were set, but also the point from which distances for cantonal mileposts were measured. In its archway, the standard measurements of meter and double meter are visible, formerly 'Elle' and 'Klafter'. Fifty-minute guided tours of the tower are given daily at 14.30 from April to October (*tickets are available at the tower, from the tourist office or at various hotels*).

The tower's bell was cast in 1405 and rung by hand for 125 years. In 1530, Casper Brunner completed work at his workshop within the tower on the astronomical clock and mechanical figure play that have made the Clock Tower such an attraction for visitors ever since. The performance starts four minutes before the hour, beginning with a rooster and continuing with a procession of bears armed with clubs and various movements of a jester, Father Time, a knight in golden armour and a lion. The calendar displays the time of day, the day of the week and month, the month itself, the zodiac and the current phase of the moon.

On the right in Kornhausplatz is Bern's most gruesome fountain, the **Ogre Fountain** (c1544). The significance of the ogre devouring a child is a matter of conjecture: that perhaps it refers to the Greek myth of Cronus (who swallowed his children at birth to thwart a prediction that one of them would supplant him); or that it alludes to the false accusation of ritual Jewish murder once thought to have been practised in the late 13th century; or simply that he represents a carnival figure.

Continuing east towards the station, you come to the **Musketeer Fountain** (1543) in Marktgasse, which has an armoured commander figure. Further on is the **Anna Seiler Fountain**, supposedly named after one of the city's early benefactors who, in 1354, gave her home and fortune to found the Insel Hospital, which began with 13 beds (today it has about 1,000). However, the subject is more likely to be an allegory of moderation or temperance, with women mixing wine and water.

Turn right into Bärenplatz. Near the junction with Waisenhausplatz is the **Dutch Tower**. Swiss mercenaries serving in Dutch armies were particularly prone to acquiring the habit of smoking, but after the fire of 1405, smoking within the old town was banned, compelling them to congregate here to indulge themselves.

Turn right into Zeughausgasse for the **French Church**, which is on the left. Bern's oldest city church was built between 1270 and 1285 for the Dominican monastery, founded there in 1269, though the west front and south aisle date from 1753 to 1754. Paintings on the rood screen date from 1495 and the choir-stalls from 1302. The huge building that faces Kornhausplatz and sits just beyond the church is the **granary**, dating from 1711 to 1718. It was rebuilt between 1894 and 1898 and houses one of the city's largest restaurants, Kornhauskeller, in its cellars and temporary exhibitions on upper floors (see *Where to eat*, page 97).

Continuing east into Rathausgasse, on the left stands the **Catholic parish church** of SS Peter and Paul, built between 1858 and 1864 from the designs of French architects as a result of a competition. Opposite is the **town hall** (Rathaus), built in 12 years after the fire of 1405 and with an imposing double staircase, though it has been much altered and rebuilt between 1940 and 1942. Nearby is the **1542 Ensign Fountain** (Vennerbrunnen). A *Venner* was a flagbearer and inspector of arms, and the second-most important official after the mayor. There were only four venners, one for each district into which the city was divided.

Further along Postgasse on the left at No 72 is the **State Chancellery** (1526–41) with lovely rib vaults in the arcade. No 66 was one of Switzerland's first **post offices**, built between 1686 and 1694 for Beat von Fischer, the founder of the Bernese postal service in 1675, whose eponymous armorial device can be seen above the door.

Mounted couriers rode to Basel, Geneva, Lausanne, Luzern, Neuchâtel, Thun and Zürich, and later extended their services over the St Bernard and Simplon passes. On each side are the posthorn emblems of the post office. No 64 was a monastery until the Reformation; its basement later became and remains a Russian Orthodox church. No 62 was built between 1492 and 1505 as the Church of the Hospital Order of the Antonites, and has subsequently been a granary, postal coach-house and antiques hall.

Return to the northwest quarter of the old city for the last few buildings, perhaps taking in the Postgasshalde, Brunngasshalde and Schüttestrasse, all of which offer views over the Aare. On Waisenhausplatz is the **Boys' Orphanage** (1782–86) for children of patrician families, but since 1941, it has been the police headquarters. Near the **Museum of Fine Arts** (*Kunstmuseum*, see page 102) and below the Lorrainebrücke is the last remnant of the fourth stage of city fortifications, built between c1458 and 1473, with a rampart and gabled roof.

Finally in Aarbergergasse is the Ryffli Fountain (c1545–46), depicting a crossbowman with a plumed headdress.

MARKETS Bundesplatz and Münsterplatz host a **produce market** (*Jan–Nov 08.00– 18.00 Tue, 08.00–16.00 Sat; Apr–Oct also 09.00–20.00 Thu*). A **crafts market** is held in Münsterplatz from March to December on the first Saturday of the month (*08.00–16.00*), and a **flea market** takes place on Mühlenplatz every third Saturday of the month from May to October (*08.00–16.00*) and on Schützenmatte on the first Sunday from May to October (*08.00–16.00*). A **geranium market** is held on Bundesplatz on two days only in late April or early May.

THE BRIDGES Until 1844, the only fixed crossing of the River Aare was by the stone **Untertorbrücke** (1461–89) which replaced an earlier wooden structure. It still survives at the eastern end of the peninsula, along with the 13th-century gate-tower on the east bank known as the Felsenburg, which was converted into a residence between 1862 and 1864.

Opened in 1844, the **Nydeggbrücke** was the first high-level bridge across the river and came equipped with a pair of customs houses. It was followed in 1858 by the first railway bridge, which stood on the same site as the present reinforced concrete bridge put up in 1941.

A British company was responsible for the 230m-long (755ft) **Kirchenfeldbrücke**, which opened in 1883 and still carries both motor traffic and trams. The Bern Land Company bought land south of the Aare, and one of the three conditions of purchase stipulated that the buyer must construct a bridge over the river.

The elegant **Kornhausbrücke** provides the longest span across the Aare at 115m (377ft); completed in 1898, it also carries both motor traffic and trams.

The reinforced concrete, 82m-span (269ft) **Lorrainebrücke** was the last road bridge to be built, completed in 1930.

ACROSS THE AARE Development of the suburbs on the opposite banks of the Aare from the old town began in earnest in the second half of the 19th century. The most important such district for the visitor is Kirchenfeld to the south, where some of Bern's principal museums cluster around Helvetiaplatz.

MUSEUMS The Bern Card (see page 95) gives free admission to the permanent exhibitions of 27 museums, libraries, archives and gardens in Bern, as well as unlimited use of public transport in the city.

The old town

Einstein House (Einstein-Haus) (*Kramgasse 49;* ✆ *031 312 00 91;* ☉ *Feb–Mar 10.00–17.00 Mon–Fri, 10.00–16.00 Sat; Apr–Sep 10.00–17.00 daily; admission charge; tram 3, 5, 9 or bus 12 to Zeitglocken*) The Nobel Prize winner's apartment where he developed his general theory of relativity. Einstein lived in Bern from 1902 to 1909, publishing 32 scientific works, including in 1905 the quantum thesis for which he was awarded the Nobel Prize in 1921. At the time of writing, the museum was closed due to severe water damage; visit www.einstein-bern.ch for the latest information.

Kornhausforum (*Kornhausplatz 18;* ✆ *031 312 91 10;* ☉ *14.00–16.00 Mon, 9.00–noon, 14.00–16.00 Tue–Thu; tram 3 or 5 to Zeitglocken*) Temporary exhibitions and collection of 20th-century applied art held in the former granary.

Museum of Fine Arts (Kunstmuseum) (*Hodlerstrasse 8–12;* ✆ *031 328 09 44;* ☉ *10.00–21.00 Tue, 10.00–17.00 Wed–Sun; admission charge; bus 11, 20 or 21 to Bollwerk*) Opened in 1879, this gallery has works by the Bernese school (c1500), Fra Angelico, Renoir, Monet, Courbet, Delacroix, Utrillo, Pissarro, Cézanne, Toulouse-Lautrec, Braque, Matisse, Van Gogh, Modigliani, Picasso, Dalí, Magritte, Léger, Chagall, Kandinsky, Ernst, Miró, Mondrian, Rousseau and Rothko. A large section is devoted to the work of the Swiss artist Ferdinand Hodler and to landscape painters such as Ludwig Aberli, Caspar Wolf, Franz Niklaus Konig and Mme Vigée-Lebrun.

Across the Aare

Art Gallery (Kunsthalle) (*Helvetiaplatz 1;* ✆ *031 350 00 40;* ☉ *11.00–18.00 Tue–Fri 10.00–18.00 Sat–Sun; admission charge; tram 6, 7 or 8 to Helvetiaplatz*) This 1918 building is the attractive setting for changing exhibitions of contemporary art.

Einstein Museum (*Helvetiaplatz 5;* ✆ *031 350 77 71;* ☉ *10.00–17.00 Tue–Sun; admission charge; tram 6, 7 or 8 to Helvetiaplatz*) Original memorabilia, written records and film documentaries describe Einstein's life. Arguably his most important years were spent in Bern. Animation films, experiments and a virtual journey through the cosmos explain Einstein's revolutionary theories in a clear and easy-to-understand way.

Historical Museum of Bern (Bernisches Historisches Museum) (*Helvetiaplatz 5;* ✆ *031 350 77 11;* ☉ *10.00–17.00 Tue–Sun; admission charge; tram 6, 7 or 8 to Helvetiaplatz*) Switzerland's second-largest historical museum is housed in a purpose-built mock medieval castle designed by André Lambert and opened in 1894. It contains a marvellous variety of displays, ranging from prehistory and early history to dioramas of 19th- and 20th-century life. Rooms are devoted to Burgundy and the republic of Bern, the Christian view of life, the growth of the city, high society under the Ancien Régime and everyday life. There are large collections of coins, armour, jewellery, glass, ceramics, utensils, bronzes, mosaics, textiles and costumes, furniture in reconstructed rooms, maps and altars. One of the most unusual exhibits is an extraordinary series of 280 portraits of men and women of rural background conceived as a single ethnographic project in the 18th century.

Natural History Museum (Naturhistorisches Museum) (*Bernastrasse 15;* ✆ *031 350 71 11;* ☉ *14.00–17.00 Mon, 09.00–17.00 Tue, Thu & Fri, 09.00–18.00 Wed,*

10.00–17.00 Sat–Sun; admission charge; tram 6, 7 or 8 to Helvetiaplatz) Founded in the early 19th century, the museum is renowned for its 220 dioramas of Swiss animals and birds in their natural settings. It has an outstanding collection of rock crystals. A popular exhibit is the stuffed St Bernard by the very un-Swiss name of Barry, who saved the lives of over 40 people trapped in snow.

Paul Klee Centre (Zentrum Paul Klee) *(Monument im Fruchtland 3; ⚲ 031 359 01 01; ⊕ 10.00–17.00 Tue–Sun; admission charge; bus 12 from station or tram 7 to Ostring)* This dramatic building, designed by Renzo Piano to reflect three gently rolling hills, was opened in 2005 and houses the world's largest collection of works by the painter and etcher Paul Klee (1879–1940), who was born in nearby Münchenbuchsee. It has over 4,000 items in its collection.

Swiss Alpine Museum (Schweizerisches Alpines Museum) *(Helvetiaplatz 4; ⚲ 031 350 04 40; ⊕ 10.00–17.00 Tue–Sun, 10.00–18.00 Wed; admission charge; tram 6, 7 or 8 to Helvetiaplatz)* A museum devoted to every aspect of the Alps, including geology, glaciology, climbing, tourism, maps, paintings, architecture, agriculture, costumes, flora and fauna, and ecology. Text accompanying the displays is in English, French, German and Italian, as is that on push-button screens which visitors can use to call up information on specific subjects. There are displays on the threats posed to the Alps by atmospheric pollution, largely caused by through road traffic and by unregulated tourism.

Communications Museum (Museum für Kommunikation) *(Helvetiastrasse 16; ⚲ 031 357 55 55; ⊕ 10.00–17.00 Tue–Sun; admission charge; tram 6, 7 or 8 to Helvetiaplatz)* Formerly the Swiss PTT Museum, this has one of the world's largest stamp collections. It is combined with the story of postal communications and telecommunications, made fascinating by the challenges posed by Switzerland's climate and topography. Amongst many pictures, artefacts and models are the first St Gotthard post coach and the first Swiss telephone exchange. Interactive installations with virtual scenes and entertaining games bring the story into the internet age.

Swiss Rifle Museum (Schweizerisches Schützenmuseum) *(Bernastrasse 5; ⚲ 031 351 01 27; ⊕ 14.00–17.00 Tue–Sat, 10.00–noon & 14.00–17.00 Sun; free admission; tram 6, 7 or 8 to Helvetiaplatz)* A large collection of firearms, including crossbows, complements the story of the country's shooting traditions immortalised by the legend of William Tell. Also displayed are pictures and trophies, some of remarkable intricacy. Air rifle and laser shooting competitions test the visitor's skill.

WALKS, PARKS AND ZOO A walk along the outer bank of the Aare from Kirchenfeldbrücke to Kornhausbrücke is largely through woods and affords the best view of the Matte, the former artisans' quarter that lines the inner bank beneath the gardens of houses on Junkerngasse. The inner bank can be reached by a pedestrian bridge beneath Kornhausbrücke.

The city's **botanical garden** *(Altenbergrain 21; ⊕ Oct–Feb 08.00–17.00 daily; Mar–Sep 08.00–17.30 daily)* can be reached by bus line 20 (alight at Gewerbeschule). Over 6,000 plant species can be seen in the 2ha site.

For a trip up Bern's mountain, the **Gurten** (858m, 2,815ft), it takes 10 minutes by Line S3 from Bern station to Wabern station or about 20 minutes by tram 9 from Bahnhofplatz to reach Wabern (alight at Gurtenbahn) to take the funicular (table

2351). There is a children's playground and two restaurants at the top, and you can walk down through the forest to a chorus of birdsong and cow bells, following signs for Waberne.

The **Zoological Garden** (✆ *031 357 15 15;* ⊕ *Apr–Sep 08.30–19.00 daily; Oct–Mar 09.00–17.00 daily; last admission half an hour before closing; Vivarium:* ⊕ *summer only 08.00–18.30; admission charge; bus 19 from station to Tierpark*) is situated beside the Aare at the southwestern end of the large wooded park of Dählhölzli. The zoo has a collection of about 300 European species, some rare, including Przewalski's horse, musk-ox, moose, otter, wildcat, lynx, Syrian brown bear, golden vulture and various species of grouse. It also has a large collection of birds.

The **Elfenaupark** (✆ *031 352 07 13;* ⊕ *11.00–21.00 Wed–Sat, 10.00–18.00 Sun*) is an 18th-century Bernese garden adjacent to a park that can be reached from Bahnhofplatz by bus 19 in the direction of Elfenau. The Elfenau estate had its heyday in the 19th century, when it provided sanctuary to the émigré Russian Grand Duchess Anna Feodorowna (1781–1860) who bought it in 1814. The house dates from 1735, and the estate was acquired in 1918 by the city of Bern, which set up the municipal nurseries there.

9

The Eastern
Bernese Mittelland

The Bernese Mittelland is the name given to the area surrounding the capital. It takes in Lake Biel to the west and the Schwarzen Burgerland to the southwest, extends to Langenthal in the northeast and embraces the Emmental almost as far as Luzern to the southeast. Bern's relatively modest population means that there is no need for an S-Bahn network on the scale of Zürich. Nonetheless, the city has numerous radiating lines. They divide quite easily into railways that serve the eastern and western parts of the region. In the eastern half, Solothurn should not be missed by those interested in architecture, while the best walking and cycling lies in the picturesque Emmental.

In the immediate vicinity of Bern are the four metre-gauge lines, each denoted by a letter and operated by Regionalverkehr Bern-Solothurn (RBS), which leave from four separate underground platforms at Hauptbahnhof. Line Z to Unterzollikofen runs parallel for most of the way with Line SE/J to Jegenstorf and Solothurn, but the other three deserve description.

BERN FISCHERMÄTTELLI–BAHNHOFPLATZ–WORB DORF
Table 295/Line G

Although it appears in the railway timetable, this suburban route is more of a long tram line, operated by modern light rail vehicles. It passes by the main station.

At **Gümligen** is a country house built between 1735 and 1736 in the Louis XV style, complete with French garden. It was constructed for Beat von Fischer, who founded Bern's first post service, and he was also responsible for the courtyard house of Hofgut, which also has fine gardens – both the house and farm buildings have *trompe-l'oeil* decoration.

Worb (Worb Dorf station) has two castles: the earlier, 13th-century castle was completely rebuilt in 1535 after a fire. A 17th-century extension houses a small museum of glassware. Schloss Neu-Worb was built in the mid 18th century. The Reformed church of St Mauritius (c1500) has glass decorated with figures and coats of arms.

From Worb Dorf station a bus service to Grosshöchstetten (table 30.793) passes the attractively situated castle of Schlosswil. The 12th-century keep is incorporated into 16th-century residential additions.

WORB
Where to stay
⌂ **Löwen*** (H)** Enggisteinstrasse 3, CH-3076; ☎031 839 23 03; e office@loewen-worb.ch; www. loewen-worb.ch

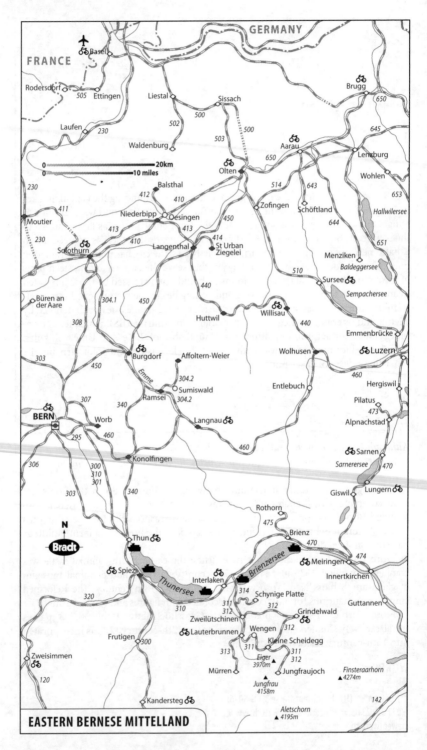

EASTERN BERNESE MITTELLAND

BERN–WORB DORF Table 307/Line S7

A surprisingly scenic metre-gauge line for a suburban service. Part of the route is mixed gauge to allow standard-gauge access to factories.

At **Ittigen bei Bern** is the Thalgut, a symmetrically planned country house of 1668. **Bolligen** has a Reformed church with Renaissance pulpit and an adjacent tithe barn. As one leaves the timber-framed houses around the station behind, the train forges into the countryside with fine views of the Bernese Alps to the southeast. From **Boll-Utzigen** a bus (table 30.781) runs to Utzigen, where there is an Italian late Renaissance-style castle of the same name set in landscaped grounds. For **Worb Dorf**, see page 105.

BERN–SOLOTHURN Table 308/Line S8

A delightful journey through rolling countryside with views of distant mountains to the east and south. The historic town of Solothurn should not be missed. RBS produces a leaflet of suggested walks from stations; though in German only, the maps and suggestions for sustenance en route can be easily understood.

Before the train leaves Bern behind, it passes Schloss Reichenbach castle at **Zollikofen**, also built for Beat von Fischer. The first part of the castle was begun in 1688 and enlarged c1719.

The modern light rail vehicles that operate this metre-gauge line are soon out in open country, though there is a sense of suburbia until after **Schönbühl** (where a second station can be found with the banal name of 'Shoppyland'). The castle at **Jegenstorf** is well worth breaking the journey to see. The early 12th-century keep has been incorporated into an 18th-century mansion in the style of Louis XIV and set in parkland. Now owned by a local foundation, it includes a museum of domestic furnishings (⊕ *mid-May–mid-Oct 13.30–17.30 Tue–Sat, 11.00–17.30 Sun; admission charge*).

Another castle may be seen but not visited at **Fraubrunnen**, where a 13th-century Cistercian convent was rebuilt as a Baroque mansion in the 18th century. It was at Fraubrunnen in 1376 that a contingent of English and Welsh mercenaries, intent on plunder under the leadership of the French noble Enguerrand de Coucy, was almost annihilated by a local force.

Bätterkinden is only a kilometre or two from the moated Schloss Landshut, which houses the Swiss Museum of Hunting and Wildlife Protection (see page 113). At **Biberist** the tower-house summer residence of the von Roll family, Schlösschen Vorder-Bleichenberg, is now a gallery of mostly local artists run by the Moos-Flury Foundation (◌ *032 672 29 89*; ⊕ *during exhibitions 16.00–19.00 Mon–Thu*). It can also be reached by bus line 6 from Solothurn to the St Elizabeth stop.

Situated astride the River Aare, **Solothurn** was founded by the Romans c370 and became the northern cornerstone of the Burgundian kingdom where the kings were crowned. It became a free imperial city in 1218, and in 1481, became the 11th canton to join the Confederation. Since then the number 11 has had a curious importance for the town, developed by the cathedral's architect, Gaetano Pisoni of Ascona in Ticino; noting also that the city's patron saints, Urs and Victor, were in the 11th Roman legion, that the town's fortifications had 11 towers, that there were 11 guilds and 11 fountains, Pisoni designed the cathedral to have 11 bells, 11 altars and three flights of 11 steps.

Although Biel/Bienne is supposedly the eastern boundary of the French language, Solothurn has long had strong connections with France and many of the town's inhabitants speak the language fluently. The town supplied mercenaries to the French kings for centuries; many returned with sufficient wealth and Francophile tastes to build houses in French style, and when the Protestant reformer Zwingli tried to abolish the practice of hired soldiers, the town opted to remain Catholic. As a consequence, from 1530 until 1792, Solothurn was the residence of French ambassadors to the Swiss Confederation.

PRACTICALITIES Bicycle hire from Solothurn station. Canton Solothurn has developed excellent cycling routes and produces a leaflet describing not only these routes, but the links with paths in neighbouring cantons. The tourist office at Solothurn offers this leaflet and also one that it produces showing local cycling and walking itineraries.

SOLOTHURN
Tourist information
🖪 Hauptgasse 69, CH-4500; 📞 032 626 46 46;
e info@solothurn-city.ch; www.solothurn-city.ch;
🕘 09.00–18.00 Mon–Fri, 09.00–13.00 Sat

Where to stay
The nearest hotel to the station is:
🏠 **Ambassador**** (H)** Niklaus-Konrad-Strasse 21, CH-4500; 📞 032 621 61 81;
e reception@ambassador-hotel.ch; www.ambassador-hotel.ch

Hotels in the old town include:
🏠 **Die Krone**** (H)** Hauptgasse 64, CH-4500; 📞 032 626 44 44; e info@diekrone.ch; www.hotelkrone-solothurn.ch
🏠 **Roter Turm*** (H)** Hauptgasse 42, CH-4500; 📞 032 622 96 21; e info@roterturm.ch; www.roterturm.ch
🏠 **Zunfthaus zu Wirthen** (H)** Hauptgasse 41, CH-4500; 📞 032 626 28 48; e info@wirthen.ch; www.wirthen.ch

Where to eat Solothurn prides itself on its gastronomy (another legacy of the French connection, no doubt) and a leaflet on the area's restaurants and their specialities is available from the tourist office.

What to see and do
Exploring the old town It is a short and pleasant walk from the station to the largely pedestrianised and exceptionally picturesque old town, though bus lines 1, 3, 4 and 7 provide transportation to it from the station across the Aare. Cross the large area in front of the station by the underground walkway in which has a sign to the centre (Zentrum). Walk along Hauptbahnhofstrasse to the bridge for pedestrians and cyclists only, the Kreuzackerbrücke; at the end of the bridge on the left is Besenval Palace, built between 1701 and 1706 for the mayor of that name for whom Schloss Waldegg was also built (see page 110). At the end of the bridge the street becomes Kroneng: on the right is the Natural History Museum (see page 110), and behind it on Klosterplatz the 17th-century St Peter's church, on which site the town's patron saints were buried after their martyrdom c300. Proceed along Kroneng into the central area in front of the cathedral. The tourist office is to the right of the cathedral steps.

The Cathedral of St Ursus was built between 1762 and 1773 on the site of a previous church (founded c910) using the local limestone known as 'Solothurn marble' – Baedeker describes the material as Portland stone. The first Neo-classical church in Switzerland, the cathedral has ornate plasterwork and very pronounced capitals on the columns. The Treasury called the *Hornbach Mass,* containing historic chalices, vestments and an illuminated manuscript dating from 983, can be visited by applying to the Sacristy at 75 Hauptgasse (*or by calling* ☏ *032 622 01 72*).

At the foot of the cathedral, steps turn right past the tourist office. Straight ahead at the east end of the cathedral is the Basel gate, a square gate-tower flanked by two bulbous cylindrical towers built between 1504 and 1535. To the north is the largest remnant of the town's defences, begun in 1667 and continued until 1727 when work was completed; the wall encloses the Riedholz tower (1548). Within sight of the wall-walk to the northwest is the Fine Art Museum (*Kunstmuseum*, see page 110).

In a square between the Riedholz tower and the cathedral is the Old Arsenal museum (*Altes Zeughaus*, see page 110); to the northwest of that lies the Gothic Franciscan church, built between 1426 and 1436 as part of a Franciscan monastery; and on the south side of the square is the Rathaus. This elaborate building was begun c1476 with the central square tower, and the last alteration, the Mannerist façade, was completed in 1711.

Return to the cathedral steps and proceed straight ahead along Hauptgasse past the Neo-classical Hotel Krone on your left. Just past the hotel on the left is the Baroque Jesuit church (1680–1705), with elaborate stucco and a broken pediment supported on scagliola columns flanking the altar.

Continue west along Hauptgasse to Marktplatz, in the middle of which stand several fountains and the clock tower (Zeitglockenturm), one of the town's oldest buildings and variously dated from the 5th to the 14th centuries! Often compared to Bern's famous clock, it has an astronomical dial and a mechanism operating a macabre figure of death, a king and a warrior. The hands of the clock are reversed: the longer is the hour hand, the shorter being installed much later when minutes began to count.

The beautiful oriel window in rich stone at No 35 Hauptgasse should not be missed. From Marktplatz, walk west along Gurzelngasse to the town's former western entrance, the 13th–14th-century Biel gate, and the nearby Buri tower (c1534). At Gurzelngasse 12 is the Kosciuszko Museum (see page 110). In Börsenplatz stands the 1548 fountain of St George slaying the dragon. Turn south towards the river to cross it by Wengibrücke. Looking east you can see on the left, jutting out into the Aare, the 1722 Landhaus alongside which boats drew up to exchange cargo. On the south bank to the east is an attractive group of buildings, including the Hospital Church of the Holy Ghost (Spitalkirche zum Heiligen Geist), built between 1734 and 1736 to the design of a French architect.

Beyond this group and near the Twisted Tower (Krumme Turm) is the landing stage for boats that operate excursions along the Aare to Biel/Bienne (*Lake Biel Navigation Company;* ☏ *032 329 88 11;* ✉ *info@bierlersee.ch; www.bielersee.ch; excursions Apr–Sep Tue–Sun; timetables available online*). The fleet includes the world's largest solar catamaran, *MobiCat*. Not only is the scenery attractive en route, but boats stop at Altreu, where Switzerland's largest stork colony of about 200 birds is only a few minutes' walk from the landing stage. The journey to Biel/Bienne takes under 2½ hours; if you would prefer to return by train, the railway station at Biel/Bienne is a short walk from the pier.

A major attraction at Einsiedelei just to the north of Solothurn is the gorge where legend has it that St Verena lived and which now bears her name. Reached by an easy walk, the site of her hermitage is marked by two 17th-century chapels. A footpath to Langendorf (see page 111) for the train back to Solothurn provides an alternative to retracing your steps.

Museums For a town of under 20,000 inhabitants, Solothurn has an outstanding collection of museums and galleries.

Fine Art Museum (Kunstmuseum) (*Werkhofstrasse 30, CH-4500;* \ *032 624 40 00;* ⊕ *11.00–17.00 Tue–Fri, 10.00–17.00 Sat–Sun; voluntary contribution*) The quality of this collection owes much to the generosity of private local collectors who have given paintings to the gallery. Although the museum now specialises in buying only the work of contemporary Swiss artists, it has paintings by Snyders, Cézanne, Van Gogh, Klimt, Renoir, Braque and Utrillo. There is a portrait of the Swiss composer Arthur Honegger, a Ferdinand Hodler of William Tell, and landscapes by the 19th-century Solothurn-born painter Otto Frölicher. Perhaps the gallery's most important painting is the Holbein *Solothurn Madonna*, painted in 1522, which shows the Virgin with St Martin and one of the town's patron saints, St Ursus.

Natural History Museum (Naturmuseum) (*Klosterplatz 2, CH-4500;* \ *065 622 70 21;* ⊕ *14.00–17.00 Tue–Sat, 10.00–17.00 Sun*) A comprehensive display of the animals, plants, geology and fossils of the region with films and videos as well as plenty of hands-on exhibits that will entertain children. There are also 150 million-year-old fossilised turtles from the town quarries.

Historical Museum Blumenstein (*Blumensteinweg 12, CH-4500;* \ *065 622 54 70;* ⊕ *14.00–17.00 Tue–Sat, 10.00–17.00 Sun; admission charge; bus 4 to Kantonsschule*) Housed in a château built c1725 in Régence style, the museum gives an insight into the life of the patrician class. On display are collections of pewter, glass, ceramics, musical instruments and religious objects.

The Old Arsenal Museum (Altes Zeughaus) (*Zeughausplatz 1, CH-4500;* \ *032 627 60 70;* ⊕ *May–Oct 10.00–noon & 14.00–17.00 Tue–Sat, 10.00–17.00 Sun; Nov–Apr 14.00–17.00 Tue–Fri, 10.00–noon & 14.00–17.00 Sat–Sun*) The political background to the Swiss Confederation meant that, until at least the 18th century, towns had to be as self-sufficient as possible with regard to arms. Solothurn had its own gun foundry and gunpowder mill, and the arsenal has survived with the second-largest collection of arms and armour in Europe. Built between 1609 and 1614, the massively gabled building contains three floors of exhibits: heavy guns, including machine guns and ammunition; small firearms and light swords; and shafted weapons, heavy swords, armour (400 suits) and uniforms.

Kosciuszko Museum (*Gurzelngasse 12, CH-4502;* \ *032 622 80 56;* ⊕ *14.00–16.00 Sat, other days by appointment only; admission charge*) Devoted to the Polish General Tadeusz Kosciuszko, who fought for his country's freedom and died in this house in 1817. The museum contains all kinds of artefacts relating to his life.

Castle Waldegg (Schloss Waldegg) (*Feldbrunnen-St Niklaus bei Solothurn;* \ *032 624 49 49;* ⊕ *Mar–Oct 14.00–17.00 Tue–Thu & Sat, 10.00–17.00 Sun; Nov–Dec 10.00–17.00 Sat; admission charge; bus 4 to St Niklaus or train to Niederbipp & alight at Feldbrunnen, 10min walk in each case*) Built between 1682 and 1713 as the summer residence of Mayor Besenval, Schloss Waldegg is the largest and most beautiful of the town's many surrounding country seats. The Baroque house contains furniture and paintings from the 17th to 19th centuries, reflecting the influence of French taste. Appropriately, a new museum is devoted to the links between Solothurn and France.

SOLOTHURN–MOUTIER Table 411

This short line to the junction at Moutier provides access to the mountain closest to Solothurn, at Weissenstein.

A footpath from **Langendorf** to Einsiedelei provides access to the St Verena Gorge and chapels (*see What to see and do*, page 109). Also an object of pilgrimage is the church of Our Lady at **Oberdorf**, an elaborately decorated building dating from 1604 which incorporates a 15th-century chapel. Only a minute's walk from the station is the two-section chairlift to **Weissenstein** (table 2026) at 1,260m (4,134ft) from where there are spectacular views of the Alps from Säntis in the east right across to Mont Blanc. There has been a spa here since 1827, visited by Napoleon III, Alexandre Dumas and the Nobel Prize winner Carl Spitteler, who portrayed Weissenstein as a home for Gods in *Olympic Spring*. A network of paths takes in a botanical garden, a geological path and a five-hour hike of the solar system by walking to Grenchenberg along the 'Path of the Planets'. In winter, the summit offers downhill and cross-country skiing and a toboggan run.

From **Gänsbrunnen** station, a postbus travels along the Dünnern valley to Balsthal station (table 50.129). For **Moutier**, see table 230, page 127.

WEISSENSTEIN
Where to stay
⌂ **Kurhaus Weissenstein***** CH-4515; ☏032 628 61 61; e kurhaus@hotel-weissenstein.ch; www.weissenstein.ch

SOLOTHURN–NIEDERBIPP–LANGENTHAL Table 413

This metre-gauge line links a series of villages in the lee of the Solothurn Jura mountains.

Trains depart from the street to the right outside Solothurn station and leave the town on a roadside tramway, crossing the River Aare and passing close to the Basel gate at **Solothurn Baseltor**. Heading east the line passes a number of fine classical houses built by the town's patrician families. **Feldbrunnen** station is ten minutes' walk from Schloss Waldegg (see opposite).

With the tree-covered slopes of the eastern Jura to the left and a broad flat valley to the right, the railway retains sufficient height on the slope to give good views to the south. Founded in 1240, **Wiedlisbach** is one of the larger places en route, its original square now altered into two streets with a charming main street. A conically topped tower is all that survives of the fortifications; the walls have been incorporated into a line of houses that can be seen from the train. The 14th-century Katharinenkapelle contains frescoes of the lives of St Catherine and St Dorothea, and there is a local museum in the granary.

At **Niederbipp**, the train pulls into a platform beside the main Solothurn–Olten line and then reverses to corkscrew underneath the standard gauge to head southeast towards Langenthal. Beyond **Bannwil**, which has a particularly attractive station with date-stone from 1907, the line descends steeply through mixed woodland to cross the Aare with lovely views down the valley on the right. Close to **Aarwangen Schloss** is the gun-ported castle from which the station takes its name. The central 13th-century keep has been absorbed by 16th-century residential accommodation.

9

At **Aarwangen** the 16th-century Gothic Reformed church has its original stained glass, and the 1767 Tierlihaus is decorated with animals commissioned by its owner, who had a travelling menagerie. A few miles alongside the streets brings the train to **Langenthal** (see table 450, page 115).

SOLOTHURN–OLTEN Table 410

The line parallels the eastern Jura which lie to the north. The riverside town of Wangen is well worth a visit from Solothurn.

The first place of note after leaving Solothurn is **Deitingen** where a tower-house was created out of the moated Schlösschen Wilihof in 1680. **Wangen an der Aare** is a delightful small town, which arose around the bridge over the Aare on the Basel–Bern road. Today's covered wooden bridge of five spans was built mostly in 1552 and is the third on the site. At the four corners of the town's medieval square plan are the castle, the bridge gate, the chancellery and the clock tower, the tower and the priest's house. The last was once a fortified Benedictine priory. The 12th-century castle was rebuilt by Beat von Fischer of Bern (see pages 100 and 105), and the 14th-century Reformed church has contemporary frescoes in the Gothic choir, which was left unaltered by the rebuilding of 1825.

On the hillside above **Oensingen** is the castle of Neu-Bechburg, built c1200 and later enlarged. The station is the junction for Balsthal (see table 412, opposite), and the town has a priest's house (1764) and an early stone Baroque house (1604), the Pflugerhaus, near the 15th-century Catholic church. A lovely 4-hour walk to Balsthal through woods and pasture is signposted from the station. The path connects to a network of routes along the ridge that lead to all three of these stations: **Egerkingen**, **Hägendorf** and **Wangen bei Olten**.

Olten is one of Switzerland's most important railway towns and contains a large works. It became the principal railway junction of central Switzerland on the recommendation of Robert Stephenson, who was invited to the country in 1850 to help plan the railway network. This choice has helped Olten to become one of the country's main conference centres. It was in Olten that the Swiss Alpine Club was founded in 1863.

The station is situated on the south bank of the Aare. To reach the small old town, turn left outside the station to walk alongside the river (Bahnhofquai) and cross the river by the early 19th-century wooden bridge which leads directly into the old town. Continue straight ahead, down Hauptgasse, past the tourist office, and turn right at the end into Graben. The old town is built on the site of a Roman citadel. Just to the north and east of Hauptgasse is the 1807 Stadtkirche, and further at Kirchgasse 8 is the Kunstmuseum (⊕ *14.00–17.00 Tue–Fri, 10.00–17.00 Sat–Sun*) with landscape paintings by Hodler and Calame and the principal collection of the 19th-century Olten-born artist Martin Disteli.

A 45-minute walk from the town is the castle of Warburg-Säli, now a restaurant with terrace. Perched on a hill overlooking the town and the Aare, the castle has been a stronghold since the 13th century. However, the reconstruction into today's white-rendered fairy-tale pastiche was commissioned by the builder of the rack railway up Mount Rigi and inventor of the rack system (after whom it is named): Niklaus Riggenbach. Riggenbach's grave can be found in the park in Olten.

PRACTICALITIES Bicycle hire from Olten station, which is on the excellent cycle network created by canton Solothurn.

WANGEN AN DER AARE
Where to stay
⌂ **Krone*** Städtli 1, CH-3380; ☎ 032 631 70 70; e hotel@krone-wangen.ch; www.krone-wangen.ch

OLTEN
Tourist information
ℹ Frohburgstrasse 1, CH-4601; ☎ 062 213 16 16; e info@oltentourismus.ch; www.oltentourismus.ch; ⏰ 09.00–noon & 13.30–18.00 Mon–Fri, 09.30–noon Sat

Where to stay
The closest hotel to the station is:
⌂ **Arte**** Riggenbachstrasse 10, CH-4601; ☎ 062 286 68 00; e reception@konferenzhotel.ch; www.konferenzhotel.ch

OENSINGEN–BALSTHAL Table 412

A standard-gauge branch that affords access to two castles and closely follows the River Dünnern for most of the way.

The 12th–13th-century castle of Alt-Falkenstein is only ten minutes' walk from the station at **Klus**. Perched on a sheer cliff, the castle was the property of the bishop of Basel before passing into the possession of Solothurn at the end of the Middle Ages, becoming a bailiff's seat. In 1922 it was bequeathed to the canton of Solothurn, and restoration of the neglected building began. The castle also contains a local history museum (⏰ *Apr–Oct 14.00–17.00 Wed–Fri, 10.00–17.00 Sat–Sun*).

The Roman origins of **Balsthal** may be glimpsed in the villa foundations of the 16th–18th-century Catholic church. The nearby chapel of St Antonius has early 17th-century vault paintings, and St Ottilien-Kapelle was founded in 1511. Herrengasse has some attractive buildings, including the early Baroque Gasthof zum Kreuz and the Biedermeier 'Rössli'. A small paper museum has been installed in the 1773 paper mill. There is a pleasant walk to Oensingen station (see opposite).

BALSTHAL
Tourist information
ℹ Goldgasse 13, CH-4710; ☎ 062 386 76 76; e info@balsthal.ch; www.balsthal.ch; ⏰ 09.00–11.30 Mon–Fri, 15.00–18.30 Tue & Thu

Where to stay
⌂ **Balsthal*** (H) Falkensteinstrasse 1, CH-4710; ☎ 062 386 88 88; e info@hotelbalsthal.ch; www.hotelbalsthal.ch

SOLOTHURN–BURGDORF Table 304.1 (S44)

The first part of a sequence of connecting trains to Bern; the line traverses a flat, fertile plain through unremarkable scenery.

The River Emme, which rises near Mount Rothorn, is crossed before **Biberist**, one of two stations for the Moos-Flury Foundation Gallery. **Utzenstorf** station is close to the delightful 17th-century Schloss Landshut; originally the residence of the provincial governor, it is now home to the Swiss Museum of Hunting and Wildlife Protection and an agricultural museum (⏰ *mid-May–mid-Oct 14.00–17.00 Tue–Sat, 10.00–17.00 Sun*). Several rooms have been furnished in 17th–19th-century style. The only moated castle in the canton of Bern, it is thought to have been built in the 12th century, although it was transformed in the 17th century.

Near **Aefligen**, the Emme is crossed again and now keeps close company most of the way to Burgdorf. At **Kirchberg** is a country house in Louis XVI style which is thought to have been designed by the Bernese architect Niklaus Sprüngli; the Tschiffeligut was commissioned by a musician and economist, Johann Tschiffeli. The village church of St Martin has early 16th-century stained glass. For **Burgdorf**, see table 450, opposite.

UTZENSTORF
Where to stay
⌂ **Bahnhof* (H)** Bahnhofstrasse 11, CH-3427;
☎ 032 665 38 38; e pedro.hanselman@bluewin.ch;
www.da-pedro.ch

BURGDORF–KONOLFINGEN–THUN Table 340

A sinuous line through attractive rolling hills with streams fringed by birch in the western part of the Emmental.

Opposite the station at **Oberburg** is Restaurant Bahnhof (☎ *0344 422 23 77*), notable for its exuberant decorative woodwork. On the left after Oberburg is a covered wooden bridge across the river, which is the longest of its kind in Switzerland. Built in 1839, it has a span of 58m (190ft). At Hasle (the junction station of **Hasle-Rüegsau**, to which there is a very frequent service from Burgdorf, table 304.2/S44), the Baroque Reformed church (1678–80) has 15th-century frescoes from an earlier church that depict the life of St Benedict.

The Reformed church at **Biglen** was built c1521 and has an elaborately carved ceiling of fantastic creatures and foliage. From **Grosshöchstetten** station, a bus (table 30.793) goes to the attractive castle of Schlosswil. As the line drops down steeply, the Bern–Luzern line comes into view far below before trains from the north twist down to cross it at the junction of **Konolfingen**. The writer Friedrich Dürrenmatt was born here in 1921; an entire centre and museum in Neuchâtel is devoted to his life and work (see page 219). The small town has a village museum with Emmental farm, a chemist shop from 1900 and collections of toys and tools.

A pretty valley with steep slopes to the west brings the line to **Oberdiessbach**, where old and new castles are within yards of each other. The old (Altes) was built c1546, the new (Neues) dates from 1666 to 1668, built in late French Renaissance style for Albrecht von Wattenwyl, to whom there is a monument in the 16th-century church.

The station at **Steffisburg** lies to the west of the town on the same side as the Neo-classical country house known as Inneres Ortbühlgut. The Reformed church was rebuilt in 1681 but retains its Romanesque tower with wooden belfry. For **Thun**, see table 300/310, page 145.

KONOLFINGEN
Tourist information
🛈 Bernstrasse 1, CH-3510; ☎ 031 790 45 45;
🕐 08.00–11.30 & 14.00–17.00 Mon–Fri

Where to stay
Close to Stalden im Emmental station, on the outskirts of Konolfingen is the attractive hotel:
⌂ **Schloss Hünigen**** (H)** Freimettingen-strasse 9, CH-3510; ☎ 031 791 26 11; e hotel@schlosshuenigen.com; www.schlosshuenigen.com. 16th-century mansion in fine grounds.

The route of stopping trains between Geneva and Zürich skirts the northern edge of the Emmental, but is scenically the least inspiring of the lines through the area. Intercity trains are routed by a high-speed line.

At **Hindelbank** stands the Baroque, horseshoe-shaped country house built between 1722 and 1725 for Mayor Hieronymus of Erlach; it is now a women's prison. His 1751 tomb may be seen in the Reformed church.

Burgdorf is regarded as the gateway to the Emmental, the fertile area to the east of the town synonymous with cheese. The region also offers good food and varied countryside highly regarded for both walking and cycling. The town and surrounding area is dominated by its magnificent castle, built on a hill with what is now the old town developing to its west, originally protected by walls punctuated with cylindrical towers. The castle was begun c1127 by Duke Konrad II of Zähringen, the keep and residential quarters being among the country's earliest brick buildings. They incorporate a Romanesque baronial hall and a chapel with frescoes from c1330. In 1218, the town passed to the Kyburgs who sold it to Bern in 1384, a governor occupying the castle until 1798.

To reach the castle and old town, through which traffic is restricted, turn left outside the station. The tourist office is just past the bicycle park on the left. Turn right into Gotthelfstrasse, which curves round to the left, then turn right and immediately left into Kornhausgasse. Opposite the Kornhaus is the house, denoted by a plaque, where the educational reformer Johann Heinrich Pestalozzi founded his first regular school in 1798, moving to Yverdon six years later. At the end of the street, turn right into Metzgergasse up the rise, and then left into Staldenstrasse and Hohengasse in which there are some fine Baroque and classical houses.

The castle also houses a local history collection (⊕ *Apr–Oct 14.00–17.00 Mon–Sat, 11.00–17.00 Sun; Nov–Mar 11.00–17.00 Sun*) with displays of ceramics, glass, church clock mechanisms, furniture and paintings.

Burgdorf gained a new gallery in 2002 with the opening of the striking buildings housing the Museum Franz Gertsch (*Platenenstrasse 3;* ⊕ *10.00–18.00 Wed–Fri, 10.00–17.00 Sat–Sun*). It displays the hyper-realistic paintings and woodcuts by Franz Gertsch, regarded as one of Switzerland's most important contemporary painters. The collection is complemented by the work of other artists.

Crossing the Emme along Wynigenstrasse, the covered Inner Wynigen bridge of 1776 is a marvellous example of truss-framed construction.

Herzogenbuchsee used to be the junction for a short branch to Solothurn, but this has been replaced by a bus (table 40.005, lines 5, 7). The town's Reformed church was built in 1728 on the remains of a Roman villa and is decorated by 20 coats of arms and a Biedermeier pulpit. .

The textile background of **Langenthal** and the surrounding area is reflected in the local history museum (Heimatmuseum) near the station (Bahnhofstrasse 11). The station is the junction for Solothurn (see table 413, page 111) and St Urban Ziegelei (table 414, page 116) for the magnificent Baroque church attached to the large Cistercian abbey. A bus from the station (table 40.052, line 52) goes to the early 18th-century manor house (referred to as a castle) at Thunstetten, built for a mayor of Bern, Hieronymous von Erlach, for whom the house at Hindelbank was also built (see above). The house is now used for concerts and banquets.

The Romanesque Reformed church of St Mauritius at Wynau (**Roggwil-Wynau** station) is a pillared basilica with frescoes from c1400 built on the site of a medieval

The Eastern Bernese Mittelland   BERN–OLTEN   9

sanctuary. The last few miles before Olten are the most attractive of the journey as the line keeps close company with the River Aare, with the finest view looking back along the river with the white rendered castle of Wartburg-Säli on a hill in the background. For **Olten**, see table 410, page 112.

PRACTICALITIES Bicycle hire from Burgdorf and Olten stations.

BURGDORF
Tourist information
🔲 Bahnhofstrasse 44, CH-3401; ✆ 058 327 50 92; e tourist-office@burgdorf.ch; www.burgdorf. ch; ⏱ 09.00–noon & 13.30–18.00 Mon–Fri, 08.00–noon Sat

Where to stay
The closest hotel to the station is:
🏠 **Hotel Berchtold*** (H)** Bahnhofstrasse 90, CH-3401; ✆ 034 428 84 28; e info@berchtold-group.ch; www.berchtold-group.ch

A little to the north of the station and offering excellent food is:
🏠 **Gasthof Emmenhof** Kirchbergstrasse 70, CH-3400; ✆ 034 422 22 75; e emmenhofburgdorf@bluewin.ch; www. emmenhof.ch

Attractively and quietly sited in the old town, but a steep walk or taxi ride from the station is:
🏠 **Hotel Stadthaus**** (H)** Kirchbühl 2, CH-3402; ✆ 034 428 80 00; e info@stadthaus.ch; www.stadthaus.ch

LANGENTHAL–ST URBAN ZIEGELEI Table 414

This metre-gauge line provides access to the remarkable former Cistercian monastery and church of St Urban.

The line has the delightful character of a roadside tramway, leaving Langenthal to cross over the main line and turning east to **Roggwil Dorf** with its pretty church near the station and a small local museum in an 18th-century storehouse.

It is only a five-minute walk from **St Urban Ziegelei** to the monastery buildings, now a sanatorium. Founded in 1194, the monastery developed a healthy business producing decorated bricks, examples of which can be seen in surviving sections of late medieval wall. The early 18th-century Baroque church was designed by the prolific Austrian architects Franz and Johann Michael Beer of the Voralberg school of artists, who built many churches in Germany, Austria and Switzerland. The pilastered hall of the church is decorated with Louis XVI stucco and elaborate carving on the choir-stalls. The wooden Rococo pulpit is richly gilded.

BERN–LUZERN Table 460

Expresses and stopping trains serve this main line through the Emmental with three different rivers for company and the delightful scenery for which the area is renowned.

Luzern-bound trains share the line to Thun as far as **Gümligen** (see table 295, page 105), where they diverge to head east through fertile farming country, the rolling hills crowned with woods and the peaks of the Bernese Oberland in view to the south. **Worb SBB** is a mile or two from Worb Dorf (see table 295, page 105). The junction at **Konolfingen** (see table 340, page 114) provides connections for Thun and Burgdorf, and has a good buffet on platform 2.

The Baroque priest's house at **Signau** was built c1738 in the style of a Bernese country house. Both the compact streets and nearby farms have attractive vernacular buildings. To the east of the village, the railway briefly follows the River

Emme to **Emmenmatt**, where it is joined by the Ilfis with the line from Ramsei at a point near the railway junction. Turning east, the Ilfis is seldom out of view of the railway for the next dozen miles.

Langnau is the main market town of the Emmental. In addition to its thriving dairies, it is known for ornamental ceramics which have been produced here since the 18th century and which can be seen in the Heimatmuseum in the Chüechlihaus on Bärenplatz (⊕ *Apr–Oct 13.30–18.00 Tue–Sat, 10.00–18.00 Sun*). This museum is housed in a 16th-century wooden building known as a Blockbau in which the load-bearing walls are made up of horizontal timbers. Also on display are tools associated with the local timber trades and crafts, glassware and displays on local history.

The Hirschenplatz is a particularly fine, largely unspoiled square, and the pulpit and font in the Reformed church dating from 1673 have ornate Baroque carving. The semi-circular wooden decoration under the gables that is characteristic of the area can be seen in some of the houses, and there are some Biedermeier houses. A bus from the station (table 30.285/line 285) takes the twisty road close to the 1,142m (3,747ft) summit of Lüderenalp (where there is an isolated hotel) and the former rail terminus of Wasen im Emmental, now served by a bus (see table 304.2 Ramsei–Huttwil, page 119).

Trubschachen has some attractive buildings from the 17th to 19th centuries, some half-timbered, others with painted façades, like the Himmelhaus of 1738 which is decorated with pictorial devices and aphorisms.

Heading east, the river is periodically spanned by covered wooden bridges, and to the south waterfalls descend from hanging valleys into the increasingly steep-sided valley of the Ilfis. Even in summer, snow-covered mountains can now be seen to the east. At the attractive village of **Escholzmatt** the Ilfis turns south towards its source and is replaced on the left by another river, the Kleine Emme, which the railway follows all the way to Luzern where it joins the Reuss.

The railway turns to the northwest along the Entlebuch valley, from which a band of peasants defeated a largely English force of 3,000 men in 1375. Under the command of Enguerrand de Coucy, who had married Edward III's daughter, the well-equipped army had invaded Switzerland in pursuit of Enguerrand's claim to a Habsburg inheritance through his mother. His force, known as the Free Companions, was defeated near Buttisholz, north of Wolhusen (see page 119). Sir Walter Scott refers to the battle in his novel *Anne of Geierstein* (1829), which is set largely in Switzerland.

From the station at **Schüpfheim**, the largest village in the Entlebuch, a bus (table 60.241) heads south along a spectacular road through the valley of the Waldemme and Lamm Gorge to the resort of Sörenberg, where there is a small cable car up to Rossweid (table 2503). Sörenberg is in the heart of the Entlebuch UNESCO-designated biosphere at an altitude of 1,165m (3,822ft). One of only 400 biosphere reserves worldwide, its fantastic moor and karst (rough limestone with underwater drainage) landscape is host to unique plant and animal life. The bus continues south to serve the cable car from Sörenberg-Schönenboden up to **Brienzer Rothorn** (table 2505). There is a choice of returning from the summit of the Rothorn to catch the same bus service, continuing east over the Glaubenbuelen Pass at 1,611m (5,284ft) to the station at Giswil (see table 470, page 187), or proceeding down the south side of the mountain by the rack railway to Brienz (see table 475, page 194).

The railway reaches **Hasle** where the Gothic ossuary attached to the parish church contains a 17th-century painted Dance of Death. The Catholic church at the pretty village of **Entlebuch** is in the Baroque style known as Singer-Purtschert, with shallow-vaulted ceiling and side altars in diagonal niches that link the nave and the choir. A bus from the station (table 60.232) goes to Gfellen, from where there is a walk over the Glaubenberg Pass at 1,543m (5,062ft) to Langis-Schwendi, where there is a hotel, and Stalden for a bus (table 60.344) down to Sarnen station (see table 470, page 187).

Riverside paths offer delightful walking along a very pretty stretch of the Kleine Emme, with fine views of craggy peaks to the southeast. At the railway junction of **Wolhusen**, the Kleine Emme and the railway turn sharply to the east.

In a glorious setting on the right, near **Werthenstein**, is a former Franciscan monastery founded in 1630 around the pilgrimage church of Unserer Lieben, which was built between 1608 and 1613. Standing on a hill with cliffs behind and a wooden bridge (1710) in the foreground, the monastery has a Tuscan-arched cloister decorated with frescoes dating from 1779.

As the line nears Luzern, the valley broadens out. Beyond **Malters** on the right is an attractive group of white-rendered buildings around the pilgrimage church of St Jost, founded c1370. The tower and eastern part of the nave remain from the original church consecrated in 1391; the rest dates from the 16th to 18th centuries. For **Luzern**, see *Chapter 12*, page 165.

PRACTICALITIES Bicycle hire from Langnau, Entlebuch and Luzern stations.

LANGNAU
Tourist information
🄸 Dorfmühle 22, CH-3550; ☎034 409 95 95; e info@langnau-tourismus.ch; www.langnau-tourismus.ch; ⊕ 08.00–noon & 13.00–18.00 Mon–Fri, 09.00–16.00 Sat

Where to stay
⌂ **Bahnhof**** Bahnhofstrasse 5, CH-3550; ☎034 402 14 95; e daluca@bluewin.ch
⌂ **Hirschen (H)** Dorfstrasse 17, CH-3550; ☎034 402 15 17; e info@hirschen-langnau.ch; www.hirschen-langnau.ch

LÜDERENALP
Where to stay
⌂ **Lüderenalp***** CH-3457; ☎034 437 16 76; e hotel@luederenalp.ch; www.luederenalp.ch

LANGNAU–BURGDORF Table 304.2/Line S4,S44

A branch line through the heart of the Emmental, closely following the course of the River Emme nearly as far as Burgdorf, though now part of the Bern S-Bahn network.

Beyond the junction of **Ramsei** (for connections to Sumiswald, see opposite) is **Lützelflüh** (station **Lützelflüh-Goldbach**). From 1832, the pastor at the Gothic Reformed church was Jeremias Gotthelf (d. 1854) whose novels portray contemporary life in the Emmental. A museum of his life and works (⊕ *mid-Apr–Oct 13.30–17.00 Tue–Fri, 10.00–17.00 Sat–Sun*) may be found next to the 1655 priest's house. The village's former grain mill (1821) is considered one of the region's finest and is now a cultural centre for the community. For the section of line beyond the junction of **Hasle-Rüegsau**, see table 340, page 114.

LÜTZELFLÜH
Where to stay
⌂ **Ochsen (H)** Gotthelfstrasse 11, CH-3432; ☎034 461 15 10; e oxberger@hotmail.ch; www.ochsen-emmental.ch

Another branch through the heart of the Emmental which provides access to the market centre of Sumiswald and to the Emmental Show Dairy. Regrettably buses have replaced trains over the onward section from Sumiswald-Grünen to Huttwil.

The Gothic Reformed church at **Sumiswald** was built between 1510 and 1512 as a church of the Teutonic Order of Knights, with later stained glass depicting the founders and patron saints. A 1225 endowment laid upon the Order an obligation to maintain a hospice for the poor and to offer hospitality to pilgrims. The Spittel is the outcome, though today's building, used as a nursing home, is the result of rebuilding following a fire in 1730.

From Sumiswald it is less than a kilometre to the south to the village of Thrachselwald, where all of the houses face south. The Reformed church from 1685 has a *trompe-l'oeil* painting based on part of Mantegna's fresco in the Camera degli Sposi of the Ducal Palace in Mantua. The oldest parts of the much-altered castle date back to the second half of the 12th century.

Sumiswald used to be the junction for a short branch to Wasen im Emmental, but the train service was also the victim of 'bustitution' (table 30.481/line 481).

Observant travellers will notice the large size of many farmsteads in the Emmental. This is largely the result of primogeniture, or at least single bequests, rather than the equal division of inheritances. This concentration of wealth has enabled farms to be run more like estates, with workers and other branches of the owning family living in a cluster of buildings around the farm rather than in neighbouring villages.

From **Affoltern-Weier** station a bus (table 30.471/line 471) runs to Affoltern where the Emmental Show Dairy (*Emmentaler Schaukäserei;* ⊕ *08.30–noon & 13.30–18.30 daily*) is situated. The cheese-making process is demonstrated daily from 08.30 to 18.30 both by the traditional method using a single vat and by the modern vat that makes four Emmental cheese wheels simultaneously. Audio-visual information is given in German, French, Italian and English. The dairy includes a bakery as well as confectionery, cheese and handicrafts shops and a restaurant.

For **Huttwil** see page 120.

GRÜNEN-SUMISWALD
Where to stay

🏠 **Gasthof Bahnhof (H)** Bahnhofstrasse 21, CH-3455; ☎034 431 15 44; e koenigmax@bluewin.ch; www.hotel-bahnhof-sumiswald.ch

🏠 **Bären*** (H)** Marktgasse 1, CH-3454; ☎034 431 10 22; e hotel@baeren-sumiswald.ch; www.baeren-sumiswald.ch

Although not the prettiest of Emmental journeys, this cross-country line serves several attractive towns and villages.

Although **Willisau** has been destroyed by fire four times, the last in 1704, it retains some older buildings, such as the Obertor from 1551 – the Untertor at the east end of the delightful Hauptgasse has been rebuilt. Outside the Obertor lies the early Baroque pilgrimage chapel (1674–75) known as the Heiliglut (Holy Blood), with biblical scenes painted on its wooden ceiling. On a hillock near the Obertor stands the Neo-classical Catholic church; though rebuilt between 1804 and 1810, it retains its 13th-century Romanesque bell tower.

Above the town is the bailiff's castle, built between 1690 and 1695 on to a watchtower in the town walls. Although used as a district court, school and for local administration, it is open for guided tours for groups on request at the tourist office.

From the station, a bus (table 60.063/line 63) goes to Sursee on the Olten–Luzern line (see table 510, page 182), calling at Ettiswil and passing just before the village the picturesque castle of Wyher; once moated, this castle was built c1510 but has been much altered.

The Reformed church at **Zell** dates from the late 15th century but there has been a church on this site since 700; it was originally the tomb of a hermit. At **Hüswil** is an 18th-century granary with finely carved door.

A town since the 13th century, the town of **Huttwil** has a unified Neo-classical appearance following its rebuilding after fire. A branch line once headed west to Ramsei, while the Langenthal line proceeds north, following the valley of the River Langeten. For **Langenthal**, see table 450, page 115.

PRACTICALITIES Bicycle hire from Willisau station.

WILLISAU
Tourist information
🛈 Hauptgasse 10, CH-6130; ☏ 041 970 26 66; e info@willisau-tourismus.ch; www.willisau- tourismus.ch; ⏰ 08.30–11.30 & 13.30–18.30 Mon–Fri

HUTTWIL
Tourist information
🛈 Marktgasse 1, CH-4950; ☏ 062 962 55 05; e info@regio-huttwil.ch; www.regio-huttwil.ch; ⏰ 08.30–11.30 Mon–Tue, Thu–Fri

Where to stay
🏠 **Kleiner Prinz*** (H)** Markgasse 5, CH-4950; ☏ 062 962 20 10; e info@kleiner-prinz.ch; www. kleiner-prinz.ch

The Western Bernese Mittelland

The area to the west of Bern is dominated by the three interconnected lakes of Biel, Morat and Neuchâtel, sandwiched between the southern range of the Jura Mountains to the north and the northwestern ranges of the Alps to the south. Despite the distance, the views of the latter on clear days can be dramatic.

It is a particularly good area for family cycling: the areas around the lakes have easy gradients, and there is an excellent network of signposted, traffic-free cycle routes.

BERN–BIEL/BIENNE Table 303

A scenically unremarkable line that links the capital with a town that sees itself as the capital of watchmaking. Biel/Bienne has a lovely old town and some of the best sports facilities in Switzerland.

The Biel/Bienne line diverges from the main line to Olten and Zürich at Zollikofen, turning northwest to **Münchenbuchsee**, birthplace of the painter Paul Klee (1879–1940). A Commandery of the Knights of the Order of St John was founded here in 1180; to the south of their surviving buildings is the Order's 13th-century Gothic church, now the Reformed church, which has stained glass from c1300. Nearby is the town bailiff's Baroque castle.

Continuing through gently undulating farmland with sugar beet as a major crop, the line reaches the junction of **Lyss**, a manufacturing town, where trains connect for Lausanne via Murten and Payerne to the southwest (tables 291/305/251) and Büren an der Aare (for buses to Solothurn) in the northeast.

Biel/Bienne is the only officially bilingual town in Switzerland, where the inhabitants switch with disarming ease from French to Schwyzerdütsch in mid-sentence and the street names appear in both languages. Founded between 1220 and 1230 by the prince-bishops of Basel, the town had semi-independent status for almost six centuries before being overrun by Napoleon's armies in 1789. It became part of the canton of Bern in 1815 and grew rapidly following the setting up of the watchmaking industry. The town is now its acknowledged centre and the home of Omega, Rolex and Swatch, the last of which sponsored an experimental car named 'The Spirit of Biel', produced by the Biel Engineers' School. Swatch joined forces with Mercedes-Benz to produce the Smart production car, though Swatch has since pulled out of the venture.

Before leaving the subway linking the station platforms, pause to look at the allegorical murals, painted by Philippe Robert, that decorate the waiting room on the right. The tourist office is the small single-storey building at the edge of the bicycle park ahead and slightly to the right as you leave the station. It has to be said

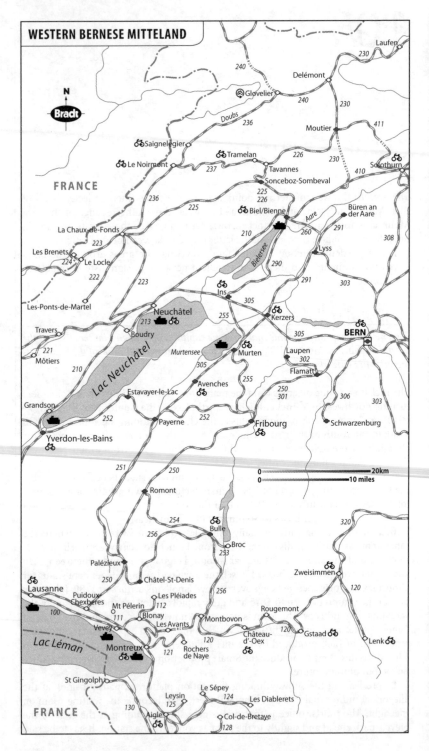

WESTERN BERNESE MITTELAND

that the area around the station is not the best part of the town, even though many of the buildings in the area are the result of an architectural competition held c1930.

To reach the attractive and refreshingly understated old town, the principal area of interest, take bus 57 or walk directly ahead down Bahnhofstrasse to a major junction and then down Nidaugasse. The old town is the largely pedestrian quarter directly ahead at the end (about 15 minutes' walk). In Burggasse are the Fountain of Justice (1714), the Zeughaus (1589–91) – once the arsenal and today a theatre – and the Rathaus (1530–34). Proceed into Obergässli to reach the Ring, the marketplace, which takes its name from the semicircle of town worthies who sat here in judgement on offenders. On the south side of the square is the Gothic Reformed Church of St Benedict; this dates from 1451 to 1492 and includes in the choir some stained glass from 1457 that depicts the life of St Benedict and Christ's Passion. Also in the square is the Standard-bearer Fountain (1557) and, opposite the church, a magnificent three-storey oriel window.

Leading north out of the square is the arcaded Obergasse. Near the Fountain of Compassion is the Gasthaus zur Krone (c1582) where Goethe once stayed. Don't miss the lovely stone carving around the windows of No 64.

To the north again, up Brunngasse, stands the station for the funicular, which runs every ten minutes up to Evilard/Leubringen (table 2023), a suburb surrounded by woods. Bus 51 from the station serves the funicular.

Three towers dating from c1405 and a suggestion of a moat are all that remain of the town's fortifications, on Jakob-Rosius-Strasse on the west side of the old town. The town's three museums are a short walk further west from these towers, right along Mühlebrücke and Seevorstadt. Museum Schwab (*Seevorstadt 50;* ⊕ *14.00– 18.00 Tue–Sat, 11.00–18.00 Sun; admission charge*) is named after the 19th-century colonel who revealed much about the region's 6,000-year-old lake settlements. These were discovered when the levels of lakes Biel, Murten (Morat) and Neuchâtel were deliberately lowered during the 19th century to reclaim land and to reduce the risk of malaria. The museum contains artefacts from the lakes and tells the story of their communities. Museum Neuhaus (*Schüsspromenade 26;* ⊕ *11.00–17.00 Tue– Sun, 11.00–19.00 Wed; admission charge*) portrays the life of 19th-century Biel, and Museum Robert (*same address*) contains work of the Robert family of painters, depicting landscapes, plants and animals.

A second funicular (table 2022) leaves from the western end of Seevorstadt, near the park adjacent to the lake. A 20-minute walk from the station (or bus 53), this one ascends to Magglingen/Macolin, where there are some of the finest sporting facilities in Switzerland. The Swiss Sports School was founded in 1944 and is a combination of school and research centre, but most of the facilities are open to the public. The earliest buildings are notable examples of modern architecture. The top of the funicular is the start of walks to Sujet at 1,382m (4,534ft) and onto the summit of Chasseral at 1,607m (5,272ft).

A short walk from the station is the landing stage for vessels on Lake Biel and along the River Aare to Solothurn (see table 308, page 107). Turn left outside the station, pass underneath the railway and then bear right down Badhausstrasse to the lake. A wide range of day, gastronomic and evening cruises is available, some using rail travel in one direction and one taking in the connected lakes of Neuchâtel and Morat. Timetables can be picked up from the tourist office or BSG (*Badhausstrasse 1a, CH-2501;* ✆ *032 329 88 11; www.bielersee.ch*).

PRACTICALITIES Bicycle hire from Biel/Bienne station. Facilities for cyclists around Biel are exceptional: a brochure with five very different circular rides is available.

10

Ranging from 38 to 62km, they include a circular tour of the lake, a riverside ride to Solothurn and a ride on the uplands above Biel to the Chasseral, the area's highest mountain at 1,607m (5,272ft). The tourist office produces a leaflet listing hotels in the area that hire bicycles or have secure covered accommodation for bicycles.

LYSS
Tourist information
☑ Hirschenplatz 1, CH-3250; ☎ 032 387 00 87; e gemeinde@lyss.ch; www.lyss.ch

Where to stay
⌂ **Weisses Kreuz*** (H)** Marktplatz 15, CH-3250; ☎ 032 387 07 40; e info@kreuz-lyss.ch; www.kreuz-lyss.ch

BIEL/BIENNE
Tourist information
☑ Bahnhofplatz/Pl de la Gare 12, CH-2501; ☎ 032 329 84 84; e info@biel-seeland.ch; www. biel-seeland.ch; ⏱ 08.00–12.30 & 13.30–18.00 Mon–Fri, 09.00–15.00 Sat

Where to stay
The hotel closest to the station, but on a busy street, is:
⌂ **Art Deco Hotel Elite****** Bahnhofstrasse/ Rue de la Gare 14, CH-2501; ☎ 032 328 77 77; e info@hotelelite.ch; www.hotelelite.ch
About 15 minutes' walk, but in a quiet location, is:
⌂ **Mercure Hotel Plaza Biel******
40 Neumarktstrasse/Rue du Marché Neuf, CH-2502; ☎ 032 328 68 68; e h6166@accor.com; www.mercure.com

LYSS–BÜREN AN DER AARE Table 291

Once part of a line on to Solothurn, the service beyond the small medieval town of Büren an der Aare has been replaced by a bus.

The principal building of interest in **Büren an der Aare** is the castle built c1620 for the governor, which is flanked by huge projecting towers. The Reformed church has a Gothic nave dating from 1510 with a painted wooden ceiling.

BIEL/BIENNE–NEUCHÂTEL Table 210

A delightful journey beside Lake Biel through a series of wine-growing villages, most of which are also served by lake boats, enabling circular journeys to be made. On clear days the Bernese Oberland seems surprisingly close.

The line emerges from a long tunnel on the outskirts of Biel to come alongside the lake, which it follows closely throughout its length, paralleling the cycle and footpath that also follows the shore. On the right, vineyards line the southern slopes of the Tessenberg, the terrace that forms the southern flank of the Chasseral, itself the southern ridge of the Jura Mountains. In places the vines come right down to the water's edge.

The picturesque village of **Twann** has been known for its wine since the Middle Ages. Some of the protruding roofs of the rendered wine growers' houses that line the main street have hoists and skylights. The Gothic Reformed church of St Martin has early Baroque carved choir-stalls from 1666 and an inlaid pulpit. Near the station is a little harbour for yachts and a children's playground.

Ligerz is also a wine centre and has a museum of viticulture offering wine-tasting events in a 1545 Gothic mansion known as the 'Hof', a minute's walk to the left from the station (⊕ *May–Oct 13.00–17.00 Sat–Sun; admission charge*). Directly opposite the station is the Tessenberg Bahn (table 2016), an unusually sinuous funicular which climbs up through vineyards, woods and meadows to **Prêles**, where there is a breathtaking view of the Bernese Oberland on clear days (it is often hazy). Various halts en route give the option of walking part of the way, or visiting the Gothic Reformed church of St Imer and Theodul, which is surrounded by vines. Built between 1470 and 1475, it has a carved wooden ceiling in the nave and stellar vaulting in the choir.

Soon after leaving Ligerz, St Peter's Island comes into view. This ceased to be an island when the lowering of the lake revealed a causeway linking the island with Jollimont near Erlach. The quality of the habitat for birds has resulted in the island being designated as a nature reserve. Its principal building is a former Cluniac monastery founded in 1127, which later became a hostelry and welcomed Goethe, Empress Josephine Bonaparte and the kings of Prussia, Sweden and Bavaria, as well as Jean-Jacques Rousseau, with whom it is particularly associated. Rousseau described the two months he spent here in 1765 as 'the happiest time of my life', and a room in today's imaginatively restored hotel contains memorabilia connected with him. The Cornishman Thomas Pitt, 2nd Baron Camelford, so enjoyed the year of his youth spent on the island that he deposited £1,000 with a Bernese banker to buy him a plot of land in which he would be buried. He died in 1804.

The language frontier is crossed before the last station near the lake, **La Neuveville**, which serves the almost square-shaped town founded in 1312 by the bishop of Basel. In addition to many 16th–19th-century houses, the town still has remnants of several towers that were part of its first fortifications and a much-altered and restored castle that pre-dates the town, having been built in 1283. There is a museum in the Hôtel de Ville at Ruelle de l'Hotel-de-Ville 11 (⊕ *Apr–Oct 14.30–17.30 Sun; free admission*), last rebuilt between 1541 and 1569, which contains art and historical artefacts, including cannon from the battlefield of nearby Grandson (1476). The imposing Maison de Bern near the small harbour was built in 1631 and once used to process the grape harvest from the Abbey of Bellelay. The White Church to the east of the centre was built in 1345 and enlarged in the 15th century; it has 14th–15th-century frescoes.

Le Landeron is another historic town, founded in 1325 by the prince-bishops of Basel. At each end of the main street stands a town gate and a fountain, while the houses flanking the street are mostly 18th-century. To the west of the clock tower is a 14th-century château, and most unusually one structure contains both the Hôtel de Ville and a chapel named the Ten Thousand Martyrs.

At **Cressier** is a château dating from 1609, now used as a parish hall and school, and the old village contains a late 16th-century lion fountain. **Cornaux** has some fine houses dating from the 15th to 18th centuries and a Reformed church with 14th-century choir tower.

For **Neuchâtel**, see *Chapter 15*, page 217.

PRACTICALITIES Bicycle hire from Neuchâtel station.

TWANN
Where to stay
⌂ **Fontana*** (H)** Moos 34/36, CH-2513;
☏ 032 315 03 03; e mail@hotelfontana.ch; www.hotelfontana.ch

LIGERZ
Where to stay
A hotel very close to the station is:

⌂ **Kreuz (H)** Hauptstrasse 17, CH-2514; ☏ 032
315 11 15; e info@ kreuz-ligerz.ch; www.kreuz-
ligerz.ch

ST PETER'S ISLAND
Where to stay
⌂ **St Petersinsel** CH-3235; ☏ 032 338 11 14;
e welcome@stpetersinsel.ch; www.st-petersinsel.
ch. Idyllic lakeside position.

LA NEUVEVILLE
Tourist information
🔲 Rue du Marché 4, CH-2520; ☏ 032 751 49 49;
e laneuveville@jurabernois.ch; www.jurabernois.
ch; ⏰ 09.00–noon & 13.30–17.30 Tue–Fri,
09.00–noon Sat

Where to stay
⌂ **J-J Rousseau***** CH-2520; ☏ 032 752 36 52;
e info@jjrousseau.ch; www.jjrousseau.ch

BIEL/BIENNE–LA CHAUX-DE-FONDS Table 225

A pretty journey through the St-Imier Valley, though part of it has been disfigured by road building.

The exit from Biel/Bienne is remarkably steep, quickly affording views to the right across the town. The line turns northeast into a well-wooded valley that joins the La Suze River, which the line follows to its source at La Creux, close to La Chaux-de-Fonds. The first station, **Frinvillier-Taubenloch**, provides access to the Taubenloch gorge, a narrow defile crossed by the railway immediately after it emerges from a tunnel. Consequently it flashes past in a glimpse, but it is well worth a special visit since a footpath was hewn out of the rock in 1890, enabling walkers to see the waterfall as well as the vertiginous gorge.

Apart from the villages and occasional town, the lovely St-Imier Valley is sparsely populated with few farms. **Sonceboz-Sombeval** is the junction for trains to Moutier and Delémont (table 226). Continuing up the valley, the predominance of mixed forest reflects the poor farming land. **St-Imier**, home of Longines watches, once had a Benedictine monastery, but all that remains is the 12th-century Romanesque collegiate church. Twelve minutes' walk from the station is a funicular up to Mont-Soleil (table 2020), opened in 1903. At the summit is the largest renewable energy park in Switzerland, with a visitor centre in the station. At **Sonvilier** is the ruined 11th-century castle of Erguel with cylindrical keep. The early 17th-century dairy at the Auberge La Grande Coronelle has a vaulted kitchen with huge pillars.

A long tunnel precedes arrival at **La Chaux-de-Fonds** (see table 223, page 220).

ST-IMIER
Tourist information
🔲 Place de la Gare 2, CH-2610; ☏ 032 942 39 42;
e saintimier@ jurabernois.ch; www.jurabernois.
ch; ⏰ 09.00–noon & 13.00–17.00 Mon–Fri; Jul–
Aug 09.00–noon Sat

SONCEBOZ-SOMBEVAL–MOUTIER–Delémont Table 226

The line provides access to the eastern terminus of the metre-gauge branch of the Chemin de Fer du Jura at Tavannes.

From the junction with the Biel/Bienne–La Chaux-de-Fonds line, the branch to Moutier climbs to a long tunnel under the pass of Pierre Pertuis; this defile was enlarged by the Romans for the movement of their legions. The railway follows the La Birse River for much of the way. **Tavannes** is another watchmaking town where many houses have the generous glazing that indicates cottage industry, like those in early English textile towns. Jura Bernois Tourism (☏ *032 494 53 43; www. jurabernois.ch*) has an excellent walking tour leaflet of the town in English. The striking Catholic church (1928–30) has a mosaic of the Resurrection over the portal.

On the approach to the junction of Moutier are some impressive cliffs above the river to the left. For **Moutier** and the line on to Delémont, see table 230, below.

TAVANNES
Where to stay
Hotels very close to the station are:
🏠 **De la Gare** Rue de la Gare 4, CH-2710; ☏ 032 481 22 21

🏠 **De la Poste** Pl de la Gare 1, CH-2710; ☏ 032 481 32 43
🏠 **Terminus (H)** Rue H-F Sandoz 26, CH-2710; ☏ 032 481 23 50

BIEL/BIENNE–DELÉMONT Table 230

Part of the main line from southwest Switzerland to Basel, the route crosses the southern massif of the Jura Mountains.

The first section to **Lengnau** shares the line to Solothurn (see table 410, page 112). At Lengnau the line turns north to pass through Grenchen before entering the 8.4km (5¼ miles) Grenchenberg Tunnel, opened in 1915, through the southern part of the Jura. The tunnel ends just before the junction of **Moutier**, a small industrial town which grew up around a monastery founded c640. The monks gave their name to one of Switzerland's best-known cheeses, Tête de Moine or Monk's Head, which is still produced in the locality (and particularly the Abbey of Bellelay) and should be eaten in fine shavings. Nothing remains of the monastery, but the Great Bible of Moutier-Grandval can be found in the British Museum.

Although the town has some 16th–17th-century houses, the most interesting building lies just outside the town to the west, passed by a bus to Souboz (table 21.231) from the station. The Romanesque Chapelle de Chalières has frescoes dating from c1020, depicting the Apostles, Christ in Glory, and Cain and Abel.

Heading north, the railway weaves through the often spectacular rock formations that line the gorge of Val Moutier, or Cluses des Roches, so narrow that the line is often in shade. The clock tower at **Courrendlin** was built as a prison and has a clock dating from 1697. Emerging from the gorge, the train bowls through fertile countryside to the capital of canton Jura, **Delémont**. In the fork of the junction at Delémont, on the right as you approach the town, is a historic steam locomotive depot which was renovated for the 150th anniversary of Swiss railways in 1997, becoming a home for various preserved steam locomotives (*www.volldampf.ch*).

Founded by the bishops of Basel, Delémont has developed on a rectangular plan. Two of its gates survive, Porte du Porrentruy and Porte-au-Loup. Near the former at 52 Rue du 23 Juin is Maison Bennot, which houses the regional art and history

10

collection of Musée Jurassien (🕐 *14.00–17.00 Tue–Fri, 11.00–18.00 Sat–Sun*). It is in front of this building that the town's public gatherings have been held. On the Grand-Rue is the early 18th-century horseshoe-shaped bishop's palace, which was used as a summer residence by church officials from Basel until 1815. Delémont's fountains date mostly from the 15th and 16th centuries.

MOUTIER
Tourist information
🄸 Av de la Gare 9, CH-2740; ☎ 032 494 53 43; e moutier@jurabernois.ch; www.jurabernois.ch;

🕐 09.00–noon & 14.00–17.00 Mon–Fri; Jul–Aug 09.00–noon, 14.00–18.00, 09.00–noon Sat

DELÉMONT
Tourist information
🄸 Pl de la Gare 9, CH-2800; ☎ 032 420 47 71; e info@juratourisme.ch; www.juratourisme.ch; 🕐 Feb 09.00–noon & 14.00–17.30 Tue–Fri; Mar–Nov 09.00–noon, 14.00–17.30 Mon–Fri, 09.00–noon Sat

Where to stay
🏠 **Le National***** Route de Bâle 25, CH-2800; ☎ 032 422 96 22; e reservation@lenational-hotel. ch; www.lenational-hotel.ch

BIEL/BIENNE–SOLOTHURN Table 410

An underwhelming section of the Neuchâtel–Olten–Zürich main line, which parallels the southern flank of the Jura Mountains.

The line climbs east out of Biel/Bienne, giving views over the town to the left. At Lengnau, the line to Basel swings north, while the Solothurn line soon reaches the industrial and watchmaking town of Grenchen. Shortly before Bellach, a loop of the River Aare can be seen to the right. For **Solothurn**, see table 308, page 107.

PRACTICALITIES Bicycle hire from Solothurn station.

GRENCHEN
Tourist information
🄸 Kirchstrasse 10, CH-2540; ☎ 032 644 32 11; e info@grenchentourismus.ch; www. grenchentourismus.ch; 🕐 13.30–18.00 Mon, 08.30–noon & 13.30–18.00 Tue–Fri

Where to stay
🏠 **Krebs**** Bettlachstrasse 29, CH-2540; ☎ 032 652 29 52; e info@hotelkrebs.ch; www. hotelkrebs.ch

BIEL/BIENNE–INS Table 290

A metre-gauge line through pleasant, market gardening country along the southern shore of Lake Biel, though views of the water are limited.

The 21km (13 miles) Biel–Täuffelen–Ins-Bahn starts from an unprepossessing concrete bunker on the southern edge of Biel station. It can only get better. For a short distance out of Biel, the line is a roadside tramway. At Hauptstrasse 6 in **Nidau** is a formerly moated castle that dates from the late 12th century, though most of the present structure was built between 1627 and 1636. It hosts a museum (🕐 *08.00–18.00 Mon–Fri, 10.00–16.00 Sat–Sun; free admission*) about the colossal engineering works required to contain the waters of the Jura Mountains. The yellow-plastered Rathaus dates from 1756 to 1760.

The line crosses the River Aare and leaves the suburbs behind after **Ipsach**. Thereafter the line runs largely through the market gardens for which the area is renowned, though towards the southern end sugar beet dominates. The first walking signs appear at **Lattrigen** and views of the lake appear to the right as the line climbs through orchards and past venerable farm buildings to **Gerolfingen**.

From **Täuffelen**, where some historic vehicles adapted for use as buffet and bar cars on special trains are kept, the line drops down steeply through orchards, running alongside the road to **Hagneck** and a bridge over the canal of the same name. Dense woodland precedes open, intensively farmed country to **Ins Dorf**. It was here that the painter Albert Anker (1831–1910) was born and died. His popularity has led to him being described as 'the Norman Rockwell of 19th-century Switzerland', and it was from the people of Ins that he drew the subjects of many of his portraits. His house at Müntschemiergasse 7 is open to visitors (⊕ *15.00–17.00 1st & 3rd Sun of the month; admission charge*). The fine town square is directly outside the station.

The line drops down steeply to the junction station of Ins, on the outskirts of the town, for trains to Neuchâtel, Bern and Murten.

PRACTICALITIES   Bicycle hire from Ins station.

LYSS–MURTEN–PAYERNE–PALÉZIEUX–Lausanne
Table 291/305/251

A long cross-country line that links several major tourist destinations, including the enchanting town of Murten, the capital of Roman Helvetia at Avenches, and Payerne, which has one of the finest Cluniac buildings in Europe.

Leaving Lyss in a southerly direction through farmland largely devoted to sugar beet, the line nears the River Aare at **Aarberg** and crosses it to the southeast of the small town. The river is also crossed at this point by a four-arched wooden bridge dating from 1568, though the stone pillars have rested on dry ground since construction of the Hagneck Canal in the 1860s (see above). The town has a late 15th–16th-century Gothic Reformed church with six Renaissance stained-glass windows and a castle thought to have been built in the late 17th century.

Traversing flat, intensively farmed land, the line reaches the junction of **Kerzers**, of interest to railway buffs for its unusual flat crossing of two lines and the rare old signal box that towers over the lines. Platforms adjoining the crossing permit easy changes with trains between Bern and Neuchâtel. A minibus operates between the station and Papiliorama (a public utility foundation), which is 20 minutes' walk from the station along Fräschelgasse. This tropical butterfly garden (✆ *031 756 04 61*; ⊕ *summer 09.00–18.00 daily; late Oct–late Mar 10.00–17.00; admission charge*) was set up using knowledge gained from butterfly gardens in Britain to create a tropical environment inside a dome. It is inhabited by 40 species of butterfly, 600 plant species, including the world's largest waterlily (*Victoria amazonica*), 25 species of tropical birds (five of them hummingbirds), tropical fish, turtles and a pair of miniature cayman. An insectarium contains numerous hair-raising creatures, and there are more overtly educational sections on the stages of butterfly reproduction and on tropical flora and fauna.

Views across the flat terrain are broken by long stands of tall columnar trees, their serried ranks providing protection from the wind for the huge areas of vegetables growing in strips of subtly different greens or purple.

10

Murten (Morat) is one of the best-preserved medieval towns in Switzerland and should not be missed. Though now in the canton of Fribourg (a legacy of Napoleon's rule), it was once administered from Bern, and for a period was under the joint rule of both towns. Founded in the late 12th century on a site overlooking the lake of the same name, Murten still has most of its defensive walls, though it is hard to tell that they were once moated. They were put to the test in 1476 when 2,000 Bernese held off a siege by 20,000 troops under the Duke of Burgundy; for 12 days they withstood artillery fire and infantry assaults, enabling a relieving force of the Swiss Confederation to engage the Burgundians and win one of the most decisive victories on Swiss soil. Five hundred English archers died in the battle.

The walled town is about ten minutes' walk from the station. Turn right outside the station and left at the roundabout into Bahnhofstrasse, following the sign to 'Zentrum'. There is a children's playground in the park on the right. Near the top of the rise the road joins Lausannestrasse. Looking across the road to the left, you can see the grounds of the Murten Museum, situated in an old mill. The leat to the mill still runs through the grounds, feeding at the side the unusual arrangement of a huge undershot wheel followed by an overshot wheel. The museum (⊕ *Apr–Oct 14.00–17.00 Tue–Sat, 10.00–17.00 Sun; admission charge*) provides a good introduction to the history of the town and surrounding area, with displays on pre-history, folk art, iconography, stamps, military history (including a diorama of the Battle of Murten), dolls and enamelware.

Visitors interested in buildings should first visit the tourist office, which has an outstandingly good booklet available in English describing the town's many historic structures.

The **old town** is entered at the top of Lausannestrasse between the castle on the left and the law court. The oldest parts of the castle date from 1255, but much of the building dates from reconstructions between the 16th and 18th centuries. Once occupied by the bailiffs of Bern and Fribourg, it became in turn a barracks, prison and hospital during the French Revolution; since 1816 it has housed the district administration.

The **walled town** is compact, comprising three parallel streets, and can only be explored on foot. The principal street, Hauptgasse, is lined with arcades similar to those in Bern, while the houses are a riot of colour with their profusion of window boxes. A street market is held on the second Saturday of the month. The street leads to the Bernese Gate, a Baroque structure finished in 1778 incorporating a clock mechanism from 1712 made in La Chaux-de-Fonds. A pleasing touch along the battered (sloping) arcades is the incorporation of stone benches at the base of some of the piers. Of particular note at the west end of Hauptgasse is No 18 with its two enormous, superimposed dormer windows. The first-floor entrances to this house and the adjacent No 16 are unique within Murten; on No 18 the ogee-headed doorcase is matched by six lovely windows.

Construction of the walls began in 1238. They were periodically strengthened and extended until the havoc wreaked by the siege in 1476, after which the roof over the wall-walk became part of the rebuilding works. The 12 towers along the wall differ in date and design, and the Zerschossener (Riddled) Tower still bears the marks of the Burgundian artillery. Beneath the staircase to the wall-walk at the western end of Deutsche Kirchgasse stands the huge mechanism of the former city hall clock built in 1816; its wrought-iron frame encases numerous brass cogs driven by heavy stone weights. The wall-walk provides a wonderful view over the town's remarkably homogeneous roofscape, the older chimneystacks having the common feature of curious open-ended gables with arched openings at the side.

Murten has separate churches for French and German speakers, the larger size of the German church close to the wall off Deutsche Kirchgasse reflecting the relative preponderance of German speakers. Dedicated to St Mary, the German church was last rebuilt in 1518 and has choir-stalls dating from 1494 to 1498 and some finely detailed stucco work on the ceiling. The pulpit is carved from a single trunk of oak and dates from 1484. Opposite the church is the German Rectory, built in 1730 by a Hungarian religious refugee.

Boats operate daily circular tours of the Murtensee from the end of May to the end of September (*www.navig.ch*). The landing stage is reached by leaving the old town through the Bern Gate, turning immediately left and crossing the road named Ryf down to the lake. Some boats also take in lakes Biel/Bienne and Neuchâtel and the River Aare to Solothurn, with the option of return by rail.

Leaving Murten, the line parallels the lake shore, though only brief glimpses of it can be seen across the fields of market gardening until **Faoug** where a large marina is close to the station. Under the Roman occupation, **Avenches** (Aventicum) was the capital of Helvetia and one of only three settlements in the province where full Roman citizens lived. It was made a colony by Emperor Vespasian after AD69, and grew to a town of 20,000 inhabitants surrounded by a wall four miles long, with four gates and 75 semicircular towers. The town never recovered from the destruction wrought by an attack in 260 by German tribes, followed by the Huns a century later, but by the end of the 4th century, it had one of the first Christian churches led by a bishop in western Switzerland. Despite being used as a quarry since the Middle Ages, Avenches has extensive Roman remains and the best-preserved Roman amphitheatre in the country.

The station is situated at the foot of the hill on which the town was built, but a bus meets trains for the short journey through today's town centre to the amphitheatre on the eastern edge of the town. Seating 12,000, the oval amphitheatre has a small section of original seating, but much of it has been replaced by concrete. Overlooking the amphitheatre is an 11th-century fortified tower, which now serves as a museum (⊕ *Apr–Sep 10.00–noon & 13.00–17.00 Tue–Sun; Oct–Mar 14.00–17.00 Tue–Sun; admission charge*) containing Roman artefacts found locally, including a replica of a gold bust of Marcus Aurelius; this was found in 1939 close to the sole remaining Corinthian column of a temple that Byron describes in *Childe Harold* (he visited Avenches in 1816). To the east and northeast of the amphitheatre are remains of baths, a theatre, the east gate and the wall. In July, an opera festival is held in this spectacular setting (⊕ *026 676 06 00; www.avenchesopera.ch*).

Avenches has many interesting buildings from later periods as well. Close to the amphitheatre is the castle, begun at the end of the 13th century by the bishops of Lausanne and enlarged with a Renaissance façade by the Bernese governor between 1565 and 1599 (Avenches fell to Bern in 1536). The tall-spired staircase tower, with handrail carved into the stone, leads to a museum that hosts changing exhibitions.

In the town centre is the three-storeyed town hall from 1438, though rebuilt between 1753 and 1755; above its arcades is a triangular gable with two Moors holding the town's coat of arms. Nearby is the Reformed church of Ste Marie-Madeleine, the oldest part of which was built at the end of the 11th century and rebuilt in 1438 and between 1753 and 1755. It has crude wall-paintings and a curious flat ceiling with large coves. Parallel with the main street on the side opposite the station is Rue des Alpes, in which can be found the 13th-century Benneville Tower, raised in the 15th century. Part of the walls have been incorporated into houses – this can be seen best by walking around the northwestern side of the town overlooking the railway. There is a children's playground near the post office at the top of the hill down to the station, and there is a Hippodrome for trotting races.

Continuing southwest, much of the flat country is given over to sugar beet farming, and in season, tractors are a more common sight at level crossings than cars. From **Domdidier**, a bus (table 20.550/line 550) goes to Gletterens, where there is a reconstructed Village Lacustre (⊕ *May–Oct 09.00–17.00 daily*), illustrating prehistoric life from 4500 to 800BC. It has plenty of activities to bring the experience to life for children: throwing an *assegai* or making a Neolithic knife. It can also be reached by boat from Lake Neuchâtel.

Payerne, situated on the River Broye, is a junction for Yverdon and Fribourg, and was a town of great importance in the 10th and 11th centuries, though there was a chapel here as early as 587. The town has a tenuous link with Glyndebourne, for a direct ancestor of the opera's founder, John Christie, emigrated from here to England in 1788.

In the 10th century an abbey was founded, soon becoming a Cluniac property. After the Reformation, the abbey became a barn and then a barracks, the choir became a gymnasium, and the west-facing entrance section was used as a prison; it is now a law court. Adjacent to it is the 11th-century abbey church of Notre-Dame, the largest Romanesque church in Switzerland and one of the finest examples of Cluniac architecture in Europe. Built on the site of a Roman villa and then an early church, the pillared basilica has a nave and two aisles with a tower topped by a slender 14th-century spire at the crossing. Of note are some interesting 11th-century capitals and wall-paintings from the 13th to 15th centuries. Art exhibitions are sometimes staged in the abbey buildings, which also contain a local history collection. The town has a number of attractive 16th-century fountains.

Intensive agriculture continues to flank the line to **Granges-Marnand**, where there is a very pretty Romano-Gothic church dating from the 12th to 15th centuries. On the right, the River La Broye is seldom out of view, its channelled banks lined with trees. At **Henniez** lies the source of the springs that produce Switzerland's best-known mineral water.

Above **Lucens** is a huge medieval stronghold with imposing cylindrical keep and numerous conical-topped turrets. Built in the 13th century by the bishops of Lausanne, it was burnt to the ground in 1476 but rebuilt and subsequently extended for the Bernese bailiff. A boys' college at the end of the 19th century, it was bought by Sir Arthur Conan Doyle's son Adrian, who created a museum devoted to his father in the castle, but the contents of the Conan Doyle museum have been moved to the Red House (La Maison Rouge) at Rue des Greniers 7 (⊕ *14.00–17.00 Sat–Sun*). A reconstruction of the Baker Street lodging of Sherlock Holmes and Dr Watson is the acclaimed exhibit created for the 1951 Festival of Britain. The room's evocative atmosphere is enhanced by the inclusion of hundreds of authentic objects – some very strange indeed. **Moudon** was a Celtic settlement before the Romans made it a staging post on the road from Avenches to the St Bernard Pass. Little remains of the original defences except the square 12th-century Tour de Broye in Rue de Château, which is in the upper part of the town. However, the town's most notable building incorporates part of the former fortifications: the belltower of the Reformed church of St Etienne. It has been described as the most important Gothic structure in the canton of Vaud after Lausanne Cathedral and contains a defensive belfry. The 13th-century church has many fragments of 13th–17th-century wall-paintings, finely carved choir-stalls and misericords from 1502.

The oldest part of the town, Quartier du Bourg, is on the hill and contains many attractive 16th- and 17th-century houses, some with turrets and pronounced overhanging roofs.

The valley narrows and impressive cliffs rise above the river on the right as the line climbs through thick woods to **Ecublens-Rue**. The latter village, on the opposite side of the valley, clusters round the hill-top castle, which was built in the 12th century, destroyed in 1237 and subsequently rebuilt and enlarged.

Equidistant between **Châtillens** and Oron station on the main line between Fribourg and Lausanne is the beautifully situated and unspoiled castle of Oron (⊕ *Apr–Sep 10.00–noon & 14.00–18.00 Sat–Sun*). It is only a short walk from either station, but there is a bus service from Châtillens station (table 10.075). The same bus going in the opposite direction (to Mézières) from Châtillens station serves the large zoo at Servion (⊕ *09.00–19.00 daily; winter 09.00–18.00 daily*), which has captive breeding programme of endangered species and is home to bison, lion, tiger, puma, lynx and many other species of mammals and birds.

The line continues to climb steeply, passing on the right near **Palézieux-Village** an interestingly designed modern school, with columned central courtyard. The line joins the Bern–Lausanne main line to the north of **Palézieux** station. For the section on to Lausanne, see table 250, page 135.

PRACTICALITIES Bicycle hire from Kerzers, Murten, Avenches and Lausanne stations.

MURTEN
Tourist information
✉ Franz Kirchgasse 6, CH-3280; ☎026 670 51 12; e info@murtentourismus.ch; www.murtentourismus.ch; ⊕ Apr–Sep 09.00–noon & 13.00–18.00 Mon–Fri, 13.00–17.00 Sat–Sun; Oct–Mar 09.00–noon & 14.00–17.00

Where to stay
Only one hotel is close to the station:
⌂ **Bahnhof** Bahnhofstrasse 14, CH-3280; ☎026 670 22 56

Hotels in the old town, only 10–15 minutes' walk from the station, include:
⌂ **Murtenhof & Krone*** (H)** Rathausgasse 1–3, CH-3280; ☎026 672 90 30; e info@murtenhof.ch; www.murtenhof.ch. A medieval building with 18th-century wing & award-winning lake terrace restaurant, built between 1991 and 1992. The formerly independent Krone is now owned by the Murtenhof & offers lower-priced accommodation.
⌂ **Ringmauer*** Deutsche Kirchgasse 2, CH-3280; ☎026 670 11 01; e welcome@ringmauer.ch; www.ringmauer.ch

AVENCHES
Tourist information
✉ Pl de l'Eglise 3, CH-1580; ☎026 676 99 22; e info@avenches.ch; www.avenches.ch; ⊕ 08.30–noon & 13.30–17.30 Mon–Fri; May–Aug 09.30–12.30 Sat

Where to stay
⌂ De la Couronne*** Rue Centrale 20, CH-1580; ☎026 675 54 14; e info@lacouronne.ch; www.lacouronne.ch

PAYERNE
Tourist information
✉ Pl du Marché 10, CH-1530; ☎026 660 61 61; e tourisme@estavayer-payerne.ch; www.estavayer-payerne.ch; ⊕ May–mid-Sep 09.00–noon & 13.30–18.00 Mon–Fri, 10.00–15.00 Sat; mid-Sep–Apr 09.00–noon & 13.30–17.00 Mon–Fri

Where to stay
⌂ **De la Croix Blanche** (H)** Grand Rue 42, CH-1530; ☎026 660 61 66; e info@hotel-croix-blanche.ch; www.hotel-croix-blanche.ch
⌂ **La Suite*** Rue du Temple 10, CH-1530; ☎026 660 56 21; e info@la-suite.ch; www.la-suite.ch

LUCENS
Where to stay
⌂ **De la Gare (H)** CH-1522; ☎021 906
81 48; e hotelgare.suter@praznet.ch; www.
hoteldelagarelucens.ch. Impressive restaurant.

MOUDON
Tourist information
ℹ Pl de l'Hotel de Ville 1, CH-1510; ☎021 905 88
66; e office.tourisme@moudon.ch; www.moudon.
ch; ⊕ 8.30–noon & 13.30–17.30 Mon–Fri, 9.00–
noon & 13.00–16.00 Sat

Where to stay
⌂ **Chemin de Fer** Pl St-Etienne 4, CH-1510;
☎021 905 70 91; www.hotel-chemin-de-fer.ch
⌂ **De la Gare** Av de la Gare 5, CH-1510; ☎021
905 45 88; e site@hoteldelagare-moudon.ch;
www.hoteldelagare-moudon.ch

BERN–NEUCHÂTEL Table 305/Line S52

Apart from being the most direct route to Neuchâtel and providing connections to Murten and Avenches, this line has little intrinsic interest.

The line heads due west out of Bern through hilly country, which proved costly for the railway builders – the viaduct before **Gümmenen**, from which there are fine views, is one of the largest in the country. This has been an important crossing point on the River Saane/Sarine since at least the 12th century. From Gümmenen station, buses leave for Laupen through the Saane valley (table 30.550), paralleling the route of the heritage Sensetalbahn.

At **Kerzers** is the unusual flat crossing and connecting platforms with the Lyss–Palézieux line, once protected by the imposing signal-box, which survives, although it is disused (for Kerzers, see page 129). The line continues across a plain of market gardening to **Ins**, where the metre-gauge line to Täuffelen and Biel/Bienne begins (table 290; for Ins, see page 129). To the west of **Zihlbrücke** station, the line crosses the Zihl Canal that threads the isthmus between the lakes of Neuchâtel and Biel. From **St Blaise**, where there are some fine 16th- and 17th-century houses, the railway climbs from lake level to join the Biel/Bienne–Neuchâtel line (table 210, page 124), from where there are good views over the lake.

PRACTICALITIES Bicycle hire from Bern, Kerzers and Neuchâtel stations.

INS–MURTEN–COURTEPIN–FRIBOURG Table 255

A short cross-country branch that connects several places of historic interest with the ancient city and cantonal capital of Fribourg.

From Ins, the line bears away to the right from the main line to Bern, passing through attractive woods between **Sugiez** and the junction with the line from Lyss and Kerzers at **Muntelier**. In the village is an 18th-century château. At Murten (see page 130), the Fribourg line bears south to **Münchenwiler-Courgevaux**, where a Cluniac priory was converted into a house in the mid 16th century. **Cressier** has a rebuilt 17th-century château opposite the church of St-Jean, rebuilt between 1842 and 1844 from a building recorded in the 12th century.

At **Givisiez** the line joins another which runs from Yverdon and Payerne to Fribourg (see table 252, page 140).

PRACTICALITIES Bicycle hire from Murten and Fribourg stations.

BERN–LAUSANNE Tables 250

The IC express route runs between St Gallen and Geneva Airport, and it is also served by stopping and regional express trains working between Fribourg and Romont. Although the principal place of interest en route is Fribourg, the line also provides access to the lovely country around Bulle and Gruyères through the junction at Romont.

The early part of the journey has little of interest to offer. **Flamatt** is the junction for the picturesque S-Bahn branch to Laupen (see table 302, page 140) and **Schmitten** has a massively-towered Catholic church, rebuilt in 1706 from a late 15th-century building. The apse of the Romanesque St Luzius's church has wall paintings that date from the second half of the 15th century. Between **Düdingen** and Fribourg the railway crosses the broad River Saane/Sarine by the Grandfey Bridge; the original 1857–62 iron bridge was encased in concrete between 1925 and 1927 when the lower-level pedestrian walkway was retained.

FRIBOURG Fribourg bears a number of resemblances to Bern. It was founded in 1157 by Berchtold IV of Zähringen, father of Bern's founder, and was also chosen for its easily defensible position on a river meander. Like Bern, its development was marked by successive lines of defence, but in contrast to the capital, Fribourg retains 2km (1¼ miles) of wall with 14 towers, mostly on the south and east sides. Fribourg joined the Confederation in 1481, three years after the end of the Burgundy Wars, by which time the fortunes of the town's textile industry were already on the wane. However, a series of alliances, purchases and conquests helped the town to grow into a city-state ruled by a patrician oligarchy. As a result of French occupation in 1798, democratic structures were gradually introduced and the formation of the canton of Fribourg began. The city's conservative nature was both cause and effect of its adherence to Roman Catholicism during the Reformation. The bishops of Geneva and Lausanne both moved to Fribourg during the 17th century, and the city remains a bastion of Catholicism. Although the Jesuit College was disbanded in 1847 under pressure from the Swiss Confederation, a Catholic university was established in 1889. The bilingual city now has a population of 40,000.

The station at Fribourg is centrally located, but the city's hills may induce all but the fittest travellers to use the occasional bus – all bus routes serve the station. Although the walking/bus itinerary suggested takes in most of the principal buildings, like most old cities Fribourg is best explored leisurely on foot. Good maps and guides to historic buildings and the museums are available from the tourist office (see page 139).

To reach the oldest part of the city or the tourist office, bear left outside the station down Avenue de la Gare or take buses 2 or 6. The tourist office is at the end of Rue de Romont on the right, off Place Georges-Python. Continue on foot along Rue de Lausanne, or on buses 2 or 6, to St Nicholas's Cathedral on Place Notre-Dame.

What to see and do **St Nicholas's** (🕘 *09.30–18.00 Mon–Fri, 09.00–16.00 Sat, 14.0-17.00 Sun*) was begun in 1283 on the site of an earlier church. The choir was completed by 1343, but it was not until 1490 that the 74m (243ft) tower was completed. It dominates the city, and its 365 steps may be climbed from mid-June to the end of September. Beneath the tower is the main entrance, which has a tympanum decorated with a late 14th-century relief of the Last Judgement. Beyond the nave and two aisles is the polygonal choir with stalls dating from 1462 to 1464 and a wrought-iron screen from 1464 to 1466. The richly carved **stone pulpit** (1513–16) and the highly regarded **organ** (1824–31) were among Fribourg's first tourist attractions. Buried at St Nicholas's is Clementina Walkinshaw, who was the mistress of Bonnie Prince Charlie, the Young Pretender, while he lived in Paris in the 1750s. She lived in Fribourg for ten years before her death in 1802.

In Place Notre-Dame stands the 1547 **Samson Fountain**, which follows a design by Dürer. Opposite the cathedral, to the northwest, is Rue de Morat along which, after a few minutes' walk, you come to the Romanesque **Church of our Lady**. This was built in the 12th century but remodelled between 1785 and 1790; it retains the choir-stalls from 1506 and a painting of the Battle of Lepanto (1571) in an early Gothic chapel at the foot of the tower, painted by Peter Wuilleret in 1635. Next door is the **Franciscan church**, which was completed by 1281 but rebuilt in the 18th century. The high altar painting of the Crucifixion (1480) and the choir-stalls (1280) are of particular note – the latter of which are among the oldest in the country.

Further along Rue de Morat is the **Art and History Museum** (⊕ *11.00–18.00 Tue–Sun, 11.00–20.00 Thu; admission charge*), which is housed in three buildings: the Ratzé Mansion (1581–84), the old slaughter house and a building designed for temporary exhibitions. The mansion was built for Jean Ratzé, who was commander of the Swiss guard at Lyons; it has been a museum since 1922 and houses paintings and sculptures, and many artefacts illustrating the political, social, military and religious life of Fribourg. The old slaughter house was built between 1834 and 1836 and converted to a museum in 1979, and it displays paintings by Courbet, Delacroix, Hodler and Marcello as well as temporary exhibitions. A former depot at Rue de Morat 2 is now a museum, **Espace Jean Tinguely** (⊕ *11.00–18.00 Wed–Sun, 11.00–20.00 Thu; admission charge*), devoted to the work of Niki de Saint Phalle and Jean Tinguely's extraordinary mechanical creations. Tinguely was born in Fribourg in 1925, and one of only three of his 'waterworks' can be seen in the city's Grand-Places.

The No 1 bus service continues along Rue de Morat past the 1622 **Capuchin church** to two more of the city's defensive towers: the Morat/Murten Gate on the edge of a gorge and the **Four-Pounder Tower** (both dating from the 1410s), named after the cannon kept here in the 15th century.

Returning to Place Notre-Dame, turn right along Rue du Pont-Muré to the magnificent **Town Hall** (Hôtel de Ville), built between 1501 and 1522. Until 1789, the ground floor was an arsenal, while above are the Grand Council Chamber and the Court Chamber, as well as the usual offices. In front of the building is the **Murten linden tree**, which is reputed to have been planted in 1476. Legend has it that the messenger bringing news of the victory over Charles the Bold at Murten expired as soon as he had gasped out the news; to commemorate his news they planted the twig of a linden tree that decorated his hat, and from this the present tree grew. His journey from Murten is commemorated by an annual race, started in 1934, from Murten to Fribourg on the first Sunday in October (there is also a signed footpath between the two towns, which takes 5½ hours to walk). On the south side of the Town Hall is a fine view overlooking the river.

From the cathedral, continue east along Rue des Chanoines and Rue des Bouchers on foot, or by buses 2 or 6, to the **Zähringen Bridge** which was the longest suspension bridge in the world for a few years after its completion in 1834.

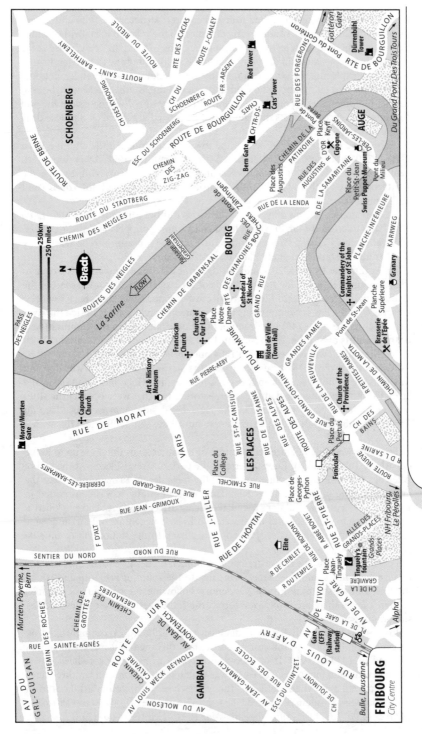

FRIBOURG
City Centre

It was replaced by a seven-arched iron and concrete structure in 1924 and affords views along the river in a southeasterly direction to the covered Bern Bridge, which dates from the mid 17th to mid 19th centuries. The oldest part of Fribourg is the area known as the **Auge** on the peninsula to the southeast of the Zähringen Bridge. It is worth exploring the streets on foot for this medieval quarter retains not only its street pattern but many of the Gothic façades to the houses. These were built to a strict building code set out in the late 14th century to reduce the risk of fire and to hamper its spread. Streets that should not be missed are Rue d'Or and Rue de la Samaritaine.

Across the Bern Bridge are five of the towers that protected the city: the **Bern Gate** (1270–90); the **Cats' Tower** (late 14th century); the **Red Tower** (mid 13th century), which is the oldest and most impressive of the surviving towers; the **Gottéron Gate** (15th and early 16th centuries) and the **Dürrenbühl Tower** (mid 13th century).

At Derrière-les-Jardins 2 in Auge is the **Swiss Puppet Museum** (⏲ *10.00–17.00 Wed–Sun; admission charge*) with a large collection of puppets and theatres from Europe, Africa, Canada, China and the Far East. The museum can be reached by bus 4 from the station (alight at Place du Petit-St-Jean).

Cross the river by the 1720 Middle Bridge (or catch bus 4) and go up Karrweg to Planche-Supérieure. On the southeast side of the large triangular open space is the **granary** dating from 1762 to 1767 with tall crow-stepped gable. It has been a winery, a barracks and a law academy, but is now devoted to archaeology. Beside the river and St John's Bridge (1746) is a group of buildings that formed the **Commandery of the Knights of St John**, established in 1224 and carrying out pastoral work until 1825. The church was consecrated in 1264 but has been much altered.

Across the river (a No 4 bus returns to the station from St John's Bridge and this walking route), bear left up Rue de la Neuveville, which has some especially attractive houses. Some had attics several storeys tall that were open at the sides for drying leather and textiles. On the right-hand side, approaching Place du Pertuis, is the **Church of the Providence**, built between 1749 and 1762 with a Louis XV façade.

From the west side of Place du Pertuis, a funicular ascends the slope up to Route des Alpes. Turn left along Rue St-Pierre to the park of Grand-Places. At the end of Allée des Grand-Places is a fine view over the meandering Saane/Sarine. Near the uninspiring pile of the Eurotel is **Jean Tinguely's fountain**. It was constructed in 1984 in memory of the sculptor's friend, the racing driver Jo Siffert, who was killed at Brands Hatch in 1971. The only other waterworks by Tinguely are in Basel and Paris.

From Grand-Places, it is only a short walk back to the station via Avenue de la Gare.

Leaving Fribourg, the railway remains at a much higher level than the La Glâne River, which flows into the Saane/Sarine just to the south of Fribourg and which the line follows south almost to Vauderens. Following the contours of the hills at such a level, there are lovely views from the train over the river valley and the surrounding uplands.

Romont is well worth a stop or day visit from Fribourg. Arrestingly sited on an exposed hill a little to the east of the station, this medieval market town was founded in 1239 by Peter II of Savoy, and retains its castle, waterwheel, tower, fortified walls and fountains. The castle was built by Peter II and still has three sides of its ring wall and cylindrical keep. The waterwheel in the courtyard dates from 1772. The Swiss Museum of Stained Glass, the Vitromusée (⏲ *mid-Mar–Oct 10.00–13.00 & 14.00–18.00 Tue–Sun; Nov–mid-Mar 10.00–13.00 & 14.00–17.00 Thu–Sun;*

admission charge) has been housed in the 16th-century part of the castle since 1981; it organises regular exhibitions of precious works of art.

Much of Peter II's town wall has also survived, and on the south side of the town is the 13th-century Tour à Boyer. The collegiate Church of Notre-Dame-de-l'Assumption is largely mid 15th century, though it incorporates part of the 13th-century church that survived the fire of Romont in 1434. The choir-stalls date from 1466 to 1469, the screen from 1478 and the older glass from the 14th to 15th centuries, though the 12 Apostles were made in 1939.

Romont is also the junction for the network of branch lines to Bulle (table 254), Broc (table 253), Gruyères and Montbovon (table 256, page 276).

South of **Vauderens** fine views open up to the right. Only a short walk from **Oron** is the most attractive castle of the same name, built between the late 12th to early 13th centuries and now a museum (⊕ *Apr–Sep 10.00–noon & 14.00–18.00 Sat–Sun*; see page 133). There is also a bus from the station (table 20.450).

Dropping down through thick woods, the railway reaches **Palézieux**, the junction for Payerne, Murten and Lyss (see tables 251/305/291, page 129) and for Châtel-St-Denis and Bulle (table 256). A bus from Palézieux station (table 20.472) serves Oron Castle and the zoo at Servion (see page 133). Beyond Palézieux, the line begins its steep descent to Lausanne, dropping 236m (775ft) in 16.4km (10¼ miles). After the junction of **Puidoux-Chexbres** (change for Vevey; see table 111, page 264), the line enters a tunnel and emerges to a breathtaking view of Lake Geneva, still 182m (600ft) below.

For **Lausanne**, see *Chapter 16*, page 253.

PRACTICALITIES Bicycle hire from Fribourg and Lausanne stations.

FRIBOURG
Tourist information
🛈 Place Jean-Tinguely 1, CH-1700; ✆026 350 11 11; e info@fribourgtourisme.ch; www.fribourgtourisme.ch; ⊕ 09.00–18.00 Mon–Fri, May–Sep 09.00–15.00 Sat, Oct–Apr 09.00–12.30 Sat

Where to stay
Hotels closest to the station are:
🏠 **NH Fribourg****** Grand-Places 14, CH-1700; ✆026 351 91 91; e nhfribourg@nh-hotels.com; www.nh-hotels.com
🏠 **Alpha*** Rue du Simplon 13, CH-1700; ✆026 322 72 72; e info@alpha-hotel.ch; www.alpha-hotel.ch
🏠 **Elite** Rue du Criblet 7, CH-1700; ✆026 350 22 60; e elitefribourg@bluewin.ch; www.elitefribourg.ch

Where to eat
Recommended restaurants are:
✗ **Auberge de la Cigogne (H)** Rue d'Or 24; ✆026 322 68 34; www.aubergedelacigogne.ch
✗ **Brasserie de l'Epée** Planche-Supériere 39; ✆026 322 34 07; www.brasserie-epee.ch; ⊕ 9.00–23.30 Mon, Wed & Thu, 9.00–15.00 Tue, 9.00–00.00 Fri & Sat, 10.00–18.00 Sun
✗ **Des Trois Tours** Rte de Borguillon 15; ✆026 322 30 69; www.troistours.ch. Closed Sun & Mon; reservations by phone.
✗ **Du Grand Pont** Rte de Bourguillon 2; ✆026 481 32 48; www.legrandpont.ch. Closed Tue, Wed & Sun evenings.
✗ **Le Pérolles** Bd de Pérolles 18a; ✆026 347 40 30; www.leperolles.ch. Gastronomic; closed Sun, Mon & Tue.

ROMONT
Tourist information
🛈 Rue de Château 112, CH-1680; ✆026 651 90 55; e info@romontregion.ch; www.romont.ch

Where to stay
🏠 **St Georges (H)** Grand-Rue 31, CH-1680; ✆026 652 44 10; e hotel-stgeorges@bluewin.ch; www.hotel-stgeorges.ch

FLAMATT–LAUPEN Table 302/Line S2

The Sensetalbahn is now part of the Bern S-bahn network. The line threads the lovely Sense valley to the scene of a major battle in 1339 in which the Bernese vanquished a Burgundian coalition. The railway used to continue on to Gümmenen – it now has another use.

The short journey from the junction with the Bern–Lausanne main line has the River Sense for company on the left for most of its length. The castle in the small town of **Laupen** has the distinction of being the oldest stone building in the canton of Bern, the oldest part dating from c930, when it was supposedly begun by King Rudolf II of Burgundy. The railway track onto Gümmenen can now be ridden on a pump trolley (*www.schienenvelo.ch*).

A connecting bus (table 30.550) takes passengers on to Gümmenen on the Bern–Neuchâtel line (see table 305.1).

FRIBOURG–PAYERNE–YVERDON Table 252

A cross-country line of limited scenic value but linking several towns of great interest.

The line heads north out of Fribourg and leaves the main line to Bern on the outskirts to swing west. Just before **Belfaux**, the branch to Murten turns off to the right. The Church of St-Etienne at Belfaux is a large church dating from the 12th century, though rebuilt between 1841 and 1852. After **Cousset**, the rolling hills around which the railway twists start to peter out as the line descends to the fertile agricultural land to the southeast of Lake Neuchâtel. The village of **Corcelles** has many wooden and stone storehouses and an 11th-century Reformed church with a Romanesque belltower.

For **Payerne**, the junction for Murten and Palézieux, see page 132. Passing through gently rolling farmland, the train pauses at the picturesque village of **Cugy**, with its outsize church, before reaching the lake at **Estavayer-le-Lac**.

This delightful small town has its origins in the late 11th century. Of its three castles, only one survives, but much of the walls erected between the three still stands, pierced by four gates. The remaining castle, Château de Chenaux, is one of the five largest castles in the country, built in the late 13th century and rebuilt in the last quarter of the 15th century after it had been badly damaged. It has three wings, a massive keep, barbican, covered bridge and two towers with machicolations. Unfortunately the castle is home to the cantonal police, though the exterior can be admired.

The Gothic collegiate church of St-Laurent was built between 1379 and 1525, though the staircase dates from 1859. The choir-stalls were carved between 1522 and 1524, and church contains some fine medieval stained glass. The church of Our Lady attached to the Dominican convent was built in 1697; the nave and two aisles are spanned by groin vaulting.

The town's Frog Museum in Rue du Musée (⊕ *Mar–Oct 10.00–noon & 14.00–17.00 Tue–Sun; Jul–Aug 10.00–noon & 14.00–17.00 daily; Nov–Feb 14.00–17.00 Sat–Sun; admission charge*) incorporates 108 sand-filled frogs arranged in human situations by an eccentric 19th-century military character in the Napoleonic Guard named François Perrier. Housed in the attractive 15th-century Maison de la Dime, the museum also has displays of regional interest, a 17th-century kitchen, weapons, embroidery and a collection of over 200 railway lamps dating from 1880.

The huge marina at Estavayer can be seen as the train turns southwest to parallel the lake shore, though it is some distance from the water. At the lakeside village of **Cheyres** is a château dating from 1773 to 1774. Views of the lake diminish as the railway enters thickening woods before **Yverdon-les-Bains** (see table 210, page 229).

PRACTICALITIES Bicycle hire from Yverdon station.

ESTAVAYER-LE-LAC
Tourist information

[i] Rue de Hôtel de Ville 16, CH-1470; ☏ 026 663 12 37; e tourisme@estavayer-payerne.ch; www. estavayer-payerne.ch; ⊕ May–mid-Sep 09.00– noon & 13.30–18.00 Mon–Fri, 10.00–15.00 Sat; mid-Sep–Apr 09.00–noon & 13.30–17.00 Mon–Fri

Where to stay

⌂ **Hotel du Port (H)*** Route du Port 3, CH-1470; ☏ 026 664 82 82; e hotel-du-port@ estavision.ch; www.hotelduport.ch

ROMONT–BULLE Table 254

A standard-gauge branch that became part of the regional express network in 2011 with fast through trains between Fribourg and Bulle. It connects with a small metre-gauge network at Bulle with branches to Broc, Montbovon, Châtel-St-Denis and Palézieux. Bulle has a historic centre and notable museum. The intermediate stations, which had particularly attractive nameboards with ornate painted lettering, were closed with the introduction of through trains.

The branch turns east from Romont towards the Gruyère district of canton Fribourg. If the heart of **Bulle** conveys the impression of a venerable town, it is an illusion since few buildings survived a disastrous fire in 1805. However, the layout of the market square was retained, and the magnificent 13th-century castle survived. The latter was built on a square plan with dominant southwest keep and corbelled turrets on the other three corners. Near the castle, another building which survived the fire is the chapel that was part of a demolished Capuchin hospital. The church of Notre-Dame-de-Compassion was built in 1454 from the remains of a fire-damaged building. The town developed as a centre of furniture making.

Also near the castle at Rue de la Condémine 25 is the Gruyère Regional Museum, *Musée Gruérien* (⊕ *Oct–May 10.00–noon & 14.00–17.00 Tue–Fri, 10.00–17.00 Sat, 13.30–17.00 Sun; Jun–Sep 10.00–17.00 Tue–Sat, 13.30–17.00 Sun; admission charge*), housed in a striking modern building. An audio-visual of surviving local traditions provides an introduction to the displays of popular art, cowbells, butter moulds, utensils and reconstructed room interiors. In addition to paintings of rural life by such artists as Courbet, Corot, Hodler and Vallotton, there is a fine collection of naïve pictures of the Poya, the ceremonial journey to and from the alpine pastures at the beginning and end of summer.

At the north end of Grand-Rue is an attractive covered market with vaulted roof.

The Gruyère region is the birthplace of the *ranz des vaches*, the cowherd's song, which is supposed to have exerted such a powerful nostalgic effect on Swiss mercenaries in French service that a minister banned it. It has also been incorporated into various operas by, amongst others, Weigl, Meyerbeer, Adam (whose *The Swiss Cottage* was performed for Queen Victoria at Windsor Castle) and Kienzl.

For the other lines from **Bulle**, see tables 253 and 256, pages 278 and 276.

10

PRACTICALITIES Bicycle hire from Bulle station.

BULLE
Tourist information

i Place des Alpes 26, CH-1630; ☎084 842
44 24; e info@la-gruyere.ch; www.la-gruyere.
ch; ⊕ 09.00–noon & 14.00–18.00 Mon–Fri,
09.00–16.00 Sat

Where to stay

🏠 **Du Tonnelier* (H)** Grand-Rue 31, CH-1630;
☎026 912 77 45; e letonnelier@bluewin.ch; www.
letonnelier.ch

BERN–SCHWARZENBURG Table 306/S6

*A standard-gauge commuter line for Bern that ends in a terminus, one of only two
such lines. It offers access to attractive walks in river valleys. Sit on the right.*

The first part of the journey is unattractive, serving suburban stations surrounded
by factories. The last station before the railway leaves the city behind is **Köniz**, where
the Reformed church of SS Peter and Paul was once part of an Augustinian priory
that was taken over by the Knights of the Teutonic Order in 1226. The Romanesque
nave has a painted wooden ceiling dating from 1503. The nearby commandery was
built as a castle in 1610.

Beyond Köniz the line climbs steeply along a ledge on the left-hand side
of a valley to reach **Moos**, where there are the first signed rural walks. Just
beyond **Niederscherli** the line crosses a ravine, but the highlight of the journey
is the breathtaking crossing of the Schwarz River by a tall bridge just before
Schwarzwasserbrücke. Looking down to the right you can see a spectacular view
of the Schwarz joining the River Sense. It is worth breaking the journey to see more
than a glimpse of it, but there is also a signed walk from here to Thurnen, a station
on the secondary line from Bern–Thun (table 303). The walk passes Rüeggisberg,
where there are the ruins of a Cluniac monastery founded in 1070, and Riggisberg,
where the Foundation Abegg has a collection of textiles and early decorative art of
international importance (⊕ *late Apr–early Nov 14.00–17.30 daily*). The walk takes
about four hours; if Thurnen is not reached, there are buses from Riggisberg back
to Schwarzenburg (table 30.611).

From Schwarzwasserbrücke, the line climbs steeply again with fine views to the
right. The town of **Schwarzenburg** has a 16th-century castle, and the Reformed
church of Maria Magdalena has a most unusual tower. Built in the second half of
the 15th century, the square, tapering tower is covered with wood shingles. To the
right of the terminus is a map of about 20 marked walking routes. To the northwest
of the town sit the clifftop ruins of Grasburg Castle, built between the 12th and 15th
centuries and abandoned in 1572.

SCHWARZENBURG
Tourist information

i Dorfplatz 22, CH-3150; ☎031 731 13
91; e info@schwarzenburgerland.ch; www.
schwarzenburgerland.ch; ⊕ 08.30–11.30
Mon–Fri

Where to stay

🏠 **Sonne**** Dorfplatz 3, CH-3150; ☎031 731
21 21; e info@sonne-schwarzenburg.ch; www.
sonne-schwarzenburg.ch
🏠 **Gasthof Bühl** Thunstrasse 1, CH-3150;
☎031 731 01 38; e info@ gasthof-buehl.ch; www.
gasthof-buehl.ch

11

Bernese Oberland

The Bernese Oberland was one of the first areas of Switzerland to be 'discovered' by tourists, or travellers as they might legitimately be called, given the relative privations and difficulties that faced the first visitors. Their principal objectives were the glacier at Grindelwald and the waterfalls around Lauterbrunnen.

The first recorded visitors arrived in the 17th century but the first guidebook to the area did not appear until c1775, written by a clergyman from Bern. It was the homes of clergymen that often provided accommodation for the earliest travellers – their houses were preferable to the few inns. Rousseau was one of the first to write of the region's beauty, and many writers followed in his wake, notably Goethe, Byron, Ruskin and Twain.

Similar to most parts of Switzerland, it was during the 19th century that the economy of the area was transformed from one largely dependent on agriculture to one reliant on tourism. Thun was at first the town used by most visitors as a base, but with the opening of the railway through to Interlaken in 1893, the balance moved decisively in favour of the latter, which has remained the springboard for the network of railways that reaches into the high-alpine heart of the Bernese Oberland.

The region's mountains have been amongst the country's favourite challenges for climbers, with the north wall of the Eiger being perhaps Europe's most notorious ascent. It also offers excellent facilities for winter sports, and the area prides itself on the welcome it gives to families and the way it caters for their needs.

BERN–BELP–THUN Table 303/S3

Known as the Gürbetal line, this commuter and local railway follows the broad valley of the River Gürbe for part of its length.

The railway shares the same exit from Bern as the Schwarzenburg line to a junction south of **Ausserholligen**, where the Thun line bears southeast. In **Kehrsatz** is a Neo-classical manor house (1782–83) known as Lohn. It was given to the Swiss Confederation in 1942 and is used as a guesthouse for visiting heads of state. The design of the park is a combination of French and English influences.

The largely Romanesque Reformed church of SS Peter and Paul at **Belp** has Gothic frescoes dating from c1455–60. At **Toffen** is a castle of medieval origins rebuilt c1671. **Burgistein** also has a fortress, dating from the 13th century, which was rebuilt in the 16th century. At Burgistein the line turns east to **Thun** (see page 145).

PRACTICALITIES Bicycle hire from Thun station.

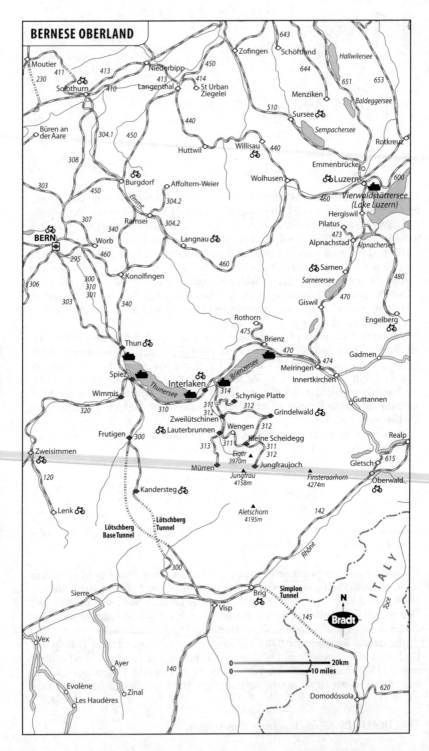

BERNESE OBERLAND

This was the first railway into the Bernese Oberland. Thun was reached via Münsingen in 1859, and two years later the line was extended to the lake at Scherzligen. It was not until 1893 that the railway along the shore of Lake Thun was opened, so Interlaken had to be reached by boat. However, from 1874 there was an extraordinary isolated railway through Interlaken connecting piers on lakes Brienz and Thun at Bönigen and Därligen respectively; called the Bödeli Railway, it used unique wine-red double-deck coaches, the upper one having open longitudinal seats so that passengers could enjoy the view. A model of one of the coaches can be seen in the Transport Museum at Luzern. Sit on the right as far as Thun, then the left.

Soon after leaving Bern, a semicircle of mountains comes into view and dominates the horizon for much of the journey. The first part of the line passes through broad, flat farming country. To the left of the station at **Münsingen** is a small 14th-century castle, rebuilt between the 16th and 18th centuries.

In Bernstrasse at **Kiesen** is the elegantly clocktowered National Dairy Museum (*Milchwirtschaftliche Museum;* ⊕ *Apr–Oct 14.00–17.00 Wed, 13.00–17.00 Sun; admission charge*) which illustrates dairy farming and cheese-making in a group of historic buildings.

The site of **Thun** has been settled since 2500BC and is the largest town on the Thunersee, the lake which takes its name from the town, situated astride the River Aare where it meets the lake. During the early years of Swiss tourism, it was the principal starting point for visitors to the Bernese Oberland. The future Napoleon III came here in 1830 as a student at the artillery school (the town retains its role as an important military training centre), and Brahms lived in the suburb of Hofstetten between 1886 and 1888, composing the *Double Concerto* among other works. Concerts are given in the castle, and an international festival of barrel organs is held in June.

The interchange between train and steamer could not be easier, the boats leaving from a pier only a few minutes' walk to the right as you leave the station, which houses the tourist office. The station restaurant features its own micro-brewery. To reach the old town and castle, bear left outside the station along Bahnhofstrasse, crossing the river twice, to Hauptstrasse. Turn left along this street of two-tiered shops to reach Rathausplatz, which has a number of splendid buildings, notably the 16th–17th-century arcaded Rathaus and one of the town's oldest buildings, the 14th-century Casa Barba in the west corner. Open-air concerts and other events are held in the square during summer. Walking around Thun is made a pleasure by extensive pedestrianisation.

Reached partly by a signed covered stairway off Hauptgasse, the castle at Thun was begun in the 12th century by Berchtold V of the powerful Zähringer family and is the only one of their castles to have survived intact. The rectangular keep with four corner turrets has the country's largest baronial hall, partly furnished with the spoils of the Battle of Grandson in 1476. The castle is now a museum (⊕ *Apr–Oct 10.00–17.00 daily; Nov–Jan 13.00–16.00 Sun; Feb–Mar 13.00–16.00, daily; admission charge*): its six floors display arms, altars, coins, toys, ceramics and folk art, and its four towers offer extensive views over the lake and mountains. Near the castle is the 18th-century Baroque Reformed church of St Mauritius, which has a 14th-century polygonal tower.

Situated in an English landscape park near the south bank outlet of the River Aare, Schadau Castle was built between 1848 and 1852 on the site of a medieval castle in a rather inharmonious mix of styles. It became the property of the city

Bernese Oberland BERN–THUN–SPIEZ–INTERLAKEN OST

11

in 1925 and is home to the Arts restaurant and the Swiss Gastronomy Museum (⊕ *14.00–17.00 Tue–Thu; admission charge*). Among the exhibits is the smallest recipe book in the world. In a building in Schadau Park between the station and the lake is a remarkable painting, the circular *Thun-Panorama*, painted between 1808 and 1814 by Marquand Wocher and the oldest painting of its kind in the world. Measuring 39 x 7.5m (128 x 25ft), it depicts the town in exceptional detail against a backdrop of the Alps (⊕ *May–Oct 11.00–17.00 Tue–Sun*).

In a striking lakeside building seven minutes' walk from the station, Thun Art Gallery (*Kunstmuseum, Thunerhof, Hofstettenstrasse 14;* ⊕ *10.00–17.00 Tue–Sun, 10.00–21.00 Wed; admission charge*) has exhibitions of Swiss and international art.

Most Swiss towns have good swimming pools, but the one at Thun deserves particular mention. It is a large complex with several pools catering for children and diving, but it is its location which makes it special: near the lake with lovely views of the mountains that ring Thunersee. The pool is at Strandbad to the south of the town.

The two intermediate stations between Thun and the major junction of Spiez are now served by bus (table 31.001). There is a lovely walk back to Thun from **Gwatt**, passing through woods as well as skirting marshes on the lake shore. At **Einigen** is the small 10th–13th-century Reformed church of St Michael.

The view of the small town of **Spiez** as you step out of the station is enchanting, looking down over fields and vineyards to the small harbour and prominent castle. Agriculture, fruit growing and viticulture were the town's mainstays before tourism.

As with so many comparable buildings, the castle's architectural history details its transformation from medieval fortress to patrician residence. Begun in the 10th century, it was progressively enlarged and rebuilt until the 16th century as the home of the von Bubenberg and later the von Erlach families. It is well worth a visit. The early kitchen has not been over-restored, and the dining-room has some very fine plasterwork dating from 1614 by the famous stuccoist from the Ticino, Antonio Castelli. The castle is now a museum (⊕ *early Apr–mid-Oct 14.00–17.00 Mon, 10.00–17.00 Tue–Sun; Jul–Aug 10.00–18.00; admission charge*).

The adjacent Romanesque church also dates from the 10th century, though it has been altered, and the spire dates from c1625. It contains murals from the 11th and 16th centuries, and an oval, unsupported crypt, which is unique in Switzerland.

Swiss public transport is so comprehensive that it is easy to forget that some railway lines have been closed. An example is the tram that once linked Spiez station with its delightful waterfront. It was eloquently described by Bryan Morgan in 1955 before its demise: '[the Spiez tram] is one of the most perfect examples, rich in squiggling iron brackets and balconies and cornices. So evocative of lost Edwardian summers is it that electricity seems too harsh a medium for it, and it should surely be travelling its three-quarters of a mile behind an old horse in a sun-bonnet which would slowly plod through the chalet-lined streets shaded by lilac and chestnut and up to the station on the hill...'

Leaving Spiez the line begins to descend to the level of the lake. The former fishing village of **Faulensee** can be seen on the hillside above a cove. The lake is at its widest point here, stretching 3.8km (2¼ miles) across to Merligen. On the opposite side of the lake, a funicular can be seen rising up to Beatenberg (see page 151). By **Leissigen**, a small resort town, the railway is right on the water's edge. At the well-wooded end of the lake, the entrance to the 2.75km (1¾ miles) canal to Interlaken, which opened in 1892, can be seen.

Interlaken West is only a few minutes' walk from the departure point for steamers on Lake Thun and the closer of the two stations to the centre of Interlaken. For the town of Interlaken, see opposite.

The section of line between Interlaken West and Ost crosses the River Aare twice. There was no need for the bridges: the railway built them purely to thwart perceived competition by preventing steamers from sailing between the two lakes. **Interlaken Ost** is the end of the standard gauge and the junction for the metre-gauge lines to Luzern, Grindelwald and Lauterbrunnen (see tables 470 and 311, pages 187 and 151).

PRACTICALITIES Bicycle hire from Thun, Interlaken West and Interlaken Ost stations.

THUN
Tourist information
🛈 Railway Station, Seestrasse 2, CH-3600; ☏ 033 225 90 00; e thun@thunersee.ch; www.thun.ch/ tourismus; 🕐 09.00–18.30 Mon–Fri, 09.00–16.00 Sat; Jul–Aug 09.00–13.00 Sun

Where to stay
None of the hotels are very close to the station. The most attractive hotels in the old town include:
🏠 **Krone**★★★★ **(H)** Obere Hauptgasse 2, CH-3600; ☏ 033 227 88 88; e info@krone-thun.ch; www.krone-thun.ch
🏠 **Emmental (H)** Bernstrasse 2, CH-3600; ☏ 033 222 01 20; e emmental@thunisst.ch; www.thunisst.ch

SPIEZ
Tourist information
🛈 Bahnhofplatz, CH-3700; ☏ 033 655 90 00; e info@thunersee.ch; www.thunersee.ch; 🕐 May–Jun & Sep 08.00–noon & 14.00–18.00 Mon–Fri, 09.00–noon Sat; Jul–Aug 08.00–18.30 Mon–Fri, 09.00–noon & 14.00–16.00 Sat; Oct–Apr 08.00–noon & 14.00–18.00 Mon–Fri

Where to stay
A hotel overlooking the lake close to the site of the sadly demolished Spiezerhof Hotel and beside the steamer pier is:
🏠 **Aqua Welle**★★★ Seestrasse 67, CH-3700; ☏ 033 654 40 44; e info@aquawelle.ch; www.aquawelle.ch

LEISSIGEN
Tourist information
🛈 Baumgartenweg 7, CH-3706; ☏ 033 847 11 36; e leissigen@thunersee.ch; www.thunersee.ch; 🕐 Jun–Sep 09.00–11.00 & 17.00–19.00 Mon–Thu; Oct–May 09.00–11.00 Tue & Fri

Where to stay
A hotel close to the station is:
🏠 **Kreuz**★★★ Dorfstrasse, CH-3706; ☏ 033 847 12 31; e info@kreuz-leissigen.ch; www.kreuz-leissigen.ch

INTERLAKEN

Interlaken is built on the deposits of the River Aare and the Lombach stream which, over millennia, separated the Wendelsee into lakes Thun and Brienz. Interlaken is the principal town of the Bernese Oberland and has long been popular as a base for day excursions in the region. Until 1891 it was known as Aarmühle. It is an old settlement, however, growing up around an Augustinian monastery founded in the early 12th century. After the Reformation, the monastery was converted into a residence for the Bernese governor until its replacement in 1750 by a château that still houses the local administration. To the west of **Interlaken Ost** station, the Gothic cloisters of the monastery survive, the only such building in the Bernese Oberland. The monastery chapel was built in 1452.

The Höhematte, a 14ha (35 acres) meadow in the middle of the town, has been protected from development by law since 1864. Part of its purpose was to ensure that

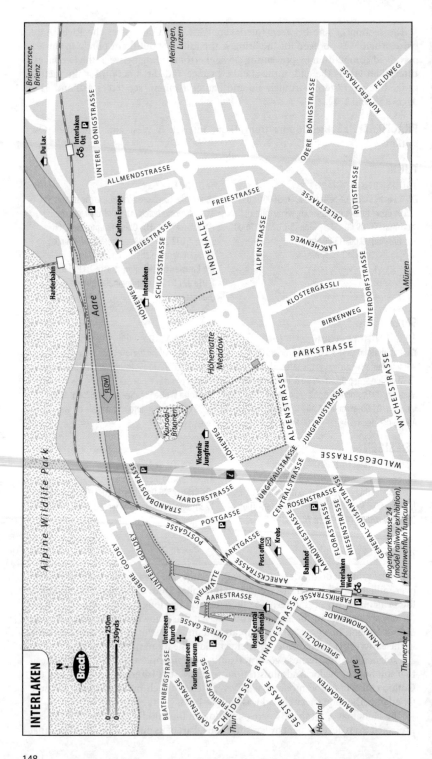

INTERLAKEN

N

Bradt

0 ——— 250m
0 ——— 250yds

Alpine Wildlife Park

Brienzersee, Brienz

Meiringen, Luzern

Aare

FLOW

Harderbahn

Du Lac

Interlaken Ost

Carlton Europe

UNTERE BÖNIGSTRASSE

ALLMENDSTRASSE

FREIESTRASSE

OBERE BÖNIGSTRASSE

FELDWEG

KUPFERSTRASSE

FREIESTRASSE

SCHLOSSSTRASSE

HÖHEWEG

Interlaken

LINDENALLEE

ALPENSTRASSE

OELESTRASSE

RÜTISTRASSE

LÄRCHENWEG

Höhematte
Meadow

KLOSTERGÄSSLI

BIRKENWEG

UNTERDORFSTRASSE

Mürren

PARKSTRASSE

Kursaal-
Brunnen

Victoria-
Jungfrau

HÖHEWEG

ALPENSTRASSE

WYCHELSTRASSE

JUNGFRAUSTRASSE

WALDEGGSTRASSE

HARDERSTRASSE

POSTGASSE

STRANDBADSTRASSE

POSTGASSE

JUNGFRAUSTRASSE

CENTRALSTRASSE

ROSENSTRASSE

FLORASTRASSE

NIESENSTRASSE

GENERAL-GUISANSTRASSE

OBERE GOLDEY

UNTERE GOLDEY

MARKTGASSE

AARECKSTRASSE

Post office

Krebs

Bahnhof

ARMUHLESTRASSE

Interlaken West

*Rugenparkstrasse 24
(model railway exhibition),
Heimwehfluh funicular*

BEATENBERGSTRASSE

GARTENSTRASSE

SCHLOFSTRASSE

FREIHOFSTRASSE

Unterseen
Church

Unterseen
Tourism Museum

SPIELMATTE

AARESTRASSE

UNTERE GASSE

Hotel Central
Continental

SEESTRASSE

BAHNHOFSTRASSE

SCHEIDGASSE

Thun

KANALPROMENADE

FABRIKSTRASSE

SPIELHOLZLI

BAUMGARTEN

Hospital

Thunersee

Aare

148

the view of the Jungfrau remained unobstructed, the grand hotels on the Höheweg benefiting from this early example of enlightened town planning. Interlaken still has a few elegant 19th-century hotels which, when sensitively modernised, have an ambience that their successors almost invariably lack.

WHAT TO SEE AND DO To the north of the Höhematte is the Kursaal (Casino), built in 1859 and rebuilt several times. It is surrounded by an attractive garden and is the venue for concerts and plays.

Unterseen is considered the loveliest part of the town, reached from Interlaken West by crossing the River Aare by Bahnhofstrasse. Unterseen's layout of two principal streets around the town hall square is the result of a fire that destroyed a third street in 1470. In the centre of the square is the old town hall, which served as a hostelry – Mendelssohn staying here in 1831. The church dates from 1853, the previous one having collapsed under the weight of snow, though the tower's foundations are early 14th century. The acoustics of the church are so good that concerts are given here during the Interlaken Music Festival (held in August). In the picturesque Unter den Häusern near the Aare, an old smithy still produces ironwork.

Anyone interested in the history of the area or tourism should spend an hour or two at the Tourism Museum at 26 Obere Gasse, Unterseen (⊕ *May–mid-Oct 14.00–17.00 Tue–Sun; admission charge*), a house built in 1686. On the ground floor are a mail coach, the first bicycle (velocipede) in Interlaken and other transport items. The upper floors describe the 'discovery' of the Alps and all that contributed to it, shipping on the lakes, the development of hotels and railways, and the growth of winter sports.

To the west of Interlaken on the shore of Lake Thun is Weissenau, where a castle guarded the approach to the Bernese Oberland and the Grimsel Pass; the ruins were restored in 1955. Beyond is the lakeside village of Neuhaus, once the steamer pier for Interlaken before the opening of the Bödeli Railway, and now known for its watersports.

Six minutes' walk from **Interlaken West** is the metre-gauge funicular to **Heimwehfluh** (table 2360), which operates from late March to late October. Turn right outside the station along Rugenparkstrasse. The walk up takes about 20 minutes. Lying on the northern slope of the Rugen, a wooded ridge to the southwest of the town, Heimwehfluh was described by the Swedish traveller Sven Hedin as 'one of the most beautiful places on earth'. The view from the observation tower is worth the ascent, and there is a restaurant, children's play area and O-gauge model railway.

Also close to Interlaken West station, at Rugenparkstrasse 24 (turn right outside the station), is a huge model railway exhibition (*Modelleisenbahn-Treff*; ⊕ *May–mid-Oct 10.00–noon & 13.30–18.00 daily*) with up to 40 trains on the move. One of the networks has 350m (1,148ft) of track, and there are rack railways and cable cars as well as conventional trains. Railway films are screened.

Five minutes' walk from Interlaken Ost beside the Aare is the funicular up the **Harder** (table 2361), which opened in 1908 and leaves from its original well-preserved station to serve another period building, the summit restaurant and hotel. The peak at 1,322m (4,460ft) provides an excellent panorama with a projecting balcony and access to some superb walks, particularly enjoyed by Mendelssohn. In common with many hotel and mountain railway companies, the Harder Railway created many of the paths, the most notable perhaps being one to the east that reaches the Brünig Pass. The difficulty of building the railway is reflected in the fact that almost half its length is built on viaduct or bridge. Operation of the funicular is limited to late April to late October.

Near the foot of the railway is an Alpine Wildlife Park with ibex and marmots. The massively horned ibex was hunted to extinction in Switzerland between the 16th and 19th centuries, and the colony here is the result of reintroduction in 1915. The park also has English-language leaflets to describe the 79 labelled trees and shrubs on the nearby Forestry Nursery Path (*Waldleherpfad*).

TOURIST INFORMATION

i Höheweg 37, CH-3800; ☏ 033 826 53 00; e mail@interlakentourism.ch; www.interlaken.ch; ☺ Jul–Aug 08.00–20.00 Mon–Fri, 08.00–17.00 Sat, 10.00–16.00 Sun; Sep 08.00–18.00 Mon– Fri, 09.00–13.00 Sat; Oct–Apr 08.00–noon & 13.30–18.00 Mon–Fri, 09.00–noon Sat; May–Jun 08.00–18.00 Mon–Fri, 08.00–16.00 Sat

WHERE TO STAY

Interlaken West

Hotels close to the station are:

⌂ **Hotel Central Continental*** (H)** Bahnhofstrasse 43, CH-3800; ☏ 033 823 10 33; e info@central-continental.ch; www.central-continental.ch

⌂ **Bahnhof** Bahnhofstrasse 37, CH-3800; ☏ 033 822 70 41

Hotels of character in the town centre not far from Interlaken West station are:

⌂ **Victoria-Jungfrau***** (H)** Höheweg 41, CH-3800; ☏ 033 828 28 28; e reservation@victoria-jungfrau.ch; www.victoria-jungfrau.ch. Interlaken's first grand hotel.

⌂ **Interlaken**** (H)** Höheweg 74, CH-3800; ☏ 033 826 68 68; e info@hotelinterlaken.ch; www.hotelinterlaken.ch. Interlaken's oldest hotel, this was once the monastic hostelry; it has a restaurant fitted out like a dining-car.

⌂ **Krebs**** (H)** Bahnhofstrasse 4, CH-3800; ☏ 033 826 03 30; e info@krebshotel.ch; www.krebshotel.ch

Interlaken Ost

Hotels close to the station are:

⌂ **Du Lac**** (H)** Höheweg 225, CH-3800; ☏ 033 822 29 22; e dulac@bluewin.ch; www.dulac-interlaken.ch

⌂ **Carlton Europe***** Höheweg 94, CH-3800; ☏ 033 826 01 60; e info@carltoneurope.ch; www.carltoneurope.ch

LAKE THUN

The maiden voyage of the first steamship, the *Bellevue*, was made in July 1835. The vessel was bought from Cave of Paris and brought to the lake in pieces by carts, and was named after the pension in Thun owned by the two purchasers of the boat. Some British visitors would doubtless have been gratified that a barrel organ on the *Bellevue* played 'God Save the King', not realising that the same tune was used by the Swiss for their national anthem until the introduction of the 'Swiss Psalm'. The instrument can be seen in the Castle Museum in Thun (see page 145). Plans are under way to raise one of Switzerland's first passenger steamboats from its watery grave at the bottom of Lake Thun.

The *Bellevue* has lain undisturbed on the lakebed since sinking in a storm in 1864 after conversion to a barge, her exact location unknown. But in summer 2004 she was found lying a few hundred metres from the landing at Oberhofen, 100m below the surface and almost entirely covered by sediment. Now there are plans to raise the vessel if sufficient funds to restore her can be found.

New vessels were added to the fleets of the two boat-operating companies, which in 1913 came into the ownership of the Bern–Lötschberg–Simplon-Bahn (BLS), which still runs them. The first motor vessels were introduced in the 1920s, and there is now a fleet of 12 and one surviving paddler, the *Blumlisalp* (1906). BLS offers various types of tickets and special packages, including such imaginative ideas as a two-day excursion from Thun to Mount Rothorn, using the paddle steamers on lakes Thun and Brienz and steam propulsion up the mountain, with an overnight stay at the hotel on the summit.

There are numerous opportunities for sailing, water-skiing, windsurfing and diving at the resorts around the lake.

Thun used to be the junction for a narrow-gauge line that ran along the northern shore of Lake Thun to Interlaken; it has been replaced by a bus service (table 31.021, line 21), and the principal villages of the northern shore are also served by steamers. For places along the south shore of the lake served by steamers, see the section on the railway between Thun and Interlaken, page 145.

HILTERFINGEN The French Renaissance-style Schloss Hünegg was built between 1861 and 1863 by a Prussian baron and has remained almost entirely unchanged since 1900. It is now an outstanding museum of social history and interior decoration (☉ *mid-May–mid-Oct 14.00–17.00 Mon–Sat, 11.00–17.00 Sun; admission charge*).

OBERHOFEN (☉ *mid-May–mid-Oct, 14.00–17.00 Mon, 11.00–17.00 Tue–Sun; park ☉ 09.30–18.00 daily*) One of Switzerland's most romantic castles, Oberhofen was built on the water's edge. The oldest part, the keep, dates from the 12th century, and it has been gradually extended, most recently in the mid 19th century. In 1940, the castle was transferred to the Oberhofen Castle Foundation by a lawyer from Pennsylvania, William Maul Measey. Apart from its important interiors, the castle houses collections of arms, toys and musical instruments. Nearby is a swimming pool with a statue of Sir Winston Churchill in the grounds. There is also a museum of mechanical musical instruments in Staatsstrasse (☉ *mid-May–mid-Oct, 14.00–17.00 Tue–Sun; mid-Oct–mid-May 14.00–17.00 Sun; admission charge*).

BEATENBUCHT This is the lower terminus of the funicular to the pretty village of Beatenberg (table 2355). Beatenbucht also provides access to the Beatus Cave (☉ *weekend before Easter–late Oct 09.30–17.00 daily*), named after the 6th-century Irish monk St Beatus who is supposed to have lived in a hermitage at the entrance. Inside are the remains of a prehistoric house and some stalactites and stalagmites, as well as the chapel created by Augustinian monks after Beatus's death.

INTERLAKEN–ZWEILÜTSCHINEN–LAUTERBRUNNEN Table 311

The construction of the first railway into the heart of the Bernese Oberland and its opening in 1890 were not universally welcomed, many having reservations about the impact that tourism would have on life in the valleys. The Bernese Oberland Bahn (BOB) operates the lines to Lauterbrunnen and Grindelwald, which share the tracks from Interlaken as far as the junction of Zweilütschinen. The lines were built to metre gauge and electrified in 1914. As the means of reaching several car-free resorts and the Jungfraubahnen, it is a very busy line. Sit on the left.

Trains for Lauterbrunnen and Grindelwald operate as one unit as far as the junction at Zweilütschinen, where the two sections separate; there is not time to transfer at Zweilütschinen, so it is important to check at Interlaken Ost that you are in the right portion of the train. Almost invariably the front section goes to Lauterbrunnen, the rear section to Grindelwald.

Leaving Interlaken, trains describe a sharp curve to head south, crossing the flat Bödeli and skirting the site of a military airfield grazed by cattle and goats as they make for an opening in the valley walls.

At **Wilderswil** trains for Schynige Platte may be seen on the left (see table 314, page 153). Beyond Schynige Platte-Bahn depot and over a covered wooden bridge across the river is the white church of Gsteig, where two daughters of Schumann and one daughter of Mendelssohn are buried. In the village is a working watermill built in 1513 which now houses a local history museum (⊕ *May–Oct 19.30–21.30 Thu, 15.30–18.00 Sat, 10.00–noon Sun; Jul–Aug also 19.30–21.30 Wed, 14.30–17.30 Sun; admission charge*). To the north of Wilderswil is the ruined castle of Unspunnen, with a cylindrical keep.

Approaching the junction of **Zweilütschinen**, the line crosses the Black Lütschine just before its confluence with the White Lütschine. At the railway workshops here, a former Rhaetian Railway tank locomotive is kept for special trains. Near the station are the remains of a 17th-century blast furnace. Beyond the station the Lauterbrunnen line forks to the right along the valley of the White Lütschine, which steadily narrows, barely leaving room for the river, railway, cycle path and road. Two rack sections lift the line to the valley level on which Lauterbrunnen is built.

Lauterbrunnen is flanked by two remarkably perpendicular walls of rock, rising on one side to the shelf on which lies Wengen and on the other, Mürren. Although the village is famous for the Staubbach Falls (which means 'dust stream') which inspired Goethe in 1779, there are 72 large and small waterfalls around the valley.

In a mill below the church is the Talmuseum (⊕ *mid-Jun–mid-Oct 14.00–17.30 Tue & Thu–Sun; admission charge*), which houses a local history collection, re-created rooms, displays on iron-ore mining, lace, mountaineering and tourism, and the 'Lötscher Bell', cast in the Valais in 1486. The building used to be a grocery store which had the valley's only supply of salt until the beginning of the 20th century. The inhabitants of outlying villages would purchase their salt after attending Sunday service.

A bus from the station goes to **Isenfluh** (table 31.142) from where a cable car rises to **Sulwald** (table 2458). Unusually, the cable car was built to help farmers with the harvest rather than carry tourists, but it is now well-used by hikers. There is a particularly fine walk from Isenfluh through alpine meadows and woods, and beside the Sausbach to Sausmatten and Winteregg where there is a restaurant (☏ 033 828 70 90).

Beyond Lauterbrunnen is **Stechelberg**, the bottom of a four-stage cable car that ascends to Mürren and then on to the **Schilthorn** (table 2460). The cable car station can be reached by bus from Lauterbrunnen station (table 31.141) in 12 minutes. For a description, see Mürren, table 313, page 154.

Near Stechelberg station are the exceptionally spectacular Trümmelbach Falls, with a volume rate of up to 20,000 litres of water per second, derived from a catchment area of 24km^2. They cascade through a chasm so narrow that it is not easy to appreciate the full spectacle, though a lift (⊕ *Apr–Oct 09.00–17.00 daily; Jul–Aug 08.30–18.00 daily; admission charge*) helps visitors reach the different levels. The lift is complemented by tunnels, bridges and walkways to enable visitors to see the majestic force of the glacier falls at close quarters. The water drains the glaciers of the Eiger, Mönch and Jungfrau.

PRACTICALITIES Bicycle hire in Lauterbrunnen from Crystal Sports (☏ 036 856 90 90) and Imboden Bike Adventures (☏ 036 855 21 14).

WILDERSWIL
Tourist information
☑ Kirchgasse 43, CH-3812; ☎ 033 822 84 55;
℮ mail@wilderswil.ch; www.wilderswil.ch;
🕐 mid-May–31 May 08.00–noon & 14.00–18.00
Mon–Fri, 15.00–18.00 Sat; Jun–mid-Sep 08.00–
noon & 14.00–18.00 Mon–Fri, 08.00–11.00 &
15.00–18.00 Sat; mid-Sep–mid-Oct 08.00–noon &
14.00–18.00 Mon–Fri, 15.00–18.00 Sat; mid-Oct–
mid-May 08.00–noon & 14.00–18.00 Mon–Fri

Where to stay
Numerous hotels; close to the station are:
🏠 **Bären*** (H)** CH-3812; ☎ 033 827 02 02;
℮ info@baeren.ch; www.baeren.ch
🏠 **Gasthof Steinbock** (H)** Gsteigwiler,
CH-3814; ☎ 033 823 30 01; ℮ info@gasthaus-
steinbock.ch; www.gasthaus-steinbock.ch

LAUTERBRUNNEN
Tourist information
☑ Stutzli 460, CH-3822; ☎ 033 856 85 68;
℮ info@lauterbrunnen.ch; www.mylauterbrunnen.
com; 🕐 Jun–Sep 08.30–noon & 13.30–18.00
daily; Oct–May 09.00–noon & 13.30– 17.00
Mon–Fri

Where to stay
Numerous hotels; close to the station are
🏠 **Silberhorn*** (H)** CH-3822; ☎ 033 856 22
10; ℮ info@silberhorn.com; www.silberhorn.com
🏠 **Schützen** Fuhren 438, CH-3822; ☎ 033
855 30 25; ℮ info@hotelschuetzen.com; www.
hotelschuetzen.com

WILDERSWIL–SCHYNIGE PLATTE Table 314

This 800mm-gauge Riggenbach-rack railway was opened in 1893 and taken over by BOB three years later. Although electrified in 1914, it still has a steam locomotive from 1894 for special trains. It is one of the most disorienting of mountain railways, its sharp curves, sometimes in tunnels, quickly destroying one's sense of direction. Its characterful though box-like locomotives are some of the oldest operating on Swiss railways, dating from 1910 to 1914; some are secondhand from the Wengernalpbahn. The frequent change of direction leaves little to choose between seats on either side of the coaches.

Leaving Wilderswil on the continuous rack, the line crosses the Lütschine, running parallel with the line to Zweilütschinen before turning abruptly east and diving into the woods. The Rotenegg Tunnel takes the railway through a horseshoe curve to emerge in almost the opposite direction. There used to be a railway-owned hotel at **Breitlauenen**, but its seasonal opening and changing fashions led to closure in 1974.

The trees thin and the views become less impeded as the railway reaches alpine meadows. There are some tremendous drops from the train, and after Grätli Tunnel, the train emerges to a spectacular view of the Eiger, Mönch and Jungfrau, which remain in sight all the way to the station at **Schynige Platte** (1,987m, 6,519ft). The view from the terminus must be one of the finest from any station in the world. At the beginning and end of the season, you may see cows being brought up or taken down the mountain by train, or sheep being transferred during the summer – the carriage of livestock by rail is now rare in Europe.

Near the summit station is the alpine garden that has delighted botanists and gardeners since 1929 – with over 500 of the 620-odd plants that exist above the tree line, it has a growing season from June to October and is open all day.

A short walk above the station stands one of the first hotels on a Swiss mountain, which opened in 1832. On two nights in mid-August, walkers gather at the hotel an hour before midnight for a guided night hike to the peak of the Faulhorn, arriving in time for sunrise. The descent is via the gondola from First down to Grindelwald.

11

The mountain slopes around the station offer some wonderful walks with some of the finest views to be had of the Bernese peaks and over lakes Thun and Brienz. An easy circular walk takes in the extraordinary domed rock known as the Daube. Even in high season you can quickly escape the crowds by taking a footpath, and by 16.00, most people have left the summit. A path also descends through the woods to Gsteig and Wilderswil via Breitlauenen.

SCHYNIGE PLATTE

Where to stay

⌂ **Berghotel Schynige Platte** CH-3801; ☎ 033 828 73 73; e hotelschynigeplatte@jungfrau.ch; www.schynigeplatte.ch

LAUTERBRUNNEN–GRÜTSCHALP–MÜRREN Table 313

When built, the section from Lauterbrunnen to Grütschalp was the steepest funicular in Switzerland; using the Riggenbach rack, the Bergbahn Lauterbrunnen–Mürren (BLM) was operated by the water/gravity principle until conversion to electric drive in 1901. Pincer brakes replaced the rack between 1948 and 1950. Water was fed into a tank underneath the upper car and gradually emptied on the descent to counteract the growing weight of the descending car's cable and the lighter cable of the ascending car. Problems with ground movement forced its replacement with a cable car in 2006. The line from Grütschalp to Mürren follows the contours along the top of the cliffs above Lauterbrunnen. Both lines were built to metre gauge, opened in 1891 and worked by the BOB from the outset. The inventor of one of the rack systems and for a time inspector of the BOB, Emil Strub, described the impact of the view from the railway: 'The scenery from Grütschalp to Mürren becomes continuously wilder, more astonishing. The passengers rise involuntarily from their seats and, intoxicated with wonder, seek to assimilate the undreamt-of, magnificent spectacle...'. Sit on the left on both lines.

A subway under the street links the BOB station at Lauterbrunnen with the station for Grütschalp. The ascent is largely through woods but there are momentary views over the Lauterbrunnen valley. At **Grütschalp** passengers and goods are transferred on to the adhesion line, a few yards from and at right angles to the cable car.

The short journey to **Mürren** is every bit as impressive as Strub's eulogy would suggest. The views over the valley and the range of towering peaks on the opposite side are unimpeded. Among the many walks in the area is a hike along the ledge to Mürren, which offers a magnificent, changing panorama of the surrounding peaks. It soon becomes evident why Mürren is so popular: it is in an incomparable position on a broad shelf above the Lauterbrunnen valley, and it has arguably the finest views of the Eiger, Mönch and Jungfrau.

Mürren is one of the larger car-free resorts, reflected in the heavy traffic on the railway, which carries over half a million people and over 5,000 tonnes of goods traffic a year. Inside the modern station is a relic from old Mürren: one of the 50cm-gauge trolleys that once ran for 450m through the village to take visitors and their luggage from the station to their hotel. Outside the station is a tablet commemorating one of the pioneers of alpine skiing, Sir Arnold Lunn (1888–1974), who had much to do with the promotion of Mürren as a winter resort.

At first the village was a summer-only resort, patronised largely by British visitors, Tennyson among them. As early as 1869, an English visitor complained that the village was 'crowded to excess with English people'. The future Archbishop of Canterbury, E W Benson, was not pleased to see British people playing tennis within sight of the Jungfrau, evidently regarding such activity as little short of sacrilegious. If this seems excessive, it was a view shared by many in the early to mid 19th century, including some of the painters of the Hudson River School: for the Bolton-born Thomas Cole, the attitude of many 'go-getting' Americans to beautiful landscapes as territory ripe for exploitation was akin to blasphemy. The redemptive power of landscape and natural forces were recurrent themes in the works of Wordsworth and other Romantics. The English church in Mürren was built in 1878 to the design of George Edmund Street (architect of the Law Courts in London). Among later eminent British visitors were Henry Morton Stanley, George Bernard Shaw, Joseph Chamberlain, Princess Mary and Field Marshal Montgomery.

In 1910, the railway was persuaded to operate a winter service for the first time; two years later, Sir Arnold Lunn officially inaugurated the first winter sports season at the Palace Hotel, where the Kandahar Ski Club (named after Earl Roberts of Kandahar) was founded in 1924. The first of the now-famous Inferno ski runs from the Schilthorn took place in 1928, and three years later Mürren was host to the first world skiing championship.

The association of Mürren with ballooning goes back to 1910 when the first crossing of the Alps by balloon began here, ending in Turin. The first annual International High Alpine Ballooning Competition was held in 1957, and it continues to provide a colourful spectacle as the big balloons rise into the clear air. An Alpine Balloon Sport and Balloon Postal Service Museum, situated in the Resort and Sports Centre, tells the story of the sport and its use as transport.

In addition to an impressive range of sports facilities, including indoor pool, a nursery is provided – ask at the tourist office (see page 156).

Above Mürren is the Allmendhubel, which can be reached by funicular (table 2463) from a station eight minutes' walk from the BLM station. Operating from June to mid-October, and for winter sports from mid-December to mid-April, the line climbs through a 183m (600ft) tunnel.

The most famous peak above Mürren is the Schilthorn, brought to world attention through its choice as the location for filming one of the most dramatic sequences of the James Bond film *On Her Majesty's Secret Service*, with Diana Rigg and George Lazenby. It was filmed just before the opening of the revolving restaurant known as Piz Gloria in 1969, which was rebuilt to increase capacity and the quality of its facilities in 1990. Now rotated by solar power, the restaurant goes through a revolution once every hour (❧ 033 856 21 56). The complex must be one of the most spectacular sites in the world for a seminar or conference – up to 340 people can be accommodated. The daily catering requirements call for four to six service lifts at the end of each day to bring up supplies, including water, and the waste discharge pipe down to Mürren has to be heated to prevent freezing. If the weather is inclement, you can see a ten-minute, multi-projector audio-visual of the surroundings and a ten-minute extract from *On Her Majesty's Secret Service*.

The summit of the Schilthorn is reached by the final stage of Europe's longest cable car route that begins at Stechelberg (see page 152; table 2460) and ascends in four stages. The first section ascends to the mountain village of Gimmelwald, passing dramatically close to the Mürrenbach waterfall. The next section rises to Mürren and then continues to Birg before the final stage to the Schilthorn at 2,970m (9,744ft).

It is from the summit that the Inferno ski race down to Mürren takes place, the record being 15 minutes for the 15.8km (10 miles) descent that has been called 'the craziest ski race in the world'. Thrills of a different but equally crazy kind can be had by bungee jumping out of a cable car on the previous cable car route between Stechelberg and Mürren, said to be the highest jump from a fixed installation in the world, at 180m (590ft).

The altitude of the mountain ensures that skiing remains possible long after lower slopes are closed. For walkers, a network of paths descends from the cable car station, but the intermediate stations might be better starting points for the less experienced.

PRACTICALITIES Bicycle hire from the tourist office in Mürren.

MÜRREN

Tourist information

ℹ️ CH-3825; 📞 033 856 86 86; e info@muerren.ch; www.mymuerren.ch; ⏱ 08.30–18.00 daily

Where to stay

Hotels close to the station are:

🏠 **Eiger****** CH-3825; 📞 033 856 54 54; e info@hoteleiger.com; www.hoteleiger.com

🏠 **Guesthouse Eiger*** CH-3825; 📞 033 856 54 60; e info@eigerguesthouse.com; www.eigerguesthouse.com

Hotels perched on the edge of the cliff with stupendous views are:

🏠 **Edelweiss***** CH-3825; 📞 033 856 56 00; e info@edelweiss-muerren.ch; www.edelweiss-muerren.ch

🏠 **Alpina**** CH-3825; 📞 033 855 13 61; e alpina@muerren.ch; www.muerren.ch/alpina

LAUTERBRUNNEN–KLEINE SCHEIDEGG Table 311

Opened in 1893, the Wengernalpbahn (WAB) was built to 800mm gauge rather than the metre gauge of the BOB, necessitating a change of train, demonstrating a rare instance of poorly planned integration. It has the distinction of being the longest continuous stretch of rack railway in Switzerland at 19.2km (12 miles). Using the Riggenbach rack, the railway was electrified between 1909 and 1910, and of the 16 steam locomotives, only one from 1891 was saved, by sale to the Brienz–Rothorn Bahn. The early coaches had open upper sections with cloth curtains that had to be opened in high winds to stop the carriages being blown over – like the injunctions in Indian narrow-gauge trains to lower the windows during storms. Thankfully most of the area served by the WAB is inaccessible to motor traffic, so the railway still plays a vital role in carrying goods traffic as well as passengers. The Swiss Pass is valid only as far as Wengen, but trains wait for passengers not holding valid onward tickets to buy them, at a discount with the Swiss Pass. Sit on the right.

The views leaving Lauterbrunnen are superb. On the left is the huge massif of the Männlichen, Tschuggen and Lauberhorn, while to the right, above the valley of the White Lütschine to the south, is the great spout of water known as the Staubbach Falls, which has a drop of 274m (900ft). On the shelf of rock from which the falls descend is the village of Mürren.

At the passing loop of Witimatte, the railway once divided, the right fork being the original line which climbed at gradients as steep as 1 in 4 through the woods and over some impressive viaducts to Wengen. Today it is disused. The line to the left is the new line that opened in 1910 with grades no steeper than 1 in 5.5. It ascends through woods punctuated by waterfalls and several tunnels to enter Wengen side by side with the older route.

Wengen is one of the largest car-free resorts, making it a perfect place for families. Like other resorts that have excluded traffic, the quality of air is an elixir for nostrils and lungs accustomed to urban pollution. The compact nature of the village makes it easy to walk everywhere, and small electric vehicles meet the trains to transport luggage and less-abled visitors to their hotels. The tourist office is a two-minute walk from the station, taking a left turn by the Hotel Eiger.

The village is a particularly good skiing resort for families, catering to a wide range of skill in 100km (62 miles) of runs, and there is a children's training area in the village. Wengen is the venue for the annual skiing contest on the Lauberhorn in late January. The village also has a natural and an artificial ice rink, and the usual complement of tennis courts, heated outdoor swimming pool and a curling hall.

A ten-minute walk from the station, past the English church dedicated to St Bernard, is the cable car to the Männlichen (table 2455) at 2,230m (7,316ft). The cable car station at the top is the start of numerous walks which help to clarify the complicated topography of the valleys. Particularly helpful is the view from the summit of the Männlichen, an easy 20-minute walk from the cable car. One of the best walks takes you along the slopes of the Tschugen and Lauberhorn to Kleine Scheidegg (*1½ hrs*). From there you can either take the train or walk back to Wengen via Wengernalp (*1½ hrs*). Another circular tour can be made by taking Europe's longest gondola down to **Grindelwald Grund** (table 2445).

The climb out of Wengen takes you steadily closer to the chain of mountains ahead, pausing at **Allmend**, an isolated halt used by hikers, after which the tree line is crossed. By **Wengernalp,** the train is so close to the massif that it inspires the feeling that you could almost reach out and touch the rock faces opposite. There is no other building near the station but the hotel, making it an exceptionally peaceful place to stay (see page 158).

It was here that Byron wrote *Manfred*, which, on publication in 1817, brought the Bernese Oberland to the attention of many through its descriptions of Wengen and the Scheidegg and Grindelwald glaciers. Tchaikovsky, Mendelssohn and Richard Wagner are amongst the guests who have stayed here in the frequently rebuilt hotel, though they would have arrived by sedan chair or on horseback.

Kleine Scheidegg is dramatically situated on the saddle between the Lauberhorn and the Jungfrau, and acts as the junction for trains to Jungfraujoch and Grindelwald (see tables 311/312, pages 158–9). The views down the valley towards Grindelwald in one direction and Mürren in the other, with the peaks of the Eiger, Mönch and Jungfrau on one side, are magnificent. The Lauberhorn to the north of the station provides one of the world's greatest skiing challenges, the World Cup Race, perpetuating the first British downhill ski races that were held here in 1921. The terrace at the station is a popular place to have lunch, and a collection of old signals adorns the station restaurant.

WENGEN

Tourist information

i CH-3823; 033 855 14 14; e info@wengen.com; www.wengen-muerren.com; ⊕ Jun–Aug 09.00–21.00 daily; Sep & Dec–Mar 09.00–18.00 daily; Oct–Nov & Apr–May 09.00–18.00 Mon–Fri

Where to stay

Numerous hotels; close to the station are:
Regina****** (H)** Dorfstrasse, CH-3823; 033 856 58 58; e reservation@hotelregina.ch; www.hotelregina.ch
Silberhorn****** CH-3823; 033 856 51 31; e hotel@silberhorn.ch; www.silberhorn.ch
Falken***** (H)** CH-3823; 033 856 51 21; e info@hotelfalken.com; www.hotelfalken.com. Delightful character.

WENGERNALP
Where to stay
⌂ **Jungfrau-Wengernalp** CH-3823; ☎ 033 855
16 22; www.wengernalp.ch

KLEINE SCHEIDEGG
Where to stay
⌂ **Bellevue des Alpes** (H) CH-3801; ☎ 033
855 12 12; e welcome@scheidegg-hotels.ch;
www.scheidegg-hotels.ch

KLEINE SCHEIDEGG–JUNGFRAUJOCH Tables 311/312

Many visionaries had toyed with the idea of a railway to the Jungfrau before Adolf Guyer-Zeller had a flash of inspiration while climbing the Schilthorn with his daughter in 1893. Staying at a hotel in Mürren, he spent much of the night sketching his ideas, which needed remarkably little alteration. Work began in July 1896, and the first section to the mouth of the tunnel opened two years later. Thereafter it was a long, arduous process to bore the tunnel to successive stations, each provided with viewing platforms on the cliff face at the end of side tunnels. Guyer-Zeller, the driving force of the project, died in 1899 but his sons continued the work. As the railway lengthened, ticket revenue increased to help fund construction. Various disasters dogged construction, the worst in 1908 when 30 tonnes of dynamite exploded, shattering windows in Grindelwald and creating a noise supposedly heard in Germany. In all seriousness, some papers reported the Eiger was wobbling. Europe's highest railway station, at 3,454m (11,332ft), opened on 1 August 1912. The metre-gauge railway was built with the Strub rack and has been electrically operated from the outset. The Swiss Pass obtains a discount on the high fares necessitated by the costs of maintaining such a railway. Because of the price, it is advisable to check that you are likely to have clear visibility from the summit. Warm clothing and sunglasses are vital. Sit on the right.

The first section of the line from Kleine Scheidegg as far as the first station is in the open, broken only by the occasional snow shelter. Beside the hotel and restaurant at **Eigergletscher** are the Jungfraubahn's husky kennels, home to the dogs which pull sledges at the summit. The station is at one end of the Eiger Trail to Alpligen, a station on the line down from Kleine Scheidegg to Grindelwald (table 312). Beyond the station are the railway's workshops, the highest in Europe, and the portal of the 7,122m (4.43 miles) unlined tunnel that ends underneath the Jungfraujoch. The journey is broken by a five-minute stop at **Eiger Wall** where passengers can walk to the former viewing platform – now regrettably converted into a picture window – on the north face of the Eiger, which has a surprisingly pastoral aspect down to Grindelwald. Seven minutes later there is another halt, at **Eismeer**, from which there is a quite different view from the previous stop. Here the window overlooks the Grindelwald and Fiescher glaciers.

Passengers arriving at **Jungfraujoch** are warned of the effects of altitude on respiration and advised to walk slowly. From the glazed hall beside the station, a lift provides access to the restaurants, Ice Palace, open-air verandas, exhibition gallery and the glacier outside, where a team of huskies gives sledge rides. A winter garden and an extension of the High Alpine Research Station were opened in 1996, and in 2012, a 250-metre subway opened to mark the centenary, lined with alcove displays about the history of the railway and tourism in the Swiss Alps. The Jungfraujoch is also home to Europe's highest manned meteorological observatory, which measures about 25 weather elements every ten minutes. This information is subsequently analysed by computer, along with that from 60 other weather stations.

A multi-projector audio-visual with commentary in German or English describes the construction of the railway and facilities on the Jungfraujoch as well as the topography of the surrounding mountains. The present buildings were erected after fire destroyed the old hotel and restaurant in 1972 and incorporate the highest grid-connected solar power plant in Europe.

The view down the Aletsch glacier is spectacular, the great tongue of ice weaving its way downhill; at 21.6km (13½ miles) it is Europe's longest glacier, stretching south towards the Rhône valley close to the Brig–Andermatt railway.

ZWEILÜTSCHINEN–GRINDELWALD Table 312

Opened in 1890, the line to Grindelwald threads the often narrow valley of the Black Lütschine, passing through the only two tunnels on the BOB.

From Zweilütschinen, the Grindelwald line curves left around the BOB workshops to head up the valley of the Black Lütschine. A long rack section raises the line between **Lütschental** and **Burglauenen**, where the valley is so narrow that it is in shade for much of the day. Cliffs with trees covering the narrowest of ledges tower above the railway. To the left, the fast-flowing river rushes down the valley, periodically crossed by covered wooden bridges, and beyond Lütschental, the railway crosses the river. Another rack section follows after **Schwendi**, after which the valley opens out as the railway nears the terminus.

Grindelwald was burned to the ground in 1892, so its reconstruction was planned with tourism in mind. The local history collection in the Talhaus near the Reformed church of St Maria (1793) provides an insight into the agricultural roots of the community, with a re-created alpine dairy and kitchen (for details, visit www.grindelwald-museum.ch). It also has many items relating to early tourism, mountaineering and winter sports.

The modern sports centre has the usual facilities – indoor pool, sauna, skating hall, games room, table tennis and restaurant.

Found at the east end of the town, the three-section gondola to **First** (table 2440) is a ten-minute walk from the station and was the world's first fully automatic gondola cableway. The summit has a restaurant and is the start of some excellent walks, one of the most popular being to **Bachalpsee**, which takes about an hour. A path continues along the ridge to the Faulhorn at 2,680m (8,793ft) where Europe's oldest surviving mountain hotel was built in 1830. You can stick to the heights by walking to Schynige Platte or descend through Bussalp back to Grindelwald (*about 5½ hrs*). Some of the best views to be had near First are from the Schwarzhorn at 2,928m (9,606ft), but this is a more difficult walk. To the east of the summit are popular ski slopes served by six lifts.

The station for the cable car to **Pfingstegg** (table 2442) to the southeast is a 15-minute walk from the BOB/WAB station and close to the Firstbahn. There are several good walks from Pfingstegg. You can walk via the old marble quarries to the Lower Glacier, which at one time stretched down to the village; it can best be appreciated by the extraordinary walk through a canyon of rock and ice known as the Gletscherschlucht (*1¼ hrs*). At Bäregg there is a Berghaus, and the Upper

11

Glacier (Oberergletscher) is overlooked by Restaurant Milchbach (*1hr*). From the Hotel Wetterhorn, you can follow the leafy trail down to the river and on the other side climb up 890 steps to the foot of the glacier.

A bus from the station heads northeast through the beautiful Rosenlaui valley to **Schwarzwaldalp** (table 31.123), where connections are made to a service to **Meiringen** (table 31.164) on the Luzern–Interlaken line (table 470). A circular ticket can be bought for the bus journey to Meiringen, followed by a train journey to Interlaken and back to Grindelwald.

To the west of Grindelwald is the Männlichen, reached by a two-section gondola from Grindelwald Grund (table 2445). This is Europe's longest gondola cableway, at 6,240m (3.9 miles). From the summit there are marvellous walks along the ridge between the valleys of the Black and White Lütschine, which can help to put the complex topography of the area in perspective. Another cable car descends to Wengen (table 2455).

PRACTICALITIES Bicycle hire in Grindelwald from Graf Sport, Haupstrasse (✆ *033 854 88 44*), about three minutes' walk from the station.

GRINDELWALD
Tourist information
🛈 Dorfstrasse 110, Postfach 124, CH-3818; ✆033 854 12 12; e touristcenter@grindelwald.ch; www.grindelwald.ch; ⏰ 08.00–18.00 daily

Where to stay
Numerous hotels; close to the station are:
🏠 **Romantik Hotel Schweizerhof**** (H)** CH-3818; ✆033 854 58 58; e info@hotel-schweizerhof.com; www.hotel-schweizerhof.com
🏠 **Central Wolter***** Hauptstrasse, CH-3818; ✆033 854 33 33; e wolter@grindelwald.ch; www.central-wolter.ch

🏠 **Derby***** CH-3818; ✆033 854 54 61; e info@derby-grindelwald.ch; www.derby-grindelwald.ch
🏠 **Hirschen*** (H)** Dorfstrasse 135, CH-3818; ✆033 854 84 84; e info@hirschen-grindelwald.ch; www.hirschen-grindelwald.ch
🏠 **Berghotel Faulhorn (H)** ✆033 853 27 13 (Faulhorn; Jul–Oct), ✆033 853 10 28 (Grindelwald); e info@berghotel-faulhorn.ch (excluding Jul–Oct); www.berghotel-faulhorn.ch. Mountain hotel located on the stunning Faulhorn summit; reservations mandatory. Contact by phone only Jul–Oct.

GRINDELWALD–KLEINE SCHEIDEGG Table 312

A short 800mm-gauge line operated by the Wengernalpbahn, which completes a circuit. Sit on the left so that you are on the right after reversal at Grindelwald Grund.

The railway drops down to the chalet-style station at **Grindelwald Grund** where the railway has its workshops and trains have to reverse, climbing out of the valley floor. The gradient is particularly severe on the ascent to **Alpiglen**, with a maximum of 1 in 4. The climb affords wonderfully open views across undulating pasture dotted with cow sheds and clumps of conifers that have survived clearance for pistes. The station is at one end of the Eiger Trail to Eigergletscher station. Although the railway is protected by snow shelters for a good length, much of the side to the right is open. For **Kleine Scheidegg**, see table 311, page 156.

SPIEZ–ZWEISIMMEN Table 320

The railway through the Lower Simmen valley is known as the Simmentalbahn and is operated by the Bern–Lötschberg–Simplon-Bahn (BLS). The heavily wooded valley is renowned for its distinctive style of chalets, and a leaflet is available from tourist offices describing a walk from Wimmis station to Erlenbach station taking in the finest examples; it is in German but the map and the gist of the text is readily decipherable. There has been a longstanding proposal to lay a third rail to metre gauge between Interlaken, Spiez and Zweisimmen to permit through running of Golden Pass metre-gauge trains between Luzern and Montreux. Gauge-changing bogies are now seen as the preferred option. Sit on the left.

Upon leaving Spiez, the Zweisimmen line shares the same route as the Thun line before turning southwest and crossing the River Kander (the White One) soon after **Lattigen bei Spiez**. At **Wimmis** there is a 10th-century Romanesque church and an imposingly sited 15th-century castle.

The railway criss-crosses the River Simme (the Mighty One), which is also crossed by attractive covered wooden bridges. A bus from **Oey-Diemtigen** station goes along the secluded valley of Diemtigtal to Grimmialp (table 31.260). The valley won the 1986 Swiss Wakker Prize for architectural heritage, Diemtigen itself having several fine farmhouses such as the Grosshaus (1805), the largest private dwelling in Simmental.

Erlenbach im Simmental has some attractive wooden houses and a much-rebuilt 10th-century church with 15th-century frescoes. About 15 minutes' walk from the station is the two-section cable car up the **Stockhorn** (table 2370) from which there is a fine panorama over Thunersee, and alpine meadows renowned for their flowers. The summit has a restaurant and is particularly popular with hang-gliders for its take-off ramp. There are 70km (44 miles) of signed paths around the 2,190m (7,200ft) peak.

One of the valley's finest wooden houses is found in **Därstetten** – the magnificent façade of the Knuttihaus was built in 1756 in the combination of Ständerbau and Blockbau principles, which is a characteristic of the area.

Beyond Därstetten, the railway crosses an impressive viaduct and continues its course along a ledge on the right-hand side of the valley. **Oberwil im Simmental** is an attractive village, its Gothic Reformed church on a hill to the right. As the valley narrows near **Enge im Simmental**, the railway drops down towards the level of the river before reaching **Boltigen**. From the station here, a bus goes over a zig-zag route across the Jaunpass to Bulle station (table 20.260) (see *Chapter 17*, page 278).

For **Zweisimmen**, see table 120, page 269.

PRACTICALITIES Bicycle hire from Zweisimmen station.

SPIEZ–BRIG Table 300

The southern section of the Bern–Lötschberg–Simplon railway (BLS) is one of Switzerland's most spectacularly engineered railways, with 25 major bridges or viaducts and 24 tunnels, most notably the 14.6km (9 miles) long Lötschberg Tunnel. The final section from Frutigen to Brig opened in 1913 and was electrically worked from the outset. In June 2007, the 34.6km (22 miles) Lötschberg Base Tunnel opened at a lower level than the original tunnel. This now carries most freight and long-distance passenger trains, saving over an hour on journey times. Because of the scenic nature of the 'old' line and the importance of Kandersteg and Frutigen (for Adelboden) stations, new trains with panoramic windows have been built for local train services between Spiez and Brig. Sit on the right.

Leaving Spiez, the line turns abruptly southeast to enter Hondrich Tunnel, which leads into the Kander valley with its characteristic grey water in the glacial river on the right. A bicycle path runs close to the river all the way from Spiez to Kandersteg.

Adjacent to the station at **Mülenen** is the bottom of the two-section funicular, opened in 1910, that goes up to Niesen Kulm (table 2405). Immediately after departure the funicular crosses the broad River Kander. Alongside the track is a flight of 11,674 steps for maintenance workers, a climb that has the distinction of being the longest staircase in the world.

The views from the top are regarded as among the finest in the Bernese Oberland. From the summit at 2,336m (7,664ft) there is a lovely, partly wooded walk down which takes about 3½ hours. Other paths descend to Frutigen (3¾ hrs), Wimmis (3½ hrs) and Oey-Diemtigen on the Spiez–Zweisimmen line (see page 160). An attractive hotel at the summit enables guests to see dawn over the Bernese Alps.

At **Reichenbach im Kandertal** are some 18th-century timber buildings with carved decoration and painted façades. From the station at **Frutigen**, an hourly bus goes up the steep-sided Engstligental to the popular resort of Adelboden (table 31.230). Halfway to Adelboden, the bus passes close to the cable car from Elsigbach to Elsigenalp (table 2417), a popular area for walks with restaurants at both ends of the cable car. The Engstligen valley also has some spectacular waterfalls.

Leaving Frutigen, the northern portal of the Lötschberg Base Tunnel can be seen and on the right are the ruins of Tellenburg Castle, which burned down in 1885. The line then crosses an imposing viaduct before looping around the remains of Felsenburg Tower. The gradients steepen to 1 in 37 for much of the next 18km (11 miles) as the line describes two huge loops to gain the next step of the valley, using viaducts and tunnels to change direction. The storm of Boxing Day 1999 brought down so many trees in this area that the line can now be seen more clearly than it has for several decades. The spectacular ascent to **Kandersteg**, much more attractive scenically than the southern ramp, prompted BLS to create a footpath down to Frutigen, opened in 1993 (see opposite).

On the platform at Kandersteg is a small steam locomotive from 1911 used in the construction of the Lötschberg Tunnel, and the station has an excellent restaurant. Kandersteg is a delightfully situated village that straggles over a broad, flat expanse ringed by mountains. A summer and winter resort, the village is a good base for walking and mountaineering holidays. In the area are 350km (219 miles) of footpaths, and in winter there are 75km (47 miles) of cross-country ski trails and 13km (8 miles) of downhill runs. The village offers the usual indoor swimming and ice rink, and has schools for mountaineering, paragliding and riding.

To the north of Kandersteg is the **Blausee**, a deep blue lake with crystal-clear water surrounded by a nature reserve and woodland. Boat trips are run on the lake, which is used as a trout farm, and St Bernard dogs are also bred here.

One of the best excursions from Kandersteg is to **Oeschinensee**: a chairlift (table 2410) ten minutes' walk from the station takes you to the level of the side valley in which the lake is situated. It is a 20–30-minute walk to the lake, spectacularly sited in a bowl of rock that forms the 3,629m (11,908ft) peak of Blümisalp and overlooked by a hotel and restaurant (see page 164). The water flows out of the lake underground and is used to generate electricity.

Also ten minutes' walk from Kandersteg station is the cable car to **Allmenalp** (table 2411), where authentic cheese making can be seen during the summer.

Much further away, about 40 minutes on foot from the station, is the cable car to **Sunnbüel** (Gemmi) (table 2412), the name of which indicates that the lift gives access to footpaths leading past isolated Daubensee and over the Gemmi Pass to the cable car down to **Leukerbad** (table 2240) (see *Chapter 18*, page 298).

The first Lötschberg Tunnel was constructed between 1906 and 1912. It was planned as a straight bore, but after two years' work, the tunnel was flooded with water and glacial debris from a fissure in the floor of the Gasterntal above. This forced the engineers to seal off 1,554m (5,100ft) of tunnel with a wall 10m (33ft) thick and build a curve to avoid the area of thin rock between the tunnel and the valley floor above. Camps for the 4,000 workers, mostly Italian, were built at Kandersteg and at **Goppenstein**, where the train emerges from the Lötschberg Tunnel. Shuttle trains for cars are run between the two stations.

The hamlet of Goppenstein is the start of the lovely Lötschental, though it is heavily visited. A bus from the station goes up the valley to **Fafleralp** (table 12.591).

Like its northern counterpart, the southern ramp of the BLS includes some of the steepest standard-gauge gradients in Switzerland with slopes of up to 1 in 37. Just after leaving Hohtenn Tunnel the line turns abruptly east to descend the north side of the Rhône valley; 400m (1,300ft) below is the SBB main line from Geneva to Brig.

The BLS has created a footpath along the southern ramp of the Lötschberg starting at **Hohtenn**. It is longer than and very different in character from the northern walk, with impressive views over the Rhône valley. The section between Hohtenn and **Ausserberg** takes about three hours. A restaurant can be found at each end and at Rarnerkumme en route. From Ausserberg runs one of the most attractive *Bisses* (see *Chapter 18*, page 281) – the irrigation water courses that have sometimes become the focus of a walkers' path. This one irrigated the now-protected Baltschiedertal. If you get tired, a bus links the post office in Baltschieder with Ausserberg and **Visp** stations (table 12.522). A small, quiet resort, Ausserberg has a climbing and riding school.

The footpath continues through **Eggerberg** to **Lalden**, the last station before Brig – see table 100, page 295.

THE BLS ADVENTURE TRAIL

The northern section of this enterprising creation by BLS starts at Kandersteg station and ends at Frutigen station, taking advantage of the natural gradient. However, it is by no means as easy a descent as the railway, since the path naturally has to drop to the foot of viaduct piers and climb up to track level again, and it sometimes climbs over the top of tunnels. Stout shoes with good grips should be worn. The path is open between April and October (as is the southern section). See www.bls.ch/e/reisen-ausfluege/ausfluege-so-wandern-bahnweg.php and www.bls.ch/e/reisen-ausfluege/ausfluege-so-wandern-suedrampe.php.

For anyone interested in the problems of operating an alpine railway, there could be no better introduction. Information boards, for which an English translation can be bought at Kandersteg station, begin at the station but the majority can be found along the main section of the trail between the closed station at Blauseemailitholz and Kandergrund. It takes about two hours to walk from Kandersteg to Blauseemitholz, an hour for the principal section, and a further two hours from Kandergrund to Frutigen. A bus runs every 1–2 hours from outside Kandersteg station to **Mitholz** (table 31.230), and you can return by the same service from Kandergrund.

The boards convey all kinds of information about the BLS and this section of track, but the most telling sight is the massive pillar of concrete that prevents an overhanging cliff from toppling into the valley, taking with it the railway's support. A platform goes round the pillar; make sure you go to the farthest point to look up at the inspection walks that have been created above. There is even a place about halfway up to have a barbecue: wood is provided with an axe (on a chain) to chop it up and a well-made grill complete with upended logs for seats.

If you want to take photographs, wait until after 11.00 as most of the line is in shade before then.

PRACTICALITIES Bicycle hire from Kandersteg and Brig stations.

NIESEN-KULM
Where to stay
⌂ **Berghaus** Niesen-Kulm Mülenen, CH-3711;
☎ 033 676 77 11; e info@niesen.ch; www.niesen.ch

KANDERSTEG
Tourist information
ℹ Dorfstrasse, CH-3718; ☎ 033 675 80 80;
e info@kandersteg.ch; www.kandersteg.ch;
⊕ Dec–Mar 08.00–noon & 14.00–18.00 Mon–
Fri, 08.30–noon & 15.00–18.00 Sat; Apr–May
08.00–noon & 14.00–17.00 Mon–Fri; Jun–Sep
08.00–noon & 13.30–18.00 Mon–Fri, 08.30–noon
& 15.00–18.00 Sat; Oct–Nov 08.00–noon &
14.00–17.00 Mon–Fri

Where to stay
Numerous hotels; closest to the station are:
⌂ **Belle Epoque Hotel Victoria*** (H)** Äusser
Dorfstrasse 2, CH-3718; ☎ 033 675 80 00; e info@
hotel-victoria.ch; www.hotel-victoria.ch
⌂ **Alpina**** CH-3718; ☎ 033 675 12 46; e info@
alpina-online.com; www.alpina-online.com

OESCHINENSEE
Where to stay
⌂ **Oeschinensee**** CH-3718; ☎ 033 675 11 19;
e info@oeschinensee.ch; www.oeschinensee.ch

AUSSERBERG
Tourist information
ℹ Sonnige Halden am Lötschberg, CH-3939; ☎
027 946 63 14; e info@sonnige-halden.ch; www.
sonnige-halden.ch

Where to stay
⌂ **Sonnenhalde*** (H)** CH-3938; ☎ 027 946
25 83; e info@sonnenhalde-ausserberg.ch; www.
sonnenhalde-ausserberg.ch
⌂ **Bahnhof**** CH-3938; ☎ 027 946 22 59;
e welcome@hotel-bahnhof.com; www.hotel-
bahnhof.com

EGGERBERG
Tourist information
ℹ See Ausserburg.

Where to stay
⌂ **Bergsonne**** CH-3939; ☎ 027 946 12 73;
e info@hotel-bergsonne.ch; www.hotel-
bergsonne.ch

12

Luzern

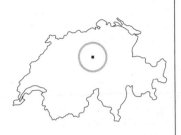

Luzern has become one of Switzerland's leading tourist centres largely by virtue of its location. Not only is it beautifully situated in a fold of gentle hills on the edge of one of Europe's finest lakes, it is also close to several of the country's best-known mountains. It grew up around a Benedictine convent founded c750 and achieved some autonomy when it became a parish in 1178, but it was the opening of the Gotthard Pass to trade that acted as a catalyst to Luzern's growth. No road existed along the lake shore until the construction of Axenstrasse in 1856, so all goods had to be shipped by barge between Flüelen and Luzern. Wealthy merchants, ambassadors, pilgrims and carriers made Luzern a place of preparation for the crossing of the Gotthard or of recovery after it. By 1450 Luzern had 400 inns.

Although this role made Luzern a cosmopolitan town, its inhabitants remained conservative and adhered to the Catholic faith during the Reformation, and later even invited the Jesuits to 're-convert' the canton. Some of the first to fight for Swiss independence came from the area around the lake, and Luzern was the first town to join the country's fledgling cantons in 1332 when it formed an alliance with the Forest Cantons of Schwyz, Uri and Unterwalden.

Contact with other cultures perhaps inclined many from the district to seek mercenary service in foreign wars, one of Luzern's most-visited monuments commemorating the Swiss who gave their lives in the defence of Louis XVI at the Tuileries in 1792 (see page 169). Another legacy of service abroad is one of Luzern's culinary specialities: the Kügelipastete, a creamed meat-filled pastry shell, was brought by returning mercenaries from Spain. Writers who came to Luzern as part of the 18th-century vogue for educational travel sometimes contributed to the town's fame, as did Goethe. Ironically Schiller, who used the William Tell legend to create a dramatic manifesto for political freedom (the play was the first production at Luzern's new theatre in 1838), never even visited Switzerland, relying on his wife's recollections of the country for background.

It was of course the construction of railways that increased significantly the number of tourists, the first railway opening from Basel in 1859. Luxurious hotels were built, many of them on Schweizerhofquai and Nationalquai along which a promenade was built. Part of this development was on land reclaimed from the lake, which entailed the destruction of a covered bridge similar in appearance to the famous Kapellbrücke. Some who had known Luzern for years were indignant at these changes. Turner chose Luzern as his base on several occasions in the 1840s and made numerous drawings and paintings of the town and the surrounding area. Retracing Turner's footsteps even in the 1860s, Ruskin could write of one of Turner's pictures as being 'a most precious drawing, all the more valuable, as the characteristic features of Lucerne are now being rapidly destroyed'.

These deplorable losses continued for much of the 19th century. Staggeringly there was a continual threat even to the Kapellbrücke. However, if Luzern's town planning was in less sensitive hands than Ruskin might have wished, much was in fact left to delight visitors a century and a half later.

GETTING THERE

Luzern station is a terminus, delightfully situated near the edge of the lake, though only a single arch remains of the original handsome station which was damaged by fire in 1971 and rebuilt in 1991. Though lacking the character of the old station, the new one is a model of convenience.

At the end of the platforms is a large concourse with the usual facilities. On a lower level, reached by escalator, and to the right are showers and banks of luggage lockers. For those catching a bus at the large terminal outside, a large board indicates the right platform (*Perron*) for the listed destinations. To the left on this lower level is a large shopping arcade and a pedestrian subway under the road to bring you up beside the post office on the corner of Bahnhofstrasse and Zentralstrasse.

The tourist office is reached by descending to the lower level under the concourse and bearing left to pass under the road, emerging near the corner of Frankenstrasse and Zentralstrasse. It has an excellent variety of publications on the city, including the *City Guide* (also found in most hotels). It is worth asking for special offers on, for example, a rail and cable car excursion to Mount Titlis.

GETTING AROUND

Steamers on the lake depart from quays on Bahnhofplatz, directly ahead from the end of the platforms and slightly to the right beyond the bus station.

The LucerneCard is available for 24, 48 and 72 hours and can be bought at the station, partner museums and the tourist office. It entitles the holder to unlimited free use of public transport in and around Luzern and a 50% discount on admission to partner museums.

Although bicycles can be hired from the station, Luzern is by no means an ideal city for cycling like Basel or Bern, partly because of the heavy traffic and a distinct lack of cycle paths, but also because it is easier to reach the main places of interest on foot. Bus tickets are discounted for more than one person, and a day card is available. The orange and white city bus is free and operates a circuit from the station, as follows: Municipal theatre–Mühleplatz–Hirschenplatz–Schwanenplatz–Kapellplatz–station.

Bus route N1 goes to Kriens, where a funicular climbs up to Sonnenberg (table 2515) and a gondola rises to Fräkmüntegg (table 2516) from where a cable car makes the leap up to Pilatus Kulm (table 2517). From there you can return to Luzern using the rack railway and either the SBB line or a steamer (see *Chapter 13*). For details of buses, see www.vbl.ch.

Bicycle hire from the station.

TOURIST INFORMATION

i Zentralstrasse 5, CH-6003; ℡ 041 227 17 17;
e luzern@luzern.com; www.luzern.com; ⊕ May–
Oct 08.30–17.00 Mon–Fri, 09.00–17.00 Sat

WHERE TO STAY

Numerous hotels; close to the station are:

⌂ **Ameron Hotel Flora****** Seidenhofstrasse 5, CH-6002; ☎041 227 66 66; e flora@ameronhotels.com; www.flora-hotel.ch

⌂ **Monopol**** (H)** Pilatusstrasse 1, CH-6002; ☎041 226 43 43; e mail@monopolluzern.ch; www.monopolluzern.ch

⌂ **Romantik Hotel Wilden Mann****** **(H)** Bahnhofstrasse 30, CH-6000; ☎041 210 16 66; e mail@wilden-mann.ch; www.wilden-mann.ch. Made up of 7 carefully renovated town houses, the oldest dating from 1517.

⌂ **Alpina***** Frankenstrasse 6, CH-6003; ☎041 210 00 77; e info@alpina-luzern.ch; www.alpina-luzern.ch

⌂ **Waldstätterhof***** Zentralstrasse 4, CH-6003; ☎041 227 12 71; e info@hotel-waldstaetterhof.ch; www.hotel-waldstaetterhof.ch

A hotel within walking distance is:

⌂ **Grand Hotel National******* **(H)** Haldenstrasse 4, CH-6006; ☎041 419 09 09; e info@national-luzern.ch; www.national-luzern.ch
Luzern's main roads are busy and noisy with traffic, so hotels on quieter streets may be preferred. A few suggestions are:

⌂ **Hotel des Balances**** (H)** Weinmarkt, CH-6004; ☎041 418 28 28; e info@balances.ch; www.balances.ch

⌂ **Rebstock**** (H)** St Leodegarstrasse 3, CH-6006; ☎041 417 18 19; e hotel@rebstock-luzern.ch; www.rebstock-luzern.ch

⌂ **Des Alpes***** Furrengasse 3, CH-6004; ☎041 417 20 60; e info@desalpes-luzern.ch; www.desalpes-luzern.ch

⌂ **Zum Weissen Kreuz***** (H)** Furrengasse 19, CH-6004; ☎041 418 82 20; e contact@altstadthotelluzern.ch; www.hotel-wkreuz.ch

WHERE TO EAT

✕ **Burgerstube** Romantik Hotel Wilden Mann, Bahnhofstrasse 30; ☎041 210 16 66
✕ **Old Swiss House** Löwenplatz 4; ☎041 410 61 71

✕ **Rathaus Brauerei** Unter der Egg 2; ☎041 410 52 57
✕ **Schiff** Unter der Egg 8; ☎041 418 52 52
✕ **Wiederkehr** Zürichstrasse 16; ☎041 410 41 44

WHAT TO SEE

EXPLORING THE OLD TOWN Luzern is a compact city, and most of its principal attractions can be reached on foot or by a short bus journey. The historic core of the city is pedestrianised and a booklet of suggested walks taking in the best buildings is available from the tourist office. Besides these buildings there are scores of smaller vernacular buildings and small courtyards with fountains, which make a stroll round the traffic-free parts of Luzern such a pleasure.

The station (and tourist office) is only a few minutes' walk from Luzern's most famous attraction, the **Chapel Bridge (Kapellbrücke)**; from both you can see the end of the main road bridge across the River Reuss where it leaves the lake. Make for it and the Chapel Bridge is to the left. Built in the first half of the 14th century and largely destroyed by a tragic fire in August 1993, the bridge formed part of the city fortifications and was named after St Peter's chapel at the northern end of the bridge. The Water Tower near the south end of the bridge was built c1300 and used at various times as a treasury, archive, prison and torture chamber.

Naturally the bridge had been rebuilt many times between its construction and the fire, but it was the loss of most of the paintings that decorated the bridge which was particularly sad. However, even these were the subject of repeated restoration and replacement. The originals were executed in the early 17th century and used Swiss history and Christianity as the principal themes. Although the bridge has been shortened by 44m (144ft) since it was built, it survived several threats of

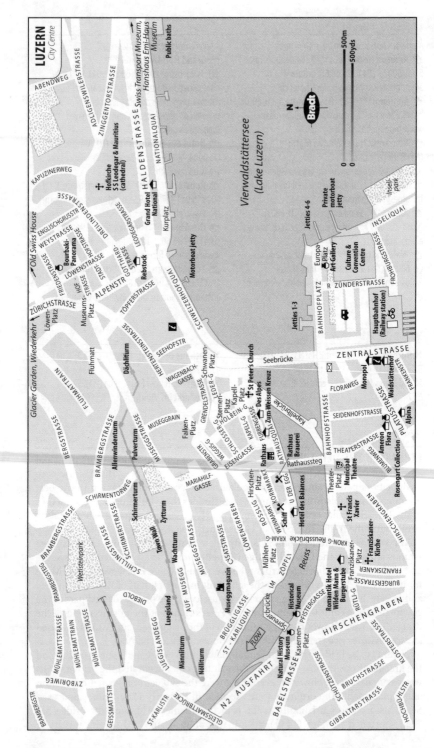

LUZERN
City Centre

Bradt

N

0   500m
0   500yds

Glacier Garden, Wiederkehr
Old Swiss House

ZÜRICHSTRASSE

ABENDWEG

ADLIGENSWILERSTRASSE

KAPUZINERWEG

ZINGGENTORSTRASSE

Swiss Transport Museum,
Hanshaus Erni-Haus
Museum

Public baths

HALDENSTRASSE

NATIONALQUAI

Hofkirche
SS Leodegar & Mauritius
(cathedral)

Grand Hotel
National

Kurplatz

Motorboat jetty

Vierwaldstättersee
(Lake Luzern)

ENGLISCHGRUSSTR

WEYSTRASSE

FRIEDENSTRASSE

DREILINDENSTRASSE

Bourbaki
Panorama

LÖWENSTRASSE

LEODEGARSTRASSE

GOTTHARD
STRASSE

STADT-
HOF-
STRASSE

MUSEUMS-
STRASSE

ALPENSTR

TÖPFERSTRASSE

Rebstock

SCHWEIZERHOFQUAI

Löwen-
Platz

Fluhmatt

FLUHMATTRAIN

Dächliturm

SEEHOFSTR

HETTENSTEINSTRASSE

WAGENBACH-
GASSE

St Peter's Church

Seebrücke

BRAMBERGSTRASSE

BERGSTRASSE

Pulverturm

MUSEGGSTRASSE

MUSEGGRAIN

Falken-
Platz

GRENDELSTRASSE

LEDER-G

STEMEN-
HOLBEIN-G

Platz

KAPELL-
Platz

KAPELLG

Des Alpes

Zum Weissen Kreuz

Kapellbrücke

Allenwindenturm

SCHLOSSER-
SCHWEBST

WEGGIS-G

GRABENSTR

EISENGASSE

FÜRENGASSE

RATHAUSQUAI

Rathaus

Rathaus
Brauerei

Rathaussteg

Jetties 1-3

BAHNHOFPLATZ

R ZÜNDERSTRASSE

Europa
Platz

Art Gallery

Culture &
Convention
Centre

Private
motorboat
jetty

INSELIQUAI

Insel-
park

FROHBURGSTRASSE

Hauptbahnhof
(Railway station)

ZENTRALSTRASSE

FLORAWEG

Monopol

Waldstätterhof

FRANKENSTR

PILATUSSTRASSE

Alpina

Ameron

Flora

Rosengart Collection

SEIDENHOFSTRASSE

THEATERSTRASSE

BAHNHOFSTRASSE

Theater-
Platz

Municipal
Theatre

BLÜMLIWEG

HIRSCHENGRABEN

St Francis
Xavier

Franziskaner-
Platz

Franziskaner-
Kirche

FRANZISKANER

BURGERSTRASSE

RÜTLI-G

HIRSCHENGRABEN

SCHIRMENTORWEG

SCHIRMERSTRASSE

SCHILLINGSTRASSE

Town Wall

Schirmerturm

Zytturm

Weinsteinpark

Wachtturm

MARIAHILF-
GASSE

LÖWENGRABEN

WEINMARKT

KORNMARKT

RÖSSLIG

HIRSCHEN-
Platz

U DER EGG

Hotel des Balances

KRON-G

Mühlen
Platz

ZÖPFLI

KRAM-G

Reussbrücke

Reuss

Romantik Hotel
Wilden Mann &
Burgerstube

Historical
Museum

PFISTERGASSE

Kasernen-
Platz

Natural History
Museum

FLOW

N2 AUSFAHRT

BASELSTRASSE

SCHÜTZENSTRASSE

BRUCHSTRASSE

GIBRALTARSTRASSE

HOCHBÜHLSTR

KLOSTERSTRASSE

Mänliturm

Nölliturm

ST. KARLIQUAI

ST-KARLISTR

GEISSMATTSTR

GLEISSMATTBRÜCKE

MÜHLEMATTSTRASSE

MÜHLEMATTRAIN

ZYBÖRIWEG

BRAMBERGSTR

BRAMBERGSTEG

DIEBOLD

AUF MUSEGG

Luegisland

LUEGISLANDEGG

IM

Spreuer
brücke

Musegg-
magazin

CSATSTRASSE

MUSEGGSTRASSE

MUSEGGGSTRASSE

168

demolition during the 19th century. After the 1993 fire, the fabric of the bridge was restored within months, a decision being taken not to use distressed materials but to allow them to weather naturally.

From the southern, Bahnhofstrasse end of the bridge continue walking along the riverbank away from the lake, past the Municipal Theatre to the **Jesuit Church of St Francis Xavier**. This was only one of many Jesuit buildings in Luzern, their college at one time teaching about 400 pupils. Work on Switzerland's first large Baroque church began in 1666, and it was consecrated in 1672. The identity of the architect is not known. Inside the shell niche on the façade stands a figure of St Francis Xavier. The Jesuit origins are evident in the absence of a choir. The transition from the dark porch into the bright white interior is striking. The stucco-work and delicate colours are restrained, creating a beautiful interior, dominated by the monumental high altar built in 1681 of red stucco marble. A detailed English guidebook is available.

The building to the west is part of the old Jesuit college, adjacent to the Ritterscher Palast, and notable for its deeply chamfered rustication. It was built in 1557 for the mayor and now houses cantonal offices. Its lovely arcaded courtyard can be visited.

Behind the college and palace is the **Gothic Franciscan church**, built c1270–80. It has one of Switzerland's most ornate pulpits, early 17th-century stucco and frescoes representing Luzern's military conquests.

Continuing along the riverbank, at the end of the **Spreuerbrücke (Mill Bridge)** is the Historical Museum. The Spreuer Bridge was built in 1408 as part of the town's fortifications; in 1626–35 Kaspar Meglinger added a series of paintings representing the Dance of Death.

A worthwhile but time-consuming diversion here was a journey to Hotel Château Gütsch on the Gütschbahn, a funicular built specially to serve the hotel in 1884. However, the hotel is currently closed. It was at a pension on a site near Hotel Gütsch in 1868 that Queen Victoria stayed with Prince Arthur and Princess Louise.

Cross the river by the Geissmattbrücke and turn right to reach the lowest of the towers on the surviving stretch of town wall, the Nölliturm. The nine surviving towers and wall between them are a fragment of the **town walls**, built in 1350–1408 and largely torn down during the 19th century. The wall is a divide between old and new Luzern, and cows still graze the slopes to the north, up which an enemy would have attacked. Some of the towers can be climbed; it is quite an ascent up the series of open steps but worth it for the view on a clear day. If you have time or energy only for one, the Zytturm is probably the most interesting on account of its 16th-century clock; the mechanism is open to view, revealing its long pulleys and crude weights in the form of lumps of rock. The Watchturm provides access to the wall-walk, but its top is sealed off.

Following the walls to the end brings you to Museumsplatz. Cross over into Hofstrasse and left into Löwenstrasse, past the Bourbaki-Panorama (see *Museums*) to the Lion Monument. Mark Twain was usually ready to satirise or pour scorn on much that he saw in his travels, but he regarded this monument as 'the most mournful and moving piece of stone in the world'. The dying lion was carved out of the rock wall of a quarry in 1821 by Lukas Ahorn to a model by Bertel Thorwaldsen, to commemorate the 796 officers and men of the Swiss guard who died in 1792 defending Louis XVI and Marie-Antoinette when the Tuileries were stormed by the mob during the French Revolution.

Retrace your steps and turn left past the Old Swiss House restaurant and then right down Weystrasse to reach the cathedral, regarded as the most important Renaissance church building in Switzerland. The site on which the Hofkirche (of SS

Leodegar and Mauritius) stands was used from the 8th century for a Benedictine monastery. The twin, finely tapering spires and their supporting square towers date from the 15th century and survived a fire in 1633 that destroyed the rest of the church. The replacement was consecrated in 1644 and contains some fine altars and carved pews. An arcaded churchyard surrounds the cathedral.

Proceed down the steps and directly ahead along Schweizerhofquai. The Neo-classical Schweizerhof was built in 1845, the first of the large hotels after part of this area was reclaimed from the lake. Tolstoy stayed here in 1857 and wrote the short story *Lucerne*. Wagner stayed two years later while finishing *Tristan and Isolde*.

Bear left towards the bridge and turn right along the pedestrianised north bank of the river (most of this quarter of Luzern has been pedestrianised). The first building is the Zur Gilgen House; this ancient and much-rebuilt house contains the country's oldest private library, preserved in its original home. Its owner, the humanist Ludwig Zur Gilgen, died in 1577. The tower was once part of the town defences.

Just beyond the Kapellbrücke is St Peter's Church which gave the bridge its name. Dating from the 12th century but much rebuilt, St Peter's is the oldest church within the town wall.

On the right just before the pedestrian bridge is the open-arcaded Rathaus, built in 1602–06 in Italian Renaissance style but with a Bernese farmhouse roof. Markets are still held here in the arcades on Tuesday and Saturday mornings. Turn right here into Kornmarkt on which the Rathaus has a tower with six-sided turrets at the corners.

Another diversion can be taken to look at the enormous storehouse that can be seen from Château Gütsch. Turn left into Weinmarkt, briefly right into Kramgasse and left into Mühlenplatz. Looking west along the river, two roads lead out of the square. Take the upper road, Brüggligasse, and turn right into Museggstrasse to one of old Luzern's largest buildings. The huge Museggmagazin was built in 1685–86 to house supplies of corn and salt.

Returning to Kornmarkt, walk along Kapellgasse to reach Kapellplatz and the Seebrücke.

MARKETS The colourful fruit and vegetable market is held on Tuesday and Saturday mornings from 06.00 under the arcades of the Rathaus beside the River Reuss. A handicrafts market is held from 07.00 to 16.00 on the first Saturday of the month (April–December) on Weinmarkt. A flea market is held every Saturday (May–Oct) from 07.00 on the Unter Burgerstrasse/Reusssteg. A Christmas Market is held in Mühleplatz from 10.00 to 21.00.

MUSEUMS

Art Gallery (Kunstmuseum) (*Europaplatz 1, immediately to right of station;* ❧ *041 226 78 00; www.kunstmuseumluzern.ch;* ⊕ *10.00–17.00 (18.00 Jul–late Oct) Tue–Sun, 10.00–20.00 Wed; admission charge*) Close to the main station, the original Art Gallery was opened in 1933 but moved in 2000 into the striking new Culture and Convention Centre designed by Jean Nouvel. Its collection focuses on Swiss art from the 16th to 20th centuries, with smaller sections on Dutch and Flemish 17th-century paintings, 20th-century German and French expressionist works, and contemporary art. However, very little if any of this permanent collection is on display, since the museum has switched to temporary exhibitions only, some of very esoteric appeal. This must disappoint many visitors, as its fine Swiss collection of portraits and landscapes provided an excellent insight into the way artists have seen the country through the centuries.

Swiss Transport Museum (Verkehrshaus) (*Lidostrasse 5;* ✆ *041 370 44 44; www.verkehrshaus.ch;* ⊕ *April–Oct 10.00–18.00 daily; Nov–Mar 10.00–17.00 daily; admission charge; bus 6 or 8 from station to Wurzenbach*) Europe's largest transport museum could easily take a full day for anyone interested in the subject. Opened in 1959 and twice enlarged since, it attracts about half a million visitors a year. It includes not only rail, air, water and road transport but also space travel, telecommunications, tourism, a Cosmorama and Planetarium. Switzerland's first IMAX film theatre opened at the museum in 1996. The rail and water sections are understandably almost entirely Swiss-oriented, but the other sections are more international, with 35 aircraft from Britain, the United States, France and the Netherlands as well as Switzerland, and cars from a similar range of countries. Labels to exhibits are in four languages, including English.

The railway section traces the history of railways in Switzerland from the first line into the country, across the border from France to Basel, to today's signalling system at Luzern station. Besides some superb, large-scale models and railway memorabilia, it has 60 original steam and electric locomotives, carriages, trams, funiculars and sectioned rack locomotive. There is a huge, working, scale model of the northern approach to the Gotthard from Erstfeld to Göschenen that children (and lots of adults) are reluctant to leave.

Hans Erni-Haus Museum (*adjacent to Swiss Transport Museum above; same details*) Over 300 works by this Swiss artist are on display, revealing the special relationship he had with technology.

Rosengart Collection (*Pilatusstrasse 10, 3min walk from main station;* ✆ *041 220 16 60; www.rosengart.ch;* ⊕ *Apr–Oct 10.00–18.00 daily, Nov–Mar 11.00–17.00 daily; admission charge*) Major collection of works by Picasso and Klee and 20 other masters, including Cézanne, Monet, Matisse, Braque, Léger and Miró, in an imaginatively converted former bank. The gallery includes the remarkably intimate portraits of Picasso *en famille*, which used to be displayed in Musée Picasso.

Bourbaki-Panorama (*Löwenplatz 18, close to Lion Monument;* ✆ *041 412 30 30; www.bourbakipanorama.ch;* ⊕ *Apr–Oct 09.00–18.00 daily; Nov–Mar 09.00–17.00 daily; admission charge; bus 1, 19, 22 or 23 to Löwenplatz*) This should not be missed by anyone interested in 19th-century history or epic canvases – it is the largest round mural in the world, covering 1,100m² (11,840sq ft). It depicts a poignant moment in the history of French arms when the Eastern Army under General Bourbaki sought asylum in Switzerland after its defeat at the hands of the Prussians in early 1871. About 88,000 exhausted men crossed the border at Les Verrières, west of Neuchâtel, where they were disarmed and given help by local people and by the recently founded Red Cross in its first act of humanitarian aid. This extraordinary canvas took seven painters two years to complete and came to Luzern in 1889 after ten years on display in Geneva. If you arrive when it opens, you are likely to have a private view and can request the English recorded commentary.

Richard Wagner Museum (*Richard Wagnerweg 27;* ✆ *041 360 23 70; www. richard-wagner-museum.ch;* ⊕ *mid-Mar–Nov 10.00–noon & 14.00–17.00 Tue–Sun; admission charge; bus 6, 7 or 8 from station to Wartegg, 10min, then follow signs, a pleasant 10min walk*) Situated at Tribschen in a house overlooking the lake and still surrounded by trees and fields grazed by cows, the museum occupies the house Wagner rented from April 1866 until 1872. He married Cosima von Bülow

(Liszt's daughter) in 1868, and the birth of their son Siegfried followed a year later. Nietzsche was staying at Tribschen the night Siegfried was born. Wagner expressed his joy in the *Siegfried Idyll* which was given its first performance at Tribschen on Christmas Day 1870. The ground-floor rooms are filled with photographs, letters, scores, paintings and other memorabilia, all labelled in German, French and English. Oddly there is no general introduction to Wagner's time in Luzern, and the only guidebook is the price of a hardback. Upstairs there is a large collection of European, African and oriental musical instruments, but labels are in German only.

Historical Museum (*Pfistergasse 24;* ✆ *041 228 54 24;* ⊕ *10.00–17.00 Tue–Sun; admission charge*) Situated in the old arsenal, this collection relating to Luzern's history includes arms and armour, sculptures, religious and secular artworks, glass and jewellery as well as a film (English commentary) about the city. Visitors are given a sophisticated hand-held device that allows you to read a barcode to display on a small screen information about the object.

Glacier Garden (Gletschergarten) (*Denkmalstrasse 4;* ✆ *041 410 43 40; www. gletschergarten.ch;* ⊕ *Apr–Oct 09.00–18.00 daily; Nov–Mar 10.00–17.00 daily; admission charge; bus 1 from station to Löwenplatz or bus 2 from Transport Museum to Luzernerhof*) Discovered in 1872, the 'garden' contains various legacies of the last ice age, such as huge boulders, the largest glacial pot-hole ever found, with a depth of over 9m (30ft), and petrified palm leaves and seashells from 20 million years ago when Luzern had a subtropical beach on the sea. A museum contains a model of the city in 1792 and the oldest relief map of the country. Children revel in the Alhambra-style labyrinth of mirrors, made in 1896 for the Swiss National Exhibition in Geneva; it has been at the Glacier Garden since 1899.

Natural History Museum (*Kasernenplatz 6;* ✆ *041 228 54 11;* ⊕ *10.00–17.00 Tue–Sun; admission charge; bus 2, 9, 12 or 18 to Kasernenplatz*) The liveliness of the presentation at this museum has won it the European 'Museum of the Year' prize. It covers archaeology and geology as well as aquariums and terrariums, an educational forest path and special exhibitions. Various animals can be seen in aquariums and terrariums, and there is a graphic display about the Alps in prehistoric times.

FESTIVALS The Luzern Festival was founded in 1932 with the help of Arturo Toscanini, who conducted the first concert. Held in August–September, the principal concerts are given in Luzern's magnificent new 1,840-seat concert hall in the Culture and Convention Centre, designed by Jean Nouvel and opened in August 1998. The Festival attracts the world's best soloists, such as Heinrich Schiff and Maria João Pires, and orchestras of the calibre of the Royal Concertgebouw, Berlin Philharmonic and Vienna Philharmonic. The centre is very close to the station. Tickets are available from late March when the programme is published. The Golden Rose television festival is also held here, in April/May, following its transfer from Montreux in 2004.

In February there is a Blue Balls Festival of eclectic music styles, with a Blues Festival and the Luzern piano festival in November.

A five-day carnival is held in February, with colourful and noisy street processions, and in June or July the Altstadtfest gives an opportunity to hear local bands, dance and eat Swiss specialities.

13

Around Luzern

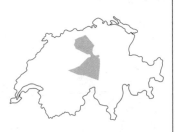

As Turner discovered, even before there was more than a rudimentary transport infrastructure, Luzern is unusually well placed for numerous excursions. Moreover, many of them are on the itineraries of first-time visitors to the country.

LAKE LUZERN (VIERWALDSTÄTTERSEE)

Lake Luzern's reputation as one of Europe's most beautiful stretches of inland water owes much to its irregular shape, creating constantly changing views, and to the grandeur of the mountains that encompass it. The shore ranges from vertiginous cliffs to gently undulating pasture grazed by cows. Although houses cover the eastern shore for some way after leaving Luzern and there are some unfortunate stretches of road visible between Brunnen and Flüelen, the lake remains remarkably unspoilt.

The lake is 38km (24 miles) long from Luzern to Flüelen, and its deepest point is 214m (702ft) between Beckenried and Gersau. It is fed principally by the River Reuss, at Flüelen, which flows out at Luzern, and also by the rivers Engelberger Aa near Buochs and the Muota at Brunnen. Although the entire lake is referred to as the Vierwaldstättersee, strictly speaking the name applies to the main body of water, the section beyond the narrows between Brunnen and Treib being known as Urner See, or the Lake of Uri, and that beyond the bridge at Stansstad being the Alpnacher See.

Its German name means 'Lake of the Four Forest States' referring to the country's original cantons – Luzern, Schwyz, Unterwalden and Uri. The opening of the Gotthard Pass and the Schöllenen gorge to packhorses in 1230–40 made the lake a major artery for traffic between Italy and northern Europe. For centuries the boatmen, organised into guilds, enjoyed privileges granted by the cantons, and their business increased with the opening of a road over the Gotthard in 1830 and the subsequent mail coach services.

A threat appeared in 1837 in the form of the first steamship, which was greeted with a hail of stones at Flüelen and a threat to the captain of imprisonment if anyone dared to land. Sense prevailed and steamship services by various companies flourished, until 1869 when they amalgamated to form the company that still runs all services on the lake. The company has the world's largest fleet of passenger-carrying ships on an inland lake, with a capacity of over 13,000 people. Besides the 15 modern vessels there are five paddle steamers: *Uri* (1901), which is the oldest working paddle steamer in Switzerland, *Unterwalden* (1902), *Schiller* (1906), *Gallia* (1913) and *Stadt Luzern III* (1928). Once coal-fired, all have been converted to oil-firing, but the engine rooms are open to view from a gallery above them and their immaculate condition is a tribute to the engineers who care for them. The *Uri* and the *Unterwalden* have telescoping funnels which enable them to pass under the rail and road bridge at Stansstad to reach Alpnachstad.

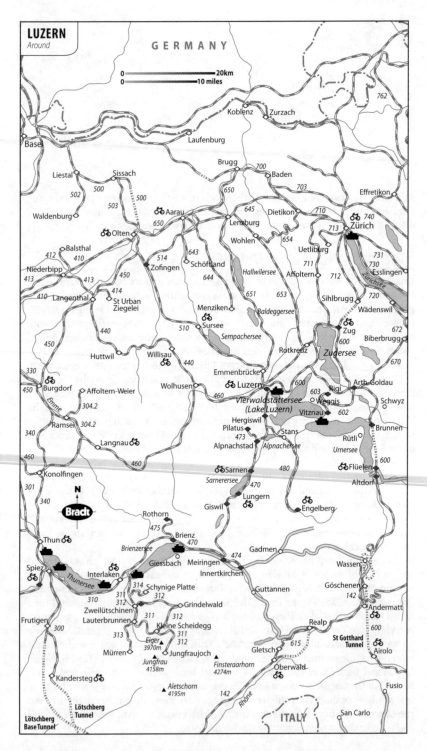

Two other paddle steamers survive as eating establishments: the *Wilhelm Tell* (1908) is moored at Luzern as a floating restaurant; and the *Rigi* (1848), which, unusually for a Swiss ship, was built in London by Ditchborne & Mare and may be seen serving as a café on dry land outside the Transport Museum (see *Chapter 12*).

Breakfast or lunch on the paddlers is a pleasure not to be missed; their Empire- or Rococo-style dining rooms have been sensitively restored and the food is remarkably good. Evening dinner cruises with music and dancing are also available on modern vessels. The shipping company even brews its own craft-brewed beer; ask for a Urbräu.

The boats serve 33 points on the lake; most are substantial villages but some are delightfully small with a cluster of chalets and footpaths radiating from a tiny pier. Eight piers serve points on the Swiss Path between Rütli and Brunnen (see page 176). An entire holiday could be spent using the steamer services to reach the numerous attractions around the lake, some of which are suggested here, taking the lake in a clockwise direction from Luzern:

- **Verkehrshaus-Lido** The pier serving Luzern Transport Museum (see *Chapter 12*, page 171).
- **Meggenhorn** Schloss Meggenhorn (⊕ *Apr–Oct tours at 12.30, 13.30 & 14.30 on Sun; admission charge; bus 24 from Luzern*) was rebuilt in the style of a French Renaissance château in 1868–70 with adjacent Gothic chapel and a romantic boathouse on the shore.
- **Meggen** On a small island is a chapel dedicated to the patron saint of mariners, St Niklaus.
- **Küssnacht** See Luzern–Airolo table 600, page 195.
- **Weggis** Mark Twain spent several months of 1897 at this summer resort, bestowing the plaudit: 'This is the most charming place we have ever lived in for repose and restfulness.' Sheltered by Mt Rigi, it has a particularly mild climate, enabling it to supply Luzern with vegetables. A cable car 15 minutes' walk from the boat goes to Rigi Kaltbad (table 2566).
- **Vitznau** Another summer resort and the lower station of the Rigi Railway (see page 177). Close to the pier is one of the world's few crossbow workshops, taking you back to the 14th century when these lethal weapons were at their zenith. You can also visit the artillery fortress built inside Mt Rigi as part of the Gotthard defence during World War II. You can even stay the night in underground accommodation with dinner and breakfast provided (*www.festung-vitznau.ch*). Tours of both can be booked through the tourist information centre (⟍ *041/398 00 35;* e *info.vitznau@wvrt.ch*).
- **Gersau** This little town was politically independent from 1390 to 1798, the smallest republic in the world. It had its own laws, tax authorities and set of gallows. Some good stone and all-wooden houses can be seen.
- **Brunnen, Sisikon** and **Flüelen** See Luzern–Airolo table 600, page 195.
- **Bauen** A village of numerous wooden houses and the birthplace of Alberik Zwyssig, composer of the Swiss national anthem.
- **Rütli** The Rütli meadow, regarded as the cradle of Swiss democracy, can be visited only by boat and the tree-shrouded landing stage. According to tradition, it was here, on 7 November 1307, that representatives of the three founder cantons took an oath confirming the Everlasting League of 1291. Schoolchildren were primarily responsible for collecting sufficient funds in around 1860 to save the meadow from having a hotel built on it (little was sacred then in the pursuit of profit). Accordingly the Rütli is considered to

belong to the children of Switzerland. It was the scene of a second symbolic meeting in 1940 when the Swiss general Henri Guisan summoned senior commanders to discuss the defence of the country against invasion. Between Rütli and Treib is the obelisk erected in 1859 to the memory of Friedrich Schiller; although the playwright never visited Switzerland, relying on his wife's recollections, it was his *Wilhelm Tell* of 1804 that did the most to propagate the legend, an invaluable contribution to 19th-century tourism in particular.

- **Treib** The boatman's house, inn and tiny harbour have offered boatmen sanctuary from storms since the 14th century. The present house dates from 1659. A funicular ascends from a station just by the jetty up to the small resort of Seelisberg (see table 2590).
- **Beckenried** A pilgrimage chapel of 1700–01 above the lake is a landmark. Five minutes' walk from the boat is the cable car to Klewenalp (see table 2556), from which the Jura and Black Forest can be seen. Skiing in winter.
- **Kehrsiten-Bürgenstock** A minute's walk from the steamer is the funicular up to the Bürgenstock (see table 2554) where there are several exclusive hotels. The journey provides open views of the lake. Providing you have a reasonable head for heights, there is a dramatic path around the mountain from the summer resort. Known as the Felsenweg, the path towards the end looks down a sheer drop of 700m (2,296ft) before turning into the cliff face to give access to Europe's tallest lift. Named the Hammetschwand-Lift and built in 1903–05, this begins inside the rock but soon emerges, rising for 165m (540ft) inside a lattice steel structure that is bracketed out from the cliff, ending at the highest point of the mountain, 1,128m (3,700ft).
- **Stansstad** See Luzern–Stans–Engelberg table 480, page 183.
- **Alpnachstad** See Luzern–Meiringen table 470, page 187.
- **Tribschen** A convenient stage for Wagner's house (see *Chapter 12*, page 171).

GETTING AROUND
Lake Luzern Navigation Co Werftestrasse 5, CH-6002; ☎ 041 367 67 67; e info@lakelucerne.ch; www.lakelucerne.ch

Tickets Eurail, Swiss Pass and Swiss Card are also valid on the boats.

WEGGIS
Tourist information
ℹ Seestrasse 5, CH-6353; ☎ 041 227 18 00; e weggis@luzern.com; www.wvrt.ch; ⊕ May–Sep 08.30–18.00 Mon–Fri, 09.00–16.00 Sat–Sun; Oct–Apr 08.30–noon & 13.00–17.30 Mon–Fri

Where to stay
Numerous hotels; close to the boat station are:
⌂ **Seehof Hotel du Lac*** (H)**
Gotthardstrasse 4, CH-6353; ☎ 041 390 11 51; e info@hotel-du-lac.ch; www.hotel-du-lac.ch
⌂ **SeeHotel Gotthard-Schönau*** (H)**
Gotthardstrasse 11, CH-6353; ☎ 041 390 21 14; e gotthard@gotthard-weggis.ch; www.gotthard-weggis.ch

THE SWISS PATH

Few of Switzerland's thousands of footpaths are given a name but an exception was made in 1991 when this 35km (22 miles) route beside the Lake of Uri was created to mark the 700th anniversary of the Swiss Confederation. Each canton assumed responsibility for a section, their lengths determined by the population of the cantons. Stretching from Brunnen to Rütli, the well-signed path can be joined or left at eight steamer piers, three SBB stations, numerous bus stops and the Treib–Seelisberg funicular. It is a wonderfully varied walk, some sections being beside the water, others giving wide panoramas over the lake and nearby mountains. Good walking boots or shoes are needed, and some sections are suitable for wheelchairs.

VITZNAU–RIGI Table 603

The Rigi is one of Switzerland's oldest tourist attractions, and has long been referred to as the Queen of the Mountains. Baedeker accorded it the seldom-awarded two stars, and encapsulated the reason for its popularity: 'Owing to its isolated situation, the Rigi commands a most extensive view, 300 M[iles, 480km] in circumference, and unsurpassed for beauty in Switzerland.' However subjective the superlative, the Rigi has seen steadily greater numbers since peace returned to Europe in 1815, the first inn being erected on the Kulm in the following year. It is therefore appropriate that this line should have been the first rack railway in Europe, opened to Rigi Staffelhöhe in 1871 and to the Kulm in 1873. The standard-gauge Vitznau–Rigi Bahn (VRB) was engineered by Niklaus Riggenbach, who had been to the United States to see the world's first mountain railway up Mount Washington. The first locomotives were vertical-boilered, built at Riggenbach's Olten workshops, but were steadily converted to horizontal-boiler machines. The line was electrified in 1937 but the most modern steam locomotives, Nos 16–17 (1923 and 1925) were kept and still work special trains up the mountain. One of the 1873-built steam locomotives survives and has been on display at the Luzern Transport Museum, but was returned to working order for special runs up the mountain on the 125th anniversary of the railway in 1996. The summer and winter resorts served by the two railways (see Arth–Rigi, page 179) have the benefit of being traffic-free – there are no roads on the mountain. Circular tickets with various permutations are available from Luzern, and unlike most mountain railways there is no surcharge for Swiss Pass holders. Sit on the left.

The location of the station at Vitznau is idyllic: close to the lake shore at an elbow in the Vierwaldstättersee, it is only a couple of minutes' walk from the steamer jetty. The climb starts from the end of the platform, the ruling gradient being 1 in 4. The line curves up through woods and across the Schnurtobel Viaduct; this was built in 1957–58 to replace Riggenbach's structure which had itself been strengthened over the years. When Mark Twain crossed, it had only two supports:

> There is nothing to interrupt the view or the breeze; it is like inspecting the world on the wing. However, to be exact, there is one place where the serenity lapses for a while; this is while one is crossing the Schnurtobel Bridge; a frail structure which swings its gossamer frame down through the dizzy air, over a gorge, like a vagrant spider-strand. One has no difficulty in remembering his sins while the train is creeping down this bridge: and he repents of them, too; though he sees, when he gets to Vitznau, that he need not have done it, the bridge was perfectly safe.

Tiny platforms for milk churns may be seen beside the line, some with old-fashioned churns that still bring the milk down from the alpine cows. On the left just before **Romiti Felsentor** a huge tree trunk has been hollowed out to create a drinking trough for cattle. The woods and meadows are threaded by paths that tempt walkers to break the journey, and at **Rigi Kaltbad-First** a footpath has been created out of a railway that ran to Rigi-First and Rigi-Scheidegg (1 hour 50 minutes). Opened in 1874 as an excursion railway that afforded wonderful views, the metre-gauge 7km (4½ miles) line closed in 1931 and its three tank engines were sold. The railway went off to the right (east) of the VRB station. It makes a good walk, with a short tunnel at Weissenegg, a viaduct at Unterstetten and a bogie coach to be seen en route. From Scheidegg, the cable car can be taken down to Kräbel (table 2568), a station on the Arth–Rigi Railway. A series of walks for the area is suggested in an English-language leaflet, listed according to the duration of the walk.

Rigi Kaltbad became a larger resort than the Kulm, where limited space and the inappropriateness of large-scale building made expansion impossible and undesirable. The beneficial properties of the water at Kaltbad were discovered in 1585, but it was not until the 18th century that it became a health resort for pilgrims, the first hostelry being authorised in 1756. Flaubert came here on doctor's orders in 1874. In 2012 a new public spa designed by Mario Botta was opened. The striking building contains mineral baths open to everyone and the spa, which is reserved for adults over 16. The baths have an indoor pool (35°C) filled with mineral-rich water from the Three Sisters Springs. The rear of the pool affords a spectacular view of the mountains and views from the outdoor pool are even more magnificent. The spa area offers the usual variety of treatments and facilities such as the herbal sauna and the crystal spa in which guests float in warm water 9m under the town square looking up through one of the 3.5m-high crystal skylights.

A cable car descends from Rigi Kaltbad to Weggis (table 2566), from where it is a 15-minute walk to the steamer.

As the summit is approached, the line from Arth can be seen swinging in on the right, and the two run side by side into **Rigi Kulm**. The mountain actually has five summits, ranging in height from 1,551 to 1,800m (5,088 to 5,905ft).

In the 19th and early 20th centuries, most tourists wanted to see at least one sunrise from the summit of a mountain, doubtless influenced by the Romantic movement and the paintings of such artists as Caspar David Friedrich. Where better than from the Rigi, with its exceptional panorama? In autumn the valleys are often shrouded in mist, the peaks rising majestically from a blanket of cloud. It was on such a visit to the Rigi that Wagner heard the alphorn that inspired the herdsman's horn in the third act of *Tristan*. Turner made several paintings of the mountain.

The idea for a hotel on the Kulm came from the painter Heinrich Keller (1778–1862) who was staying down at Klösterli; he suggested to his landlord that he build a hotel at the top so that he wouldn't have to go up and down each day to paint. The landlord obliged and the first hotel opened in 1816. The grandest hotel on the Kulm was the Hotel Schreiber, completed in 1875 with accommodation for about 300 guests. Both Escoffier and Ritz worked there, Ritz having the idea of keeping guests warm by heating stones in the ovens and placing them under cushions. Ludwig II of Bavaria was an early guest, and the hotel flourished in the years before World War I. Sometimes families would come for the whole summer, bringing servants with them. On 8 August 1903, for example, 237 people were staying from 17 countries: 72 Germans, 47 French, 30 Americans, 21 Russians, 12 Dutch, 11 Swiss, ten Austrians, nine Italians, six Belgians, five English, four Poles, two Egyptians, two Spanish, two from then semi-independent Trieste, two Danes, one Brazilian and one Czech. In the same month the hotel required 14,100 small loaves of bread, 1,980kg (nearly 2 tonnes) of chicken and 4,500 litres of beer.

Changing fashions and economic circumstances meant that the capacity of the old hotel exceeded demand, so the present hotel was built in 1950–54 and the old one dismantled. Some of the fittings from the old hotel, such as mirrors and posters, were used in the new one. For those in search of quiet and a sense of being 'away from it all', a night on the bare mountain would be hard to better (once the last train has descended).

VITZNAU
Tourist information
🛈 Bahnhofstrasse 1, CH-6354; ☎041 227 18 10; e vitznau@luzern.com; www.wvrt.ch; ⊕ May–Sep 08.30–noon & 13.00–17.30 Mon–Fri, 09.00–13.00 Sat–Sun; Oct–Apr 08.30–noon & 13.30–17.30 Mon–Fri

Where to stay
Numerous hotels; closest to the station are:
🏠 **Rigi***** Seestrasse, CH-6354; ☎041 399 85 85; e info@rigi-vitznau.ch; www.rigi-vitznau.ch
🏠 **Hobby Hotel Terrasse** (H)** Schiffstation, CH-6354; ☎041 397 10 33; e ferien@hobbyhotel. ch; www.hobbyhotel.ch

RIGI KATLBAD-FIRST
Tourist information
🛈 Casa Margherita, CH-6356; ☎041 227 18 20; e rigi@luzern.com; www.wvrt.ch; ⊕ 09.00–12.30 & 14.00–17.00 Mon–Fri, 09.00–12.30 Sat–Sun

RIGI STAFFELHÖHE
Where to stay
🏠 **Edelweiss***** CH-6356; ☎041 399 88 00; e willkommen@edelweiss-rigi.ch; www. edelweiss-rigi.ch

RIGI KULM
Where to stay
🏠 **Rigi-Kulm** CH-6410; ☎041 880 18 88; e hotel@rigikulm.ch; www.rigikulm.ch

Vitznau also has two of Switzerland's best hotels, dating from the Belle Epoque
🏠 **Park Hotel Vitznau***** (H)** Seestrasse, CH-6354; ☎041 399 60 60; e info@parkhotel-vitznau.ch; www.parkhotel-vitznau.ch. Reopened in 2012 as a suite hotel, residence, medical centre and research facility. The film of Anita Brookner's novel Hotel du Lac was shot here.
🏠 **Vitznauerhof***** (H)** Seestrasse 80, CH-6354; ☎041 399 77 77; e info@vitnauerhof. ch; www.vitznauerhof. Hermann Hesse, Richard Strauss and Paul Klee were among the early guests after opening in 1901. It has been completely renovated recently to combine the Art Nouveau features with modern amenities, including a spa.

Where to stay
🏠 **Bergsonne***** CH-6356; ☎041 399 80 10; e info@bergsonne.ch; www.bergsonne.ch
🏠 **Alpina**** CH-6356; ☎041 397 11 52; e hotel@alpina-rigi.ch; www.alpina-rigi.ch
🏠 **Rigi First**** CH-6356; ☎041 859 03 10; e info@rigifirst.ch; www.rigifirst.ch

ARTH–RIGI Table 602

For trains to Arth-Goldau, and the town, see Luzern–Airolo. Less well known than the ascent from Vitznau, the standard-gauge line from Arth was opened only two years after its rival, in 1875. It does not enjoy the open views of the Vitznau line until near the Kulm but it provides access to good walks and a different aspect of the Rigi. The railway has the oldest cogwheel railcar in the world, described as the Rigi-Pullman, which operates special trains. The iron bridge at the foot of the railway in Arth-Goldau is a National Monument. Sit on the right.

Passing the depot on the left, the line climbs through woods to **Kräbel** from where a cable car ascends to Rigi Scheidegg (table 2568); the abandoned railway from there to Rigi Kaltbad can be walked (see page 177). The tall rock faces on the left indicate the amount of excavation required to build the railway. Numerous walking paths radiate from **Fruttli** and from a point just below the station.

A waterfall crashes down on the left just before the next tunnel (heralded by the carriage lights coming on). There is quite a village at **Rigi Klösterli**, with several hotels and a church. Several ski lifts rise into the meadows above. The gradient steepens as the last woods are penetrated before emerging to marvellous views to the right before **Rigi Staffel**.

The Vitznau line joins from the left and the two run parallel into the terminus at **Rigi Kulm** (see page 178).

KLÖSTERLI
Where to stay
⌂ **Rigi Klösterli (H)** Klösterliweg 17, CH-6410; ☏ 041 855 05 45; e hotel@kloesterli.ch; www. kloesterli.ch

RIGI STAFFEL
Where to stay
⌂ **Berggasthaus Staffel-Stubli** CH-6410; ☏ 041 855 02 05

LUZERN–LENZBURG Table 651

The line known as the Seetalbahn skirts two minor lakes and provides access to two great castles. Passing through pleasant rolling hills, fields and woodland, the line provides connections with the main Geneva–Zürich line at Lenzburg. Running alongside or even on roads for much of the way, the railway is like an inter-urban tram. Curiously it was built by an English contractor for a company whose chairman was MP for Cirencester and opened in 1883.

Trains leave the terminus at Luzern in a southerly direction, but with one exception all loop round to head north, passing through the modern suburbs of the city. The Lenzburg branch turns off the main Olten line at **Emmenbrücke**, where trains for Lenzburg reverse, and reaches **Eschenbach**, where the rebuilt buildings and twin-towered church of a 13th-century Cistercian convent can be seen.

The Catholic church at **Ballwil** is something of a curiosity, being built in 1847–49 in a Romanesque style and regarded as the first ecclesiastical structure to be built in a historical style in central Switzerland. The industrial town of **Hochdorf** has an imposing mid 18th-century Baroque Catholic church and adjacent priest's house and ossuary.

A glimpse of the Baldeggersee can be had to the west just before the village of **Baldegg**. The 5.6km-long lake is unusual in not having any significant resorts on its shore. At the northeastern corner of the lake is the pretty village of **Gelfingen**, above which is Schloss Heidegg, a medieval stronghold transformed into a fortified residence in the early 16th century. The tower was raised in height in around 1680–90 and given a Baroque makeover in the early 18th century. Now a museum (☉ *Apr–Oct 14.00–17.00 Tue–Fri, 10.00–17.00 Sat–Sun*) with displays of local history as well as furnishings, the Schloss comprises a massive tower, chapel, outer

One of the most beautifully situated châteaux in Vaud, the majestic Aigle Castle is surrounded by lush vineyards (S/DT) page 281

left The Swiss capital, Bern, has abundant arcaded shopping streets filled with fountains, small, specialist shops and antique dealers (DB/DT) page 93

below The Cathedral of St Pierre, Geneva, features myriad different styles, from its Neo-classical portico to its Romanesque and Gothic nave (MBL/DT) page 244

bottom The Grossmünster towers over Zürich's attractive Old Town, which fills a peninsula in the Limmat River (UM/DT) page 37

above With its beautiful setting, historic Kapellbrücke (Chapel Bridge) and quaint old town streets, Luzern has attracted tourists for centuries (AC/S (inset) and B123/S) page 165

right Lugano's mild climate has ensured a thriving café culture (SS) page 319

below Basel's sienna-coloured Rathaus is decorated with frescoes and ornate carvings (MW/BT) page 205

above — Brightly coloured masked musicians feature in the morning procession through Basel during the three-day *Fasnacht* (Carnival) (FRV/BT) page 207

left and below left — Every September, goats and elaborately garlanded cows are led from alpine meadows down to the valley by farmers in traditional dress, and their arrivals are celebrated by festivals in the villages below (AT)

below — Every year the shores of Lake Léman play host to the famous Montreux Jazz Festival (PR/A) page 267

above Alpenhorn players demonstrate their skills in Fribourg's main square (SS) page 135

right Villagers in traditional Appenzell dress (*Tracht*) (AT) page 73

below The village of Urnäsch is renowned for its woodcarving and has a number of elaborately decorated house fronts (AT) page 76

above   The Schilthorn, famous as one of the locations for the James Bond film *On Her Majesty's Secret Service*, offers sweeping views over the Lauterbrunnen Valley (OD/DT) page 155

left   The Appenzell region is a Mecca for outdoors types, with countless cycle routes and 1,200km of footpaths (AT) page 73

below   The Lavaux Vineyard Terraces cover the northern shores of Lake Geneva, and visitors can sample wines in the cellars of the *vignerons* (EC/F) page 259

above Founded in 1480, the Franciscan monastery of
Madonna del Sasso is built on a precipitous rock-face
above Locarno. Once only accessible via an arduous
footpath from the shore of Lake Maggiore, it can now
be reached by a funicular (AC/S) page 328

right Passing through dramatic and varied scenery, as here
in the Flims Gorge, the Glacier Express is the slowest
and yet one of the most popular express routes in the
world (ML/S) page 26

below The Castle of Chillon is one of Europe's best-
preserved medieval fortifications (AC/S) page 278

Mark Twain described the village of Weggis as 'the most charming place [...] for repose and restfulness'. Its warm climate and beautiful setting on Lake Luzern have secured its popularity as a tourist destination to the present day (T/S) page 175 wall, rose garden and attractive approach. The banqueting hall is particularly impressive.

After leaving the lake the train comes to **Hitzkirch** where there is a former Commandery of the Knights of St John, founded in 1236 and rebuilt in the mid 18th century. Beyond **Mosen** the railway runs along the west shore of Hallwilersee, an attractive lake 8.4km (5¼ miles) long, and this station is the closest to the lake for intending walkers.

Beinwil am See used to be the junction for Beromünster, but the train has been replaced by a bus (table 50.398) which also serves Reinach. At Beromünster is a 14th-century tower in which the first book in Switzerland was printed in 1470; it is now a museum (☉ *May–Oct 14.00–17.00 first Sun of month*) with a reconstruction of the printing room.The town of Beinwil has a Baroque Catholic church of 1619–20 with fine ceiling paintings and stucco, and Schloss Horbin, a small mansion built c1700 as a rest home for Muri monastery. Trees screen the lake from view until the northern end, when the steamer that plies the lake may be seen. The boat can be caught from a pier which is 15 minutes' walk from the station at **Birrwil**. The station at **Boniswil** is 15 minutes from Schloss Hallwyl, a magnificent and picturesque group of buildings that has been in the same family for over 800 years and is now open to visitors (☉ *Apr–Oct 10.00–17.00 Tue–Sun; admission charge*). One of the family's ancestors, Hans of Hallwyl, commanded the Confederate army at the Battle of Murten in 1476. Built on two walled islands linked by drawbridge, the moated medieval castle comprises a ruined keep, residence, towers, gatehouse, granary and stables. The castle provides the spectacular setting for a month-long opera festival from late July (*www.operschlosshallwyl.ch*).

Lenzburg was an important Roman town, as evidenced by the 1st-century theatre for 4,000 people on the northeast outskirts of the town. Today it is a centre of jam making and canning of fruit and vegetables, but it has an attractive old town with elegant Baroque houses and town hall – a fire in 1491 destroyed most older houses. The main reason for visiting the town, however, is its castle, a massive hill-top agglomeration of buildings that was begun in the 11th century. It can be reached from the station by bus 93 or by a 20-minute walk. Some of the buildings are strikingly positioned on overhanging rocks, and a perimeter walk gives a clearer idea of the various building periods. Built around a pretty courtyard with formal garden and trees, the castle was briefly the headquarters of the bellicose German Emperor Barbarossa. The German dramatist Frank Wedekind lived here in 1886 when his father owned the castle. In 1892 it was bought by August Edward Jessup from Philadelphia, who restored the castle. Jessup was married to Lady Mildred Bowes-Lyon, daughter of the 13th Earl of Strathmore and Kinghorne from Glamis Castle in Scotland, and her monogram can be seen in the ceiling plasterwork above her bed. In 1911 the castle was bought by the wealthy Chicago mine owner and banker James W Ellsworth, and it was at Lenzburg Castle that his son, Lincoln Ellsworth, and Amundsen planned their 1920s polar expeditions. Besides the fortifications, the castle contains a large history collection from the canton of Aargau (☉ *Apr–Oct 10.00–17.00 Tue–Sun; admission charge*). A good English-language leaflet is available.

LENZBURG

Tourist information

🛈 Kronenplatz 24, CH-5600; ☎062 886 45 45; e tourismus@lenzburg.ch; www.lenzburg. ch; ☉ 09.00–11.45 & 13.30–17.30 Mon–Fri, 09.00–13.00 Sat

Where to stay

Several hotels; the closest to the station is:
🏠 **Lenzburg***** Aavorstadt 26, CH-5600; ☎062 888 87 87; e info@hotellenzburg.ch; www. hotellenzburg.ch

A main line taken by trains from Italy to Basel, it serves several historic sites and towns, passing through gently undulating country.

It takes some time to leave Luzern behind, the line looping round **Rothenburg** before reaching the south end of the Sempachersee at **Sempach-Neuenkirch**. The station is equidistant between the two towns, and served by buses to Sempach and Sursee station (table 60.084).

It was at Sempach in 1386 that one of the most famous battles on Swiss soil took place, marked by a monument in the church square and by the chapel of St Jakob near the village of Hildisrieden. A force of just 1,500 Swiss infantry defeated a larger force of Austrian knights in armour so heavy that the heat of the day helped to sap their fighting abilities. The Austrian commander, Archduke Leopold III, was killed in the battle, but historians have cast doubt on the main reason for the battle being so well known: a soldier named Arnold von Winkelried is supposed to have saved the day for the Swiss by deflecting enough of the long Austrian lances for the Swiss to break through. Unfortunately the story of this national hero seems to have been 'lifted' from a battle near Milan two centuries later.

The town of Sempach retains some of its medieval defences and a fine half-timbered Rathaus of the 17th century.

Neuenkirch is worth visiting for its medieval appearance and the remains of its fortifications in the form of parts of the town wall and a tower. The medieval castle, now a local museum, was enlarged in the 16th century and dominates part of the old town.

The railway now runs right beside the Sempachersee, an 8km-long lake, an example of what determined action to halt environmental degradation can achieve. The lake was badly polluted until strict laws were applied and the water artificially oxygenated.

A bus from **Nottwil** station (table 60.062/line 62) goes to the pilgrimage village of Buttisholz where there is a mound known as the 'English Barrow' in which the remains of Enguerrand de Coucy's English soldiers are said to have been buried in 1375 (see page 117). Schloss Tannenfels at Nottwil is a hipped-roof house of 1688. Shortly after Sempachersee is left behind, most trains stop at the attractive town of **Sursee**. Founded in the 13th century it still has two of its medieval towers, numerous fine houses of the 16th–18th centuries and a particularly splendid Rathaus of 1539–45.

On the hill above the village of **Reiden** stand the 16th–18th-century remains of a former Commandery of the Knights of St John, founded c1280.

Not much remains of the fortifications of **Zofingen**, but it has a palatial late Baroque Rathaus of 1795, a market hall of 1725 and a Gothic Latin School of 1600–02 that now houses the library and archive. The Reformed church of St Mauritius dates from the 12th century and retains some stained glass of c1400 but has been substantially rebuilt. Zofingen is the junction for the branch that turns east to Lenzburg.

In a spectacular position above **Aarburg-Oftringen** stands the castle of Aarburg, built in the 17th century on the site of an older fortification. To the west of the town stands a wooden bridge across the River Aare that dates from 1568.

For **Olten**, see table 410, page 112.

PRACTICALITIES Bicycle hire from Sursee and Olten stations.

SURSEE
Tourist information

ℹ Theatrerstrasse 9, CH-6210; ✆041 920 44 44; e info@sempachersee-tourismus.ch; www. sempachersee-tourismus.ch; ☉ 08.00–noon & 13.30–17.00 Mon–Wed, 08.00–noon & 13.30–18.00 Thu, 08.00–noon & 13.30–16.00 Fri

Where to stay

⌂ **Sursee***** Bahnhofstrasse 15, CH-6210; ✆041 922 23 23; e info@hotel-sursee.ch; www. hotel-sursee.ch
⌂ **Eisenbahn und Bären (H)** Bahnhofplatz 5, CH-6210; ✆041 921 13 57

ZOFINGEN
Tourist information

ℹ Stadthaus Kirchplatz, CH-4800; ✆062 745 71 72; e verkehrsbuero@zofingen.ch; www.zofingen. ch; ☉ 07.30–noon & 13.30–17.00 Mon–Tue &

Thu–Fri, 07.30–noon & 13.30–18.45 Wed, 09.00–noon Sat

ZOFINGEN–LENZBURG Table 514

A local line that crosses the two modernised metre-gauge branch lines running south from Aarau. At Suhr the line crosses the metre-gauge Aarau–Menziken line before proceeding to Lenzburg. It serves no tourist attractions of note.

LUZERN–STANS–ENGELBERG (LSE) Table 480

A pleasant journey up the Engelberger Aa valley to the monastery town of Engelberg. It serves funicular/cable car excursions from Stans up the Stanserhorn and from Engelberg to Titlis. Sit on the right leaving Luzern.

Leaving from platform 15 at Luzern, the metre-gauge Zentralbahn (ZB) trains for Engelberg share the Brünig line as far as **Hergiswil**, where the Engelberg line turns east through a long tunnel and crosses Lake Luzern by the Achereggbrücke to reach the town of **Stansstad**. A crenellated square tower dating from 1280, the Schnitzturm, stands beside the harbour, which has been a port since medieval times; it is now served by lake steamers. Buses leave Stanstaad station for Bürgenstock (table 60.321).

Stans, the capital of canton Nidwalden, has a fine central square, Dorfplatz, which is only five minutes' walk from the station. From the station subway follow the sign for the funicular to turn right up the stairs. Turn left to reach the main road and turn left again for the square, which owes its appearance to planning following a fire in 1713. Its dominant building is the early Swiss Baroque Catholic church of St Peter, built 1641–47 and noted for its black and marble stucco. In the church is a tablet commemorating the death at the hands of the French of over 400 people from Nidwalden following their rejection of the Helvetian constitution in 1798. An orphanage was subsequently opened in Stans at the St Klara convent by Pestalozzi (see page 231). A painting of Pestalozzi and his children at Stans hangs in the Kunsthaus in Zürich. Beyond the square, in Engelbergstrasse, is the Winkelriedhaus, a cultural museum in a 16th–17th-century patrician home.

The town's principal museum is the Höfli on Alter Postplatz (☉ 11.00–17.00 Sat–Sun). Retrace your steps from the square towards the station and the museum is on the left-hand side of the main road. Its three floors contain historic paintings of the area, reconstructed rooms, military ephemera, coins and tiled floors and decorated ceilings. Beams cut by passing visitors activate video programmes in several rooms,

13

but the commentary and the labels to exhibits are in German only. The lower floor is a gastronomic restaurant.

From Stans you can take one of Switzerland's most delightful funiculars up the Stanserhorn at 1,924m (6,310ft) (table 2550). To reach this period piece, follow the sign in the station subway to turn right up the stairs. Turn left, cross the main road and then walk past the Höfli Museum into a car park; the station is the sienna chalet-style building on the far left (five minutes' walk from the Zentralbahn station). The 24-minute journey is in two sections: funicular to Kälti, an ascent of 263m (862ft); and a cable car to the summit, rising another 1,184m (3,882ft). It operates from early April to mid-November.

The funicular section has changed little since it was opened in 1893, its elderly wooden cars creaking softly as they crawl through orchards and farms. Two upper sections were also funicular until in 1970 lightning struck a cable and set fire to the 100-bed hotel on the summit. It was decided to replace these two sections with a cable car, and this opened in 1975, followed the next year with a new restaurant, open terrace and shop on the foundations of the hotel. The remains of the funicular and its tunnels can be seen from the cable car.

When it opened in 1893 the Stanserhornbahn was the world's first mountain railway to be powered by electricity. One of the partners, Franz-Joseph Bucher, was a farmer's son who went on to build railways and hotels all over the world, including the Semiramis in Cairo, and died in 1906 leaving a fortune of SFr14 million in cash alone. Although the Stanserhornbahn never paid a dividend, its shareholders proudly framed their share certificates – one can be seen on the wall of the buffet at Stans Zentralbahn station, along with historic photographs of the local railways.

In 2012 the Stanserhorn cable car hit the headlines by becoming the world's first double-deck cable car with a roofless upper deck. The lower level of the CabriO has space for 60 people, from where an elegant staircase leads up to the sun deck, which has room for about 30 people.

The 360-degree panorama from the Stanserhorn is magnificent, the summit being ten minutes' walk from the station. Numerous paths descend from the summit, enabling you to gain solitude in minutes after your arrival. Amongst the signposted routes from the summit are walks to Alpnach (4 hours, station), Dallenwil (3 hours, station) and Wirzweli (3½ hours, cable car to Niederrickenbach ZB).

Buses from Stans station can be taken to: Emmetten and Seelisberg station (table 60.311); Beckenreid and Flüelen station (table 60.310).

At **Dallenwil** is the Catholic parish church of St Laurentius, built 1697–98, with black stucco. It is a 15-minute walk to the cable car for Wirzweli (table 25450) for signed paths to the Stanserhorn. From **Niederrickenbach** it is two minutes' walk to the east for the cable car to the village of Niederrickenbach (table 2546); 15 minutes' walk to the west is the car to Wirzweli. Between these stations the line crosses the Engelberger Aa river, which remains on the right all the way to Engelberg, crossed by a series of wooden-covered bridges.

In the village of **Wolfenschiessen** is the Catholic parish church of St Martin, built between 1775 and 1777. On the west bank of the river, before **Dörfli**, is a fine example of a lord's house dating from 1586: the Höchhaus has an attic room for entertaining like that in the Höfli at Stans – it can be viewed on request. Beyond Dörfli on the right is the dramatic Fallenbachfall, a three-stage waterfall. On the right, adjacent to the station at **Grafenort**, is the huge Herrenhaus of 1690, the summer residence of the abbots of Engelberg. At the edge of the platform is a pretty gazebo, and on the opposite side of the line is the curious octagonal Heiligkreuz chapel, dating from 1689. Today the Herrenhaus is a holiday home for Benedictine monks. The railway enters a tunnel, opened in 2010 to cut out a section of rack railway which climbed steeply through woods at a gradient of 1 in 4, making it the steepest section of Riggenbach rack line anywhere in the world. Journey time between Luzern and Engleberg was cut by 19 minutes. Emerging from the 4km tunnel, the valley opens out to give fine views of the mountains that surround **Engelberg**, the terminus of the line. The station bookstall sells maps of the area, and to the left of the station on the opposite side of Bahnhofstrasse is a map of the town with tourist information.

Engelberg is a summer and winter sports resort with good opportunities for walking and mountain biking. The first hotels were built in 1850 but it was the opening of the railway in 1898 that spurred its development. However, since 1120 it has been the site of a Benedictine abbey which gave the parish the status of an independent state until 1798. The abbey still dominates the town, the extensive buildings and monastery church dating from 1730 to 1737 when they were rebuilt after the third fire in the abbey's history. One of its 19th-century abbots went on to found two abbeys in the United States, at Conception, Missouri, and Mount Angel, Oregon.

The light, barrel-vaulted nave of the monastery church is flanked by side chapels, each with an altar, and its ceiling is decorated with seven frescoes depicting scenes from the life of Mary. Smaller panels along each side are of the life of St Benedict. The spatial division between monks and laymen is marked by two altars which frame the high altar.

Tours of the monastery, one of only five Benedictine monasteries in Switzerland, at 10.00 and 16.00 (*Wed–Sat*) enable visitors to see the Great Hall, Library and the guests' refectory. The corners of the main building have *trompe-l'oeil* decoration to suggest chamfered rustication. The monastery is still home to about 30 monks, and it incorporates a cheese factory (⊕ *09.00–18.30 Mon–Sat, 09.00–17.00 Sun*).

Near the tourist office (Klosterstrasse) at Dorfstrasse 6 is the Tal Museum in the Wappenhaus, which was built in 1786–87. The museum portrays the history of the town and the surrounding valleys through pictures, documents and a wide range of artefacts (⊕ *14.00–18.00 Wed–Sun; admission charge*).

Most day visitors to Engelberg come to take the cable car up Mt Titlis (tables 2535.1 and 2535.2), reached in 40 minutes. This excursion is on the coach-trip circuit and is crowded even out of season; those who dislike tourist throngs might prefer the Stanserhorn. To reach the cable car station, turn right outside the ZB station to pass in front of the Hotel Eden. Cross over the main road and then the river before turning right along a small path to follow a line of trees beside the river. The station is straight ahead, less than ten minutes' walk. The first of three stages takes passengers to Gerschnialp at 1,300m (4,264ft) and to Trübsee at 1,800m (5,900ft) in six-seater gondolas; doors open and close automatically, but remain seated at Gerschnialp unless you want to break the journey. The funicular which was superseded by the cable cars can be seen below; it has been retained to carry supplies up the mountain.

Beyond Gerschnialp, a second cable car route offers bungee jumping with drops of 70 or 140m (459ft) between mid-April and mid-October (*Outventure, ☎041 611 14 41; www.outventure.ch*). Both cable cars descend for a short distance over cow meadows before rising up to Trübsee, which takes its name from the lake close to the station. Although the lake is in a striking position, tarmac paths and rather ugly surrounding buildings mar its appearance. The chairlift to Jochpass (table 2537) is a 15-minute walk past the lake. From Jochpass you can take the chairlift down to

13

Engstlensee (table 2538) from which there are footpaths down the Gental valley to Meiringen, and the train back to Luzern (table 470, page 187).

From Trübsee a larger gondola ascends to Stand (2,450m, 8,000ft) for the final section to Titlis (3,020m, 10,000ft) in the world's first revolving gondola, which was introduced in 1992. This is no gimmick, since it enables all passengers (near the windows) to enjoy the 360-degree panorama and to look down into the deep crevasses of the blue-grey Titlis Glacier – like most alpine glaciers, in steady retreat. From Titlis station, you can walk to the summit in about 45 minutes.

The excursion to Titlis is one of the most expensive cable car journeys, but its cost can be reduced by the usual discounts with various cards or by descending on foot from Stand (July–September only, 1¼ hours to Trübsee) or from Trübsee (1½ hours to Engelberg).

On the opposite side of the valley is the cable-car up to Brunni (Ristis) (table 2530). Turn left outside the ZB station and right into Dorfstrasse. Pass a park with children's playground on the left, and shortly after Hotel Engelberg turn left up Hinterdorfstrasse to the cable car station (five minutes' walk). At the summit are a network of footpaths, a small children's zoo and several restaurants.

PRACTICALITIES Bicycle hire from Engelberg station.

STANS
Tourist information
🛈 Bahnhofplatz 4, CH-6371; ☏ 041 610 88 33; e info@lakeluzern.ch; www.lakeluzern.ch; ◷ 09.00–noon & 14.00–17.00 Mon–Fri

Where to stay
⌂ **Engel*** (H)** Dorfplatz 1, CH-6371; ☏ 041 619 10 10; e info@engelstans.ch; www.engelstans.ch
⌂ **Linde*** (H)** Dorfplatz 7, CH-6370; ☏ 041 619 09 30; e info@hotel-linde.ch; www.hotel-linde.ch
⌂ **Stanserhof***** Stansstaderstrasse 90, CH-6370; ☏ 041 619 71 71; e info@stanserhof.ch; www.stanserhof.ch

ENGELBERG
Tourist information
🛈 Tourist Centre, Klosterstrasse 3, CH-6390; ☏ 041 639 77 77; e welcome@engelberg.ch; www.engelberg.ch; ◷ 08.00–17.30 Mon–Sat

Where to stay
Hotels close to station are:
⌂ **Bellevue-Terminus (H)** Bahnhofplatz, CH-6390; ☏ 041 639 68 68; e welcome@bellevue-perminus.ch; www.bellevue-terminus.ch

⌂ **Crystal***** Dorfstrasse 45, CH-6390; ☏ 041 637 21 22; e info@crystal-engelberg.ch; www.crystal-engelberg.ch
⌂ **Ski Lodge Engelberg** Erlenweg 36, CH-6390; ☏ 041 637 35 00; e info@skilodgeengenberg.com; www.skilodgeengenberg.com

TRÜBSEE
Where to stay
⌂ **Berghotel Trübsee***** CH-6390; ☏ 041 637 13 71; e info@truebseehof.ch

JOCHPASS
Where to stay
⌂ **Mountain hostel** ☏ 041 637 11 87; e info@jochpass.ch; www.jochpass.ch

This was the only metre-gauge line operated by Swiss Federal Railways (SBB) until 2004 when it became independent, becoming the Zentralbahn (ZB) the following year. It is one of the country's most popular journeys for visitors, passing through glorious scenery between the two major resorts. It provides access to the resort of Meiringen and two major mountain railways, up Pilatus and Rothorn. Golden Pass trains with special panorama cars and swivel armchairs are operated over the line. The railway opened fully between Luzern and Brienz in 1889, but it was not until 1916 that the section beyond Brienz to Interlaken was completed, passengers and freight being carried by steamer on Lake Brienz until then. Sit on the right.

Interlaken-bound trains share the same route out of Luzern as Engelberg trains to the junction and lakeside resort of **Hergiswil**, beyond which a tunnel takes Brünig trains to the shore of the Alpnachersee with the Stanserhorn overlooking the far shore. Wooded hills rise out of the lake as the train approaches **Alpnachstad**, from where the rack railway up Pilatus begins (see page 191).

The railway follows the River Sarner Aa through rolling farmland and past the slender spire of the Catholic church at **Alpnach** to the capital of the Forest Canton of Obwalden at **Sarnen**. An early 13th-century foundation, Sarnen has a ruined castle on the west bank of the river. The imposing white building on the hill is a shooting lodge dating from 1752. The town is dominated by the diagonally placed towers of the hill-top Catholic church of St Peter, built by Franz and Johann Singer between 1739 and 1742 on 11th-century foundations. An older church is the chapel of Maria Lauretana, its tower dating from 1556 and its last reconstruction between 1658 and 1662. Near the lake is an early 17th-century convent and a Benedictine college built between 1745 and 1750, also by Johann Singer. The Rathaus of 1729–32 contains the *White Book of Sarnen*, which is the oldest account of the inception of the Swiss Confederation, written c1470.

Soon after leaving Sarnen the lake of the same name comes into view on the right, a footpath following the shoreline. **Sachseln** is a good place from which to walk beside the lake. Boats can be hired and there is a children's playground beside the lake to the south of the station. The Catholic church of St Theodul, built between 1672 and 1684, is well worth a visit for its extraordinary contrast in the use of black and white marble. The supporting columns of the arches and the archivolts are in black. The village also has numerous fine houses, such as the three-storey, half-timbered Alte Krone, dating from 1674. Above Sachseln is Flüeli where the patron saint of Switzerland, St Nicholas of Flüe, farmed.

Beyond the reed-covered end of the Sarnersee is **Giswil**. Its Catholic church, built between 1630 and 1635, stands on a mound once occupied by a castle – in 1629 the village was swept away by the Lauibach torrent. Giswil is the destination of steam-operated excursions from Interlaken that run on some Sundays during the summer; it is also the start of the climb to the Brünig Pass, trains engaging the Riggenbach rack soon after leaving the station. Buses from the station go over the Glaubenbüelenpass to Sörenberg, Rothornbahn (table 60.241), where a cable car goes up the Brienzer Rothorn (table 2505). The bus continues on to Schüpfheim on the route of Panorama Route Express postbus. Above Giswil is the skiing village of Mörlialp, served by skiing season postbus (table 60.362).

The steep ascent lifts the train to views over the almost turquoise water of the reservoir of Lungernsee on the right. The line climbs along a ledge with rock walls on the left to **Kaiserstuhl**, overlooking the lake. At the end of the lake is the charming small resort of **Lungern**. Just to the west of the village is a cable car to

13

Turren (table 2520.1), from where a gondola ascends to Schönbüel (table 2520.2). The lower cable car is 20 minutes' walk from the ZB station, which is at a higher level than the village.

As the line climbs into a remote, unspoilt valley with nothing more than a track and a few attractive farmsteads, look out for wood carvings of mammals beside the railway. From the summit station of **Brünig-Hasliberg**, a bus (table 31.151) goes along the ridge through woods and meadows to Ballenberg open-air museum in one direction and in the other to Hasliberg Reuti, which serves the gondola from Twing to Käserstatt (table 2485). The area is popular with walkers and there is an antique emporium opposite the station.

The Brünig Pass marks the cantonal boundary between Obwalden and Bern. As the train drops down to the valley of the Aare, glimpses open up between the trees of the Bernese Oberland peaks to the southwest. On the extraordinarily flat valley floor, the broad, channelled Aare can be seen flowing towards Lake Brienz, paralleled by the railway.

Meiringen is itself on the edge of the Bernese Oberland and a good place to break a journey, since there are some major attractions in the vicinity. The town is strategically situated between several mountain passes: the Brünig to the north, and the Susten and Grimsel passes to the east. The town's name was bestowed on the culinary creation of a local early 17th-century patissier named Gasparini: the French version of the word, 'meringue', has become its usual name. In 1985 the town made the world's biggest meringue, which had to be baked in a sauna and weighed in at 64kg. The tourist office can arrange for children to visit a bakery to make their own meringues, which can be collected the following day after baking.

Another reason for its fame and popularity with tourists is that Sir Arthur Conan Doyle chose the nearby Reichenbach Falls as the setting for the death of his best-known creation, Sherlock Holmes. It has long been a popular resort for walkers and mountaineers, King Albert of the Belgians being a regular visitor on account of his love of rock climbing.

The resort has good facilities for skiing and other sports, with indoor and outdoor swimming pools. However, it is probably walkers and mountain bikers who will find the area exceptionally attractive. The four-stage Meiringen–Hasliberg-Bahnen provides access to 300km (187½ miles) of footpaths along the Hasliberg: the cable car station in Meiringen is ten minutes' walk from the railway. The first stage goes to Hasliberg Reuti (table 2480.1); the second and third are gondolas to Bidmi and Mägisalp (table 2480.2); and the final chairlift goes to 2,245m (7,385ft) at Alpen tower (Planplatten) (table 2480.3). Each level provides walks of a different kind, the higher the more rugged.

For cyclists, the tourist office produces an excellent map showing the 420km (262 miles) of signed routes, some of which use flowers as symbols, as well as numbers. A well-produced English-language leaflet provides a guide to the distinctive farms and houses along the Hasliberg.

The town's connection with Sherlock Holmes is commemorated by a museum (⊕ *May–mid-Oct 13.30–18.00 daily; mid-Oct–Apr 16.30–18.00 Wed & Sun*), appropriately situated in the basement of the English church near the Park Hotel. Its main feature is a reconstruction of the sitting room of Holmes's house in Baker Street, but there are other fascinating items of memorabilia about Conan Doyle and Holmes's time, such as a large map of London c1840. An English-language guide is available.

The falls where Holmes plunged to his death after a struggle with Professor Moriarty lie to the southeast of the town and were chosen by Sir Arthur Conan

Doyle because of their sheer impressiveness. They can be reached by a delightful funicular (20 minutes' walk from the station) from Reichenbach to Reichenbachfall (table 2475), which operates from mid-May to early October. It was opened in 1899, and the funicular still has a period charm: the roof of its glass-walled train shed is supported by wood columns with chamfered edges. Besides taking passengers to the viewing platform where the duel took place, the funicular can be used for walks through the Rosenlaui valley to Gross Scheidegg, First and Grindelwald, the last stage of which could take advantage of the gondola down from First. Buses serve part of this route, running from Meiringen station to Schwarzwaldalp (table 31.164) for onward connection to Grindelwald (table 31.123). From Rosenlaui a path opened in 1903 goes to the glacier gorge (Gletscherschlucht, *www.rosenlauischlucht.ch*), offering spectacular views (⊕ *May/Oct 10.00–17.00 daily; Jun–Sep 09.00–18.00 daily; admission charge*).

To the east of Meiringen is the second magnificent natural feature close to the town. The Aare between Innertkirchen and Meiringen squeezes through a gorge of astonishingly narrow width, the sky often nothing more than a slit of colour between vertical rock walls only a metre or two apart in places. A footpath runs through the gorge, sometimes through a tunnel, and on to Innertkirchen, from where a train returns to Meiringen (see page 192). The gorge (⊕ *Apr–Oct 08.30– 17.30 daily; admission charge; www.aareschlucht.ch*) is lit on Wednesday and Friday nights in July and August between 21.00 and 23.00. There is a restaurant at the entrance to the gorge. A bus runs hourly from the station to the gorge in July to September.

Meiringen station is at one end of some notable postbus journeys. To the south a bus goes over the Grimsel Pass to Oberwald station on the Brig–Andermatt line and then on over the Furka Pass to Andermatt station (table 31.161). To the east a service crosses the Susten Pass to Göschenen and Andermatt stations (table 31.162). Finally, from June to early October a bus goes up the Gental to the unspoilt village of Engstlenalp (table 31.163); from beside nearby Engstlensee you can either walk or take a chairlift up to the Jochpass (table 2537), from where you can walk or take a chairlift down to Trübsee and Engelberg (see page 185).

The bus to Oberwald (table 31.161) calls at Handegg, the lower station of the Gelmer funicular which has the distinction of being the world's steepest, at 106% (1 in 0.94). And it certainly feels like it. You have to hang on to the bar that holds you in as the car climbs at an alarming (though perfectly safe) angle to the lonely Gelmersee, which you can walk round in about two hours. Built for the construction and maintenance of a hydroelectric dam, the funicular was opened in 2001. Near its lower station is a cable suspension bridge spanning the Handeck Falls; it leads on to Hotel Handeck, passing a cheesemaker.

Of note in Meiringen is one of the few buildings to survive the devastating fires of 1879 and 1891, the Reformed church of St Michael, which has the country's oldest-dated bell, thought to have been forged in 1351, in its Romanesque tower. The rest of the church was rebuilt in 1684 but incorporating fragmentary frescoes of c1300. Excavations in 2005 revealed the foundations of three previous churches up to 5m below the present floor, some from the 10th century; they are open to visitors. Unusually the organ is placed directly behind the altar with the choir-stalls on either side. It is situated at the top of Kirchgasse close to the Hasli Museum (*Museum der Landschaft Hasli, Kapellan 1;* ⊕ *Jun–mid-Oct 15.00–18.00 daily*), which has a focus on local history.

PRACTICALITIES Bicycle hire from Sarnen and Meiringen stations.

HERGISWIL
Tourist information
🛈 Seestrasse 54, CH-6052; ☎ 041 632 65 65;
e info@hergiswil.ch; www.hergiswil.ch;
🕐 08.00–noon & 13.45–17.00 Mon–Fri

SARNEN
Tourist information
🛈 Hofstrasse 2, CH-6060; ☎ 041 666 50 40;
e info@sarnen-tourism.ch; www.sarnen-tourism.
ch; 🕐 Jun–mid-Sep 08.00–noon & 13.30–18.00
Mon–Fri, 08.00–noon Sat; Jan–May, mid-Sep–
Dec 13.30–18.00 Mon–Fri

SACHSELN
Where to stay
🏠 **Kreuz**** (H)** Bruder-Klausen-Weg 1, CH-6072; ☎ 041 660 53 00; e info@kreuz-sachseln.
chwww.kreuz-sachseln.ch

GISWIL
Tourist information
🛈 Brünigstrasse 49, CH-6074; ☎ 041 675 17 60;
e info@giswil-tourismus.ch; www.giswil-
tourismus.ch; 🕐 09.00–noon & 14.00–18.00
Mon–Fri, 09.00–noon Sat

Where to stay
🏠 **Bahnhof** Brünigstrasse 49, CH-6074;
☎ 041 675 11 61; e info@bahnhofgiswil.ch; www.
bahnhofgiswil.ch

KAISERSTUHL
Where to stay
🏠 **Kaiserstuhl** CH-6078; ☎ 041 678 11 89;
e hotelkaiserstuhl@gmx.ch; www.
hotelkaiserstuhl.ch

LUNGERN
Tourist information
🛈 Bahnhofstrasse 33, CH-6078; ☎ 041 678 14
55; e tourismus@lungern.ch; www.lungern-
tourismus.ch; 🕐 08.00–20.00 daily

Where to stay
🏠 **Löwen***** Brünigstrasse 72, CH-6078; ☎ 041
678 11 51; e wimfield@hotel-loewen-lungern.ch;
www.hotel-loewen-lungern.ch

MEIRINGEN
Tourist information
🛈 Bahnhofstrasse 12, CH-3860; ☎ 033 972 50 50;
e info@haslital.ch; www.haslital.ch;
🕐 08.00–18.00 Mon–Fri, Mar–early Apr, Jun, late
Aug–late Oct also 08.00–18.00 Sat; late Jun–late
Aug also 08.00–18.00 Sun

Where to stay
Numerous hotels; close to the station are
🏠 **Alpin Sherpa****** Bahnhofstrasse 3, CH-3860; ☎ 033 972 52 52; e welcome@haslitalhotels.
ch; www.alpinsherpa.ch

🏠 **Park Hotel du Sauvage******
Bahnhofstrasse 30, CH-3860; ☎ 033 972 18 80;
e info@sauvage.ch; www.sauvage.ch
🏠 **Baer***** Bahnhofstrasse 2, CH-3860; ☎ 033 971
46 46; e info@hotel-baer.ch; www.hotel-baer.ch
🏠 **Meiringen***** Bahnhofplatz 1, CH-3960;
☎ 033 972 12 12; e info@hotel-meiringen.ch;
www.hotel-meiringen.ch
🏠 **Victoria***** Bahnhofplatz 9, CH-3860; ☎ 033
972 10 40; e info@victoria-meiringen.ch; www.
victoria-meiringen.ch
🏠 **Brunner** Bahnhofstrasse 8, CH-3860; ☎ 033
971 14 23; www.hotel-brunner.ch

HANDECK/GUTTANEN
Where to stay

⌂ **Handeck** CH-3864; ☏ 033 982 36 11;
e welcome@grimselhotels.ch; www.grimselwelt.ch

ALPNACHSTAD–PILATUS Table 473

This 4.3km (2½ miles) line has the distinction of being the world's steepest rack railway. Its fame makes it one of the busiest mountain railways, and deservedly so. Apart from the railway being a marvellous feat of engineering, the views from the summit are spectacular, and a variety of walks quickly takes unhurried visitors away from the crowds that throng the station area in season. The railway's operation is limited by snow to the months of May to mid-November. Alpnachstad can be reached by rail or steamer from Luzern, and the return can be made by cable car down to Kriens followed by bus 1. The Swiss Card obtains a 50% reduction, Eurail 35%. Dress warmly.

Visitors have been ascending the 2,132m (7,000ft) summit of Pilatus from long before the 800mm-gauge railway was opened in 1889, arriving by foot, horseback or even sedan chair, two hotels catering for their needs from 1860. Amongst the early visitors were Wagner, Tolstoy and Queen Victoria, who rode to the summit on a pony she had brought from England, accompanied by Highland attendants. The solution to the challenge of building a railway up Pilatus was found by the experienced railway builder Edward Locher. He devised an ingenious mechanism whereby the locomotive drive was transmitted by bevel gears to a pair of horizontal cog wheels; these engaged a double-sided rack placed centrally between the two rails. Underneath these cogs a disc overlapped the teeth to fit underneath the rack and prevent vertical movement. This mechanism gave sufficient power to lift the carriage up the fearsome gradient of 48% (1 in 2) and a safeguard against strong winds that might topple a train using one of the other types of rack mechanism. Unique steamcoaches – a locomotive combined with a coach on a chassis incorporating a water tank – struggled up the mountain until 1937 when the railway was electrified.

The journey starts at Alpnachstad where the Pilatus station is just across the road from the ZB station. The coaches are stepped so that passengers sit on the level; this is a common device on funiculars but not on rack and pinion lines. Sensational views vie for attention with the railway's rate of ascent as the cars climb through meadows, beech woods and a series of short tunnels to the loop at Amsigenalp, where the traversers at each end are original. Unless you can pose as a convincing shepherd, you are not allowed to get off the train here.

The final section to the top is awe-inspiring, the train clawing its way up a ledge blasted out of the face of a sheer wall of rock. The station is in the lee of the Esel, one of several peaks that form Mount Pilatus. Most unusually the point at the station throat rotates to change track. Directly outside is the Bellevue Hotel, built in 1963; it is not an aesthetic contribution to the mountain. The older Pilatus Kulm Hotel, built in 1890, is a much more agreeable place to stay or eat, particularly after the creation of a new gourmet restaurant in 1999, incorporating sandstone arches and a glass wall overlooking the panorama of surrounding peaks.

One of the best vantage points is from the top of the Esel, which is reached by a path that begins beside the Bellevue Hotel. One of several paths continues past the Kulm Hotel along a gallery cut into the rock, part of it through a tunnel. To reach the other side of the ridge, you can climb through a passage hollowed out of the rock, past the observatory to a ledge looking west. Beneath, on the Klimsenhorn, is a tiny chapel, beside which the foundations of the hotel built in 1860 can just be made out.

Another way of returning to Luzern is to take the cable car down to Fräkmüntegg (table 2517) from where a gondola descends to Kriens (table 2516). At Fräkmüntegg is the Pilatus Rope Park, a 1,350m-long all-weather toboggan run and a 60m tubing slide. Bus route N1 from Kriens returns to the main bus terminal beside the station.

PILATUS
Where to stay
⌂ **Pilatus-Kulm and Bellevue*** (H)** Kriens-Pilatus, CH-6011; ☏ 041 329 12 12; e hotels@pilatus.ch; www.pilatus.ch

MEIRINGEN–INNERTKIRCHEN Table 474

Opened as late as 1926, this 5km (3 miles) line was built in connection with the extensive hydroelectric works of the area to the east of Meiringen. It includes one of Switzerland's most extraordinary stations – Aareschlucht Ost not only has the country's shortest platform at 2m (6ft), but it is located in a tunnel. Sit on the right.

The trains of the Meiringen–Innertkirchen Bahn (MIB) leave from Track 13 at the east end of Meiringen station. The train climbs gently up the valley with the River Aare on the right, diving into a long tunnel while the river negotiates the famous gorge (see table 470, below). Inside the tunnel is **Aareschlucht Ost**; passengers exit the platform by an automatic sliding door which affords access to a new suspension bridge across the river and a path to the eastern entrance to the spectacular gorge, 1,400m (1,531yds) long, and its footpath. The river is in exactly the same position on leaving the tunnel and is soon crossed by a covered wooden bridge. You may see llamas in a field near **Innertkirchen Post**, the station close to the village's hotels. The line continues on to **Innertkirchen MIB** where the railway's shed contains some of the old trams and battery cars that used to operate the line.

INNERTKIRCHEN
Where to stay
⌂ **Alpenrose*** (H)** Hauptstrasse, CH-3862; ☏ 033 971 11 51; e info@alpenrose-innertkirchen.ch; www.alpenrose-innertkirchen.ch

⌂ **Hof und Post**** CH-3862; ☏ 033 971 19 51; e reception-hof@bluewin.ch; www.hotel-hof-post.ch

Luzern–MEIRINGEN–INTERLAKEN Table 470

Trains have to reverse at Meiringen, but since it is now better to sit on the left, through passengers from Luzern who have sat on the better, right side thus far will not have to move. The view of Lake Brienz looking west as the train approaches the large expanse of turquoise water is one of the loveliest views from a train in Switzerland. Brienz is the start of the mountain railway up Mount Rothorn and also the station for one of the country's finest museums.

The River Aare is not far away on the left as the train leaves behind the railway's workshops at Meiringen and bowls along the flat valley floor past orchards to the country's cleanest lake, once renowned for its oarswomen who rowed tourists to Giessbach for the falls. The first steamer was launched in 1839, and a paddle steamer still plies the lake – the *Lötschberg* of 1914. The railway skirts the northern shore of the lake, the first station being the wood-carvers' village of **Brienz**. Apart from a tradition of wood carving with several workshops open to visitors, Brienz has a school for making stringed instruments.

Opposite the station in this attractive village is the start of the Brienz Rothorn Bahn (see page 194). A bus meets all trains at Brienz to take visitors to the Swiss Open-Air Museum at Ballenberg (*Freilichtmuseum;* ⊕ *early Apr–Oct 10.00–17.00 daily; for daily programme* ☏ *033 952 10 30; www.ballenberg.ch; admission charge*), which opened in 1978 on a 60ha (148 acres) site. Over 100 buildings threatened with destruction on their original site have been carefully dismantled and re-erected to form a museum of rural architecture and décor. Drawn from almost all cantons, they have been placed in an appropriate setting that strives to be as authentic as possible – for example, using grasses or cereals that were once common but are no longer grown commercially.

The museum preserves not only buildings but also the crafts of the rural economy. Accordingly you may see demonstrations of such skills as the making of bread, baskets, lace, shingles, fountain troughs, pack baskets, brush bundles and wood carving. Rare breeds can be seen in farmyards, a herb garden has been created behind a house, and there are various exhibitions explaining different aspects of the museum's work. The museum's three restaurants offer regional dishes, and there is an exceptionally good English-language guide.

The museum name is given to occasional steam trains along this route, including the rack section, marketed under the name 'Ballenberg Dampfbahn'. Details from tourist offices or www.ballenberg-dampfbahn.ch.

The village of Brienz is in a delightful position beside the lake, its Reformed church with 12th-century tower standing on a knoll. Steamers from the pier near the station serve seven others, including Giessbach, where an enchanting funicular near the jetty goes up to the spectacular falls from early April to mid October (table 2470). Nearby is the historic Grandhotel.

Brienz West, a delightful chalet-style station festooned with hanging baskets, is popular with walkers. The village of **Oberreid am Brienzersee** has some characteristic wooden houses, and there is a lovely 1.1km lakeside walk from **Niederried** to **Ringgenberg** where the 17th-century church stands on a knoll and incorporates masonry from a mid 13th-century castle.

Interlaken Ost is the more important of the town's two stations, being the interchange point between metre and standard gauges, and between the metre-gauge lines from Luzern and into the Bernese Oberland. However, Interlaken West is more convenient for the town centre. For Interlaken, see *Chapter 11*.

PRACTICALITIES Bicycle hire from Interlaken Ost station.

BRIENZ

Tourist information

🛈 Hauptstrasse 143, CH-3855; ☏ 033 952 80 80; e info@brienz-tourismus.ch; www.brienz-tourismus.ch; ⊕ May–mid-Jun 08.00–noon & 14.00–18.00 Mon–Fri, 09.00–noon & 14.00–17.00 Sat; mid-Jun–Sep 08.00–18.00 Mon–Fri, 09.00–13.00 & 14.30–18.00 Sat, 10.00–13.00 & 15.00–17.00 Sun; Oct–Apr 08.00–noon & 14.00–17.00 Mon–Fri

Where to stay

Numerous hotels; close to the station is:
🏠 **Weisses Kreuz*** Hauptstrasse 143, CH-3855; ☏ 033 952 20 20; e hotel@weisseskreuz-brienz.ch; www.weisseskreuz-brienz.ch

GIESSBACH
Where to stay
🏠 **Grandhotel Giessbach**** (H)** CH-3855;
📞033 952 25 25; e grandhotel@giessbach.ch;
www.giessbach.ch

RINGGENBERG
Tourist information
✉ Hauptstrasse 170, CH-3852;📞033 822 33
88; e mail@ringgenberg-goldswil.ch; www.
ringgenberg-goldswil.ch; ⏰ Jun–Sep 08.00–
11.00 & 14.00–18.00 Mon–Fri, 09.00–noon Sat;
Jul–Aug, also 16.00–18.00 Sat; Oct–May 08.00–
noon & 14.00–17.30 Mon–Fri

Where to stay
🏠 **Milan** Hauptstrasse, CH-3852;📞033 828 15
20; e milan@quicknet.ch

BRIENZ–ROTHORN Table 475

This rack railway has the distinction of running the most steam locomotives in regular service of any Swiss railway, and is now one of the most heavily used mountain railways. It was not always so – the original company went bankrupt and the railway was closed between 1915 and 1930, doubtless contributing to the survival of the steam locomotives at a time when many other railways were adopting electric traction. It also has the distinction of climbing a greater vertical distance than any other rack railway in the country, 1,678m (5,505ft), in just 7.6km (4¾ miles). The railway operates only between early June and late October, and the single journey takes one hour.

The Brienz Rothorn Bahn (BRB) was built using the Abt rack system and formally opened to a station near the summit of the 2,350m (7,710ft) mountain in June 1892. The journey starts at the original delightful station at Brienz, which was carefully restored for the railway's centenary. Most departures are made up of several trains which form a procession up the mountain. Some are likely to be diesel-propelled, as the number of passengers often exceeds the capacity of its eight working steam locomotives. The five oldest steam engines (Nos 1–5) were built between 1891 and 1892, although only three are currently in use, No 6 dates from 1933, No 7 from 1936, Nos 12 and 16 from 1992 and Nos 14 and 15 from 1996 – the last three in batches of new locomotives built in Winterthur for several railways in Switzerland and Austria.

Passing the railway's depot and workshops on the left, the railway twists up a series of horseshoe bends through farmland and deciduous woods with ever-broadening views over the lake. There is a passing loop at Geldried between two tunnels, but the only station is at **Planalp**, where there is a restaurant and from where numerous walks are signed. Steam locomotives take water here, so there is a chance to photograph them. The slopes above and below the railway are astonishingly steep after the trains have passed through the upper loop at Oberstafel and claw their way up the last switchback curves into the summit station, which was rebuilt in 1991.

Hotel Rothorn Kulm was opened in 1893 to replace an earlier structure destroyed by fire, though it has been rebuilt and extended so many times that it does not look its age. From the summit a cable car descends to Sörenberg Schönenboden (table 2505), from where a bus (table 60.241) can be taken to either Schüpfheim station on the Bern–Luzern line (table 460, page 116), or to Giswil station (see table 470, page 187). Alternatively there is a delightful four-hour walk east along the Höhenweg

Wileralp to the Brünig Pass and the Zentralbahn station at Brünig-Hasliberg (see page 188).

BRIENZ-ROTHORN
Where to stay

🏠 **Rothorn Kulm*** CH-3855; ✆033 951 12 21; e hotel-rothorn@brb.ch; www.brienz-rothorn-bahn.ch

🏠 **BRB** CH-3855; ✆033 952 22 22; e info@brb.ch; www.brienz-rothorn-bahn.ch

LUZERN–AIROLO–Lugano–Chiasso Table 600

A wonderfully varied journey that takes in several lakes and the Gotthard route through the Alps. Some trains between Luzern and Arth-Goldau are routed via Rotkreuz rather than the lakeside route through Küsnacht. The section from Flüelen to Lugano forms the railway part of the William Tell Express, so named because many of the places associated with the legend are served by this line. Sit on the right.

Leaving Luzern the train loops round the town to head east, running close to the shore of Vierwaldstättersee. The chapel of St Niklaus can be seen on its small island near **Meggen**, where Schloss Meggenhorn is built in the style of a French Renaissance château. Attached to it is an ornately decorated neo-Gothic chapel.

On the approach to **Küssnacht** is a chapel dedicated to the memory of Queen Astrid of the Belgians who was killed in a car crash in 1935 near the site. The village has some fine half-timbered buildings, such as Gasthaus Engel in Hauptplatz. A 15-minute walk from the station is the cable car to Seebodenalp from where there is a path up the Rigi.

It was near a chapel, the Tellskapelle, in a wooded, sunken lane outside Küssnacht on the way to Immensee that the Austrian Gessler was supposed to have been shot by William Tell. Goethe visited the site and suggested the story to Schiller, leading to Schiller's play (1804) and later to Rossini's opera (1829).

A line comes in from the north before **Immensee**, which overlooks the Zugersee. The lake remains in view for much of the way to the major junction of **Arth-Goldau**. The village of Goldau was destroyed on 2 September 1806 when part of the Rossberg collapsed to engulf the whole village, an event commemorated in Byron's verse drama *Manfred*, published in 1817. Turner painted the replacement village in around 1842. The Bergsturz-Museum near the Tierpark (see below) in Goldau (☉ *mid-Mar–Oct 14.00–17.30 Wed, Sat; admission charge*) describes the landslide, which was the first scientifically recorded collapse of its kind in the world.

When the railway was built, Goldau was simply a junction with a branch to the more important lakeside village of Arth; Arth had grown through being a port on the north–south Gotthard route, in much the same way as Flüelen on Vierwaldstättersee. Today the branch to Arth is closed and Goldau is the larger of the two. The bus terminus in Arth (from Arth-Goldau station see table 60.621) is on the site of the old station, also indicated by Gasthof Bahnhof. Arth's Catholic church was one of the first large Baroque churches to be built in central Switzerland, between 1695 and 1696, though the Gothic tower is 14th century. Arth-Goldau station is the junction for services north to Zürich, northeast to Einsiedeln and Rapperswil, and for the Arth–Rigi Bahn, which leaves from its own platform.

Only three minutes' walk from the station is the entrance to the Tierpark (☉ *Apr–Oct 09.00–18.00 Mon–Fri, 08.00–19.00 Sat–Sun; Nov–Feb 09.00–17.00*

13

daily; www.tierpark.ch; admission charge), a wildlife reserve for animals native to Switzerland. Some are wandering around freely, which always delights children, and safe enclosures contain bears, wolves, wild boar, lynx, racoons and marmots.

With views over the small Lauerzersee to the right, the train continues through **Steinen** to the capital of the eponymous canton of **Schwyz**. The station is poorly sited for the town, but numerous buses link the two (tables 60.501/503). The stop for the centre is Postplatz. The tourist office inside the post office has good leaflets on the town's exceptional wealth of patrician houses, two of which are open to visitors in summer.

The fame of the town rests on it giving the country its name and coat of arms. It was after the victory over the Habsburgs at nearby Morgarten in 1315 that Helvetia adopted the name of Schweiz, the canton being one of the three founders of the Confederation, the Forest Cantons of Uri, Unterwalden and Schwyz. It was in Schwyz that the spring-loaded Swiss Army Knife originated, in 1897.

The cobbled main square (Hauptplatz) is the focal point of public life. On it stand the Catholic parish church of St Martin, built by the Singer brothers between 1769 and 1774, and the Rathaus, built from 1643 to 1645, with murals depicting events in Swiss history on two façades and some splendid interiors. The most important collection in Schwyz is the Bundesbriefmuseum (Swiss Federal Archives) at Bahnhofstrasse 20 (⊕ *09.00–11.30 & 13.30–17.00 Tue–Fri; May–Oct also 09.00–17.00 Sat–Sun; Nov–Apr also 13.30–17.00 Sat–Sun*). This contains all the charters of the Confederacy between 1291 and 1513, the copy of the very first charter being the only one in existence. Murals in the 1936 building illustrate seminal events and themes on Swiss history.

A museum on Hofmatt near the post office, Forum Schweizer Geschichte Schwyz (⊕ *10.00–17.00 Tue–Sun*), traces the development of the Swiss lifestyle and what one might term the collective unconscious, including the attitude to nature and landscape.

At Rickenbachstrasse 24 is the Ital Reding Estate (⊕ *May–Oct 14.00–17.00 Tue–Fri, 10.00–noon & 14.00–17.00 Sat–Sun; admission charge*), an outstanding group of buildings reflecting life in the often-turbulent 17th century, though the oldest building is the late 13th-century Bethlehem House, with a muralled banqueting hall.

Beyond Schwyz the line crosses the River Muota that flows into the lake to the west of **Brunnen**. Before the opening of the Axenstrasse in 1865, Brunnen was an important port where goods were trans-shipped between horse-drawn wagons and boats that plied between the town and Flüelen at the southern end of the lake. The opening of the Gotthard route in 1882 acted as a great stimulus to tourism in the area, and a number of new hotels were opened in Brunnen. Most of them tried to take advantage of the wonderful views over the lake, the town being situated at the elbow between the Vierwaldstättersee and the Urnersee. Its position makes it an ideal centre for watersports – sailing, waterskiing and windsurfing.

It was here that Shelley and Mary Godwin almost ran out of money in 1814 and had to return to England after only two days. Turner spent a considerable time here and at Schwyz in 1841–43. Several watercolours in the Tate Gallery depict the Bay of Uri and its boat traffic in the pre-railway age, while one of his more detailed watercolours of Brunnen is in a gallery at Williamstown, Massachusetts. Winston Churchill spent his honeymoon at Brunnen.

Above Brunnen is the alpine resort of Morschach, reached by bus from the station (table 60.504). This service passes the cable car up to Stoos (table 2572), from where another car ascends to Fronalpstock (table 2571) for a view that almost rivals the Rigipanorama. A chairlift from Stoos ascends the Klingenstock (table 2571.1). The Stoos ridge hike from Klingenstock to Fronalpstock offers a view of over ten lakes and countless peaks.

The railway runs along the lake though the views are interrupted by numerous tunnels. From the station at the small resort of **Sisikon** a bus goes up a narrow gorge on the short journey to Riemenstalden (table 60.541). To the south of Sisikon is a small pier near the Tellskapell, the chapel built on the site where William Tell is supposed to have leapt to freedom from the floundering boat in which he was being taken to a dungeon in Küssnacht. A storm had blown up, and his captors had untied Tell so that with his knowledge of the lake he could steer them to safety. He said there was shelter to be had near the shore, and when near enough he grabbed his crossbow, leapt ashore and dived into the forest. The chapel was erected in 1879–80 on the site of an earlier commemorative building; the frescoes of the legend are by the Basel painter Ernst Stückelberg. A painting of the earlier chapel by Turner hangs in the Yale Centre for British Art at New Haven, Connecticut.

Flüelen was once a thriving port for trans-shipping goods on the north–south road over the Gotthard. Today passengers on the William Tell Express leave the boat at this small resort and take the train on to Lugano. In the village are the disused church of SS George and Nikolaus, built in 1665–66, and the multi-gabled tower of Rudenz Castle; both buildings were prominent in one of Turner's watercolours of the settlement. When he stayed here, the marshes around the Reuss delta were regarded as a source of pestilence, which, according to Murray in 1838, gave the locals 'pale faces, crippled limbs, and goitred necks'.

A 15-minute walk from the station takes you to the cable car to Eggberge (table 2592), popular with mountain bikers and paragliders.

South of Flüelen the railway enters the broad valley of the Reuss, the land on either side a mix of arable and pasture overshadowed by the snow-covered pyramid of the Bristenstock. The mountains become so high that the valley floor is in shadow from mid-afternoon in autumn. The station for the cantonal capital of Uri, **Altdorf**, is on the edge of the town, but frequent buses link them (tables 60.402/403). The town's fame rests on the William Tell legend, for it was in the main square that Tell shot the apple from his son's head on the orders of the Austrian governor, Gessler, in 1307. A huge statue of Tell erected in 1895 stands in the square beside a 13th-century tower. Tradition has it that Tell was born in nearby Bürglen, where a museum has been set up in the 13th-century Wattigwillerturm (⊕ *May–Jun 10.00–11.30 & 13.30–17.00 daily; Jul–Aug 10.00–17.00 daily; www.tellmuseum.ch; admission charge*) telling the story of the legend over six centuries. Bürglen can be reached from Altdorf Telldenkmal by a bus starting at Flüelen station (tables 60.408/409).

Altdorf lost many of its older buildings in a fire which broke out in 1799 during the Revolutionary Wars, when the armies of France, Austria and Russia fought in and around the town. Among the older buildings that survived are Switzerland's oldest Capuchin monastery, of St Karl, founded in 1579 to the northeast of the town, and the mid 16th-century Suvarov House just off the main square to the southeast. This acquired its name from the Russian general who made it his headquarters in 1799 after forcing a passage of the Schöllenen gorge against fierce French resistance (see page 311).

A neo-Gothic building dating from 1905 at Gotthardstrasse 18 houses a regional museum (⊕ *May–Jun, mid-Aug–mid-Oct, Dec 13.00–17.00 Wed, Sat–Sun*) with collections of art, porcelain, furniture, textiles and arms.

A bus from Altdorf station goes to Schloss A Pro at Seedorf (table 60.403), an enchanting manor house built between 1556 and 1558 which has been described as one of the finest mansions in Switzerland, with an impressive knights' hall. Now owned by the canton of Uri, it has a display on minerals as well as changing exhibitions and a gastronomic restaurant (*www.schlossapro.ch*). The castle is open at the same time as the restaurant (🕘 *09.30–23.00 Wed–Thu, 09.00–24.00 Fri–Sat, 09.00–17.00 Sun*) and is freely accessible to all.

With the Reuss still to the right, the railway reaches the railway town of **Erstfeld** where assisting engines were stationed for the northern ascent of the Gotthard, which begins here. Over the next 28km (17¾ miles) the railway has to climb a vertical height of 634m (2,080ft). To achieve this it has to be taken through one spiral tunnel, the Pfaffensprung, and two horseshoe loops around the Catholic church at Wassen. The views as the railway forges up the gradient are spectacular, spoilt only by the new road. At Amsteg there is a fine view up the Kärstelenbach gorge to the east. The old packhorse route can be seen at several places, crossing the Reuss by elegant masonry arches. After the horseshoe curves the line enters the 1,570m (5,150ft) long Naxberg Tunnel which brings the railway to **Göschenen**, junction for the short rack line up to Andermatt (see *Chapter 18*).

It is no longer possible to hire bikes at Göschenen station but a footpath has been created to pass the most spectacular features of the railway; it links Göschenen with Erstfeld, and a similar path and bike route has been devised for the south ramp from Airolo down to Biasca (see page 316).

Immediately beyond Göschenen station the line enters the Gotthard Tunnel. Work began on the tunnel in June 1872, using compressed-air rock drills and working from both ends. For nearly eight years an average of 2,500 men toiled night and day to bore the 15km tunnel. Apart from a single curve at the southern end the tunnel is straight; when the tunnellers met up in 1880, the centre lines of the bores were only 18cm (7in) out horizontally and 10cm (4in) vertically. The tunnel opened to full traffic in June 1882. Tragically the tunnel's engineer, Louis Favre, died of a heart attack in the tunnel in 1879 and is buried in the cemetery beside the church at Göschenen.

It takes ten minutes to travel through the tunnel; before its opening the journey between Göschenen and Airolo took a whole day.

KÜSSNACHT
Tourist information
ℹ️ Unterdorf 6, CH-6403; ☎ 041 850 33 30; e info@hohlgassland.ch; www.hohlgassland.ch; 🕘 08.30–noon & 13.30–18.00 Mon–Fri

Where to stay
🏠 **Du Lac Seehof*** (H)** Seeplatz 6, CH-6403; ☎ 041 850 10 12; e seehof@remimag.ch; www. du-lac-seehof.ch

🏠 **Zum Hirschen*** (H)** Unterdorf 9, CH-6403; ☎ 041 854 33 33; e info@zumhirschen.ch; www. zumhirschen.ch

ARTH
Where to stay
🏠 **Seehotel Adler Garni**** Zugerstrasse 2, CH-6415; ☎ 041 855 12 50; www.hri.ch/6415-adler

🏠 **Hofmatt** Schulweg 10, CH-6415; ☎ 041 855 10 33

SCHWYZ
Tourist information
ℹ️ Bahnhofstrasse 4, Postfach 655, CH-6431; ☎ 041 855 59 50; e info@schwyz-tourismus.

ch; www.schwyz-tourismus.ch; 🕘 08.00–noon Mon–Fri

BRUNNEN
Tourist information
🖃 Bahnhofstrasse 15, CH-6440; 📞041 825 00 40; e info@brunnentourismus.ch; www. brunnentourismus.ch; ⏰ Jun–Sep 08.30–18.00 Mon–Fri, 09.00–13.00 Sat; Jul–Aug 08.30–18.00 Mon–Fri, 0900–15.00 Sat–Sun; Oct–May 08.30– noon & 13.30–17.30 Mon–Fri

Where to stay
Numerous hotels; closest to the station is:
🏠 **National*** Bahnhofstrasse 47, CH-6440; 📞041 820 18 78; e gasthaus.national@ swissonline.ch
A hotel overlooking the lake and adjacent to the steamer pier is:
🏠 **Seehotel Waldstätterhof***** (H)** Waldstätterquai, CH-6440; 📞041 825 06 06; e info@waldstaetterhof.ch; www.waldstaetterhof. ch. Winston Churchill stayed here on his honeymoon.

SISIKON
Where to stay
🏠 **Tellsplatte***** CH-6452; 📞041 874 18 74; e info@tellsplatte.ch; www.tellsplatte.ch

FLÜELEN
Where to stay
Several hotels; near the station is:
🏠 **Weisses Kreuz**** Axenstrasse 2, CH-6454; 📞041 870 17 17; e info@weisseskreuz-fluelen.ch; www.weisseskreuz-fluelen.ch

ALTDORF
Tourist information
🖃 Schützengasse 11, CH-6460; 📞041 874 80 00; e info@uri.info; www.uri.info; ⏰ 09.30–11.30 & 13.30–17.30 Mon–Fri, 09.00–11.30 Sat

Where to stay
🏠 **Bahnhof*** Rynächstrasse 2, CH-6460; 📞041 870 10 32; e hotel.bahnhof@bluewin.ch; www. hotel-bahnhof.ch

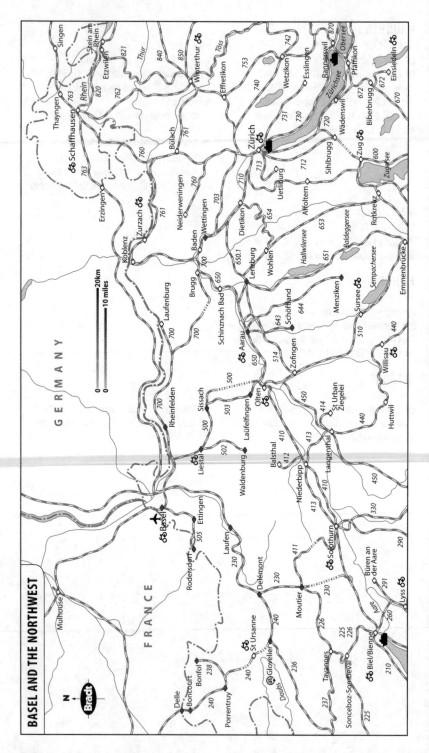

BASEL AND THE NORTHWEST

14

Basel and the Northwest

This populous corner of Switzerland has a concentration of heavy industry in some of the urban centres, such as Basel and Olten. But it also has the eastern end of the Jura Mountains and the Black Forest across the border in Germany, easily reached by S-Bahn trains from Basel. The main reason for visiting Basel is its museums, which are outstanding in scope and quality, especially in art.

BASEL

Basel is Switzerland's second-largest city with a population of 200,000 and owes a long history of trading links to its strategic position on a bend in the Rhine between the barriers of the Jura and Black Forest ridges. Even by the time the town's first bridge (of wood) across the Rhine was opened in 1226, the place had established a reputation for scholarship. Its university was founded in 1460, and Basel became a part of the Helvetic Confederation in 1501. The city became a crucible of Humanism, adopting the Reformation in 1529 and providing a refuge for many skilled tradesmen exiled from France and Italy by the Counter-Reformation.

Silk ribbon weaving began in the 16th century, becoming important in the 17th when much of the work was done by outworkers in surrounding villages. The profits from silk weaving and dyeing went into the Blue House and White House – Nos 16 and 18 on Rheinsprung near the cathedral – which are rare examples of Baroque architecture in Basel. It spawned the chemical industry that has become a major part of the city's economy.

Basel was not only the first community in Switzerland to have a railway when the line from St Louis in France opened in 1844, it also had the world's first international station. After the arrival of the last train each evening, the gates of the walled city were closed by a sentry paid for by the railway company. By the late 19th century Basel had become a major railway junction, and its chemical industries emerged as one of the city's principal activities. It is also a great centre for trade exhibitions and fairs, at which time hotel accommodation can be at a premium.

The Dutch Humanist Erasmus (1466–1536) spent about ten years of his life in Basel, where many of his books were published. Prince Charles Edward, the Young Pretender, spent the years 1754–56 here with his mistress Clementina Walkinshaw (who died in Fribourg) and their daughter Charlotte Stuart. Nietzsche was professor of classical philosophy at the university from 1869 to 1879. Hermann Hesse (1877–1962) spent much of his childhood here, becoming a bookseller and antiquarian in the city between 1895 and 1902 as well as writing his first successful novel, *Peter Camenzind*.

It is said that the people of Basel, despite receiving influences from the three countries on their doorstep, are restrained and introspective. 'English

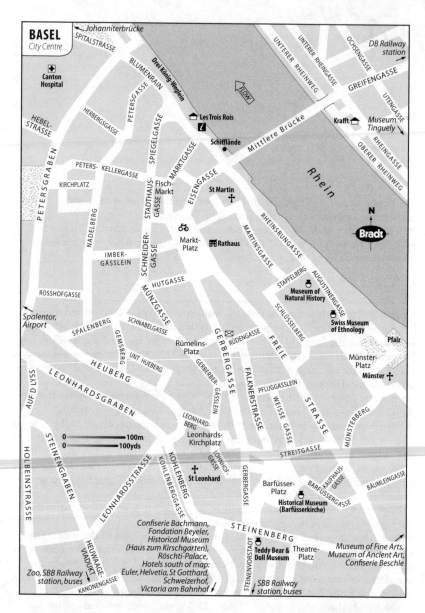

BASEL
City Centre

understatement looks like megalomania when compared with that of the people of Basel', as someone put it. They have also been known for their pitiless realism and iconoclasm – Erasmus departed from the city in horror when the art treasures of the churches and monasteries were destroyed in three bonfires on the cathedral square.

Basel has become a major centre for art and particularly modern art and architecture, with galleries designed by architects of the calibre of Renzo Piano, Mario Botta and Herzog & de Meuron. Contemporary buildings have been designed by Diener & Diener, Frank Gehry, Zaha Hadid, Richard Meier and Álvaro Siza Vieira.

Many of its old town shops are small and unusual: you may find whole shops devoted to African jewellery, tea, philately, ink stamps, teddy bears and travel memorabilia. The city has 170 fountains, all with potable water.

GETTING THERE The airport is situated in France but frequent buses link it with the SBB station without border formalities. A tram link is under consideration. Basel is served by more direct trains from cities outside the country than any other Swiss city. Trains for French and Swiss destinations use the SBB station on the south side of the Rhine; those for most German destinations leave from the DB station in Kleinbasel, linked with the SBB station by tram line 2 (destination Eglisee travelling to the DB station; destination Binningen Kronenplatz travelling from the DB to SBB station).

The SBB station has all the usual facilities, including money change and a branch of the main tourist office (⊕ *08.30–18.30 Mon–Fri, 09.00–17.00 Sat, 09.00–16.00 Sun*).

Before leaving the station, spare a moment to look at the mechanical toy by Jean Tinguely in one of the concourses.

GETTING AROUND

Using public transport Basel has an outstandingly good public transport network with 11 tram lines and 46 bus routes (*www.bvb.ch*). Clear maps are available free from the tourist offices or the city transport office in Barfüsserplatz. Every visitor who stays in Basel overnight receives a Mobility Ticket allowing free use of public transport, and a hotel reservation confirmation guarantees a free public transport transfer from the station or airport to your hotel.

Fares are determined by the zones, but most of the city is covered by zone 10, with outlying suburbs on the longer tram and bus lines covered by zones 11 and 12. Multi-journey cards are available, giving 12 journeys for the price of 10. Day cards offering unlimited travel are a better buy if you are making numerous journeys on a single day. Regional passes for the whole of northwest Switzerland are also available; these allow a one-way journey on a Rhine steamer between Basel and Rheinfelden (see page 215). All these cards have to be stamped in a ticket machine before commencement of the first journey, by inserting them in the slot marked *Entwerten*.

The longer tram lines such as 10 to Rodersdorf and 11 to Aesch go out into the country. Bus and tram routes cross the border into France and Germany.

On Sundays a historic tram operates an hour-long guided city tour; contact the tourist office for details.

Using bicycles Cyclists in Basel enjoy one of the most comprehensive networks of cycle lanes in Europe. There are numerous segregated routes, and at junctions the needs of cyclists are not forgotten, overhead direction signs even having a separate sign for cycle lanes. Most one-way streets are open for two-way bicycle traffic, and speed humps have flat sections for cyclists.

These measures form part of a co-ordinated policy to reduce car traffic, especially by commuters. Only 21% of the population now travels to work by car.

Bicycle hire (⊕ *daily 07.00–21.00*) from Basel station.

TOURIST INFORMATION

⛵ Railway station Aeschenvorstadt 36; ⊕ 08.30–18.00 Mon–Fri, 09.00–17.00 Sat, 09.00–15.00 Sun

⛵ Stadtcasino Barfüsserplatz, Steinenberg 14, CH-4051; ☏ 061 268 68 68; e info@basel. com; www.basel.com; ⊕ 09.00–18.30 Mon–Fri, 09.00–17.00 Sat, 10.00–15.00 Sun & public holidays

WHERE TO STAY

Numerous hotels; close to the station are:

🛏 **Euler***** Centralbahnplatz 14, CH-4002;
📞061 275 80 00; ℮ reservation@hoteleuler.ch;
www.hoteleuler.ch

🛏 **St Gotthard**** Centralbahnstrasse 13, CH-4002;📞061 225 13 13; ℮ reception@st-gotthard.ch; www.st-gotthard.ch

🛏 **Victoria am Bahnhof**** Centralbahnplatz 3–4, CH-4002;📞061 270 70 70; ℮ hotel-victoria@balehotels.ch; www.victoria.balehotels.ch

🛏 **Helvetia*** Küchengasse 13, CH-4051;
📞061 272 06 88; ℮ info@hotelhelvetia.ch; www.hotelhelvetia.ch

🛏 **Schweizerhof*** Centralbahnplatz 1, CH-4002;📞061 560 85 85; ℮ info@schweizerhof-basel.ch; www.schweizerhof-basel.ch

A hotel in the old city is:

🛏 **Les Trois Rois***** (H)** Blumenrain 8, CH-4001;📞061 260 50 50; ℮ info@lestroisrois.com; www.lestroisrois.com. Claims to be Switzerland's oldest hotel. Built on the site of a house where in 1026 the Emperor Conrad II met the last king of Burgundy, Rudolf III. In a fine position overlooking the Rhine.

Just across the Mittlere Brücke is:

🛏 **Krafft*** (H)** Rheingasse 12, CH-4058;
📞061 690 91 30; 061 690 91 31; ℮ info@krafftbasel.ch; www.krafftbasel.ch. Modern bedrooms, historic common rooms & excellent restaurant.

WHERE TO EAT

Restaurants and cafés near the station are:

✕ **Atlantis** Klosterberg 13;📞061 228 96. Unique ambience with excellent cuisine – with terrace in summer – combined with a friendly bar culture.

✕ **Café Confiserie Beschle** Aeschenvorstadt 56;📞061 295 40 40. Famous café with own pastry.

✕ **Caspar's** Hotel Euler, Centralbahnplatz 14;📞061 275 80 00. Regional and seasonal specialities & a daily changing lunch.

✕ **Confiserie Bachmann** Centralbahnplatz 7;📞061 271 26 27. Coffee, snacks & pastry, legendary müesli.

✕ **Le Train Bleu** Centralbahnplatz 3-4;📞061 270 78 17. Swiss & regional cuisine, bistro restaurant with spacious terrace.

✕ **Restaurant Aeschenplatz** Aeschenplatz 4;📞061 271 38 55. Swiss & American cuisine with courtyard bbq in summer, cellar restaurant with fireplace in winter.

✕ **Restaurant Elsbethenstübli**
Elisabethenstrasse 34;📞061 272 11 05. Swiss cheese fondue & typical Basel cuisine.

✕ **Ristorante Da Robert** Küchengasse 3;📞061 205 85 50. Italian cuisine.

✕ **Röschti-Palace at the Brasserie**
Centralbahnstrasse 14;📞061 295 39 50. Rösti in different styles.

WHAT TO SEE

Exploring the city A good starting place is the Schifflände – the quay for steamers along the Rhine. A variety of cruises and excursions along the Rhine is offered by four boat operators, visiting such places as the Roman town of Augusta Raurica in Kaiseraugst and Rheinfelden (details from the tourist office). From outside the railway station take tram 8 (direction Kleinhüningen) or 11 (direction St-Louis Grenze). Much of the centre is pedestrianised, and there are colour-coded walking routes taking in the old town's historic buildings. Each walk is named after an historic figure associated with Basel, such as Erasmus or Holbein; details can be obtained from the tourist office, which also organises guided walks between April and October.

If time is short, the area to the southeast embraces Basel's principal old buildings, and it is a lovely walk parallel with the river, past timber-framed buildings, to the red sandstone cathedral on Münsterplatz. From Schifflände, walk up the narrow Rheinsprung. No 11 was an old university building where the secretary of state to Elizabeth I, Sir Francis Walsingham, and the founder of the Bodleian Library in Oxford, Thomas Bodley, were educated.

As you approach the cathedral square you pass the Museum of Natural History (see *Museums*, page 207).

The oldest part of the cathedral is a section of the choir's foundations, which date from an early 9th-century building destroyed by the Huns. The next structure was founded in 1019 by the Holy Roman Emperor Henry II, but fire in 1185 destroyed much of it. Reconstruction began in a part-Romanesque, part-Gothic style based on Modena Cathedral, which had been consecrated the year before, but this was badly damaged by the severe earthquake of 1356 that brought down the tower situated at the crossing. This was dispensed with in the rebuilding that produced the building we see today (after various restorations): instead of a crossing tower, two slightly asymmetrical towers were put up at the west end, the northern tower dedicated to St George and the southern to St Martin. Equestrian statues of the saints can be seen at the foot of each tower. The west portal contains a statue of Henry II and his wife, Kunigunde, and of a Foolish Virgin and her seducer.

The interior of the nave has little decoration, except for the ornate pulpit on tapering base of 1486. At the east end of the choir are the Schaler chapel, in which Erasmus was reburied in 1928, and the Fröwler chapel with a relief of six Apostles that dates from c1100.

At the east end of the cathedral is the tree-shaded Pfalz from which there is a fine view over the Rhine. South of the cathedral, along Rittergasse, is the Kunstmuseum (see *Museums*, page 206).

Parallel to Rheinsprung is Martinsgasse which leads, at its northern end, into Martinsplatz: the Reformed church of St Martin was built between the 13th and 15th centuries on the site of a 6th-century church. It was here that the first Protestant services in Basel were held.

Steps beside the church lead down into Marktplatz, dominated by the sienna-coloured Rathaus. The three-storey central section with clock was built between 1503 and 1507, the left-hand part with oriel window from 1606 to 1608 and the tower from 1898 to 1904. Its courtyard is decorated by frescoes executed in 1608 by Hans Block.

South of Marktplatz, reached by Gerbergasse, is Leonhardskirchplatz, a small square in which stands the Reformed church of St Leonhard. Once part of an Augustinian foundation, the present Gothic church was built in 1481–1528. The interior has a fine stellar vault.

Slightly outside the pedestrianised part of the old city, at the end of Spalenvorstadt on tram route 3 (direction Burgfelden Grenze), is Basel's finest surviving city gate, the 14th-century Spalentor. Two round towers flank a massive square tower.

The career of Jean Tinguely began in Basel, so it is appropriate that the city has two public works by the Swiss sculptor, as well as a museum devoted to him. One is in the station concourse; the other, his fountain of 1977, is outside the theatre on Theaterplatz.

Museums Basel has 39 museums, including some of Switzerland's most important, in particular the Fine Arts Museum (Kunstmuseum) and the Historical Museums. For visitors wishing to visit a number of museums, there is a three-day museum pass entitling the holder to free admission to permanent and special exhibitions in the canton of Basel-Stadt. The pass can be bought at the main and station tourist offices.

Fondation Beyeler (*Baselstrasse 101; ⟍ 061 645 97 00; ⊕ 10.00–18.00 daily, Wed 10.00–20.00; tram 6 to Riehen Dorf or Fondation Beyeler; admission charge*) This beautifully designed museum by Renzo Piano (who also designed the Paul

Klee Centre in Bern) provides a home to the collection of 20th-century art created by Hildy and Ernst Beyeler. It includes work by Bacon, Cézanne, Monet, Picasso, Rothko, Van Gogh and Warhol.

Museum of Fine Arts (Kunstmuseum) (*St Alban-Graben 16;* ☎ *061 206 62 62;* ☉ *10.00–18.00 Tue–Sun; during special exhibitions only: also 10.00–19.00 Wed; tram 2 or 15 to Kunstmuseum; admission charge*) This contains the most distinguished collection of paintings in Switzerland and is one of the oldest galleries in the world. As early as 1679 the art historian Joachim von Sandrart could write: 'Of all the towns of the Swiss Confederation none deserves more praise than the City of Basel and its worthy elders for their great expenditure and diligence in collecting and highly honouring studies and the arts, especially excellent paintings, drawings and the like.'

The tradition was already two centuries old when von Sandrart was writing, for works had been bought from two artists resident in Basel in the 15th century: Konrad Witz, the first great Swiss painter, who lived in Basel from 1435 to 1446, and Hans Holbein the Younger who resided here from 1515 to 1532, when he moved to London and became the favourite court painter of Henry VIII.

The city of Basel bought 20 Holbeins in 1661, but these early collections have almost been eclipsed by the Kunstmuseum's modern art collection. This includes a small collection of Impressionists (but 200 works on paper by Cézanne), an outstanding collection of Cubist paintings and a large holding of American art.

Amongst the many other painters whose work can be seen are Altdorfer, Grünewald (there is a larger collection of his work across the border in Colmar, less than an hour on the train from Basel), Cranach, Holbein the Elder, David, Rembrandt, Teniers the Younger, Böcklin, Goya, Gauguin, Renoir, Van Gogh, Braque, Picasso, Chagall, Klee, Kline, Newman, Noland and Still.

Museum of Contemporary Art (Museum für Gegenwartskunst) (*St Alban-Rheinweg 60;* ☎ *061 206 62 62;* ☉ *11.00–18.00 Tue–Sun; tram 2 or 15 to Kunstmuseum; admission charge*) Built for the principal shareholder in the pharmaceutical firm Hoffman-La Roche, Maya Sacher, the museum's collection contains two Picassos bought in 1967 after a referendum; Picasso was so touched by the people's decision that he gave the museum several other canvases.

Museum of Ancient Art (Antikenmuseum und Sammlung Ludwig) (*St Alban-Graben 5;* ☎ *061 201 12 12;* ☉ *10.00–17.00 Tue–Sun; trams 2 or 15 to Kunstmuseum; admission charge*) Housed in two adjacent mansions of 1826 and 1828, the museum contains Greek and Roman sculpture, glass, sarcophagi, vases, masks, caricatures and coins.

Historical Museum (Barfüsserkirche) (*Barfüsserplatz;* ☎ *061 205 86 00;* ☉ *10.00–17.00 Tue–Sun; trams 3, 6, 8, 11, 14, or 16 to Barfüsserplatz or 10 to Theatre*) The 14th-century Franciscan church was used as a salt store until conversion to a museum in 1894. It contains a heterogeneous collection relating to the history of Basel and the surrounding area, such as furniture, glass, pewter, metalwork, sculpture, arms and armour, medals and coins.

Historical Museum (Haus zum Kirschgarten) (*Elisabethenstrasse 27;* ☎ *061 205 86 00;* ☉ *10.00–17.00 Tue–Fri & Sun, 13.00–17.00 Sat; tram 2 to Kirschgarten*) Near Theaterplatz is one of Switzerland's principal museums of domestic life during the 18th and 19th centuries, with large collections of porcelain, stoves, ironwork, glass, furniture (some in re-created rooms), tapestries, silver, musical instruments and shop signs. A room tells the story of the remarkable life of the explorer Johann Ludwig Burckhardt, whose father originally owned the house. It was Burckhardt who 'discovered' Petra in 1812 and was the first European to make the pilgrimage to Mecca.

Museum of Natural History (Naturhistorisches Museum) (*Augustinergasse 2;* ☎ *061 266 55 00;* ☉ *10.00–17.00 Tue–Sun; trams 6, 8, 11, 14, or 16 to Schifflände or trams 2 or 15 to Kunstmuseum*) A journey to all corners of the earth, covering all aspects of the natural sciences, from extinct to living mammals.

Museum Tinguely (*Paul Sacher-Anlage 1;* ☎ *061 681 93 20;* ☉ *11.00–18.00 Tue–Sun; bus 31 or 36 to Tinguely Museum; admission charge*) Mario Botta designed this museum, devoted to the life and work of Jean Tinguely, iron sculptor extraordinaire.

Teddy Bear and Doll Museum (Spielzeug Welten Museum Basel) (*Steinenvorstadt 1;* ☎ *061 225 95 95;* ☉ *10.00–18.00 daily; trams 3, 6, 8, 11, 14, or 16 to Barfüsserplatz or tram 10 to Theatre*) Over 6,000 teddy bears, dolls, doll's houses and miniatures in imaginatively arranged scenes.

Vitra Design Museum (*Charles-Eames-Strasse 2;* ☎ *07621 702 32 00;* ☉ *10.00–18.00 daily; bus 55 from Claraplatz to Vitra; admission charge*) The Vitra Design Museum is housed in a spectacular building designed by Californian architect Frank Gehry and his first structure outside the US. Other buildings include Zaha Hadid's Fire Station (1990–93) and a building designed by Herzog & de Meuron in 2010. The museum is home to one of the world's leading collections of industrial furniture design and architecture. Along with a changing programme of exhibitions, the museum organises workshops and produces special edition pieces.

The subjects of other museums include sports, applied arts, architecture, cartoons, paper, Swiss folk art, toys, cats, Jewish history, coaches and sleighs, cars, musical instruments, fire brigade, pharmacy, navigation and plaster cats.

Zoo Close to the SBB station is the highly regarded zoo (*Binningerstrasse 40;* ☉ *Mar–Apr & Sep–Oct 08.00–18.00 daily; May–Aug 08.00–18.30 daily; Nov–Feb 08.00–17.30 daily; tram 10 or 17 to Zoo; admission charge*), which covers 11ha (27 acres) and has some rare species among its 6,000 animals, from 600 different species. After the falls at Schaffhausen, it's the most visited attraction in Switzerland. An aquarium offers shelter if it's raining. At the entrance is a table of feeding times.

Festivals Basel has what is probably the most idiosyncratic of Swiss festivals, the Fasnacht, which was first recorded in 1376. The atmosphere during part of this spring carnival is almost sombre, reflecting its self-deprecating and mocking undertones. The first event takes place in January when three mythological figures – the griffin (*Vogel Gryff*), savage (*Wilde Mann*) and lion (*Leu*) – appear to chase winter away. Then, at 04.00 precisely on the Monday after Ash Wednesday, all lights in the city are extinguished and the morning parade (*Morgenstreich*) begins. The shrill sound of piccolos contrasts with the rumble of heavy Basel drums as groups of outlandishly dressed musicians move through the streets. The music, weird masks and lanterns combine to create an eerie, timeless atmosphere, accentuated by the lanterns developed after open torches were banned in 1845. The festival continues for three days, fuelled by all-night opening of cafés and bars, where satiric verses are recited, and by the special trains operated by SBB to bring in more participants. Parades of floats take to the streets on Monday and Wednesday afternoon, and on Tuesday afternoon the children have their own parade.

Trade fairs During the full calendar of trade fairs, the two most important (when hotel rooms are harder to find) are the Swiss Industries Fair in spring and the Autumn Fair at the end of October.

BASEL–RODERSDORF Table 505/Line 10

This is the longest of Basel's tram lines and takes you right out into the country.

Set in an attractive park at **Binningen** is a former moated castle built in the late 13th century.

At **Bottmingen** is a magnificent moated castle. Thought to have been constructed in the 13th century, it was restored in Baroque style in the 17th century and became a hotel and restaurant in 1890. Now the property of the city, it is still a restaurant (✆ 061 421 15 15; *www.schlossbottmingen.ch*) and open to visitors for dinners, including jazz dinner-dances.

From the stop at **Flüh**, a bus runs to Mariastein (table 50.069/line 69), where there is a Benedictine monastery around the church and sanctuary of Our Lady, a place of pilgrimage from the 15th century. The present church was built between 1830 and 1834. Mariastein is also the start of a 30-minute walk to the rebuilt medieval fortress of Rotberg. The castle was built in the 13th century and restored voluntarily by unemployed workers from Basel during the 1930s. Today it is the Mariastein-Rotberg youth hostel and open to visitors (✆ 061 731 10 49).

BASEL–DELÉMONT Table 230

The route of trains from Basel to Geneva follows the sinuous valley of the River Birse.

The first two stations on the line both serve suburbs of Basel which have a number of interesting buildings. At **Münchenstein** are the country houses of Bruckgut (1759–61), and the Neo-classical Ehinger (1828–31). On the St Alban pool is a large hammer mill.

The local history museum at Dornach (station **Dornach-Arlesheim** or tram 10 to Arlesheim Dorf) is housed in the former Catholic church of St Mauritius. Between Dornach and Arlesheim is a curious ferro-concrete structure (1924–28) known as the Goetheanum which serves as the headquarters of the Anthroposophical Society founded by Rudolf Steiner.

The Rococo Arlesheim Cathedral stands in an imposing forecourt and has the last playable organ built by Johannes Andreas Silbermann (1712–83) in Switzerland. It dates from 1761. Afterwards take a stroll through the Ermitage Arlesheim, the oldest English landscape garden in Switzerland, with mill, ponds, grottoes, hermitage and the ruined 13th-century castle of Birseck. A 30-minute walk uphill from the town is the castle of Dorneck. The 13th-century castle was destroyed by an earthquake in 1356, rebuilt in 1360 and largely destroyed after it was sacked in 1798 during the French Revolution. However, there are extensive remains of the curtain walls, keep and various towers (⊕ *May–Sep 10.00–noon & 13.30–18.00 Sun*). After the walk, stop for irresistible cakes and tea at Confisserie Brändli at Dorfplatz 9.

Some buildings that made up the early 17th-century Blarer Schloss at **Aesch** have survived, including the barn, which is now a local history museum (🕐 *10.00–noon & 15.00–17.00 1st Sun in month*). At Aesch the valley begins to narrow, forcing the railway to become single track for a section. From the station at **Grellingen** a postbus (table 50.116/line 116) goes to Seewen where there is a large and extraordinary museum of mechanical musical instruments (🕐 *11.00–18.00 Tue–Sun; admission charge*), ranging from a musical tobacco box to immense church organs.

One of the area's most attractive and best-preserved castles is at **Zwingen** where the walls rise above the River Birse, which is crossed by a bridge that springs from the gatehouse-tower. The buildings date from the 14th to 17th centuries.

The railway continues through the well-wooded valley, which is a glorious kaleidoscope of browns and yellows in autumn, to **Duggingen**. On the cliff to the right the imposingly sited ruins of the castle of Pfeffingen can be seen; sections of the keep and much of the walls remain of this 12th–13th-century fortress.

Laufen was founded in 1295 by the bishop of Basel, and the town retains three gateways and a good length of the town walls. Near the Untertor is the Baroque church of St Katharina with mid 18th-century Rococo stucco.

Above **Soyhières** is the ruined castle of the same name, but buses from the village to Delémont (tables 21.213/lines 13 & 14) can reduce the walk. The castle was built in the 11th century and destroyed during the Swabian War in 1499. It was rebuilt in the 16th century.

For **Delémont** see table 230, page 127.

DORNACH
Where to stay
🏠 **Kloster Dornach (H)** Amtshausstrasse 7,
CH-4143; ☎ 061 701 12 72; 📧 info@klosterdornach.
ch; www.klosterdornach.ch

DELÉMONT–PORRENTRUY–BONCOURT Table 240

An initially dull journey suddenly comes to life as the railway skirts the River Doubs. St Ursanne is an undervisited ancient town.

The only thing of interest on the scenically unexciting line between Delémont and Glovelier is the Catholic church of St Germain d'Auxerre in **Courfaivre**, which has stained glass of 1954 designed by Fernand Léger. At **Glovelier**, the metre-gauge line of the CF Jura leaves for La Chaux-de-Fonds from just outside the standard-gauge station. If you are changing trains, spend a minute and 20¢ in the waiting room (see table 236, page 224).

The long tunnel that follows after Glovelier provides one of those dramatic transitions that rail travellers soon become accustomed to in Switzerland. The line emerges high up on the right-hand side of the magnificent valley of the River Doubs as it describes a semicircle, with lovely views to the left as the line also sweeps round to the left across the huge Combe Maran Viaduct. Just before another long tunnel, under the Col de la Croix, is **St Ursanne**, which is worth breaking the journey to see. The station has a buffet and terrace overlooking the valley.

The town beside the River Doubs is a four-minute bus journey from the station (table 21.161). The settlement grew up around a monastic community based on the cell of the Irish monk Ursicinus, and the 12th-century concentric plan can still be seen, overlaid by the straight streets to the east created after fire swept through the town in 1403. The three town gates that were rebuilt in the 16th–17th centuries still survive, that of St Jean guarding the early 17th-century bridge across the river. The Romanesque collegiate church has a 12th-century choir under which there is a hall crypt that once held the bones of St Ursicinus. The tower dates from 1442, and the church has finely carved choir-stalls, pulpit and capitals.

The second tunnel provides another emphatic change in the landscape, the train emerging into farmland. The approach to **Porrentruy** is despoiled by a motorway that dominates the landscape, but the town, though industrial, has much of interest.

Dominating the old town is the castle, a stronghold built by the bishop of Basel in the 13th century. The oldest part is the cylindrical Réfouss Tower (⊕ 08.00–18.00 *daily*); the rest of the buildings are used by local government. The residence, chancellery and Cock tower (the cock was the bishop's emblem) were built in the 16th century. The castle ceased to be an ecclesiastical residence from 1792 and would have been demolished but for the intervention of local people.

The old town beneath the castle was built on an island in the river, but little of the fortifications remains other than the 16th-century French Gate. Even by the 11th century the town had two churches. The oldest today is the Romanesque Catholic church of St Germain, which dates from the 12th to 17th centuries and has a notable Gothic font. The Catholic parish church of St Pierre is mid 14th-century Gothic with fine side altars, and the galleried church of the Ursulines dates from the early 17th century. The Hôtel-Dieu (former hospital) in Grand-rue houses the tourist office and a museum of local history.

North of Porrentruy the railway follows the River l'Allaine closely through an attractive valley, particularly between **Courchavon** and **Courtemaîche**. Beside the prettily sited station at **Buix** are a three-arched stone bridge across the river and the church, with striking coloured tiles. Trains used to terminate at **Boncourt**, the last station on Swiss soil, but the line across the French border to **Delle** has been rebuilt for a resumption of passenger services in conjunction with the new high-speed line serving Belfort, to which Delle trains will be extended as part of a new service between Delémont and Belfort.

PRACTICALITIES Bikes can be hired at St Ursanne station and also returned to Glovelier station.

ST URSANNE
Tourist information
◪ Place Roger Schaffter, CH-2882; ✆ 032 420 47 73; e stursanne@juratourisme.ch; www. juratourisme.ch; ⊕ Apr, Oct 10.00–noon & 14.00–17.00 Mon–Fri, 10.00–noon, 13.30–17.30 Sat–Sun; May–Sep 09.00–noon & 14.00–18.00 Mon–Fri, 10.00–noon & 13.30–17.30 Sat–Sun; Oct–mid-Nov 10.00–noon & 14.00–17.00 Mon–Fri, 09.00–noon Sat

Where to stay
⌂ **Demi-Lune** ** (H)** Rue Basse 2, CH-2882; ✆ 032 461 35 31; e info@demi-lune.ch; www. demi-lune.ch

COURGENAY
Where to stay
⌂ **Hôtel-Restaurant de la Petite Gilberte (H)** Rue de la Petite Gilberte 2, CH-2950; ✆ 032 471 22 22; e petitegilbert@bluewin.ch; www. lapetitegilberte.ch. The work in the restoration of this classic station hotel has been commended. The annexe for entertainment purposes, built in 1909 by the building's owner, Gustave Montavon, was amply used by his daughter who has gone into Swiss lore as Gilberte de Courgenay, famous for entertaining the Swiss troops who were stationed here. Her exploits were incorporated in a film made in the early 1950s.

PORRENTRUY

Tourist information

✉ Grand Rue 5, CH-2900; ☎ 032 420 47 72; e porrentruy@jouratourisme.ch; www.juratourisme.ch; ⏲ Feb 09.00–noon & 14.00–17.30 Mon, Wed–Fri; Mar–Nov 09.00–noon & 14.00–17.30 Mon–Fri, 09.00–noon Sat

Where to stay

Hotels opposite the station are:

⌂ **Terminus**** Rue du Jura 31, CH-2900; ☎ 032 466 26 43

⌂ **De la Gare** Place de la Gare 45, CH-2900; ☎ 066 466 20 30; e contact@hoteldelagareporrentruy.ch; www.hotelgareporrentruy.ch

PORRENTRUY–BONFOL Table 238

An undistinguished branch that serves a military establishment beyond the terminus. Oddly it is operated by CF du Jura, though of standard gauge and quite separate from the rest of its system.

Leaving Porrentruy on a parallel course with the Delémont line, the branch then veers to the left through a mix of pretty woods and fields of sugar beet in season, with sparse habitation.

BASEL–OLTEN Table 500

A principal north/south artery, the line carries heavy passenger and freight traffic. Many of the places it serves depend on industry, and the only scenery of note is between Liestal and Sissach.

The suburbs of Basel are heavily industrialised but there is a surprising survival at **Muttenz**: in the centre of the upper village is a walled enclosure with a complex of largely 15th-century buildings surrounding the Romanesque and Gothic church of St Arbogast. In the choir of the church are some Renaissance murals. Muttenz can also be reached by tram route 14.

The castle at **Pratteln** was built in the late 13th century and rebuilt between 1470 and 1476. It survived use as a workhouse in the 19th century.

Liestal is the capital of the half canton of Basel-Landschaft (the 'rural' part of the canton as opposed to the city), and was the birthplace of the novelist and poet Karl Spitteler who was awarded the Nobel Prize for literature in 1919. The station is the junction for Waldenburg (see page 212). The town's compact centre has some interesting buildings only a short walk from the station. On Rathausgasse, approached at the southern end by the medieval Obertor, is the Gothic Rathaus that dates largely from c1568. The Reformed church in Kirchplatz dates largely from the 16th and 17th-century, and the nearby 17th-century Zeughaus (arsenal) was later used as a granary.

In Zeughausplatz is the cantonal museum (⏲ *10.00–17.00 Tue–Sun*), which has archaeological, natural history and cultural collections.

From the station at Liestal buses run to Reigoldswil (table 50.070, line 70) where a gondola ascends to Wasserfallen (table 2029) for hiking trails. Bikes can be hired for a descent through rock-hewn tunnels.

The village of **Itingen** has some fine vernacular buildings (16th–19th centuries). At **Sissach** is an opulent Baroque country house built in 1773–75 known as Schloss Ebenrain, set in landscaped grounds in the English style. A footpath to it is signed from the station, and it is approached by a long avenue.

From **Gelterkinden**, which has an attractive village square, there is a good walk to the massive ruined fortress of Farnsburg, built c1320 and plundered by the local population in 1798 (⊕ *at all times*).

Immediately before Olten is the second Hauenstein Tunnel through the Jura range, built between 1912 and 1916; although at 8,134m (5 miles) it is considerably longer than the original tunnel on the Sissach–Olten line (see below), it avoids the steep 1 in 38 gradient of the earlier route.

For **Olten**, see table 410, page 112.

PRACTICALITIES Bicycle hire from Liestal and Olten stations.

LIESTAL
Tourist information
i Rathausstrasse 30, CH-4410; ☎ 061 921 01 25;
e poetennest@datacomm.ch; www.myliestal.ch

LIESTAL–WALDENBURG Table 502/Line 19

The Waldenburgerbahn has the distinction of being the only 750mm (2ft 5½in) gauge railway in Switzerland. Opened in 1880, the 14km (8¾ miles) line serves the communities that are spread along the attractive valley of the River Frenke. The railway still has a tank locomotive which was built for the line in 1902 and still operates special excursions.

The railway parallels the main line to the south as they leave Liestal before the narrow gauge turns southwest. In **Bubendorf** the Dinghof of 1600 has stepped gables and decorated windows. The valley gradually narrows, woods replacing fields of sunflowers. Above the small town of **Waldenburg** stand the remains of a late 12th-century fortress, which include a lofty crenellated tower.

BUBENDORF
Where to stay
⌂ **Bad Bubendorf*** (H)** Kantonsstrasse
3, CH-4416; ☎ 061 935 55 55; e hotel@
badbubendorf.ch; www.badbubendorf.ch

SISSACH–OLTEN Table 503

A secondary line through the Homburgertal that was the original main line from Basel to Olten. The first Hauenstein Tunnel through the Jura was built by the British engineer Thomas Brassey in 1853–58. At the time it was the longest tunnel in Europe, at 2,495m (1½ miles).

The route holds little of interest other than the remains of castles at **Läufelfingen** and **Trimbach**.

OLTEN–BRUGG Table 650

The route of some Bern- and Biel/Bienne–Zürich trains, this is a busy stretch of line and serves the historic city of Aarau. It follows the valley of the Aare though is seldom in sight of the river.

In **Schönenwerd** the Romanesque former collegiate church of St Leodegar dates from the 11th century, though it has since been altered several times. In the town park is a reconstruction of a prehistoric lake dwelling. The 18th-century Villa Felsgarten at Oltnerstrasse 6 was once the home of the Bally family and now houses a museum of footwear from ancient times to the present (⊕ *summer & last Sun in month; guided tours 14.30 & 16.00*).

Aarau, the capital of canton Aargau, has long been an industrial town: its bell foundries are thought to have supplied a quarter of Switzerland's church bells. The town was founded in the mid 13th century and its early concentric plan may still be made out, helped by the survival of sections of the town walls and several towers. One of the latter has been incorporated into the largely 18th–20th-century Rathaus. Nearby is the 15th-century Reformed church. The surrounding old town has several streets of attractive 17th–18th-century houses, some with painted decoration on the upper façades and in the eaves.

The oldest building in Aarau is the small castle which was founded in the 11th century. Gradually extended over the next three centuries, the castle housed a boarding school in the 19th century and was given to the town in 1930 by the last private owners. Over 20 rooms are now open as the Stadtmuseum Aarau (⊕ *14.00– 17.00 Wed–Sun*), with re-created rooms and displays of weaponry, local history, handicrafts and industry, including Aarau pewter figures.

The Kunsthaus in Aargauerplatz (⊕ *10.00–17.00 Tue–Sun, 10.00–20.00 Thu; admission charge*) has a fine collection of mostly Swiss paintings from the 18th century by such artists as Ferdinand Hodler, Arnold Böcklin, Paul Klee and Giovanni Giacometti. The building was extended in 2003 by the Swiss architectural firm Herzog & de Meuron, and there is a café in the attractive foyer.

Aarau is the junction for the branch lines to Schöftland and Burg-Menziken (see page 214).

Beyond **Rupperswil** the direct line to Zürich branches off to the south through Lenzburg while the Brugg line continues its easterly course to **Wildegg**. On a hill overlooking the village, about 20 minutes' walk from the station, is a dramatic fortress built in around 1200 by the Habsburg family. From 1484 until 1912 it was owned by 11 generations of the Effinger family who bequeathed it and most of the contents to the Swiss Confederation. Twenty-five rooms are now open (⊕ *Apr–Oct 10.00–17.00 Tue–Sun*), illustrating interior furnishings from the 16th to 19th centuries. There are extensive formal gardens, vineyard, woodland, farm and an aviary.

About 25 minutes' walk from **Schinznach Bad** is a very large garden nursery, the Baumschule, in which there is a 3km (1.87 miles) railway in a figure of eight around the grounds (*www.schbb.ch*). This 60cm (1ft 11½in) gauge line was built in 1928 to provide internal transport for the nursery, but now gives rides to visitors behind steam engines on Saturdays and Sundays between mid-April and mid-October, and diesels on Wednesday afternoons. The locomotive fleet includes an articulated Beyer Garratt from South Africa and industrial engines from Poland and Germany. Alternatively, continue to Brugg and take the postbus (table 50.371), alighting at Schinznach Baumschule.

The town of Schinznach Bad has the strongest sulphur baths in Switzerland, which are part of the health industry that has grown up around the medicinal spring. A classical semicircular building erected in 1828 and set in parkland is the principal hotel.

On the summit of the Wülpelsberg to the right of the line is the picturesque medieval stronghold of Habsburg, the original seat of the family which became such an important part of European dynastic history. With an 11th-century keep and 16th-century residential wing, the castle became the property of the canton of Aargau in 1804 and shortly after a restaurant was opened in the residential part. It is still open (throughout the year), and the keep can be climbed for a fine view. It can be reached by bus from Brugg station (table 50.366).

For **Brugg**, see table 710, page 49.

PRACTICALITIES Bicycle hire from Aarau station.

AARAU
Tourist information
☑ Schlossplatz 1, CH-5000; ☎ 062 834 10 34;
e mail@aarauinfo.ch; www.aarauinfo.ch;
⊕ 13.00–18.00 Mon, 09.00–18.00 Tue–Fri,
09.00–noon & 13.00–17.00 Sat

Where to stay
⌂ **Sorell Aarauerhof***** Bahnhofstrasse 68,
CH-5000; ☎ 062 837 83 00; e info@aarauerhof.ch;
www.aarauerhof.ch

WILDEGG
Where to stay
⌂ **Aarhof***** Bahnhofstrasse 5, CH-5103;
☎ 062 887 84 84; e empfang@aarehof.ch; www.
aarehof.ch

SCHINZNACH BAD
Where to stay
⌂ **Kurhotel im Park*** (H)** CH-5116;
☎ 056 463 77 77; e info@bs-ag.ch; www.bad-
schinznach.ch

⌂ **Rössli** Aarauerstrasse 39, CH-5116; ☎ 056
443 11 23; www.roessli-schinznach-bad.ch

AARAU–SCHÖFTLAND Table 643/S14

A metre-gauge line operated by modern light rail vehicles, which leave from platform 13 or 14, simultaneously with the jointly operated line to Menziken-Burg (see below). The initials 'WSB' on the vehicles stand for Wynental- und Suhrentalbahn, named after the two valleys served by the lines.

After leaving the suburbs of Aarau, the line parallels the River Suhre to **Oberentfelden** where it crosses the standard-gauge line from Zofingen to Lenzburg. A 15-minute walk from the station at **Muhen** is a 16th-century Ständerbau building (the walls having vertical wooden supports) with a steeply angled thatched roof. This has been turned into a museum of rural life (*Strohdachhaus, Hardstrasse*; ⊕ *Apr–Oct 14.00–17.00 1st & 3rd Sun in month*).

The local administration at the terminus of **Schöftland** occupies a Baroque castle dating from 1660.

AARAU–MENZIKEN Table 644/S14

A metre-gauge line operated by modern light rail vehicles, which leave from platform 13 or 14, simultaneously with the jointly operated line to Schöftland (see above). The initials 'WSB' on the vehicles stand for Wynental- und Suhrentalbahn, after the two valleys served by the lines. For much of the way the line is a roadside tram, well used by commuters and shoppers. Most stations are served by bike routes and footpaths, and covered accommodation for bikes is provided.

At **Gränichen** is Schloss Liebegg, a mélange of the foundations of a castle, Gothic house (1561–62), early 17th-century farm building and a Neo-classical residence (1817). Beyond Gränichen the suburbs recede and are replaced by pleasant farming country through which walks are signed from most stations.

The Romanesque church at **Unterkulm** has early 14th-century frescoes that were revealed during restoration of the building in 1968. Various walks are suggested from **Menziken**, including paths to the lake at Sursee and to Beinwil on the Luzern–Lenzburg line (for both, see table 651, page 180).

BASEL–BRUGG–ZÜRICH Table 700

Local trains on this main line serve one of Switzerland's most important Roman sites.

The service shares the same route out of Basel as the Olten line through **Muttenz** to **Pratteln** (for both, see page 211) where the lines divide. The Brugg line swings northeast to **Kaiseraugst**, a village on the site of the Roman town of Augusta Raurica, which was founded c15–10BC. During the 2nd century it developed into a flourishing commercial town with a population of 20,000 and opulent public buildings. It was destroyed by the Alemanni c260.

It is only ten minutes' walk from the station to the reception area and Roman Museum (⊕ *Mar–Oct 13.00–17.00 Mon, 10.00–17.00 Tue–Sun; Nov–Feb, 13.00–17.00 Mon, 11.00–17.00 Tue–Sun*), which is probably the best place to start. The museum contains the most interesting of the 900,000 items found on the site, the most notable being a hoard of 4th-century silver which is thought to have belonged to the commander of the nearby fortress on the Rhine. It was found in 1961 and contained 68 items of an ornate table service, a candelabrum, a statuette of Venus, three silver ingots and 186 coins and medallions.

Nearby is a reconstructed Roman merchant's house with kitchen, dining room, bedroom, bathroom, workshops and a shop; some of the rooms are furnished with original objects.

The site, incorporating 24 points of archaeological interest, includes the remains of a theatre for 8,000 people, a bakery, tavern, temple, forum, baths, pottery, town walls, baptistery and tile workshop. Some of the outlying sites require a walk of 15–20 minutes. There is also a Roman Farm Animal Park, which has rare breeds that were farmed by the Romans: wool-haired pigs, Nera Verzasca goats, Grisons highland sheep, Italian chickens and peacocks.

The line continues to run parallel with the Rhine to **Rheinfelden**, which was built with stone salvaged from Augusta Rurica. Sections of the town wall and several towers survive. The Catholic church of St Martin dates from 1477 with 17th–18th century alterations, and the mid 15th-century chapel of the Order of St John has numerous wall paintings from the same century.

RHEINFELDEN

Tourist information

📋 Marktgasse 16, CH-4310; ☎ 061 833 52 00; e tourismus@rheinfelden.ch; www.tourismus-rheinfelden.ch; ⊕ 13.30–17.00 Mon, 08.00–noon & 13.30–17.00 Tue–Thu, 08.00–noon & 13.30–18.30 Fri, 08.00–noon 1st & 3rd Sat of the month

Where to stay

🏠 **Ochsen***** **(H)** Kaiserstrasse 2, CH-4310; ☎ 061 831 51 01; e hotel-ochsen@bluewin.ch; www.ochsen-rheinfelden.ch

🏠 **Schützen***** Bahnhofstrasse 19, CH-4310; ☎ 061 836 25 25; e willkommen@hotelschuetzen.ch; www.hotelschuetzen.ch

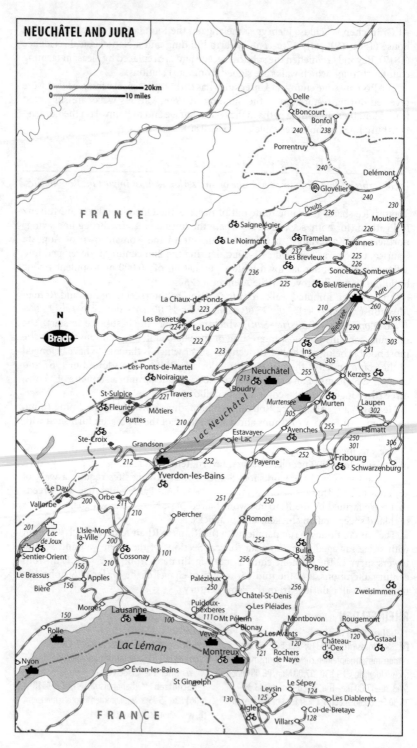

NEUCHÂTEL AND JURA

Delle
Boncourt
Bonfol
240   238
Porrentruy
240
Delémont
Glovelier   240   230
Moutier
Doubs   236   226
Saignelégier
Le Noirmont   Tramelan   Tavannes
Les Brevleux   237   225
226
Sonceboz-Sombeval
236   225
Biel/Bienne
La Chaux-de-Fonds   223   210   260   Aare
Les Brenets   Lyss
224   Le Locle   290
222   Ins   251   303
223   305
Les-Ponts-de-Martel   Kerzers
Noiraigue   Neuchâtel   255
213
St-Sulpice   Boudry
Travers   Murtensee   Murten   Laupen
Fleurier   221   305   302
Môtiers
Buttes   210   Avenches   255   Flamatt
Ste-Croix   Estavayer-   250   306
Grandson   le-Lac   252   301
212   252   Payerne   Fribourg
Yverdon-les-Bains   Schwarzenburg
Le Day   251   250
Vallorbe   200   Orbe
211   210   Bercher   Romont
201   254
Lac   L'Isle-Mont-   256   Bulle
de Joux   la-Ville   200   253
Sentier-Orient   210   Cossonay   101   Broc
156   Palézieux
Le Brassus   Apples   250   256   Zweisimmen
Bière   156   Châtel-St-Denis
150   Puidoux-   Les Pléiades
Morges   Chexbres   Montbovon   Rougemont
Lausanne   100   1111 Mt Pélerin   120
Rolle   Vevey   Blonay   Château-   120
Les Avants   d'-Oex   Gstaad
Nyon   Lac Léman   Montreux   121   Rochers
de Naye
Évian-les-Bains   Leysin   Le Sépey
St Gingolph   125   124   Les Diablerets
130   Aigle   Col-de-Bretaye
Villars   128

FRANCE

FRANCE

N
Bradt

0   20km
0   10 miles

216

15

Neuchâtel and Jura

The western part of Switzerland lying close to the French border is probably one of the areas less well known to tourists, with the exception perhaps of Neuchâtel. The proximity to France has given the area a legacy of fine castles, many to the Savoyard plan of a square or quadrangle with corner towers. Many of the towns are involved with watchmaking, and have museums with some of the finest collections of historic watches and clocks in the world.

Dominated by the Jura Mountains, the region offers wonderful walking country, with far fewer visitors than the Alps. The area around La Chaux-de-Fonds known as the Neuchâtel Montagnes is excellent for cycling, with 1,760km (1,100 miles) of bike paths, and the country served by the CF de Jura from La Chaux-de-Fonds has many routes of varying difficulty signed from stations.

NEUCHÂTEL

The name of Neuchâtel appears for the first time in an act of 1011 when it was part of the Burgundian Empire. During the 12th century the counts of Neuchâtel emerged as the leading family, while the people of the town allied with the Swiss leagues. It was placed under the authority of the French sovereign until 1707 when a dispute arose over the succession, which was settled in favour of the Prussian king. Between 1752 and 1760 the city's governor was the exiled Jacobite Lord George Keith, 10th Earl Marischal of Scotland, thanks to his friendship with Frederick the Great. The Prussian connection was not ended until 1856–57, although the principality had become a Swiss canton from 1815.

TOURIST INFORMATION
Hôtel des Postes, Case Postale 3176, CH-2001; 032 889 68 90; e info@ne.ch; www.neuchateltourisme.ch; 09.00–noon & 13.30– 17.30 Mon–Fri, 09.00–noon Sat; Jul–Aug 09.00–18.30 Mon–Fri, 09.00–16.00 Sat, 10.00–14.00 Sun

WHERE TO STAY
The closest hotel to the station is:
Alpes et Lac*** (H) Place de la Gare 2, CH-2002; 032 723 19 19; e info@alpesdulac.ch; www.alpesetlac.ch

A hotel in a lovely position beside the lake is:
Beau-Rivage***** Esplanade du Mont-Blanc 1, CH-2001; 032 723 15 15; e info@beau-rivage-hotel.ch; www.beau-rivage-hotel.ch

WHERE TO EAT
A short bus ride from the station but full of character and with excellent food is:

La Maison du Prussien Rue des Tunnels 11, CH-2000; 032 730 54 54; e info@hotel-prussien.ch; www.hotel-prussien.ch

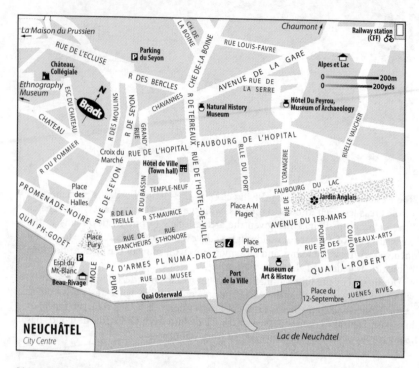

NEUCHÂTEL
City Centre

✕ **Maison des Halles** Rue du Trésor 4, CH-2000; ☎032 724 31 41; e maison-des-halles@bluewin. ch; www.maisondeshalles.ch. Café & gourmet restaurant in one of Neuchâtel's finest buildings.

WHAT TO SEE Arriving at the large station, built on the hillside overlooking the town, take the funicular 'Fun'ambule' from the station down to the English Garden beside the lake. The tourist office is in the post office building at the west end of Place du Port.

Directly inland from Place Pury is the old city, which is largely pedestrianised and well worth exploring at leisure to appreciate the buildings, statues and market. From Place Pury proceed inland into Rue du Seyon and turn right into Rue du Temple-Neuf; on the right is the galleried Temple du Bas (1695–96). The street leads into Place de l'Hôtel-de-Ville; the town hall was built between 1784 and 1790 to the design of Louis XVI's architect, Pierre-Adrien Paris, and paid for by David de Pury. The gable of the Neo-classical building has an allegory of war and peace. The ground floor is open to the public and contains a model of the 18th-century town.

Turn left into Rue de l'Hôpital, which has 18th-century houses and a fountain of justice carved between 1545 and 1547, and proceed straight ahead into Place de la Croix-du-Marché. In the square is the Renaissance Hôtel du Banneret of 1609, with elaborately decorated door and first-floor windows, and banner fountain of 1681. On the far corner with Place des Halles is Maison des Halles of 1570, a glorious building with corner oriel, polygonal staircase tower, and decorative banding and doorcase. Corn was sold on the ground floor, cloth above. It is now a restaurant.

Walk up the steep Rue du Château out of the northwest corner of the square, following signs to the château. On the right-hand side of Escalier du Château is the 12th–13th-century Tour de Diesse, partly rebuilt in 1715. The château itself was founded in the 12th century but repeatedly altered and restored. The group of

218

massive buildings is best appreciated from the railway to the west of the station; from below or the terrace beside the collegiate church it is hard to appreciate its size. It is now the seat of the cantonal government, but the courtyard is open to the public and there are tours of the castle (*Apr–Sep 10.00, 11.00, noon, 14.00, 15.00 & 16.00 Tue–Fri; 14.00, 15.00 & 16.00 Sat–Sun*).

The collegiate church of **Notre-Dame** was begun before 1185 and dedicated in 1276. A fire that devastated part of the town in 1450 destroyed the church's timber work, stained glass and ornaments. Further damage was inflicted during the Reformation, brought to Neuchâtel by Guillaume Farel (a statue of whom stands outside the west front), when soldiers returning from Geneva in 1530 sacked the chapels and altars. The rose window was created in the 18th century, and the spire of the steeple was added in 1869.

The three apses at the altar end of the church are notable examples of fine Norman decoration. The nave is surprisingly narrow for such an important church, and the heavy use of stained glass makes the interior dark, except where the tower lantern casts a pool of light. Under the arch of the choir is the church's great treasure – the cenotaph of the counts of Neuchâtel, which was started in 1372 and represents knights and ladies of the city's ruling family.

Outside, the terrace provides a wonderful view of the town, lake and the Bernese Oberland. Descend by steps beyond the statue of Farel to reach the Rue Jehanne de Hochberg. To the right, in Rue St Nicholas, is the **Ethnography Museum** (✆ 032 717 85 00; ⊕ 10.00–17.00 Tue–Sun; admission charge except on Wed); founded in 1834, it displays the finds of several local collectors and therefore reflects their interests – Africa, Bhutan and Oceania. Descending the hill along Rue Jehanne de Hochberg you pass a series of lovely houses with elegant street lamps.

Neuchâtel has four other museums (*admission free Wed*). To the east of Place Pury, on the east side of the harbour, is the **Museum of Art and History** (*1 Esplanade Léopold-Robert;* ✆ 032 717 79 20; ⊕ 11.00–18.00 Tue–Sun; admission charge). On the ground floor are exhibits of local interest – topographical pictures and portraits, silver, watches, coins, ceramics, furniture, jewellery, costumes, arms and glass. On the first Sunday of the month, on the hour at 14.00, 15.00 and 16.00, three incredibly intricate automata – the writer, the musician and the draughtsman – created in the 18th century by three local watchmakers, come to life. The writer, for example, is animated by 120 revolving internal discs, assembled to tolerances of 0.1mm. On the first floor are rooms of Swiss paintings by such artists as Hodler, Anker and Amiet, and a collection of French, mostly Impressionist, pictures by Corot, Monet, Pissaro, Renoir and Sisley.

On the corner of Rue des Therreaux and Avenue de la Gare is the **Natural History Museum** (✆ 032 717 79 60; ⊕ 10.00–18.00 Tue–Sun; admission charge), which has dioramas of Swiss birds and animals, displays of live fish and reptiles, and displays on animals of the world, minerals, fossils and rocks.

In a striking lakeside position at Espace Paul Vouga is Laténium, the large **Museum of Archaeology** (✆ 032 889 69 17; www.latenium.ch; ⊕ 10.00–18.00 Tue–Sun; admission charge), which has some fascinating finds made at the sites of early dwellings along the shore of Lake Neuchâtel. From the centre, take bus 1 in the direction of Marin and alight at Musée d'Archéologie.

Bus 9 or 9b from the station to stop Ermitage takes you to the **Centre Dürrenmatt Neuchâtel** at 74 Chemin du Pertuis-du-Sault (✆ 032 720 20 60; ⊕ 11.00–17.00 Wed–Sun), located in the house where Friedrich Dürrenmatt wrote and painted. One of his novellas formed the basis of Sean Penn's 2001 film *The Pledge*, starring Jack Nicholson, Helen Mirren and Vanessa Redgrave.

15

Also to the east of the city is a funicular to Chaumont where there is an unusual viewing tower from which there are magnificent views of the Bernese Oberland on a clear day. Take bus 7 from Place Pury to La Coudre, from where the funicular ascends on the half-hour (table 2011). There are some lovely walks from Chaumont, one of them to the attractive old village of Valangin (2 hours) with a main street of 16th–18th-century houses and dominated by a 12th–14th-century castle. After being a possession of the bishops of Basel, it became the administrative seat of the counts of Neuchâtel. It was equipped with several rooms used as torture chambers and prisons for persons condemned as witches. The fortress is now a local museum (✆ 032 857 23 83; ⊕ Mar–Oct 11.00–17.00 Wed–Sun; admission charge) with furniture, arms, clothing, old kitchen, and temporary exhibitions.

Finally, boat services provide access to other places of interest around the lake, and on the connected lakes of Biel and Morat. The company operating nine boats on the lakes of Neuchâtel and Morat operates daily all year round. Boats leave from the harbour just to the east of Place Pury (✆ 032 729 96 00; www.navig.ch).

NEUCHÂTEL–BOUDRY Table 213/Line 5

This metre-gauge line leaves from a terminus at Place Pury and is worked by light rail vehicles. As a separate system operated as part of the city's public transport network, it is something of an anomaly in that it appears in the railway timetable. It runs along the lake for much of the way.

The village of **Auvernier**, now part of the suburbs of Neuchâtel, is famous for the lake dwellings from the Neolithic and Bronze ages that have been excavated here. The attractively sited château dates from 1559 with late 17th-century extensions and wrought ironwork in the garden. The village has many 16th–17th-century houses.

The multi-towered castle at **Colombier** should not be missed. The huge building dates from the 12th to 16th centuries and was successively the property of the lords of Colombier and the counts of Neuchâtel. Jean-Jacques Rousseau was received here by Lord George Keith (see page 217) while he was governor of Neuchâtel. It now houses two museums: a military museum with a large collection of firearms (some from the 14th century) and uniforms; and a museum of woodblock printing and printed fabrics (⊕ Mar–Nov 10.00–noon & 14.00–17.00 Tue–Sun).

Boudry was the birthplace of the chocolate manufacturer Philippe Suchard (1797–1884). The once-walled market town has two museums: one about wine and viticulture (⊕ 14.00–18.00 Wed–Sun) in the delightful 13th–16th-century castle; and in Avenue du Collège the Museum of the Areuse (⊕ Apr–Nov 14.00–17.45 Tue–Sun; admission charge) with a collection of local and African objects, and exhibitions on natural history.

NEUCHÂTEL–LA CHAUX-DE-FONDS Table 223

A short but spectacular line with a most unusual railway feature – a single standard-gauge reversing point, necessitated by the need to cross the southern range of the Jura Mountains. This operating and schedule handicap has prompted plans for a new tunnel to obviate it and accelerate services. The steep climb up the slope affords steadily more impressive views over Lake Neuchâtel to the Alps. Stopping and fast trains from Bern serve the line.

Trains head west out of Neuchâtel and bear right at a junction beyond **Corcelles-Peseux**; the main street of the former village of Corcelles has some fine 16th–18th-century houses and a 15th-century Reformed church, and Peseux has a 16th-century château with three polygonal towers. Climbing steeply, the line enters a tunnel and emerges high up on the hillside, passing through vineyards and then woods to the reversing station at **Chambrelien**.

Seven minutes are allowed for the locomotive/driver to change ends. In the Andes and Himalayas, where narrower-gauge railways employ a similar mountain-climbing device, the need for the locomotive to change ends is usually avoided by having a zig-zag so that the train can be propelled after the first reversing point and then continue with the engine at the 'right' end after the second.

The steepness of the climb is evident when the train pulls into **Les Geneveys-sur-Coffrane**, where level sidings are first seen above your carriage roof. Beyond the ski resort of **Les Hauts-Geneveys** the line enters a long tunnel, with the station at Convers sandwiched between it and another tunnel from which the train emerges on the outskirts of **La Chaux-de-Fonds**.

LA CHAUX-DE-FONDS This city of 37,500 people is the highest (at 1,000m, 3,281ft) in Switzerland and the third largest in the French-speaking part of the country. It is renowned as a centre of upmarket watchmaking and as a prime example of idealistic early 19th-century town planning and architecture. This was reflected in the Federal government classifying the city as being of national importance, with Switzerland's only significant collection of later Art Nouveau.

Part of the reason for this heritage is that the village on the site was completely destroyed by fire in 1794; the town was then rebuilt on a grid pattern. The other reason is that one of the best-known figures of modern architecture was born here: Charles Edouard Jeanneret (1887–1965), better known as Le Corbusier (the name of his maternal grandfather, which he adopted in 1920). This pioneer of modern architecture studied and designed his first buildings here. He admired the English Arts and Crafts movement, and his first houses, built in 1906, incorporated decorative motifs based on the works of John Ruskin and Owen Jones. Later his designs were to exert a powerful influence on a whole generation of architects. The house he built for his parents in 1912, Maison Blanche (*Chemin de Pouillerel 12;* ⏂ *10.00–17.00 Fri–Sun; bus 4 from station; admission charge*), has been rescued from neglect and restored with original and appropriately period furnishings.

Leaving the large station, proceed directly ahead into the broad, tree-lined Avenue Léopold-Robert and turn right to reach the tourist office. Le Corbusier's Turkish House (1916–17) is at Rue du Doubs 167 (\ *032 912 31 233;* ⏂ *13.00–17.00 1st & 3rd Sat of each month*).

Tourist information

▪ Espacité 1, CH-2302; \ 032 919 68 95; e info.cdf@ne.ch; www.neuchateltourisme.ch; ⏂ Sep–Jun 09.00–noon & 13.30–17.30 Mon–Fri, 09.00–noon Sat; Jul–Aug 09.00–12.15 & 13.45–18.30 Mon–Fri, 10.00–16.00 Sat; May & Oct 11.00–noon & 13.00–16.30 daily; Nov–Apr 13.00–16.00 daily

Where to stay

Hotels near the station are:

⌂ **Club***** Rue du Parc 71, CH-2300; \ 032 910 01 01; e reservations@hotel-club.ch; www.hotel-club.ch

⌂ **De France** Daniel-Jeanrichard 46, CH-2300; \ 032 913 11 16; e info@hoteldefrance.ch; www.hoteldefrance.ch

What to see

Museum of Fine Art (Musée des Beaux-Arts) (*Rue des Musées 33, CH-2300;* \ *032 967 60 77;* ⊕ *10.00–17.00 Tue–Sun; admission charge*) This Art Deco construction was built between 1925 and 1926 with a bas-relief of one of the architects, Charles L'Eplatinier, on the façade. It contains portraits of and by Le Corbusier and furniture designed by him, as well as the work of other local and Swiss artists.

The International Clock Museum (Musée International d'Horlogerie) (*Rue des Musées 29, CH-2301;* \ *032 967 68 61;* ⊕ *10.00–17.00 Tue–Sun; admission charge*) This striking museum was founded in 1902 and contains over 3,000 items, now housed in a largely underground museum opened in 1974. Beginning with the sundial and concluding with the atomic clock, the museum traces the development of timepieces through paintings, machines and an outstanding collection of rare clocks and watches. There is also a restoration workshop where visitors can see craftsmen at work. In the park above ground is a unique carillon in polished steel which comes to life every quarter-hour with music, movement and changes of colour.

The History Museum (Musée d'histoire) (*Rue des Musées 31, CH-2300;* \ *032 967 60 88;* ⊕ *14.00–17.00 Tue–Fri, 10.00–17.00 Sat–Sun; admission charge*) This was set up in 1876 in a nobleman's residence, and includes reconstructed interiors, furniture, pewter, glassware, portraits, topographical pictures, coins and weapons as well as medals.

The Museum of Natural History (Musée d'Histoire Naturelle) (*Av Léopold-Robert 63, in post office building opposite railway station, CH-2300;* \ *032 967 60 71;* ⊕ *14.00–17.00 Tue–Fri, 10.00–17.00 Sat–Sun; admission charge*) This museum has numerous dioramas of Swiss and African wildlife, as well as marine life, fossils and palaeontology.

Museum of Farming and Crafts (Musée Paysan et Artisanal) (*Crêtets 148, CH-2300;* \ *032 926 65 60;* ⊕ *Apr–Oct 14.00–17.00 Tue–Sun; Nov–Feb 14.00–17.00 Wed & Sat–Sun; bus 4 to Polyexpo on Rue l-J Chevrolet; admission charge*) This is in the opposite direction from the other museums, to the southwest of the station, and is situated in one of the city's oldest buildings, a late 16th–early 17th-century farmhouse. Furniture, tools, clothing and other artefacts illustrate the way of life of the *Montagnons* (mountain people). There is also an information centre on the preservation of the region's architectural heritage.

Le Bois du Petit-Château (*Rue Alexis-Marie Piaget 82, CH-2300;* \ *032 967 60 94;* ⊕ *Apr–Oct 08.00–18.00 daily, Nov–Mar 08.00–17.00 daily; bus 4 from station to Bois du Petit-Château; admission charge*) In 'the wood of the small château' is a zoo and vivarium, situated at the northwestern end of Rue Docteur-Coullery.

LA CHAUX-DE-FONDS–LE LOCLE Table 223

The line forms the last section of express workings from Bern, providing connections with an international service across the French border to Besançon. Le Locle also provides access to the metre-gauge line to Les Brenets.

Heading southwest out of La Chaux-de-Fonds, it soon becomes apparent that the city and the railway are built on something of a plateau, for beyond **Le Crêt-de-Locle** the line drops steeply downhill to the watchmaking town of **Le Locle**.

It was here in 1709 that an anonymous travelling Englishman unwittingly provided the stimulus for the Swiss watch industry in this part of the country. Until then small numbers of very expensive watches had been produced in Geneva, but the ability to produce reliable, inexpensive watches was then largely the preserve of London clocksmiths. The traveller's watch had stopped working, so when he called at the blacksmith's shop of Daniel Jean-Richard in Le Locle and saw him mending a clock, he asked whether he could mend his watch; Jean-Richard did so, and made a drawing of the movement. He produced a replica and set up a business that dramatically undercut the competition in Geneva, spawning an industry that has been one of Switzerland's most important ever since. The town's debt to Jean-Richard is commemorated by a statue in the centre.

Like La Chaux-de-Fonds, Le Locle was largely laid waste by fire, in 1833, after which it was also rebuilt on a grid pattern. Only the 16th-century square tower with turret of the Reformed church is left of an earlier chapel, the nave being rebuilt in 1758–59. The elegant Château des Monts at Route des Monts 65, built in 1785–90 for the watchmaker Samuel Du Bois, houses a Museum of Clocks and Watches (*Musée d'Horlogerie;* ⊕ *May–Oct 10.00–17.00 Tue–Sun; Nov–Apr 14.00–17.00 Tue–Sun; admission charge*), which displays some of the collection in appropriate room settings. There are also some automata, including an old lady shuffling with two sticks.

At Le Col 23 near **Le Locle-Col-des-Roches** station on the line to Besançon, to the west of the town, is a most extraordinary museum of underground mills, Moulins souterrains du Col-des-Roches (⊕ *May–Oct 10.00–17.00 daily; Nov–Apr 14.00–17.00 Tue–Sun; admission charge*). At this point, the River Bied, which flows into the River Doubs, flows for 2.5km (1½ miles) underground. In the mid 17th century Jonas Sandoz had the idea of harnessing this power and set about opening up huge caverns in the rock, sometimes creating waterfalls to extract more power. By the end of the century the mountain contained an oil mill, a thresher, two flour mills and a sawmill. During the 19th century the sawmill was moved outside by the use of two 50m (164ft) wooden axles to transmit power, but shortly before 1900 the mills closed and the caverns began to fill in. In 1973 volunteers began to excavate them, and today visitors can walk through the galleries and see various exhibitions illustrating the mills and the power of hydraulics.

Trains for Besançon leave from platform 3. Buses leave from the station for Les Ponts-de-Martel and Neuchâtel (table 21.080).

LE LOCLE

Tourist information

🛈 Moulins Souterraines, Le Col 23, CH-2400; ☎032 889 68 92; e info.ll@ne.ch; www.neuchateltourisme.ch; ⊕ May–Oct 09.00–noon & 13.30–17.30 Mon–Fri, 10.00–noon & 13.00–17.00 Sat; Nov–Apr 09.00–noon & 13.30–17.00 Tue–Fri, 14.00–17.00 Sat

Where to stay

🏠 **Des Trois Rois***** Rue du Temple 29, CH-2400; ☎032 932 21 00

LE LOCLE–LES BRENETS Table 224

Though short, this metre-gauge line should not be missed since it provides a glimpse of, and access to, the gorge known as Les Bassins du Doubs.

Trains leave from platform 4, which is at the west end of platform 2. The line passes through a very long tunnel before **Les Frêtes** from which there are numerous signed walks. The gorge can be seen through the trees to the left before the train dives into more tunnels, the last just before the station at **Les Brenets**. It is a 15-minute walk to the pier from which boats leave for a 1 hour 20 minute journey between the limestone cliffs of Les Bassins du Doubs; at a point near the French border passengers disembark for a path to the spectacular Doubs waterfall (Le Saut-du-Doubs), 27m (88ft) high. The boats run from April to late October (℡ *032 932 14 14; www.nlb.ch*). Alternatively it is a one-hour walk from the station to the falls.

LES BRENETS
Where to stay

⌂ **Les Rives du Doubs** *** Pré-du-Lac 26, CH-2416 ; ℡ 032 933 99 99; e rives-du-doubs@ bluewin.ch; www.rives-du-doubs.ch

LA CHAUX-DE-FONDS–GLOVELIER Table 236

The metre-gauge lines of the CF du Jura deserve to be much better known, since they serve some delightful walking, riding and cycling country. Besides its natural beauty, this area, known as the Franches-Montagnes, has some of the cheapest accommodation, largely because it is away from the alpine honeypots. Nearly all the stations have large numbers of signed walks and many have cycle routes. A leaflet is available showing the routes marked from the stations at Le Noirmont and Saignelégier, where bikes can be hired by telephoning the stations.

The railway leaves La Chaux-de-Fonds as though it were a tram line, mixed up with traffic, though on mostly quiet streets. It climbs steeply above the town, affording views to the left over it, and into woodland, reaching a summit at **Bellevue**. Most railways were built along valley floors, but this line clings to the higher contours, at this point at the same height as the top of the hills on the opposite side of a deepening valley.

The area is renowned for its Freiberger ponies, and it would be rare in clement weather not to see groups of riders from the train. The gentle nature of the region's horses has encouraged the setting-up of equestrian centres where horses can be hired by the hour or the week (see *Saignelégier tourist informaton* below).

The village of **La Ferrière** has a pretty little square, and cycle routes as well as footpaths signed from the station. Long avenues of mature trees become a feature of the almost entirely pastoral landscape, and the varied timbre of cowbells is sometimes the only sound to be heard as the train pauses at the smaller halts. Heavily booted walkers are the most likely passengers to board the train at **Le Creux-des-Biches**. The sparsely populated country is farmed from solid, often white rendered buildings, the door and window jambs and lintels of rough-hewn stone left unpainted as though to emphasise their strength.

Le Noirmont is the junction for the branch to Tavannes and a town of some importance. The Catholic basilica of St Hubert dates from the early 16th century, while to the east of the town is an aggressively modern church. The Tavannes line goes off to the south as the railway forges round the hills to the largest town on the line, **Saignelégier**, which is the railway's headquarters and the venue for an annual national horse show in early August. It was once the residence of the bishop's representative, who lived in the attractive 16th-century Préfecture which has a hipped roof and stone lock-up tower on one end. Numerous walks are signed from the station.

Beyond **Pré-Petitjean** a collection of elderly railway vehicles may be seen on the left-hand side, some from other metre-gauge railways. Occasional steam-hauled excursions using locomotives from Portugal are operated (☏ *032 952 42 90; www. la-traction.ch*). Shortly after, the character of the line changes suddenly, the railway plunging into woods with steep rock cuttings. **La Combe** offers woodland walks (with a buffet by the station), and soon after a lake, near **Bollemont**, the line enters the first tunnel. The railway joins a river fringed by rocky cliffs on the opposite side and drops down to the isolated station of **Combe-Tabeil**. Here the train reverses direction to continue its descent, burrowing down an exceptionally narrow, wooded valley that would seem familiar to anyone who has travelled the forestry railways of Transylvania.

The departure from beech woods is as sudden as the earlier entry into forest, the railway threading through farmland on the final leg of the journey to the junction with the standard-gauge at **Glovelier**. If you have a few minutes' wait for a connection here, the waiting room contains a delightful old music box; for a 20¢ coin three ladies dance round while three musicians at the back tap bells.

PRACTICALITIES Bicycle hire from Le Noirmont and Saignelégier stations, and return only to Glovelier.

LA FERRIÈRE
Where to stay
🏠 **Auberge La Puce (H)** CH-2333; ☏ 032 963 11 44; e Zwingli.simoes@bluewin.ch; www. auberge-lapuce.ch

LE NOIRMONT
Where to stay
🏠 **Georges Wenger Hotel**★★★★ Rue de la Gare 2, CH-2340; ☏ 032 957 66 33; e info@georges-wenger.ch; www.georges-wenger.ch. Home to 1 of Switzerland's outstanding restaurants, with 2 Michelin stars & 18–20 GaultMillau points.

A hotel also close to the station is:
🏠 **Du Soleil** CH-2775; ☏ 032 953 11 11; e info@ lesoleilaunoirmont.ch; www.lesoleilaunoirmont.ch

SAIGNELÉGIER
Tourist information
🛈 Rue de la Gruère 6, CH-2350; ☏ 032 420 47 70; e info@juratourisme.ch; www.juratourisme. ch; ⏲ 09.00–noon & 14.00–18.00 Mon–Fri, 09.30–13.30 Sat–Sun

Where to stay
🏠 **De la Gare**★★★ 4 Rue Gruère, CH-2350; ☏ 032 951 11 21; e info@hotel-la-gare.ch; www. hotel-la-gare.ch

LE NOIRMONT–TAVANNES Table 237

A steeply graded metre-gauge branch off the 'main line' of the CF Jura which drops down to a junction with the Moutier–Sonceboz–Sombeval–Biel/Bienne line.

Leaving Le Noirmont the line climbs sinuously across the rising valley floor in the first of two crossings of the ridges of the Jura Mountains that run southeast/northwest. Having crossed the open grassland, the train dives into woods before dropping down through delightful pasture, liberally broken up by spruce and

Douglas firs. This is marvellous walking country, testified by the large numbers of walkers that use **Les Breuleux**.

The line climbs again to the attractive village of **Les Reussilles**, where there is a riding school near the station and a tea room to fortify returning walkers. The line now begins a fearsome descent through a series of horseshoe curves to the large town of **Tramelan**. Its long main street, Grand Rue, has many fine buildings including a Blue Cross Hotel of 1889, built to help alcoholics. Falling more gently, the line crosses upland meadows and then finds a well-wooded narrow valley to reach the junction at **Tavannes** (see table 226, page 127).

PRACTICALITIES Bicycle hire from Tramelan station.

LA CHAUX-DE-FONDS–LES PONTS-DE-MARTEL Table 222

A well-used metre-gauge line that serves a broad, flat-bottomed valley with heavily wooded hills to either side.

The line leaves from the metre-gauge platforms of the CF Jura at the eastern end of La Chaux-de-Fonds station. The line has to describe a 180-degree curve out of the town which it does by climbing steeply and twisting round over the standard-gauge lines to Biel/Bienne and Neuchâtel. For half a mile or so it keeps company with the latter before turning southeast down the curiously shaped valley towards Les Ponts-de-Martel. Despite the well-wooded slopes on each side of the valley, there are few trees on the valley floor, and those are usually in clumps.

The village of **La Corbatière** has some good examples of Jura houses and farms, with their characteristic heavy stone window and door lintels and jambs, the massive stones usually left unpainted in contrast to the coloured render of the walls. **La Sagne** has a late 15th-century Gothic Reformed church, its numerous vaults having carved keystones. It also has some fine houses, as does **Les Coeudres**.

The popularity of the valley for walking and cycling is evident from the large numbers of walkers who use the railway and in the generous provision for bicycles on the trains. At **Les Ponts-de-Martel** a cheese factory can be visited, and the surrounding peat bogs are now largely a nature reserve. A bus service from the station goes north to Le Locle and south to Neuchâtel (table 21.080).

LES PONTS-DE-MARTEL
Where to stay
⌂ **Hôtel-Restaurant du Cerf** Major-Benoit 3, CH-2316; ☏ 032 937 11 08

NEUCHÂTEL–TRAVERS–BUTTES/PONTARLIER Table 221

A line of unexpected scenic beauty through the lovely valley of the River l'Areuse, with several sites of cultural and scenic interest. TGVs between Bern and Paris used to use the line as far as Travers where they climbed the north side of the valley slope to the border beyond Les Verrières, but now only secondary international trains use the route. Steam locomotives sometimes work special trains over the line between Travers and St Sulpice. The valley offers good walks and cycling routes. Sit on the left.

Heading west out of Neuchâtel, the line shares the same tracks as the Yverdon line as far as the junction west of **Auvernier**. This village has a main street of 16th–17th-century houses, and below it an attractive château dating from 1559 with 18th-century wrought ironwork in the garden.

Beyond **Bôle** the line enters a steeply sided valley with impressive views of mountains to the left. The River l'Areuse flows through the valley and is seldom out of sight all the way to Buttes. Clinging to the hillside on a shelf, the railway enters the spectacular limestone Gorge de l'Areuse, with waterfall near Pont-Dessus, which can be explored on foot from **Champ-du-Moulin**. Rousseau stayed at a nearby house in September 1764 (see below).

The valley opens out before **Noiraigue**, from where it is only a short walk to the Creux du Van. This extraordinary bowl, forming a natural amphitheatre in the mountains, should not be missed; its scale and the views over the surrounding countryside are stupendous, and it has been described as the most impressive feature of its kind in Europe. It is also the highest of the Jura peaks in the area, at 1,465m (4,806ft), and has a nature reserve for roe deer and chamois. There is a cycle route and footpath around it, forming part of a longer walk to Môtiers station (see below).

Travers is the junction for the lines to Butte and Les Verrières. A four-arched stone bridge of 1665 crosses the river, and there is a large 17th–18th-century château near the 13th–17th-century Reformed church. Just to the east of the village is a well-presented museum based on the asphalt mines that were in use from 1712 until 1986, for some of the time under British ownership. The story of this versatile substance is described, and 1km (⅝ mile) of the underground workings is open to visitors (warm clothing advised). The tunnels total about 100km (62 miles), and their output was exported to places as distant as New York and Sydney. The museum (✆ 032 964 90 64; *guided tours Apr–mid-Oct 10.30 & 14.30 daily; Jul–Aug, also 12.30 & 16.00; Nov–Mar 12.30 & 14.30 Sun; admission charge*) also has a historic watchmaker's workshop and a restaurant in the miners' canteen; this offers local specialities, including the ham, wrapped in tinfoil, that the museum boils in asphalt for four hours at 220°C and serves with potatoes.

Leaving Travers the line crosses the river soon after the line to Les Verrières bears to the right. The river runs right through the centre of **Couvet**, which has some attractive 18th-century houses and a Reformed church (1657). The town of **Môtiers** had a Benedictine priory from the 11th century; its secularised buildings and staircase tower form an attractive courtyard. The part-Romanesque, part-Gothic Reformed church dates from 1460–90, the choir and tower from 1669–79, while the lovely round-arched market hall was built in 1612. The town has two museums, housed in a group of buildings just five minutes' walk from the station.

One of a number of fine 18th-century houses, Maison des Mascarons at Grand-Rue 14, is the Regional Museum of History and Crafts (⊕ *May–mid-Oct, 14.30–16.30 Tue, Thu & Sat–Sun; admission charge*), with reconstructed rooms such as a cheese factory, absinthe distillery (produced in the area during the 19th century from the locally grown wormwood), a clockmaker's workshop, rustic kitchen, lace-making workshop and a bistro dating from 1900. The Jean-Jacques Rousseau Museum (⊕ *May–Oct 14.30–16.30 Tue, Thu & Sat–Sun; admission charge*) occupies the house where the political philosopher and essayist lived between 1762 and 1765 after his expulsion from Geneva following the furore over the publication of his didactic novel *Emile*. While living in Môtiers under the protection of Frederick the Great, he was visited by James Boswell in 1764 and wrote *Lettres de la Montagne*. He left to take up an invitation to stay at Wootton Hall near Ashbourne in Derbyshire. Amongst the exhibits associated with Rousseau is the desk at which he wrote, and visitors can see the peepholes through which he could watch passers-by.

Fleurier is the junction where a branch to **St Sulpice** swings off to the right. The service over this line has been replaced by a bus (table 21.090, also shown in railway timetable) which serves some stations on the line between Travers and Pontarlier in France. It is now the only way to visit Les Verrières, the pine-forested border crossing where General Bourbaki's retreating and exhausted army sought asylum in February 1871 during the Franco-Prussian War. The scene of this epic event is depicted in the vast painting on display in the Bourbaki-Panorama at Luzern (see page 171).

At St Sulpice is a railway museum depot which houses a large collection of steam locomotives, including massive examples from France and Germany. On various weekends of the year, special trains are operated over the line down the valley to Travers and Neuchâtel (*Vapeur Val-de-Travers, www.vvt.ch*).

The hill above Fleurier to the west is known as Le Chapeau de Napoleon (Napoleon's hat), from which there are fine views down the valley. From Fleurier station there is also a bus to the small skiing resort of La Brévine (table 21.083), known as the Siberia of Switzerland for its low winter temperatures, which has particularly good cross-country skiing. The French writer André Gide stayed here long enough in 1894 to write *Paludes* and some of *La Symphonie Pastorale*.

Walks back down the valley are signed from the terminus at **Buttes**. At Ruelle de la Consommation is a Salt Museum (⊕ *Jun–Sep 14.00–17.00 first Sun of month; admission charge*). Five minutes' walk from the station is the seasonal chairlift to La Robella (table 2008). Le Chapeau de Napoleon can be reached in 1 hour 25 minutes, St Sulpice in 2 hours. A bus (table 21.092) leaves from the station for that at Ste-Croix (see table 212), passing through Mont de Buttes, the village beneath the eponymous peak.

PRACTICALITIES Bicycle hire from Noiraigue and Fleurier stations.

NORAIGUE
Tourist information
🛈 Place de la Gare, CH-2103; ☎ 032 889 68 96; e info.vdt@ne.ch; www.grandson.ch; ⊕ 08.00–18.00 daily, Jul–Aug –19.00

TRAVERS
Where to stay
⌂ **Crêt-de-l'Anneau** Crêt-de-l'Anneau 1, CH-2105; ☎ 032 863 11 78; 032 863 40 38; e cret@hotmail.ch; www.lecret.ch

COUVET
Where to stay
⌂ **De l'Aigle*** (H)** Grand-Rue 27, CH-2108; ☎ 032 864 90 50; e info@gout-region.ch; www.gout-region.ch

⌂ **Central** Grand Rue 2, CH-2108; ☎ 032 864 90 55; www.hotelcentral-vdt.ch

ST SULPICE
Where to stay
⌂ **Du Moulin** Bas du Village, CH-2123; ☎ 032 861 26 98

BUTTES
Where to stay
⌂ **Auberge des Fées** Place de l'Abbaye 2, CH-
2115; ☎ 032 861 52 55; e info@auberge-des-fees.
ch; www.auberge-des-fees.ch

LES VERRIÈRES
Where to stay
⌂ **De Ville** Rue de la Croix-Blanche 48, CH-
2126; ☎ 032 866 10 00; e hoteldeville@hotmail.ch

NEUCHÂTEL—YVERDON-LES-BAINS Table 210

Part of a main route between Zürich and Lausanne/Geneva that follows the castle-lined lake shore for part of the way. It passes the site of one of the most celebrated military victories on Swiss soil, at the Battle of Grandson in 1476.

Leaving Neuchâtel there is a good view of the castle and collegiate church on top of the hill above the old town. For **Auvernier**, **Colombier** and **Boudry** see table 213, page 220 (they are served by the light-rail transit line to Boudry). The height of the railway above the lake continues to afford good views to the south, although the line turns away from the shore and begins to drop steadily to the water level.

At **Bevaix** is a Baroque château dating from 1722 and a Reformed church (1605) with Romanesque decoration on the west portal that was retrieved from the church of a nearby Benedictine priory. To the east of Gorgier (station **Gorgier-St-Aubin**) is a much-altered 13th-century castle. **Vaumarcus** has an imposing 13th-century castle which was burnt after the Battle of Grandson but rebuilt with a massive sloping buttress that reaches the machicolation under the roof. The castle is open only for guided tours of eight or more people, but there is a café in the castle (☎ 032 836 36 36; ⊕ 08.00–noon, 14.00–18.00 daily, until 17.00 Sat–Sun).

Look out to the right before the next station at **Concise** to catch a glimpse of a lovely château shaded by mature trees and screened to the north by woodland. Before the station, the railway has returned to the lake shore and runs alongside the water for most of the way to Yverdon. In the pretty village of Concise is an 11th–12th-century Romanesque Reformed church with late 15th-century Gothic additions. A bus from the church to Provence passes the site of the Battle of Grandson, commemorated by a stone and tablet; the bus starts at Yverdon station and calls at Grandson station (table 10.630).

The battle was fought in March 1476, war having broken out between the Austrians and the Burgundians in 1468 in which the Swiss sided with the Austrians. The castle of Grandson (see page 230) had been taken by the Burgundian forces under Charles the Bold, but two days later a Swiss force drawn from many parts arrived to give battle. It was an inconclusive fight in that it was a victory through Burgundian confusion rather than Swiss supremacy, and most of the French force quit the field to fight another day. However, they left behind loot so rich that one wonders what place it had in a military campaign. Today's Swiss museums are the beneficiaries, since many have on display trophies from Grandson. If a decisive victory eluded the Swiss at Grandson, Murten/Morat almost four months later was another matter (see page 130).

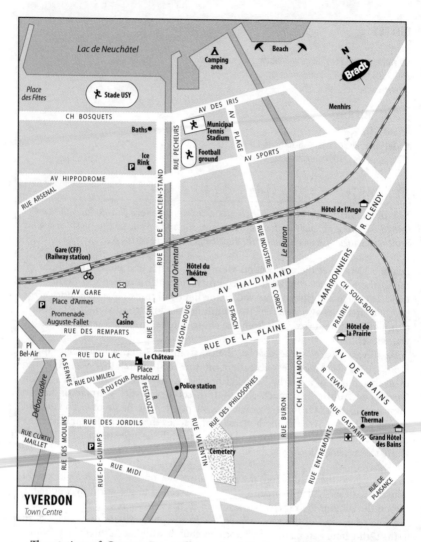

YVERDON
Town Centre

The station of **Onnens-Bonnvillars** serves the two villages. The Reformed church at the former has high Gothic wall-paintings of the Entombment and St Peter at the Gates of Paradise and Hell in the 14th-century choir.

Grandson should not be missed. The massive 11th-century castle is one of the largest fortresses in Switzerland, though most of the present structure was built in the 13th. Its protection of three circular and two semicircular towers, gatehouse and outer defence works proved unable to withstand the assault of the Burgundian Charles the Bold in February 1476, and its garrison was killed. Today a large part is open to the public (by courtesy of its private owner), with a display of arms and vintage cars (including a white Rolls-Royce owned by Greta Garbo and Winston Churchill's 1938 Austin Cambridge), and a museum of military history (⊕ *Apr–Oct 08.15–18.00, daily; Nov–Mar 08.15–17.00 daily; www.chateau-grandson.ch*).

The only part of a Benedictine monastery still to be seen at Grandson is the Reformed parish church (St-Jean-Baptiste). Once under the abbey of La Chaise-Dieu in the Auvergne, the 11th-century church owes much to the Auvergne Romanesque. The capitals of the columns have been described as some of the finest in the country.

Yverdon-les-Bains is the capital of the North Vaudois and has a long history of settlement going back to the 5th century BC, when Celts lived by the shore of the lake. It was strategically sited at the crossing on the main road between central France and Italy via Pontarlier, Vevey and the St Bernard Pass, and the short section of road between Yverdon and Vidy near Lausanne that linked the river systems of the Rhine, Aare and Rhône. The Romans named the town Eburodunum and established thermal baths to exploit the sulphurous springs on which stands today's impressive Thermal Centre.

The town lost its importance and for centuries was little more than a village until Peter II of Savoy chose it as the site of a new fortress in 1251 to defend the town on its most vulnerable side, the east. The castle was built in 1250–60 by one of England's most famous castle builders, Master James of St George. He had been brought to Savoy when Peter finally returned there after 23 years at the English Court, during which time he was made Earl of Richmond and carried out diplomatic missions for Henry III. Master James was to return to England and become in 1286 Master of the King's Works in Wales, building many of the Principality's best-known castles and later becoming Constable of Harlech Castle.

After the castle was burnt in an accidental fire in 1378 and an intentional one in 1476 when the castle was embroiled in the Burgundian wars, it was conquered by the Bernese in 1536. Part of the castle became home to the first museum in the canton in 1761, and the building achieved some fame in 1805–25 as the home of Heinrich Pestalozzi's institute for poor or abandoned children.

Pestalozzi (1746–1827) is one of those historical characters whose reputation exceeds his achievements. Influenced by Rousseau and equally impractical (he once said that with 200 disciples he could change the world), his previous efforts at running homes at Stans and Burgdorf had not met with much success. However, his published writings had made him well known, and space in Yverdon Castle was offered to him. Here he was visited by educationalists and reformers such as Robert Owen and Henry Brougham, but the establishment was no more of a success than the others and it was forced to close.

PRACTICALITIES Bicycle hire from Yverdon-les-Bains station.

GORGIER
Where to stay
⌂ **Des Tilleuls** Rue du Centre 18, CH-2023; ☏ 032 835 16 64; e hotellestilleuls@bluemail.ch; www.gorgier.ch

CONCISE
Where to stay
⌂ **Hotel du Lac et Gare (H)** Rue de la Gare, CH-1426; ☏ 024 434 18 36; e info@holaga.ch; www.holaga.ch. The restaurant has 13 GaultMillau points.

ONNENS
Where to stay
⌂ **Bellevue*** (H)** Rue des Fontaines 20, CH-1425; ☏ 024 436 13 26; e info@bellevue-onnens.ch; www. bellevue-onnens.ch

GRANDSON

Tourist information

🛈 Rue Haute 13, CH-1422; ☎024 445 60 60;
e tourisme@terroirs-region-grandson.ch; www.
grandson-tourisme.ch; ⊕ 09.00–19.00 (Nov–Apr
until 18.00) Mon–Fri, 10.00–18.00 Sat, 11.00–
18.00 Sun

Where to stay

🏠 **Du Lac** Rue Basse 36, CH-1422; ☎024 446
26 76; e info@hoteldulacgrandson.ch; www.
hoteldulacgrandson.ch

YVERDON

Tourist information

🛈 Av de la Gare 2, CH-1401; ☎024 423 61
01; e info@yverdon-les-bains.ch; www.
yverdonlesbainsregion.ch; ⊕ Sep–Jun
09.00–noon & 13.30–18.00 Mon–Fri; Jul–Aug
09.00–18.00 Mon–Fri; Apr–Oct 09.30–15.30 Sat;
Apr–Sep 09.30–15.30 Sun

Where to stay

🏠 **Hôtel de la Prairie ****** Av des Bains 9, CH-
1400; ☎024 423 31 31; e contact@laprairiehotel.
ch;www.hoteldelaprairie.ch. The restaurant has 12
GaultMillau points.

🏠 **Hôtel du Théâtre (H)** Av Haldimand 5, CH-
1400; ☎024 424 60 00; e info@hotelyverdon.ch;
www.hotelyverdon.ch. The hotel was opened in
2005, created in a 'gentlman's residence'.

🏠 **De L'Ange*** Rue du Clendy 25, CH-1400;
☎024 425 25 85
The hotel adjacent to the Centre Thermal is:

🏠 **Grand Hotel des Bains**** (H)** Av des
Bains 22, CH-1401; ☎024 424 64 64;
e reservation@grandhotelyverdon.ch; www.
grandhotelyverdon.ch. The building is 18th-
century.

What to see Leaving the station (the tourist office is in the same street), proceed
directly ahead across the park (with children's playground) known as Place d'Armes,
with the white, Belle Epoque-style Casino and Theatre of 1898 on the left. Cross
Rue des Ramparts and proceed down Rue de Ruelle into Rue du Lac. Turn left to
reach Place Pestalozzi, the heart of the old town, on which stand the Town Hall of
1766–73 and to the left of that the castle.

Little remains of the moat that once surrounded the castle, but otherwise it
remains a fine and little-altered example of a quadrangular Savoyard castle, with
four cylindrical towers, one a massive keep. Today it houses an eclectic museum,
the Pestalozzi Records and Research Centre (⊕ *14.00–17.00 Tue–Sun; Jun–Sep
11.00–17.00 Tue–Sun; www.musee-yverdon-region.ch; admission charge*), a theatre
and conference facilities. The museum includes displays on: the history of Yverdon,
with a model of the Roman 4th-century AD fort, mosaics, decorative carvings, early
pots, tools and utensils; weapons and firearms; bicycles; a collection of Egyptian
remains, with the rather gruesome mummy and sarcophagus of Nesshou (3rd–1st
century BC), the body still wrapped in a papyrus Book of the Dead and wearing
amulets (shown by X-ray) to ward off evil spirits; and birds. Although labels are
in French, a returnable English guide is available on request at the entrance. There
is also an independent Swiss Fashion Museum with over 5,000 garments and
accessories from two centuries, which can be seen as part of the tour through the
castle. In the Guards' Tower is the carefully preserved living room of Pestalozzi.

Opposite the castle at Place Pestalozzi 14 is a museum devoted to science fiction,
called The House of Elsewhere (*La Maison d'Ailleurs*; ⊕ *14.00–18.00 Wed–Fri,
11.00–18.00 Sat–Sun*). Unique in Europe, it explores the great themes of the genre
through magazines, comics, toys, works of art, posters, film stills and models.

On the other side of the square is the striking Baroque façade of the Reformed
church (1753–57), with a curved pediment above the blue-faced clock. The interior
layout is unusual in that the altar is placed on the longest side, with a gallery around

the other three sides; this contains an organ on one side and seating on the other two. There are some elaborately carved stalls dating from c1500, which came from an earlier Gothic church on the site.

The vernacular buildings on the square are a few of many lovely houses and old shops which line the streets of the pedestrianised old town. Rue du Four (No 17 has an almost Italian courtyard with murals, No 18 a curious corner extension with identical coats of arms above the door and window), Rue du Milieu, Rue du Lac and Rue de la Plaine (the last has traffic) are particularly well endowed with fine buildings.

The Centre Thermal (⊕ *08.00–22.00 Mon–Sat, 08.00–20.00 Sun; www.cty.ch; admission charge*) off Avenue des Bains offers a wide range of treatments for various muscular and respiratory disorders, with indoor and outdoor pools supplied by water from 500m (1,640ft) below ground, and saunas and massage rooms. It is attractively designed and used by 1,200 people a day, making it one of Switzerland's most popular spas.

YVERDON-LES-BAINS–STE-CROIX Table 212

This spectacular metre-gauge line climbs 631m (2,070ft) in just over 24km (15 miles) without any rack assistance. It climbs up a dramatic gorge and offers magnificent views – on clear days you may be able to see as far as Mont Blanc. Some of the trains are bizarrely decorated with clowns on the outside and like a nursery ceiling inside, with a starlit sky. Sit on the right.

The line leaves Yverdon on the same alignment as the Biel/Bienne line until it bears off to the left, passing the railway's workshops on the outskirts of the town. Some of the small stations are no longer staffed, but the title 'Chef du Gare' can still be seen in fading paintwork on the stone lintels.

The railway heads up a narrow valley, following a stream through orchards, before the country flattens out to reveal an agricultural plain leading gently up to hills on the right. Sugarcane is carried out by rail, huge standard-gauge wagons riding on diminutive bogies. A bus goes from **Essert-sous-Champvent** (table 10.617) to Champvent, where there is one of the finest Savoyard castles in Switzerland, built in the 13th century and unusually sited on a hill. It is not open to the public but can be seen from the surrounding countryside. **Vuiteboeuf** is popular with walkers, and **Baulmes** is a delightfully unspoilt village. In the tower of the Reformed church is a Roman altar dedicated to Apollo, and the former Maison de la Dîme is a local history museum open on request (☎ *024 459 25 32*).

Just before **Six-Fontaines** the line describes a 180-degree bend and climbs so steeply that passengers are looking down on the rooftops of Baulmes as the train passes by the village for the second time, in the opposite direction. There follows a breathtaking section of line that twists its way along a ledge on the edge of woods in which you may be lucky enough to glimpse a chamois near the isolated station of **Trois-Villes**. Shortly after, the line turns away from the views towards the Alps and heads up the deep Gorges de Coratanne, where the line is covered by the occasional avalanche shelter.

Suddenly the railway comes out of the trees on to an open plateau and into **Ste-Croix**. This ski and hiking resort lays claim to be the world capital of the music box and has a number of factories making them, so it is little wonder that there are two museums on the subject. The Music Box and Automata Museum (*Musée de Boîtes à Musique et d'Automates, Rue de l'Industrie 2;* ⊕ *Jun tours at 14.00 & 15.30 Tue–Sun; Jul–Sep tours at 15.00 on Mon, at 10.30, 14.00 & 15.30 Tue–Sun; admission*

15

charge) is four minutes' walk from the station and has a collection of exquisitely made early boxes, automata such as an acrobat with chairs and Pierrot the writer, and phonographs which were also made at Ste-Croix. An annexe houses craftsmen who preserve the traditional skills. Guided tours take about 75 minutes (notes in English available).

Beyond Ste-Croix and reached by a bus from the station (table 10.510) through the Col des Etroits is the village of L'Auberson, close to the French border, where Musée Baud (☺ *Jul–Sep 14.00–17.00 daily; mid-Sep–Jun 10.00–noon & 14.00–18.00 Sun; www.museebaud.ch; admission charge*) may be found. This family-run museum is the result of three generations practising the craft of making mechanical objects that reproduce music. Drawn from many countries, the huge collection ranges from a Gavoili fair organ and an extraordinary Phonoliszt Violina – a piano and three violins in an elaborate wood case – to a robotic accordionist made in 1930. Guided tours last about an hour.

Around Ste-Croix/Les Rasses are 200km (125 miles) of marked footpaths, which include a stretch of the Jura Summits Path. Marvellous views can be had of the Alps from Mount Chasseron at 1,607m (4,833ft), about a two-hour walk from Ste-Croix. In February dog-sledding competitions are held here. From the station there is a bus service to the station at Buttes (table 21.092) (see table 221, page 228).

PRACTICALITIES Bicycle hire from Ste-Croix station.

STE-CROIX
Tourist information

🛈 Hôtel de Ville, Rue Neuve 10, CH-1450; ☏024 455 41 42; e ot@sainte-croix.ch; www.sainte-croix-les-rasses.ch; ☺ 08.30–noon & 13.15–16.30 Mon–Wed & Fri, 08.30–noon & 13.15–17.30 Thu

Where to stay

⌂ **De France*** (H)** Rue Centrale 25, CH-1450; ☏024 454 38 21; e info@hotel-defrance.ch; www.hotel-defrance.ch

⌂ **Auberge de Jeunesse** Rue Centrale 16, CH-1450; ☏024 454 18 10

Hotels in nearby Les Rasses, reached by bus from Ste-Croix station (table 212.25):

⌂ **Grand Hotel Residence*** (H)** CH-1452; ☏024 454 19 61; e info@grandhotelrasses.ch; www.grandhotelrasses.ch

⌂ **Du Chasseron** CH-1450; ☏024 454 23 88; e hotel@chasseron.ch; www.chasseron.ch

YVERDON-LES-BAINS–LAUSANNE Table 210

Scenically unremarkable, but providing access to two interesting branches and the main line across the French border used by Lausanne–Paris TGVs.

For much of the way, the railway uses a broad valley with long stands of tall trees fringing the fields. At **Chavornay**, the junction for Orbe (see opposite), the main street has some attractive 16th–17th-century houses. Above the village of **Bavois** is a medieval castle rebuilt in the 19th century, and the village's part-Romanesque, part-Gothic Reformed church has a centrally placed belltower. Shortly after **Eclépens**, the line from France and Vallorbe trails in on the right.

The valley narrows at **Cossonay**, where the old town is on such a tall hill that it is served by a funicular from the station (table 2003). Although the original castle that was once home to a powerful local family has disappeared, Cossonay retains its old concentric plan and has an 18th-century château on the site. The largely 13th-century Reformed church has a tower surmounted by a 15th-century watchtower, and the clocktower of a school in Petite Rue was once one of the town gates. Cossonay was the limit of the canal that Dutch engineers built from Yverdon, reaching here in 1648, when the goal of reaching Lake Geneva was abandoned. The canal was last used in around 1829, but some impressive stone-lined stretches can still be walked.

For **Lausanne**, see *Chapter 16*.

PRACTICALITIES Bicycle hire from Lausanne station.

CHAVORNAY–ORBE Table 211

A very short branch, of only 4km (2½ miles), but serving an interesting town dating back to Roman times. The railway is independently operated and offers a remarkably full travel service, as well as carrying a healthy freight traffic. Most trains connect with services to and from Lausanne; fewer connect with services from Yverdon.

Known by the Romans as Urba, **Orbe** expanded from the 11th century and was the scene of a stout resistance by the Savoyard defenders in 1475 during the Burgundian wars, when the town was taken and largely destroyed by Bern. Little remains of the 13th-century castle but the cylindrical keep and a square wall-tower. The Reformed church dates largely from the 15th century, and has an extraordinary tower which was once part of the town walls; it was given a bellcote and four corner turrets (bartizans). Inside is some fine stone carving. The town has many attractive 18th-century buildings, including the Hôtel de Ville (1786–89) which overlooks a banner fountain (1543).

Just to the north of the town, about 2km (1¼ miles) out on the Yverdon road and served by buses from the post office at Orbe (table 10.680), are Roman mosaics that are claimed to be the most important in Switzerland. They were found at La Boscéaz in 1841 and date from the 3rd century AD. Four small pavilions also remain from the large villa. To visit, apply at the tourist office (see *Orbe*).

ORBE
Tourist information
⚿ Grand-Rue 1, CH-1350; ☎ 024 442 92 37; e tourisme@orbe.ch; www.orbe-tourisme.ch; ⊕ 14.00–17.00 Mon, 08.30–noon & 14.00–17.00 Tue–Fri; Jul–Aug also 10.00–15.00 Sat

LAUSANNE–COSSONAY–VALLORBE
Table 200/Line S2 of Vaud RER

The line is used by TGVs between Paris and Lausanne as well as local trains. Travelling from the north, the first station south of the junction is Cossonay. The railway provides access to several places of interest and the branch along the Vallée de Joux.

From the junction to the north of Cossonay (see table 210, opposite), the line to Vallorbe turns to the northwest. At **La Sarraz** is a magnificent fortress dating back to the mid 11th century, though the oldest surviving parts, including two square towers, are 13th century. The castle was rebuilt after being badly damaged in 1475 and 1536, and was given by the family that had owned it for 850 years to a charitable society, which now runs it as a museum (⊕ *Mar–May & Sep–Oct 13.00–17.00 Sat–Sun; Jun–Aug 13.00–17.00 Tue–Sun*) with collections of porcelain, silverware, furniture and antiquities. In the attractive grounds of the castle is an Equestrian Museum (*Musée du Cheval; same hours as castle*) which has a reconstructed smithy and saddlery, and displays of horse-drawn vehicles and smaller artefacts.

In the 14th-century church of St Antoine is the gruesome tomb of Franz I of La Sarraz, who died in 1363. The effigy of the naked man is carved in a state of decomposition which is being accelerated by nibbling toads and worms.

La Sarraz has one of Switzerland's last three bell foundries, and the abandoned canal from Yverdon to Cossonay (see table 210, page 234) passes by the village.

The line describes a long meander before **Croy-Romainmôtier**, which should not be missed by anyone interested in churches – the latter has the most important Romanesque monastery church in Switzerland. The church was part of the Abbey of SS Pierre and Paul, which is thought to have been founded in the 6th century. Today's building was begun in the early 11th century based on the layout of Cluny and retains many original features such as columns, capitals and the nave arcade. Frescoes of the 14th century decorate the vault of the porch, of the 15th-century north chapel (⊕ *07.00–18.00 daily*). Little of the cloisters remains, but the clocktower opposite the church was once part of the abbey's protective walls. Also open is the former prior's house (⊕ *Apr–Nov 08.30–18.30 daily*) and the tithe barn, La Maison de la Dîme (◌ *024 453 14 65;* ⊕ *Easter–Oct 09.00–noon & 13.30–18.00 daily*), featuring a tape/slide presentation (with English commentary as well as French and German) using nine projectors.

Soon after **Le Day**, the junction for Le Brassus and the closest station to Vallorbe Fort (see below), the railway crosses the valley of the River Orbe and the river itself and swings to the west to reach the last station before France at **Vallorbe**. Its prosperity was created through the establishment of metallurgical industries, with crude beginnings in the 13th century. By 1670 it had three blast furnaces and about 30 forges, developing into tool, nail, lock, gun and file manufacture. During the last century, Vallorbe turned to more sophisticated products, and today about 700 French people cross the border each day to work here.

The town has two notable museums. The Iron and Railway Museum (*Musée du Fer and Chemin de Fer, Grandes Forges 11; www.museedufer.ch;* ⊕ *Apr–Oct 14.00–18.00 Mon, 10.00–18.00 Tue–Sun; Nov–Mar 14.00–18.00 Tue–Fri*) is based on the site of Les Grandes Forges, only ten minutes' walk from the station, near the bridge over the Orbe, from which the foundry drew power and water. This site was first developed for metallurgy in 1495. Besides four large waterwheels, the smithy is still used to illustrate ancient skills and produce objects for sale. The railway part of the museum illustrates the strategic position of Vallorbe and the nearby Jougne Pass in the crossing of the Jura by the railway that arrived in 1870. There is a large exhibition of railway memorabilia and pictures, and an O-gauge layout of the station which is built to an exceptionally realistic standard.

It is quite a hike to the other museum at Pré-Giroud – an hour from Vallorbe and 40 minutes from Le Day – but there is nothing else quite like it in Switzerland. Inside a mountain facing the Jougne Pass three connected forts known as the Vallorbe Fort were hollowed out in 1937–41, underground galleries linking observation posts, gun emplacements, magazines, control room, refectory, kitchen, dormitory and infirmary. It was abandoned and sold to the commune for just SFr1 as recently as 1988. The whole warren is open to visitors by guided tour, for rather more (*www.pre-giroud.ch;* ⊕ *May–Oct first tour 11.30, last tour 16.30 Sat–Sun; Jul–Aug first tour 11.00, last tour 17.00 daily*).

To the southwest of the town is a half-hour walk through a gorge of the Orbe to the river's source at the foot of a cliff. The network of subtly lit caves from which it emerges was opened to visitors in 1974 (*www.grottesdevallorbe.ch*; ⊕ *Apr–Oct 09.30–16.30 daily; Jun–Aug until 17.30 daily*); besides stalagmites and stalactites, panels provide information at stages in the underground circuit.

ROMAINMÔTIER
Tourist information

☑ Rue du Bourg, CH-1323; ☎ 024 453 38 28; e tourisme@romainmotier.ch; www. romanmotier-tourisme.ch; ⊕ Apr–Jun, Sep–Nov

10.00–noon & 13.30–17.00 Tue–Sun; Jul–Aug
10.00–noon & 13.30–18.00 daily

VALLORBE
Tourist information

☑ Grandes Forges 11, CH-1337; ☎ 021 843 25 83; e contact@vallorbe-tourisme.ch; www.vallorbe-tourisme.ch; ⊕ Apr–Oct 14.00–18.00 Mon,

10.00–18.00 Tue–Sun; Nov–Mar 09.30–noon & 13.30–18.00 Tue–Fri

VALLORBE–LE DAY–LE BRASSUS Table 201

A most attractive standard-gauge branch line of 13km (8 miles) that runs for most of its length beside Lac de Joux. Vallée de Joux means valley of forest, and many of the slopes are still covered in woods; the valley has developed a reputation for the high quality of its watchmakers. There are 250km (156 miles) of marked walks in the area, and Le Brassus and Le Sentier are ski resorts. Sit on the left.

From the junction at Le Day you can look back across the valley to Vallorbe and see the line climbing steeply towards the long tunnel underneath the Jura into France. From the broad open valley, the line enters a narrow valley with the cliffs from which the River Orbe emerges on the right.

Before the small resort of **Le Pont** the tiny Lac Brenet can be seen on the right. On the Vallorbe side of Le Pont on Route Vallorbe is a park which is home to bears, wolves and a herd of North American bison. From Le Pont, steam-hauled trains, including fondue specials, operate on certain days between June and September (*reservations* ☎ *021 845 55 15; www.ctvj.ch*); they are hauled by one of two six-coupled tank engines dating from 1909 and 1915. From the station a bus crosses the Col du Mollendruz on summer Sundays only (table 10.733), terminating at Morges on Lake Léman. Le Pont is also the departure point for a boat service on Lac de Joux (☎ *021 841 12 03; www.nlj.ch; Jun & Sep Sat–Sun; Jul–Aug daily*).

As the line reaches the shore of Lac de Joux, the largest lake in the Jura, the huge tower at L'Abbaye can be seen across the water, all of any substance that is left of the Premonstratensian abbey.

Sentier-Orient is the largest town in the valley, both it and **Le Brassus** having specialist watchmaking industries. In 1969 a mammoth skeleton from around 10,300BC was found near Le Brassus; it may be seen in the Palais de Rumine in Lausanne. From Le Brassus station a bus runs on summer weekends to Nyon on Lake Léman, crossing the Col du Marchairuz (table 10.820).

LE PONT
Where to stay

⌂ **De la Truite***** CH-1342; ☎ 021 841 17 71; e hoteltruite@bluewin.ch; www.hoteltruite.com

LE ROCHERAY
Where to stay
⌂ **Bellevue***** CH-1347; ☎ 021 845 57 20;
✉ info@rocheray.ch; www.rocheray.ch

SENTIER-ORIENT
Tourist information
🗺 Office du tourisme de la Vallée de Joux, Rue
de l'Orbe 8, CH-1347; ☎ 021 845 17 77; ✉ info@
valleedejoux.ch; www.myvalleedejoux.ch;
🕓 09.00–noon & 13.00–18.00 daily

Where to stay
⌂ **De Ville**** Grand Rue 29, CH-1347;
☎ 021 845 52 33; ✉ info@hotelsentier.ch; www.
hotelsentier.ch

LE BRASSUS
Where to stay
⌂ **De la Lande** Pl de la Lande, CH-1348;
☎ 021 845 44 41; ✉ info@hotellalande.com; www.
hotellalande.com. Family-run hotel in the centre
of the town.

16

Geneva and Lausanne

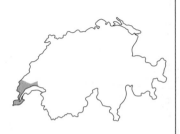

The southwestern corner of Switzerland is dominated by Lake Léman, commonly known as Lake Geneva, rather to the irritation of those living elsewhere along its shores. This French-speaking area has the benefit of the western end of the Jura Mountains as well as wonderful views across western Europe's largest lake to the French and Swiss Alps. It is also one of the most populous areas, partly due to the important international role played by Geneva and, to a lesser extent, Lausanne. The area's natural beauty has also attracted foreign visitors and affluent residents for centuries, and the tourist boards can call on a litany of famous names who have made their home in the area.

GENEVA

Geneva has long been Switzerland's most cosmopolitan city. For centuries, exiles from religious or political persecution have chosen the city as their refuge. Today, the headquarters of over 200 international organisations are based here, raising an always numerous foreign community to one-third of the population. The city is also a major banking centre – a 'city of wealth by stealth' as the British actor Robert Morley put it. These roles have contributed to it being an expensive city in which to live or stay, but it has much to offer the visitor, principally the old town and some fine museums.

Situated at the southwestern end of Lac Léman, Geneva is the departure point for lake steamers, and only an arrival by water can convey just how well sited the city is, with foreground hills against a backdrop of mountains.

There has been a settlement here since Neolithic times, which became one of some importance in Roman times, judging by contemporary remains found near the cathedral. After becoming an imperial city under Emperor Conrad II in 1032, it was for five centuries the subject of a struggle for dominance between the local bishops and lords. Alliances with the cantons of Fribourg (1519) and Bern (1526) helped the city to achieve independence in 1530. This was reinforced by the adoption of Protestantism in 1535 and the arrival of the austere and intolerant theologian Jean Calvin, who lived here from 1541 until his death in 1564.

It was Calvin who fostered the birth of watchmaking in Geneva, but it was the influx of Protestant refugees, particularly Huguenots, that did most to develop this and other industries such as banking. Following the French Revolution, Geneva became a part of France from 1798 until 1813, joining the Swiss Confederation the following year. Switzerland's neutrality since 1815 has encouraged many international organisations to establish their headquarters in the country, principally in Geneva. Among them are the International Labour Organization, the World Health Organization and the International Telecommunications Union.

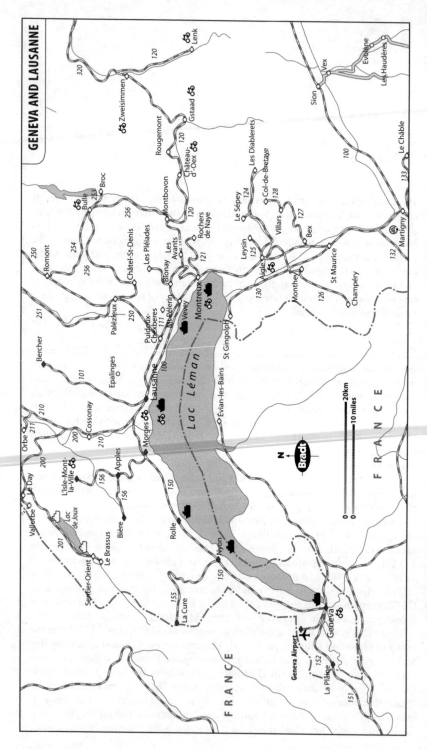

GENEVA AND LAUSANNE

The outcome of an international conference in 1864 was the Geneva Convention, which established the Red Cross and a code of conduct for the care of the victims of war by the Red Cross, using the Swiss flag with transposed colours as its emblem. In 1920 Geneva became the headquarters of the League of Nations, followed in 1946 by the European headquarters of the United Nations.

Geneva's reputation as a refuge for religious and political exiles led to many well-known figures making it their home or visiting friends who had. Amongst the hundreds that could be listed were John Knox (who became the first British pastor here in 1555), Robert Devereux (Elizabeth I's favourite), Milton, Richard Cromwell, Thomas Gray, John Evelyn, William Beckford, Disraeli, George Eliot, Tolstoy, Dostoyevsky (who wrote *The Idiot* here), General Ulysses Grant, Thomas Hardy, Lenin and Joseph Conrad. Sir Humphry Davy, who is credited with the invention of the eponymous mining lamp, is buried in the Plainpalais Cemetery.

Geneva's reputation, connected with the Academy established by Calvin (now the university), made the city a popular choice for the sons of prominent British families to finish their education, either formally or as part of the Grand Tour. During the 1730s, for instance, a group of such aristocratic visitors formed a loose club known as the Common Room, which put on plays and organised expeditions, notably to the Mer de Glace above Chamonix; they surveyed the little-known glacier and produced a pamphlet about it. Later Geneva became a popular refuge for Russian revolutionaries prior to the 1917 revolution, the life of anarchists in the area known as La Petite Russie being described in Conrad's *Under Western Eyes*.

Some visitors were highly critical of the destruction of ancient buildings during the 19th century. Ruskin, for example, spent many long visits to Switzerland trying to identify the precise subjects and angles of Turner's paintings; he was so angered by contemporary developments in Geneva that he included only one picture of the city in his exhibition catalogue of 1857, hoping that 'Geneva will be properly humiliated at being left out of the list, as too much spoiled to be worth notice'. However, if the universal ogre of insensitive redevelopment has destroyed much, the old town still has many lovely streets and squares of 18th-century houses, a good number thankfully pedestrianised.

The city straddles the Rhône, the northern part being referred to as the right bank (*rive droit*) and the southern the left bank (*rive gauche*).

GETTING THERE Those arriving by air at Geneva have only a short journey from Geneva Airport station from which all Swiss expresses depart rather than from the city's central and principal station at Gare de Cornavin, built in 1913–16. Cornavin has all the facilities one would expect, including an office providing details and tickets for public transport, operated by Transports Publics Genevois (*www.tpg. ch*; ⊕ *07.00–19.00 Mon–Fri, 09.00–18.00 Sat*). There is a press-button map with telephone to locate and book accommodation near the tourist office.

The main locker area is adjacent to the main ramp to platforms 2–3, and another bank of lockers may be found by the ramp to platforms 4–6.

Most bus routes and the six tram routes serve the station from various stops close to Place de Cornavin, immediately outside the station. A map from the public transport office shows the precise locations.

GETTING AROUND Since 2007 everyone staying at a hotel, hostel or campsite in Geneva has received a Geneva Transport Card conferring free use of trams, buses and boats for the duration of their stay.

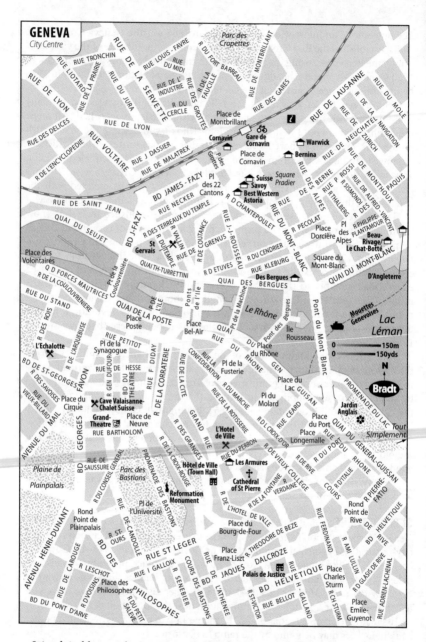

It is advisable to pick up a map and guide to the bus and tram routes (constantly being extended) at the separate public transport office at the station. Routes serving the city area are designated by a number; those reaching into the suburbs are given letters.

It is essential to buy tickets before you board a tram or bus – no tickets are sold on them and there is a penalty for ticketless travel. You can buy a ticket for one hour's duration, irrespective of changes, from the vending machines at stops. For numerous trips, 1-, 2- and 3-day passes can be bought from the office at Cornavin station or the Transports Publics Genevois office at Rond-Point de Rive. You must validate all tickets using the vending machines at stops.

The Swiss Pass covers all journeys.

Bicycle hire from Cornavin station, and a map showing cycle routes is available.

TOURIST INFORMATION
i 18 Rue du Mont-Blanc, CH-1211; ☎022 909 70 00; e info@geneve-tourisme.ch; www.geneve-tourisme.ch; ⏰ 10.00–18.00 Mon, 09.00–18.00 Tue–Sat; 10.00–16.00 Sun

The region is also covered by www.lake-geneva-region.ch.

WHERE TO STAY
Hotels around Place de Cornavin, on to which the station fronts, are:

🏠 **Cornavin****** Gare de Cornavin, CH-1201; ☎022 716 12 12; e cornavin@fhotels.ch; www.fassbinhotels.com

🏠 **Warwick****** 14 Rue de Lausanne, CH-1201; ☎022 716 80 00; e res.geneva@warwickhotels.com; www.warwickhotels.com

🏠 **Best Western Hotel Astoria***** 6 Pl Cornavin, CH-1211; ☎022 544 52 52; e hotel@astoria-geneve.ch; www.astoria-geneve.ch

🏠 **Savoy***** 8 Pl de Cornavin, CH-1201; ☎022 906 47 00; e info@hotel-savoy.net; www.hotels-savoy.net

🏠 **Suisse***** 10 Pl de Cornavin, CH-1201; ☎022 732 66 30; e reservation@hotel-suisse.ch; www.hotel-suisse.ch

🏠 **Bernina**** 22 Pl de Cornavin, CH-1201; ☎022 908 49 50; e info@bernina-geneve.ch; www.bernina-geneve.ch

Hotels overlooking Lac Léman are:

🏠 **D'Angleterre******* **(H)** 17 Quai du Mont-Blanc, CH-1201; ☎022 906 55 55; e bookan@rchmail.ch; www.dangleterrehotel.com

🏠 **Beau-Rivage******* **(H)** 13 Quai du Mont-Blanc, CH-1201; ☎022 716 66 66; e info@beau-rivage.ch; www.beau-rivage.ch

🏠 **Four Seasons Hotel Des Bergues******* **(H)** 33 Quai des Bergues, CH-1201; ☎022 908 70 00; www.fourseasons.com/geneva

In the old town:

🏠 **Les Armures******* **(H)** 1 Rue Puits-Saint Pierre, CH-1204; ☎022 310 91 72; e reception@hotel-les-armures.ch; www.hotel-les-armures.ch

WHERE TO EAT
✕ **Brasserie-Restaurant de l'Hotel-de-Ville** Grand-Rue 39; ☎022 311 70 30

✕ **Café du Centre** Pl de Mollard 5; ☎022 311 85 86

✕ **Cave Valaisanne-Chalet Suisse** Bd Georges-Favon 23; ☎022 328 12 36

✕ **Dix Vins** Rue Jacques-Dalphin, Carouge; ☎029 342 40 10

✕ **Epiapres** Rue Saint-Joseph 37, Carouge; ☎022 342 03 32

✕ **Le Chat-Botté** Quai du Mont Blanc 13, Hôtel Beau Rivage; ☎022 716 66 66

✕ **L'Echalotte** Rue des Rois 17; ☎022/320 59 99

✕ **Le Moulin a Poivre** Ruelle du Midi 5; ☎022 700 27 27

✕ **St Gervais** Rue des Corps-Saints 4; ☎022 732 39 34

✕ **Tout Simplement** Rue de Soleure 2; ☎022 736 28 28

WHAT TO SEE
Exploring the old town The old town is a delightful area to explore on foot. The streets and squares comprise mainly 18th-century façades of dressed stone with restrained classical decoration. In common with many Swiss cities, the sound of water playing in fountains can be frequently heard. The tourist offices sell and rent an MP3 audio guide in English describing sites of interest in the old town, lasting about 2½ hours. Take bus 6, 8 or 9 from the station to the stops of Molard, Longemalle or Place du Port respectively.

The tourist office in Place du Molard is a good place to start, situated in a lively, pedestrianised square of flower stalls and numerous cafés that was once the city's economic centre. The tower was built in 1591.

The heart of the old town is the surprisingly small Cathedral of St Pierre, built between 1160 and 1289 on the site of a 4th–6th-century church. To the original Romanesque and Gothic elements was added a Neo-classical portico in 1752–56. By this time, however, it had lost many of its ornaments and holy objects during the iconoclasm of the Reformation. As a consequence, there is an austere appearance to the body of the church, the decoration being limited to the capitals, some blind arcading and the chancel stained glass. So it is rather a shock to enter the Maccabean chapel: built in 1406, it was turned into a warehouse at the Reformation, but in 1878 it was refurbished in neo-Gothic style by the best-known French restorer, Viollet-le-Duc. The ceiling panels between the vault ribs have elaborate gilded decoration on blue and red grounds that would have appealed to the contemporary British Gothicist William Burges and his principal client, the 3rd Marquess of Bute.

If you feel energetic, a climb of 157 steps takes you to the top of the north tower (⊕ *Jun–Sep 09.30–18.00 Mon–Sat, noon–18.30 Sun; Oct–May 10.00–17.30 Mon–Sat, noon–17.30 Sun; admission charge*) from which there are fine views over the old town and lake. The cathedral's carillons change their tune every month of the year.

Underneath the cathedral is an archaeological site that provides an insight into the cathedral's past, including the remains of a 4th-century baptistry and 5th-century mosaics (⊕ *10.00–17.00 Tue–Sun; admission charge*).

Just to the southeast of the cathedral is Auditoire Calvin, once the 13th-century parish church of Notre-Dame-de-la-Neuve. Here Calvin lectured and Knox preached to the English and Scottish communities in 1554–59. It was in Geneva that Knox worked with Thomas Bodley (after whom the Bodleian Library at Oxford was later named) and others to revise the Coverdale Bible of 1535; the new version was first published in 1560 and known as the Geneva Bible.

To the west of the cathedral is Rue du Puit-St-Pierre in which is situated the 15th-century Town Hall (Hôtel de Ville), which houses Geneva's parliament. The Renaissance street façades date from 1617 to 1630. The cobbled ramp in the square tower of 1556 facilitated the arrival of dignitaries on horseback. Off the inner courtyard, in which concerts are held in summer, is the Alabama Chamber; it is named after the settlement by arbitration of the Alabama Dispute between Britain and the US in 1872, though this scarcely remembered incident was of little consequence compared with the signing eight years before in the same room of the first Geneva Convention. Outside the Town Hall in 1762 the public executioner burnt Rousseau's polemical novel on education, *Emile*, after which he was forced to flee Geneva for Môtiers (see page 227).

Opposite is the arcaded Armoury; this was built in the 16th century as a corn hall, altered in 1629–34, converted into an arsenal in 1720 and now houses the state archive. Under the pronounced eave is a pictorial frieze of 1893 telling the story of Geneva.

In the same street, at No 6, is Maison Tavel, the oldest private dwelling in the city and now a museum (see page 248).

To the east of the cathedral is Place du Bourg-de-Four, which is the oldest public square in Geneva and thought to have been built on the site of the Roman forum. To the east of the square is the Palais de Justice, with pronounced rusticated columns. Built in 1707–12 as a convent, it became a hospice until 1857 when it was converted into the judiciary.

Other sights on the left bank To the south of the old town is a park, the Promenade des Bastions, in which stands the Reformation monument (1909–17), a massive group of figures associated with the Reformation, Knox and Oliver Cromwell among them. It stands on a long wall with a moat below. Overlooking it is the Promenade de la Treille where you can sit and admire the view from the world's longest bench, at 122m (400ft).

To the south again is the Parc des Bastions in which the university is situated, housed in a Neo-classical building (1868–72). To the northwest is Place Neuve, a focal point of Geneva's musical life. The Grand-Théâtre (1874–79) was inspired by the Paris Opera and is home to the Orchestra de la Suisse Romande, founded by Ernest Ansermet (1883–1969). The façade of the Florentine-style Conservatoire, built in 1857–58, is decorated with statues and niches. Just south of the square, in Rue Général-Dufour, is the Victoria Hall, a concert hall named after Queen Victoria.

Tram 13 from the station to Palettes will take you south across the River Arve to a district named Carouge (also the name of the bus stop) that was once the property of Sardinia. It was planned and designed in the 18th century by Piedmontese architects, and retains a Mediterranean feel. The main square, Place du Marché, is shaded by plane trees, and on its northeast corner, by Rue Vautier, is the former mansion of the Count of Veyrier which has a lovely courtyard. The area is full of small shops and crafts, some being practised in shops open to view.

In Cologny and Montalègre, reached by bus E from Rive (bus 8 from the station), are the villas where Byron, Shelley, Mary Godwin and her stepsister Claire Clairmont lived during the summer of 1816. Byron lived with his companion-physician John Polidori at Villa Diodati, 9 Chemin de Ruth; the others at Maison Chapuis, where Mary Godwin began *Frankenstein*, published two years later. The two households created some scandal, the result of which was Claire Clairemont having a child by Byron. The proprietor of the Hôtel d'Angleterre made money out of it by charging to look through a telescope trained on Byron's bedroom in the villa across the water from his hotel.

The right bank Most of Geneva's international organisations are located near the Place des Nations, reached by bus F, V or Z from the station. The large park adjacent to the Place is dominated by the Palais des Nations, European headquarters of the United Nations and the largest building in Europe after the Palace of Versailles. It was designed by five architects of different nationality and built for the League of Nations in 1929–37. The lobby of the Council Chamber (*open for guided visits: Apr–Jun 10.00–noon & 14.00–16.00 daily; Jul–Aug 10.00–17.00 daily; Sep–Mar 10.00–noon & 14.00–16.00 Mon–Fri; admission charge*) has bas-reliefs by Eric Gill.

To the east of the Palais des Nations at Chemin de l'Impératrice 1 are the Botanical Gardens (☉ *Nov–Mar 09.30–17.00 daily; Apr–Oct 08.00–19.30 daily; bus 1 from the station to Jardin Botanique, also on bus routes 11 and 28*), which contains an animal park devoted to conservation as well as over 16,000 plant species.

Musée Ariana and the Museum of the Swiss Abroad at Château de Penthes (see page 248) are both close by.

Continuing to the north by bus F you can cross the frontier into France to visit the château at Ferney-Voltaire where the French writer Voltaire lived from 1758 to 1778. His bedroom and antechamber contain their original furniture. He was visited at Ferney by Boswell in 1764, John Wilkes the following year, and Adam Smith in 1766.

On the western outskirts of Geneva is the Science and Technology Exhibition ✆ *022 767 76 76; e cern.reception@cern.ch; www.cern.ch; from the main station take tram 13 to CERN; 3-hour tours in English at 10.30 Mon–Sat*) at CERN (European Council for Nuclear Research), where the world's largest scientific instrument is located. Built in 1983–89, the large electron-positron collider (LEP) and its successor, the Large Hadron Collider (LHC), which was completed in 2008, are housed in a 17-mile tunnel that enables sub-microscopic particles to be accelerated to near the speed of light so that scientists can analyse the results to discover more about the origins of the universe. There has been much talk of the quest for the Higgs Boson particle. The Microcosm exhibition provides an insight into the science behind the machine and the whole field of space research and cosmology. Visits (*09.00 & 14.00 Mon–Sat*), which last half a day and are unsuitable for those under 14, must be pre-booked; long notice is advised, given their popularity and the limits on numbers.

The lakefront The view from any point is dominated by the fountain (*Jet d'Eau*) which shoots a jet of water 145m (476ft) into the air. It was inaugurated in 1886 and improved in 1891 and 1947, and visitors soon learn to be wary of the spray on windy days. From Pont du Mont Blanc, where the Rhône leaves the lake, there is a lovely walk along the south shore. To the right is the Île Rousseau with its statue of the seated philosopher by Pradier (1835). You soon reach the Jardin Anglais with its famous flower clock. Just beyond the harbour are the large Parc La Grange and Parc des Eaux-Vives; in the former park is a fine Neo-classical villa of 1766–67.

The proprietor of one of the early lakefront hotels, Hotel d'Angleterre, in 1816 cashed in on human prurience by training a telescope on Villa Diodati on the other side of the lake and charging to watch the goings-on between Byron, Shelley, Mary Godwin and her stepsister Claire Clairmont, who later gave birth to Byron's child. It was a bet made then between Byron and Godwin about who would first write a horror story that produced *Frankenstein*, first published in 1818. A plaque on the villa, still privately owned, recalls Byron's tenure.

Mont Salève Geneva's local mountain is actually in France, but easy to reach by bus 8 from Cornavin station to Veyrier. It is only a ten-minute walk across the border (take your passport) to the cable car and the start of paths up the mountain. The 1,100m (3,608ft) mountain affords fine views over the city, lake, Rhône and surrounding mountains.

Museums

International Red Cross and Red Crescent Museum (Le Musée International de la Croix-Rouge et du Croissant-Rouge) (*17 Av de la Paix, CH-1202; ☎ 022 748 95 25; www.micr.org; ⏰ 10.00–17.00 Wed–Mon; admission charge; bus 8 or F from station*) The superbly presented story of the Red Cross and the men and women who have devoted their lives to the service of mankind, with audio-visual presentations.

Museum of Science History (Musée d'Histoire des Sciences) (*Villa Batholoni, 128 Rue de Lausanne, CH-1202; ☎ 022 418 50 60; ⏰ 10.00–17.00 Wed–Mon; bus 1 from station to Sécheron*) Unique to Switzerland, the subject of this museum is the numerous scientific instruments created by previous generations, their application and the story of the people who created and used them. Housed in a villa built in 1828–31, it focuses on Geneva and the brilliant 18th century, when great progress was made in the city.

Natural History Museum (Musée d'Histoire Naturelle) (1 Route de Malagnou, Case Postale 6434, CH-1211; ☎ 022 418 63 00; ⏰ 10.00–17.00 Tue–Sun; bus 1, 8 or 27 to Museum or tram 16 to Villereuse from station) Switzerland's largest museum of its kind, with dioramas, collections of fossils, invertebrates and minerals, and live creatures in aquariums and vivariums.

The Museum of Art and History (Musée d'Art et d'Histoire) (2 Rue Charles Galland, CH-1206; ☎ 022 418 26 00; ⏰ 10.00–18.00 Tue–Sun; bus 1, 8 to Tranchées or 3, 5 to Athénée, or tram 16 to Rive from station) This museum has a collection so large that much is not on display or has been transferred to satellite museums. The most notable picture is the *Miraculous Draught of Fishes*, which is the earliest European painting of an identifiable landscape. Painted in 1444, it depicts Lac Léman. Other subjects of interest are the Battle of Murten/Morat, portraits of Diderot, Maria Theresa and Rousseau, a hunt scene at Brocket Hall in Hertfordshire, and many topographical views of Switzerland as well as Geneva and its environs. There are works by Wouwerman, Maes, Pourbus the Younger, Jean-Etienne Liotard, Pieter Brueghel the Younger, Hobbema, Fuseli, Corot, Hodler, Cézanne, Renoir, Sisley, Monet, Calame and Félix Vallotton, who was born in nearby Lausanne. Some English portraits by Romney, Lawrence, Raeburn and Hoppner were bequeathed to the state of Geneva by Lord Michelham of Hellingly (1900–84), who lived in the city for 35 years. Other rooms contain furniture, arms and armour, pewter, stained glass and a large collection of archaeological finds (including Roman treasures from Martigny, see pages 287–8).

International Museum of the Reformation (Musée International de la Réforme) (Maison Mallet, Rue du Cloître 2; ☎ 022 310 24 31; ⏰ 10.00–17.00 Tue–Sun; admission charge; tram 16 to Molard from station) In a building on the very site where the Reformation was proclaimed, this museum uses traditional and modern techniques such as holograms to portray one of the most important religious transformations in the last millennium.

Collection Baur (8 Rue Munier-Romilly, CH-1206; ☎ 022 704 32 82; ⏰ 14.00–18.00 Tue–Sun; admission charge; bus 1, 8 to Florissant from station) Situated close to the Art and History Museum, this exhibition of 8th–19th-century Chinese and Japanese treasures forms by far the most important collection of Far Eastern objects in Switzerland. Created by Alfred Baur (1865–1951), it includes ceramics, jade, lacquerwork, prints, netsuke and ceremonial weapons.

Voltaire Museum and Institute (Institut et Musée Voltaire) (25 Rue des Délices, CH-1203; ☎ 022 344 71 33; ⏰ 14.00–17.00 Mon–Sat; bus 6 or 26 to Prairie or bus 27 to Musée Voltaire from station) Voltaire owned this house from 1755 to 1765, living here for the first four years. Numerous books and objects associated with, and manuscripts by, Voltaire.

Jean-Jacques Rousseau House (Espace Jean-Jacques Rousseau) (Grand-Rue 40, CH-1211; ☎ 022 310 10 28; ⏰ 11.00–17.30 Tue–Sun; admission charge; bus 36 to Hôtel de Ville) Jean-Jacques Rousseau was born in this house on 28 June 1712. A 25-minute audio-visual traces the life of the famous writer and philosopher of the Enlightenment, bringing his works and personality to life.

Musée Barbier-Mueller (10 Rue Jean-Calvin, CH-1206; ☎ 022 312 02 70; ⏰ 11.00–17.00 daily; admission charge; bus 2 or tram 16 to Molard from station)

The first items in this collection were bought in 1907 by Josef Mueller, whose descendants continued to purchase items of classical and tribal sculpture, textiles and ornaments. The African and Indonesian collections are the largest. Close to the cathedral.

Musée Ariana (*10 Av de la Paix, CH-1206;* ☏ *022 418 54 50;* ⏱ *10.00–18.00 Wed–Mon; admission charge; bus F or Z to Place des Nations and then bus 18*) Seven centuries of ceramics, from Geneva and Nyon, elsewhere in Switzerland and from the Orient.

Museum of the Swiss Abroad (Musée des Suisses dans le Monde) (*Château de Penthes, 18 Chemin de l'Impératrice, Pregny-Genève, CH-1292;* ☏ *022 734 90 21;* ⏱ *10.00–noon & 13.00–17.00 Tue–Sun; admission charge; bus V or Z from station to Penthes*) The story of the Swiss abroad, focusing on the centuries when Swiss mercenaries were the most prized soldiers that could be hired. Other displays look at the achievements of Swiss architects, engineers, industrialists, explorers etc. It is situated in a lovely house that was a family home until 1972, when it was sold to the state of Geneva. In the grounds is a pavilion containing a museum devoted to the military history of Geneva.

Maison Tavel/Museum of Old Geneva (*6 Rue du Puits-St-Pierre, CH-1204;* ☏ *022 418 37 00;* ⏱ *10.00–18.00 Tue–Sun; bus 2 or tram 16 to Bel-Air from station*) Appropriately this museum is housed in the city's oldest dwelling. Although parts of the house were built in the 12th century, its façade dates from the 17th and there is a round tower on the northeast corner. The museum describes life in the city from the 14th to 19th centuries and has Switzerland's largest relief map on the top floor, as well as a model illustrating Geneva when it was a walled city before 1850. The oval model, measuring 7m x 6m, took a Genevan architect 18 years to make in zinc and copper.

Musée Rath (*Place Neuve 2, CH-1204;* ☏ *022 418 33 40;* ⏱ *10.00–18.00 Tue, Thu–Sun, noon–21.00 Wed; admission charge; buses 3, 36 or tram 12 to Place de Neuve*) This was the first Swiss museum to be devoted to the fine arts, given to the city by the Rath sisters and opened in 1826. It was conceived as a 'Temple of the Muses' embodying both French taste and the Italian style and displays temporary exhibitions organised by the Art and History Museum.

Festivals Among the city's festivals are the Carnival in March and the International Music Competition in October, but the most dramatic is the Escalade over a mid-December weekend. It commemorates an attempt to storm the city walls in 1602. The old city becomes the scene of torchlit parades of costumed figures, some on horseback, with country markets, folk music, Rabelasian banquets and a bonfire in Cathedral square.

LAC LÉMAN

Its name derived from the Roman Lacus Lemanus, Lac Léman (or sometimes Lac Genève) is the largest lake in Switzerland and western Europe. Shaped like a croissant, the north shore is 72km (45 miles) long and its widest point is 14km (8¾ miles) across. Three-fifths of the lake belongs to Switzerland, the rest to France. In contrast to the blue-green of most Swiss lakes, Léman is much bluer. Its Swiss shore, to the east of Nyon particularly, is lined with terraced vineyards, backed by mountains that grow in height from west to east.

The marvellous views that are enjoyed from its northern shore, coupled with the attractiveness of the towns and villages between Geneva and the lake's eastern end at Villeneuve, have long made the region a favourite place to live for many eminent and famous people. Amongst those who have chosen the area to live in are the composers Tchaikovsky, Liszt, Stravinsky, Ravel, Strauss and Hindemith; the writers Byron, Voltaire, Dickens, Tolstoy, Gibbon, Goethe, Simenon, Nabokov and Greene; film stars Charlie Chaplin, Noël Coward, Audrey Hepburn, Yul Brynner, Richard Burton, James Mason and Peter Ustinov; singers and musicians Arthur Rubinstein, Clara Haskil, Joan Sutherland, Barbara Hendricks and David Bowie; artists Kokoschka, Courbet and Balthus.

BOAT SERVICES ON LAC LÉMAN AND THE RHÔNE The first steamer on the lake, in 1823, was owned by an American and inappropriately named *William Tell* (Lake Luzern has a better claim). Today there are still five steam-driven paddle steamers: *Montreux* (1904), *La Suisse* (1910), *Savoie* (1914), *Simplon* (1920) and *Rhône* (1928), and three paddlers that are diesel-electric driven: *Vevey* (1907), *Italie* (1908) and *Helvetie* (1926). It is necessary to check the timetable (table 3150) to see which services the older ships are operating, as most are worked by the 12 modern diesel ships.

Services leave from near the Jardin Anglais and serve 35 piers, including the French resorts of Thonon-les-Bains and Evians-les-Bains. Most services operate only between May and September, and excursions range in duration from one to 11 hours, some with gourmet, Belle Epoque and firework themes (*Compagnie Générale de Navigation sur le Lac Léman, Avenue de Rhodanie 17, Case postale 116, Lausanne 6, CH-1000; infoline* 0848 811 848; e *info@cgn.ch; www.cgn.ch*).

Swiss Boat operates a variety of themed cruises down the Rhône (*Swiss Boat*, 022 732 47 47; *www.swissboat.com*) between April and September. Boats leave from Quai du Mont Blanc.

It was while leaving Hôtel Beau Rivage to board a boat at Geneva that Elizabeth of Bavaria (known as 'Sisi'), wife of the Austrian Emperor Franz Joseph I, was fatally stabbed in 1898 by an anarchist whose intended victim was a visiting member of the French royal family.

COPPET–GENEVA–ANNEMASSE–EVIAN

This cross-city service is expected to start operation in 2016 once a missing link is built between Lancy-Pont-Rouge (terminus of suburban trains from Coppet on the Lausanne line since 2002) and Eaux-Vives, allowing through trains to Annemasse. The service will open up new possibilities for exploring the French side of the lake.

GENEVA–LA PLAINE–BELLEGARDE Table 151

Operated by light rail vehicles rather than conventional trains, the stopping service on the line to Lyon provides access to a few attractive villages, some surrounded by vineyards.

At the village of **Satigny** was a Benedictine priory founded in the 10th century. The Reformed church was attached to it, the Gothic choir dating from the 13th century. To the north of the church is a 15th–16th-century house and nearby, the 18th-century priest's house.

16

This is the first section of the important main line to Brig, where the line turns south through the Simplon Tunnel into Italy. It was built by the Irish engineer Charles Vignoles. Its scenic quality may be judged by the late Alan Clark, politician and historian, citing it as his favourite journey. There are many villages and towns of interest along the way, and hardly a station does not afford access to at least one castle or château.

Leaving Geneva the railway affords few glimpses of the lake for the first few miles, and the western end of the journey depends upon the visibility of the French Alps to be inspiring. The line passes the Botanical Gardens with its large palm house visible to the right. At **Genthod-Bellevue** (also on bus line V from Cornavin station) are a number of 18th-century mansions, such as the Maison de Saussure, named after the alpinist Horace-Bénédict Saussure. A largely 17th-century château was the home of the lords of Genthod. A vain attempt was made to develop **Versoix** into a rival to Geneva when it was owned by France.

The small town of **Coppet** is graced by arcaded houses, but it is also worth a visit on account of the château of 1767 and its connection with the writer and political hostess Mme de Staël. An 1809 portrait of her by Elizabeth Vigée-Lebrun hangs in Geneva's Museum of Art and History. She inherited the house from her father, Jacques Necker, who was born in Geneva and became Louis XVI's minister of finance. He was caught up in the maelstrom of the Revolution, but resigned in 1790 and retired to the château he had bought six years before. It was after his death in 1804 that Mme de Staël held her famous literary salons, like those she had held in Paris. Here they were attended by such figures as Genevese historian Sismondi, Mme Récamier and Chateaubriand. Byron visited her here in 1816. Set in a large French-style park, the U-shaped house (✆ *022 776 10 28;* ⊕ *Easter–Oct 14.00–18.00 daily; English-language tours*) is approached through a courtyard with stables and orangery. It is still owned by Mme de Staël's descendants and contains the original fine furniture and paintings.

The Reformed church at Coppet was once part of a Dominican monastery; built c1500 it has 16th-century carved choir-stalls. In the late Gothic Maison Michel at Le Port is a regional museum (*Musée Régional du Vieux-Coppet; Grand Rue 30;* ✆ *022 776 36 88;* ⊕ *May–mid-Oct 14.00–17.00 Tue–Thu*).

Château de Garengo at **Céligny** was built in 1722 and enlarged in the 19th century. Visible from the road at **Crans** is a large U-shaped château built in 1764–67.

Nyon was the first town to be founded by the Romans in western Switzerland, in 45BC by Julius Caesar, but it was destroyed by the Burgundians and was not revived until the 11th century. The 12th-century castle with five cylindrical towers was much altered in the 16th–18th centuries; today it houses a newly renovated museum (✆ *022 363 83 61;* ⊕ *Apr–Oct 10.00–17.00 Tue–Sun; Nov–Mar 14.00–17.00 Tue–Sun; admission charge*) devoted to the history of the town and the products of its once-famous porcelain factory which turned out high-quality ware from 1781 to 1813. Children like the prison cells.

The town's Roman past is well presented in the Roman Museum (*Basilique et Musée Romains, Rue Maupertuis;* ✆ *022 361 75 91; www.mrn.ch;* ⊕ *Apr–Oct 10.00–17.00 Tue–Sun; Nov–Mar 14.00–17.00 Tue–Sun; admission charge*) near the castle. Beside the lake is the Musée du Léman (*Quai Louis-Bonnard 8;* ✆ *022 361 09 49;* ⊕ *same as Roman Museum*), which houses displays on the history and natural history of the lake and the vessels that have used it. A ticket is available to cover all three museums.

The 12th–15th-century Reformed church has paintings on the north wall of the choir that date from c1300. The 18th-century building of the former porcelain factory still stands at 13 Rue de la Porcelaine.

Nyon is the junction for the line to La Cure (see page 253).

The 18th-century château at **Prangins** was briefly occupied in 1755 by Voltaire, and in 1814 by Napoleon's elder brother Joseph Bonaparte, who after Waterloo in the following year escaped to the United States, taking out citizenship and becoming a farmer in New Jersey. The château is now the Swiss National Museum for the French-speaking part of Switzerland (\ *022 994 88 90; www.museenational.ch;* ⊕ *10.00–17.00 Tue–Sun; admission charge*), focusing on the cultural, social, political and economic aspects of the 18th and 19th centuries. The attractive Neo-classical Reformed church of 1761 in Prangins was given a belltower in 1860.

The two villages of Gilly and Bursinel share a station (**Gilly-Bursinel**). Each has a château, Bursinel of medieval origin though largely 18th century, and Gilly a modestly sized building with two low wings dating from 1724–93. On the lakeshore at **Rolle** is a late 13th-century castle that was altered in the 16th and 18th centuries, but the medieval appearance of the four corner towers belies their years. The Grand-Rue has many fine 16th-century buildings. The obelisk on the tiny island is to Général César de la Harpe who secured independence from Bern for the canton of Vaud in 1798.

The Reformed church at **Perroy** dates back to at least the 12th century, though the nave was altered c1828. There are two châteaux, dating from the 16th and 17th centuries, on the outskirts of the village on the road to **Allaman**, where a castle from the 15th–16th century was restored in the 18th as a rather austere château. Near the 14th-century Reformed church of St Jean is the fortified Maison de Rochefort, with cylindrical tower. A bus from the station goes to 'Aubonne, gare' (table 10.720), recalling the branch line that used to run from Allaman through Aubonne to Le Prunier-S, close to Gimel. According to Byron, Aubonne has 'by far the fairest view of the Lake of Geneva'; it also has a prominent château and well-preserved old town where Michael I, the exiled last king of Romania, found a home.

St Prex is a delightful lakeside town that was once walled. Only the entrance gate survives, and the château has also been reduced to a square tower and residence. The 12th–13th-century Reformed church of St Protais stands outside the settlement.

The town of **Morges**, junction for Bière and L'Islemailont-la-Ville, was founded in 1286 when work began on the huge square castle that sits right by the lake and was originally protected by moats. Modelled on Yverdon, the castle has four cylindrical corner towers, one acting as a keep and rising above the others. It is home to the Vaud Military Museum (*Musée Militaire Vaudois;* \ *021 316 09 90;* ⊕ *10.00–noon & 13.30–17.00 Tue–Fri, 13.30–17.00 Sat–Sun; Jul–Aug 10.00–17.00 daily; admission charge*) containing uniforms, weapons and an outstanding collection of lead toy soldiers. The cellars of the castle are an artillery museum with over 40 pieces on display.

Beside the castle is the harbour, today full of yachts and motor boats but built for naval vessels by the Bernese in 1696. The Hôtel de Ville in the square of the same name was built with a staircase tower in 1518–20 and given a Baroque portal in 1682. At Grand Rue 54 is Musée Alexis Forel (\ *021 801 26 47;* ⊕ *mid-Mar–Nov 14.00–18.00 Wed–Sun*), a collection of furniture, tapestry, paintings, dolls and antiquities set in a 16th-century house that was rebuilt in Baroque style in 1670.

Changing exhibitions of photographs, postcards and prints are displayed in the medieval town house of Fondation Bolle at Rue Louis-de-Savoie 73–75 (\ *079 349 22 91;* ⊕ *mid-Mar–Nov 14.00–18.00 Wed–Sun*).

It was on the Tolochenaz estate on the outskirts of Morges that the Polish statesman and pianist Paderewski, a prodigy from the age of three, spent the last years of his life. Stravinsky stayed here in 1915, completing *The Wedding*. The environmental charity WWF has its origins in Morges; the Morges Manifesto was signed here in 1961 with a prominent role played by Sir Julian Huxley.

Paderewski's near 40 years in Morges are commemorated in a museum at Place du Casino 1 (↘ *021 811 02 78*; ⊕ *14.00–17.00 Tue, Thu*).

Beyond Morges the line soon enters the outskirts of Lausanne and is joined by the main line coming south from Yverdon and Neuchâtel. For **Lausanne**, see opposite.

PRACTICALITIES Bicycle hire from Morges and Lausanne stations.

NYON
Tourist information
🛈 Av Viollier 8, CH-1260; ↘ 022 365 66 00; e info@nrt.ch; www.nyon-tourisme.ch; ⊕ mid-May–mid-Sep 08.30–noon & 14.00–17.30 daily; mid-Sep–mid-May 08.30–12.30 & 13.30–17.30 Mon–Fri

Where to stay
A hotel very close to the station is:
🏠 **Hotel Des Alpes*** Av Viollier 1, CH-1260; ↘ 022 994 30 00; e info@alpes-nyon.ch; www.alpes-nyon.ch
A hotel overlooking the lake is:
🏠 **Beau-Rivage**** Rue de Rive 49, CH-1260; ↘ 022 365 41 41; e info@beaurivagehotel.ch; www.beaurivagehotel.ch

MORGES
Tourist information
🛈 Rue du Château 2, CH-1110; ↘ 021 801 32 33; e info@morges-tourisme.ch; www.morges-tourisme.ch; ⊕ Apr–Sep 09.00–18.00 Mon–Fri, 09.30–17.00 Sat; Jul–Aug also 10.00–15.30 Sun; Oct–Mar 09.30–12.30 & 13.30–17.30 Mon–Fri

🏠 **De Savoie*** (H)** Grand-Rue 7, CH-1110; ↘ 021 801 21 55; e info@hotelsavoie.ch; www.hotelsavoie.ch
Hotels overlooking the lake are:
🏠 **La Fleur du Lac**** Route de Lausanne 70, CH-1110; ↘ 021 811 58 11; e hotel@fleur-du-lac.ch; www.fleur-du-lac.ch
🏠 **Romantik Hotel du Mont-Blanc au Lac*** Quai du Mont-Blanc 1, CH-1110; ↘ 021 804 87 87; e info@hotel-mont-blanc.ch; www.hotel-mont-blanc.ch

Where to stay
Hotels in the pedestrianised old town are:
🏠 **De La Nouvelle Couronne*** (H)**
2 Passage de la Couronne, CH-1110; ↘ 021 804 81 81; e info@couronne-morges.ch; www.couronne-morges.ch

NYON–LA CURE Table 155

A 27km (17 miles) metre-gauge line that opened as recently as 1916 and until 1958 used to extend across the border with France to Morez. Crossing an impressively large viaduct before La Givrine, it serves some of the closest ski resorts to Geneva.

The line leaves from an underground platform reached from the underpass beneath the SBB station. The line curves north, soon affording views over Lake Léman and the French Alps and describing great U-shaped curves past dairy farms after **Genolier**. Vineyards give way to woods of beech and birch as the line climbs steeply towards **St Cergue**, which the scholar and Rugby headmaster Thomas Arnold credited with a view of the Alps he 'never saw surpassed' when he was here in

1829. After the skiing resort of **La Givrine** and the col of the same name at 1,232m (4,041ft), the line drops down through fields of yellow flowers to the terminus at **La Cure**. It is said that there was once a hotel here that straddled the border, enabling the proprietor to hire out a room to newly married couples who could then bemuse family and friends by saying that they spent their first night in different countries.

MORGES–BIERE/ L'ISLE-MONT-LA-VILLE Table 156

These metre-gauge branches divide at the junction of Apples. The line is little used by tourists but it serves a very different Switzerland from the popular resorts around Lac Léman. Traversing pleasant arable and well-wooded countryside, the line also affords a fine view of one of Switzerland's most idiosyncratic castles.

The huge, towering keep of the castle of Vufflens is visible for some distance before the train describes a U-shaped curve around it to reach the station of **Vufflens-le-Château**. Unfortunately the bizarre structure is not open to visitors. It was built of brick between 1395 and 1430 by Henri de Colombier, the keep echoed by four similar, smaller towers and linked by an inner courtyard to a rectangular residence with circular corner towers. The appearance of the two disparate parts is unified by the crenelles and the slender machicolations.

On the branch to L'Isle-Mont-la-Ville is Pampigny (station **Pampigny-Sévery**) where the late 15th-century Reformed church has contemporary wall-paintings in the choir. The village of **Montracher** had to be rebuilt after a fire in 1828, though a tower surviving from the defensive walls has been converted into a belltower. At L'Isle (station **L'Isle-Mont-la-Ville**) is a château (1696) which now serves as a school.

BIÈRE
Where to stay
⌂ **Des Trois Sapins* (H)** Pl de la Tilette, CH-1145; ☎021 809 51 23; e accueil@lestroissapins. ch; www.lestroissapins.ch. Has a good organic restaurant.

LAUSANNE

The capital of the French-speaking canton of Vaud is built on the slopes of Mont Jorat, though the earliest settlements were beside the lake; Neolithic remains have been found at Vidy to the west of Ouchy. The Roman town on the lake was destroyed by the Alemans in 379, and the next settlement was on the hill where the cathedral now stands. The town gained in importance when Bishop Marius transferred his see here from Avenches in 590. The area was then part of the Burgundian kingdom, becoming part of the Holy Roman Empire in 1032.

Probably the greatest ceremony ever held in the town was in 1275 when the consecration of the cathedral was combined with the coronation of Rudolf of Habsburg, attracting secular and religious dignitaries from all over Europe, including Pope Gregory X. Having gained a degree of independence, the city was overrun by Burgundian troops in 1476. Protestantism was introduced after the Vaud was taken over by Bern in 1536, which retained its control until 1798. The bishopric was translated to Fribourg in 1663. Lausanne was made capital of the new canton of Vaud in 1803.

During the 20th century Lausanne hosted a number of international conferences, most notably that in 1922–23 in which Lord Curzon played a key role in achieving the Treaty of Lausanne (1923), which produced a post-war settlement between

Turkey and Greece. In 1915 the city became the headquarters of the International Olympic Committee.

Lausanne's lovely position and its liberalism has for centuries attracted writers and artists. As the poet Robert Southey put it: 'were I to settle anywhere on the Continent, Switzerland would be the country, and probably Lausanne the place.' In the 1750s Voltaire staged his plays at his home, to which the recently arrived Edward Gibbon was invited. It was in a summer-house in the city, on a June evening in 1787, that Gibbon wrote the final words of the most celebrated historical work in the English language, *The Decline and Fall of the Roman Empire*. Gibbon had lived for 15 years in a 'country which I have known and loved from my early youth. Under a mild government, amidst a beauteous landscape, in a life of leisure and independence, and among a people of easy and elegant manners.'

Dickens wrote much of *Dombey and Son* and *The Battle of Life* during six months in a villa overlooking the lake during 1846, where the family was visited by Tennyson, Thackeray and Marc Isambard Brunel amongst many others. Arnold Bennett wrote part of *Clayhanger* here in 1910. The final part of *The Waste Land* was written here in 1922 when T S Eliot came to convalesce after a breakdown.

Among notable natives of the city are J L Burckhardt (1784–1817), who 'discovered' Petra and was the first European explorer to enter Mecca, and the painter Félix Vallotton (1865–1925). The Russian jeweller Fabergé died here in exile in 1920, and the creator of Maigret, the writer Georges Simenon, in 1989.

GETTING AROUND The main hall of the station has a branch of the main tourist office (⊕ *09.00–19.00 daily*). The m2 Métro, extended and rebuilt in 2008, runs from Ouchy (see page 258) through the main station before continuing to the northern terminus in **Les Croisettes**. Its gradients and sharp curves necessitated adoption of rubber-tyred tramcars like those on some Paris metro lines.

The city has an excellent network of buses and trolleybuses, and there is a standard-gauge metro from Lausanne-Flon to Renens, serving 13 stations en route, with extensions under construction. Passes covering all public transport are available for a day or, for tourists, a three-day card.

Bicycle hire from Lausanne station.

TOURIST INFORMATION

i Av de Rhodanie 2, CH-1007; ☏021 613 73 73; e info@lausanne-tourisme.ch; www.lausanne-tourisme.ch; ⊕ 08.00–17.00 Mon–Fri
i Railway Station, Pl de la Gare; ⊕ 09.00–19.00 daily

i Pl de la Navigation (Métro: Ouchy); ⊕ Apr–Sep 09.00–19.00 daily; Oct–Mar 09.00–18.00 daily

WHERE TO STAY

Hotels very close to the station are:
⌂ **Continental****** 2 Pl de la Gare, CH-1001; ☏021 321 88 00; e reservation@hotelcontinental.ch; www.hotelcontinental.ch
⌂ **Victoria****** Av de la Gare 46, CH-1001; ☏021 342 02 02; e info@hotelvictoria.ch; www.hotelvictoria.ch
⌂ **A la Gare***** Rue du Simplon 14, CH-1006; ☏021 612 09 09; e info@alagare.com; www.alagare.com

⌂ **Elite***** Av Sainte-Luce 1, CH-1003; ☏021 320 23 61; e info@elite-lausanne.ch; www.elite-lausanne.ch
⌂ **Jeunotel** Ch du Bois-de-Vaux 36, CH-1007; ☏021 626 02 22; e lausanne@youthhostel.ch; www.youthhostel.ch/lausanne. This innovative concept offers no-frills but comfortable & modern accommodation, designed for young people on a budget. From Ouchy station take bus 2 to Bois de Vaux (direction Bourdonnette).

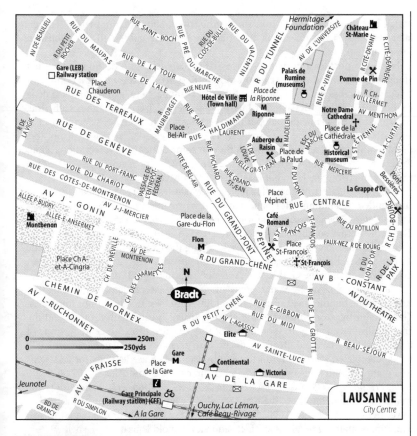

LAUSANNE
City Centre

WHERE TO EAT

✕ **À la Pomme de Pin** Rue Cité Derrière 11; ☎ 021 323 46 56

✕ **Auberge du Raisin** Pl de l'Hôtel de Ville 1, Cully; ☎ 021 799 21 31

✕ **Café Beau-Rivage** Pl du Général-Guisan 18, Ouchy; ☎ 021 613 33 39

✕ **Café Romand** Pl St-François 2; ☎ 021 312 63 75

✕ **La Grappe d'Or** Rue Cheneau-de-Bourg 3; ☎ 021 323 07 60

See also under Ouchy, page 258.

WHAT TO SEE

Exploring the old city Lausanne is a hilly city, but the principal buildings and museums of the old city are not far from the station. From the station's main exit, in Place de la Gare, either use the m2 Métro to Flon and walk along Rue du Grand-Chêne to Place St François, or proceed directly ahead into Rue du Petit-Chêne which climbs to the right of the square to reach Place St-Francis. It is dominated by the church of the same name, the sole remnant of a Franciscan monastery that was founded in 1258; however, it has been frequently rebuilt, and the main interest is the choir-stalls, dating from 1387.

The post office opposite St François's church stands on the site of the house in which Edward Gibbon lived from 1783, and where stood the summer-house in which he completed *The Decline and Fall of the Roman Empire* in 1787 (Byron later sent a sprig of an acacia tree that grew in the garden to his publisher, John Murray).

From the northeast corner of Place St François take Rue de Bourg, turn left along Rue Caroline and left again on to Pont Bessières. This is one of a number of bridges that cross valleys to link the hills of Lausanne, here leading to Place de la Cathédrale (m2 stop Bessières or bus 16 stop Pierre Viret). Lausanne's cathedral, still called Notre-Dame despite periodic Protestant objections, was begun in 1173 and consecrated by Pope Gregory X in 1275. It is regarded as one of, if not the, finest Gothic building in Switzerland, though some critics have reservations about the exterior restoration work of Viollet-le-Duc, which was begun in 1877 – he died in Lausanne two years later, but his plan was finally completed in 1926.

Built to a cruciform plan, with a nave and two aisles before a raised apsidal choir surrounded by an ambulatory and flanked by two side towers, the cathedral has a tower above the crossing. One tower of the main façade was never completed. The 13th-century southern entrance is referred to as the Apostles' Doorway or the Painted Portal and contains sculptures depicting the Death and Assumption of the Virgin Mary, Christ in Majesty, prophets and apostles. The richly decorated west doorway, though in the Gothic style, was not built until the 16th century.

The interior is austere and some monuments were damaged during the Reformation, but the sheer size of the building with over 1,000 columns impresses. The glass in the rose window of the south transept is early 13th century, and the choir-stalls placed along the south wall of the nave are also 13th century, some of the oldest in Switzerland. Regular concerts are given on the organ of almost 7,000 pipes, completed in 2003. From the south aisle a staircase ascends for 232 steps to a platform with stupendous views over the city, lake and Alps (⊕ *07.00–19.00 Mon–Fri, 08.00–19.00 Sat–Sun; Oct–Mar 08.00–17.30 Mon–Fri*). Maintaining the tradition of the nightwatch, the hour is called by an 'All's well' from the cathedral tower between 22.00 and 02.00. To the southwest of the cathedral is the Historical Museum containing religious artefacts and views of old Lausanne (see below).

On the northeast corner of Place de la Cathédrale, Rue Cité Derrière runs north between attractive buildings to Place du Château, in which stands a huge square sandstone and brick building that was put up in 1397–1431 as the residence of the bishop. The Château St-Marie has four corner turrets and narrow machicolations. Enlarged and altered, the building became the seat of the Bernese governors and now that of the cantonal government.

From the southwestern corner of Place de la Cathédrale, Avenue de l'Université leads to Place de la Riponne, on which stands the colossal Palais de Rumine, named after the benefactor who bequeathed the money to build it. The building houses the university headquarters and library, and various geological, zoological and palaeontological museum collections (see opposite).

Continuing south, Rue Madeleine leads to Place de la Palud, on which markets are held. On the west side of the square is the Renaissance-style façade of the rebuilt 17th-century town hall, with two storeys built over arcades. Mozart gave two concerts here when he was ten, in 1766.

Rue de la Louve leads south out of Place de la Palud, into Rue Centrale. Continue into Rue Pépinet to return to Place St François. By turning right to Le Grand-Pont of 1844, there is a good view of Pont Chauderon-Montbenon further west.

Museums The first four museums are all housed in the Palais de Rumine (*Place de la Riponne 6, CH-1014; bus 5, 6 or 9 to Riponne*).

Museum of Fine Arts (Musée Cantonal des Beaux-Arts) (↘ 021 316 34 45; ⊕ 11.00–18.00 Tue–Wed, 11.00–20.00 Thu, 11.00–17.00 Fri–Sun; admission charge) Includes French and Swiss artists of the 18th–20th centuries, including Anker, Bonnard, Cézanne, Ducros, Gleyre, Hodler, Marquet, Matisse, Renoir, Utrillo, Vlaminck, Vallotton and Vuillard.

Museum of Archaeology and History (Musée Cantonal d'Archéologie et d'Histoire) (↘ 021 316 34 30; ⊕ 11.00–18.00 Tue–Thu, 11.00–17.00 Fri–Sun) A rich collection of Neolithic and Bronze and Iron Age artefacts. It also has the golden bust of Marcus Aurelius that was discovered at Avenches in 1939.

Geological Museum (Musée Géologique Cantonal) (↘ 021 692 44 70; ⊕ 11.00–18.00 Tue–Thu, 11.00–17.00 Fri–Sun) Regional geology museum with a palaeontology room. Of particular interest is the skeleton of a mammoth dating from c10,300BC found in 1969 near Le Brassus. A major attraction is the Welcome Nugget, the largest gold nugget ever recorded, weighing in at 57.3 kg. Sadly it is only a replica as the original Australian nugget was melted down in London in 1859.

Zoology Museum (Musée Zoologique Cantonal) (↘ 021 316 34 60; ⊕ 11.00–18.00 Tue–Thu, 11.00–17.00 Fri–Sun) Three galleries dealing with animals from all over the world.

Olympic Museum (Musée Olympique) (*Quai d'Ouchy 1, CH-1006*; ↘ 021 621 65 11; ⊕ 09.00–18.00 daily; admission charge; m2 Métro station Ouchy; buses 2 (alight Navigation) or 8 (alight Musée Olympique)) Opened in 1993, the museum stands in a park overlooking the lake and tells the story of the Olympic idea and its revival by Pierre de Fredi, Baron de Courbetin in 1896. The quality of the displays and the techniques used to tell the history of a century of the games helped the museum to win the 1995 European Museum of the Year Award. It has special exhibitions on a wide range of subjects – from Technology in Sport to Sport in Art. Lausanne's most visited museum is undergoing a modernisation which should be completed in late 2013.

Hermitage Foundation (*2 Route du Signal, CH-1008*; ↘ 021 320 50 01; ⊕ 10.00–18.00 Tue–Sun, 10.00–21.00 Thu; admission charge; bus 3 from station, direction Bellevaux (alight La Motte) or bus 16 from city centre, direction La Clochatte (alight Hermitage)) Changing exhibitions of paintings and sculptures, focusing on Impressionism and French art, are held in this attractive old house set in an English park.

Elysée Museum (*Av de l'Elysée 18, CH-1006*; ↘ 021 316 99 11; ⊕ 11.00–18.00 Tue–Sun; admission charge; m2 Metro, direction Ouch (alight Jordils) or bus 2, direction Bourdonnette (alight Croix-d'Ouchy), or bus 4, direction Pully CFF (alight Montchoisi) or bus 8, direction Paudex/Verrière (alight Musée Olympique)) Set in an 18th-century house within a park, this is Switzerland's principal museum of photography, illustrating both artistic and technical aspects. It has a collection of over 120,000 original prints.

Lausanne Historical Museum (Musée Historique de Lausanne) (*Ancien-Evêché, Pl de la Cathédrale 4, CH-1005*; ↘ 021 315 41 01; ⊕ 11.00–18.00 Tue–Thu, 11.00–17.00 Fri–Sun; Jul–Aug also 11.00–18.00 Mon; admission charge; m2 (alight

Bessières) or bus 7 *(alight Caroline)* or 5 *(alight Riponne)* or 16 *(alight Pierre-Viret))* Housed in a remnant of the bishop's palace is a museum devoted to the city's history, which includes a huge model of the town in the 17th century, complete with sound and lighting effects. It also contains religious artefacts and a collection of pewter.

'Art Brut' Collection *(Château de Beaulieu, Av des Bergières 11, CH-1004; ☏ 021 315 25 70; ⊕ 11.00–18.00 Tue–Sun; Jul–Aug, also open Mon; admission charge; bus 2 or 3 (alight Beaulieu))* Created by a local painter Jean Dubuffet, this extraordinary collection of naïve art first opened in 1976. The creations are all by people on the margins of society and therefore idiosyncratic and highly original.

Vidy Roman Museum *(24 Chemin du Bois-de-Vaux, CH-1007; ☏ 021 315 41 85; ⊕ 11.00–18.00 Tue–Sun; admission charge; bus 1 or 4 (alight Maladière) or 2 (alight Bois-de-Vaux) or m1 Métro (alight Bourdonette))* A museum illustrating the Roman past of the area, with displays of tools, vessels, coins, ceramics and bronzes unearthed by digs.

Musée Bolo *(Faculty of Information and Communication, Ecole Polytechnique Fédérale de Lausanne, CH-1015; ☏ 078 748 21 16; ⊕ 08.00–18.00 Mon–Fri; m1 Métro to EPFL)* A huge display of computers and computing from the earliest home computers in 1981 and the first Macs in 1984.

Claude Verdan Foundation – Museum of the Hand *(Rue du Bugnon 21, CH-1011; ☏ 021 314 49 55; ⊕ noon–18.00 Tue–Fri, 11.00–18.00 Sat–Sun; admission charge; m2 to CHUV, direction Les Croisettes)* The museum is dedicated to scientific and medical culture with exhibitions on aspects related to the human body and to medicine. It aims to raise awareness of issues relating to biotechnological innovations.

OUCHY–LES CROISETTES

This 5.9km (3¾ mile) line had the distinction of being the world's shortest metro until its extension opened in 2008. The steepest part of the climb from the lakeshore is 1 in 8, though the average is 1 in 16. The end-to-end journey time is 18 minutes, and has 14 stations, including one underneath Lausanne main station and another at Flon which connects with the Lausanne–Echallens–Bercher (LEB) line (see opposite). The trains are rubber-tyred and based on those operating Line 14 in Paris.

In most cities of the world, the view from such a line would be an eyesore, passing through embankments of litter and the ugly backs of buildings. Here the section above Ouchy is planted with trees and shrubs. Trains run every 7–8 minutes for most of the day, serving the main station en route, at **Lausanne-Gare CFF**. There are 14 stations, some open, most underground.

It was at 9 Place du Port in Ouchy that Byron wrote *The Prisoner of Chillon*.

OUCHY
Where to stay
Hotels close to Ouchy station on the lake shore are:
⌂ **Angleterre & Résidence**** (H)** 11 Pl du Port, CH-1006; ☏ 021 613 34 34; e ar@brp.ch; www.angleterre-residence.ch

⌂ **Aulac*** (H)** Pl de la Navigation 4, CH-1000; ☏ 021 613 15 00; e aulac@cdmgroup.ch; www.aulac.ch

⌂ **Château d'Ouchy*** (H)** 2 Pl du Port, CH-1006; ☎ 021 331 32 32; ℮ info@chateaudouchy.ch; www.chateaudouchy.ch

⌂ **Hotel du Port***** Pl du Port 5, CH-1006; ☎ 021 612 04 44; ℮ info@hotel-du-port.ch; www.hotel-du-port.ch

LAUSANNE FLON–ECHALLENS–BERCHER Table 101

This 23km (15½ miles) line has the distinction of being Switzerland's first narrow-gauge railway, opening in 1873. Its original terminus in Lausanne, at Chauderon, has been superseded by a new station at Flon which is more convenient for the city centre and provides an interchange with the m2 Métro Ouchy–Les Croisettes and light rail line to Renens. The line traverses scenery that is pleasant rather than spectacular, but there are good walks from some of the stations. Some of the 70 waymarked walks from the railway's stations are illustrated on side tables in the carriages and in a leaflet published by the railway. Steam-hauled excursions are operated by a 0-6-0 tank engine from 1910, usually on Sundays from August to mid-September, for which reservations are obligatory (☎ 021 886 20 15; www.leb.ch).

Once the line emerges from its tunnel under the city, it runs alongside the Yverdon–Neuchâtel road. A large park overlooking the lake is served by the station at **Montétan**, but it takes several miles to leave behind the factories and suburbs of Lausanne.

From **Romanel** there are two walks to **Cheseaux**, where a 17th-century château can be seen on the left-hand side of the train. It is not until after **Etagnières** that the last traces of Lausanne are left behind; once out into the country, the landscape is a broad plain of cultivated fields rarely punctuated by trees except in stands of woodland, reflecting the area's role in cereal production. The centre of this district is **Echallens**, where the Wheat and Bread Museum (*La Maison du Blé et du Pain;* ☉ *08.30–18.00 Tue–Sun; admission charge*) is a working museum at which you can bake bread or produce the perfect croissant yourself. Covering 8,000 years of agrarian activity, the museum is situated at 5 Place de l'Hôtel de Ville. The Hôtel de Ville itself was built in 1781 with a clocktower. Near it is a rebuilt castle (1273) with two surviving cylindrical towers and a north wing (1719).

The railway's depot is situated at Echallens and the historic carriages for the steam train, dating from 1873 to 1916, may usually be seen. It is worth looking out for the attractive station buildings on the line, with decorative keystones to the arched openings.

Numerous walks are signed from the terminus at **Bercher**, where there is a buffet on the station and Hotel/Restaurant de la Gare.

BERCHER
Where to eat
✕ **De la Gare** Pl de la Gare, CH-1038; ☎ 021 887 70 50. Gourmet cuisine.

LAUSANNE–VEVEY Table 100

This section of the Geneva–Brig main line is dominated by terraced slopes of vines, which often reach right down to the water's edge. The Lavaux Vineyard Terraces were designated a World Heritage Site in 2007 by UNESCO. They stretch for 30km east from Lausanne to the castle of Chillon, embracing the villages of Chexbres, Cully and Lutry where the Lavaux wines can be sampled in the cellars of the vignerons. A network of footpaths threads the vineyards and links the caveaux and village inns.

Geneva and Lausanne LAUSANNE–VEVEY

16

259

The terraces date from the 11th century when the area was controlled by Benedictine and Cistercian monasteries. The line descends from the high level of Lausanne station down to the level of the lake, running right beside the water or separated from it by only a few feet of vines. Sit on the right.

Before leaving Lausanne, the line to the east divides, the northerly fork climbing towards Puidoux-Chexbres on its way to Fribourg and Bern, the Vevey line dropping down towards the lake. Local trains call at **Pully** (also reached by bus 4, 8 or 9 from Lausanne), where there is a restored Roman villa at Av Samon-Reymondin 2 (☉ *May–Sep 14.00–18.00 Sun; admission charge*); it contains the most significant 1st-century fresco discovered north of the Alps.

At **Lutry** the 13th–16th-century Reformed church has nave and choir vaulting painted in 1577, and on Rue du Bourg stands an imposing entrance to the 15th–16th-century castle. The gables of some of the older houses are decorated with monkeys' heads; this commemorates the occasion when Lutry was overrun by the Bernese, and the inhabitants, lacking any weapons, resorted to climbing trees and roofs and pelting the enemy with stones. This earned them the epithet *les singes de Lutry* (the monkeys of Lutry). In the vineyards to the south of the line stands a squat cylindrical tower, the Tour Bertholod. The vineyards in this area are interlaced by networks of monorails which help to transport the grapes up the steep slopes.

Cully has a delightful little harbour and a number of 16th–18th-century houses. To the north of the line just beyond **Epesses** is the crenellated Tour de Marsens, documented since the 12th century but much restored in the 19th. As the train skirts the lake, you can see small gardens created on headlands that are reached by footbridges across the railway. To the east of **Rivaz** is the castle of Glérolles, thought to date back to the 12th century and once the summer retreat of the bishops of Lausanne.

St-Saphorin is renowned as one of the loveliest villages in the area; it also has one of the best-sited stations in Switzerland from the point of view of waiting passengers – the westbound platform is right over the water of the lake. Among the village's old houses is the 16th-century arcaded priest's house, and the porch of the 16th-century Reformed church of St Symphorien is flanked by a 1st-century Claudian milestone and a Roman altar.

For **Vevey**, see *Chapter 17*.

LUTRY

Tourist information
☑ Quai Gustave-Dolet, CH-1095; ✆ 021 791 47 65; e info@montreuxriviera.com; www.montreuxriviera.com; ☉ mid-Mar–mid-Oct 08.00–22.00 daily

Where to stay
⌂ **Le Rivage***** Rue du Rivage, CH-1095; ✆ 021 796 72 72; e info@hotelrivagelutry.ch; www.hotelrivagelutry.ch

CULLY

Tourist information
☑ Pl de la Gare 4, CH-1096; ✆ 021 962 84 54; e info@montreuxriviera.com; www.montreuxriviera.com; ☉ 09.00–noon & 14.00–18.00 Mon–Fri (closed Wed pm)

Where to stay
⌂ **Auberge du Raisin (H)** Pl de l'Hotel de Ville 1, CH-1096; ✆ 021 799 21 31; e info@aubergeduraisin.ch; www.aubergeduraisin.ch. A distinctive & beautifully appointed small hotel with excellent cuisine.
⌂ **Au Major Davel***** Pl d'Armes 8, CH-1096; ✆ 021 799 94 94; e info@hotelaumajordavel.ch; www.hotelaumajordavel.ch

17

Vevey and Montreux

Few districts have as interesting a history of tourism or as much to offer today's visitor as the contiguous towns of Montreux and Vevey. Some of the country's best railway journeys are on their doorstep, the surrounding country offers excellent walking, both towns are served by lake steamers, there is a wealth of museums in the area, excellent food and local wines, and arguably Switzerland's best-known building – the Castle of Chillon – is a short walk from Montreux.

In common with many of the towns and villages along the shore of Lac Léman, Vevey and Montreux have attracted foreign visitors and residents for centuries. These rich associations are developed in an English leaflet produced by the joint tourist office entitled 'On the Trail of Hemingway', which guides the visitor to places and buildings connected with 20 personalities in each town. Hemingway himself visited the area in 1922 and describes it in both *A Farewell to Arms* and *For Whom The Bell Tolls*.

Both towns are renowned for their international festivals. The Montreux Jazz Festival is held in July, when Vevey hosts the International Film Festival of Comedy. In September the Montreux–Vevey International Music Festival is held.

Equally the area offers a host of sporting opportunities, from waterskiing to paragliding, and the combination of walking, cycling or journeys by train, bus and steamer offer a limitless range of excursions. The tourist offices have separate walking maps for the Vevey and Montreux regions.

VEVEY

The artist and author Edward Lear wrote in 1861 that 'Vevey...is Paradise, and I don't see how people there and at Lausanne can have the impudence to suppose that they can go to Heaven after death.' Most people have been attracted by the view of the lake and mountains, but for some of the earliest foreign residents, it was protection from extradition that drew them to Vevey. Several of the English regicides lived here from the 1660s, including Lt-Gen Edmund Ludlow (whose memoirs were published here in 1698) and Andrew Broughton, who read the death sentence to Charles I.

The town's origins go back to Roman times when it was called Vibiscum and was an important port. Chocolate manufacture began in the 17th century, and the town is now the international headquarters of Nestlé. Henri Nestlé (1814–90) discovered in the 1860s how to make powdered milk, which made the company's fortune. He sold the company in 1874 and is buried in Vevey, with his wife Clementine. The area's vineyards are celebrated in an elaborate festival held every 25 years (next in 2024), the Fête des Vignerons, which takes place in the Grande Place beside the lake.

The literary and artistic associations with the town are numerous. Rousseau came to Vevey 'to cheer himself up' and used the town as the setting for *Julie ou*

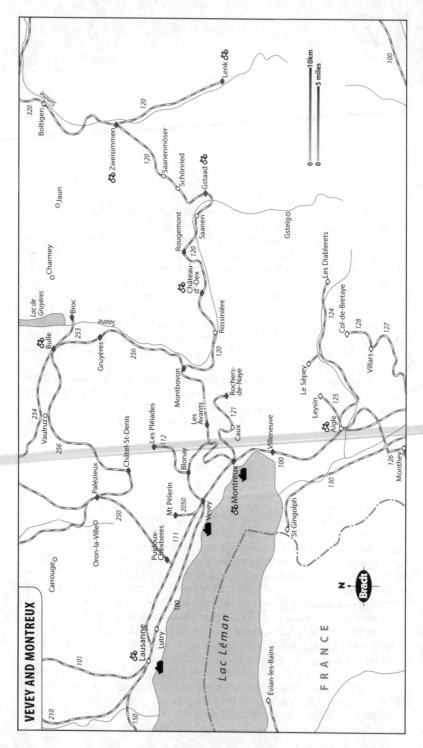

VEVEY AND MONTREUX

Lac Léman

FRANCE

Lausanne
Lutry
Carrouge
Oron-la-Ville
Puidoux-Chexbres
Mt Pèlerin
Vevey
Montreux
Évian-les-Bains
St Gingolph
Monthey
Villeneuve
Aigle
Leysin
Le Sépey
Villars
Col-de-Bretaye
Les Diablerets
Caux
Rochers-de-Naye
Les Avants
Blonay
Les Pléiades
Châtel-St-Denis
Palézieux
Vaulruz
Bulle
Broc
Gruyères
Montbovon
Rossinière
Château-d'Oex
Rougemont
Saanen
Gsteig
Gstaad
Schönried
Saanenmöser
Zweisimmen
Jaun
Charmey
Boltigen
Lenk

Lac de Gruyères
Sanne
Simme

210
101
150
100
250
256
254
253
256
111
2050
112
100
121
100
130
126
125
124
128
127
120
120
120
120
120
320

N
Bradt

10km
5 miles
0
0

262

la Nouvelle Héloïse, written in 1756–9. Gogol began *Dead Souls* here. The novelist W M Thackeray wrote part of *The Newcomes* during a visit in 1852, and Dostoyevsky stayed here for part of 1868 while working on *The Gambler*. Henry James set in Vevey the opening chapter of the novel that established his reputation, *Daisy Miller*, following his stay here in 1872. In 1908 Arnold Bennett wrote *The Card* in Vevey. The musicologist and author of *The Oxford Companion to Music*, Percy Scholes, died here in 1958, as in 1977 did Charlie Chaplin, who had lived here since 1952, and Graham Greene in 1991 (he is buried in nearby Corseaux).

TOURIST INFORMATION

⊠ Grand Place 29/La Grenette, CH-1800; ☎ 0848 86 84 84; e info@montreuxriviera.com; www.montreuxriviera.com; ☉ mid-May–mid-Oct

09.00–18.00 Mon–Fri, 09.00–13.00 Sat–Sun; mid-Oct–mid-May 09.00–noon & 13.00–17.30 Mon–Fri, 09.00–noon Sat

WHERE TO STAY

Vevey has numerous hotels; those closest to the station are:

🏠 **Astra****** Pl de la Gare 4, CH-1800; ☎ 021 925 04 04; e info@astra-hotel.ch; www.astra-hotel.ch

🏠 **De Famille***** Rue des Communaux 20, CH-1800; ☎ 021 923 39 00; e reservation@ hotelfamille.ch; www.hotelfamille.ch

WHAT TO SEE

Exploring the town Close to the station is the Russian church, its gilded dome visible from passing trains. Turn left outside the station to reach it, in Rue des Communaux. The church was the gift of Prince Schouvalow and consecrated in 1878. Musée Jenisch, of fine arts, is opposite (see below), and close by on a terrace is St Martin's church, repeatedly altered and rebuilt since its 13th-century origins, and included in Turner's 1841 watercolour of Vevey. Here are buried the regicides Andrew Broughton and Edmund Ludlow. The belltower is distinguished by its balustrade and four bartizans.

In the Grand Place by the lake is the old grain market, the Grenette, dating from 1808. A market of local crafts is held in the square on Saturdays in July and August. The old town lies to the east of the square.

To the west of Vevey, at Route de Lavaux 21 in Corseaux, is Villa Le Lac, the lakeside house built in 1923 by Le Corbusier for his parents (☎ *021 923 53 63;* ☉ *13.30–17.00 Wed or by appointment*). The Jeanneret family lived there until 1973.

Notable walks from Vevey include a 10km (6¼ miles) hike beside the lake to Villeneuve known as the 'Flowered Path', for which a leaflet is available, giving the botanical name of many of the trees and rare flowers along the way.

Alimentarium (Musée de l'Alimentation) (*Rue du Léman;* ☎ *021 924 41 11;* ☉ *10.00–17.00 Tue–Fri, 10.00–18.00 Sat–Sun; admission charge*) Opened in 1985 and funded by Nestlé, the museum is devoted to all aspects of food. Its three sections focus on the scientific, ethnological and historical aspects of food. Temporary exhibitions, films and audio-visual programmes, and interactive computers enliven the displays.

Musée Jenisch: Musée des Beaux-Arts (*Av de la Gare 2;* ☎ *021 925 35 20;* ☉ *10.00–18.00 Tue–Sun, until 20.00 Thu; admission charge*) Fanny Jenisch of Hamburg made her home in Vevey and bequeathed it to the town. It has a rich collection of Swiss paintings and a substantial part of the Oskar Kokoschka Foundation.

Print Museum (Musée Jenisch: Cabinet Cantonal des Estampes) (*Av de la Gare 2;* ✆ *021 925 35 20;* ⊕ *as above*) A remarkable collection of art on paper, including woodcuts and engravings by Dürer, etchings by Rembrandt, Lorrain, Canaletto and Tiepolo, and contemporary lithographs and screenprints.

Swiss Camera Museum (Musée Suisse de l'Appareil Photographique) (*Grande-Place 99;* ✆ *021 925 34 80;* ⊕ *11.00–17.30 Tue–Sun; admission charge*) A strikingly designed museum about the development of the camera, photographic studios and processing, with interactive exhibits and computer games; one floor is set aside for changing exhibitions of photographs.

Vevey Historical Museum/Museum of the Brotherhood of Wine Growers (Musée Historique du Vieux-Vevey/Musée de la Confrérie des Vignerons) (*Rue du Château 2;* ✆ *021 921 07 22;* ⊕ *11.00–17.00 Tue–Sun; Nov–Mar 14.00–17.00*) Housed in a château of 1599, these museums portray the district's past and its oldest industry. Restaurant.

VEVEY–MONT PÈLERIN Table 2050

The station of this funicular is 15 minutes' walk from the main station, or five minutes by trolleybus. It takes you to a terrace with spectacular views over the lake on which several hotels have been built, set in a peaceful, rural spot very different from the bustle of Vevey. During the 11-minute ascent, the funicular passes through lovely woods and pauses at the wine village of **Chardonne**. Numerous signed paths thread the woods and uplands, and the energetic can climb Mont Pèlerin at 1,080m (3,543ft). On the summit the Plein Ciel lift takes visitors to the top of a telecoms tower, 65m above ground, for a spectacular panorama over the lake and mountains.

MONT PÈLERIN
Where to stay
⌂ **Le Mirador Kempinski Lake Geneva*****
(H) Ch du Mirador 5, CH-1801; ✆ 021 925 11 11; e fo.lemirador@kempinski.com; www.mirador. ch. One of Switzerland's outstanding hotels, built in 1904 as a medical establishment where the composer Maurice Ravel was one of many famous patrons. It has tremendous views over the lake & French Alps. The Mont Pèlerin Society was formed here in 1947 when Professor Friedrich von Hayek called an international meeting largely made up of economists.

VEVEY–PUIDOUX–CHEXBRES Table 111

The 'Train des Vignes' provides a useful link that obviates the need for passengers travelling from eastern Switzerland to go into Lausanne to head north, unless they are intent on catching an express. The line climbs steeply from Vevey to provide impressive views over the vineyards beside Lac Léman and the Alps.

The one intermediate station of **Chexbres-Village** serves this wine-producing village and small resort, noted for its sunny position.

CHEXBRES-VILLAGE
Tourist information
🇮 Pl de la Gare, CH-1071; ✆ 021 962 84 64; e info@montreuxriviera.com; www. montreuxriviera.com; ⊕ 13.30–17.30 Mon, Tue, Thu, Fri, 08.30–12.30 Wed, Sat–Sun; mid-May– mid-Sep also 09.00–13.00 Sat

Where to stay and eat

🏠 **Baron Tavernier** Route de la Corniche, CH-1071; ☎ 021 926 60 00; e info@barontavernier.ch; www.barontavernier.ch

🏠 **Préalpina** Route de Chardonne 35, CH-1071; ☎ 021 946 09 09; e info@prealpina.ch; www.prealpina.ch

✕ **Du Lion d'Or** Grand-Rue 10, CH-1605; ☎ 021 946 11 51

VEVEY–LES PLÉIADES Table 112

A journey not to be missed, climbing at almost alarming gradients to a terminus close to the summit of Les Pléiades. Sit on the right.

Trains leave from platform 7 at Vevey and turn through 90° to parallel the course of La Veveyse as it rushes down to the lake from its defile north of the town. The exit from Vevey is somewhat uninspiring, but after twisting through a tunnel the line emerges in orchards and vineyards with good views to the right overlooking Vevey.

Near **Hauteville** is a lovely avenue of trees leading to a mid 18th-century château with a pretty rotunda in the grounds; another avenue has been destroyed by the nearby motorway. **St-Légier Gare** used to be the junction for a metre-gauge line to Châtel-St-Denis, which closed in 1969. At the Reformed church of St Légier at **La Chiésaz**, the German composer Paul Hindemith is buried. The approach to **Château-de-Blonay** is dominated by the imposing building after which the station takes its name; the castle has been much altered and extended since it was begun in 1175 by the same family that still owns it. It is not open to the public.

Blonay is the starting point for the preserved CF-Musée Blonay–Chamby (see page 266). The rack section that continues all the way to Les Pléiades begins at the end of the platform at Blonay. There is a fine view of the castle as the train leaves, starting its formidable climb through woods. It sometimes stops at stations on a steep part of the line, as at **Bois-de-Chexbres**, demonstrating on restarting the extraordinary power of the rack mechanism. There are numerous walks waymarked through the woods (boots or walking shoes advised), and in winter the area provides plenty of skiing. Just beyond **Ondallaz-L'Alliaz** is a delightfully unspoilt chalet with chestnut roof tiles.

From **Lally** you can hire mountain bikes for an easy 9km (5½ miles) route taking less than an hour or a more challenging 37km (23 miles) route via Les Paccots and Châtel-St-Denis. A leaflet is available and the routes are signed.

The terminus at **Les Pléiades** is only a few minutes' walk from the summit and nearby children's playground and restaurant (*closed Mon*). From the summit at 1,360m (4,462ft) there are panoramic views with only Rochers de Naye of the nearby peaks exceeding Les Pléiades in height. There are waymarked paths down to Blonay (1 hour 20 minutes), Montreux (4 hours 10 minutes) and Châtel-St-Denis (2 hours) (see table 256, page 277). One walk, down to Lally station, is known as the Botanical Path and takes 1½ hours.

BLONAY
Where to stay

🏠 **Bahyse*** 11 Rte du Village, CH-1807; ☎ 021 943 13 22; e bahyse@bluewin.ch; www.hotelbahyse.ch

BLONAY–CHAMBY

One of Switzerland's best-known preserved railways, operating trains on Saturdays and Sundays from late April until the end of October, and on Friday afternoons in July and August. The museum buildings that house one of Europe's largest collections of metre-gauge steam and electric locomotives and rolling stock would be the envy of most preserved railways. The collection includes locomotives from France, Germany, Spain and Italy as well as Switzerland. Run entirely by volunteers, the line is only 3.2km (2 miles) but is full of interest with a tunnel, a graceful, curved masonry viaduct over the Baye de Clarens and a gradient of 1 in 20 that has steam locomotives barking noisily. The depot and museum, with café and shop, is at Chaulin near Chamby. Two hours should be allowed for a journey and museum visit (✆ *021 943 21 21; www.blonay-chamby.ch*).

Geneva–VEVEY–MONTREUX–Brig Table 100

This short section is away from the lake and either largely screened from it by buildings or in a tunnel.

La Tour-de-Peilz, served by the first of three intermediate stations, is where the English writer, collector and builder William Beckford took up refuge at the château in 1785 to escape a scandal. Here he finished his novel *Vathek*, and later bought Gibbon's library in Lausanne. It is also where the painter Gustave Courbet died, having fled France to avoid punitive fines for his role in the Commune in 1871. A bust by him decorates the Fountain of Liberty near the church.

The Swiss Museum of Games (*Musée Suisse du Jeu;* ✆ *021 977 23 00;* ⊕ *11.00–17.30 Tue–Sun; admission charge; bus 1 from Vevey to Place du Temple*) is housed in the lakeside château, created in the 18th century out of a castle built by Peter II of Savoy in 1251–57. This unusual museum looks at the history of games throughout the world and at the various types of game, involving education, strategy, risk, memory, role playing etc. Visitors can play games both inside and in the garden, so the museum is ideal for children.

Clarens now forms the western suburb of Montreux, its many elegant villas rising up the hillside above the railway. On the hill above Clarens is Châtelard Castle, the large 15th-century refuge built for the people of Montreux. Clarens has had its share of famous residents, including the Russian anarchist Bakunin, and the composers Wagner and Tchaikovsky (the 4th Symphony was finished here). Stravinsky wrote *The Rite of Spring* at his house in Clarens in 1913. It is also the setting for Rousseau's novel *Julie, ou la nouvelle Héloïse*, published in 1761, though it is impossible today to correlate places and descriptions. Adolf Loos built his first private house here, the Villa Karma, in 1904–06.

The station at **Montreux** is one of the very small number in the world that is served by railways built to three different gauges: the standard gauge of the main line; the metre gauge of the Montreux–Oberland Bernois Railway; and the 800mm (2ft 7½in) gauge of the Montreux–Glion–Rochers-de-Naye line. For **Montreux**, see opposite.

LA TOUR-DE-PEILZ
Where to stay
⌂ **La Vieille Tour*** 43 Grande-Rue, CH-1814;
✆ 021 944 10 10; e info@vieilletour.ch; www.
vieilletour.ch

The town of Montreux has been formed by the gradual joining of neighbouring villages that were once separated by vineyards. Montreux's past is portrayed in the Museum of Montreux (*Musée du Montreux; Rue de la Gare 40;* \ *021 963 13 53;* ⊕ *Apr–Oct 10.00–noon & 14.00–17.00 daily*). Situated in the former convent of Sâles, it traces the town's history from Palaeolithic times with displays of Roman finds, local furniture and artefacts of everyday life, the growth of tourism and the way its environs have served as an inspiration for writers, artists and musicians. A Riviera Museum Card covering over 10 museums in Vevey and Montreux, and the Castle of Chillon, is available from participating museums.

Hans Christian Andersen wrote *The Ice Maiden* in Montreux in 1861, and the painter Oskar Kokoschka died here in 1980.

The first two hotels opened their doors in 1835; before then visitors had lodged in private homes. The following year Hotel Byron opened. By 1850 the town offered 250 hotel beds, by 1860 there were 810 beds in 18 hotels, and by 1912, 7,525 beds in 85 hotels. Part of the reason for Montreux's success, apart from its lovely position, was its comparatively mild winter and spring climate, plus the fact that it was close to good skiing for those who wanted it. Funiculars and rack railways were built to provide access to mountain walks and ski slopes, and the Kursaal (casino) was opened in 1883.

World War I was a crushing blow to Montreux, and to Swiss tourism generally. The days of receiving families, and often their servants, for stays of months' duration from all over Europe and the United States were over, as were the days of SFr25 for £1. Some hotels closed or were adapted to other uses; some, like the National Hotel with its lovely interiors, still stand empty. Today there is less than half the 1912 number of beds.

Yet the popularity of the area for tourists remains, and the exceptional conference facilities have proved a tremendous success. Amongst such buildings is the Stravinsky Auditorium, named in honour of the Russian-born composer who spent many productive years here. The impressive and acoustically outstanding hall is now the setting for the annual jazz festival in July as well as regular concerts.

In Place du Marché by the lake is the well-restored market hall in which flea markets are held on Tuesday and Friday mornings. The older part of Montreux is up the hill from the station, reached by turning right from the station and right again into Rue de la Gare, continuing into Rue du Pont. The yellow building with covered staircase and a bear on a ledge (No 3) was an early hospital. One of the area's best walks begins (or, for those who prefer walking downhill, ends) off this street, in Rue de la Baye: turn right after crossing the river and follow the road round. Connecting the area of Les Planches with Les Avants, the signed path crosses a Roman bridge and threads the boulder-strewn gorge of Chauderon through which flows the Baye de Montreux. It is about 2 hours to Les Avants, 4 hours to the Col de Jaman and 5¾ hours to Les Rochers-de-Naye; there are restaurants at all three destinations.

PRACTICALITIES Bicycle hire from Montreux station.

TOURIST INFORMATION

☑ Pl de l'Eurovision, CH-1820; \ 0848 86 84 84; ℮ info@montreuxriviera.com; www. montreuxriviera.com; ⊕ mid-May–mid-Oct

09.00–18.00 Mon–Fri, 09.30–17.00 Sat–Sun; mid-Oct–mid-May 09.00–noon & 13.00–17.30 Mon–Fri, 10.00–14.00 Sat–Sun

WHERE TO STAY

Montreux has numerous hotels; the closest to the station are:

⌂ **Grand Hotel Suisse Majestic**** (H)** 45 Av des Alpes, CH-1820; ☎ 021 966 33 33; e hotel@ suisse-majestic.ch; www.suisse-majestic.ch

⌂ **Parc et Lac***** Grand-Rue 38, CH-1820; ☎ 021 963 37 38; www.montreux.ch/parc-et-lac

⌂ **Splendid*** (H)** Grand-Rue 52, CH-1820; ☎ 021 966 79 79; e info@hotel-splendid.ch; www. hotel-splendid.ch

MONTREUX (TERRITET) – GLION Table 2054

This funicular ascends from the Montreux suburb of Territet (in which the English church, St John's, is situated); the SBB station, two minutes' walk from Territet funicular station, is off Rue de Chillon. From 1883 until 1975 the funicular to Glion used to be powered by water, a system designed by the great mountain railway engineer Niklaus Riggenbach. A tank under the car was filled at the top and emptied at the bottom, the amount of water required being determined by the number of passengers in each car. The number ascending was telephoned from the lower station to the operator controlling the volume of water at the top, who was able to calculate the quantity, knowing the number of descending passengers. The water also served to cool the rack and pinion mechanism, which was used as a brake.

This was not only the first mountain railway in the French-speaking part of Switzerland, it was also the first railway in the world to climb at a gradient as steep as 1 in 1.8. One of the cars survives at Territet station and another in the Transport Museum in Luzern.

The funicular to Glion links with a station on the line up Rochers-de-Naye (see opposite). Glion is the starting point for a signed walk of 1–2 hours called the Panoramic Path to the Heights of Caux, where there is a restaurant.

MONTREUX–ROCHERS-DE-NAYE Table 121

This 800mm (2ft 7½in) rack railway, built as the CF Montreux–Glion–Rochers-de-Naye (MGN), should not be missed: the 55-minute journey and the views from the summit are stupendous. The Swiss Pass is valid as far as Caux; there is a 50% discount on tickets to the summit. Sit on the right.

The rack (Abt system) and steep gradient start as soon as the line leaves the station at Montreux, tunnelling under the town and soon climbing through woods and orchards to a tunnel that describes a semicircle before **Glion**. The reason for the large size of the station at Glion is not simply that this is the railway's headquarters, but also that this was before 1909 the start of the line up Rochers-de-Naye. Until then passengers reached Glion by the funicular from Territet (see page 278) and had to change trains; a link with Montreux station was then built. It was at Glion in 1926 that the Austrian poet Rainer Maria Rilke died, while attending a clinic.

Numerous walks are signed from Glion, including the Panoramic Path (see section on Glion funicular, above). From Glion, the line turns away from the lake, climbing along the ridge overlooking the deep valley of the Chauderon, on the other side of which the Montreux–Oberland Bernois Railway can be seen climbing to Les Avants. Huge retaining walls protect the MGN as it turns east, frequently crossing mountain streams and passing piles of neatly stacked logs protected by a sheet of corrugated iron.

Caux is an old resort which once had several large hotels. Today they fulfil other purposes. The enormous Caux Palace Hotel, for example, was opened in July

1902 with 350 bedrooms furnished by the Paris branch of Waring & Gillows of Lancaster. The hotel offered lawn tennis, tobogganing, skating, hydro and electric therapy, a telegraph, library and daily concerts. It was patronised by such people as John Rockefeller, the Maharajah of Baroda and the writers Scott Fitzgerald, Edgar Wallace and Kipling. The 1930s Depresssion, followed by World War II, ruined the hotel, forcing its closure. It was bought by a group of Swiss and is now a European Centre of Moral Re-Armament. Caux is also now a popular skiing centre.

The line climbs through pines in a fairly straight line towards the Dent de Jaman, by which time the tree line has been left behind. From Jaman a footpath known as the 'Riviera's High Road' follows the ridges to Les Pléiades, which takes about 5½ hours. Alternatively there is a shorter walk of 2 hours to Les Avants.

A tunnel takes you into a different world of often bare rock, the line protected by snow shelters and barriers. At this height you may be lucky enough to see chamoix or marmots, and in summer there are myriad butterflies. The train approaches the summit along a saddle of rock and describes a semicircle into the station at **Rochers-de-Naye** beside the hotel, discreetly tucked into a fold of the mountain beneath the summit. The view from the small viewing platform on the summit at 2,045m (6,709ft) is spectacular, encompassing the Swiss and French Alps, Lac Léman and even the Jura.

From the station a 220m (722ft) tunnel takes you under the peak to the Plein Roc restaurant with a wall of glass overlooking the views to the south. In bad weather screens descend over the windows and an eight-projector slide presentation shows what you are missing outside. One of many paths descending from the station turns upwards to one of the oldest alpine gardens, La Rambertia, founded in 1896. Allow 30–45 minutes to see the thousand-odd species, some extremely rare. It is about 15 minutes' walk from the station. Marmots' Paradise tells you about these endearing creatures, and you can see five species in a large compound.

You can spend the night on the bare mountain inside a Mongolian yurt. Seven white Mongolian yurts accommodating up to eight can be rented, and the MGN (*www.goldenpass.ch*) offers a package of train journey, yurt rental, a 'Mongolian Plancha' and breakfast.

GLION
Where to stay
⌂ **Righi Vaudois****** CH-1823; ☎ 021 966 18 18
⌂ **Victoria****** Rte de Caux 16, CH-1823;
☎ 021 962 82 82; e info@victoria-glion.ch; www. victoria-glion.ch

⌂ **Des Alpes Vaudoises***** Rue de Bugnon 15, CH-1823; ☎ 021 963 20 76; e reception@ hotel-alps.ch

CAUX
Where to stay
⌂ **Hostellerie de Caux** Rte des Monts 31, CH-1824; ☎ 021 961 25 91; e contact@hostellerie-caux.com; www.hostellerie-caux.com

⌂ **Les Rosiers*** Ch de l'Impératrice, CH-1824; ☎ 021 963 61 73

MONTREUX–ZWEISIMMEN–LENK Table 120

This is one of the best-known and most popular train journeys in Switzerland, reflected in the unique panoramic trains that operate some services. It forms a section of the Golden Pass Express between Zürich and Geneva, and serves some of the country's most popular ski resorts. At Zweisimmen trains connect with the standard-gauge branch from Spiez, while metre-gauge trains have to reverse there to reach Lenk im Simmental. It has always been a railway for tourists, opening in stages between 1901 and 1905 and powered by electricity from the outset. Sit on the right.

The line is operated by the Montreux–Oberland Bernois Railway (MOB), a company which owns other railways in the Montreux area as well as eight hotels and restaurants. It has a long tradition of running luxury trains for tourists, having the distinction of running the only narrow-gauge Pullman service in Europe from 1931. However, it was a victim of the Depression, and the carriages were sold in 1939 to the Rhaetian Railway on which they still operate. Since the prototype panoramic coach appeared in 1976, the MOB has invested heavily in outstanding air-conditioned coaches, progressively improving the quality from the Panoramic to the Superpanoramic in 1985 and from 1993 the Crystal Panoramic Express, designed by Pininfarina. The train is now called the Golden Pass Panoramic. The trains have driving trailers at each end with the driver seated in a cockpit above a saloon; this allows passengers to enjoy a driver's-eye view of the line ahead (or behind). Reservation of seats in these trains is no longer mandatory, but advance booking is usually vital to secure a seat in the end coaches. The Panoramic stops at Les Avants, Château-d'Oex, Rougemont, Gstaad and Zweisimmen on its way to Lenk; the Crystal Panoramic (to Zweisimmen only) at Château-d'Oex and Gstaad. In 2005 the MOB introduced the Golden Pass Classic with Belle Epoque-style coaches offering an at-seat meal.

There is also a Chocolate Train from Montreux, which visits a cheese factory at Gruyères and allows time for lunch and a walk round the town before continuing on to the Nestlé Cailler chocolate factory at Gruyères-Broc. Using first-class Belle Epoque coaches and/or panoramic coaches, this train operates every Monday, Wednesday and Thursday from June to October, and every day in July and August (✆ +41 840 245 245 *from outside Switzerland,* 021 989 81 90 *within;* e info@ goldenpass.ch; www.goldenpass.ch).

Stopping trains serve all stations between Montreux, Zweisimmen and Lenk and there are additional trains to various places at each end of the line, such as Les Avants from Montreux and Saanen from Zweisimmen.

Trains begin the 75.5km (47 miles) journey to Lenk in a spiral tunnel, climbing at 1 in 15 to escape the suburbs and reach the vineyards above Montreux. A series of horseshoe curves follows as the train climbs 575m (1,886ft) in height to Les Avants. At **Châtelard** is the 15th-century castle with its massive keep, built as a refuge for local people. The view becomes ever more spectacular as the train gains height; in the reverse direction the view from the summit of the climb is, without hyperbole, breathtaking.

At **Chamby** weekend travellers may be lucky enough to catch a glimpse of a steam train on the preserved line from Blonay. The train twists through more U-shaped curves, flanges squealing, to reach the winter resort of **Les Avants**. Noël Coward took the train to Les Avants in 1959 to look at a chalet that was for sale; he bought it and lived there until his death in 1973. From Les Avants, a funicular ascends every 20 minutes to Sonloup (table 2057), where the first bobsleigh championship was held in around 1929, although it had been a popular sport when the funicular opened in 1910. A circular 1½-hour walk begins here, known as the Narcissi Path, which is naturally best walked in the spring.

The gradient stiffens through pine and beech woods to the steepest on the entire line, an astonishing 1 in 13.7 – the MOB is entirely operated by adhesion. The train is still climbing as it enters the line's longest tunnel just beyond **Jor**; passing under the Col de Jaman it is 2,424m (2,560yds) long and dead straight. The summit is reached just before the end of the mostly unlined tunnel, the line emerging at the lonely station of **Les Cases**. The tunnel often marks an abrupt change of weather, the train leaving grey skies on one side to emerge in bright sunshine – or vice versa! The descent from Les Cases is down one of the remotest valleys of the journey, the pasture dotted with only occasional unspoilt chalets linked by ribbons of unpaved tracks. Beyond **Les Sciernes** is one of the sharpest curves of the railway, the line crossing the River Hongrin before it joins the Sarine/Saane.

At the foot of the descent is the junction of **Montbovon** (change for Gruyère and Bulle), which Byron described as 'a pretty, scraggy village, with a wild river and a wooden bridge'. Below the neo-Romanesque Catholic church of St Grat, built in 1896–98, is a group of attractive old houses, one with an inscription listing the owners on its façade.

In places protected by avalanche shelters, the railway climbs through the wooded gorge of the Sarine to **La Tine**, entering the open district known as the Pays d'Enhaut. After crossing over the Sarine/Saane and passing the tiny Lac du Vernex on the right, the railway reaches **Rossinière**, with some pretty chalets in the square and one of the largest and finest chalets to be found in Vaud, close by the railway. Built in 1754, it has 113 windows and is decorated with carvings, paintings and inscriptions.

The railway loops north away from the river to serve the winter and summer sports resort of **Château d'Oex**, where the actor David Niven made his home and is buried. Three churches, all on the right below the line, are passed before reaching the station: the first is the Catholic church, the second the English church of 1902, and beyond that the Reformed church of St Donat which is built on the site of, and probably using the masonry of, the castle from which the town takes its name.

Château d'Oex has made a speciality of hot-air ballooning, and in the last week of January the town hosts the world's leading hot-air championships. Visitors can experience the unique thrill of a balloon flight over the mountains, summer or winter (℡ *026 924 22 20;* e *info@ballonchateaudoex.ch; www.ballonchateaudoex.ch*).

Turning left outside the station and walking parallel with the railway, at Route du Clôt 2 you come to the Pays-d'Enhaut Museum (⊕ *Dec–Oct 14.00–17.00 Tue–Sun*), established in 1922, with some fine reconstructed interiors and displays of local crafts such as lace making and weaving. One room is devoted to early tourism.

There are 250km (156 miles) of waymarked paths in the district, and the tourist office has maps for walkers and mountain bikers.

Close to the railway, beyond Hôtel de la Poste, is the bottom of the two-stage (cable car and chairlift) cable journey up to La Montagnette (table 2060). Close by is Le Chalet, where demonstrations of cheese making are given (the tourist office also organises overnight stays in genuine cheese-maker's chalets in the mountains); Le Chalet also contains a model railway and a fondue restaurant.

From the station a bus (table 12.174) makes a mountainous journey through a spectacularly narrow gorge via L'Etivaz, where the cheese cellars storing the eponymous cheese can be visited, to Col-des-Mosses. It continues to the station at Le Sépey (see table 124, page 284). This service connects with another bus to continue to Leysin (table 12.171).

The line continues on its hillside shelf with good views across the valley to the right – one of the reasons for the popularity of the journey is the almost continuously high level at which the railway runs, affording far better views than any parallel roads below. A tributary of the Sarine/Saane is crossed by a viaduct just before **Flendruz**, and the end of the French-speaking area is reached at the last station in Vaud, **Rougemont**, the Sarine becoming the Saane.

To the west of this attractive village stands an 11th-century Romanesque church that was once part of a Cluniac priory dissolved in 1555. Concerts are held here as part of the Menuhin Festival (see below). The choir is 16th century, the tower 17th century. Near it is the château, built on the site of an 11th-century castle, but rebuilt several times, most recently after a fire in 1974; it retains a curtain wall punctuated by turrets. On the opposite side of the river, six minutes' walk from the station, is a two-section gondola lift up to La Videmanette (table 2062).

Saanen is another small village of wooden chalets, pronounced overhangs to the eaves being the local characteristic. The village is known in Switzerland for the quality of its Vacherin cheese and for the Menuhin Festival, which is held each year between late July and early September. Although the symphony concerts are held in Gstaad, most of the chamber or solo performances are given in the mid 15th-century church of St Mauritius. In the choir are frescoes of the life of Mary and of St Mauritius.

The train bowls along the valley, making the most of the last stretch of fast track before the climbing starts in earnest after the well-known summer and winter sports resort of **Gstaad**. The resort is renowned for attracting the famous, though it is less exclusive than St Moritz and the better for it. Development has been carefully controlled, and the town's hotels are all of chalet style. The tourist office is on Hauptstrasse; turn right on to it from the station. The district around Gstaad has 71 ski lifts and 250km (156 miles) of ski runs, mostly for intermediate levels of skill; the ski facilities are covered by the Gstaad Super Ski Pass. There is an exceptionally good sports centre with attractive indoor swimming pool, as well as an outside pool.

The area around Gstaad is known as the Saanenland and is a good centre for walking, the skiing infrastructure being equally useful in other seasons to reach alpine walks, such as the gondola lift to Höhi Wispile (table 2393), 20 minutes' walk from the station. The tourist office produces an excellent leaflet suggesting walks and giving details of the region's transport, including bus and train timetables, and mountain restaurants. Particularly recommended are walks in Lauenental; the pretty village of Lauenen (served by bus, table 12.181) has attractively carved and painted decoration to its 18th-century chalets and an early 16th-century Gothic church. Beyond the village is the tiny Lauenensee, served by some of the buses along the valley, southeast of which is a pair of impressive waterfalls at the head of a small valley, the Geltental.

From Gstaad Kapälliplatz a new trail follows the River Saane to the Mauritiuskirche in Saanen; the Yehudi Menuhin Philosopher's Trail has 12 boards with quotes by Lord Menuhin (1916–99) and takes about one hour.

Gstaad hosts a CinéMusic Festival in March, the Swiss Open Tennis Championships at the beginning of July, and the larger events in the Menuhin Festival and Alpengala, which combine to form a music festival from late July to early September.

From the station there are bus services to Les Diablerets (table 12.180) via Feutersoey and Gsteig.

The climb out of Gstaad into a side valley is at 1 in 25, the line looping round to cross an imposing three-span truss viaduct that has been repeatedly featured in publicity material since the line opened. Only a few minutes' walk from the station at the small resort of **Schönried** are a chairlift to Horneggli (table 2388) and a two-section gondola to Rellerligrat (table 2389). From Horneggli there is a good walk around the Hornfluh. The summit of the whole line, at 1,275m (4,183ft), is reached before **Saanenmöser**, another small resort. Its station building has white, green and red painted decoration.

From there it is a steady descent down through the new Moosbach Tunnel, built after the previous tunnel was filled with debris washed down by a storm in 1983, to the junction for Spiez at **Zweisimmen**. This is the main village in the Simmental, and has a small folk museum at the Kirchstalden in Kirchgasse (⊕ *late May–late Oct 14.00–17.00 Wed & Sat–Sun*). The mid 15th-century Reformed church of St Maria has late 15th-century frescoes, and the village has some decorated wooden houses characteristic of the valley.

Just two minutes' walk, turning left from the station, is the longest gondola in Switzerland, at 5,102m (5,580yds), in two sections, up to Rinderberg (table 2375). There is a good walk back to the village. Attractive canopies with carved brackets shelter passengers at the multi-platformed station, at which trains for Lenk have to reverse. The line to Lenk opened in 1912, turning the small agricultural hamlet into a tourist resort. Near the first station, at **Blankenburg**, is a Baroque castle dating from 1767, built on the site of an older castle, and a covered bridge across the Simme may be seen soon after leaving the station.

The railway parallels an excellent signed bike route all the way to Lenk which is often on the other side of the river, the railway remaining on the east bank after crossing it on the outskirts of Zweisimmen. Evidence of the area's forestry can be seen at some stations such as **St Stephan**, where the church has a Romanesque nave and 17th-century wooden tunnel-vaulted roof.

On the approach to **Stöckli** a wonderful range of distant snow-covered mountains comes into view, growing as the train nears journey's end at **Lenk**, where the station is close to the centre. This summer and winter resort is attractively situated in a bowl of mountains dominated by the Wildstrubel at 3,243m (10,639ft) – 'a grand termination to the valley' as Baedeker puts it. Its location at the head of a valley means that it does not suffer from through traffic and is therefore quieter than most resorts. It offers a surprising variety of activities and events, and was a favourite resort of Field Marshal Montgomery, who stayed here (at Hotel Wildstrubel) in 1937 and again after the war.

The resort achieved recognition through its 'well fitted-up sulphur-baths and grounds', as Baedeker noted in 1895 (in those days Lenk was reached by an eight-hour journey by diligence from Thun). Astonishingly Lenk had already been a spa for over two centuries by then, having been authorised by Bern in 1689 to set up a spa to exploit the strongest alpine sulphur springs in Europe. Even today 30% of summer guests use the sulphur spa, which has the usual options of solarium, massages, beauty parlour and fitness training as well as specialist treatments.

There is a wide choice of sporting activities with indoor and open-air swimming pools, sports hall, open-air ice rink, tennis, fishing, river rafting, mountain biking and walking. Bike and walking route maps are available from the tourist office, and there is a guided walk for familes to the Jaunpass on Tuesday mornings (Jun–mid-Oct). During the winter there are 51 cable cars and chairlifts in the local skiing area, which includes Adelboden. An arrangement exists whereby a six-day pass entitles skiers to one free day ticket from a neighbouring area, such as Gstaad. This opens up access to 180 lifts and 610km (381 miles) of runs. The local area has a good balance between the three grades of ski runs, and there are also good cross-country routes. For those who eschew skis, 30km (19 miles) of paths are cleared for winter walks.

One of the finest walks in the area is to the impressive Simmenfälle and Siebenbrunnen, the seven springs, which is the source of the Simme; a bus from/to the station (table 31.283) can be used for one leg of the walk. This bus also takes you to the cable car up to Metsch (table 2382). A two-section gondola to Betelberg (table 2380) is a ten-minute walk from the station. There are also buses along a serpentine road to Bühlberg (table 31.281) and to Iffigenalp (table 31.282), which provides access to the highest waterfall in the area, the Iffigfall. It is about a four-hour walk to Adelboden over the Hahnenmoos Pass.

Sport is not the only attraction. For ten nights in July the town is given over to New Orleans jazz, with bands and guest musicians from other countries in Europe and from the United States. In August, the International Summer Academy of Music brings together up to 200 students from all over the world who attend classes on individual instruments, workshops and lectures by visiting professors. Concerts are held every night.

Lenk makes a point of catering for families, with babysitting and kindergarten services, and even toy rental! It has also pioneered a concept for people with impaired hearing, providing a variety of inductive hearing systems in relevant buildings, training courses and staff trained in effective communication.

PRACTICALITIES Bicycle hire from Château d'Oex, Gstaad, Zweisimmen and Lenk stations.

LES AVANTS
Where to stay
🏠 **De Sonloup** (H)** Col de Sonloup, CH-1833; ☎021 964 34 31; e hotel.sonloup@bluewin.ch; www.sonloup.ch

🏠 **Helioda**** Rte des Narcisses, CH-1833; ☎021 964 39 50

MONTBOVON
Where to stay
🏠 **De la Gare** Rte de l'Intyamon 332, CH-1669; ☎026 928 10 88; e emal@hotel-gare.ch; www. hotel-gare.ch

ROSSINIÈRE
Tourist information
🛈 Rossiniere Animation, CH-1658; ☎026 924 42 42; www.chateau-doex.ch; ⏱ 10.00–noon & 13.30–17.00 Mon–Fri daily

Where to stay
🏠 **De Ville* (H)** CH-1658; ☎026 924 65 40; e info@hotel-rossiniere.ch; www.hotel-rossiniere.ch

CHÂTEAU-D'OEX
Tourist information
🛈 La Place, CH-1660; ☎026 924 25 25; e info@chateau-doex.ch; www.chateau-doex. ch; ⏱ 08.00–noon & 14.00–18.00 Mon–Fri, 09.30–15.30 Sat

Where to stay
Numerous hotels; close to the station are:
🏠 **Hotel Buffet de la Gare** Route de la Gare 8, CH-1660; ☎026 924 77 17; e buffet-doex@ bluewin.ch; www.buffet-doex.ch
🏠 **De la Poste*** Route de la Ray 32, CH-1660; ☎026 924 62 84; e roslysarl@bluewin.ch; www. hoteldelaposte.ch

ROUGEMONT
Tourist information
🛈 Route de la Croisette 16, CH-1659; ☎026 925 11 66; e info@rougemont.ch; www.rougemont. ch; ⏱ 08.30–noon & 14.00–17.30 Mon–Fri, 10.00–noon Sat

Where to stay
A hotel close to the station is:
🏠 **Hotel de Commune** Rue des Allemans 7, CH-1660; ☎026 925 11 00; e hotel.commune. rougemont@bluewin.ch

SAANEN
Tourist information
ℹ️ Gstaad Saanenland Tourismus, CH-3792; 📞 033 748 81 81; ✉ gst@gstaad.ch; www.gstaad.ch; 🕐 08.30–noon & 14.00–17.30 Mon–Fri, 09.00–noon & 13.30–17.00 Sat (only during the high season)

GSTAAD
Tourist information
ℹ️ Promenade 41, CH-3780; 📞 033 748 81 81; ✉ info@gstaad.ch; www.gstaad.ch; 🕐 08.30–18.00 Mon–Fri, 09.00–noon & 13.30–17.00 Sat–Sun; Jul–early Sep & mid-Dec–early Mar 08.30–noon & 13.30–18.00 Mon–Fri, 10.00–noon Sat

Where to stay
Very expensive, but a historic hotel and the best in Gstaad, is:
🏠 **Palace******* **(H)** CH-3780; 📞 033 748 50 00; ✉ info@palace.ch; www.palace.ch

SCHÖNRIED
Where to stay
🏠 **Kernen***** Hauptstrasse, CH-3778; 📞 033 748 40 20; ✉ info@hotel.kernen.ch; www.hotel-kernen.ch

SAANENMÖSER
Where to stay
🏠 **Hotel des Alpes** Saanenmöserstrasse 168, CH-3777; 📞 033 748 04 50; ✉ info@desalpes.ch; www.desalpes.ch

ZWEISIMMEN
Tourist information
ℹ️ Thunstrasse 8, CH-3770; 📞 033 722 11 33; ✉ tourismus@zweisimmen.ch; www.zweisimmen.ch; 🕐 08.30–noon & 14.00–17.30 Mon–Fri; mid-Jun–mid-Oct also 08.30–noon & 13.30–16.30 Sat

LENK
Tourist information
ℹ️ Rawilstrasse 3, CH-3775; 📞 033 736 35 35; ✉ info@lenk-simmental.ch; www.lenk-simmental.ch; 🕐 08.30–noon & 14.00–17.30 Mon–Fri, 09.00–noon & 14.00–17.00 Sat; Jul–late Oct 09.00–noon & 14.00–17.00 Sun

Where to stay
All hotel guests at Lenk receive a Visitors Card, which gives discounts to a wide range of goods

Where to stay
Numerous hotels; close to the station is:
🏠 **Saanerhof***** CH-3792; 📞 033 744 15 15; ✉ hotel@saanerhof.ch; www.saanerhof.ch

Numerous hotels; close to the station are:
🏠 **Bernerhof****** Promenade, CH-3780; 📞 033 748 88 44; ✉ info@bernerhof-gstaad.ch; www.bernerhof-gstaad.ch
🏠 **Christiania****** Unter Gstaadstrasse, CH-3780; 📞 033 744 51 21; ✉ info@christiania.ch; www.christiania.ch
🏠 **Sporthotel Victoria***** Promenade, CH-3780; 📞 033 748 44 22; ✉ info@victoria-gstaad.ch; www.victoria-gstaad.ch

Where to stay
A hotel opposite the station in a quiet position is:
🏠 **Post***** **(H)** CH-3770; 📞 033 729 30 40; ✉ info@hotel-post-ag-zweisimmen.ch; www.hotel-post-ag-zweisimmen.ch

and services, including bike hire and free use of bus transport in the town. Numerous hotels; close to the station are:
🏠 **Simmenhof****** Lenkstrasse 43 CH-3775; 📞 033 736 34 34; ✉ info@simmenhof.ch; www.simmenhof.ch
🏠 **Wildstrubel***** **(H)** Lenkstrasse 8, CH-3775; 📞 033 736 31 11; ✉ info@wildstrubel.ch; www.wildstrubel.ch

17

A metre-gauge line linking several major tourist towns, the first section through the district known as Haute Gruyère. Sit on the right.

Leaving Montbovon, the railway careers down the streets of the town before reaching its own right of way on the outskirts. On the right is a narrow packhorse bridge, the Pontet, which can be reached by signed footpath from the station. Also on the right is a small lake, one of several through which the River Saane/Sarine runs. **Lessoc** is a lovely village with an onion-domed fountain (1796) at its centre; some of the farms in the village are decorated with poyas, naïve paintings of the celebrated transhumance of cows.

Beyond **Neirivue**, the river is just to the right of the railway for some miles, and a frequent sight on the parallel road is cows on their way to or from milking, cowbells clattering. The village of **Grandvillard** has many fine 17th-century houses and a 1930s church. Beyond **Enney**, with its wood-ceilinged early 17th-century church, railway and river part company as the former turns to the west into a narrower, more wooded valley.

It is best to try to visit **Gruyères** out of season. This deservedly popular medieval town is overrun in the summer months, when the town receives the majority of its one million annual visitors. An alternative is to stay the night to savour the atmosphere once the day visitors have left, but the limited accommodation puts a premium on the price of rooms. Needless to say cars have no place in such a town and are confined to the foot of the hill on which the walled town is built. It is a ten-minute walk from the station to the old town.

The town's walls and towers date from the 12th to 15th centuries and encompass an oval-shaped marketplace surrounded by some well-designed houses, mostly dating from the 15th to 17th centuries. In summer the scene resembles a flower show in its profusion of window boxes and tubs. Older than most is the 14th-century Maison de Chalamala, which is believed to have belonged to a contemporary court jester at the castle. The church of St Théodule was founded in the 13th century but the tower dates from 1680, the choir from 1731 and the nave from 1860. The views from the town and castle are magnificent.

The castle was built by the 12th century for the counts of Gruyère who held sway over the area until 1544 when the indebted Michael I was forced to sell the estates. The castle became the residence of the bailiffs and then prefects of Fribourg before being sold to the Bovy family in 1848. It was bought back by the canton of Fribourg in 1938 and opened to the public (✆ 026 921 21 02; www.chateau-gruyeres.ch; ⊕ Apr–Oct 09.00–18.00 daily; Nov–Mar 10.00–16.30 daily; admission charge).

Of the original castle only the 13th-century dungeon and round Savoy keep remain, a fire in 1493 having destroyed the living quarters. It was reconstructed by the widow of Louis II; he had fought on the Swiss side at the Battle of Murten (1476) and brought back as booty the three copes bearing the arms of defeated Charles the Bold which now hang in the Burgundy Room. On the ground floor are the guardroom and kitchen. On the first floor are Gobelin tapestries in the Count's Room, landscape paintings by Corot and original 17th-century painted décor in the Bailiff's Room. The second floor has some good pieces of Louis XV furniture. The Arsenal Room is used for temporary exhibitions, and the lovely Chapel of St John has 15th-century stained glass.

The name of Gruyères is famous because of cheese, although it is the area rather than the town that lends its name to the product. Opposite the station is La Maison du Gruyère, a dairy which welcomes visitors (✆ *026 921 84 00; www.lamaisondugruyere.ch;* ⊕ *Jun–Sep 09.00–19.00 daily; Oct–May 09.00–18.00 daily; production usually about 09.00–11.00 & 12.30–14.30; admission charge*). Since it takes 12 litres of milk to produce 1kg of cheese, it's no wonder that the dairy uses 13,000 litres of milk a day. A tape/slideshow with English commentary illustrates the process in which milk is warmed and stirred before rennet is added to curdle the milk. The firm mass is cut into tiny granules that float in whey before being pumped into round presses for compaction. A day's submersion in a saline bath is followed by ripening, which can take anything from four months to a year.

A few yards from the castle is Château St Germain which has become a permanent gallery (⊕ *Apr–Oct 10.00–18.00 daily; Nov–Mar 13.00–17.00 Tue–Fri, 10.00–18.00 Sat–Sun; admission charge*) for the bizarre paintings and sculptures of Chur-born artist H R Giger, who won an Oscar for Best Visual Effects in *Alien*.

A bus from Gruyères station runs to Moléson-Village (table 20.263/line 263) where there is a 17th-century dairy listed as a historic monument (✆ *026 921 10 44;* ⊕ *May–Sep 09.30–19.00 daily; admission charge*). Only a minute from the bus stop is the small cable car up Le Moléson (table 2045).

On a rock at **La Tour-de-Trême** stands a large 13th-century tower which protected the village founded by the counts of Gruyère. On the outskirts of **Bulle** the branch line from Broc trails in on the right. Change here for Broc and Romont. For the town of Bulle see table 254, page 141.

A few miles after leaving Bulle, the line turns to the southwest into the area known as the Veveyse, in which the largest town is **Châtel-St-Denis**. The neo-Gothic church of St Denis was built in 1872–76. Near the church are the remains of a 13th-century castle, which was incorporated in 18th-century alterations. A walking map showing signed routes in the area is available from the tourist office. A bus from the station serves the winter resort of Les Paccots (table 20.492/line 492) which has a network of ski lifts.

PRACTICALITIES Bicycle hire from Bulle station.

GRUYÈRES
Tourist information
🛈 Rue du Bourg 1, CH-1663; ✆ 0848 424 424; e tourisme@gruyeres.ch; www.la-gruyeres.ch; ⊕ Jul–Aug 09.30–17.30 daily; Sep–Jun 10.30–noon & 13.00–16.30 daily

Where to stay
⌂ **Hostellerie des Chevaliers***** Ruelle des Chevaliers, CH-1663; ✆ 026 921 19 33; e info@chevaliers-gruyeres.ch; www.chevaliers-gruyeres.ch

⌂ **Hostellerie St-Georges***** (H) CH-1663; ✆ 026 921 83 00; e info@st-georges-gruyeres.ch; www.st-georges-gruyeres.ch
⌂ **Hôtel de Ville**** CH-1663; ✆ 026 921 24 24; e info@hoteldeville.ch; www.hoteldeville.ch
⌂ **La Fleur-de-Lys**** Rue du Bourg 14, CH-1663; ✆ 026 921 82 82; e hotelfleurdelys@bluewin.ch; www.hotelfleurdelys.ch

CHÂTEL-ST-DENIS/LES PACCOTS
Tourist information
🛈 Les Paccots, Rte des Paccots 215, CH-1619; ✆ 021 948 84 56; e info@les-paccots.ch; www.les-paccots.ch; ⊕ Jun–Sep 09.00–noon & 15.00–17.30 Mon–Fri, 09.00–14.00 Sat–Sun; Oct–May 09.00–noon & 16.30–17.30 Mon–Fri, 09.00–noon Sat

Where to stay
⌂ **Corbetta*** Rte des Paccots 163, CH-1619; ✆ 021 948 71 20

BULLE–BROC Table 253

A metre-gauge branch line that serves the resort of Broc on the south tip of Lac de la Gruyère.

Broc-Village is best known for the Nestlé chocolate factory founded in 1898 by Alexandre Cailler. Factory visits have had to be replaced by a film. At the entrance to the village is a 14th-century fortified house, Château-d'En Bas. A bus from the station goes up the east side of the lake to Corbières (table 20.262/line 262), where there is a château in the centre of the village.

From the station a bus service goes to the beautifully situated village of Charmey (and on to Jaun) (table 20.260/line 260) past the artificial Lac de Montsalvens. In the woods above stand the impressive ruins of the 12th-century castle of the same name that was abandoned in 1671.

The chalet that houses the tourist office at Charmey also contains a museum of rural artefacts (⊕ *10.00–noon & 14.00–18.00 Mon–Fri, 10.00–noon & 14.00–16.00 Sat, 14.00–18.00 Sun*), particularly those relating to the dairy industry and cheese making, Carthusian monasticism, weapons, flora and local history. Two minutes from the bus stop is a cable car to Vounetse (table 2042). At Jaun is a ruined castle, destroyed in 1407.

The same bus service (table 20.260/260), from Bulle station, which calls at Jaun, proceeds over the Jaunpass to Boltigen station on the Spiez–Zweisimmen line (see table 320, page 160).

CHARMEY
Tourist information

🛈 Les Charrières 1, CH-1637; ☎026 927 55 80; e office.tourisme@charmey.ch; www.charmey.ch; ⊕ 09.00–noon & 13.30–17.00 Mon–Fri, 09.00–noon & 13.30–16.30 Sat

Where to stay

⌂ **Le Sapin*** CH-1637; ☎026 927 23 23; e info@hotel-le-sapin.ch; www.hotel-le-sapin.ch

Geneva–MONTREUX–AIGLE–Brig Table 100

This section of the main line between Geneva and Brig covers the transformation from the eastern end of Lac Léman to the fertile Rhône valley, along which orchards of apples and pears cover the broad valley floor while vines climb the eastern slopes. It passes close to the world-famous Castle of Chillon, immortalised by Byron's poem.

The first station, **Territet**, is a suburb of Montreux from which two funiculars ascend, to Glion and Mont-Fleuri (see page 268). **Veytaux-Chillon** is the station adjacent to the castle, but there is a delightful footpath along the lakeshore from west of Clarens through Montreux to the castle and beyond.

Even if Byron had not written *The Prisoner of Chillon*, the castle would still be the outstanding attraction it has become; not only is its position on a peninsula strikingly picturesque, but it is one of Europe's best-preserved examples of medieval military architecture. The rock on which it is built has supported a settlement since the Bronze Age, the Romans fortified it, and the defences were developed in the 9th century. The present castle was begun in the mid 13th century by Peter II of Savoy (London's Savoy takes its name from him) who employed the military architect Pierre Mainier to create strong defences on the side of the road and mountain with the residential parts overlooking the lake.

The castle was held by the lords of Savoy until 1536 when an army of 6,000 Bernoise and some vassals from Geneva forced the castle's surrender. It was this that effected the release of Chillon's most famous prisoner, the prior François Bonivard (1493–1570). A supporter of the Reformation and of Geneva in its struggles with the Catholic dukes of Savoy, Bonivard was imprisoned in Chillon in 1530, spending four of the six years incarcerated in the dungeons, chained to a pillar. It was his plight, and the poem Bonivard wrote ('Lamentation in Captivity at Chillon'), that inspired Byron to write his poem following a visit to the castle with Shelley in 1816.

After the seizure by the Bernois until the early 18th century, Chillon was the residence of the Bailiff of Vevey. The castle was then used as a prison and hospital before being restored at the end of the 19th century, having become one of the most visited, painted and engraved castles in the world. Flaubert waxed lyrical about seeing Byron's name carved in the stone of the dungeon; he was deluded – it is a forgery.

There is an excellent English-language guide to the castle (⊕ *Apr–Sep 09.00–18.00 daily; Oct & Mar 09.30–17.00 daily; Nov–Feb 10.00–16.00 daily; these are last entry times; admission charge*), which has 28 rooms and areas open to visitors, with a fine banqueting hall and collection of armour. The castle can be very crowded in summer, but it is justly popular. The best viewpoint of the castle was probably from the lake until marred by one of the country's most insensitively sited motorways (regrettably it is not without serious competition), which rises on piers out of the wood behind the castle. There is a landing stage by the castle for lake steamers.

Villeneuve was for centuries an important staging post on the route from Italy to Gaul over the Grand St Bernard Pass. As late as 1800 Napoleon used it as his advance base for getting the Army of Reserve across the Alps at the start of what became the Marengo campaign, depicted in David's painting of *Napoleon Crossing the St Bernard Pass* in the Musée National de Malmaison, Paris. Remains of fortifications can be seen near the church.

At Le Bouveret, along the shore towards the French border and where the Rhône enters Lac Léman, is the Swiss Vapeur Parc (⊕ *mid-Mar–mid-May, mid-Sep–Oct 13.30–18.00 Mon–Fri, 10.00–18.00 Sat–Sun; mid-May–mid-Sep 10.00–18.00 daily; www.swissvapeur.ch*): up to ten trains at a time are in use on 2km (2,190yds) of superbly laid-out 5in- and 7¼in-gauge track, with scale buildings, tunnels, viaducts and an impressive variety of locomotives based on prototypes from different countries. Children (and most adults) are invariably reluctant to leave.

Unfortunately Vapeur Parc is no longer easy to reach by rail since most trains on the branch line between St Monthey and St Gingolph, serving Bouveret, have been replaced by buses (table 130, page 291). The easiest way to reach it from the west is by steamer, since it is only a short walk to the Steam Park from the pier at Bouveret. The alternative is to take the train to Bouveret from St Maurice (table 130, page 291). Some services are operated by buses.

There was also a steam train, the 'Rive-Bleu Express', over the standard-gauge line from Bouveret to St Gingolph and across the border to the well-known source of bottled water, Evian. The scenery along the 22km (13¾ miles) is superb, the train running along the lake for most of the way, interrupted only by the odd tunnel and cutting. However, the track is in poor condition, and services have been suspended.

As Lac Léman comes to an end, there is a sudden transition as the line enters the broad Rhône valley, the hills to the west lined with vineyards and orchards of apples and pears. For **Aigle**, see *Chapter 18*, page 281.

VILLENEUVE
Tourist information
🛈 Pl de la Gare 5, CH-1844; ☎021 960 84 81;
📧 info@montreuxriviera.ch; www.
montreuxtourism.ch; ⏱ mid-May–mid-Sep
13.00–18.00 Mon, 09.00–noon & 13.00–18.00
Tue–Fri, 09.00–13.00 Sat; mid-Sep–mid-May,
08.30–noon & 13.00–17.30 Mon–Fri

Where to stay
🏠 **Du Port***** Rue de Quai 6, CH-1844; ☎021
960 41 45; 📧 hotel@duport.ch; www.duport.ch

18

Southeast Vaud and the Valais

This region contains many of Switzerland's best-known ski resorts, mostly situated in the mountains that line the Rhône valley and easily reached by railway, cable car and postal bus. An astonishing 18% of the canton of Valais is covered by glacier so it is little wonder that there should be such good skiing, served by an extensive network of cable cars and ski lifts. Forty-seven of the mountains in the canton are over 4,000m (13,123ft) high; there are 'only' 65 in the whole of the Alps. It is also one of the finest areas for walking, with tens of thousands of kilometres of paths.

The area produces the largest quantity of Swiss wines – more than 80% of Swiss wine is grown in the Rhône Valley – and the regional dish of raclette (melted cheese with potatoes) is found in many restaurants. The Valais has one of the lowest rainfall rates amongst the Swiss cantons, and the need to bring water to the vines and other crops has created a feature found in many valleys; the *Bisses* are irrigation channels that were created as long ago as the 13th century. Some are in extraordinarily vertiginous locations, and many are in such attractive settings that they are often followed by walkers' trails.

AIGLE

This centre of viticulture is a major junction, the station outside and to the east of the main line station being the start of three metre-gauge railways that serve resorts in the mountains above the Rhône valley. Each has a very different character, both scenically and in the resorts at their terminus – Leysin, Les Diablerets and Champéry. Sometimes pulling a four-wheel van for post and newspapers, the trains play an important transport role in valleys whose roads are slow and dangerous in winter.

The town of Aigle dates back to Roman times and was held by Savoy from 1076 until the Bernese captured the town and destroyed the 11th-century castle in 1475. After being rebuilt the castle was the residence of the governor until 1798, becoming a prison until 1972. The following year work began on its restoration and conversion into a magnificent museum of the vine and wine, with some of the state rooms adapted for dinners. The museum (⊕ *Apr–Jun & Sep–Oct 11.00–18.00 Tue–Sun; Jul–Aug 11.00–18.00 daily*) looks at the industry's history, equipment, bottles, barrels and the position of wine in society using reconstructed rooms as well as displays. The castle itself is one of the most picturesque in the canton, situated on the outskirts of the town surrounded by vines and a vast 17th-century barn. This barn, the Dîme House, has been adapted for use as an art gallery displaying the landscape paintings of Frédéric Rouge (1867–1950), who captured every season, scene and mood of the Vaudois Alps, where he spent most of his life.

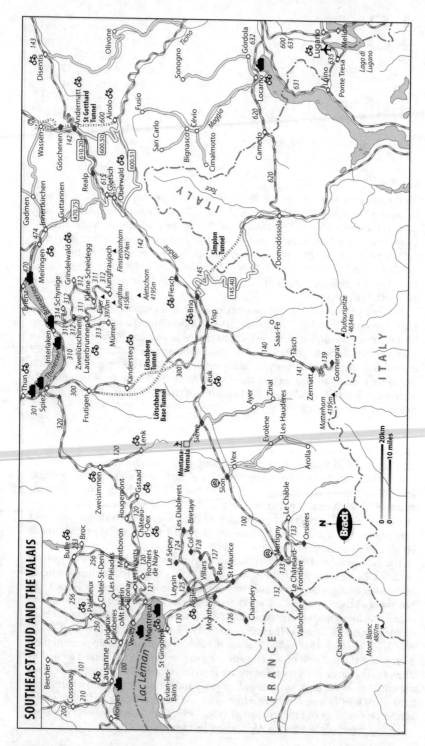

SOUTHEAST VAUD AND THE VALAIS

The town itself has a pedestrianised centre, and the medieval German Reformed church of St James was where the famous reformer Guillaume Farel (whose statue stands beside the collegiate church at Neuchâtel) preached when he lived in Aigle. The unusual arcades of the attractive alley named Rue de Jérusalem should not be missed.

TOURIST INFORMATION

Rue Colomb 5, CH-1860; 024 466 30 00; info@aigle-tourisme.ch; www.aigle-tourisme.ch; Apr–Oct 08.30–noon & 13.30–18.00

Mon–Fri, 08.00–noon Sat; Nov–Mar 08.30–noon & 13.30–17.00 Mon–Fri

WHERE TO STAY

Closest to the station is:

Hotel Le Suisse Rue de la Gare 28, CH-1860; 024 466 22 07; hotel-suisse@bluewin.ch; www.hotelcafesuisse.ch

AIGLE–LEYSIN Table 125

Serving the summer and winter sports resort of Leysin, the line is the shortest of the three private railways from Aigle, at 6.2km (4 miles).

For anyone unfamiliar with street-running trams, the line to Leysin will be an eye-opener in the way the train glides through the streets of Aigle before a horseshoe bend brings it to the railway's depot. Here it reverses, engages the rack and begins the fierce climb through vineyards and then forest to **Leysin**.

This was a completely isolated village, accessible only by footpath until a road was built in 1875. Its people were largely self-sufficient, growing nearly all their food and even making wine. Their long life expectancy came to the notice of the British economist Thomas Malthus, who devoted six pages of his *Essay on the Principle of Population* to the village. Its healthy climate and reputation attracted people in search of a cure, and the first large hotels were clinics, especially for those suffering from tuberculosis; the large balconies on to which beds could be wheeled and their protective glass screens can still be seen on many of Leysin's buildings. Oskar Kokoschka came here in 1909, painting a view of the Dents du Midi.

The railway opened in 1900 to Leysin-Feydey, being extended 15 years later to the present terminus at Grand Hôtel. During World War II Leysin was one of the places where British servicemen who managed to escape to Switzerland were interned. It was only after the war that Leysin became a major winter sports centre with the construction of chairlifts and cable cars. In 1962 the American School moved to Leysin, boosting demand for the excellent sports facilities the town has progressively developed. Amongst them, and ten minutes' walk from the station, are gondola lifts up the Berneuse (table 2070). Plans exist for a 3.87km (2½ miles) extension of the railway from the Grand Hôtel to the Berneuse where it would terminate in an underground station beneath the Kuklos (Greek for turning) revolving restaurant, which is situated on the peak of the Berneuse at 2,048m (6,719ft) above sea level and provides a wonderful panorama of the surrounding Alps in its 90-minute revolution. The restaurant is said to have been designed to mirror the shape of two nearby mountains, the Tour Mayern and Tour d'Ai, in order to blend into the natural surroundings; some visitors may feel the simple structures of earlier generations, using a local stone, do less to announce their presence.

LEYSIN
Tourist information
ℹ️ Pl Large, CH-1854; ☎ 024 493 30 00; ✉ info@
leysin.ch; www.leysin.ch; ⏱ 08.00–20.00 daily

Where to stay
Numerous hotels; close to the station are:
🏠 **Mercure Classic****** CH-1854; ☎ 024 493 06
06; ✉ info@classic-hotel.ch; www.classic-hotel.ch
🏠 **Hotel Le Grand Chalet***** CH-1854; ☎ 024
493 01 01; ✉ hotel.grand-chalet@bluewin.ch;
www.grand-chalet.ch

AIGLE–LES DIABLERETS Table 124

Probably the most scenic of the three lines from Aigle, it serves the smallest population and, despite the gradients, the climb through the Ormont valley is made without rack assistance. The cable car journeys from the winter and summer sports resort of Les Diablerets are particularly impressive. Sit on the right until Le Sépey and then move to the left.

Like the line to Leysin, the railway to Les Diablerets leaves Aigle through the streets, passing, even in the town, tiny stone-walled areas of vines, as though no patch of ground can be wasted that might produce grapes for the celebrated white wines that Aigle vignerons produce. Shortly after the station it crosses the line to Champéry at a right angle on the level. As soon as the railway's depot is passed on the right, the castle comes into view. The railway describes a series of horseshoe curves to gain height, affording marvellous views of three sides of the castle.

A tunnel leads into the thickly wooded, steep-sided valley of the Grande-Eau, the railway keeping to its southern flank except where it crosses the river on a long bridge to reach Le Sépey. Passing through pine and beech with sheer rock cuttings, the drop to the valley floor becomes progressively more spectacular. Small mountain farms are linked by paths, some discreetly signed, as from **Les Fontanelles**.

Les Planches is a junction, though served by only a tiny hut. Here alternate trains proceed to the small resort of **Le Sépey** where they reverse, return to Les Planches and proceed up to Les Diablerets; the other trains are met at Les Planches by a postbus for Le Sépey, the train proceeding directly to Les Diablerets. From Le Sépey station a bus runs to Château d'Oex over the Col des Moses (table 12.174).

Streams tumble down from side valleys to join the Grande-Eau as the line drops down to **Les Aviolats**, after which the valley narrows before the first ski lifts are seen at **Vers-l'Eglise**. The lovely church after which the village is named was built in around 1456 with a square stone tower, but was altered in the 18th century. Next to the church is a large inn (1833) named The Bear. The line drops down further to **Les Diablerets**, where the station is close to the unspoilt village centre. In summer the resort offers various sports such as climbing, tennis, swimming, riding, rafting and mountain biking. There are numerous good walks: to Col de Bretaye in 3 hours 20 minutes, Gryon in 4 hours 40 minutes and L'Etivaz (boots essential) in 5 hours 20 minutes, for example.

The bus from the station to Gstaad (table 12.180) stops at Col-du-Pillon for the Glacier 3000 two-section gondola and cable car up to the Glacier-des-Diablerets (table 2085); this should not be missed – the views are exceptionally fine, and there is almost year-round skiing at this height (3,000m, 9,843ft), as well as excellent food at Restaurant Botta 3000, designed by Mario Botta. A great adrenalin rush is provided by the world's highest bobsleigh run; the railed sleds on the 1km Alpine Coaster reach speeds of 40km/h and negotiate a 520° loop, waves, jumps and bridges. The glacier is also served by a two-section cable car that comes up from Reusch (table 2398), which is on the same bus route.

Only six minutes' walk from Les Diablerets station is the gondola lift to Isenau (table 2080), and there is also a bus over the Col de la Croix to Villars (table 12.162).

In winter Les Diablerets offers 120km (75 miles) of varied ski runs with 50 lifts, skating and curling rinks and an indoor swimming pool.

From Les Diablerets you can experience what it is like to build and sleep in an igloo. A bus takes you to the Glacier 3000 cable car in the Pillon Pass from which you ascend to 3,000m (9,843ft). Guides take you across the glacier to the Quille du Diable (Devil's Bowling Skittle) where you are instructed in the art of ice construction, with the incentive of having to spend a night in the result. A traditional alpine meal helps to fend off the cold before bed, and the trek down after breakfast takes in the beauties of the Martisberg nature reserve; details from the tourist office.

Another thrill can be had through Mountain Evasion (✆ *024 492 12 32; www. mountain-evasion.ch*) in Les Diablerets. It takes 'monster bikes' to Isenau for a long descent down farm tracks and across fields, the fat tyres absorbing the bumps.

LES DIABLERETS
Tourist information
🛈 Rue de la Gare, CH-1865; ✆024 492 00 10; e info@diablerets.ch; www.diablerets.ch; ⊕ 09.00–12.30 & 13.30–18.00 Mon–Sat, 09.00–12.30 & 13.30–17.00 Sun

Where to stay
Numerous hotels, though none is adjacent to the station; within five minutes' walk is:

🏠 **Auberge de la Poste* (H)** CH-1865; ✆024 492 31 24; e info@aubergedelaposte.ch; www.aubergedelaposte.ch. Delightful chalet dating from 1789; family-run.

Where to eat
✖ **Restaurant Le Terminus** ✆024 492 31 44. Opposite the station. Excellent local dishes such as wild mushrooms.

AIGLE–CHAMPÉRY Table 126

The principal place on the line is the industrial town of Monthey, where the train reverses to head up the Val d'Illiez through which runs La Vieze. The Strub rack system is employed on the steeper sections to the ski resort at the terminus. Sit on the right.

Trains for Champéry leave from the two bay platforms closest to the main line. The train runs alongside the road for much of the way to Monthey. Above **St-Triphon-Village** are the substantial remains of a 12th-century castle destroyed in 1476 during the Burgundian wars. Just to the north are the ruins of an 11th–14th-century chapel.

The line climbs sharply up to the attractive village of **Ollon**, where the Reformed church has a 15th-century frieze depicting the Apostles. From the post office in Ollon a bus goes up to Panex (table 12.145) where the remains of Switzerland's first salt mine, operated between 1554 and 1797, can still be seen, including the Maison des Salines.

Dropping down, the railway traverses the Rhône valley, crossing the Geneva–Brig railway and the river which forms the boundary between the cantons of Vaud and Valais. Near these crossings an extraordinary Italianate villa can be seen to the right, perched on a large outcrop of rock. After crossing over the line to St Gingolph, the railway turns abruptly south along the main street of **Collombey**, overlooked by the Monastery de Bernardine. The 17th-century buildings were built on to the keep of a 13th-century castle.

The train enters the modern terminus at **Monthey**, passing the railway's depot, which also maintains its buses. Near the station is a château rebuilt in the 17th century incorporating a medieval tower; it now houses a museum about old Monthey. The town also has several interesting defensive buildings, including an arsenal and a walled residence in Avenue du Crochetan. From the station a postbus climbs to Les Cerniers (table 12.063) where you can stay in a Whitepod, a domed tent on a wooden platform with wood-burning stove; the pod is accessible only by snow shoes or skis, so it provides an unusual experience (*www. whitepod.com*).

The train reverses (do not change sides – the best views are now to the left) and swings west to engage the rack and climb steeply out of the town to reach the Val d'Illiez, along which it holds to the west bank at a height that provides good views for most of the way to Champéry. Just before **Hôpital (Monthey)** on the right is a huge rock precariously balanced on another with wedges to prevent it from moving. Near **Croix-du-Nant** is an attractive small church with tiny belltower. Beyond the station is a viaduct across the Val de Morgins which joins the main valley at this point. Morgins is a ski resort close to the French border, reached by a bus (table 12.061) that starts at Monthey station and calls at **Troistorrents** station before tackling the hairpin bends up to Morgins at 1,400m (4,593ft).

Glorious views of the Dents du Midi can be seen to the left, and the chalets thin out as the valley sides steepen, those on the opposite side being reached by zig-zag tracks. On the right before **Fayot** is a lovely old bridge with the characteristic shrine incorporated into a parapet. **Val d'Illiez** is a picturesque village with ornately carved decoration to the chalet balconies; its white-rendered Catholic church has a distinctive spire to the façade tower. A bus ascends from Val d'Illiez to the tiny village of Champoussin (table 12.082). Before **La Cour** there are stupendous views down to the river hundreds of metres below, though the valley is wooded and the views in summer are more limited.

The station at **Champéry** was rebuilt in the mid-1990s, the line being slightly extended to incorporate the cable car station to Planachaux (table 2110), from where there are marvellous views of the Dents du Midi, Dents Blanche and other ranges. Many other lifts on the slopes to the west of the resort cater principally for skiers capable of intermediate runs.

CHAMPÉRY
Tourist information
🄴 Residence Opaline, CH-1874; ☎024 479 20 20; e info@champery.ch; www.champery.ch; ⏰ 08.00–noon & 14.00–18.00 daily

Where to stay
Numerous hotels. None is adjacent to the station; within 10 minutes' walk are:

🏠 **Beau-Séjour***** Rue du Village 114, CH-1874; ☎024 479 58 58; e booking@beausejour.ch; www.bo-sejour.com

🏠 **Suisse***** Grand Rue 55, CH-1874; ☎024 479 07 07; e hotelsuisse@netplus.com; www. hotel-champery.ch

🏠 **Hotel des Alpes**** Rue du village 9, CH-1874; ☎024 479 12 22; e hoteldesalpes@bluewin. ch; www.hotel-desalpes.ch

Geneva–AIGLE–MARTIGNY–Brig Table 100

This fast stretch of the main line runs almost north–south, paralleling the Rhône once south of Bex. It is best to keep the eyes on the valley slopes and mountains beyond, as industrial activity is evident along the valley floor for much of the remaining journey to Brig. The railways that branch off the Rhône valley are all more attractive.

The first station, at **Bex**, is the junction for the delightful rack railway to Villars. The station is on the outskirts of the town, but the centre can be reached by trains to Villars (see page 290).

Soon after crossing the Rhône the railway reaches **St Maurice**. Tradition has it that the warrior-saint Maurice was martyred here for refusing to fight fellow Christians. The abbey named after him was built on the site of a 4th-century chapel erected on the tomb by St Theodore, first bishop of the Valais, and is the oldest Christian site in the country. Switzerland's oldest monastery was founded in 515 by the Burgundian King Sigismund, the kings residing in the town until the ninth century. The monastery became an Augustinian possession in 1128. Situated in the north of the town, the abbey has been repeatedly rebuilt but contains several important examples of art, including an exquisite goblet thought to date from the 1st or 2nd century BC.

In the castle is the cantonal museum of military history (⊕ *late Apr–Oct 13.00–18.00 Tue–Sun; admission charge*), focusing on the development of arms, uniforms and regimental colours from 1815 to the present. A later military position (1940–46) can be visited by guided tour, at Fort Cindey (⊕ *mid-Mar–Jun, Sep–mid-Nov 14.00 Sat–Sun; Jul–Aug at 10.30, 13.30 &16.00 daily*), one of many forts built during the early 1940s. On four days a year there are also tours of Fort du Scex at 13.30; reservations through the tourist office essential.

In 1863 a huge underground lake fed by a waterfall was discovered at St Maurice. The Grotte aux Fées (◊ *024 485 10 45*; ⊕ *mid-Mar–mid-Nov 10.00–17.00 daily; Jul–Aug 10.00–18.00 daily; admission charge*) is open to visitors, but wear a pullover – it's cold 914m (3,000ft) inside the rock.

The approach to **Martigny** is heralded by the cylindrical keep of the castle at La Batiaz on a rock to the right of the train. It dates from the first half of the 13th century, and the castle has an exhibition of medieval war machines. Situated on an elbow of the Rhône and at its junction with the Drance valley that leads to the Great St Bernard Pass, Martigny has been an important crossroads for 2,000 years. Little remains of the Roman capital of the region, except for the foundations of an elliptical amphitheatre for 5,000 spectators. Christianity arrived in around 300, and the first bishopric in Switzerland was established here.

The town's oldest building is the 13th-century castle of La Batiaz, which was painted by Turner. It can be reached by crossing the Drance on a covered bridge. The first part of the castle was built by the bishop of Sion, but the cylindrical keep was commissioned by Peter II of Savoy. The castle was sacked in 1475 and slighted after a siege in 1518. At the foot of the hill to it is the Notre-Dame de Compassion chapel of 1595 with a collection of beautiful 18th- and 19th-century votive pictures.

In the centre of the town is the 17th-century Baroque Catholic church of Notre-Dames-des-Champs, with fine carved door, and behind it the Provostry where Napoleon stayed in 1800. At Place Centrale 7 (near the tourist office) is the much-altered, mid 16th-century Grande-maison, a former hotel that welcomed Rousseau, Goethe, Stendhal, Byron and Alexandre Dumas, amongst others.

Martigny's principal attraction, however, is close to Martigny-Bourg station on the branch to Orsières/Le Châble (see table 133, page 293). The Pierre Gianadda Foundation (◊ *027 722 39 78; www.gianadda.ch; ⊕ Nov–May 10.00–18.00 daily; Jun–Oct 09.00–19.00 daily*) would be worthy of a city and is a surprise to many visitors. It is the creation of Leonard Gianadda, a civil engineer who was building housing in Martigny when his brother Pierre was killed in an air crash in Italy. When a Roman temple was discovered on the site of the housing, Leonard Gianadda decided to create a memorial to his brother on the site. The result is a cultural centre that hosts exhibitions of an astonishing quality, sometimes in association with museums of the stature of the Metropolitan Museum of Art in New York, and concerts in an impressive hall. On an upper level is a Gallo-Roman museum displaying artefacts found in the town, notably a three-horned bull.

A passage underneath the adjacent road is used as a photographic gallery and links the main building with the largest collection of Swiss-made motor cars, including a Martigny. The Delaunay-Belleville was built to order for Tsar Nicholas II, intended for use on hunting expeditions, but never delivered because of the October Revolution. All are in working order. There is a small section devoted to the Swiss inventor Isaac da Rivaz (1752–1828), who came up with the idea of an explosion in a cylinder and who died in nearby Sion.

In the park around the Foundation are sculptures by Giacometti, Modigliani, Rodin, Toulouse-Lautrec and others, and a swimming pool.

On the other side of the branch line, on Rue du Levant, are the remains of the amphitheatre, where the annual cowfight takes place in early October. Locals are adamant that there is no cruelty involved and that the cows are very seldom hurt in this popular event. The amphitheatre is one of the places on the archaeological walk that starts at the tourist office (leaflet available) and takes in the various sites of interest.

Close to the amphitheatre is the St Bernard Dog Museum (*Route de Levant 34; www.museesaintbernard.ch;* ⊕ *10.00–18.00 daily*), in a former arsenal. Above the dogs' enclosure are two floors of exhibitions about the role of the breed in saving countless lives over the last three centuries.

Martigny is a good centre for walking with three railway branch lines up surrounding valleys, which provide access to the gorges of the Durnand, Trièg and Trent (see page 293). Asparagus and apricots are grown in quantity in the area, and there is an annual apricot market in early August.

ST MAURICE
Tourist information
🄸 Av des Terreaux 1, CH-1890; ☎ 024 485 40 40; e info@saint-maurice.ch; www.saint-maurice.ch; ⊕ 15.00–18.00 Mon, 09.00–noon & 15.00–18.00 Tue–Fri; mid-Jun–mid-Oct also 10.00–noon Sat

Where to stay
🏠 **Hotel Restaurant La Dent du Midi*****
Av du Simplon 1, CH-1890; ☎ 024 485 12 09; www. torrente.ch

MARTIGNY
Tourist information
🄸 Av de la Gare 6, CH-1920; ☎ 027 720 49 49; e info@martigny.ch; www.martigny.com; ⊕ May–Jun & Sep–Oct 09.00–noon & 13.30– 18.00 Mon–Fri, 09.00–noon & 13.30–17.00 Sat; Jul–Aug 09.00–18.00 Mon–Fri, 09.00–17.00 Sat, 10.00–13.00 & 14.00–17.00 Sun; Nov–Apr 09.00– 12.30 & 13.30–17.30 Mon–Fri, 09.00–12.30 Sat

Where to stay
Numerous hotels; close to the station is:
🏠 **Forclaz-Touring***** 15 Rue du Léman, CH-1920; ☎ 027 722 27 01; e contact@ hotelforclaztouring.ch; www.hotelforclaztouring.ch
Near Martigny-Bourg station is:
🏠 **Forum***** Av Grand S-Bernard 72, CH-1920; ☎ 027 722 18 41; e info@hotel-forum.ch; www. hotel-forum.ch. Excellent restaurant.

BEX–BÉVIEUX–VILLARS Tables 127/129

This is one of the loveliest of Switzerland's mountain railways, with great character for those who appreciate such things. There are a couple of trains a day between Bex and Bévieux and between Gryon and Villars in addition to the through trains. The former were worked until recently by a venerable tram car.

Trains leave from directly outside the station at Bex (pronounced Bé), the Villars train standing at right angles to the main line.

The train proceeds directly up the road to the town centre, twisting through narrow streets to **Bex-Place-du-Marché**. The prosperity of Bex was built on salt, which the Bernese began to exploit in the 16th century. In the 19th century this was augmented by the development of the town as a spa – its full name is Bex-les-Bains – which was patronised by Victor Hugo, Tolstoy and Rimski-Korsakov. The huge tower of the Reformed church of St Clément is the oldest part, dating from 1501; the classical nave and choir are early 19th century.

The line continues as a roadside tramway to **Bévieux**, where the railway's depot is situated on the right. A 50-minute 3.2km (2 miles) walk from Bévieux station to the mine is one of Switzerland's most unusual and fascinating museums. The subject of salt may not sound enthralling, but the experience of riding on a mine train through 3.2km (2 miles) of the 50km (31 miles) of tunnel, and seeing the vast, ingeniously lit and interpreted chambers, will never be forgotten. Although the salt deposits were discovered in the 16th century, the first tunnel was not dug until 1684, and the mines were developed with painful slowness because of the hard rock and limited tools of the time. For example, there is an unfinished passage of 734 steps 1,500m (1,640yds) long that was abandoned after 13 years' digging. The reason for such Herculean endeavour was, of course, the price of salt, which was compared with gold. The toll on health was severe: miners started work at the age of 12 and seldom lived beyond 35.

The salt was dissolved in underground chambers and then piped along larch logs to intensifying plants where it was boiled, requiring huge amounts of timber, followed by evaporation. The discovery of salt-impregnated rock in 1867 and cheaper methods of extraction was a breakthrough. Today nine men produce about 40,000 tonnes of salt a year, half of which goes to chemical works and most of the other half to the kitchens of Switzerland. About 10 million tonnes of salt remain.

Conducted tours (📞 024 463 03 30; www.mines.ch; late Mar–May & late Sep–Oct 09.45, 11.15, 14.15 & 15.45 Tue–Sun; Jun–late Sep daily; tours can be pre-booked on the website; admission charge) begin in a huge chamber with a central pillar of rock supporting a 30m (100ft) wide roof; in the centre is a model of the mines in a lake of brine, and around the perimeter are dioramas of the extraction process. A three-projector tape/slide presentation about three centuries of salt mining is shown (with headphone commentaries in English, French and German), followed by the train journey into the heart of the mine for a walk through some of the tunnels and such demonstrations as the flammability of methane gas. The tour lasts just over two hours. A pullover should be worn as the temperature is a constant 17°C (63°F). For the more adventurous, there are TrekkMine tours of the older galleries, lasting from 3½ to 5½ hours. There is also a restaurant at the mine.

The first section of Abt rack starts just beyond Bévieux station, the line heading into a gorge with sheer walls of rock on the other bank of the river. The fields in spring and summer are a mass of wildflowers, appearing days after the last crystals of snow have soaked into the ground so that residual tongues of melting snow can be surrounded by brilliant colours. The line twists so much that it is difficult to keep track of the compass, tunnels sometimes masking the passage from one valley to another.

Gryon is a small resort, principally of interest for winter sports but a good base for mountain walks, notably that to the ancient and isolated village of Taveyannaz. Besides its local slopes, Gryon is connected with the Villars ski runs. The lovely chalet-style station has a restaurant and café with a view that would be hard to beat.

Just before Gryon the railway joins the road to Villars and continues running alongside it all the way to the terminus. During the summer a bus leaves **La Barboleuse** (table 12.161) for the remote village of Solalex from where there is a path to Derborence for a postbus to Sion (table 12.332). Five minutes' walk from the station at La Barboleuse is a gondola to Les Chaux (table 2089), from which it is a short walk to Taveyannaz.

Villars is a major skiing resort with 120km (72 miles) of signed pistes, mostly for beginner to intermediate levels, served by 45 ski lifts, with 44km (27½ miles) of cross-country trails. The ski kindergarten here is excellent.

However, there is much to do in summer with riding, climbing, paragliding, tennis, ice skating, swimming and 300km (187 miles) of signed walks on offer. The main access to the upland walks or pistes is by the rack railway to Col-de-Bretaye (see below), and four minutes' walk from the station there is a gondola to Roc-d'Orsay (table 2090) from which you can walk to one of the area's principal viewpoints at Le Chamossaire at 2,113m (6,932ft).

BEX
Where to stay
⌂ **Hotel Le Cèdre****** Av de la Gare 24, CH-1880; ☏ 024 463 01 11; e cedre@hotel-cedre.ch; www.hotel-cedre.ch

GRYON
Tourist information
ℹ Pl de la Barboleuse, CH-1882; ☏ 024 498 00 00; e information@gryon.ch; www.villars.ch; ⏱ 08.15–18.00 Mon–Sat, 09.00–18.00 Sun

Where to stay
⌂ **Le Bois-Gentil** CH-1882; ☏ 024 498 11 37

VILLARS
Tourist information
ℹ Rue Centrale, CH-1884; ☏ 024 495 32 32; e information@villars.ch; www.villars.ch; ⏱ 08.00–18.30 daily

Where to stay
Numerous hotels; close to the station are:
⌂ **Du Golf & Spa**** (H)** Rue Centrale, CH-1884; ☏ 024 496 38 38; e info@hoteldugolf.ch; www.hoteldugolf.ch
⌂ **Ecureuil *** (H)** Rue Centrale, CH-1884; ☏ 024 496 37 37; e ecureuil@bluewin.ch; www.hotel-ecureuil.ch

VILLARS–COL-DE-BRETAYE Table 128

This short line is a scenic delight at any season, though it is busiest in winter, ferrying skiers to the principal pistes near Villars. In summer you may see milk churns being loaded on to a wagon attached to the train, a sight long since vanished from most European railways. The Swiss Pass is not valid for the journey.

The climb starts from the end of the platform at Villars, which is adjacent to that for trains from Bex. Climbing through woods the train reaches **Col de Soud**, where the *auberge*/restaurant overlooks the valley. Shortly beyond is what must be one of the world's most majestically sited golf courses, though some may prefer to see it in winter when the clubhouse is concealed under a blanket of snow. It is so peaceful up here that in summer you may see a fox content to stand in a field as the train passes.

At the summit the train swings through a right angle to the terminus, unusually crossing over a ski lift on the approach. The walks from here are legion, and there is a lovely old chalet hotel beside one of the three small lakes for those who wish to make the most of them.

COL DE SOUD
Where to stay
⌂ **Auberge du Col de Soud** CH-1884; ☏024 495 26 40; e auberge@col-de-soud.ch; www.col-de-soud.ch. Peaceful hotel.

COL-DE-BRETAYE
Where to stay
⌂ **Hôtel du Lac Bretaye (H)** CH-1884; ☏024 495 21 92; www.bretaye.ch. Remote hotel in wonderful location, accessible only by train.

Sion–ST MAURICE–ST GINGOLPH Table 130

The usefulness of this line has been reduced by the replacement of some trains by buses.

The branch leaves the Geneva–Brig main line just north of St Maurice station and proceeds north along the west bank of the Rhône. For **Monthey** see table 126, page 286. At **Vouvry** the belltower of the 15th-century church stands near the Neo-classical Catholic church built in 1820; the older building has some original stained glass.

Unless approaching from the south, it is much easier to visit the Steam Park at **Bouveret** (see page 279) by steamer, since the pier is close to the park.

MARTIGNY–VALLORCINE–Chamonix–St Gervais Table 132

This international metre-gauge railway deserves to be better known as one of Switzerland's great mountain railways. The views along the valley of Le Trient are stupendous, and it provides access to numerous walks and to some of the best views of the highest mountain in the Alps, Mont Blanc. At one time all passengers had to change trains at the frontier stations, at either Le Châtelard-Frontière or Vallorcine, but today's trains work the whole length of the line. The service is marketed as the Mont-Blanc Express, and an excellent leaflet is available describing some of the best walks, sometimes using a combination of train and bus, including the Orsières/Le Châble lines which are operated by the same company. Sit on the left.

Trains for Vallorcine leave from a bay platform at the west end of Martigny station. For the first section the line parallels the main line to Geneva, passing the castle of Le Batiaz on the left, orchards and rows of poplars. At **Vernayaz**, where the main depot is on the right, a footpath bracketed out from the rock heads up the extraordinarily narrow defile of the Gorge du Trient down which the water boils in its rush to join the Rhône. The path leads up to the next station at Salvan (the descent is obviously easier). The line swings southwest, engages the Strub rack and climbs at an almost alarming gradient.

Twisting through tunnels and sheer rock cuttings, the line affords impressive views down the Rhône valley before reaching the summit of the climb and the end of the rack section before the pretty station at **Salvan**. Opposite the church

18

in Salvan is Le Musée Marconi (☉ *Jul–Aug 14.00–18.00 Fri–Sun*), devoted to the story of Marconi's experiments with the telegraph between Salvan and Les Marécottes in 1895.

Five minutes' walk from the station at **Les Marécottes** is an alpine zoo with most species of mammals in a generous natural setting; it also has a large natural swimming pool with nearby restaurant (☉ *09.00–19.30 daily*). Seven minutes' walk from the station is the gondola to La Creusaz (table 2140), from where there is a walk to Emaney and back down to Les Marécottes.

Trétien is a delightful village clinging to the mountainside, its roofs a marvellous mélange of stone. From here a footpath goes up the Gorges du Triège, a spiral staircase giving access to a spectacular waterfall and to three caves. Trétien is the start of the most spectacular part of the journey as the line is perched on a ledge with a sheer drop of 426m (1,400ft) to the valley floor. Its scale is made all the more breathtaking by the short tunnels from which the train emerges with no visible means of support.

From **Finhaut** you can either take a bus from the station (table 12.230) or walk to Lac d'Emosson (see below). On the opposite side of the Trient, hanging valleys can be seen descending from the peak of Pointe Ronde at 2,655m (8,711ft). Some of the railway's historic vehicles are kept in the tunnel before **Châtelard**. A funicular three minutes' walk from the station provides another way of reaching the Emosson dam (table 2143); the funicular was built by Swiss Federal Railways in 1920 to take materials up to build the Barberine dam, which generated electricity for the railways. The funicular is one of the most complicated in Switzerland because of the special devices needed to overcome the many curves, depressions and humps. However, the dam was itself submerged by the construction in 1967–75 of the huge Emosson dam.

The funicular to Château-d'Eau is a 12-minute journey. From there, an electric 60cm-gauge 'panoramic' train (occasionally steam-hauled) takes you on a ten-minute journey along the course of a steam railway that was built during construction of the Barberine dam. The views of the Mont Blanc range and the Gorges du Bouqui are magnificent. The Emosson-Minifunic then takes you up to La Gueulaz near the top of the dam, providing an impressive view of the curving dam wall. There is a restaurant here, and numerous walks, including a one-hour walk to the largest dinosaur footprints in Europe, which are on the path beside the shore of the lake to the old Emosson dam (Barrage de Vieux-Emosson). From La Gueulaz you can take the bus down to Finhaut (see above).

In the days before through trains, transfer to SNCF trains took place either at **Le Châtelard-Frontière** or amongst the lupins on the platform at **Vallorcine**, the two stations a contrast in appearance. From Le Châtelard, a bus returns to Martigny via Col-de-la-Forclaz (table 12.213), offering spectacular views and access to strenuous walks. The railway proceeds to Chamonix, where the CF Chamonix–Montenvers rack line climbs 5.4km (3½ miles) to the terrace over the Mer de Glace; this sinuous glacier is overlooked by the Grandes Jorasses at 4,206m (13,799ft). Beyond is Chamonix, and the journey's end at St Gervais-les-Bains-Le-Fayet. This large station offers connections with the standard gauge for trains to Annecy and Lyons, and with the Tramway du Mont-Blanc to Le Nid d'Aigle for spectacular views of Mont Blanc.

SALVAN
Tourist information
🛈 As for Les Marécottes

LES MARÉCOTTES
Tourist information
🛈 La Gare 1, CH-1923; 📞 027 761 31 01; e info@
marecottes.ch; www.marecottes.ch; ⊕ 08.15–
12.15 & 13.30–17.00 daily

Where to stay
⌂ **Aux Mille Etoiles** 9 Pl des Télécabines, CH-
1923; 📞 027 761 16 66; e info@mille-etoiles.ch;
www.mille-etoiles.ch

FINHAUT
Tourist information
🛈 **Responsable Maison du Tourisme** Pl de
la Gare 1, CH-1925; 📞 027 768 12 78; e info@
finhaut.ch; www.finhaut.ch; ⊕ 08.30–12.15 &
13.30–17.45 daily

Where to stay
⌂ **Beau-Sejour** (H)** CH-1925; 📞 027
768 11 01; e beausejour@bluewin.ch; www.
hotelbeausejour.ch

LE CHÂTELARD
Tourist information
🛈 As for Finhaut

Where to stay
⌂ **Suisse**** CH-1925; 📞 027 768 11 35;
e hotelsuisse@bluewin.ch

MARTIGNY–ORSIÈRES/LE CHÂBLE Table 133

These standard-gauge branches share the same line between the bay platform at the east end of Martigny station and the junction at Sembrancher. Since the branch to Orsières serves the larger community, trains are normally run through from Martigny while passengers for Le Châble have to change at Sembrancher. The ski resort of Verbier is reached by cable car or bus from Le Châble.

Leaving Martigny the River Drance is on the right as the train skirts the town to **Martigny-Bourg**, close to the Foundation Pierre Gianadda and the amphitheatre. As the train begins to climb, the valley bifurcates; the railway takes the right-hand valley but there are lovely views along the cliffs of the left-hand valley along which a road ascends the Col des Planches, served by a bus from Martigny station (table 12.215). Ten minutes' walk from **Bovernier** is the hamlet of Les Valettes, where a footpath can be taken to the Gorges du Durnand. This canyon of rock, through which a noisy torrent of water cascades over 14 waterfalls, was made accessible in 1877 by the construction of a gallery bracketed out from the rock. It takes about an hour to explore the gorge, either returning by a footpath or continuing up a steep road to Champex and its lake (see below).

The line criss-crosses the river to the junction at **Sembrancher**, where the village has some attractive stone houses and, overlooking the village to the south, the ruins of a 12th-century castle destroyed in 1575.

The **Orsières** line enters a tunnel and turns south up the Val d'Entremont to the attractive town. From the station a bus climbs up to Champex (table 12.271) where the resort is clustered round a smallish lake. A botanical alpine garden has been created with over 3,000 species, the foundation working with the universities of Geneva and Neuchâtel. Ten minutes' walk from the bus is the chairlift to La Breya (table 2150). This has the distinction of being the steepest chairlift in Switzerland, climbing at an angle of almost 45˚.

The branch from Sembrancher to Le Châble crosses the river and starts to climb steeply up a broad pleasant valley with snow-covered peaks ahead. **Le Châble** is the station for the ski resort of Verbier, reached by a gondola (table 2160) from a huge circular building adjacent to the station, which has a café/restaurant on the platform.

18

Buses leave from the station to Verbier (table 12.251), Bruson and Moay (table 12.252), and up the Val de Bagnes to a protected area that is closed in winter due to avalanches, but glorious in summer. At the end of the valley is the Mauvoisin dam, the tallest concave dam in Europe and second highest in the world.

The relatively new resort of Verbier has one of the largest skiing areas in Europe, with 400km (250 miles) of runs served by 100 lifts. It also boasts Europe's largest cable car, which can take 150 passengers up to Mont Fort at 3,000m (9,840ft), and it is a good base for walking in summer when accommodation is cheaper.

A high reputation has been gained by the festival of concerts and masterclasses held in the second half of July (*www.verbierfestival.com*). Verbier is promoting electric vehicles and there are free buses around the town all winter and during the Verbier Festival.

ORSIÈRES
Tourist information

☑ Rte de la Gare 34, CH-1937; ☎ 027 775 23 81; ℮ orsiere@v-sb.ch; www.st-bernard.ch; ⊕ 09.00–noon & 14.00–18.00 Mon–Fri, 09.00–noon Sat

Where to stay
A hotel adjacent to the station is:
🏠 **Terminus*** (H)** Pl de la Gare, CH-1937; ☎ 027 783 20 40; ℮ info@grosminus.ch; www.grosminus.ch

VERBIER
Tourist information

☑ Carrefour Centrale 2, CH-1936; ☎ 027 775 38 88; ℮ info@verbier.ch; www.verbier.ch; ⊕ 08.00–12.30 & 14.00–18.30 Mon–Fri, 08.30–19.00 Sat, 09.00–noon & 15.00–18.30 Sun

Where to stay
Numerous hotels; near the cableway from Le Châble is:
🏠 **De la Poste**** Rue de Médran 12, CH-1936; ☎ 027 771 66 81; ℮ hoteldelaposte@verbier.ch; www.hotelposteverbier.ch

THE GREAT ST BERNARD Bus table 12.211

A bus from Orsières station (starting at Martigny, table 12.211) continues along the Val d'Entremont and provides an international service to Italy over the Great St Bernard Pass, though most buses terminate at Bourg St-Bernard. It was through this valley that Napoleon's Army of Reserve passed on its epic crossing of the pass in 1800 at the beginning of the Marengo campaign against Austria. Stendhal was amongst the 40,000 men, who had to carry sufficient provisions to last from the army's supply base at Villeneuve near Montreux to the Aosta valley. However, the unexpectedly doughty defence by just 300 soldiers of Fort Bard, which commanded the road down the Aosta valley, threatened the whole campaign. Supplies could not be brought up because the army blocked the track through the pass, which was only 45cm (18in) wide in places. The fort finally surrendered, but Napoleon's difficulties suggest that the Gotthard would have been the better pass to have chosen.

Before the bus enters the tunnel under the pass, it stops at Bourg-St-Pierre where the tower of the Catholic church dates from around 1000 and there is an alpine garden. The concave wall of the Toules dam near Bourg-St-Pierre offers the adrenalin rush of a 'rap jump': standing on the edge of the drop, wearing harness and with a rope over a frame on the dam wall, you lean forward until you are horizontal and then pull yourself down the rope until you become heavier than it, your descent being braked by someone at the foot (*No Limits Canyon Company;* ☎ 027 395 45 45; *www.nolimitscanyon.ch*).

Further on, at the Col du Grand St Bernard, is the famous hospice where about 10 of the even more famous breed of dog can be seen at the kennels attached to the monastery and hospice. Introduced between 1660 and 1670, they were used by the monks to seek out lost travellers, saving hundreds of lives – 22m (72ft) of snow can fall over a winter. The Augustinian hospice is supposed to have been established in around 1050 by St Bernard, archdeacon of Aosta, but the buildings have been much altered and rebuilt over the centuries. The older buildings, which may be visited, contain a library, a chapel with great organ loft supported on barleytwist columns, and a room with a Broadwood piano presented by Edward VII in 1904. The museum tells the story of the pass, the hospice and the natural history of the surrounding area. The bus continues over the border to Aosta, a station on the line from Pré St-Didier to Turin.

There is a wonderful walk from the Col to the Fenetre de Ferret at 2,689m (8,882ft) before dropping down to Lac du Fenetre and Ferret for the postbus (table 12.272) down to Praz-de-Fort and Orsières.

Geneva–MARTIGNY–BRIG Table 100

This fast stretch of line along the Rhône valley serves some of Switzerland's most popular skiing resorts, reflected by the through TGV service with Paris on winter Saturdays. The broad valley itself alternates between fruit growing and industry, while the slopes are largely planted with grapes.

At the attractive village of **Saxon** the partly Romanesque chapel of St Maurice stands beneath the ruins of the castle. Shortly after Saxon the magnificent ruined walls of the castle at Saillon may be seen on a hill to the left. Regarded as one of the best-preserved 13th-century fortifications in Switzerland, it was partly built by Peter II of Savoy to the design of Chillon's architect, Pierre Meinier. Next to the Catholic church is a 13th-century priest's house.

Eight minutes' walk from **Riddes** is the cable car to Isérables (table 2173), a fascinating village perched on a ledge of rock 610m (2,000ft) above the valley. Below the village are some venerable wooden granaries. A bus (table 12.392) also takes a serpentine road from the station to the gondola at La Tzoumaz to Savoleyres (table 2171). From there another gondola descends to Les Creux (table 2170) which is 20 minutes' walk from Verbier. There is also an easy 5½-hour walk from Mayens-de-Riddes (where food is available) following the course of the ancient Saxon *Bisse* through Boveresse to Col des Planches, from where there is a bus to Martigny (table 12.215).

The station named **Chamoson** is some way from the village of that name but close to St-Pierre-de-Clages, where the eponymous church is one of the most highly regarded Romanesque buildings in the Valais. Thought to have been built in the early 12th century, the triple-apsed church had an octagonal tower added over the crossing later in the century. Remains of another castle built by Peter II of Savoy can be seen at Conthey (station **Châteauneuf-Conthey**).

It would be quite wrong to judge **Sion** by the view from the railway: apart from the castles on top of the two hills that overlook the town, Sion looks a bland, modern town. In fact, the main town of the Valais has a historic centre and much of interest to visitors. Evidence of a settlement here dates back to 3500BC, but it was the choice of Sion as the political and ecclesiastical capital of the Valais in the 6th century that created the status it still enjoys.

To reach the tourist office, proceed directly ahead from the station along Av de la Gare, and the office is on the right in Place de la Planta. As the town map reveals, the principal places of interest are close together and easily visited on foot. The furthest away are the two castles, Tourbillon to the north, Valère to the south. The latter is the older and more extensive group of buildings, the castle dating from at least the early 10th century and the Romano-Gothic collegiate church of Notre-Dame from the 12th to 13th centuries. The church contains fine 12th-century carved capitals, a 13th-century rood screen, decorative choir-stalls of 1662–64 and some remarkably well-preserved, gruesome early 15th-century wall-paintings, one depicting the martyrdom of St Sebastian. The pulpit-like structure jutting out from the rear wall is claimed to be the oldest playable organ in the world, dating from the late 14th century and used for occasional concerts. Its restoration in the early 1950s was begun by an English music teacher from Eton, and it is played on Saturdays in July and August at 16.00. A guided tour is the only way to see the church following vandalism of a 15th-century wall-painting.

In Château de Valère is the **Cantonal Museum of History and Ethnography** (⊕ *Jun–Sep 10.00–18.00 daily; Oct–May 10.00–17.00 Tue–Sun; admission charge*), which has some rare medieval chests and sculptures as well as a good collection of arms and armour.

Tourbillon Castle was built c1294 and frequently rebuilt or altered until 1788 when it was ruined by fire, which destroyed most of the castle but left the walls. It is quite a steep climb to the castle (⊕ *mid-Mar–Apr, Oct–mid-Nov 11.00–17.00 daily; May–Sep 10.00–18.00 daily; admission charge*) but the view from the hill towards Brig is impressive.

Returning to the old town via Rue des Châteaux, you pass on the right the **Cantonal Art Museum** (*Musée Cantonal des Beaux-Arts; Place de la Majorie 19;* ⊕ *Jun–Sep 11.00–18.00 Tue–Sun; Oct–May 11.00–17.00 Tue–Sun; admission charge*), which is housed in a 16th-century episcopal building and concentrates on work by Valaisian artists from the Middle Ages. On the corner with Rue du Grand-Pont is the Hôtel de Ville (1657–65) in which is displayed one of the oldest Christian inscriptions, and the oldest in Switzerland, dating from 377. Outside is an astronomical clock (1667) and decorative downpipes at the corners.

Nearby, in Rue de Conthey, is **Maison Supersaxo** (⊕ *08.00–noon & 14.00–18.00 Mon–Fri*), built between 1503 and 1505 for a local potentate. A Gothic staircase leads to its chief feature, the lavishly decorated ceiling of a second-floor hall.

A little to the north is the **Cathedral Notre-Dame-du-Glarier**, a largely 15th-century building incorporating a 12th-century belltower, and close by the Catholic church of St Théodule. This early 16th-century building in the Flamboyant style was built on much older foundations and has good vaulting in the choir and carved angels at the foot of the pillars of the triumphal arch. Curiously all the glass is modern.

To the northwest of these churches is the last remnant of the town's 12th-century fortifications, the Tour des Sorciers. Round the corner from it, at the north end of Avenue de la Gare (no. 42), is the **Natural History Museum** (⊕ *Jun–Sep 13.00–18.00; Oct–May 13.00–17.00 Tue–Sun; admission charge*), which focuses on the flora and fauna of the Alps.

Sion boasts the largest postal bus station in Switzerland, reflecting the number of side valleys that join the Rhône valley, and can be reached by bus from the station. Amongst the services are ones to the Sanetsch See over the Col du Sanetsch at 2,251m (7,385ft) (table 12.344); Dixence (table 12.373), where the world's tallest dam towers 284m (932ft) above the valley floor and requires a cable car to take visitors to the Lac-des-Dix (table 2190); the remote valley of Derborence (table 12.332), from where there is a path over the Pas de Cheville to Solalex for a bus to La Barboleuse (see tables 127/129); the major ski, hiking and biking resort of Nendaz (table 12.362); and buses to a string of delightful villages in Val d'Hérens (tables 12.381/2/3), including the larch-wooded resort of Arolla, passing through the extraordinary pyramids of rock at Euseigne, and the villages of Evolène and Les Haudères, which are both part of the Inventory of Swiss Heritage Sites.

Characteristic of many of these valleys are the *Bisses*, watercourses built for irrigation as long ago as the 13th century, which offer some of the best and most level walks in the region with plenty of diverting things for children. The walking on offer in the region is astonishing: there are 7,000km (4,375 miles) of signed paths.

Finally, an excursion to the east from Sion that should not be missed: the lake of St Léonard, which was discovered as recently as 1943. The station that once served the village has been closed but a bus (table 12.411) from Sion station goes to the largest underground lake in Europe, on which rowing boats are used to explore the illuminated chambers (⊕ *mid-Mar–Oct 09.00–17.00 daily; www.lac-souterrain. com; admission charge*). Wear warm clothing.

Continuing east along the valley, with the Rhône close to the railway on the right, the line reaches **Sierre**, which is said to enjoy more hours of sun than any other Swiss town. Smaller than Sion, the town has some buildings of note and the tourist office has a leaflet, *Promenade des Châteaux*. They include the 16th-century Château des Vidames with a massive square tower, and the 13th-century Tour de Goubing in a vineyard southeast of the town. Off Avenue du Château is the 15th-century Church of Notre-Dame-des-Marais with 16th-century frescoes.

In the northeast of the town, reached by Rue du Manoir, is Château de Villa, which forms one part of the Valaisian Wine Museum (⊕ *Mar–Nov 14.00–17.00 Tue–Sun; Rue Ste Catherine 6; www.museevalaisanduvin.ch; admission charge*). The exhibition features wine presses, the cellar, and the social aspects of wine; it is linked to the other part in the well-preserved village of Salgesch by a Wine Path. This meanders through vineyards with 45 explanatory panels about viticulture and its associated buildings. The walk takes about two hours.

To the left of the station, seven minutes' walk away, is the lower station of a two-stage funicular that has the distinction of being the longest single haulage cable of any funicular in Switzerland, from Sierre–Montana Gare (table 2225). The first section has 1½ miles of moving cable, and the two stages lift passengers up a vertical height of 930m (3,054ft) to the modern winter and summer sports resort of Montana. It spreads inseparably along the mountain side to Crans, the two places being marketed as Crans Montana and projected openly as an 'upmarket' resort. Its stature as a winter sports centre was confirmed by hosting various world ski championships. It has the usual broad range of sports facilities, but is especially proud of its three golf courses.

Buses run from Sierre station to **Crans Montana** and from the top of the funicular to Crans and a host of neighbouring villages (tables 12.353 and 12.421/2). There are some particularly spectacular gondola and cable car journeys from Crans Montana, for example to Glacier de la Plaine-Morte (table 2231) and Cry-d'Er (tables 2221 and 2227). In Crans is a model railway museum with a collection of over 1,300 historic railway items from tinplate to the present, and six different layouts (⊕ *10.00–13.00, 15.00–19.00 daily; www.trains-miniatures.ch*).

Buses serving the south side of the Rhône valley include the lake at Moiry (table 12.452) and the long Val d'Anniviers through eight picturesque villages to Zinal (table 12.453). From Zinal a cable car ascends to Sorebois (table 2203). A six-day walking package through the valley is available in pre-arranged hotels with luggage transferred between them.

Leaving Sierre the railway parallels the Wine Path to **Salgesch**, where the Wine Museum is situated in the attractive Zumofen House (⊕ *Mar–Nov 14.00–17.00 Tue–Sun*), focusing on viticulture rather than wine. This district reputedly produces the best Swiss reds, which is thought to have been one reason why the Knights of St John established a hospice here in the 13th century. The village of Salgesch is a pleasure to explore on foot, being full of historic timber buildings.

Between Sierre and Leuk the railway used to negotiate a section of the Rhône valley engulfed by massive landslides. Since November 2004, the section has been in a tunnel on a new alignment away from the river. The undulating topography has helped to keep the area in a state of relative wildness, and the Bois de Finges is now regarded as one of the most important pine forests in Europe. A path through it has been created by the Swiss League for the Protection of Nature.

Around **Leuk** (or **Loèche**) the language changes to German, marking the former border between the Burgundians and the Alemanni. The town is some way from the station, but there is a good bus service between the two (table 12.472). The town has some remarkably fine buildings, on some of which the town's symbol of a dragon carrying a sword may be seen. The square-towered Bishop's Palace is a much-altered 15th-century building that houses a local history and folk museum (⊕ *Jul–mid-Sep 14.00–16.00 Sat*). The tower is now crowned by a dome designed by Mario Botta. Another massive tower, with corner turrets, is the Rathaus, formerly the Château des Vidames, which was founded c1254 and last rebuilt between 1541 and 1543.

The Ringackerkapelle is regarded as one of the canton's most outstanding Baroque buildings. Constructed between 1690 and 1694, it has a most unusual arcaded porch that belies the building's role as a church. Inside are lavish stucco decoration, an imposing high altar and a Baroque organ. The Catholic church of St Stéphane was built in around 1497 incorporating a fine 12th-century Romanesque belltower.

Buses from Leuk station serve the popular spa and sports resort of **Leukerbad** (table 12.471) in a glorious position within a horseshoe of mountains. A branch line once ran to Leukerbad from Leuk, but this closed in 1967 and the station is now an arts centre. It has 65 springs delivering 3.9 million litres of water a day which has taken 40 years to percolate through the ground after falling as rain. Leukerbad offers an impressive variety of baths and pools, and the Swiss Olympic Medical Centre is located here. Some pipes of hot spring water have been cleverly channelled under the road to keep the street near the church free of snow, and it is perfectly normal to see people walking the streets in dressing gowns between hotel and one of the spas. Mark Twain described the sight of valetudinarians in the baths here, submersed for hours up to their chins and occupied by floating trays of coffee, books and chessboards. (There is a picture depicting such scenes in the museum at Valère Castle in Sion.)

Around Leukerbad are 300km (187½ miles) of signed walks, 14 ski lifts and two cable cars, to Gemmipass (table 2240) and Rinderhütte (table 2242). But the walk up to the Gemmipass should not be missed: this extraordinary zig-zag track up an almost sheer wall of rock was built in the 18th century as a trading route by the Austrians, and any time under two hours is considered 'acceptable'. The upper station of the Gemmipass lift is close to the small lake of Daubensee which is an easy walk.

Beside the Wildstrübel restaurant at the summit is a new viewing platform jutting out over the immense drop; its open metal floor sometimes enables you to experience the powerful updraft of air against the mountain. For those who want to spend more time on the Gemmi and Dauberhorn, there is a via ferrata classified as 'extremely difficult' and a new shorter adventure via ferrata.

Along the Gemmi Pass is Berghotel Schwarenbach, which inspired Maupassant's short story 'L'Auberge'. The path continues to Sunnbüel, the upper station of a cable car from Kandersteg (table 2412).

Continuing east from Leuk, the line crosses the duck-egg blue Rhône, remaining on the south bank of the river all the way to Brig. The next station, **Turtmann**, is five minutes' walk from the cable car to Oberems (table 2246) from where there is a walk up Turtmanntal to Meiden and the glacier of the same name. From **Gampel-Steg** it is a 15-minute walk to the cable car to Jeizinen (table 2247).

Looking up to the left the south ramp of the Bern–Lötschberg–Simplon Railway (BLS) can be seen beginning its descent to Brig. In the graveyard beside the 16th-century Catholic parish church of St Romanus at **Raron** is buried the Austrian poet Rainer Maria Rilke, who spent the last five years of his life in the Valais in a medieval-looking tower at Muzot. He died in 1926. The church is in a spectacular hill-top position next to the 12th-century tower that was once the seat of the lords of Raron. In the nave of the church is an early 16th-century painting of the Last Judgement.

Less than ten minutes' walk from Raron station are the cable cars to Eischoll (table 2250) and Unterbäch (table 2253) in the Augstbord region; the latter is an excellent centre for walking with 500km (312½ miles) of hiking trails and for mountain biking with 60km (37½ miles) of trails.

At **Visp** the metre-gauge Matterhorn Gotthard Bahn (MGB) curves in from the south to run parallel with the standard gauge to Brig. The station was rebuilt for the opening of the Lötschberg Base Tunnel in 2007 when it became the major interchange between the MGB and the main line.

Between 1250 and 1365 Visp was under Italian control, but there are only two buildings from that time: the much rebuilt Catholic church of Heiligen Drei Könige ('The Three Wise Men') with Romanesque belltower and the square tower of the Lochmatterturm. The area around this and the Catholic church of St Martin has some attractive 14th–16th-century houses.

Brig has been an important road junction for centuries, and its history is inseparable from its location at the upper end of the main Rhône valley and at the junction of the roads over the Furka and Simplon passes. Even the town's most imposing building was financed from the profits of trade: the Stockalper Palace was built in 1658–78 by Kaspar von Stockalper, by all accounts an arrogant and autocratic man who so alienated the people of Brig that he was forced to leave the town and seek refuge in Italy. Much of his money came from salt, but also from a trade in mercenaries, especially with France.

Nonetheless the building he left behind is the most important Baroque palace in Switzerland and was the country's largest private residence. The palace takes the form of two- and three-storey arcades of different heights arranged around a courtyard, which is overlooked by three tall square towers crowned by bulbous gilded onion domes. The tallest is nine storeys high, and they are said to recall the three wise men. The living quarters are arranged on four floors with two levels of cellars beneath. The palace is connected to a rebuilt 16th-century house put up by an ancestor, Peter Stockalper. Various rooms including the chapel are open to visitors, there is a local museum on an upper floor and a horse-drawn postbus from the Grimselpass route in the courtyard (⊕ *the courtyard and garden are always open; the castle by guided tour only, May–Oct 09.30, 10.30, 13.30, 14.30, 15.30 & 16.30 Tue–Sun; admission charge*).

It is worthwhile to wonder through the attractive alleyways and pedestrianised streets of the old part of Brig. Much of the town had to be restored in 1993 following a devastating flood after which people could walk on compacted mud at first-floor level. The town is well endowed with churches, the most notable being the 17th-century Catholic collegiate church of Spiritus Sanctus on Simplonstrasse and the Chapel of St Sebastian (1636–37) in the eponymous central square. Also in the square is a statue and fountain in memory of the Peruvian pilot Georges Chavez, who crashed and was killed after being the first person to fly over the Alps, in 1910.

It is worth taking the postbus over the Simplon Pass (table 12.631, see opposite) and returning to Brig by train from either Iselle or Domodóssola stations at which the bus stops (see opposite). Another bus route serves the region at the foot of the Aletsch glacier, starting from beneath the Jungfrau, as it curves southwest towards Belalp. The bus goes from Brig station through the historic village of Naters to Blatten bei Naters (table 12.624). From here a cable car ascends to Belalp (table 2325) for a fine view of the glacier. The first non-Swiss known to have visited Belalp was Ruskin, in 1844.

PRACTICALITIES Bicycle hire from Brig station.

SION
Tourist information
🛈 Pl de la Planta 2, CH-1950; ✆ 027 322 77 27; e info@siontourisme.ch; www.siontourisme.ch; ⏱ 09.00–12.30 & 13.30–18.00 Mon–Fri, 09.00–12.30 Sat; mid-Jul–mid-Aug 09.00–18.00 Mon–Fri, 09.00– 16.00 Sat; mid-Jun–Sep also 09.00–12.30 Sun

Where to stay
Numerous hotels; closest to the station are:
🏠 **Hotel du Rhône*** Rue du Scex 10, CH-1950; ✆ 027 322 82 91; e durhonesion@netplus.ch; www.durhonesion.ch
🏠 **Elite** Av du Midi 6, CH-1950; ✆ 027 322 03 27; e info@hotelelitesion.ch; www.hotelelitesion.ch

SIERRE
Tourist information
🛈 Pl de la Gare10, CH-3960; ✆ 027 455 85 35; e info@sierre-salgesch.ch; www.sierre-salgesch.ch; ⏱ 08.30–18.00 Mon–Fri, 09.00–17.00 Sat; 09.00–13.00 Sun

Where to stay
Numerous hotels; close to the station is:
🏠 **Terminus*** 1 Rue du Bourg, CH-3960; ✆ 027 455 13 51; e info@hotel-terminus.ch; www.hotel-terminus.ch. One of Switzerland's outstanding restaurants.

CRANS MONTANA
Tourist information
🛈 CH-3983; ✆ 027 485 04 04; e information@crans-montana.ch; www.crans-montana.ch;

⏱ Jul–Aug 08.30–18.00 Mon–Sat; Sep–Jun 10.00–noon & 14.00–17.30 Mon–Sat

SALGESCH
Where to stay
🏠 **Rhone*** Bahnhofstrasse 80, CH-3970; ✆ 027 455 18 38; e info@hotelrhone.ch; www.hotelrhone.ch

LEUK
Tourist information
🛈 Bahnhof 5, CH-3952; ✆ 027 473 10 94; e info@leuktourismus.ch; www.leuktourismus.ch

LEUKERBAD
Tourist information
i Rathaus, CH-3954; ☎ 027 472 71 71; e info@ leukerbad.ch; www.leukerbad.ch; ⊕ Jul–Oct & Dec–Apr 09.00–noon & 13.15–18.00 Mon–Fri, 09.00–18.00 Sat, 09.00–noon Sun; May–Jun & Nov 09.00–noon & 13.15–17.30 Mon–Sat

UNTERBÄCH
Tourist information
i Dorfplatz, CH-3944; ☎ 027 934 56 56; e info@ unterbaech.ch; www.unterbaech.ch; ⊕ 08.30– 11.00 Mon–Fri, 14.00–17.00 Mon, Thu & Fri

VISP
Tourist information
i Balfrinstrasse 3, CH-3930; ☎ 027 946 18 18; e info@visp.ch; www.vispinfo.ch; ⊕ 08.30–noon & 13.30–18.00 Mon–Fri; Jun–Aug, also 09.00– noon Sat

Where to stay
Hotel close to the station is:
🏠 **Visperhof*** *** Bahnhofstrasse 2, CH-3930; ☎ 027 948 38 00; e info@visperhof.ch; www. visperhof.ch

BRIG
Tourist information
i Bahnhofplatz 1, CH-3900; ☎ 027 921 60 30; e info@brig-belalp.ch; www.brig-belalp.ch; ⊕ 08.30–noon & 13.30–18.00 Mon–Fri; Jul–mid-Sep also 09.00–13.00 Sat

Where to stay
Numerous hotels; close to the station are:
🏠 **Europe Garni*** *** Viktoriastrasse 9, CH-3900; ☎ 028 923 13 21; e info@hotel-europe-brig.ch; www.hotel-europe-brig.ch
🏠 **Victoria*** (H)** Bahnhofstrasse 2, CH-3900; ☎ 027 923 15 03; e hotel_victoria@swissonline.ch; www.victoria-brig.ch

BRIG–DOMODÓSSOLA Table 145

Trains from western and northern Europe for Milan converge on Brig where the northern portal of the Simplon Tunnel is entered shortly after leaving the station. The first Simplon Tunnel was opened in June 1906, completing the Simplon Railway to Italy, and was followed by a second slightly longer bore in 1922. It was the longest railway tunnel in Europe (the Channel Tunnel apart), at 19.8km (12.55 miles) until the opening in 2007 of the Lötschberg Base Tunnel. All are easily eclipsed in the world listings by Japan's Siekan Tunnel at 53.85km (33.8 miles), which in turn will be overtaken by the Gotthard Base Tunnel, scheduled to open in December 2016, at 57km (35.6 miles). The Swiss/Italian frontier is about halfway through. Besides through passenger and freight trains, the tunnel handles car-carrying trains between Iselle di Trasquera and Brig. Bicycles are also carried on these shuttles.

At Domodóssola, connections are made with trains over the marvellous Centovalli line to Locarno (see table 620, page 331).

BRIG–DOMODÓSSOLA Bus table 12.631

One of the country's most impressive roads, enlarged in 1801–08 from a track by 30,000 labourers working to Napoleon's orders, though the current road takes a different route in many places. Besides the pass at 2,006m (6,581ft), the road negotiates the Gondo Gorge on the descent into Italy. It was after crossing the pass in 1646 that the

18

diarist and author John Evelyn nearly died in Brig, having been given the bed of the innkeeper's sick daughter and promptly contracting smallpox. During the 1810s, a former London–Dover mail coach was in use, still with its English route painted on the panels. Sit on the right.

The climb starts almost immediately to offer ever more impressive views over the Rhône valley and the dramatic rock formations that overlook the road. The old road built by Napoleon can be seen below; it makes a perfect route for cyclists. Small mountain villages can be seen as the bus approaches Rothwald, one of a number of places where the bus driver drops off and picks up a sack of mail. The road passes through a succession of avalanche shelters, which are camouflaged by grass on their roofs to minimise their intrusion on the landscape.

At the summit is the hospice begun in 1801 but not completed until 1831 by the canons of Great St Bernard. It replaced a hospice that dated from 1235. The Simplon eagle commemorates the mobilisation of the country in 1939–45, to defend Switzerland against attack by the Axis countries.

Hardly a house in Simplon Dorf is without geranium-filled window boxes. The descent through the narrow Gondo gorge is spectacular and very different in character from the northern ascent. Black striations on the rock look as though a giant has taken a tar brush to the defile.

The peaceful station at Iselle is a more pleasant place to wait for a train, and there is a good café and restaurant on the platform.

BRIG–ZERMATT Table 140

The western section of the Glacier Express route is operated by the Matterhorn Gotthard Bahn (MGB) and was constructed between 1886 and 1891 when the first steam train pulled into Zermatt station. During the 1880s, when it was possible to reach Zermatt only by mule track, the village received 12,000 visitors a year. In the first year of the railway, it received 33,695 people. The reason for its fame was, of course, the tragic first ascent of the Matterhorn by Edward Whymper in 1865, coupled with the magnificent views of the striking mountain that can be had from Zermatt. Of the 44km (27½ miles) between Brig and Zermatt, 7.7km (4¾ miles) are rack assisted, the steepest gradient being 1 in 8. Sit on the left.

The metre-gauge trains of the MGB parallel the main line to Geneva as far as **Visp** (see table 100, page 299) where they turn south to follow the River Vispa through a narrow, steep-sided valley with vines on the slopes.

Stalden-Saas has long been an important crossing point of the valley, testified by the graceful stone bridge that has for centuries carried travellers across the river. The village is situated at the confluence of the Matter Vispa and Saaser Vispa rivers, the latter flowing down the Saastal that leads up to the car-free resort of Saas-Fee. Above the railway are the highest vineyards in Europe.

Frequent buses leave from Stalden-Saas station (table 12.511) for a resort that some believe would have eclipsed Zermatt in fame had it not been for the Matterhorn. Saas-Fee lies in a glorious position at the foot of the highest mountain entirely within the Swiss frontier, the Dom at 4,545m (14,911ft) – the higher Dufourspitze is shared with Italy. Although the first hotels were built in the mid 19th century, the first road to Saas-Fee was built only in 1951, on condition that the village itself would remain traffic-free. Consequently it has a quality of air and an atmosphere of tranquillity that are unknown to many visitors and a distant memory to others. Luggage is transported by electric vehicles, and concern for the environment extends to other facets of tourism in Saas-Fee.

It has become a popular winter resort, offering 100km (62½ miles) of ski runs, winter hiking trails, cross-country runs, day and night toboggan runs and the usual range of all-weather sports facilities. The world's highest underground railway takes skiers to the Mittelallalin at 3,456m (11,339ft), where there is an Ice Pavilion explaining glaciers and their significance. The summit is famous for the world's highest revolving restaurant and the world's largest ice grotto. There are also five cable cars and gondolas from Saas-Fee (tables 2300–6). In summer 350km (219 miles) of paths are open for hikers and mountain bikers, and the height of Saas-Fee makes summer skiing possible – many national ski teams spend several weeks of the summer here.

The final part of the road up to Saas-Fee climbs from Saas Grund, the starting point for a bus up to the dam and lake of Mattmark (table 12.513). There are some marvellous walks from here, including one over the Monte Moro Pass from which you can take a cable car down to Macugnaga in Italy.

Another bus service running between Stalden and Saas takes the incredibly sinuous road to Moosalp (table 12.518), and the two-section cable car to Staldenried and Gspon (table 2270) provides excellent views along the Saastal and Mattertal.

Continuing south from Stalden-Saas, the train begins its journey up the Mattertal. The quality of the landscape and sheer size of the mountains that tower above the train soon explain the reason why the Glacier Express is one of Switzerland's most popular journeys. From **Kalpetran**, which has an attractive station building, a cable car ascends to Embd (table 2272) where the steeply sited village quarries green quartzite roofing slates and pavement slabs. Ropeways lower 5,000 tonnes a year. From Embd another cable car continues to Schalb (table 2273) where there is a restaurant. From Kalpetran there is a walk of almost six hours to the Augstbordpass at 2,894m (9,495ft).

The railway continually alternates between riverbanks, waterfalls periodically drop to the Matter Vispa and the first scree slopes appear as the valley broadens out. From the station at **St Niklaus**, buses serve Gasenried (table 12.553) and Grächen (table 12.5520) where a gondola rises from this sun terrace to Hannigalp (table 2275).

On the left you may glimpse a small barn elevated by staddle stones to deter nibbling mammals, and a modern chalet with a huge mural of St Niklaus. The sound of cow bells may be heard beyond **Herbriggen**, where, on the right, you may see the vast hole in the flank of rock that descends from the Brunegghorn; here, in 1991, part of the mountain collapsed, necessitating construction of a new alignment for the railway and road.

Randa is a village rich in mountaineering traditions and the starting point for several ascents. The vulnerability of this part of the valley is reflected in the number of times that Randa has been damaged by glacial slides. The valley broadens again before the village of **Täsch**, beyond which access by motor vehicles is severely restricted as part of the necessity of making Zermatt a car-free resort. The huge area of car and coach parking is not a pretty sight.

A shuttle service operates between Täsch and Zermatt, supplementing the through trains from Brig. This section through the narrow Nikolai valley is the most vulnerable to avalanches – hence the numerous shelters over the line.

Journey's end at **Zermatt** is in a large modern station fronting on to a square in which the tourist office is situated, on the right. It contains an illustrated accommodation board that displays the availability of rooms and enables you to make immediate bookings.

The reason why Zermatt now has 115 hotels with over 7,000 beds goes back to 1865, when the rivalry between British and Italian climbers to be the first to plant their national flag on the summit of the Matterhorn was finally ended by Whymper's successful climb. Human nature being what it is, his achievement would probably not have received the same publicity had four of his party not plunged to their deaths on the descent. The controversy that surrounded the fatalities kept the name of Zermatt in the news, and tourists from all over the world came to see the scene of the tragedy and the objective of the fateful climb. Amongst them was Thomas Hardy who came in 1887 and wrote a sonnet about Whymper entitled *To the Matterhorn*.

One may speculate on whether an Italian village would have become as popular as Zermatt had the Italian climber J A Carrel beaten Whymper to the summit. But Zermatt's appeal lies not only in its historical associations and tradition, but of course its location. Tourism had begun in 1820, and the first inn opened in 1838. As Baedeker put it, with admissible hyperbole: 'In no other locality is the traveller so completely admitted into the heart of the alpine world, the very sanctuary of the "Spirit of the Alps". The views of the Matterhorn from Zermatt itself are splendid enough, but a network of mountain railways and cable cars allows an exceptional choice of viewpoint.

As for the town itself, it has retained a surprising number of unspoilt buildings and in places still retains the character of an alpine village – no mean achievement given its long history of mass tourism. It is consequently a real pleasure to explore on foot, quite unlike some modern resorts that offer little but the bland trappings of tourist retailing. Anyone interested in the story of the climbers and the objects of their endeavours should not miss the fascinating Matterhorn Museum (*Kirchplatz 11*; ☉ *Jul–Sep 11.00–18.00 daily; 1 week after Easter–Jun, Oct 14.00–18.00 daily; mid-Dec–1 week after Easter 15.00–19.00 daily; admission charge*), which uses a sunken village with reconstructed spaces and rooms to convey the story of the mountain's origin and history as well as varied memorabilia collected by the Seiler family (famous hoteliers), as well as displays on natural history, geology and social history. The toll taken by local mountains is obvious from the memorials in St Peter's English church, which was consecrated by the suffragen bishop of Dover in 1871 and still has Sunday services. It's just off the main street behind the Snow and Alpine Centre. Among the countless climbers who came here was Winston Churchill, who climbed Monte Rosa in 1894.

Zermatt's narrow streets and the sheer number of visitors make it immediately apparent why motor vehicles had to be excluded from the town. It inevitably adds to the pleasure of walking around the town, the only 'threat' being from the electric vehicles that ferry luggage between station and hotels. Towards the arrival time of trains, the square outside the station is lined with these vehicles, slightly smaller than British milkfloats, which each serve a particular hotel. The drivers wear identifying caps, and load the luggage on to the back platform while passengers seat themselves in the cab. The five-star hotels Mont Cervin and Zermatterhof have horse-drawn open carriages, which are lavishly decorated with flowers for newly married couples.

The area is famous for the length of the skiing season, having the largest all-year skiing area in the Alps. In winter there are 350km (219 miles) of runs for all degrees of skill, served by an exceptional winter network of 54 mountain railways and cableways of various kinds (23 in summer). A kindergarten is available. In summer there are 400km (250 miles) of walking routes, and sports facilities in abundance.

The network of transport up the adjacent slopes is impressive. In addition to the Gornergratbahn, there is an underground railway called the Sunneggabahn which opened in 1980; it is followed by a cable car to Blauherd and a gondola to reach the Rothorn (all covered by table 2290). Others climb from Zermatt to Schwarzsee and Trockener Steg (table 2280), from Furi to Trockener Steg and on to Klein Matterhorn (tables 2285/6), the second part being the highest-altitude cableway in Europe, at 3,818m (12,526ft).

SAAS-FEE
Tourist information
▮ Obere Dorfstrasse 2, CH-3906; ☎027 958 18 58; e to@saas-fee.ch; www.saas-fee.ch; ◷ 08.30–noon & 14.00–18.00 Mon–Fri, 08.00–noon Sat, 09.00–noon Sun

TÄSCH
Tourist information
▮ CH-3929; ☎027 967 16 89; e taesch@zermatt.ch; www.zermatt.ch; ◷ 08.00–noon & 13.30–18.00 Mon–Fri; mid-Jun–Sep & mid-Oct–mid-Apr, also 08.00–noon & 13.30–18.00 Sat

ZERMATT
Tourist information
▮ Bahnofplatz 5, CH-3920; ☎027 966 81 00; e info@zermatt.ch; www.zermatt.ch; ◷ mid-Apr–mid-Jun, Oct–mid-Dec 08.30–noon & 13.30–18.00 Mon–Sat, 09.30–noon & 16.00–18.00 Sun; mid-Dec–mid-Apr 08.30–noon & 13.30–18.00 Mon–Fri, 08.30–18.00 Sat, 09.30–noon & 16.00–18.00 Sun; mid-Jun–Sep 08.30–18.00 daily

Where to stay
Hotels close to the station are:
⌂ **Schweizerhof****** Bahnhofstrasse 5, CH-3920; ☎027 966 00 00; e schh.reservation@seilerhotels.ch; www.seilerhotels.ch/schweizerhof
⌂ **Gornergrat Dorf***** Bahnhofstrasse 1, CH-3920; ☎027 966 39 20; e info@gornergrat.com; www.gornergrat.com

Where to eat
For outstanding cuisine:
⌂ **Waldhotel Fletschhorn** H-3906; ☎027 957 21 31; e info@fletschhorn.ch; www.fletschhorn.ch

Where to stay
⌂ **Täscherhof***** Bahnhofstrasse, CH-3929; ☎028 966 62 62; e info@taescherhof.ch; www.taescherhof.ch

Hotels of character and interest are:
⌂ **Mont Cervin****** (H)** Bahnhofstrasse 31, CH-3920; ☎027 966 88 88; e mcp.reservation@seilerhotels.ch; www.seilerhotels.ch. Originally built in 1852.
⌂ **Zermatterhof****** (H)** Bahnhofstrasse 55, CH-3920; ☎027 966 66 00; e info@zermatterhof.ch; www.matterhorn-group.ch/zermatterhof/. Built in 1879.
⌂ **Monte Rosa***** (H)** Bahnhofstrasse 80, CH-3920; ☎027 966 03 33; e mr.reservation@seilerhotels.ch; www.monterosazermatt.ch. Built in 1855, Zermatt's 1st hotel & where Whymper stayed before his ascent of the Matterhorn.
A hotel with an exceptional restaurant is:
⌂ **Mont Mirabeau***** Unteremattenstrasse 12, CH-3920; ☎027 966 26 60; e info@hotel-mirabeau.ch; www.hotel-mirabeau.ch

ZERMATT–GORNERGRAT Table 139

The appeal of the Matterhorn (4,478m, 14,692ft) is such that it is no surprise that this remarkable metre-gauge railway was Switzerland's first electric rack and pinion line, opened in 1898 and climbing a vertical distance of 1,484m (4,868ft) in 9.4km (5.9 miles). There are five tunnels, five bridges and five viaducts, one of which is a particularly impressive structure – the Findelenbach, which is 50m (164ft) high. This is the most popular mountain railway in Switzerland, carrying up to 3.3 million people a year, but less busy after mid-afternoon. It is advisable to wear sunscreen on a bright day. The Swiss Pass obtains a 50% discount. Good views on both sides.

The station of the Gornergratbahn (GGB) in Zermatt is just to the east of the station. Trains quickly climb above the rooftops of the town and into spruce trees, huge drops opening up as the railway sails over mountain torrents with vast boulders beneath. The line twists up through tunnels and horseshoe curves, pausing at four intermediate stations, including **Riffelalp,** to serve several wonderfully positioned hotels. A 800mm gauge tramway built by Alexander Seiler served his isolated Riffelalp Hotel, because the local authorities would not sanction a road – an early instance of green local planning. From 1961, it lay derelict following a fire that destroyed the hotel, but the tramcars survived and were stored in Zermatt. With the opening of a new hotel at Riffelalp, it was briefly replaced by a tiny caterpillar dray, but in 2001 a new 800mm-gauge electric tram was opened to transport guests, their luggage and supplies to the hotel.

Gornergrat is the highest open-air station in Europe, at 3,089m (10,125ft). The solidly built and crenellated building at the summit is close to the combined hotel and observatory, surrounded by balconies from which can be seen 19 of Switzerland's 47 peaks over 4,000m (13,123ft).

During the summer a weekly trip is operated to enable visitors to watch the sun rise from Gornergrat. Breakfast is available at the hotel.

RIFFELALP
Where to stay

⌂ **Riffelalp******* CH-3920; ☏ 027 966 05 55; e reservation@riffelalp.com; www.riffelalp.com. Opened in 1884, but the original hotel tragically burnt down during restoration. New hotel in traditonal style.

⌂ **Riffelberg*** (H)** CH-3920; ☏ 027 966 65 00; e riffelberg@zermatt.ch; www.riffleberg.ch. First opened in 1854 & since extended.

GORNERGRAT
Where to stay

⌂ **Kulmhotel Gornergrat**** CH-3920; ☏ 027 966 64 00; e gornergrat.kulm@zermatt.ch; www.gornergrat-kulm.ch. The highest hotel in the Alps.

BRIG–ANDERMATT Table 142

This section of the Glacier Express continues up the Rhône Valley into the eastern part of the Upper Valais known as the Goms, with the first spiral tunnel of the journey. Opened as late as 1926, it was originally operated by the Furka-Oberalp-Bahn (FO), taking its name from the Furka and Oberalp passes which the railway has either to cross or tunnel under. The FO amalgamated with the Brig–Visp–Zermatt Railway in 2003 to form the Matterhorn Gotthard Bahn. All the way to the Furka Tunnel, the railway forges up a broad, steep-sided valley with numerous side valleys that afford excuses to break the journey at almost every station. The river is a constant companion on the south side of the line. Along the ridge to the north of the railway is the lovely Arolla pine forest of Aletsch, which offers fine walking. Some of the villages are also small ski resorts. It is also on this section that lunch is served on eastbound trains. To have the pleasure of eating in the 1925-built coach that was originally built for the Montreux–Oberland Bernois Railway, you will almost certainly have to join an excursion. It has beautiful walnut panelling, brass bottle-holders, hooks, lights and racks, and each section of roof is coved. Sit on the right.

Until December 2007, trains had to reverse at Brig but a new alignment along the south side of the River Rotten/Rhône created a through station. For Brig, see table 100, page 299.

The much-rebuilt medieval Catholic church at **Mörel** has 16th- and 17th-century wall-paintings, and a walk of one or three minutes from the station are two cable cars to the car-free resort of Riederalp (tables 2330 and 2331), where there is an alpine dairy and a small museum in an authentically furnished 17th-century chalet. Two chairlifts continue to Moosfluh (table 2333) and Hohfluh (table 2334).

Just before **Betten** the train crosses the Rhône by the Nussbaum Viaduct and then engages the first MGB rack section. Above the valley and reached by two cable car routes from Betten station (table 2337.1/2) is another car-free resort, Bettmeralp, forming with Riederalp Europe's largest pedestrian area. The district is also noted for its large number of days of sunshine. Bettmeralp is a good summer and winter sports resort, especially for those with children. The rack continues to **Grengiols** where the train crosses a 91m-high viaduct just before entering a spiral tunnel to gain height.

You emerge to a marvellous view looking down on Grengiols Viaduct and the confluence of the Rhône and Binna rivers, while the train continues on the rack as far as **Lax**, another good departure point for walks. To the right you can look up the Binntal, a lovely valley of particular interest for its terminal moraines left by the retreating Fiescher glacier. It can be reached by bus from the next station, at **Fiesch** (table 12.652). The buses stop at Ernen, regarded as one of the Valais's most beautiful villages with many 15th–18th-century houses and a sumptuously decorated and wonderfully sited Catholic church of 1510–18, which has a notable organ of 1679 on which recitals are given. The south front of the Tellenhaus of 1576 is decorated with the earliest known representation of the William Tell legend. The bus continues through a nature reserve (because of the outstanding flora) and a long tunnel to Binn, another delightful village with a small museum; it contains some fine crystals for which the area is renowned.

Five minutes' walk from Fiesch station is the cable car to Eggishorn (table 2343) from which there are outstanding views along the great Aletsch Glacier, Europe's longest at about 24km (15 miles). In contrast to the view of the glacier from Jungfraujoch, from here you get a much better idea of its immense size.

Leaving Fiesch another rack section climbs through the Fiesch forest to **Fürgangen-Bellwald** from where a cable car ascends to Bellwald (table 2345), a sports resort which claims to have protected itself from 'real estate madness'. The hamlets that make up Bellwald have no less than eight chapels, mostly from the 17th–18th centuries, and the village is at one end of the hiking trail along the Goms ridgeway that leads to Oberwald (see page 308). At the village of Mühlebach across the Rhône is one of the oldest wooden buildings in the Valais, which was the birthplace of Cardinal Matthäus Schiner, the bishop of Sion and Pope Julius II's military leader; he campaigned in Italy and became a familiar figure at European courts.

The valley now becomes broader still, with the village of Steinhaus to the right before the train reaches **Niederwald** and its closely packed, almost black chalets. This was the birthplace of the famous hotelier César Ritz (1850–1918), who managed the Savoy in London soon after it opened, then went on to build the Ritz in Paris and lend his name to the Ritz in London. Edward VII called him 'the hotelier of kings and king of hoteliers'. Ritz was but one of many people from the area who emigrated in the 19th century, a large proportion to the USA. The Catholic church of St Theodul has an elaborate Baroque interior, and the village has many attractive traditional buildings.

Altars and pulpit in the onion-domed Baroque Catholic church at **Reckingen** have the most vivid, varied colours one is likely to see in a church, fortunately set against largely plain white walls. It also has an ossuary with a gruesome skeleton decorated with glass medallions, and the village has some fine black barns, the oldest of which dates from the 17th century. The village once had a bell foundry, casting many of the bells that can still be heard in cantons Valais, Uri and Luzern, and there is a covered bridge across the river just beside the railway. **Münster** is another picturesque village with vernacular buildings as old as the 15th century. The mill's waterwheels may still be seen and some of the buildings are mounted on staddle stones. The white-painted Catholic church of St Maria has a Gothic altar of 1509 that is regarded as second in beauty only to that of Chur Cathedral in all Switzerland. It also has a fine ceiling and choir-stalls of 1670. The area offers river rafting and excellent opportunities for mountain biking.

The valley floor is now broad and flat, and you may see herds of goats on the track beside the railway. More dark-wood houses and barns can be seen at **Geschinen**. From **Ulrichen** station you can take one of the most impressive bus journeys in Switzerland (table 62.111), over the Nufenen Pass at 2,478m (8,129ft) to Airolo station at the south end of the Gotthard Tunnel in the Ticino. The bus starts in Andermatt and also calls at Oberwald station (see below).

The different appearance of the village at **Obergestein** is due to the fire that devastated it in 1868. Some of it was rebuilt in stone rather than the wood characteristic of Goms. **Oberwald** is the highest village in the Upper Valais, and one end of the Goms ridgeway path that extends all the way to Bellwald (see page 307) and the riverside path along the Rhône down to Ernen. There is also a notable cross-country skiing trail from here to Niederwald. The station is a stop on the spectacular bus route between Meiringen and Andermatt that takes in the Grimsel and Furka passes (table 31.161).

The passes crossed by the road beyond Oberwald open only in the summer months, so for eight months of the year the car-carrying trains through the Furka Base Tunnel are the only way to proceed east. The single-bore 15km (9½ miles) tunnel was opened in 1982 and was the longest metre-gauge tunnel in the world, with two passing places, until eclipsed by the Vereina Tunnel (see page 351). It avoids the notorious climbs up to the old Furka Tunnel, which were susceptible to avalanches and forced the railway to close in winter. Above the new tunnel are the headwaters of the Rhône, the boundary between Valais and Uri, and the intersection of old east–west and north–south trade routes, the Grimsel Pass leading north towards Meiringen.

The train emerges from the tunnel into a very different landscape, with few trees and fewer farms, and the hills covered with gorse. One could be in a Scottish glen. Soon after returning to daylight, the train passes **Realp**, the start of a steam-operated preserved railway over part of the old line to the Furka Tunnel and down to Gletsch (see table 615, page 310).

The young River Reuss appears on the left as the train bowls along the Urseren Valley, past the tiny hamlet of Zumdorf and across the Richleren bridge to the attractive village of **Hospental**, where the 12th-century tower of the Hospental family stands. Part of the village is not visible from the train, but it contains a large Baroque church of 1705–11 and the St Karl chapel of 1719.

Andermatt is an important railway junction, providing a connection with the Zürich–Milan main line at Göschenen where the main line enters the northern portal of the Gotthard Tunnel, the route of which lies directly underneath the MGB station at Andermatt.

The town is both a summer and winter resort, helped by a reputation for sun and clear air: with 500km (312 miles) of paths, it is an excellent centre for walking, and there is canoeing, hang-gliding, fishing and mountain biking, as well as the usual facilities for such sports as swimming and tennis; in winter 56km (35 miles) of ski runs are served by ten lifts, a chairlift to Nätschen (table 2596.1) and Stöckli (table 2596.2), and a cable car to the impressive viewpoint of Gemsstock (table 2597), at 2,961m (9,714ft). About 600 peaks can be seen from the mountain. In summer there is a path back to Andermatt from the Gemsstock, which takes about 5½ hours.

Andermatt's attractive arcaded Rathaus of 1767 incorporates part of an older building, and the town has a 17th-century Baroque Catholic parish church. On the southern outskirts of the town is the pilgrimage church of Maria-Hilf, built in 1739–42 and standing in a commanding position overlooking the town. From the chapel a path leads southeast to the Gurschenbach Falls. The Talmuseum (⊕ *16.00–18.00 Wed–Sat*) is one of the loveliest houses in the Ursern valley; it was built in 1786. The sound of small arms fire is periodically heard around Andermatt as the district is an army training centre – as is usually obvious by military movements on the railway and roads – and some areas are off-limits.

Andermatt offers some of the best postbus journeys in Switzerland. It is linked to Meiringen by the splendid bus journey over the Furka and Grimsel passes (table 31.161), affording magnificent views over the Rhône Glacier, which is at its best in early summer when the shoulders of the valley are bright with alpine flowers. To the south is a journey over the Gotthard Pass (see page 312).

For the next section of the Glacier Express, see table 920 on page 339.

PRACTICALITIES Bicycle hire from Fiesch, Oberwald and Andermatt stations.

FIESCH
Tourist information
ℹ Furkastrasse 44, CH-3984; ☎ 027 970 60 70; e info@fiesch.ch; www.fiesch.ch; ⊕ 08.30–noon & 13.30–17.30 Mon–Fri; mid-Dec–mid-Apr & Jul–mid-Oct also 09.00–16.00 Sat

Where to stay
⌂ **Des Alpes*** Furkastrasse, CH-3984; ☎ 027 971 15 06; e info@des-alpes.ch; www.des-alpes.ch

MÜNSTER
Tourist information
ℹ Furkastrasse 53, CH-3985; ☎ 027 974 68 68; e tourismus@obergoms.ch; www.obergoms.ch; ⊕ Jun–Oct, Dec–Mar 08.00–noon & 14.00–18.00, 09.00–17.00 Sat; Apr–May, Nov 09.00–noon, 14.00–18.00 Mon–Fri

Where to stay
⌂ **Croix d'Or & Poste*** (H) CH-3985; ☎ 027 974 15 15; e info@hotel-postmuenster.ch; www.hotel-postmuenster.ch. Goethe stayed here in Jun 1779.

REALP
Where to stay
⌂ **Hotel Post** CH-6491; ☎ 041 887 15 45; e mail@posthotel.ch; www.posthotel.ch

⌂ **Hotel-Pension Furka** CH-6491; ☎ 041 887 14 24; e infanger@pension-furka.ch; www.pension-furka.ch

ANDERMATT
Tourist information

ℹ️ Gotthardstrasse 2, CH-6490; ☎041 888 71 00;
✉ info@andermatt.ch; www.andermatt.ch;
🕐 09.00–noon & 14.00–17.30 Mon–Sat

Where to stay

Numerous hotels; closest to the station is:
🏠 **Badus**** Gotthardstrasse 25, CH-6490;
☎041 887 12 86; ✉ info@hotelbadus.ch; www.
hotelbadus.ch
A hotel in the town centre is:
🏠 **Activ Kronen***** Gotthardstrasse 64, CH-
6490; ☎041 887 00 88; ✉ info@kronenhotel.ch;
www.kronenhotel.ch

REALP–GLETSCH–OBERWALD Table 615

When the old section of line between Realp and Oberwald closed for the last time in October 1981, it seemed as though that would be the end of rail access to the Rhône Glacier. The reason for building the new Furka Base Tunnel was to end the seasonal availability of the line, which had had to be closed in the winter, and a particularly vulnerable bridge, the Steffenbach Bridge, dismantled until the threat of snow damage had passed in the spring.

However, a preservation society was formed, the Dampfbahn Furka Bergstrecke (DFB), which took over the line and commenced operations to Tiefenbach in July 1992, followed by reopening to Furka, the entrance to the tunnel, in July 1993. In July 2000 the section through the 2km-long tunnel and down to Gletsch was opened. The final stretch on to Oberwald, with its spiral tunnel, was reopened in 2011. The rack line is worked by four steam locomotives: two that were built for the line in 1913, sold to Vietnam when the FO was electrified, and repatriated in 1990; and two locomotives that were built for the Brig–Visp–Zermatt Railway. The railway (☎ 0848 000 144; www.furka-bergstrecke. ch) operates Friday–Sunday from mid-June to early October and daily from mid-July to mid-August; a one-way trip takes just over 2 hours. In bad weather services are reduced. Ideally sit on the left to the summit tunnel and then move to the right and back to the left from Gletsch to Oberwald – though trains are usually sold out.

The DFB station at Realp is a ten-minute walk from the FO station, following the road on the north side of the line that parallels the railway towards the new tunnel. Trains are made up of four-wheel coaches, one a more generously windowed bar coach. Some do not have lights so the passage through the tunnels is atmospheric for those close to the locomotive, the orange glow of the fire illuminating the swirling steam.

The scenery is truly spectacular, the railway forging up a desolate, steep-sided valley that is like a Scottish glen writ large when mist obscures the mountains that tower over the line to the north. The postbus route over the Furka Pass can be seen snaking its way round the contours hundreds of feet above the railway. The Furkereuss River keeps close company with the railway all the way to the summit, periodically tumbling over boulders beneath a sturdy bridge. There is a loop at **Tiefenbach** and trains take water there, enabling passengers to photograph the train. At the summit station, **Furka**, passengers can patronise the buffet, set into the hillside to protect it from snow.

The single-bore tunnel under the pass is 1,874m (6,148ft) long, and the line emerges at Muttbach station to begin the descent to **Gletsch**, offering a magnificent panorama over the Rhône Glacier to the right. Overlooking the glacier is the boarded-up Belvedere Hotel which featured, along with the still-electrified railway, in the 1964 James Bond film *Goldfinger*, with Goldfinger's yellow and black Rolls-Royce climbing past the hotel towards the Furka Pass. Near the station is the historic Glacier du Rhône Hotel, a huge building which once had stables for 250 horses.

Soon re-engaging the rack after leaving Gletsch, the line emerges from the 548m spiral tunnel to cross the Rhône and follow the western slope of the valley through forest where sprinklers have been installed to dampen any sparks from ascending trains. The western portal of the Base Tunnel comes into view as the train nears Oberwald, and the locomotive whistles for the level crossing and crosses over the MGB to the new terminus on the south side of the main line.

GLETSCH
Where to stay
⌂ **Glacier du Rhône** CH-3999; ☎027 973 15 15; e hotel@glacier-du-rhone.ch; www.   glacier-du-rhone.ch. A vast 1860-built hotel full of character.

ANDERMATT–GÖSCHENEN Table 142

This useful link between the Matterhorn Gotthard Bahn and the Zürich–Milan main line is also an extraordinary if short journey and worth doing just for the experience. The rack railway drops down the Schöllenen gorge past the famous Teufelbrücke (Devil's Bridge). Sit on the right.

Trains heading for Göschenen leave Andermatt in an easterly direction and immediately turn north to enter the exceptionally narrow and deep defile of the Schöllenen gorge in which there is only just room for the railway and road. The first path through the gorge was created by suspending planks from the valley sides. The construction of the bridge across the River Reuss that flows through the gorge was a crucial event in opening up north–south communications. Two successive old bridges can be seen on the right at the head of the gorge: the still-usable (by pedestrians and cyclists) 1830 bridge and below it the fragments of its 15th-century predecessor which was swept away. The falls near here sometimes send spray over the Devil's Bridge, so named because legend has it that the structure was built through a Mephistopholian pact whereby the devil would have the soul of the first to cross the bridge; the builder sent a goat. In 1799 the sound of the falls would probably have been drowned out by the clash of arms as Austrian and Russian troops under Suvarov fought two savage battles here against the French.

Although the railway clings to the west bank and is often protected by avalanche shelters, there are occasional long views down the gorge. However, the best way to appreciate the gorge is on foot or by bicycle. Another graceful stone arch can be seen over the river at the lower end of the Schöllenen, and just before Göschenen, the train twists over the river into the station with the northern portal of the Gotthard Tunnel on the right. For **Göschenen**, see table 600, page 198.

PRACTICALITIES Bicycle hire from Andermatt station.

OBERWALD–MEIRINGEN Bus table 31.161

The postbus journey over the Grimselpass is regarded as one of the most spectacular, requiring a double-decked postbus to meet demand. But it also serves a useful purpose in linking two east–west railways separated by the massif that parallels the northern flank of the Rhône. Sit on the left.

From Oberwald the bus climbs alongside the track of the old railway over the Furka Pass, which is gradually being reopened by a preservation society (see table 615, page 310). On the approach to Gletsch the spiral tunnel can be seen on the right. The bus winds its way through a seemingly endless succession of hairpin bends, its unique horn demanding the right of way as it takes up the full width of the road to negotiate the turn. At the summit the bus stops long enough for passengers to have a beverage in the summit café or hotel.

The air is so clean at this altitude that the rocks covering the hillsides of the descent are covered in pale green lichen. Two dammed lakes are passed before the bus negotiates a tunnel that once required a deviation.

GRIMSELPASSHÖHE
Where to stay
⌂ **Grimsel-Blick***** CH-3999; ☎ 027 973 11 77; e grimselblick@rhone.ch; www. grimselpasshoehe.ch

OBERWALD–AIROLO Bus table 62.111

A postbus journey to the south of Oberwald takes the route over the Nufenen Pass completed as recently as 1969. The broad valley sides on the northern side are covered in hardy bushes and rocks. The bus passes the Griesser reservoir on the right, beyond which is the Griespass, an old 'wine road' between Switzerland and Italy. The bus stops at the summit for refreshment in the café-restaurant, before the long, straight descent down the Val Bedretto to Airolo. A small force of French retreated this way and north over the Nufenen Pass in 1799 after being defeated by Suvarov's superior Russian army.

AIROLO–ANDERMATT Bus table 62.111

The Gotthard Pass is perhaps the most famous of the Swiss alpine passes and for centuries has been associated with hazardous and punishing travel. As long ago as 1402 Adam of Usk crossed the pass in an ox cart with eyes blindfolded. The coach road was built in 1819–30, heralding the era of epic postbus journeys, replaced by postal sleighs when conditions were so bad that coaches could not get through. The importance of the road diminished when the rail tunnel was opened in 1882.

The climb out of Airolo begins immediately, the old road twisting its way upwards to the east as the newer and less sinuous new route uses tunnels and shelters to gain height with fewer bends.

At the 2,108m (6,916ft) summit is a group of buildings of mostly 19th-century origin that derive from the first use of the pass in the 13th century. A hospice and chapel were built by Capuchin fathers who assisted travellers until 1799. One of the buildings houses the National St-Gotthard Museum (☎ *091 869 15 25; www. museen-uri.ch;* ⊕ *Jun–Oct 09.00–18.00*), which vividly portrays the history of the pass, its geographic significance and the hard life of those who provided transport over it. An excellent guidebook and history of the Gotthard in English is available. For bus tickets or bookings (advisable in high season), apply at the tourist office.

Although this postbus journey parallels the old route of the Matterhorn Gotthard Bahn, now reopened to Gletsch, the views offered by the higher road are different enough to justify the experience of both.

The ascent to the Furka Pass affords good views over the railway and the very Scottish character of the scenery in the valley of the Furkareuss. Near the summit is the massively built, traditional Hotel Belvedere. To the right is the Rhône Glacier, one of the most photographed of glaciers, though it has shrunk considerably since it was first recorded on glass plates. The road follows the railway down to Gletsch, an intermediate station of the DFB (see page 310), to Oberwald station.

18

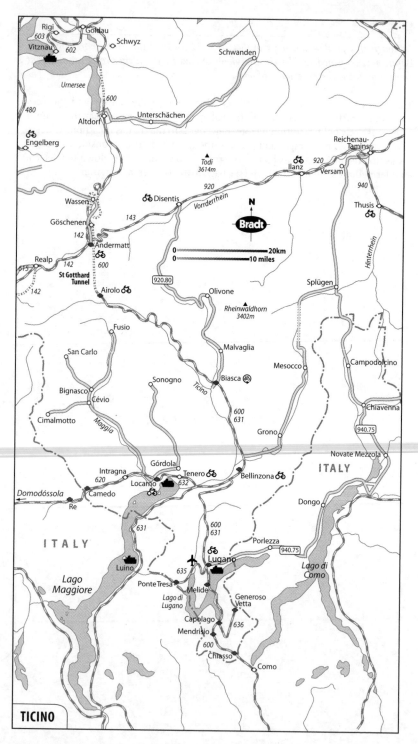

19

Ticino

The only Swiss canton to lie wholly on the southern side of the Alps, Ticino was the result of a consistent policy by the Confederation to incorporate the area south of the great trade route across the mountains. The canton became part of the Confederation in 1803 and is the fourth largest. It is noted for the extraordinary variety of its flora and fauna which inevitably reflect the exceptional difference in altitude between the lowest and highest parts – from just under 200m (656ft) to over 3,400m (11,155ft).

AIROLO—LUGANO Tables 600/631

The southern section of the Gotthard main line is one of the busiest arteries in Europe, handling over 120 passenger and freight trains a day in each direction. As the Alpine Museum in Bern puts it, 'since the opening of the Gotthard motorway in 1980, the magical word "Gotthard" has lost its lustre. It has become a synonym for transit and queues, and arouses feelings of anger and loss'. The unobtrusive railway remains a marvel of engineering, but the view of stark concrete road viaducts from the train window is a sad reminder of misplaced priorities. The pollution caused by the motorway was one of the reasons behind the referendum vote in favour of building new railway tunnels through the Alps to rid the country of transit lorries.

The Gotthard Tunnel crosses the boundary between the cantons of Uri and Ticino and marks the transition between the German- and Italian-speaking parts of the country. Trains emerge from the tunnel at the station of **Airolo**, the highest on the Swiss Federal Railways' network, at 1,142m (3,747ft). The town grew up as a staging post for packhorse trains, waggons and coaches crossing the perilous Gotthard Pass. The town was almost totally destroyed by fire in 1877, while tunnelling work was in progress, and was devastated by a landslide in 1898, so few old buildings survive. On the left near the station buildings is the bronze monument by Vincenzo Vela to the 177 men who died building the tunnel.

Buses from Airolo station travel through the dramatic Val Bedretto and over the Nufenen Pass to Oberwald station on the Brig–Andermatt line and over the Gotthard Pass to Andermatt (both table 62.111, page 312) (see *Chapter 18*). The funicular from Piotta to Ritom (table 2603) can be reached by bus from Airolo station (table 62.191); opened to the public in 1921 in connection with a hydroelectric project and one of Europe's steepest funiculars at 87%, it serves a sanatorium, the village of Altanca and the artificial lake of Ritóm, on the shore of which is an alpine park with an estimated 500 species of flora. The railway takes 12 minutes to rise 785m (2,575ft).

A good way to explore the villages as far as Biasca is to avail oneself of the special bicycle-hire system at Airolo whereby combined tickets cover bike hire and a return journey by train. Bicycles are returned to Biasca station.

Walking routes can be followed along both sides of the valley to Biasca: the eastern one known as the Strada Alta is the more developed (with the regrettable and thankfully rare use of asphalt for sections of the path); the western route passes through villages such as Prato and Chironico, the latter having a beautiful Romanesque church with frescoes dating from 1338.

The south ramp of the Gotthard is gentler than the northern approach, with a vertical drop down to Biasca through the Val Leventina of 849m (3,747ft) in 45.6km (28½ miles). Nonetheless it calls for four spiral tunnels and gradients of 1 in 37, as well as repeated crossings of the River Ticino, which the railway follows all the way to Giubasco. Both pairs of spirals were required by steep falls in the valley at points where the river crashes through gorges. The first pair of tunnels is just below Rodi Fiesso on the approach to **Faido**.

The principal town of the Val Leventina, Faido has some fine 16th-century wooden houses as well as typical Ticinese stone dwellings. To the south of the town is a Capuchin monastery and church of San Francesco, built in 1608. Samuel Butler stayed here in 1880 while writing *Alps and Sanctuaries of Piedmont and the Canton Ticino*, published two years later.

South of Faido chestnut and mulberry trees and vines appear as the train approaches the second pair of spiral tunnels beyond the closed station of Lavorgo. Three levels of track can be photographed together as the tightly compressed loops skirt the adjacent river as it gushes through the Biaschina ravine.

The descent from the Gotthard is marred by the ugly motorway that has been ruthlessly driven down the valley without regard to the landscape. The Val Leventina is a textbook example of the way railway engineers were able to integrate their narrow threads of steel into the landscape, building bridges of elegance out of local materials, whereas the functional concrete motorway structures obtrude horribly into what was a lovely valley. Moreover, the electric railway produces no pollution while traffic on the St Gotthard route emits 30 tonnes of nitrogen each weekend. As a result the air quality in many alpine valleys bordering the motorway is now worse than that in cities like Zürich and Basel.

It is well worth making the effort to visit **Giornico**. It was here in 1478 that a Swiss force outnumbered 10 to 1 defeated a Milanese force by rolling stones down the hillside. But the reason for visiting the village is its two famous churches, especially San Nicolao, which is regarded as the loveliest Romanesque church in the canton. Dating from the second half of the 12th century, it has a timeless atmosphere, since there is almost no evidence of anything having been done to alter the church since it was built, with three apses and no transepts. Even the bench pews and rudimentary choir-stalls seem original. A crude lion and the head and shoulders of a cow flank the doorway, and just two tiny round-headed windows on each side of the nave light the bare stone walls. Up the hill the church of Santa Maria di Castello stands beside the ruins of a Milanese castle destroyed in 1518; it too has 15th-century frescoes. The 16th-century Casa Stanga, festooned with colourful armorial devices, contains a museum about the Levintina (⊕ *Apr–Oct 14.00–17.00 Tue–Sun; Jul–Aug 14.00–17.00 Wed–Sat*).

The valley has widened by the time **Biasca** is reached at the foot of the descent. This is the southern ramp equivalent of Erstfeld where an additional locomotive was attached for the ascent. Looking up the valley side to the east, you can see a spectacular waterfall which may be reached by a panoramic path called the Via

Crucis. It begins at the collegiate church of Santi Pietro e Paolo, which is thought to have been built at the end of the 11th/early 12th centuries and contains an exceptionally fine collection of frescoes. Ask for the key at the parsonage before climbing the hill.

The Via Crucis takes you over a Roman bridge to the oratory of St Petronella and continues past several lovely waterfalls, the remains of an aqueduct carved out of rock and the ruins of Orelli Castle.

Buses from Biasca serve the Blenio Valley along which a metre-gauge railway used to run to Acquarossa-Comprovacco (table 62.131, page 343) which continues on to Olivone. Between mid-June and mid-October the Olivone bus is extended all the way to Disentis station between Andermatt and Chur (table 90.481, page 343). The Blenio Valley is noted for its walking, and maps and suggested itineraries are available from the Biasca tourist office.

From **Castione** a preserved metre-gauge electric railway operated by Ferrovia Mesolcinese FM (also known as the Misoxerbahn) runs for 13km up Val Mescolcina to Cama. Trains usually run on varying Sundays between April and October (*timetable* ✆ *079 262 39 79 or 091 825 21 31; www.seft-fm.ch*). Astonishingly both the local and cantonal authorities seem indifferent to the operation.

Leaving Biasca the train races along a straight section to the capital of the Ticino at **Bellinzona**, which developed from Roman times thanks to its strategic position at the entrance to three passes – Gotthard, Lukmanier and San Bernardino. To reach the tourist office from the station, turn left along Viale Stazione to arcaded Piazza Nosetto on which the office may be found. This, with the adjacent Piazza Collegiata, is the heart of the old town in which a colourful market is held on Saturday mornings. The latter takes its name from the large collegiate church of Santi Pietro e Stefano, a much-rebuilt largely Renaissance church which has elaborate 17th–18th-century stucco.

Beside the church is a pedestrian alley that climbs the hill to one of Bellinzona's three castles, all of which have survived largely intact and which constitute some of Switzerland's most dramatic military buildings. Their importance is reflected in the three being a World Heritage Site. The three are also known by the names of the three cantons which prosecuted the policy of bringing the canton under Swiss hegemony and which installed their bailiffs in them. The Castello di Montebello (Castle of Schwyz) was begun at the end of the 13th century and progressively enlarged to consist of two multi-towered curtain walls surrounding a rectangular five-storey keep and a gate-tower. The fortress's slender and uniform machicolations belie the different building periods. It houses the Civic Museum of archaeological and historical artefacts (*Castle* ⊕ *mid-Mar–Oct 08.00–20.00 daily; admission charge; Museum* ⊕ *mid-Mar–Oct 10.00–18.00 daily; admission charge*). One ticket covers all three castles.

On the other side of Piazza Collegiata is Castelgrande (Castle of Uri), the oldest and largest of the three, dating from the 12th century. The castle is dominated by two tall 13th-century towers, one a keep, the other residential. The museum is devoted to interpreting the site through the 6,500 years of its occupation, from Neolithic times to the present (*Castle* ⊕ *10.00–18.00 Mon, 09.00–22.00 Tue–Sun; Museum* ⊕ *Apr–Oct 10.00–19.00 daily; Nov–Mar 10.00–17.00 daily*). It has a restaurant reached by a lift shaft through the rock as well as by steps. One of its walls was built to close off the valley, being crenellated on both sides and the wall 'walk' wide enough for four horses to ride abreast.

The third castle, Castello di Sasso Corbaro (Castle of Unterwalden), lies outside the old town and is approached by a winding road leading to its two working drawbridges. Reputed to have been built in just six months by Sforzas following the defeat of Milanese troops at Giornico (see page 316). Some walls are 4.7m thick. In the castle is a museum of folk art, including a beautiful 17th-century panelled room with stove from a house at Olivone in the Blenio Valley (*castle* ⊕ *Apr–Nov 10.00–18.00 Mon, 10.00–22.00 Tue–Sun; museum* ⊕ *late Mar–Nov 10.00–18.00 daily*).

Along Via Lugano is a church that once came under a Franciscan monastery: Santa Maria delle Grazie was built in 1481–85 and has an exceptionally intricate fresco decorating the rood screen. The central scene of the Crucifixion and 15 surrounding scenes of the life of Christ were executed by an unknown artist in the late 15th century, but they have been compared with the fresco by Bernardino Luini in the Santa Maria degli Angioli in Lugano.

Not far from Santa Maria delle Grazie, on the other side of the railway, is the 13th-century church of San Biagio, with a huge 14th-century fresco of St Christopher on the façade and 14th–15th-century frescoes inside.

One of the country's longest postbus journeys, the San Bernardino Route Express, leaves from Bellinzona station for Thusis and Chur stations (table 90.171), crossing the San Bernardino Pass.

Beyond **Giubiasco** is the junction where the lines to Locarno and Luino (in Italy) veer to the right, while the line to Lugano and Chiasso climbs to the south. Five minutes' walk from **Rivera-Bironico** is the gondola up to Alpe Foppa (table 2640) on Monte Tamaro where there are good walks with views over lakes Maggiore and Lugano.

PRACTICALITIES Bicycle hire from Airolo, Biasca (drop-off only), Bellinzona and Lugano stations. A good cycle track runs from Bellinzona to Lake Maggiore, Locarno and Ascona, running beside the River Ticino.

AIROLO
Tourist information
🛈 Via Stazione, CH-6780; ☎091 869 15 33; e info@leventinaturismo.ch; www.leventinaturismo.ch; ⊕ 08.00–18.00 Mon–Fri; Jun–Aug 08.00–noon Sat, 08.00–noon Sun

Where to stay
🏠 **Forni*** Via Stazione, CH-6780; ☎091 869 12 70; e info@forni.ch; www.forni.ch. Opposite station.

BIASCA
Tourist information
🛈 Contr Cavalier Pellanda 4, CH-6710; ☎091 862 33 27; e info@biascaturismo.ch; www.biascaturismo.ch; ⊕ 08.30–noon & 14.00–18.00 Mon–Fri; May–Oct 08.30–11.30 Sat

Where to stay
🏠 **Al Giardinetto*** Via Pini 21, CH-6710; ☎091 862 17 71; e info@algiardinetto.ch; www.algiardinettoe.ch
🏠 **Nazionale** Via Bellinzona 24, CH-6710; ☎091 862 13 31; e info@albergonazionale.ch; www.albergonazionale.ch. Opposite station.

BELLINZONA
Tourist information
🛈 Palazzo Civico, CH-6500; ☎091 825 21 31; e info@bellinzonaturismo.ch; www.bellinzonaturismo.ch; ⊕ summer 09.00–18.30 Mon–Fri; winter 09.00–noon & 13.30–18.30 Mon–Fri, 09.00–noon Sat

Where to stay
🏠 **Internazionale*** Viale Stazione 35, CH-6500; ☎091 825 43 33; e info@hotel-internazionale.ch; www.hotel-internazionale.ch
🏠 **Unione*** Via G Guisan 1, CH-6500; ☎091 825 55 77; e info@hotel-unione.ch; www.hotel-unione.ch

LUGANO

Lugano is the principal resort of Ticino, Switzerland's third banking city thanks to its proximity to Italy, and a good base for exploring one of Switzerland's two Italian-speaking cantons. Visitors are attracted by its extremely mild climate, glorious scenery and luxuriant vegetation. The Swiss record for hours of sun is held by the nearby hill village of Agra, but the humidity of July and August does diminish visibility. Its location on the oddly shaped lake of the same name is complemented by a long, tree-shaded promenade along the water's edge, created in the late 1840s by sweeping away numerous villas and gardens; a few relics survive, such as the bust of George Washington that once graced the garden of a villa built by a returning emigré. The views are dominated by the peaks of Monte Brè to the east and Monte San Salvatore to the south.

The local people share the Italian love of showing off in motor cars, so traffic levels and accident rates are relatively high. However, extensive pedestrianisation makes the historic core of the city a delight to walk round: trees, shrubs and fountains enhance the attractive stone sets, and many of the old villas and arcades have been carefully conserved. A range of themed guided walks is organised from late March to mid-October by the tourist office. Lugano has also become a centre of modern architecture, and the tourist office has an illustrated leaflet for a walk taking in its contemporary buildings. The city is particularly proud of its most famous modern architect, Mario Botta, who has designed buildings in North America as well as Europe. In Lugano he has designed one of the many banks, several residences and the library of the Capuchin monastery. Although his work and a number of other modern structures in Lugano are striking and exciting, others – especially some of the banks – are as sadly lacking in merit as their counterparts the world over, despite, in some cases, their position next to a historic building.

The station is on high ground overlooking the city and connected to the pedestrian centre by a frequent funicular that runs from under the platform canopy as you leave the station, down to Piazza Ciocarro. Alternatively, across the main road and directly ahead is a zig-zag path that drops down the hill, past the Federale Hotel and the Cathedral of San Lorenzo to the pedestrian area. This walking route is a delight, the streets graced by fountains, trees and tubs of flowers and shrubs. Arcades line many of the shopping streets. Markets are held in the main square of Piazza della Riforma on Tuesdays and Fridays from 07.00 to noon.

Among Lugano's many churches are two that should not be missed. A church has stood on the site of the Cathedral of San Lorenzo since at least the 9th century, but the Romanesque building has been progressively enlarged. The fine Renaissance façade dates from 1500 to 1517, and the interior has frescoes in varying states of completeness from the 13th to 16th centuries.

Overlooking the lake on Piazza B Luini and best reached from the pedestrian area by walking along Via Nassa is the Santa Maria degli Angioli. Once part of a Franciscan monastery, the church was built in 1499–1515. Its crowning glory is the vast fresco that occupies the whole wall above three arched openings that link the nave and choir. Painted by Bernardino Luini (c1475–1532) towards the end of his life, the fresco portrays the Passion and Crucifixion of Christ. The church has other frescoes, some also by Luini.

Near the church are the Belvedere Gardens (Giardino Belvedere) in which works by local and international sculptors stand beneath sub-tropical trees. Another park worth visiting is Parco Tassino (*bus routes 9, 10*), just to the southwest of the railway station. Once owned by Swiss Federal Railways, it is laid out in the form of anEnglish garden and contains 300 rose bushes of 80 varieties. It also contains some red and fallow deer and a children's playground.

GETTING AROUND
Ticino Discovery Card This affords unlimited use of public and tourist transport within the Canton Ticino and free admission to several tourist attractions. The price is roughly half for children aged between six and 16. The cards can be purchased at the counters of transport companies as well as travel agencies, affiliated hotels and local tourist offices.

By bike Bicycle hire from Lugano station.

TOURIST INFORMATION
■ Palazzo Civico, Riva Albertolli, CH-6901; ☎091 913 32 32; e info@lugano-tourism.ch; www.lugano-tourism.ch; ⏱ Apr, Oct 09.00–19.00 Mon–Fri, 09.00–17.00 Sat, 10.00–17.00 Sun;

May–Sep 09.00–19.00 Mon–Fri, 09.00–18.00 Sat, 10.00–18.00 Sun; Nov–Mar 09.00–noon & 13.30–17.30, Mon–Fri, 10.00–noon & 13.30–17.00 Sat

WHERE TO STAY
Numerous hotels; closest to the station are:
🏠 **Continental-Parkhotel***** Via Basilea 28, CH-6900; ☎091 966 11 12; e info@continentalparkhotel.com; www.continentalpark.ch

🏠 **Federale***** Via Paolo Regazzoni 8, CH-6903; ☎091 910 08 08; e info@hotel-federale.ch; www.hotel-federale.ch. Quiet location.

WHERE TO EAT
✘ **Cristallo** Viale S Franscini 8; ☎091 923 53 14
✘ **Motto del Gallo** Via Bicentenario 10; ☎091 945 28 71
✘ **Ristorante Grand Café Al Porto** Via Pessina 3; ☎091 910 51 30

✘ **Romantik-Hotel Ticino** Piazza Cioccaro; ☎091 922 77 72
✘ **Trattoria Anema & Core** Via Capelli 2; ☎091 971 24 36

WHAT TO SEE
Museums
Cantonal Art Museum (*Via Canova 10;* ☎ *091 910 47 80;* ⏱ *14.00–17.00 Tue, 10.00–17.00 Wed–Sun; admission charge; bus 4*) Collection of 19th- and 20th-century artists, including Hodler, Klee, Nicholson, Degas and Renoir, as well as numerous local artists. The museum is also the headquarters of the Swiss Photography Foundation in the canton, and regular exhibitions of its collection are held.

Cantonal Museum of Natural History (*Viale Cattaneo 4, near Parc Civico;* ☎ *091 815 47 61;* ⏱ *09.00–noon & 14.00–17.00 Tue–Sat; admission free; bus 1, 2, 11 or 12*) Collections and displays of zoological, botanical, palaeontological and geological interest.

Historical Art Museum (*Villa Ciani, Parco Civico;* ☎ *091 866 72 14;* ⏱ *10.00–18.00 Tue–Sun; bus 1, 2, 11 or 12*) Housed in a villa of 1840–43 built by a prominent Lugano family, the museum represents the centre of cultural life in the region with international exhibitions about a wide variety of changing subjects as well as a collection of paintings that includes Matisse, Monet and Rousseau.

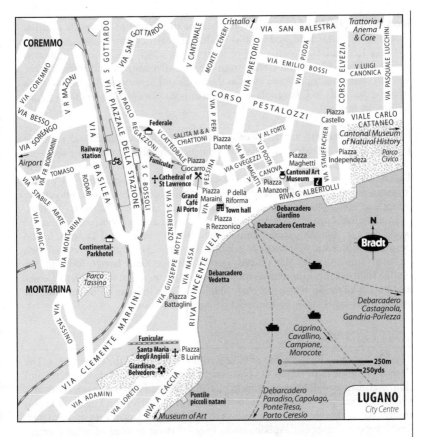

Museum of Art (*Viale Malpensata, Riva Caccia 5;* ☏ *058 866 72 14;* ⊕ *only during exhibitions; admission charge; bus 2*) Changing exhibitions of 20th- and 21st-century art, drawing on the municipal collection.

Monte San Salvatore (Table 2652)

The attractive station at the foot of the two-stage funicular can be reached from the first station south of Lugano, **Lugano-Paradiso**, or by bus 9 or 10. It opened in 1890 and operates from mid-March to early November. Unusually the funicular crosses over the standard-gauge Chiasso line close to Paradiso station. The second stage is especially steep, climbing through woods and rock cuttings.

Although the top of the mountain is disfigured by a huge communications mast, it is an excellent place from which to work out the complicated shape and topography of Lake Lugano. Standing close to the 912m (2,992ft) summit is a chapel of 13th-century origin; the present building dates from 1705, the materials having been carried up the mountain by the women of Pazzallo and Carabbia as voluntary offerings. The church has an adjacent tower and viewing platform; walk round the side of the chapel to the stairs.

An Italianate villa at the top has a restaurant and picnic terrace. During July and August dances are held at the restaurant, with the last funicular down at 23.00. There is a good walk to Carona (for the bus back to Lugano, table 62.434/line 34) or down to Melide with the possibility of returning by steamer or train.

Ticino LUGANO

19

321

Monte Brè (Table 2653) Monte Brè has the distinction of being the sunniest mountain in Switzerland, and the two-section funicular operates year-round.

Buses 1, 2 and 11 pass the end of Via Pico on which the funicular station is situated, only a few minutes' walk from the bus. A restaurant and terrace at the summit offer panoramic views as far as the Valais and Bernese Alps, and a network of paths descends to Castagnola and Gandria; both places have piers for a return journey by boat.

FESTIVALS From mid-June to the end of August, the lakeside is given back to people by banning cars on Friday and Saturday evenings, so that the city can come alive with concerts, plays and dance performances, film screenings and activities for children. During the 11 weekends there are 170 events – many of them free – at various locations which can be reached by a walk beside the lake. Some of the concerts are performed in churches and public halls in and around Lugano. All concerts are free.

In early July Lugano Estival Jazz draws fans from all over Switzerland and the world for the canton's premier music event, set in the heart of Lugano, in the beautiful 19th-century Piazza della Riforma. The open-air setting has featured such legendary musicians as Miles Davis, Dizzy Gillespie, Keith Jarrett, Ray Charles, Herbie Hancock, BB King and Wynton Marsalis. In late August it's the turn of Blues and Bop to fill the air with more than 40 hours of free, live music on four different stages, with gospel music finding a slot on Sunday afternoon.

LAKE LUGANO

The lake also goes by the name of Lake Ceresio – the lake of the cherry trees. The fleet of 11 motor ships serves 14 points on the lake. Options include lunch, tea and dinner cruises as well as excursions to piers that offer connections with buses and trains. For example, Ponte Tresa is the terminus of a branch from Lugano, and two trains a day up Monte Generoso connect with boats from Lugano at Capolago pier. There are even shopping expeditions to Italy for those in need of retail therapy. Services are operated by the Navigation Co of Lake Lugano (✆ 091 971 52 23; e info@lakelugano.ch; www.lakelugano.ch).

Passing through Lugano c1900, Hilaire Belloc observed boats that 'were strange, unlike other boats; they were covered with hoods, and looked like floating waggons. This was to shield the rowers from the sun.'

A footpath skirts most of the lake. Taking the villages in a clockwise direction from Lugano:

- **Castagnola/Museo Heleneum** This delightful park was designed in 1931 at the same time as Villa Heleneum, which is a faithful copy of Petit Trianon at Versailles. In 1989 the Villa became the Museo delle Culture Extraeuropee (Museum of Extra-European Cultures) with objects from Oceania, Indonesia, and Africa. The generous and well-treed garden surrounding the building is packed with an amazing variety of tropical and subtropical plants and flowers which survive the winter thanks to the area's favourable microclimate. There are lemon trees, orange trees, kumquats and grapefruit trees, date and Chile palms. There are also rare camellias, blue and white agapanthus, and yellow orange false-ginger plants with an incredible perfume, as well as wisteria and antique climbing roses.
- **Gandria** One of the most charming villages of the Ticino, helped by being car-free, Gandria is best reached on foot or by boat. Since the village clings

precariously to a steep slope from the water's edge, it has no roads, only twisting alleyways along which all provisions have to be carried. Out of season this is delightful; choose a quiet time (early or late) during the high season.

- **Cantine di Gandria** The unusual Swiss Customs Museum (*Museo Doganale Svizzero*; ⊕ *Palm Sunday–late Oct 13.30–17.30 daily; free admission*) can be reached only by lake steamer (13.15 departure from Lugano Giardino) or by footpath. It is housed in a four-storey building put up in 1904, though there had been a customs post on the site since 1856. The displays look at the lives of customs officers, but the most fascinating display is the incredible ways people have tried to smuggle drugs by creating compartments in all manner of seemingly innocuous objects. Outside there is a small submarine which was seized with a ton of salami. A section looks at the use of technology by both sides to try to outwit the other.

- **Campione** An enclave of Italy surrounded by Switzerland. Swiss money is preferred and there are no border formalities, though it is wise to take your passport. The pilgrimage church of Santa Maria dei Ghirli dates principally from the 13th to 14th centuries and contains some important 14th- and 17th-century frescoes.

- **Bissone** The birthplace of Francesco Borromini (1599–1667), described as the most original genius of high Baroque architecture in Rome. Much of the picturesque village remains unspoilt. Casa Tencalla is a typical and beautifully furnished 17th-century Ticinese house, but is no longer open to visitors.

- **Capolago** The start of two trains a day up Monte Generoso (most start at the junction station with the main line). Only a short walk from the pier is the very old settlement of Riva San Vitale (see Lugano–Chiasso, table 600, page 195).

- **Brusino** Two minutes' walk from the jetty is the cable car from Brusino Arsizio to Serpiano (table 2680), a health resort and the start of woodland walks and with good views over the lake. The cable car takes you some of the way towards the World Heritage Site of pyramid-shaped Monte San Giorgio, reached through chestnut woods. Its status is due to the fossils of fish from 230 million years ago found here; some of the best fossils can be seen in the Meride Fossil Museum.

- **Ponte Tresa**, **Caslano** and **Agno** See Lugano–Ponte Tresa table 635, page 325.

- **Morcote** One of the most delightful villages of the Ticino, which lies at the foot of the Ceresio peninsula. A pretty row of buildings lines the waterfront, many of the villas decorated with elaborate stucco or frescoes. The campanile of the much- rebuilt 14th-century church of Santa Maria del Sasso towers above the houses; it is decorated with 16th-century frescoes. The chapel of San Antonio Abate is part of a group of medieval buildings and has 15th-century frescoes. The Ticinese Poster Museum (⊕ *Apr–Oct 14.00–18.00 Tue–Sat*) opened in 2007, displaying over 100 original posters about the canton, housed in the ancient Casa della Torre. Parco Scherrer (⊕ *Mar–Oct 10.00–17.00 daily; Jul–Aug 10.00–18.00*) is an extraordinary park, founded by the proprietor of an embroidery business from St Gallen who died in 1956. He had opened the park to the public and his widow donated it to the municipality of Morcote. Besides the fine cedars, Mexican pines, camphor trees, Chinese magnolias and palms, the park is full of original works and copies of objets d'art from around the world, such as a Siamese tea house, Greek statues and an Arab house. It can also be reached by bus from Lugano (table 62.431/line 31).

- **Melide** For the village, see Lugano–Chiasso, table 600, page 334. There is an attractive lakeside walk starting near the pier which passes Swissminiatur.

19

GANDRIA
Where to stay
⌂ **Moosmann***** CH-6978; ☎ 091 971 72 61;
✉ hotel_moosmann@bluewin.ch; www.hotel-
moosmann-gandria.ch

MORCOTE
Where to stay
⌂ **Carina-Carlton*** (H)** Riva da Sat Antoni,
CH-6922; ☎ 091 996 11 31; ✉ carina@enjoyticino.
com; www.carina-morcote.ch. Close to pier.

⌂ **Albergo Della Posta (H)** CH-6922; ☎ 091
996 11 27; ✉ info@hotelmorcote.com; www.
hotelmorcote.com

AROUND LUGANO

The tourist office in Lugano organises a series of guided walks of half- and full-day duration throughout the surrounding area, some with a particular theme.

Parts of the Malcantone to the northwest of Lugano, and the Ceresio (the peninsula to the southwest of the town), can be reached only by bus from Lugano. Many bus routes start in Via San Balestra and call at the station before leaving the town.

Cademario in the Malcantone is served by the bus to Aranno (table 62.424/line 424) and its botanical garden is home to Switzerland's finest collection of cacti. Just below the village of Cademario is the church of San Ambrogio, which dates from the 12th century and has some exceptional wall-paintings from the first half of the 13th century. Continuing on to Aranno, the village has an old water-powered forge with the only trip hammer in the Ticino. Malcantone means 'area of hammer mills', and the area was once famous for its water-powered ironworks. The region has some exceptionally fine walks, including two – the Trail of Wonders (*Sentiero delle meraviglie*) and the Green Trail (*Sentiero verde*) – that follow the banks of the Magliasina; details can be obtained from the tourist office in Caslano, a station on the line from Lugano to Ponte Tresa (see opposite).

To the northeast of Lugano is the village of Tesserete, once the terminus of a branch line from Lugano and now served by bus (table 62.442/line 42). Just before Tesserete is Ponte Capriasca where the Catholic parish church of San Ambrogio has a 1550 copy of Leonardo da Vinci's *Last Supper*; it is of great value to art historians because the original masterpiece in the Refectory of Santa Maria delle Grazie in Milan is badly damaged.

To the south of Lugano is the hill-top village of Carona, reached by bus from the main bus station in Via San Balestra (table 62.434/line 434). Carona is notable for Botanical Park San Grato, which is open (free) all year and has large collections of conifers, azaleas, rhododendrons and heathers. Carona also has three fine churches: San Giorgio with 15th-century relief sculptures; Santa Marta with 15th-century frescoes; and the picturesquely sited pilgrimage church of Santa Maria d'Ongero with mid 16th-century stucco.

Admirers of the novels of Hermann Hesse can see his house, Casa Camuzzi (privately owned) at Montagnola, where he lived from 1919 to 1926, and his grave at nearby San Abbondio di Gentilino. The village can be reached by the bus from Lugano to Agra (table 62.436/line 36). The museum about Hesse's life and work in Torre Camuzzi at Ra Cürta 2 (⏰ *Mar–Oct 10.00–18.30 daily; Nov–Feb 10.00–17.30 Sat–Sun*) has also created a walk of the area. A rare piece of film records Hesse's fear that excessive motor traffic would one day damage the quality of life around Lugano. The Austrian conductor Bruno Walter is also buried at San Abbondio.

Opened in 1912, this metre-gauge railway provides access to the area lying to the north of the line known as the Malcantone. This beautiful area is made up of the main and side valleys of the River Magliasina which flows from Mount Lema into Lake Lugano at Magliaso. Gold has been mined in the area on and off for two centuries, with little success, but it has left a rich legacy of industrial archaeology in a glorious setting. The regional tourist office in Caslano produces a map of the area's footpaths and an exceptionally good English guide to a circular walk from Novaggio, taking in many sites of historic and archaeological interest. Bicycles cannot be carried on this line.

The station for Ponte Tresa is on the opposite side of the main road outside the main station at Lugano and a minute's walk to the right. There is an attractive café in the station. The railway dives underneath the main line and soon leaves the town behind, though it serves a populous area all the way to the Italian border. Near **Sorengo** the line skirts the small Laghetto di Muzzano in which the fish are dying; no explanation has been found for their demise. The lake is unusual in that no streams flow in or out.

From **Cappella-Agnuzzo** there is a walk along the ridge of the Collina d'Oro to the hilltop village of Agra, which holds the Swiss record for hours of sunshine. The railway then drops down and describes a U-bend around Lugano airport to reach the largest town on the line at **Agno**. Here the railway reaches the shore of Lake Lugano where Garibaldi landed after his troops were defeated near Varese in 1848. There is a small museum about the local railway in Agno (⊕ *13.30–17.00 Mon, Fri*).

From **Magliaso** station connecting buses (tables 62.425/7; lines 425/427), take you to Miglieglia, where the church of San Stefano has a fine Romanesque tower and Gothic frescoes. The paintings of the 12 Apostles form part of a service conducted here at least seven or eight times a year at the request of infertile couples. Candles are lit in front of each of the Apostles; following Mass, a special prayer is said on behalf of the couple who then vow to give the anticipated child the name of whichever apostle is the last to be lit by a candle.

The bus from Magliaso to Novaggio serves Curio (table 62.425/line 425) where a museum of the district, Museo del Malcantone (⊕ *Apr–Oct 14.00–17.00 Fri*), occupies the attractive old high school, built in 1855. The bus continues to Novaggio, the start of a signed, circular walk, the *Sentiero delle meraviglie*. An illustrated leaflet in English describes the walk and objects of interest on the way, such as mills (including the Aranno forge and a hammer mill), mines, kilns, woods, agricultural terraces and a castle. The walk takes four to six hours depending how long one lingers. Curio can also be reached by bus from Ponte Tresa (table 62.428/line 428).

From Miglieglia a chairlift goes up Monte Lema (table 2660) at 1,624m (5,328ft) from which there is a panorama over the Malcantone to Lake Lugano and to the Grisons and Bernese Alps. You can walk along the ridge from Monte Lema to Monte Tamaro, where a gondola descends from Alpe Foppa to Rivera (table 2640), five minutes' walk from Rivera-Bironico station on the Bellinzona–Lugano line.

Zoo 'Al Maglio' at Magliaso (⊕ *Apr–Oct 09.00–19.00 daily; Nov–Mar 10.00–18.00 daily; admission charge*) has over 100 animals from all over the world. Leaving Magliaso the railway cuts across the golf course on the way to the resort of **Caslano**, where there is a museum that chocaholics should not miss, though it's rather short on interpretation and long on sales promotion. Schokoland Alprose (⊕ *09.00–17.30 Mon–Fri, 09.00–16.30 Sat–Sun; admission charge*) is devoted to

19

the subject of chocolate and its culinary development and is situated alongside a factory producing 8,000 tonnes a year under the brand name Alprose.

Ponte Tresa is Switzerland's smallest municipality, with an area of only 0.28km² (69 acres), and the bridge over the River Tresa, which flows from Lake Lugano into Lake Maggiore, is the border. From Ponte Tresa station a bus goes to Luino (table 62.421/line 421), following the river for much of the way. There are plans to extend the railway to Luino. Bridges periodically cross the river, each one a border post. The border of the bus route is a few miles before Luino on Lake Maggiore; from there a steamer or train can be caught to Locarno in the north (see opposite) or Sesto Calende in the south.

CASLANO
Tourist information
✏ Piazza Lago, CH-6987; ☎ 091 606 29 86; e info@malcantone.ch; www.malcantone.ch; ⏰ 08.00–noon & 14.00–18.00 Mon–Fri; Jul–Aug, also 09.00–noon & 14.00–17.00 Sat

Where to stay
🏠 Gardenia**** (H) Via Valle 20, CH-6987; ☎ 091 611 82 11; e info@albergo-gardenia.ch; www.albergo-gardenia.ch

PONTE TRESA
Where to stay
🏠 Tresa Bay**** Via Lugano 18, CH-6988; ☎ 091 611 27 00; e info@tresabay.ch; www. tresabay.ch

LUGANO–ST MORITZ Bus table 90.631

The Palm Express leaves from a bus stop just outside the station and to the right. Almost half the journey is through Italy, and the stop for refreshments is in Italy. Reservations are required (St Moritz, ☎ 058 448 35 35; e stmoritz@postauto.ch; www. postbus.ch/alps). Sit on the right.

The 3¼-hour journey begins along the north shore of Lake Lugano, overlooking the lakeside villas and villages. The bus squeezes through gaps with barely an inch to spare either side of its wing mirrors. The border is crossed before the end of the lake, and a series of unremarkable Italian towns precedes the first glimpse of Lake Como as the bus descends to the pretty lakeside town of Menággio.

The bus then follows the lake shore for much of the way to its northern end, through the town of Dongo where Mussolini and other Fascists were caught in April 1945. The isthmus between Como and Lago di Viezzola is crossed before turning north to the historic town of Chiavenna, which thrived while the road over the Splügenpass was still an important international artery. The town is the terminus of a branch railway from Cólico with the odd through train to Milan. A stop is made here for refreshments.

The road follows the River Mera on the south side of the road. The stone bridge in Promontogno dates from 1390, and many of the village houses are decorated with sgraffito; also known as scratch work, this process entails overlaying a coat of coloured plaster with a white coat which is then scratched off to create a pattern out of the colour underneath. Vicosoprano is just off the main road and has several good restaurants. Deciduous woodland gives way to conifers as the bends tighten during the bus's climb to the Malojapass at 1,815m (5,955ft). The stretch of road alongside Silser See is delightful, with a rugged shoreline on the opposite shore and streams tumbling down the hills. Sils Maria benefits from being off the main road, and has numerous hotels. The smaller Silvaplaner See is followed by the even smaller Champfèrer See, after which the road drops down towards St Moritz.

LUINO–CADENAZZO–Bellinzona Table 633

A delightful journey for most of which Lake Maggiore is in view. Sit on the left.

Although the line follows the lakeshore all the way, the railway remains at a level high enough to afford good views over the lake, looking down on tiny harbours like that at **Maccagno** or on the villas that occupy some of the headlands. The station at **Pino-Tronzano** is particularly delightful, its well-tended garden screened by palms and shrubs. The border is crossed before **Ranzo-San Abbondio**, which is followed by a string of lakeside villages before the line drops down to the Bolle of Magadino. This protected marshland that surrounds the deltas of the Ticino and Verzasca rivers is an area of great ecological interest, forming a transitional zone between land and water that is home to 300 kinds of birds and many rare species.

For Locarno, change trains at the junction of **Cadenazzo**.

BELLINZONA–LOCARNO Table 632

Although obviously of less importance than the Lugano line, the branch to Locarno has through trains to Basel, Luzern and Zürich.

The Locarno line bears to the right leaving Giubiasco as the Chiasso line climbs away to the left. Market gardening is much in evidence as the train follows the River Ticino across the broad Magadino Plain to **Cadenazzo**, the junction station for the line along the eastern shore of Lake Maggiore into Italy. The Locarno line swings to the right, crossing the Ticino River and the Plain of Magadino. Lake Maggiore is reached at **Tenero**, which is the gateway to Val Verzasca and linked during the summer by a free boat to **Locarno**, Switzerland's principal town on the lake. Locarno station is situated right in the centre, only a few minutes' walk from the lake and many of the hotels.

PRACTICALITIES Bicycle hire from Tenero and Locarno stations.

TENERO
Tourist information
i Via ai Giardini, CH-6598; ☏ 091 745 16 61; e info@tenero-tourism.ch; www.tenero-tourism. ch; ⏱ 09.00–noon, 14.00–18.00 Mon–Fri; | Jul–Aug 09.00–noon, 13.30–17.30 Sat; Jun, Sep 09.00–noon Sat

LOCARNO

Like Lugano, Locarno was once the property alternately of the bishops of Milan and Como, becoming a part of Switzerland in 1512 with a victory by a force from cantons Uri, Schwyz and Unterwalden. The town earned a place in the history books through hosting the Locarno Peace Conference of 1925, but is best known today for its International Film Festival in August. The mildness of the climate has spawned a rash of developments around Locarno and Lake Maggiore; few have done the appearance of the area any favours.

The centre of the town is Piazza Grande, a few minutes' walk west of the station; en route is the tourist office. Attractive houses over arcades line the north side of the piazza, in which films are screened in the open during the festival. To the west of the square is Via F Rusca, off which narrow streets to the right lead to Via Cittadella and Piazza Castello, where the medieval palace that was once the home of the ruling Visconti family can be found. Work on the building is thought to have started in 1342, though conflict and rebuilding have substantially altered the structure. The museum it houses (⏲ 10.00–noon, 14.00–17.00 Mon–Fri, 10.00–17.00 Sat–Sun) contains Bronze Age and Roman items, a fine collection of medieval glassware and an exhibition on the Locarno Treaty.

The town's oldest church is San Vittore, just north of the railway along Via Collegiata. Although much altered, the church dates from at least the 9th century. The 11th-century Romanesque crypt has sculptured capitals, and the tower has a marble relief of St Victor brought from the castle.

The patrician 18th-century house of Casa Rusca on Piazza San Antonio is now an art gallery (⏲ 10.00–noon & 14.00–17.00 Tue–Sun) with work by Jean Arp, a founder of Dadaism who is buried in Locarno, and by Ticino and French artists.

TOURIST INFORMATION

🅕 Lago Zorzi 1, CH-6600; ☎0848 091 091; e info@ascona-locarno.com; www.ascona-locarno. com; ⏲ mid-Mar–Oct 09.00–18.00 Mon–Fri,

10.00–18.00 Sat, 10.00–13.30 & 14.30–17.00 Sun; Nov–Mar 09.30–12.30 & 14.00–18.00 Mon–Fri

WHERE TO STAY

Numerous hotels; close to the station are:
🛏 **Rosa-Seegarten*** Viale Verbano 25, CH-6600; ☎091 743 87 31; e rosa-seegarten@ bluewin.ch; www.rosa-seegarten.ch

🛏 **Garni du Lac*** (H)** Via Ramogna 3, CH-6600; ☎091 751 29 21; e info@du-lac-locarno.ch; www.du-lac-locarno.ch

WHAT TO SEE
Locarno–Madonna del Sasso (Table 2620) The funicular to Locarno's most
important group of religious buildings is two minutes' walk from Locarno station; from the end of the platforms turn left and the funicular station is on the right.

The first halt is for the Grand Hotel, the town's oldest hotel and the building in which some of the meetings leading to the Locarno Peace Treaty of 1925 were held, confirming the German borders of France and Belgium and the demilitarisation of the Rhineland. Mussolini and Joseph Chamberlain stayed at the hotel during the conference. The halt is linked to the hotel by an elegant iron bridge. The second halt is for Hotel Belvedere.

Construction of the Franciscan monastery beside the terminus at Orselina must have been a difficult task. As you near the top of the funicular you can see the supporting arches built on near-perpendicular rock. The monastery was founded in 1480 after a monk had had a vision of the Virgin Mary and was reached by pilgrims ascending a path from the lake shore representing the Way of the Cross. On the way up to the church, a room with grille door contains life-sized terracotta figures that once occupied the shrines along the path. Attributed to Francesco Silva, they date from 1625 to 1650. The church itself was built in the 16th–17th centuries but much altered at the beginning of the 20th. Its low ceiling painted blue-black makes the church dark and the frescoes difficult to see. On the high altar is a miraculous image of the Madonna of 1485–87, and in the south aisle a 1522 painting by Bramantino of the flight to Egypt. A small museum (⏲ *Easter–Oct 14.00–17.00 Sun–Fri or*

\091 743 62 65) containing religious treasures and paintings of rural life is attached to the monastery.

Beyond the church and sanctuary is the cable car to Cardada (table 2621) followed by a chairlift to Cimetta (table 2622) from where there is a splendid panorama over the Alps and over Lake Maggiore to the Italian plains.

Where to stay
🏠 **Belvedere****** Via ai Monti 44, CH-6601;
\091 751 03 63; e info@belvedere-locarno.com;
www.belvedere-locarno.com

LAKE MAGGIORE

A fifth of the 212km² (82 square miles) of Lake Maggiore is in Switzerland, and it stretches for 66km (41 miles) from Magadino in the north to Sesto Calende in the south, the points at which the River Ticino enters and leaves the lake respectively. The lake water's cleanliness makes it a great centre for watersports, but local winds sometimes make navigation difficult for the vessels on Lake Maggiore run by Gestione Navigazione Laghi (\ 091 751 61 40; e navigazione@maggiore.ch; www.navigazionelaghi.it). The company has an unusually diverse fleet of vessels, ranging from the 1904 paddle steamer *Piemonte* to the 1989 hydrofoil *Lord Byron* and 2002 catamaran *Leopardi*, though most of its boats are conventional motorships. Day passes are available (unusually, the Swiss Pass is not valid), and boats operate from late March to mid-October.

The services call at 36 places on the lake, and there are some outstanding attractions. It is advisable to take your passport. There is a range of cruises and special offers, some involving rail travel, such as the Lago Maggiore Express which takes the Centovalli (see table 620, page 331) from Locarno to Domodóssola, where a Milan-bound Cisalpino is caught to Stresa for the boat journey back to Locarno via Isola Bella.

Taking first the places in Switzerland served by boat from Locarno, in a clockwise direction:

- **Magadino** A nature reserve of particular interest to ornithologists is the Bolle di Magadino, an area of marsh and waterways where over 300 species of bird have been recorded. A path enters the reserve from the village of Magadino. Tours of the reserve are operated from Locarno by Gambarogno Turismo (\ 091 795 18 66; www.gambarognotourismo.ch) on Thursday mornings.
- **Brissago** On the lakeshore stands the Baroque Palazzo Branca-Baccalà (1740–50). In the middle of the village is the Renaissance Catholic parish church of Santi Pietro e Paolo, 1526–1610. The Italian operatic composer Leoncavallo (1858–1919) made his home here, and there is a museum about his life and works in the Palazzo (⊕ Mar–Oct 10.00–noon, 16.00–18.00 Tue, Wed, Fri, Sat). Offshore are the islands of the same name; on the main island of San Pancrazio is a botanical garden (⊕ Mar–Oct 09.00–18.00 daily; www.isolebrissago.ch; admission charge) and a 1927 villa that houses a small museum of African ethnography. The church on the smaller island dates from the 11th to 12th centuries. Boat trips are run to the islands every hour from Brissago and every half hour from Porto Ronco.

Places of interest on the Italian part of the lake include, again in clockwise direction from the northeast:

- **Laveno** where the 18th-century buildings along the waterfront have retained a homogeneous appearance.
- **Stresa** A resort since the mid 19th century, with many elegant 18th-century villas. The Sanctuary of Santa Caterina on the other side of the lake from Stresa is built on a shelf of rock in sheer cliffs; a separate boat service takes visitors from Stresa. Stresa offers marvellous views over the lake and the three Borromeo Isles, which are linked with Stresa by a half-hourly boat.
- **Isola Bella** Probably the lake's *pièce de résistance*, it has an outstanding mansion and 17th-century garden created by the Borromeos. The palazzo has a gallery (⊕ *late Mar–late Oct 09.00–noon & 13.30–17.30 daily*) with works by Tiepolo and Zuccarelli amongst others, and the garden is a series of ten terraces arranged as a pyramid.
- **Isola dei Pescatori** The first of the three islands to be inhabited, by fishermen. Today it is a labyrinth of alleys, houses covering the tiny island to the extent that there is barely room for a dozen trees.
- **Baveno** The garden shore has attracted many famous guests, such as Byron, Lamartine, Wagner, Queen Victoria and Churchill.
- **Isola Madre** was transformed in the mid 16th century by Lancillotto Borromeo's villa and garden, described by Flaubert as 'a terrestrial paradise'.
- **Pallanza** Nearby is the island of San Giovanni where for several decades the conductor Arturo Toscanini had his summer residence in a 17th-century palace.
- **Villa Taranto**, between Pallanza and Intra, was built at the end of the 19th century and bought in 1931 by a Scot, Captain Neil MacEacharn. He helped create one of Europe's richest botanical gardens (⊕ *Apr–Sept 08.30–19.30 daily; Oct 08.30–17.00*) with over 30,000 specimens and donated it to the Italian state in 1939.

Italian railways serve Stresa, Arona and Laveno, and both Luino and Maccagno are on the line that runs up to Bellinzona.

AROUND LOCARNO

Ascona, easily reached by bus from Locarno (table 62.316/line 316), by boat or on foot along the lake, should not be missed. It was made famous by perhaps Europe's most remarkable colony of intellectuals in the early 20th century; it included the dancer Isadora Duncan, the painters Paul Klee and Jean Arp, and the writers Hermann Hesse, James Joyce and Erich Maria Remarque who were joined by such unlikely figures as the Russian anarchists Mikhail Bakunin and Piotr Kropotkin.

Ascona has retained the attractiveness of the old village by the careful conservation of its buildings and extensive pedestrianisation of the old quarter and the piazza on the lake shore. Art galleries, antique shops and craft shops proliferate in the warren of narrow streets, the lakeshore promenade lined with pollarded plane trees.

The church of Santa Maria has 15th–16th-century frescoes, and the Collegio Papio to the south of it has a lovely two-storeyed cloister dating from the 16th and 17th centuries.

Among the subjects of Ascona's festivals are New Orleans jazz (end of June) and classical music (late August–mid-October). In the Palazzo Pancaldi at Via Borgo 34 is a modern art gallery (⊕ *Mar–Dec 10.00–noon & 15.00–18.00 Tue–Sat, 10.30–12.30 Sun*) which includes works by Paul Klee, Jean Arp and Ben Nicholson.

Buses continue beyond Ascona to Porto Ronco (where Erich Maria Remarque, author of *All Quiet on the Western Front*, lived) and Brissago (table 62.316/line 316); for both places, see *Lake Maggiore*, page 329. A free bus service connects the two villages every hour.

To the northeast of Locarno is the Verzasca Valley, reached by bus from the station (table 62.321/line 321). The valley encapsulates vineyards, chestnut forests, beechwoods and pine forest with views of the valley's tallest mountain, Pizzo Barone, at 2,864m (9,396ft). At the head is the Verzasca Dam, which was used in the opening sequence of *GoldenEye* when Pierce Brosnan as James Bond bungee jumps off the top; many have paid to follow his 220m drop, reaching up to 100mph (☉ *Apr–Oct Sat–Sun pm; mid-Jul–mid-Aug, also Wed–Fri pm; www.trekking.ch*). At Vogorno the church of St Bernard has Byzantine-style frescoes dating from around 1200. It is worth stopping off at Bivio per Corippo, at the northern end of Lago di Vogorno, to take the track up to the village of Corippo, designated a national landmark for the cluster of carefully restored houses on a mountain ledge. A little further up the valley, at Lavertezzo, is a double-arched medieval bridge across the River Verzasca with an adjacent 18th-century chapel. The church of Santa Maria at Brione has some highly regarded frescoes dating from around 1350, depicting scenes from the Life of Christ, including the Last Supper. The 17th-century castle of Marcacci near the church is now a restaurant. Overlooking the village square in Sonogno at the end of the valley is a local museum in Casa Genardini (☉ *May–Oct 13.00–17.00 daily*). A footpath, the *Sentierone*, runs the length of the valley, and there are good walks into lonely side valleys, such as Val d'Osola from Brione.

ASCONA

Tourist information

🛈 Viale Papio 5, CH-6612; ☎0848 091 091; e info@ascona-locarno.com; www.ascona-locarno.com; ☉ Mar–Oct 09.00–18.00 Mon–Fri, 10.00–18.00 Sat, 10.00–14.00 Sun; Nov–Feb 09.30–12.30 & 14.00–17.30 Mon–Fri

Where to stay

Numerous hotels; in traffic-free area on lakeside promenade is:

🏠 **Castello Seeschloss****** **(H)** Piazza Motta, CH-6612; ☎091 791 01 61; e hotel@castello-seeschloss.ch; www.castello-seeschloss.ch. Delightful hotel, part of which is converted from a medieval castle.

Hotels also in quiet locations are:

🏠 **Eden Roc******* CH-6612; ☎091 785 71 71; e info@edenroc.ch; www.edenroc.ch. One of Switzerland's great hotels, decorated by Carlo Rampazzi

🏠 **Ascona****** Via Collina, CH-6612; ☎091 785 15 15; e booking@hotel-ascona.ch; www.hotel-ascona.ch

🏠 **Tobler****** Strada Collina 28, CH-6612; ☎091 785 12 12; e info@hotel-tobler.ch; www.hotel-tobler.ch

🏠 **Al Porto***** Piazza G Motta, CH-6612; ☎091 785 85 85; e info@alporto-hotel.ch; www.alporto-hotel.ch

LOCARNO–DOMODÓSSOLA Table 620

From either end this glorious journey starts unpromisingly in a concrete bunker. Opened as recently as 1923, the metre-gauge international line is known as the Centovalli – a hundred valleys – which refers to the numerous side valleys that join the main valley of the River Melezza. These forced the railway's builders to span them with 17 major bridges or viaducts that are as impressive today as they must have been to the local people when new – it is their spectacular locations as well as the engineering that attracts admiration. The elements in the area can be destructive – in 1978 a storm did so much damage to the line that it was shut for three years, the opportunity being taken to modernise it. This must have caused real hardship to the communities along the railway for it is a vital lifeline to many isolated communities as well as one of Switzerland's finest journeys for tourists. The line is operated by the Ferrovie Autolinee Regionali Ticinesi, which uses the unfortunate acronym. Nine of the 12 stations in Switzerland are request stops, requiring intending passengers to press a button in the shelter, or if there is none to give a hand signal to the driver. Bicycles cannot be taken on the trains. Sit on the left to Camedo, then on the right.

The bunker in Locarno, with its statue of the patron saint of miners, St Barbara, may be reached by steps from platform 3. For the first few miles, the railway has the character of a modern light rail transit, with two more underground stations before the modern train rushes up a steep gradient into the open. Soon after the first above-ground station at **San Martino**, the railway joins the River Maggia which it follows to the point where it is joined by the Melezza.

Ponte Brolla is at the confluence of the Maggia with the Melezza, the defile beneath the bridge a jumble of enormous rocks. The excellent Restaurant della Stazione is another good excuse to break the journey here. Ponte Brolla used to be the junction for a branch up the Valle Maggia to Bignasco that has sadly closed. Trains have been replaced by buses, and the beauty of the valley makes it an outstanding excursion. The main bus service up the valley leaves from the station at Ponte Brolla (table 62.315/line 315) to Cavergno. The village of Maggia has a notable church, St Maria della Grazia, with some early 16th-century frescoes. From Cevio, shortly before Cavergno, there is a bus service which climbs up a side valley to Cerentino where the road again divides: the southern arm goes to Cimalmotto (table 62.332/line 332); the northern fork goes to the highest village in Ticino and the only place where German is the principal tongue, Bosco/Gurin (table 62.331/line 331). The area is made up of larch forests, and one of the village's oldest houses, the Walserhaus, accommodates a local museum (⊕ *Easter–Oct, Tue–Sat 10.00–11.30, 13.30–17.00, Sun 13.30–17.00*).

In Cevio is the Valmaggia Museum (⊕ *Apr–Oct 10.00–noon & 14.00–18.00 Tue–Sat, 14.00–18.00 Sun*), housed in the 17th-century Palazzo Franzoni and Casa Respini-Moretti; these two elegant buildings were once home to Chancellor G A Franzoni. Continuing up the main valley of the Maggia, at the former railhead of Biagnasco, the valley bifurcates, the western fork following the River Bavona to San Carlo (table 62.333/line 333) where a cable car goes up to Robiei (table 2627) from June to early October. The Bavona valley is inhabited only in summer. The eastern fork winds up innumerable hairpins along the valley of the Maggia to Fusio (table 62.334/line 334) via Mogno, famous for the marble and granite church of San Giovanni Battista, designed by the Ticinese architect Mario Botta and built in 1994–96 on the site of a 350-year-old predecessor swept away by an avalanche in 1986. Mogno also has some watermills. The western fork goes to Piano di Peccia (table 62.335/line 335), renowned for its white marble.

The Maggia valley is of interest to ecologists because its vegetation is an unusual amalgam of alpine and sub-tropical, the former brought down by flood waters. Consequently the woods comprise oak, birch, lime, ash and chestnut, the last best seen during blossom time in late June.

Returning to the Centovalli, the line soon reaches **Tegna** where the villas exhibit the stucco and painted decoration that can be seen along the valley. The tree-covered hills to the north rise higher and higher, bare patches of rock outcropping amongst the trees. At **Verscio** the church of San Fedele, topped by an octagonal tower, is clearly visible from the train just before the station. The 13th–14th-century building was rebuilt in 1743–48 into a lovely Baroque church with liberal use of marble. The choir of the old church, with its intricate and beautifully coloured 15th-century Gothic frescoes, was incorporated into the new building.

The railway has climbed high above the river by **Cavigliano**, beyond which an immense bridge can be seen ahead; this is the first of several spectacular iron bridges, leaping 91m (300ft) across the River Isorno 70m (230ft) below. The railway organises bungee jumping from this bridge (either contact FART, see page 334, or the tourist office in Locarno). On the hill overlooking the bridge is the village of **Intragna**, where the church tower of San Gottardo is the highest in Ticino at 65m (213ft). Five minutes' walk from the station is the cable car to Costa (table 2624) from where there is a 2½-hour walk through a wood of walnut trees to the hamlet of Cremaso and down through the village of Pila back to Intragna. If there is a wait for the next train, visit the museum in the 17th-century Casa Maggetti devoted to the Centovalli (☉ *Easter–Oct 14.00–18.00 Tue–Sun*), which includes paintings, agricultural implements, re-created rooms and costumes. There is also a lovely walk along the river to Corcapolo.

Beyond Intragna the valley becomes remoter and even more densely wooded, the occasional farm isolated in a clearing in the forest. The river can be glimpsed below, the banks periodically joined by stone arches with a shrine at the apex of their parapets. Waterfalls punctuate the great folds of hills that stretch into the distance, the intensity of their colour receding to a misty horizon. The trees are mostly deciduous, so the valley clothed in the colours of autumn is spectacular.

Right by the station at the picturesque village of **Verdasio** is the cable car up to the unspoilt hill village of Rasa (table 2625), which is inaccessible to motor traffic and whose tiny church has the oldest playable organ in Ticino. From Rasa you can walk in an easterly direction down to the earlier station at Corcapolo. As you leave Verdasio the views down to the river hundreds of feet below are breathtaking.

Some of the houses in the village of **Palagnedra** are decorated with paintings, and the largely 17th-century church of San Michele has late 15th-century Gothic frescoes from an earlier building. Below the railway are the turquoise waters of an artificial lake which winds along the valley floor to **Camedo**, the last station in Switzerland and the site of another huge iron bridge on the eastern approach. The walking possibilities from Camedo are legion, indicated on the walking map at the station. Sustenance before or after walks can be had at Restaurant Vittoria, which is reached by a flight of steps at the end of the platform and which produces ham sandwiches with slices of meat as thick as the bread. One of the walks, taking about four hours, climbs briefly to Lionza and then follows an old mule path through Verdasio down to Intragna.

The railway somewhat redeems its refusal to carry bicycles by hiring them at Camedo for a return on two wheels to Ponte Brolla. Since the track/road is at a much lower level than the railway it gives a very different perspective.

Half a mile beyond Camedo, through a broader stretch of the valley, the railway comes to the border with the old road bridge on the right. Once in Italy the line goes through a long stretch of shelters which interrupt views of the boulder-strewn river before the Vigezzo valley opens out at **Folsongo-Dissimo**, where some attractive villas can be seen from the train.

Leaving the large station at **Re** the pilgrimage church can be seen on the hillside; for 500 years pilgrims have come here following the miracle when the Madonna is supposed to have shed blood for 21 days after an enraged young man threw a stone at her forehead. Some of the farm buildings in the area have the distinctive characteristic of stone steps leading to the first floor. The highest station on the line is reached at **Santa Maria Maggiore**, the largest community served by the railway. The village's popularity as a home for artists is evident from the number of galleries, and the square is bordered by some elegant palazzi. It has a tiny museum devoted to, of all things, chimney sweeps. It was also the home of the inventor of eau de Cologne, Giovanni Maria Farina (1685–1766).

Conifers replace deciduous trees and the hills diminish in height as the train presses west to the delightful village of **Gagnone-Orcesco**. The homogeneous character of the stone-walled buildings, usually roofed in stone too, is a feature of a succession of villages as the river threads another gorge and the hillsides steepen. The natural beauty of this area is reflected in the name given to the valley, 'Valley of Painters'. After the pretty village of **Marone** the line starts to descend, twisting down the contours to the level of the first vines, at **Verigo**.

Near the station at **Trontano** is a fine group of religious buildings with separate, tall belltower. Beyond the village the railway and the Val Vigezzo join the broad valley of the River Toce, Val Antigório, though the railway is still high above the valley floor, requiring a tortuous, flange-squealing descent through horseshoe curves. One of the curves circumscribes the lovely garden of a tower-house that stands in a commanding position on the valley slope.

Once reached, the valley floor is unattractive, the train passing through a mile or so of scruffy industrial activity before reaching the terminus in a bunker beside the main Simplon line at **Domodóssola**. Here direct trains can be caught to Brig, Thun, Bern, Olten, Basel, Sierre, Montreux and Lausanne to the north, and Milan, Genoa, Florence and Rome to the south. The old town is delightful and well worth exploring.

GETTING AROUND

FART Via Domenico Galli 9, CH-6601; 091 756 04 00; e fart@centovalli.ch; www.centovalli.ch

TEGNA
Where to stay
Garni Barbatè** CH-6652; 091 796 14 30; e info@garnibargate.ch; www.garnibarbate.ch. Peaceful, with good food & close to station.

INTRAGNA
Where to stay
Garni Antico** (H) CH-6655; 091 796 11 07; e info@hotelantico.ch; www.hotelantico.ch

Garni Intragna (H) Piazza, CH-6655; 091 796 10 77; e info@garni-intragna.ch; www. garni-intragna.ch

LUGANO–CHIASSO–Milan Tables 600/631

The line offers excellent views over Lake Lugano, but beyond the junction for Monte Generoso at Capolago the line passes through a series of industrial towns to the border station at Chiasso.

Trains leaving Lugano's hillside station provide good views along the eastern limb of the lake as they descend through **Lugano-Paradiso**, where the San Salvatore funicular crosses over the line, to the water's edge. For much of the way to Melide the train skirts the lake shore. **Melide** is famous for the Swissminatur Melide (☉ *mid-Mar–Oct 09.00–18.00 daily*), which contains many of the country's most famous buildings in one-twenty-fifth scale, with examples from all the cantons. The railway that threads the park comprises a network of 3.5km (1.87 miles) of track and includes rack railways and cable cars. There is also a passenger-carrying miniature railway and a children's playground.

From Melide the railway crosses the manmade causeway, built in the 1840s, over the lake to proceed along the eastern shore of the lake to **Capolago-Riva San Vitale**. A short walk from the station, the village of Riva San Vitale has Switzerland's oldest-surviving Christian building. The baptistery dates from c500 and has an octagonal interior and drum dome although its ground plan is square. Until the 9th or 10th century, baptisms were performed by immersion in the octagonal basin in the centre; the huge font was then installed. Niches around the apse contain 12th-century paintings. Adjacent to the baptistery is the Catholic parish church of San Vitale, a 10th-century (or earlier) foundation rebuilt in 1756–59. The Catholic church of Santa Croce, designed by G A Piotti, is regarded as one of the country's finest Renaissance buildings, and has a prominent rotunda with drum dome.

The station is the junction for the rack line up Monte Generoso, although two trains a day run over the short section down to the boat pier to connect with sailings from Lugano. The run on to **Mendrisio** is uninspiring, though Monte Generoso and the railway up it can be seen to the left. The large town of Mendrisio is an old settlement with some fine houses in the square and a belltower that may date from the 12th century. The Catholic church of Santi Cosma e Damiano is a vast 19th-century structure, its rather fussy façade and portico leading to a colossal rotunda with octagonal dome and lantern.

From Mendrisio station a bus starting in Lugano (table 62.523, line 523) goes to Stabio where the Rural Heritage Museum of the Mendrisiotto is housed in a 19th-century school on Via al Castello. Its three floors of displays cover rural transport, agricultural equipment, rustic crafts and temporary exhibitions (☉ *14.00–17.00 Tue, Thu, Sat & Sun*).

A preserved steam-worked railway between Mendrisio station and Cantello, across the border in Italy, is set to become part of the fastest route between Britain and Ticino. SBB and Italian railways are working on restoration of the line on to Varese to create a direct Malpensa airport–Gallarate–Varese–Lugano service, expected to start in late 2013. It would also allow a new Geneva/Lausanne–Lugano service, cutting two hours off the current journey time. In the meantime, this rare example of an international heritage railway operates on various summer Sundays (*Mendrisiotourism;* ⟍ *091 971 05 43; www.clubsangottardo.ch*).

At Via Stefano Franscini in Mendrisio is the Baumgartner Model Railway Gallery (☉ *09.30–noon & 13.30–17.30 Tue–Fri, 09.30–17.30 Sat–Sun; www.galleriabaumgartner.ch*). The goal of the Baumgartner Gallery is to safeguard private collections of model railways and other types of models, promoting the hobby of model railroads as an intelligent pastime for both young and old. The Baumgartner Gallery exhibits about 8,000 railway models, dioramas, layouts as well as ship and motor car models.

The much-altered 12th-century church at **Balerna** has an adjacent baptistery in which there is a 16th-century fresco of the Virgin and Child and a Renaissance triptych of c1500. Immediately beyond **Chiasso** the railway enters a tunnel which marks the border with Italy. Milan is only 40 minutes away.

PRACTICALITIES Bicycle hire from Capolago station.

MELIDE
Where to stay
🏠 **Art Deco Hotel Del Lago*** (H)** Lungolago
G Motta 9, CH-6815; ☎091 649 70 41;
📧 welcome@hotel-dellago.ch; www.hotel-
dellago.ch

🏠 **Riviera***** Lungo Lago Motta 7, CH-6815;
☎091 640 15 00; 📧 info@hotel-riviera.ch; www.
hotel-riviera.ch

MENDRISIO
Tourist information
ℹ️ Via Luigi Lavizzari 2, CH-6850; ☎091 641
30 50; 📧 info@mendrisiottotourism.ch; www.
mendrisiottotourism.ch; 🕐 Sep–Jun 09.00–noon
& 14.00–18.00 Mon–Fri, 09.00–noon Sat

Where to stay
🏠 **Stazione***** Pazziale Della Stazione, CH-
6850; ☎091 646 22 44; 📧 stazionemendrisio@
gmail.com; www.stazionemendrisio.com

CHIASSO
Where to stay
🏠 **Garni Centro** Corso San Gottardo 80, CH-
6830; ☎091 682 36 86; 📧 info@hotelgarnicentro.
ch; www.hotelgarnicentro.ch

CAPOLAGO–GENEROSO Table 636

The only rack line in the south of the country was opened in 1890 with steam propulsion. The 800mm-gauge railway suffered financial difficulties during the 1930s and closed in 1939, to be reopened two years later under the new ownership of the founder of the supermarket chain Migros, Gottlieb Duttweiler. Diesel replaced steam in 1953, but the line was not electrified until 1982. A steam locomotive, built by SLM in 1890, and a diesel survive for special workings. The railway operates between early December and early January and between mid-March and October. The journey takes 35 minutes. Sit on the right.

To connect with steamers from Lugano, the 9km (5½ miles) railway begins at **Capolago Lago** on the lake shore. Using the Abt rack even on almost level sections, trains have to travel only a few hundred metres to the junction with the Lugano–Chiasso line at **Capolago-Riva San Vitale**. Near the station is a display of the different types of rack system used in Switzerland. The Monte Generoso line then twists over the standard gauge and climbs steeply up the hillside away from the lake. As so often happens on mountain railways, a tunnel masks a transition into very different terrain by describing a horseshoe bend to take the railway into another valley.

The station at **San Nicolao** is named after the nearby grotto, which is a 15-minute walk. A climb through thick woods interlaced with paths brings the railway to **Bellavista**, where there is an alpine garden on the south flank of the mountain. Its slopes are of particular interest to botanists as it is home to flowers that are rare or seen only here in Switzerland. The station has a restaurant with terrace and a kiosk adapted from an old tramcar. Numerous paths are signed from the station area. The views become much more open as the railway approaches the summit, for a while traversing the ridge to give views in both directions.

The summit at 1,704m (5,590ft) offers unrivalled views over the Ticino, northern Italy and the Tyrolean Alps, but the hotel and restaurant building is devoid of character. Edward Lear, the painter and writer of nonsense verse, spent summers from 1878 to 1883 on the mountain; his atmospheric oil painting of *The Plains of*

Lombardy from Monte Generoso is in the Ashmolean Museum, Oxford. Among many routes from the summit there is a walk down the eastern flank of the mountain towards Scudellate and Muggio which gives an insight into the past and present of the rural economy and way of life. You pass mills, wash-houses, bird-hunting towers and water troughs. A bus from Muggio takes you along the Ticino's southernmost, unspoilt valley to Chiasso station (table 62.515/line 515). A booklet is available suggesting 25 other walks.

MONTE GENEROSO
Where to stay
⌂ **Vetta Monte Generoso**   CH-6825; ☎091 630 51 11; e info@montegeneroso.ch; www. montegeneroso.ch

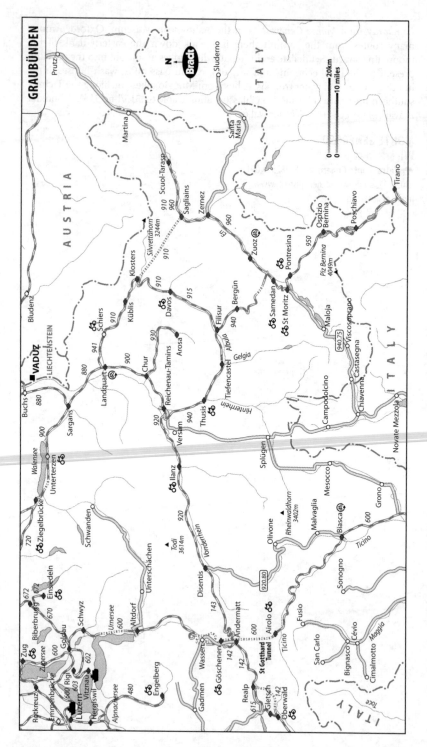

GRAUBÜNDEN

338

20

Graubünden

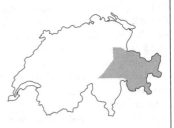

The history of Graubünden, or Grisons, reflects its location at the crossroads of different cultures to the north and south of the Alps. The alpine passes gave it an importance difficult to appreciate today, though the scenic grandeur that surrounds them now makes the canton one of the most visited by tourists.

Graubünden became a canton in 1803 and is the largest in Switzerland, though also the most sparsely populated. About one-seventh of the inhabitants speak Romansch, the language derived from vernacular Latin.

The canton has many of the most popular winter sports resorts, such as St Moritz, Arosa, Klosters and Davos (the metre-gauge Rhätische Bahn which serves them once had a special hospital-car for those injured in skiing accidents); it also has wonderful opportunities for cycling, ranging from hard-going climbs for mountain bikers to easy routes through the Engadine Valley. An excellent map showing recommended cycling routes in the canton is available from tourist offices.

The Engadine is unquestionably one of Switzerland's outstandingly beautiful valleys as well as being so long that it is divided into the Upper Engadine – Maloja–Zernez, taking in St Moritz, Celerina and Samedan – and the Lower Engadine, stretching from Zernez to the Austrian border.

Graubünden was also the last canton to hold out against the motor car, refusing on eight occasions to allow the 'precarious vehicle' on to its territory, finally relenting in June 1925.

ANDERMATT–CHUR Tables 143/920

The next section of the Glacier Express continues on the Matterhorn Gotthard Bahn (MGB) as far as Disentis where the Rhätische Bahn (RhB), translated as the Rhaetian Railway, takes over. The line passes through remote country, entering the area in which Switzerland's fourth national language, Rhaeto-Romansch, is spoken. Sit on the right.

The departure east from Andermatt is nothing if not dramatic – eastbound trains can be watched from the platform for about ten minutes as they snake their way up four half spirals, three of which are through a tunnel. The views from the train are magnificent as it climbs higher than the summits of some chairlifts. Shingle-roofed farm buildings dot the fields of tussock grasses, and tiny streams and bogs glint fleetingly in the sun. It is for sections of climb like this 1 in 9 ascent that the restaurant car has special glasses with angled stems so that they can be turned to avoid spilling the wine (they are also sold as souvenirs).

The rack continues through **Nätschen**, past Lake Oberalp on the right and beyond it the summit of the Pazzolastock, to the summit of the Oberalp Pass, the highest point on the MGB at 2,033m (6,670ft) and the boundary between cantons

Uri and Graubünden. At this point there is a station, **Oberalppasshöhe**, from which there is a fine walk to the source of the Rhine at Toma Lake; where the branch of the Rhine known as the Vorderrhein leaves the small lake you can cross it in a single step. In winter the snow can be so high here that the train passes through a sheer-sided canyon of it that almost blocks out direct light, and the line is shielded by periodic avalanche shelters.

From the pass the line drops down, still on the rack, into a long tunnel. This is the moment the head waiter on the Glacier Express often chooses to do his party trick – pouring grappa with a metre gap between glass and bottle. The train emerges into daylight at **Tschamut-Salva**, the first village on the Rhine, which enters a narrow defile visible from the train. To the south the dam holding back the waters of Lai da Curnera can be glimpsed up a side valley. The chairlift from **Dieni** to Milez (table 2908) operates only in the winter for skiers. Young forests overlook the line, planted as a protection against avalanches as the line continues to drop down the attractive valley of the Vorderrhein, twisting through sharp curves and rock cuttings to the winter and summer sports resort of **Sedrun**. The church here dates back to 1205 and has a fine Baroque altar.

The track of a branch line may be seen dropping down to the former AlpTransit Base Tunnel workings to the east of **Bugnei**. It was sufficiently steep to require rack working.

Locomotives are changed at the summer and winter resort of **Disentis**, a town dominated by the imposing white Benedictine monastery of St Martin, said to have been founded by an Irish monk named Sigisbert c700. The Baroque monastery church was completed in 1712 to the design of Caspar Moosbrugger of Einsiedeln.

From the post office a series of postbuses, starting with the service to Lukmanier Passhöhe (table 90.481), heads south through attractive valleys to Biasca on the Gotthard route. The cable car to Caischavedra (table 2905) is 15 minutes' walk from the station.

The desolate character of the line since Andermatt gives way to pasture and more woodland as the train descends at a higher speed through several small stations, with the Rhine close to the line on the right, to **Trun**. Near the chalet-style station is the Baroque chapel of St Anna, built in 1704; inside is a wall-painting which was executed to mark the 500th anniversary of an important local event that took place beside the maple tree outside in 1424. In that year an alliance of farmers was formed, for the first time giving political ascendancy to the communes over feudalism. The tree that stands today is actually a cutting of the original tree, which was destroyed by a storm in 1870. Meetings of the confederation took place in the attractive Disentiser Hof at the west end of the village which is now the Sursilvan Museum and Museum of the Grey League (🕐 mid-Apr–Oct 14.00–17.00 Mon, Wed, Sat & 2nd and 4th Sun in month; admission charge). It has a spectacularly decorated meeting room with hundreds of brightly coloured coats of arms around the walls and frescoed ceiling.

On the hillside above the village of Brigels (**Tavansa-Breil/Brigels**) is the small, white-rendered pilgrimage church of St Sievi which has exterior and interior wall-paintings dating from the 15th century.

Before **Ilanz** the railway crosses the Vorderrhein. Ilanz has been a town since the late 13th century and is the first town on the Rhine. Two towers of its fortifications have survived. The Reformed church of St Margarethen was finished in 1518, incorporating an earlier defensive tower that had been adapted as a belltower in 1438. Some fine 15th–16th-century houses testify to the town's early prosperity.

Ilanz is the starting point for one of the best stretches of river in Europe for white water rafting, if dramatic scenery is as important as the thrill. The Flims gorge can be seen from the train but you get a very different perspective from a raft in the middle of the river. Most trips go as far as a shingle beach just before Reichenau-Tamins (*Swiss Raft Adventures,* ✆ *081 911 52 50; www.swissraftadventures.ch*).

From the station a bus goes to Waltensburg (table 90.424) where the Reformed church (c1100) has wall-paintings dating from the 14th to 15th centuries, one showing a gruesome martyring of St Sebastian. Two castles are each within about 30 minutes' walk of Waltensburg: the curious 12th-century stronghold of Kropfenstein, which incorporated a cave into the structure; and the substantial and dramatically sited remains of Jörgenberg, which was first mentioned in 765 and last inhabited in the late 16th century.

Frequent buses from Ilanz station (table 90.411) serve the resort of Flims with its extensive network of chairlifts and cable cars (tables 2885, 2892 and 2893). Flims and the snowboarders' paradise of Laax have an equally good service from Chur (table 90.081).

Leaving Ilanz the valley broadens and arable fields break up the pasture. If there is a spare seat on the left-hand side of the train, take it. Near **Valendas-Sagogn** the valley divides, the railway following the Rhine along the right-hand valley which soon becomes one of the scenic highlights of the journey. The dimensions of the gorge of Flims are exceptional: huge, almost white cliffs tower over the railway on its ledge above the river, the rock faces above often contorted into peculiar shapes. If you want to explore the gorge on foot, local trains stop at **Versam-Safien**, where there is a small restaurant. Perhaps the best view of the gorge is from the 'Il Spir' observation platform built out over the cliff wall near Conn, which can be reached by bike or on foot from Flims and where there is an excellent restaurant.

The railway crosses the river, and soon after **Trin** the railway from St Moritz can be seen to the right swinging in to join the line to Chur shortly before the confluence of the Vorderrhein and Hinterrhein, which can be seen on the left. Hereafter the river is known simply as the Rhine. On the opposite bank of the river is Reichenau Castle, which dates from the early 17th century. A century later it became a school for the upper classes where the future king of France, Louis-Philippe, taught in 1793–94, before he went to the US for four years and then to England. Although **Reichenau-Tamins** is the junction station, it is usual for Glacier Express coaches on the direct service to St Moritz to proceed to Chur and return here on a St Moritz-bound train. The Glacier Express that runs to Davos continues through Chur to Landquart.

The train now races along a broad valley past a huge chemical works to **Chur**, the capital of Graubünden. Admirers of London's Waterloo International station may want to spare a moment to look at the similar, striking station roof at Chur, which won for Ove Arup & Partners the 1994 Brunel Award for outstanding visual design in rail transportation in the Major Civil Engineering Projects category. The bus station is accommodated on a raft built over the platforms.

There has been a settlement on the site of Chur since Neolithic times, c2500BC. It was an important Roman town and became a bishopric by the end of the 4th century. As princes of the Holy Roman Empire, the bishops ruled the town until forced to surrender their power in 1464. The Reformation was accepted in 1524.

Chur was the birthplace of the painter Angelica Kauffmann (1741–1807) who in 1766 emigrated to England where she had a brilliant career as a portrait painter, becoming a Royal Academician. Her birthplace, at Reichsgasse 57, still stands.

To explore the principal sites of the old town, the tourist office organises a two-hour guided tour every Wednesday at 14.30 from April until the end of October (no booking required). Alternatively it can supply an English audio guide or MP3 download to inform you about the most important buildings and sights. With plenty of pedestrianised areas and numerous old houses, the old town is a pleasure to wander round.

From the station proceed directly ahead along Bahnhofstrasse; at No 35 is the Bündner Kunstmuseum (⊕ *10.00–17.00 Tue–Sun,10.00–20.00 Thu; admission charge*). This art gallery, housed in an elegant villa of 1874–76, contains pictures and sculptures from the 16th century, a self-portrait by Angelica Kauffmann, and works by Hodler, Calame, Giovannia, Augusto and Alberto Giacometti. There is a portrait of Alberto, the most famous of the three, whose Surrealist work achieved international acclaim.

To continue to the old town, which is grouped around Martinsplatz, return to Bahnhofstrasse and turn left into Poststrasse. On the left is the arcaded Rathaus – two buildings dating from 1464 linked by a hall with groin vaulting (1540). Further south is the Reformed parish church of St Martin, largely completed in 1491 though the tower was added in 1526. On the right as you enter are three windows painted by Augusto Giacometti in 1919.

Beside the church is the Rätisches Museum (*Hofstrasse 1;* ⊕ *10.00–17.00 Tue–Sun; admission charge*) in a house put up in 1675 for the family of Baron Paul von Buol. Since 1876 it has been a museum about the canton's archaeology, history and culture. It has Neolithic, Bronze Age and Roman finds, paintings and maps of the area, and collections of arms and armour, silver, furniture, pewter, costumes, wood carvings, pottery and musical instruments.

To the east of the museum is the Hof-Torturm, the entrance tower to the court beside the 17th–18th-century palace of the bishops of Chur. The cathedral was founded in the 8th century; fragments of this Carolingian-style building were incorporated into the present cathedral, built in 1150–1272. Largely Gothic, it has some Romanesque embellishments, and the tower with Baroque dome was added c1600. Beyond the massive piers of the nave, the choir is at an unusually higher level. The vault of the crypt is supported by a single column that rests on a man squatting on a lion.

At Masanserstrasse 31 is the Natural History Museum of Graubünden (⊕ *10.00–17.00 Tue–Sun; admission charge*) with displays and changing exhibitions about the flora and fauna, geology and ecology of the canton.

To the east, on a vine-covered hill, stands the former monastery church of St Luzi, an often- and over-restored partly Romanesque building dating from the 12th century.

For the next section of the journey to St Moritz or Tirano, see table 940, page 345.

PRACTICALITIES Bicycle hire from Disentis, Ilanz and Chur stations.

SEDRUN
Tourist information
🛈 Sedrun Disentis Tourism, Via Alpsu 2, CH-7188; ☎ 081 920 40 30; e info@disentis-sedrun.ch; www.disentis-sedrun.ch; ⊕ mid-Dec–mid-Apr,

Jul–mid-Oct 08.00–17.30 Mon–Fri, 10.00–16.00 Sat–Sun

DISENTIS
Tourist information
🛈 As for Sedrun

TRUN
Where to stay
⌂ **Casa Todi*** (H)** Via principala 78, CH-7166;
☎ 081 943 11 21; e casa-toedi@casa-toedi.ch;
www.casa-toedi.ch

ILANZ
Where to stay
⌂ **Casutt** (H)** Glennerstrasse 18, CH-7130;
☎ 081 925 11 31; e hotel@hotelcasutt.ch; www.
hotelcasutt.ch

CHUR
Tourist information
🅸 Bahnhofplatz 3, CH-7002; ☎ 081 252 18 18;
e info@churtourismus.ch; www.churtourismus.ch;
🕘 08.00–20.00 Mon–Fri, 09.00–12.15 & 13.15–
18.00 Sat, 10.00–12.15 & 13.15–18.00 Sun

Where to stay
Numerous hotels; closest to the station is:
⌂ **ABC Terminus****** Ottostrasse 8, CH-7000;
☎ 081 254 13 13; e abc@hotelabc.ch; www.
hotelabc.ch
Hotels with character in or near the old town are:
⌂ **Freieck*** (H)** Reichsgasse 44/50, CH-7002;
☎ 081 255 15 15; e hotel@freieck.ch; www.freieck.ch

⌂ **Romantik Hotel Stern*** (H)** Reichsgasse
11, CH-7000; ☎ 081 258 57 57; e info@stern-chur.
ch; www.stern-chur.ch
⌂ **Rebleuten** (H)** Pfisterplatz 1, CH-7000;
☎ 081 255 11 44; e contact@rebleuten.ch; www.
rebleuten.ch

Where to drink
For a drink in unforgettable surroundings, try:
V Giger Bar Comercialstrasse 23, CH-7000;
☎ 081 253 75 06; 🕘 08.00–20.00 Mon–Thu,
08.00–24.00 Fri–Sat. Designed by H R Giger who
won an Oscar for Best Visual Effects in Alien. Giger
was born in Chur.

DISENTIS–BIASCA Bus tables 90.481/62.131

The Lukmanier Pass at 1,914m (6,280ft) is one of the lower of the alpine passes but quite different and varied in character from the others, being far more wooded on the lower slopes. The first bus terminates at Olivone for onward connections to Biasca. Sit on the right.

The departure south from Disentis follows the fast-flowing Medel River as it rushes down to join the Rhine. The landscape is pastoral with the occasional tended herds of goats and sheep. Long avalanche shelters are pierced by openings to allow something of a view. Spruce and pines cover the hillsides around Olivone, where the 12th-century Romanesque tower of the church survived an 18th-century rebuilding.

At Acquarossa the bus pauses at the former railway station on the line that ran up the Val Blenio. The journey ends at Biasca station, to the east of which is a large waterfall visible from the platform.

CHUR–BELLINZONA Table 90.171

One of Switzerland's finest postbus journeys, involving a long climb to the San Bernardino Pass, now reduced by a tunnel under the highest part, and a dizzyingly sinuous descent into Ticino. Naturally the architecture makes the transition from German to Italian styles.

20

After Thusis the road looks down on the mouth of the Via Mala (see table 940, page 345) before stopping at the village of Zillis, which has one of Europe's outstanding art treasures. In the church of St Martin are 153 square wooden panels painted c1150 and depicting subjects ranging from sea monsters and fishermen to the lives of Christ and St Martin. It is the oldest completely painted wooden ceiling in Europe. On the climb lies **Splügen**, one of the oldest and most authentic alpine pass villages in Graubünden, and today a small summer and winter sports resort. Just south of the tunnel underneath the pass, the bus pauses near the domed rotunda of the 1867 Neo-classical church of San Bernardino in the eponymous village. On the seemingly endless descent of Valle Mesolcina, following the River Moesa, the bus passes to the north of Mesocco a strikingly situated ruined citadel above the village; within the walls and towers is the seven-storey campanile of San Carpoforo.

SPLÜGEN
Where to stay
⌂ **Bodenhaus** CH-7435; ☏ 081 650 90 90; e info@hotel-bodenhaus.ch; www.hotel-bodenhaus.ch. Built in 1722 as a warehouse for goods in transit, it became a hotel in 1828 and hosted Nietzsche, Turner and Prince Louis Napoleon Bonaparte.

CHUR–AROSA Table 930

A railway journey that has much of interest and some marvellous walks from its stations. It opened as late as 1914, by which time Arosa was already a thriving resort with 16 hotels. Before the railway the twice-daily diligence took six hours from Chur; the railway takes one hour. Sit on the right.

Trains for Arosa leave from outside the station at Chur and are found standing in the road like a tram. Indeed, for the first couple of miles the train behaves like a tram, ploughing through the streets to the road that follows the tree-lined banks of the River Plessur. There was a plan to re-route the railway to avoid this street running but it seems that better ways have been found of spending the money than eradicating a feature of character just to save a few seconds on a car journey.

Between the street halt at **Chur Stadt** and **Sassal** the line parts company with the road and begins to climb up the immensely impressive gorge of the Schanfigg Valley with the River Plessur often far below as the railway gains height along its ledge on the steep valley side. Short tunnels and avalanche shelters periodically interrupt the view of the long drops to the meandering river. After **Untersax** the line crosses the Castiel Viaduct which leads directly into a tunnel in a wall of rock. Eventually upland meadows are reached, affording some views to the left.

It is worth breaking the journey at **Lüen-Castiel** to savour the landscape and to visit one of Switzerland's oldest churches in Lüen; the small Reformed church dates from 1084 and has wall-paintings dating from c1350. Unobstructed views take the train to **St Peter-Molinis** where the village can be seen below the pretty station. It is quite a climb up from the station at **Peist** to the village above. Tiny wooden-roofed huts and barns dot the landscape as a huge bridge comes into view. **Langwies** is a particularly attractive village from which there are good walks, including one to the Büelenbach gorge and waterfalls, and vantage points over the Langwies Bridge. When first built, this was the longest reinforced concrete span in the world, with a 96m (315ft) span and a total length of 287m (942ft).

After leaving the station, the line turns sharply south to cross the bridge, followed by a long climb through woods away from the river. The train pauses at **Litzirüti** before continuing to climb through horseshoe curves set in pine woods to the tunnel that precedes arrival at **Arosa**.

In 1851 the population of Arosa was just 56. Within 50 years it had become a major resort with sanatorium as well as hotels, and skiing had begun. Today it is best known as a skiing resort with 70km (44 miles) of downhill runs and 25km (15 miles) of cross-country routes, along with the usual ice rinks, indoor swimming pools and even balloon flights. However, in summer it offers 200km (125 miles) of walking paths, horseriding, mountain biking, golf and tennis. Between July and October, the tourist office offers special hiking packages, starting in Lenzerheide or Davos, in which your luggage is taken care of by hotels en route and carried by train or bus to your next destination. Maps, route descriptions and vouchers for cable cars and mountain railways are included.

The station is close to the Obersee, one of Arosa's three lakes, which help to give the town a village atmosphere by spreading out the town's hotels – it never looks big enough to have 6,000 beds. There is a small local history museum in the Egga House (⊕ *late Dec–early Apr 14.30–16.30 Tue & Fri; mid-Jun–late Oct 14.30–16.30 Mon, Wed, Fri; admission charge*); one of its rooms is a bedroom where a family was taking vespers by oil light in around 1550.

Close to the station is a two-section cable car up the Weisshorn (table 2910) from where you can walk over the Carmenpass and down to Tschiertschen to catch a postbus to Chur station (table 90.042) for the train back to Arosa. A free bus service around Arosa makes it easy to reach the gondola to Hörnli (table 2912); the bottom is a 40-minute walk from the station.

Arosa has few old buildings but the walk up to the famous mountain chapel at Innerarosa built in 1492–93 should not be missed. The walls are battered (tapered) and above the wooden roof shingles rises a wooden tower.

AROSA

Tourist information

🛈 Poststrasse, CH-7050; ☎ 081 378 70 20; e arosa@arosa.ch; www.arosa.ch; ⊕ mid-Jun–mid-Oct 08.00–18.00 Mon–Fri, 09.00–13.00 Sat, 09.30–13.00 Sun; winter 09.00–18.00 daily

Where to stay

Numerous hotels; close to the station are:
🏠 **Posthotel****** Oberseepromenade, CH-7050; ☎ 081 378 50 00; e mail@posthotel-arosa.ch; www.posthotel-arosa.ch

🏠 **Vetter*** Seeblickstrasse, CH-7050; ☎ 081 378 80 00; e info@arosa-vetter-hotel.ch; www.arosa-vetter.ch. Rooms refurbished 2008.
Hotels in a quiet location are:
🏠 **Tschuggen Grand******* Sonnenbergstrasse, CH-7050; ☎ 081 378 99 99; e info@tschuggen.ch; www.tschuggen.ch. Outstanding hotel with spa designed by Mario Botta.
🏠 **Astoria***** Alteinstrasse, CH-7050; ☎ 081 378 72 72; e hotel@astoria-arosa.ch; www.astoria-arosa.ch

CHUR–ST MORITZ Table 940

As though the journey of the Glacier Express thus far has not been dramatic enough, the final leg surpasses the earlier sections both in terms of railway engineering and in scenic splendour. The final part of the continuous climb to the Albula Tunnel has been described as one of the railway engineering wonders of the world, recognised by UNESCO in 2008 when the railway was made a World Heritage Site. Appropriately the climax comes towards the end, as it does for the westbound working with the prospect of the Matterhorn at journey's end. One of the astonishing aspects of this part of the journey is that there is not a single rack section – all the climbs are achieved by adhesion. This is also the first part of the Bernina Express which runs between

Chur and Tirano. Seat reservations and a surcharge are required on both trains. In November 1999 the 18.4km (11½ miles) Vereina Tunnel opened to provide a direct railway link between Klosters and the St Moritz–Scuol line at Sagliains/Susch. This has greatly reduced the fastest times between Chur and St Moritz, though passengers wanting the most scenic route should choose the slower trains using the Albula line. There is a good service of stopping trains between Chur and Thusis. Sit on the right.

The Glacier Express retraces its steps to **Reichenau-Tamins**, swings to the left at the junction and starts climbing steeply, affording good views along the Vorderrhein valley to the right. The railway stays on the west bank of the Hinterrhein as it heads south into a fertile area known as the Domleschg. The throat of the valley was guarded by several impressively sited castles on the east slope, the ruins of which can be seen from the train. **Rhäzüns** has three churches, all worth visiting: the Catholic parish church of 1697 has an unusual octagonal nave and polygonal choir; and the churches of St Paul and St Georg both have particularly good wall-paintings. Some regard the 14th-century frescoes in St Georg as the finest in Switzerland.

More castles can be seen to the east as the valley narrows, but none is open to visitors. **Thusis** has a large new station and is an attractive town, divided into an area that survived the fire of 1845 and a new village. A postbus journey leaves from Thusis station, skirting the Via Mala (see below) and taking the San Bernardino Pass, ending at Bellinzona station (see table 90.171). Europe's highest settlement can be reached by postbus (table 90.552) from Thusis station: Juf lies at 2,126m (6,976ft) and has been continuously inhabited for almost 800 years. Just 30 people now live on the steep meadows, and there is one pension (*www.pension-edelweiss.ch*).

Leaving the station, the train climbs and turns to the east to cross the Hinterrhein, allowing a quick glimpse of the Via Mala to the right. This extraordinary road was first built in 1473, negotiating a defile barely 10m (33ft) wide with sheer cliffs of limestone soaring above. Murray's *Hand-book* described it as 'the most sublime and tremendous defile in Switzerland', and Turner made several paintings of it. The view from Thusis has been ruined by a utilitarian motorway bridge thrown across the gorge, seemingly without regard for the beauty of the surroundings.

On the right-hand side, but too high to be seen easily, is the 12th-century castle of Hohenrätien which appears in at least two of Turner's paintings. It is quite a climb from the lovely village of Sils im Domleschg, but the view from the ruins is well worth it. In the village of Sils is a former palace with Italian-style terraced garden. A 15-minute walk to the south of the village is the 13th-century castle of Ehrenfels, now a youth hostel (✆ *081 651 15 18; only groups of 10 or more may stay*), which may be visited.

The train passes through a succession of tunnels along the wild Schyn ravine, which is shared with the Albula River. The railway crosses the river immediately after Solis by a graceful masonry arch of 42m (138ft) at a height above the river of 89m (292ft), the arch being approached on either side by viaduct. For a better view of the gorge, you can walk from Solis station; the Solis-Brücke restaurant is by the bridge.

After further tunnels there are glorious views to the right as the valley opens out on the approach to the prettily sited village of **Tiefencastel**, dominated by the spire of the Baroque Catholic parish church of St Stefan, built between 1650 and 1652. A postbus from Tiefencastel (starting in Chur) goes south through Savognin (where the painter Segantini lived and worked for ten years) to Bivio and over the Julierpass at 2,284m (7,493ft) to St Moritz (table 90.181).

The valley grows wilder and more heavily forested, trees seeming to crown every ledge. Near Surava a waterfall can be seen to the right, and a mile or so after Alvaneu is a structure on which miles of film must have been expended. The combination of a spectacular location and an elegant, curving design have given the Landwasser Viaduct a rare status for a railway viaduct. The final arch is sprung from the wall of rock into which the train burrows to reach the junction of Filisur, where the line from Davos trails in on the left. (For Filisur–Chur, see page 359.)

Filisur is in a pleasant position and the village itself has some attractive houses decorated in the Engadine style with painted motifs, sgraffito and window grilles. Its hotels make a perfect base for walkers, not least because the footpath that has been created to view the civil engineering triumph of the railway is only a few miles to the south.

Leaving Filisur the train begins the climb to the Albula Pass, negotiating a single spiral tunnel, though the real drama does not begin until after **Bergün**. This mountain village has a 12th-century Reformed church with Romanesque nave and wall-paintings dating from c1500. Even earlier wall-paintings, from the early 14th century, can be seen by taking a bus from the station to Stugl/Stuls (table 90.591) to see the Reformed church. Preserved inside the large wooden goods shed at Bergün is one of the old 'Crocodile' electric locomotives that once hauled trains over the line. The shed contains a museum about the region and its railway, with a rustic-style café. The locomotive has been fitted with a driver's footplate simulator to give an impression of the line (⊕ *Jun–Oct, Dec–May 10.00–17.00 Tue–Fri, 10.00–18.00 Sat–Sun*).

To reach the Albula Tunnel without rack assistance, the railway's engineers contrived an ingenious series of loops and spiral tunnels, raising the line a vertical height of 416m (1,364ft) in 13km (7.9 miles). The 8km (5 miles) historic rail trail from Bergün to the next station at **Preda** enables walkers to see the four spirals, two galleries and seven viaducts at close quarters, with information boards and seats at suitable points. Immediately after the station at Preda the line enters the Albula Tunnel, which took 1,300 workers four years to build from 1898 and is 5,865m (3.6 miles) long. When first opened, guards were posted to prevent people trying to walk through the tunnel. The tunnel needs so much remedial work that a new tunnel is being bored alongside it. In winter, sledges can be hired at Preda station so that people can toboggan for 12.6km down the most popular run in the canton along the road to Bergün, which is closed to traffic. In order to offer the special experience of a moonlit run, with lamps at intervals, the railway obligingly ferries passengers up to Preda until 22.15!

Emerging at the extraordinarily isolated and attractive station of **Spinas**, from where there is a cycle- and footpath down to Bever, the train drops down the Val Bever to join the Engadine. A small river, the Beverin, joins the River Inn at **Bever**, eventually flowing into the Danube near Passau in Germany and ultimately into the Black Sea. At Bever, the line from Scuol-Tarasp trails in from the left. The church here has an exterior wall-painting of a knight fighting a dragon, painted in the 14th–15th centuries.

The upper Engadine is quite different in character from the narrow valleys since leaving Reichenau-Tamins, being much broader and with gentler contours to the lower mountains. **Samedan** is another junction, where a curve goes off to Pontresina and Tirano, forming a triangle of lines with the direct line from St Moritz to Pontresina. The village has some imposing houses, including one that belonged to the influential Planta family and is now a Rhaeto-Romansch cultural centre.

Leaving Samedan you can see to the left a partially ruined group of church buildings, standing in a picturesque setting of trees on a low hill. The church of San Gion (John the Baptist) dates from the 11th to 12th centuries, though the taller tower was added in 1478. In 1682 it was struck by lightning and never restored. The 1938 painting of this striking subject by the German painter Otto Dix hangs in the Art Gallery in Chur. Inside the choir are some 15th-century wall-paintings. The key is held at Celerina tourist office. The church is closest to Celerina Staz station on the line between St Moritz and Pontresina.

About six minutes' walk from **Celerina** is the gondola to Marguns (table 2976). Celerina is the bottom of the Olympic bob-run and Cresta run, on which speeds of 140km/h (87mph) have been reached. Many new buildings in Celerina continue the local tradition of sgraffito work (painted decoration). A short tunnel precedes arrival at the world-famous resort of **St Moritz**.

There is some evidence that the springs for which St Moritz became famous were used in pre-Roman times, and by 1519 Pope Leo X promised full absolution for every Christian visitor to the spa. But it was not until the 1830s that visitors began to come here in some numbers. Even then, accommodation was limited until the first hotel of consequence was built in 1856–59 by Johannes Badrutt. It was he who began the vogue for the British to winter in Switzerland by offering a group of British tourists free winter accommodation to prove that winter in the mountains could be a pleasure. They agreed to both propositions, and thousands followed. (Badrutt also switched on the first electric lightbulb in Switzerland at his Engadine Kulm Hotel.)

Curling was introduced from Scotland, and in 1884 the Cresta run was built through the initiative of three Englishmen. In 1928 and 1948 St Moritz hosted the Winter Olympic Games. It has become immensely fashionable, in part because of its marvellous winter climate, when four months of mostly uninterrupted clear, dry weather are the norm. However, exclusivity has its price, and if it is Switzerland you have come to see, rather than other people, one of the neighbouring resorts is likely to be cheaper and less rarefied. It is also less likely to be choked with traffic and fumes, which have become serious problems for St Moritz at certain times of year.

Of interest in the town is the leaning tower (1672) that was once part of the former parish church of St Mauritius. The Engadine Museum (*Via dal Bagn 39;* ☉ *10.00–noon & 14.00–17.00 Sun–Fri; closed May & Nov*) gives a good idea of what life was like in the area through a number of reconstructed rooms and collections of furniture and stoves. The Segantini Museum (*Via Somplaz 30;* ☉ *mid-May– mid-Oct & early Dec–mid-Apr 10.00–noon & 14.00–18.00 Tue–Sun*) is devoted to the paintings of Giovanni Segantini (1858–99), who specialised in mountain landscapes. The museum was renovated for the 100th anniversary of Segantini's premature death. In the heart of the town is the Berry Museum (*Via Arona 31;* ☉ *10.00–13.00 & 16.00–19.00 Wed–Mon*) devoted to the oils, pastels and drawings of the Upper Engadine and its people by Dr Peter Berry (1864–1942).

In the centre of the town, 15 minutes' walk from the station, is the rebuilt funicular to Corviglia followed by a cable car to the top station at Piz Nair (table 2970), from which it is a short walk to the 3,055m (10,026ft) summit and panoramic views. The route forms part of the Clean Energy Tour, which promotes renewable energy sources such as the solar power cells that line part of the track.

The River Inn near St Moritz offers some of the best canoeing and river-rafting waters in Europe, and there are over 500km (312 miles) of signed walking routes. Local walking and cycling maps are available.

In January/February each year a Gourmet Festival is held in St Moritz, attracting leading chefs from all over the world. Taking a lead from this festival, the Rhaetian Railway operates regular gourmet excursions during the winter from Chur to St Moritz using a special dining car, which can also be chartered.

From St Moritz there are several outstanding postbus journeys. By the Palm Express postbus to Lugano (table 90.631) you can reach the Italian town and railway terminus of Chiavenna (see page 326). The road passes the two lakes of Silvaplanersee and Silsersee (which has Europe's highest lake boat service), and serves the village of Sils-Maria, location of the house in which Nietzsche spent his summers from 1881 to 1888 (⊕ *mid-Jun–mid-Oct & mid-Dec–mid-Apr 15.00–18.00 Tue–Sun*). It contains a collection of memorabilia. The bus also stops at the village of Stampa, home of the Giacometti family.

PRACTICALITIES Bicycle hire from Thusis, Samedan and St Moritz stations.

THUSIS
Tourist information
🛈 Bahnhofstrasse, CH-7430; ☎ 081 651 11 34; e info@myviamala.ch; www.viamala.ch; ⊕ 08.00–noon & 13.30–17.30 Mon–Fri; Sat (Dec–May, Jun–Oct)

Where to stay
🏠 **Weiss Kreuz***** Neudorfstrasse 50, CH-7430; ☎ 081 650 08 50; e info@weisskreuz.ch; www.weisskreuz.ch

FILISUR
Where to stay
🏠 **Grischuna Am Bahnhof** CH-7477; ☎ 081 404 11 80; e hotel.grischuna.filisur@bluewin.ch; www.grischuna-filisur.ch

🏠 **Rätia Bahnhofstrasse** CH-7477; ☎ 081 404 11 05; e hotel.raetia@bluewin.ch; www.raetia.ch

BERGÜN
Tourist information
🛈 Dienstleistungszentrum, Plazi 2A, CH-7482; ☎ 081 407 11 52; e info@berguen-filisur.ch; www.berguen-filisur.ch; ⊕ 08.00–noon & 13.30–18.00 Mon–Fri

Where to stay
🏠 **Albula**** Dorfplatz, CH-7482; ☎ 081 407 11 26; e albula@berguen.ch; www.hotelalbula.ch
🏠 **Weisses Kreuz** Dorfplatz, CH-7482; ☎ 081 407 11 61; e weisseskreuz@berguen.ch; www.weisseskreuz-berguen.ch

SAMEDAN
Tourist information
🛈 Haus Bernina, CH-7503; ☎ 081 851 00 60; e samedan@estm.ch; www.engadin.stmoritz.ch; ⊕ 08.45–noon & 13.30–18.00 Mon–Fri; mid-Jun–mid-Oct also 08.45–noon & 13.30–17.30 Sat; mid-Dec–early Apr, also 08.45–noon & 15.00–18.00 Sat

Where to stay
Numerous hotels; closest to the station is:
🏠 **Donatz*** (H)** Plazzet 15, CH-7503; ☎ 081 852 46 66; e info@hoteldonatz.ch; www.hoteldonatz.ch

CELERINA
Tourist information
🛈 Via Maistra, CH-7505; ☎ 081 830 00 11; e celerina@estm.ch; www.engadin.stmoritz.ch; ⊕ opening hours constantly changing – see website

Where to stay
Hotels of character are:
🏠 **Cresta Palace**** (H)** Via Maistra, CH-7505; ☎ 081 836 56 56; e mail@crestapalace.ch; www.crestapalace.ch

🏠 **Chesa Rosatsch (H)** Via San Gian 7, CH-7505; 📞 081 837 01 01; e hotel@rosatsch.ch; www.rosatsch.ch

🏠 **Garni Trais Fluors (H)** Via Miastra 113, CH-7505; 📞 082 833 88 85; e hotel@traisfluors.ch; www.traisfluors.ch

ST MORITZ
Tourist information

🔲 Via Maistra 12, CH-7500; 📞 081 837 33 33; e stmoritz@estm.ch; www.stmoritz.ch; ⊕ mid-Dec–mid-Apr & mid-Jun–mid-Sep 09.00–18.30 Mon–Fri, 09.00–12.30 & 13.30–18.30 Sat, 16.00–18.00 Sun; mid-Apr–mid-Jun & mid-Sep–mid-Dec 09.00–noon & 14.00–18.00 Mon–Fri, 09.00–noon Sat

Where to stay
Numerous hotels; closest to the station are:
🏠 **La Margna****** **(H)** Via Serlas 5, CH-7500; 📞 081 836 66 00; e info@lamargna.ch; www.lamargna.ch. Delightful period hotel.

🏠 **Waldhaus am See***** Via Dim Lej 6, CH-7500; 📞 081 836 60 00; e info@waldhaus-am-see.ch; www.waldhaus-am-see.ch. Quiet location overlooking lake, with the largest selection of whiskies in the world (according to the Guinness Book of Records). Also voted best 3-star hotel in Switzerland.
In a quiet location:
🏠 **Kempinski Grand Hotel des Bains******* Via Mezdi 27, CH-7500; 📞 081 838 38 38; e info.stmoritz@kempinski.com; www.kempinski.com/en/st-moritz
Right in the town centre:
🏠 **Steffani** Sonnenplatz, CH-7500; 📞 081 836 96 96; e info@steffani.ch; www.steffani.ch

ST MORITZ–SCUOL-TARASP Table 960

The railways travelled by the Glacier and Bernina expresses quite rightly receive lavish praise and promotion. But this line through the Upper and Lower Engadine deserves to be far better known: although the landscape is less obviously dramatic, it has about it a softer, immensely pleasing quality that is hard to convey. The broader views, gentler slopes, forests, river and delightful villages with distinctive Engadine style of architecture combine to produce an idyllic setting. It is the perfect valley to explore by bicycle, with a cycle route for much of its length. Sit on the right.

The train shares the railway with services to Chur as far as the junction just beyond **Bever**, the Scuol line following the River Inn the whole way and keeping mostly to the north side of the valley. The first station building at **La Punt-Chamues** is typical of those that follow, with attractive round-headed doors and windows, usually festooned with bright window boxes. Another characteristic of the Engadine is sgraffito decoration. The white Reformed church at La Punt has an octagonal choir, and the large white rectangle of Casa Mereda, with crenellated gables, is an example of the combination of farm buildings and living accommodation under one roof that is common to the Engadine.

Zuoz was once the main village of the Upper Engadine, and the original home of the influential Planta family whose curious three-storey tower can be seen near the ugly new station. This was part of their mansion, one of many patrician houses in the village which is well worth exploring. The bear's claw crest of the Planta family can be seen on buildings throughout the area. The Gothic Reformed church has glass from 1929–33 by Augusto Giacometti, and the now-secularised chapel of St Sebastian, which was built c1250, has some fine 15th-century wall-paintings.

Several houses in **S-chanf** have the sgraffiti decoration characteristic of the Engadine. Access to the western end of the huge national park, described under Zernez, opposite, can be gained to the east of S-chanf station.

Shortly after **Cinuos-chel-Brail**, which also affords access to the park, the railway crosses the river on a viaduct with a single span across an impressively deep gorge. A section with tunnels and mushroom-covered cuttings follows before Carolina. After a few miles, the railway turns sharply to the west, crossing the River Spöl, which flows into the Inn just before the wide loop into **Zernez**. The uniformity of this village is the result of a fire in 1872, after which similar square houses with gently pitched roofs were built as replacements. The Reformed church incorporates a Romanesque tower (c1200) and has fine stucco work in the choir and a pierced wooden parapet to the gallery. Schloss Wildenberg was the home of the Planta family for 450 years from c1400, and is arranged around a court with a corner tower of 1280. Zernez is home to the headquarters of the Swiss National Park, the country's largest reserve, and the new National Park Centre opened in 2008, which is a 10-minute walk from the station.

A postbus from Zernez station goes over the Ofenpass to the frontier village of Müstair (table 90.811), the most easterly in Switzerland, where the Benedictine convent is a World Heritage Site on account of its 8th–9th-century frescoes (though unfortunately some have been repainted). The bus crosses into Italy and continues through the medieval village of Glurns to Mals where the Vinschg Railway from Meran terminates. Connections are available in Meran for Bozen, Verona and Venice.

The village of **Susch** was almost completely destroyed by fire in 1925, but it was rebuilt in traditional style. Between its attractive station, overlooked by the remains of a tower, and **Sagliains** is the triangular junction for the 19km Vereina Tunnel line to Klosters. In high summer 3,000 cars an hour used to cross the Flüela Pass, and the tunnel enables car-carrying trains to reduce this unacceptable level of pollution. For Scuol the impact has been dramatic, reducing the journey time by train with Zürich from 4 hours 50 minutes to 2 hours 40 minutes.

After **Lavin**, where the Reformed church (c1500) has extensive wall-paintings in the choir, the scenery becomes even more attractive. A covered bridge crosses the tree-lined Inn with forest and mountains beyond. **Guarda** is another typical Engadine village which is well worth wandering round; in 1975 it won the Wakker Prize for architecture. **Ardez** has as many buildings of interest and a marvellous view from the hillside nearby. Sgraffiti and wood carvings decorate many of the houses in the village which climbs up the hill above the station. The village has received European recognition for the way it has conserved its heritage. The church dates from 1577 and is curiously asymmetrical. The best viewpoint is from the ruined keep of Steinsberg Castle on its knoll of rock, which can be seen to the left as the train leaves Ardez.

The line drops steeply to a tunnel from which the train emerges to glorious views over the valley with a glimpse of Tarasp Castle, surely one of the most beautifully sited castles in all Europe. A longer tunnel follows to bring the train to **Ftan**, the station some way below the village which is served by a bus from Scuol (table 90.911). From Ftan you enjoy a clear view of Tarasp Castle on its rocky eminence, before proceeding to journey's end at Switzerland's most easterly station, **Scuol-Tarasp**.

Scuol is the main town of the Lower Engadine and is one of the country's most celebrated spas. It is also a skiing resort, with the longest downhill run in the Engadine, and enjoys 300 days of sunshine and only 1.4 days of fog a year. Mountain bikes can be hired to explore the designated routes, and there are 1,000km (625 miles) of footpaths in the area. River rafting and white-water canoeing are available on the Inn. From a building close to the station a gondola rises to Motta Naluns (table 2993).

The spa and health centre, Bogn, is spectacular. Clever use of daylight, materials of the highest quality, such as north Italian marble, and the subtle use of the six colours of Graubünden have produced an exciting yet restful building. All the equipment is state of the art, with computer-programmed whirlpools. Apart from the benefits to be derived from the ten different types of mineral springs, part of the purpose of the spa is to promote preventive medicine, with diet one of several areas on which advice is available. The spa has the only Roman-Irish bath in Switzerland in which steam and water baths are alternated, followed by soap-and-brush massage and relaxation periods. One of the pools leads outside, enabling you to soak up the mountain scenery as well as the salts.

Scuol is divided into upper and lower parts; both are worth exploring on foot, having numerous elegant houses with sgraffiti, paintings and even coats of arms for decoration. The old centre of upper Scuol is delightful: farm buildings are still interspersed with houses of massive walls, their deeply recessed windows splayed like gunports. Some have balconies supported by poles, and oriel windows are a feature of the village, perhaps the finest being on La Plazzetta. There, a fountain offers two types of drinking water: normal and red, iron water. The nearby street named Somvi also has some attractive houses. The Reformed church in the lower part dates from 1516 and has been little altered since.

The Museum of the Lower Engadine (⊕ *Jun–Oct 16.00–18.00 Tue–Fri*) focuses on the lifestyle and culture of the predominantly agricultural region and has a Romansch Bible, first translated in 1679.

Beside the river, on the opposite side from Scuol Palace Hotel in Nairs, is the Neo-classical Trinkhalle, built in the 1840s for people to drink a specifically prescribed mineral water. The interior is rather like a temple, with malachite obelisks and arched doorways in front of each of the waters. It has become the NAIRS Centre for Contemporary Art with exhibitions, concerts, readings, films and guided walks.

A frequent bus service from Scuol post office to the pretty village of **Tarasp** (table 90.912) makes it easy to reach the castle. Built c1040 by the lords of Tarasp, the castle was briefly the summer retreat of the bishops of Chur before becoming for several centuries an Austrian possession. Following the upheaval of the Napoleonic Wars, ownership passed to the newly created canton of Graubünden, but the cost of upkeep prompted its sale in 1827. A series of irresponsible owners allowed its fabric to deteriorate, and the contents were gradually sold off or dispersed. Salvation came in 1900 with its purchase by a wealthy German from near Dresden, Dr Karl Lingner, who had made his money principally from a mouth freshener named Odol. He spent a fortune restoring the building, but tragically he died just as he was about to take up residence, in 1916. The castle was bequeathed to the king of Saxony, but for practical reasons he declined it. It was then offered to a grandson of Queen Victoria, Grand Duke Ernest Ludwig of Hesse, who accepted it, and it remains in the care of his family.

The interior is as fascinating as one would hope from such a romantic edifice. Guided tours begin with the shrine dedicated to St John of Nepomuk which was built in 1720. Then follows the armoury near the entrance, stuffed with muskets, crossbows, pikes, halberds and helmets. The tour takes in the chapel, with 15th-century frescoes, the water cistern fed by the castle's inward-sloping roofs, staircase, a room used as an assize court, dining room, now used for organ recitals and concerts, concert room, battlements, bedrooms and kitchen. The castle (✆ *081 864 93 68*; ⊕ *daily guided tours, Jun–mid-Jul 14.30 & 15.30; mid-Jul–mid-Aug also 11.00 & 16.30; admission charge*) has been restored by using salvaged ceilings, panelling, doorcases, locks and other items of the highest quality, which extends to the sympathetically chosen collection of furniture and paintings. An excellent English guidebook is available. Open-air concerts are sometimes given in the courtyard.

Between late May and late October, there is a bus service between Scuol and S-charl (table 90.913). Silver and zinc used to be mined in the Middle Ages, but today the tiny village of S-charl is at the heart of some wonderful walking country in Val S-charl and Val Mingèr where the last wild bear was shot in Switzerland, in 1904. It has the highest forests of Arolla (or cembra) pines in Europe. You would be unlucky not to see chamois or deer as they graze on the slopes of Piz Pisoc and Piz Mingèr, or the nutcracker which feeds on the seeds of the pines. The Schmelzra S-charl in the Woods Museum (⊕ *Jun–Oct 14.00–17.00 Tue–Fri, Sun)* has an exhibition about bears and illustrates the lives of the miners with a guided visit of the tunnels.

The tourist office organises various walks, including one to mine workings.

LA PUNT-CHAUMES-CH
Where to stay
⌂ **Hotel Gasthaus Krone***** CH-7522; 📞081 854 12 69; e info@krone-la-punt.ch; www.krone-la-punt.ch

ZUOZ
Tourist information
ℹ Via Staziun 67, CH-7524; 📞081 854 15 10; e zuoz@estm.ch; www.engadin.stmoritz.ch; ⊕ high season 09.00–noon & 14.00–18.00 Mon–Sat, 16.00–18.00 Sun; low season 09.00–noon & 14.00–18.00 Mon–Fri

Where to stay
Numerous hotels; close to the station is:
⌂ **Posthotel Engiadina**** (H)** CH-7524; 📞081 851 54 54; e mail@hotelengiadina.ch; www.hotelengiadina.ch
An exceptional hotel, reopened in 2004
⌂ **Castell (H)** CH-7524; 📞081 851 52 53; e info@hotelcastell.ch; www.hotelcastell.ch. Hammam spa.

ZERNEZ
Tourist information
ℹ Chasa Fuschina, CH-7530; 📞081 856 13 00; e zernez@estm.ch; www.engadin.stmoritz.ch; ⊕ frequent changes to times – see website

Where to stay
⌂ **Sport Hotel Bettini***** Röven 51, CH-7530; 📞081 856 11 35
⌂ **Filli-Bäckerei*** (H)** Röven 61, CH-7530; 📞081 851 51 51; e info@hotelfilli.ch; www.hotelfilli.ch
⌂ **Baer & Post** CH-7530; 📞081 851 55 00; e info@baer-post.ch; www.baer-post.ch

GUARDA
Tourist information
ℹ Dorfstrasse, CH-7545; 📞081 862 23 42; e guarda@engadin.com; www.engadin.com; ⊕ 09.00–11.00 & 16.00–18.00 Mon–Fri

Where to stay
⌂ **Meisser*** (H)** Dorfstrasse 42, CH-7545; 📞081 862 21 32; e info@hotel-meisser.ch; www.hotel-meisser.ch

ARDEZ
Tourist information
ℹ CH-7546; 📞081 862 23 30; e info@ardez.ch; www.ardez.ch; ⊕ 16.00–18.00 Mon–Wed & Fri, 08.30–10.30 Thu

Where to stay
⌂ **Muntanella*** (H)** Brölet 34, CH-7546; 📞081 860 00 23; e info@hotelmuntanella.ch; www.hotelmuntanella.ch

SCUOL
Tourist information
ℹ Stradun, CH-7550; 📞081 861 22 22; e info@engadin.com; www.engadin.com;

⊕ May 08.00–noon & 13.30–18.00, 09.00–noon & 13.30–17.30 Sat, 09.00–noon Sun; Jun–late Oct 08.00–18.30 Mon–Fri, 09.00–noon

& 13.30–17.30 Sat, 09.00–noon Sun; late Oct–mid-Dec 08.00–noon & 13.30–18.00 Mon–Fri, 09.00–noon Sat

Where to stay

Numerous hotels; closest to the station are:

🏠 **Bellaval*** Ftanerstrasse, CH-7550; ☎ 081 864 14 81; e hotel@bellaval-scuol.ch; www.bellaval-scuol.ch

🏠 **Garni Panorama*** Ftanerstrasse 491A, CH-7550; ☎ 081 862 10 71; e rezeption@panorama-scuol.ch; www.panorama-scuol.ch

Hotels of character are:

🏠 **Belvedere**** (H)** Stradun, CH-7550; ☎ 081 861 06 06; e info@belvedere-scuol.ch; www.belvedere-scuol.ch

🏠 **Chasa Sofia*** (H)** CH-7550; ☎ 081 864 87 07; e info@chasa-sofia.ch; www.chasa-sofia.ch

🏠 **Engiadina*** (H)** Rablüzza 152, CH-7550; ☎ 081 864 14 21; e info@hotel-engiadina.ch; www.hotel-engiadina.ch

BAD TARASP-VULPERA

Where to stay

🏠 **Schlosshotel Chastè**** (H)** CH-7552; ☎ 081 861 30 60; e chaste@schlosshoteltarasp.ch; www.schlosshoteltarasp.ch

FTAN

Where to stay

🏠 **Haus Paradies** CH-7551; ☎ 081 861 08 08; www.paradieshotel.ch. This is 1 of Switzerland's most superbly sited hotels, with a restaurant serving exceptional cuisine.

THE SWISS NATIONAL PARK

Although Switzerland has numerous nature reserves, it has only one national park. It was created in 1914 after eight years of discussion, becoming Europe's first national park. It now covers 16,870ha (41,686 acres) around the Ofenpass in the Lower Engadine, thanks to periodic additions from the surrounding communes, and there are plans to enlarge it still further. A much higher level of protection is given to the park than its equivalents in either Britain or the United States. No grazing of animals is allowed, no trees have been felled and visitors must stick to the 80km (50 miles) of authorised, marked paths. No camping is allowed, and the customary country codes of not picking fruit or flowers, disturbing animals etc, are enforced. Walking in the park is permitted as soon as the snow melts in late spring and forbidden once snow covers the footpaths in autumn.

The result is a unique environment in which nature has been allowed to take its course unchecked by human intervention. There are over 600 plant species in the park, thanks to the great difference in altitude and the variety of rock types within the park. Larch, spruce, mountain pine, dwarf pine, alpine alder, alpine rose bush and the majestic cembra pine dominate the forest. Among the flowers are spurred violet, gentian, catch-fly, saxifrage, alpine ranunculus, mountain crowfoot, hawkweed, yellow Rhaetian mountain poppy, bearberry, androsaca and primroses. June and early July are the best times for flowers. Visitors may see red and roe deer, ibex, marmot, bearded vultures, common vipers and nutcrackers, but the last lynx was shot in 1872 and the last bear in 1904. For the first time in over a century, bearded vultures bred again in the park in 1988, and there are now about 1,500 chamois in the park.

Campsites are provided just outside the park, and it is possible to stay within the park at Chamanna Cluozza, an old inn set amid larches above Ovada Cluozza, or on the edge of the park at Hotel Il Fuorn on the Ofenpass road. Booking is essential. A visit to the exhibition at the new National Park House in Zernez (✆ *081 851 41 11;* e *info@nationalpark.ch; www.nationalpark.ch;* ⊕ *Jun–Oct 08.30–18.00 daily*), which opened in 2008, is strongly recommended before venturing into the park. There is also an exhibition on bears and mining (⊕ *Jun–Oct 14.00–17.00 Tue–Fri & Sun*) at S-charl, which can be reached by seasonal bus from Scuol (table 90.913). The Scuol Tourist Office (see page 353) organises guided tours of the Mot Madlain mining galleries that were exploited in the Middle Ages. A miner's snack is provided at the end of the tour. The tour lasts one hour and reservations must be made in advance.

WHERE TO STAY

⌂ **Chamanna Cluozza** ✆ 081 856 12 35
(Jun–mid-Oct) or 081 856 16 89; e cluozza@
nationalpark.ch

⌂ **Hotel Il Fuorn (H)** ✆ 081 856 12 26; e info@
ilfuorno.ch; www.ilfuorn.ch

Bookings can be made through the tourist office at Zernez (see page 353).

ST MORITZ/SAMEDAN–TIRANO Table 950

This line is the highest rail crossing of the Alps, helping to make it one of Europe's outstanding train journeys. In summer open-air cars enable passengers to experience the views and glorious air without the interference of glass, making it perfect for photographers. The climb is made even more astonishing by the fact that it is achieved without rack assistance, compelling the builders to devise tortuous loops and spirals to gain or lose height. Sit on the right.

Leaving St Moritz, the train crosses the River Inn, curving away from the Samedan line to head for Pontresina through the Charnadüra Tunnel, at 689m (2,260ft) the longest on the line. The line passes close to the church of San Gion (see Celerina, page 348) which can be reached from **Celerina Staz** (though the keys are held at Celerina tourist office); the chalet station building here has the date 1720 carved on it, a very rare instance of a much older building being adapted for use as a station. The halt at **Punt Muragl Staz** is only a short walk from **Punt Muragl** station on the chord between Samedan and Pontresina. From Punt Muragl a funicular climbs up to Muottas Muragl (table 2980) from which there is a scenic 9km (5½ miles) Climate Path with periodic information boards about climate change and its impact on the Alps. It ends at Alp Languard, from where a chairlift descends to Pontresina (table 2982).

From Punt Muragl the two lines run parallel to the large year-round resort of **Pontresina**, an excellent base for winter sports, walking, cycling and mountaineering. In winter there are 350km (219 miles) of ski slopes served by 60 cable cars and ski lifts, and 150km (94 miles) of cross-country runs.

The first inn was opened in 1850 and had become a sufficiently popular resort by 1879 for an English church to be opened. It was here that Elizabeth Gaskell wrote *Wives and Daughters*.

A path from the upper town leads to the town's principal building of interest, the Reformed church of Sta Maria on which an informative booklet in English is produced by the tourist office. It has some quite exceptional wall-paintings dating from c1230 and 1495. Nearby is a pentagonal Moorish tower.

The Museum of the Alps, in a house dating from 1716 at Via Maistra 199 (⊕ *late Dec–mid-Apr & Jun–late Oct 16.00–18.00 Mon–Sat*), is a fascinating collection of photographs, furniture, alpine equipment, natural history and reconstructed rooms.

Leaving Pontresina the train climbs through woods of larch and sweet-scented cembra pine with the River Bernina on the left. A few minutes' walk from **Surovas** is an open-air concert site in the Tais Forest where occasional performances are given.

Bicycle and walking routes are liberally provided in the area, and one of the most popular walks is the half-hour stroll to Morteratsch Glacier from **Morteratsch**. From the glacier you can climb to viewing points on either side. A waterfall plummets down on the right as you leave the station, where the railway describes a horseshoe bend, providing a lovely view of the glacier. Beyond are the snow-covered peaks of the Bernina range, the tallest of which is Piz Bernina at 4,049m (13,284ft). Cheese making using traditional methods has been revived at an alpine dairy at Alp Morteratsch which closed in the 1950s. The dairy is open to visitors (☏ *081 842 62 73; www.alp-schaukaeserei.ch;* ⊕ *Jun–early Oct 09.00–17.00 daily*) and for light meals incorporating its produce. It is located 100m from Morteratsch station in the direction of Pontresina. Meal reservations must be made at the latest by 17.00 the day before.

From **Bernina Diavolezza** a cable car ascends over the green waters of the eponymous lake to Diavolezza (table 2985) where there is a 'view of surpassing grandeur', as Baedeker puts it, along the Bernina range and over the ice field that merges with the Morteratsch Glacier. At the summit there is a basic hotel for walkers and those who want to watch the sun rise over the mountains. Another cable car goes southeast from Curtinatsch near **Bernina Lagalb** to Piz Lagalb (table 2987) from where you can look over Lago Bianco towards Italy.

Now above the tree line, the terrain is desolate and rugged, and it is little wonder that this pass was seldom used until a road was built to replace a bridlepath in the mid 19th century. As the train climbs towards the summit, it begins to skirt the large, dammed lake known as Lago Bianco, its pale green water only a few feet from the train. Some of the rocks around the lake are covered in lichens, a sign of unpolluted air – the road over the range takes a different valley. The solidly built summit station of **Ospizio Bernina** at 2,253m (7,329ft) is popular with walkers, and there is a fine two-hour walk on to the next station at Alp Grüm, passing Restaurant Sassal Masone en route. As the highest rail crossing of the Alps, at 2,257m (7,405ft), this can be spectacular in winter when the train can pass through walls of snow, the track cleared by rotary snowploughs. Near the summit is Galleria Scala, the first of many snowsheds.

The descent into Italy begins gently but steepens as the train drops down through two tunnels to **Alp Grüm**, another popular place to break the journey. The main reason to do so is the viewing point over the Palü Glacier and down Val Poschiavo. The station has a restaurant and adjacent terrace from which the view can be savoured while you have lunch.

The descent to Poschiavo is one of the greatest sections of railway in the world. Without rack, trains drop down at the astonishingly steep ruling gradient of 1 in 14, negotiating curves so severe and numerous that the direct distance between the two points is doubled by rail. In many places the railway follows the route of an old Roman road. The experience is, of course, made exceptional by the views, though the elbows of the curves are often in tunnels and trees cover the slopes in a landscape very different from the barrenness of the pass. With flanges squealing on the curves, the train reaches a short flat section through **Cavaglia**. The most sinuous part of the descent follows **Cadera**, the line resembling a child's fantasy as it twists through tunnels and crosses numerous watercourses by viaduct. Italian-influenced buildings are now in evidence and the linguistic divide is crossed. At Ospizio Bernina you may see the station official rush in to get his binoculars to see a rare bird; here you are more likely to see hunting rifles.

Linking the Engadine to the north and the Italian Valtellina to the south, it is not surprising that the valley of Poschiavo has been fought over by Etruscans, Romans and the troops of the bishops of Como and Chur. It became part of Graubünden in 1494.

As the railway approaches **Privilasco**, the road over the pass can be seen on the left, later joining the railway in following the Poschiavino River down the valley. Before they meet, the railway arrives in the valley's main town, **Poschiavo**. Curiously the Reformation was brought to Poschiavo by two Italians in the first half of the 16th century, when the second printing press in what is now Switzerland was set up here, printing the first book published in Romansch, a catechism, in 1552. In an early spirit of ecumenicalism, Catholics and Protestants used the same church. In 1803 Graubünden joined the Swiss Confederation.

Architecturally, Poschiavo is a gem. As you leave the station for the centre, notice the stonemason's yard on the left – a rare sight in the 21st century. The fountained central piazza (in which the tourist office is situated and where the Wednesday market is held from July to early September from 13.00) is surrounded by many fine patrician houses as well as the old town hall with square Romanesque tower (c1300). Behind it is the Reformed church (1642–49) with tall tower. On its south side is the Catholic church of San Vittore with a rose window and tracery dating from 1503. On the west side is Albergo Albrici, built in 1682, which has old furniture and portraits, tunnel-vaulted corridors and a coffered ceiling.

On the opposite side of the river is Palazzo Mengotti, built in two stages between the mid 17th and early 18th centuries, which now houses a local museum ($\oplus$ *Jun–Oct 14.00–17.00 Tue & Fri; Jul–Aug, also Wed*) with all kinds of artefacts, some in reconstructed rooms, as well as the police station and local administration.

Casa Console at Via da Mez 32 has recently been restored to its 19th-century glory as the Museum of Romantic Art ($\oplus$ *mid-Dec–Oct 11.00–16.00 Tue–Sun*), a gallery of over 100 Swiss and German paintings from the 19th century, including works by Anker, Calame, Hodler and Segantini.

In the southern part of the town is the delightful Spanish quarter, built c1830 with the savings of returning emigrants who had made money as hotel keepers, brewers and pastrycooks. Standing alone to the south of the town is the Baroque Catholic church of Sta Maria Assunta. Built in 1692–1709, it has a *trompe l'oeil* painting in the dome and an outstanding Renaissance pulpit from 1634.

The tourist office organises various walks and visits as well as numerous printed suggestions for walks, one to the station of Brusio (see page 358).

The train runs right beside the road through the cultivated, fertile valley beyond Poschiavo, woods covering the steep mountain slopes. At **Le Prese** the railway reaches Lake Poschiavo, overlooked by the superbly sited Le Prese Hotel, which is close to the station. There is a particularly fine walk from Le Prese to the remote hamlet and pilgrimage chapel of San Romerio perched on the edge of a precipice overlooking Val Poschiavo. Family-run Ristoro Alpe San Romerio serves a hearty lunch of stew and polenta cooked in a cauldron.

The railway skirts the western shore of the lake with nothing more than a cycle- and footpath between water and railway. Looking north from **Miralago** where the lake ends, there is a lovely view of the mountains the railway has descended. There is a popular restaurant at the station with a perfect view over the lake.

Since Poschiavo, the gradient has been gentle, but beyond Miralago it joins the river in a headlong descent to Tirano. Twisting down the hill with vines, tobacco, corn and maize appearing beside the line, the railway reaches **Brusio**, dominated by two tall campaniles. Beyond the station is the famous open-air spiral, in which the line crosses itself on a steeply angled nine-arched viaduct, looping around three modern sculptures. **Campocologno** is the last station in Switzerland, but border formalities are carried out on the train.

The valley opens out to join the Valtellina; the train then drops steeply down through orchards and market gardens to **Tirano** where the railway runs through the streets before terminating alongside the FS station (no luggage lockers). From here trains can be taken to Colico on Lake Como and on to Milan. Tirano's streets are shaded by palm trees, in extraordinary contrast to the landscapes of the 61km (38 miles) from St Moritz. There are plenty of restaurants and hotels close to the station.

PRACTICALITIES Bicycle hire from Pontresina station.

PONTRESINA
Tourist information
ℹ Rondo Congress Centre, CH-7504; ☏ 081 838 83 00; e pontresina@estm.ch; www.engadin. stmoritz.ch; ⏱ mid-Dec–early Apr 08.30–18.00 Mon–Fri, 08.30–noon & 15.00–18.00 Sat, 15.00–18.00 Sun; early Apr–mid-Jun & mid-Oct–mid-Dec 08.30–noon & 14.00–18.00 Mon–Fri, 08.30–noon Sat; mid-Jun–mid-Oct, 08.30–18.00 Mon–Fri, 08.30–noon & 15.00–18.00 Sat, 16.00–18.00 Sun

Where to stay
Numerous hotels; closest to the station is:
⌂ **Bahnhof*** Cuntschet 1, CH-7504; ☏ 081 838 80 00; e hotel-stay@station-pontresina.ch; www. station-pontresina.ch
Hotels of character are:
⌂ **Grand Hotel Kronenhof***** (H)** Via Maistra, CH-7504; ☏ 081 830 30 30; e info@ kronenhof.com; www.kronenhof.com
⌂ **Walther**** (H)** Via Maistra 215, CH-7504; ☏ 081 839 36 36; e info@hotelwalther.ch; www. hotelwalther.ch

BERNINA DIAVOLEZZA
Where to stay
⌂ **Berghaus Diavolezza** CH-7504; ☏ 081 839 39 00; e berghaus@diavolezza.ch; www.engadin. stmoritz.ch

OSPIZIO BERNINA
Where to stay
⌂ **Albergo Ospizio Bernina** CH-7710; ☏ 081 844 03 03; e info@bernina.hospiz.ch; www.diavolezza.ch

ALP GRÜM
Where to stay
⌂ **Albergo Ristorante Alp Grüm** CH-7710; ☏ 081 844 03 18; e alpgruem@bluewin.ch; www. alpgruem.ch

⌂ **Belvedere** CH-7710; ☏ 081 844 03 14; e info@belevedere-alpgruem.ch; www.belvedere-alpgruem.ch

POSCHIAVO
Tourist information
ℹ Stazione, CH-7742; ☏ 081 844 05 71; e info@ valposchiavo.ch; www.valposchiavo.ch;

⏱ summer 08.00–noon & 14.00–18.00 Mon–Fri, 09.00–noon Sat; winter 09.00–noon & 14.00–17.00 Mon–Fri

Where to stay

Numerous hotels; closest to the station are:

⌂ **Croce Bianca***** Via da Mez 178, CH-7742; ☎081 844 01 44; e relax@croce.bianca.ch; www.croce-bianca.ch

⌂ **Suisse*** (H)** Via da Mez, CH-7742; ☎081 844 07 88; e hotel@suisse-poschiavo.ch; www.suisse-poschiavo.ch

⌂ **Albrici a la Poste (H)** Plaza da Cumün 137, CH-7742; ☎081 844 01 73; e welcome@albricihotel.ch; www.hotelalbrici.ch. A 17th-century mansion.

LI CURT

Where to stay

⌂ **Pensione Restorante Capelli** CH-7745; ☎081 844 01 92; e giovanni.capelli@bluewin.ch; www.pensione-capelli.ch

LE PRESE

Where to stay

⌂ **Le Prese**** (H)** CH-7746; ☎081 844 03 33; e info@hotelleprese.com; www.hotelleprese.com. Spa hotel built in 1857 close to station & offering fine organic cuisine. Closed for renovation at the time of writing; expected to reopen 2013.

MIRALAGO

Where to stay

⌂ **Albergo Miralago** CH-7743; ☎081 839 20 00; e info@miralago.ch; www.miralago.ch

FILISUR–DAVOS–CHUR Tables 915/910

Serving the two major skiing resorts of Davos and Klosters, this line is busy in winter. The section between Landquart and Klosters has become still busier since the Vereina Tunnel opened to the Upper Engadine in 1999. The line provides access to some fine walks, especially from Wiesen and Cavadürli stations. Sit on the left.

Leaving Filisur in a northerly direction, the line soon turns to the northeast along the south bank of the River Landwasser, which gives its name to the famous bridge on the Thusis line. The railway remains high through the gorge, providing fine views to the left, culminating in the crossing of the great masonry arch at **Wiesen**. Beside the station is a café to serve the many walkers who come to enjoy the spectacular walks along the valley, following the footpath beside the river. You can also walk back from Wiesen station over the viaduct, with terrific views into the gorge.

The railway enters a long tunnel and by its end the river lies only 50m (164ft) below the line. Davos must be one of Switzerland's most linear communities, strung out along the valley for miles, but this side of Davos is relatively unspoilt with old chalets dotting the slopes. Near **Davos Monstein** is the Bergbaumuseum (☉ *Jun–mid-Oct 12.45–17.00 Wed, 14.00–16.00 Sat; admission charge*), devoted to the history of mining. A local bus from the station climbs up to Monstein which has the distinction of having the highest brewery in Europe at 1,626m (5,335ft). Monstein's shareholders are paid dividends in beer, and they have to come and collect it, so the AGM usually lasts several days. Unlike many of Switzerland's 96 microbreweries, it tries to use local ingredients and has revitalised the cultivation of barley. Visitors are welcome, and there is a good restaurant at Hotel Ducan. **Davos**

Glaris is opposite the cable car to Jatzmeder (table 2878) for the Rinerhorn. After **Davos Frauenkirch** (where the Reformed church has a wedge-shaped avalanche deflector on one wall) and **Davos Islen**, the train finally arrives at the famous skiing resort's principal station, **Davos Platz**.

Davos was a large village until the 1860s when a Dr Alexander Spengler promoted its favourable climate for the cure of tuberculosis – dry, sunny, sheltered from wind and with clear air. Sanatoria and hotels were put up, winter visitors arrived and with them the first pair of skis, brought by a Colonel Napier in 1888.

Davos was not short of famous visitors from the beginning: *Treasure Island* was finished here while Robert Louis Stevenson was convalescing in 1881. He first came to Davos the year before, when there was still no railway, so the final leg of the journey was an eight-hour sleigh ride. Conan Doyle, too, wrote here while accompanying his consumptive wife, and laid out the first golf course. It was during a visit in 1912 that Thomas Mann conceived the story of *The Magic Mountain*, based on Davos and published in 1924. The town's role as a centre for medical treatment is all but over: in 1950 there were 24 sanatoria; by 2005 there were just four left.

The town has remained a prime destination thanks to the quality of its skiing, boasting some of the longest downhill runs and enough hardware on the slopes to carry 35,000 people an hour. It has also built a vast skating rink, conference facilities that cater for the kind of gatherings that appear on the main television news, and a good array of other sports facilities. Yet the situation of the town lacks the beauty of so many other Swiss resorts, and there are few buildings to lift the spirits. Even the Rathaus of 1564 was spoilt by a hamfisted reconstruction during the 1930s.

In the Kirchner Museum on Ernst Ludwig Kirchner Platz (⊕ 14.00–18.00 Tue–Sun; early Dec–mid-Apr & late Jun–mid-Oct 10.00–18.00) is the world's largest collection of paintings by the Davos resident from 1917 until his death in 1938. He was a major influence on German Expressionism. A local history museum can be found at Museumstrasse 1 (⊕ 15.00–17.00 Tue–Sun).

From Davos Platz station a bus goes over the Flüelapass to Susch (table 90.331) on the St Moritz–Scuol railway (see table 960, page 350).

A funicular from Platz (table 2872) rises to Schatzalp and the famous sanatorium opened in 1900 which stands on a shelf of the hillside with magnificent views to the south. As tuberculosis ceased to be common, tourism took over. Today Hotel Schatzalp retains its Jugendstil features and even period fittings in the bathrooms, and the hotel's famous garden, Alpinum Schatzalp, is open to visitors. It has 3,500 species from as far afield as Tibet, Nepal and New Zealand. The Alpinum (⊕ mid-May–mid-Nov 09.00–18.00 daily; www.alpinum.ch) includes a garden of medicinal plants and is best visited in June and July.

Close to Davos Platz station is a cable car to Ischalp and Jakobshorn (table 2875) at 2,580m (8,464ft). However, the highest peak is ascended by a funicular from near the next station towards Chur, **Davos Dorf**. The Parsennbahn (table 2865) has unique 140-seater double cars and is the highest funicular in Switzerland, reaching 2,663m (8,737ft) at Weissfluhjoch, from where a cable car goes up to the top of the Weissfluh, Weissfluhgipfel (table 2866), at 2,844m (9,331ft).

The railway continues around the edge of the small Davoser See through more stations named after Davos, though the town has been left behind: **Davos Wolfgang** and **Davos Laret**. Open country with clumps of conifers precedes the Wolfgangpass, where the line drops down steeply through woods which surround the sunflower-gardened station at **Cavadürli** from where there is a choice of woodland walks. The mountain farms beyond are delightful, ancient barns housing goats and horses in scenes that seem light years from dreary factory farming.

After a horseshoe loop **Klosters** comes into view below, the train passing the northern portal of the Vereina Tunnel on the right just before the station. Like Davos, Klosters is divided into Platz around the station and Dorf served by another station towards Chur. Unlike Davos, Klosters has much more of the atmosphere of an alpine village, though it attracts large numbers for skiing, and the resort is Prince Charles's favourite.

The tourist office is to the right outside the station, and opposite is the Gotschnabahn, a two-section cable car to Gotschnagrat (table 2860) that crosses over the railway on its way to the 2,293m (7,523ft) summit, where there is good walking and one of the most dangerous ski runs in the world, the Gotschnawang. A free bus service for guests links Klosters with the spa of Serneus, which has indoor sulphur baths. A regional ticket expands the local skiing to the Davos area, producing a total of 480km (300 miles) of runs. In Mülliweg is a working water-powered grain mill with demonstration days.

The railway drops quite steeply to **Klosters Dorf**, which has retained more of its older chalets than the area around Platz. A tunnel underneath the road outside the station leads to the gondola lift to Madrisa (table 2855). The railway now descends the wooded Prättigau Valley, following the River Landquart down to its confluence with the Rhein. A waterfall can be seen on the right just before **Saas** where there are lovely views across the valley, small villages being perched on bluffs that protrude from the slopes.

The old part of **Küblis** can be seen from the train, the Rathaus and Gothic Reformed church of 1472, with fine interior vaulting, clustered around the square. A lovely section of line follows the crossing by the railway of the Landquart, the river now flowing through a gorge on the right, white water frothing. The valley broadens out and becomes more populous as the train nears **Grüsch**, where the huge mid 17th-century patrician house known as the Haus zum Rosengarten contains a local history museum (⊕ *Apr–Nov 14.00–17.00 Sat–Sun*). A long tunnel precedes the wine-growing village of **Malans**, with many 17th-century houses, a Rathaus (1690) and the huge Schloss Bothmar. Its garden is regarded as the finest surviving French Baroque garden in the country. From the station it is a 20-minute walk to the gondola lift to Alpli (table 2848).

The valley broadens still further until the train is speeding through a flat landscape with the mountains steadily more distant. The railway joins the standard-gauge line from Zürich at **Landquart**, where the workshops of the Rhätische Bahn are situated and the railway's three surviving steam locomotives are kept (these and a vintage train with period Pullman coaches can be hired). Although metre and standard gauge follow a roughly parallel course, they are separate, the RhB serving local stations while the main line expresses press on to journey's end at Chur.

In the village of **Igis** is the canton's only moated castle, with corner towers; although built in the 13th century, most of the structure dates from the 17th. **Zizers** has two castles, the lower one an imposing square 17th-century building with a five-storey, domed octagonal tower. The upper castle is late 17th century. It was in a convent here that Zita, the widow of the last Habsburg emperor, Karl I, who had died in 1922, herself died in 1989.

The metre gauge crosses over the main line just before **Untervaz**. The last station before Chur, **Haldenstein**, has a 16th–18th-century castle, partly commissioned by a French ambassador. Above it, on a pinnacle of rock, stands the ruined keep of the 12th-century castle of Haldenstein. For **Chur**, see table 920, page 341.

PRACTICALITIES Bicycle hire from Davos Dorf, Landquart and Chur stations.

DAVOS PLATZ
Tourist information
🆔 Talstrasse 41, CH-7270; 📞 081 415 21 21;
📧 info@davos.ch; www.davos.ch; 🕐 Jul–late Oct
08.30–18.00 Mon–Fri, 09.00–18.00 Sat, 09.00–
13.00 Sun; mid-Oct–Jun 08.30–18.00 Mon–Fri,
09.00–18.00 Sat, 10.00–noon & 16.00–18.00 Sun

Where to stay
Numerous hotels; close to the station is:
🏠 **Grischa*** Talstrasse 3, CH-7270; 📞 081 414
97 97; 📧 info@hotelgrischa.ch; www.hotelgrischa.ch
A historic hotel with fine views over the town is:
🏠 **Waldhotel Davos**** Buolstrasse 3, CH-
7270; 📞 081 415 15 15; 📧 info@waldhotel-davos.
ch; www.waldhotel-davos.ch. Thomas Mann &
his wife Katja stayed here in 1912 & the hotel is
described in The Magic Mountain, though it has
been rebuilt beyond recognition.

DAVOS DORF
Tourist information
🆔 Bahnhofstrasse 8, CH-7260; 📞 081 415 21 21;
📧 info@davos.ch; www.davos.ch; 🕐 Jul–mid-Oct
08.30–18.00 Mon–Fri, 13.00–18.00 Sat, 09.00–
13.00 Sun; mid-Oct–Jun 08.30–18.00 Mon–Fri,
13.00–18.00 Sat, 10.00–noon & 16.00–18.00 Sun

Where to stay
Numerous hotels; close to the station is:
🏠 **Flüela Davos***** Bahnhofstrasse 5, CH-
7260; 📞 081 410 17 17; 📧 hotel@fluela.ch
🏠 **Montana*** Bahnhofstrasse 2, CH-7260;
📞 081 416 17 75

KLOSTERS
Tourist information
🆔 Alte Bahnhofstrasse 6, CH-7250; 📞 081 410 20
20; 📧 info@klosters.ch; www.klosters.ch;
🕐 July–late Oct 08.30–18.00 Mon–Fri,
09.00–18.00 Sat, 09.00–13.00 Sun; late Oct–Jun
08.30–18.00 Mon–Fri, 09.00–18.00 Sat, 10.00–
noon & 16.00–18.00 Sun

Where to stay
Numerous hotels; close to the station is:
🏠 **Alpina**** Bahnhofstrasse 1, CH-7250;
📞 081 410 24 24; 📧 hotel@alpina-klosters.ch;
www.alpina-klosters.ch

MALANS
Where to stay
🏠 **Weisskreuz (H)** Dorfplatz 1, CH-7208; 📞 081
322 81 61; 📧 info@weisskreuzmalans.ch; www.
weisskreuzmalans.ch

CHUR–ZIEGELBRÜCKE–Zürich Tables 880/900/905

Chur can be reached by direct train from Basel and Zürich. The line is seldom out of view of mountains through a part of Switzerland less frequently visited by tourists. Sit on the right.

For the section between Chur and the junction with the Rhätische Bahn at **Landquart**, see tables 915/910, page 359. **Maienfeld** has some fine houses and a Rathaus, but its main attractions are two large castles: Brandis began as a medieval castle of which the 13th-century residential tower survives; and the largely 17th–18th-century Salenegg, fronted by a Baroque garden. Nearby is Steigwald, where the 'Heidi' novels of Johanna Spyri (1827–1901) are set.

Before **Bad Ragaz** the railway crosses the cantonal boundary into St Gallen. The town has some interesting buildings, such as the Chapel of St Leonhard with unique (for Switzerland) Italianate painting dating from 1414 to 1418 in the choir, and the spa hotel that was converted from a Benedictine monastery building in 1840. But the principal reason for breaking the journey here is to explore the extraordinary gorge of the River Tamina.

A bus from the station to the small resort of Vättis and Gigerwald (table 80.451/ line 451) goes up the wooded defile, in which there is barely room for river and road, to Bad Pfäfers. This village has a huge monastery church built in 1688–93 and spa buildings from 1704–18. Beyond is the Taminaschlucht in which hot springs rise; early patients were lowered into the gorge by ropes. There is a signed walk back to Bad Ragaz, via Pfäfers, with fine views over the Rhein Valley, and the ruins of 13th-century Wartenstein Castle.

A five-minute walk from Bad Ragaz station is the gondola lift to Pardiel (table 2805) for good views over the Rhein Valley and surrounding mountains.

The railway and Rhein part company, the river turning east before continuing north to the Bodensee while the railway heads northwest. For the junction of **Sargans** see page 91. Change here for trains to Rorschach. **Mels** has numerous good 18th–19th-century buildings. Opposite the station is the Gothic Heiligkreuz chapel with wall-paintings from the late 15th century. The Landsgemeindeplatz (the main square) is remarkably unspoilt; it includes a mid 17th-century Capuchin monastery and a row of 17th-century wooden buildings.

The village of **Flums** still has evidence of the iron smelting that was carried on here in the surviving ironmaster's house (Eisenherrenhaus) from 1567. The Romanesque former parish church was rebuilt in the 12th century and has 15th-century painting in the choir. From the station a bus twists up a hairpin road to Flumserberg Tannenbodenalp (table 80.441/line 441) from where a gondola ascends to Maschgenkamm (table 2792) for views over the Walensee. A cable car descends from Tannenbodenalp to Unterterzen (table 2790) beside the lake and only one minute from the railway station.

To the northwest of Flums is the spectacularly sited ruined castle of Burg Gräpplang and the St Jakob chapel with wall-paintings from c1300.

Passing through pleasant farming country along the level floor of the valley, the railway reaches **Walenstadt** and the eastern end of Walensee, where the railway skirts part of the southern shore. The views across the lake are dramatic, since steep cliffs rise directly out of the lake along the northern shore, culminating in the Churfursten ridge. A cycle-path and footpath run along the south shore of the lake, on which there are boat services in summer.

From **Unterterzen** a cable car climbs to Tannenbodenalp (table 2790), and at **Murg** there is a small pier 300m west of the station for the service across Walensee to the tiny village of Quinten, surrounded by woods and vineyards and dominated by limestone cliffs on the north shore. It is one of the few settlements in Switzerland with no road access, so it can be reached only by boat or a 7km walk from Walenstadt. The ferry service is operated by a German-built vessel from 1919, MS *Alvier*. At **Mühlehorn** a working water-powered hammer can be seen as a relic of the 18th-century iron industry. A long tunnel brings the railway to **Weesen**, a resort at the western end of Walensee. The Catholic Heiligkreuz church dates from the 13th century and forms an attractive group with the Dominican convent buildings, which were last rebuilt in around 1690.

A bus from Weesen post office (starting at Ziegelbrücke station) climbs up on to the western end of the Churfirsten at Amden (table 80.650/line 650), another small resort with superb views over the lake. There is also a good walk from Weesen along the northern shore of the lake to Betlis, and from there to the Serebach Falls.

For **Ziegelbrücke** and the journey on to Zürich see *Chapter 6*.

Graubünden CHUR–ZIEGELBRÜCKE

20

363

PRACTICALITIES Bicycle hire from Landquart, Bad Ragaz, Sargans, Unterterzen and Ziegelbrücke stations.

MAIENFELD
Tourist information
🖪 Bahnhofstrasse 1, CH-7304; ☏ 081 330 18 00; e maienfeld@heidiland.ch; www.heidiland.ch; ⊕ 09.30–noon & 13.30–17.00 Mon–Fri, 09.00–noon & 13.00–16.00 Sat

Where to stay
🏠 **Swiss Heidi Hotel** Werkhofstrasse 1, CH-7304; ☏ 081 303 88 88; e info@swissheidihotel.ch; www.swissheidihotel.ch

BAD RAGAZ
Tourist information
🖪 Am Platz 1, CH-7310; ☏ 081 300 40 20; e spavillage@heidiland.ch; www.heidiland.ch; ⊕ 08.30–18.00 Mon–Fri, 09.00–14.00 Sat

Where to stay
Numerous hotels; close to the station is:
🏠 **Garten-Hotel Sandi******
(H) Bahnhofstrasse 47, CH-7310; ☏ 081 303 45 00; e info@hotelsandi.ch; www.hotelsandi.ch

UNTERTERZEN
Tourist information
🖪 Infostelle Walensee, CH-8882; ☏ 081 720 17 17; e unterterzen@heidiland.ch; www.heidiland.ch; ⊕ 09.00–noon & 13.00–17.00 Mon–Fri; mid-May–mid-Oct also 09.00–13.00 Sat

Where to stay
🏠 **Churfirsten***** Bahnhofstrasse 41, CH-8880; ☏ 081 736 44 44; e info@hotelchurfirsten.ch; www.hotelchurfirsten.ch

WEESEN
Where to stay
🏠 **Parkhotel Schwert am See*** (H)**
Hauptstrasse 23, CH-8872; ☏ 058 616 14 74; e info@parkhotelschwert.ch; www. parkhotelschwert.ch. Building dates from the mid 15th century.

Appendix 1

LANGUAGE

DAYS AND MONTHS

	German	French	Italian
Sunday	*Sonntag*	*dimanche*	*domenica*
Monday	*Montag*	*lundi*	*lunedì*
Tuesday	*Dienstag*	*mardi*	*martedì*
Wednesday	*Mittwoch*	*mercredi*	*mercoledì*
Thursday	*Donnerstag*	*jeudi*	*giovedì*
Friday	*Freitag*	*vendredi*	*venerdì*
Saturday	*Sonnabend/ Samstag*	*samedi*	*sabato*
January	*Januar*	*janvier*	*gennaio*
February	*Februar*	*février*	*febbraio*
March	*März*	*mars*	*marzo*
April	*April*	*avril*	*aprile*
May	*Mai*	*mai*	*maggio*
June	*Juni*	*juin*	*giugno*
July	*Juli*	*juillet*	*luglio*
August	*August*	*août*	*agosto*
September	*September*	*septembre*	*settembre*
October	*Oktober*	*octobre*	*ottobre*
November	*November*	*novembre*	*novembre*
December	*Dezember*	*décembre*	*dicembre*

NUMBERS

	German	French	Italian
1	*eins*	*un(e)*	*uno/una*
2	*zwei*	*deux*	*due*
3	*drei*	*trois*	*tre*
4	*vier*	*quatre*	*quattro*
5	*fünf*	*cinq*	*cinque*
6	*sechs*	*six*	*sei*
7	*sieben*	*sept*	*sette*
8	*acht*	*huit*	*otto*
9	*neun*	*neuf*	*nove*
10	*zehn*	*dix*	*dieci*
11	*elf*	*onze*	*undici*
12	*zwölf*	*douze*	*dodici*

13	dreizehn	treize	tredici
14	vierzehn	quatorze	quattordici
15	fünfzehn	quinze	quindici
16	sechszehn	seize	sedici
17	siebzehn	dix-sept	diciassette
18	achtzehn	dix-huit	diciotto
19	neunzehn	dix-neuf	diciannove
20	zwanzig	vingt	venti
100	hundert	cent	cento
1,000	tausend	mille	mille

USEFUL VOCABULARY

arrivals	Ankunft	arrivées	arrivo
departures	Abfahrt	départs	partenza
information	Auskunft	renseignements	informazioni
left luggage	Gepäckaufbewahrung	consigne	il deposito bagagli
platform	Bahnsteig, Perron	quai	binario
station	Bahnhof	gare	stazione
ticket office	Fahrkarten-schalter	bureau de vente des billets	l'ufficio prenotazioni
timetable	Kursbuch	horaire	orario

GERMAN WORDS USED IN TEXT

Bad	spa, bath
Bahnhof	station
Burg	castle, citadel
Brücke	bridge
Dorf	village
Fälle	waterfall
Gasthaus	guesthouse
Gasthof	inn
Gondelbahn	gondola lift
Graben	trench, often site of former moat
Hauptgasse	main street
Heimatmuseum	local/folk museum
Hauptbahnhof	main station
Jugendstil	German/Austrian form of Art Nouveau
Kirche	church
Kulm	summit, peak
Luftseilbahn	ski lift
ober	upper, main
Perron	platform
Platz	square
Rathaus	town hall
Rhoden	medieval tax district
Schloss	castle
See	lake
Standseilbahn	funicular
Stöckli	accommodation for retired farmers
Tal	valley
Tor	gate

Turm	tower
Turmhof	tower-house
unter	lower/secondary
Verkehrsbüro	tourist office
Zentrum	centre
Zeughaus	arsenal
Zunfthaus	guildhall

FRENCH WORDS USED IN TEXT

hôtel de ville	town hall
train à grande vitesse	high-speed train

Wanderlust
SUBSCRIBE TODAY

SAVE 25%
ONLY £22.80 FOR 8 ISSUES
PLUS
» Subs Club discounts and offers every issue
» Subscriber-only features and articles at **wanderlust.co.uk**

Visit www.wanderlust.co.uk/shop
☎ Call our subscriptions team on 01753 620426

*"There simply isn't a better magazine
for the serious traveller"* Bill Bryson

Appendix 2

SWITZERLAND TOURISM OFFICES

Australia & New Zealand Switzerland Tourism, Level 3, Market St 46, AU-Sydney, NSW 2000; 029 262 1377; e info.aus@myswitzerland.com

Austria & Hungary Schweiz Tourismus, Haldenbachstrasse 9, Zürich, CH-8006; 00800 100 200 29; e info@myswitzerland.com

Benelux Suisse Tourisme/Zwitserland Toerisme, Rue Belliard 20/Postbus 1600, BE-1040 Bruxelles/Brussels; 0123 43 87 95; e info@myswitzerland.com

Brazil Switzerland Tourism, Avenida Paulista, 1754 - 4º Andar, Edifício Grande Avenida, BR-01310-200 São Paulo-SP; 00800 100 200 29; e info@myswitzerland.com

Canada Switzerland Tourism, 480 University Ave., Suite 1500, CA-Toronto, ON M5G 1V2; 011 800 100 200 30 (English), 011 800 100 200 32 (French); e info.caen@myswitzerland.com (English), info.cafr@switzerland.com (French)

China *Beijing* Switzerland Tourism, Prosper Center, Tower 1, Office 609, Guanghua Road 5, CN-10020 Beijing; 010 6512 5427; e info@myswitzerland.com. *Shanghai* Switzerland Tourism, Room 1208 West Gate Tower, 1038 Nan Jing Xi Lu, Shanghai 200041; e info@myswitzerland.com

Czech Republic Schweiz Tourismus, HST Obchodni komora, Svycarsko-Ceska republika, Jankovcova 1569/2c, CZ-179 00 Praha 7; 02 22 52 11 25; e info@myswitzerland.com

France Suisse Tourisme, 11 bis, rue Scribe, F-75009 Paris (closed to the public); info/res: 00800 100 200 29; e info@myswitzerland.com

Germany Schweiz Tourismus, Rossmarkt 23, DE-60311 Frankfurt; info/res: 00800 100 200 29; e info@myswitzerland.com. *Also has offices in Berlin, Düsseldorf, Hamburg and Munich.*

Hong Kong Switzerland Tourism, Suite 1116, 11/F Ocean Centre, Harbour City, 5 Canton Road, Tsim Sha Tsui, Kowloon; 000852 2865 6505; e info@myswitzerland.com

India Switzerland Tourism, c/o Swiss International Airlines, Urmi Estate, 10th Floor, 95 Ganpatrao Kadam mar, Lower parel (west), IN-400013 Mumbai; info/res: 022 6128 2500; e info@switzerland.com

Israel c/o Embassy of Switzerland, 228 rue Hayarkon, IL-63405 Tel Aviv; 0507 878 199; e info@myswitzerland.com

Italy Svizzera Turismo, Via Palestro 2, IT-20121 Milano; info/res: 00800 100 200 29; 02 760 011 63; e info@myswitzerland.com. *Also office in Rome.*

Japan Toranomon Daini Waiko Bldg. 3F, 5-2-6 Toranomon, Minato-ku, JP- Tokyo 105-0001; 03 5401 5426; e info@my switzerland.com

Malaysia c/o Embassy of Switzerland, 16 Persiaran Madge, MY-55000 Kuala Lumpur; 03 2148 0622; e info@myswitzerland.com

Netherlands Zwitserland Toerisme, Postbus 17400, NL-1001JK Amsterdam; info/res: 00800 100 200 29; e info@myswitzerland.com

Nordic Countries c/o Embassy of Switzerland, Valhallavägen 64, PO Box 26143, SE-10041 Stockholm; 08 676 7924; e info@my switzerland.com

Poland c/o Ambasada Szwajcarii, Aleje Ujazdowskie 27, PL-00-540 Warszawa; 022 628 04 81; e info@myswitzerland.com

Singapore 1 Swiss Club Link, SG-288162 Singapore; 06468 5788; e info@myswitzerland.com

South Korea 13Fl., Dongbu Dadong Bldg, 103 Da-Don, Juung-Gu, KR- Seoul 100-800; 03789 3200; e info@myswitzerland.com

Spain/Portugal Suiza Turismo, c/o Disputación 289, ES-08009 Barcelona; ☎ 093 467 20 19; e info@myswitzerland.com
Taiwan as Australia
Thailand c/o Swiss International Airlines, 18th Floor, q House Asoke Building, 66 Sukhumvit 21 Road (Asoke), TH-Bangkok 10110; ☎ 0204 7777; e info@myswitzerrland.com

EUROPEAN RAILWAYS
Rail Europe Ltd 193 Piccadilly, London W1J 9EU; ☎ 0844 848 4078; www.raileurope.co.uk.
Deutsche Bahn (German Rail) PO Box 687A, Surbiton, Surrey KT6 6UB; ☎ 08718 808066; e sales@bahn.co.uk; www.bahn.com/uk

SPECIALIST SWISS TRAVEL AGENTS
Inghams Mountain House, Station Rd, Godalming, Surrey GU7 1EX; ☎ 01483 791111; www.inghams.co.uk
Kuoni Travel Kuoni House, Deepdene Av, Dorking, Surrey RH5 4AX; ☎ 0844 488 0414; e holidays@kuoni.co.uk; www.kuoni.co.uk
The Swiss Holiday Company 45 The Enterprise Centre, Cranborne Rd, Potters Bar, Herts EN6 3DQ;

MISCELLANEOUS
Swiss Railway Society Membership Secretary Steve Buck, 55 The Boulevard, Wylde Green, Sutton

United Kingdom 30 Bedford St, London WC2E 9ED; ☎ 020 7845 7681; e info.uk@myswitzerland.ch
United States Switzerland Tourism, Swiss Center, 608 Fifth Av, NY 10020; ☎ 011 800 100 200 30 (toll free) or 1-212 981 1177; e info.usa@myswitzerland.com

Swiss Federal Railways 30 Bedford St, London WC2E 9ED; ☎ 0800 100 200 30 (freephone), 020 7420 4900; e sales@stc.co.uk; www.switzerlandtravelcentre.co.uk or www.swisstravelsystem.co.uk

☎ 0844 901 1100; e info@swissholidayco.com; www.swissholidayco.com
Switzerland Travel Centre 30 Bedford St, London WC2E 9ED; ☎ 020 7420 4900; e sales@stc.co.uk; www.stc.co.uk
Swiss Travel Service Locksview, Brighton Marina, Brighton, Sussex BN2 5HA; ☎ 0844 879 8813; www.swiss-holidays-lakes-mountains.co.uk

Coldfield, Birmingham B73 5JB; e membership@swissrailsoc.org.uk

If you would like information about advertising in Bradt Travel Guides please contact us on +44 (0)1753 893444 or email info@bradtguides.com

Appendix 3

POSTBUS

Appendix 4

FURTHER INFORMATION

Allen, Cecil J *Switzerland's Amazing Railways* Thomas Nelson & Sons, 1953
Bewes, Diccon *Swiss Watching* Nicholas Brealey Publishing, 2010
Bonjour, E, Offler, H S and Potter, G R *A Short History of Switzerland* Oxford, 1952
Brown, Karen *Swiss Country Inns & Itineraries*, Travel Press, 1984
Charles, Scott *All About Geneva*, Georg 1985
Lieberman, Marcia and Philip *Walking Switzerland The Swiss Way* The Mountaineers (Seattle), 1987
Morgan, Bryan *The End of the Line* Clever-Hume Press, 1955
Robertson, Ian *Switzerland, Blue Guide* A & C Black, 1992
Rosenkranz, Paul et al *Discover Lucerne* Werd Verlag, 2001
Rossberg, Ralf Roman *The Jungfrau Region* Hallwag Edition, 1991
Rubli, Walter H *Bern* Lausanne, 1954
Soloveytchik, George *Switzerland in Perspective* Oxford University Press, 1954
Wade, Paul, and Arnold, Kathy *Charming Small Hotel Guide: Switzerland* Duncan Petersen, 1993
Warrell, Ian *Through Switzerland with Turner* Tate Gallery Publications, 1995
Wraight, John *The Swiss and the British* Michael Russell, 1987

Switzerland Insight Guides, 2008
Switzerland, A Phaidon Cultural Guide Phaidon, 1985
Zermatt U Guides, 1995

Details of steam railways and steamers or other forms of preserved transport are given in an annual publication, *Schweizer Ferien mit Dampf und Nostalgie* (℡ 061 338 16 38; e schweizerferein@laupper.ch; www.laupper.ch – click on Schweizer Ferein).

Index

Page numbers in **bold** indicate main entries; those in *italics* indicate maps.